Kālī Kaula

Published by Avalonia

BM Avalonia
London
WC1N 3XX
England, UK

www.avaloniabooks.co.uk

KALI KAULA

ISBN (10) 1905297-37-8
ISBN (13) 978-1-905297-37-5

First Edition, September 2010
Design by Satori

British Library Cataloguing in Publication Data. A catalogue record for this book is available from the British Library.

Kālī Kaula

A Manual of Tantric Magick

Jan Fries

Published by Avalonia
www.avaloniabooks.co.uk

Figure 1 - Tigerblossom.

Acknowledgements

This book took quite a while to develop, and then a further few years to find its way to print. In the process, a good many people influenced, supported and inspired the project. There are many whom I want to thank.

Thanks are due to all those who shared in the weaving, who contributed, provided literature, agreed, disagreed, made me happy or mad and otherwise did their share to make this book much better than I could have made it on my own. It's been a difficult journey and many of us underwent considerable changes in the process. I am very grateful to all of you.

This goes for my personal deities, who encouraged, confused and amazed me many times as I transformed with the writing, but it also goes for the many kind and dedicated souls who participated in this communion.

First of all, I would like to thank Astrid and Gavin for their friendship and the wonderful job they did in streamlining the manuscript, designing the front cover and helping me to find a new editor. Without their untiring help, this book would still be unpublished.

In the years between writing and publication, the manuscript went through the hands of several dedicated friends, each of whom contributed in one way or another to its final publication.

Heartfelt thanks and blessings go to Mogg Morgan of Mandrake of Oxford, Robert Ansell of Fulgur and Nigel Saunders.

Finally, thanks to Marina, it found its way to Avalonia.

Sorita D'Este and David Rankine proved to be a pair of inspired, patient and reliable co-workers, for whose excellent efforts I am very grateful.

Then there are my dear friends who supplied ideas, criticism, encouragement, books, inspiration, practical advice, support, provocation and much needed diversions.

Thank you (in alphabetical order), Alex, Anad, Dieter, John, Julia, Kenneth, Maggie (Nema), Mike and Volkert.

I am very grateful to Louise Finn for her advice on shaking in literature, a very special mantra and her kindness in allowing me to quote from her writings. May your work prosper.

Thanks are due to the gurus of my childhood, my parents, grandmother and to Gisela Eberlein, who taught me much more than she knew.

Greetings and thanks to my main Wushu teachers Kim Dagu Nee and Little Lee: some of your lore has gone into the chapters on posture and breathing. Wherever you are: blessings.

Thanks are due to the local Bengali community for allowing me to participate in many of their annual rituals. Jay Durgā!

Special thanks to Xiaonan. Your laughter was essential for the completion of this book (and the foundation of the next).

Many thanks to Richard Bandler, whose pioneering insights on hypnosis, submodalities and innovative trance induction are a mind-blowing source of fresh inspiration. Your work has transformed my magick and my life.

More than three decades ago, Kenneth Grant's gloriously darksome writings aroused my interest in the Nightside of tantric magick. And Maggie (Nema) taught me how to discover this magick in any ancient religion I came upon. Indeed, Maat goes across time and space on wings of nothingness. Thank you both for this blessing.

While writing this book, Maxine Hong Kingston's books were a delightful source of fresh ideas. I admire her passionate way of blending alternate realities and the many practical and poetic references to subconscious thought processes. Peace be with you.

At the same time, I discovered the unique movies of Hayao Miyazaki. They helped me through some difficult times and gave new enthusiasm to my work. If you want to see real magick, shamanism and modern mythology, the Studio Ghibli movies are a must.

Next, I would like to express my deep gratitude to all the magnificent indologists and tantric scholars whose exemplary work has made this book possible. Your names appear in the bibliography, which ought to inspire all readers to buy your books and enjoy them. It's a great boon that there are academics who struggle with eldritch manuscripts (instead of, say, sitting in the sunshine at the beach) and share them with the world. I have quoted from your work and hope that I have not misinterpreted your insights. Let me apologise for errors, misspellings and misunderstandings; they are my own responsibility. And I can only ask my readers to study your works in full length. There is no shortcut to enlightenment, and all who really wish to understand what a fascinating, multi-layered subject Tantra is, are invited to read up on the subject in full length. All I have written is a brief introduction to a huge subject: be assured that a lot of exceptional material, well worth exploring in body and mind, remains to be discovered.

Finally, I wish to thank all of you who go beyond reading and develop something new and wonderful. Tantra is a living art, and it is you who make it so. Here's to the future!

Dedicated to five living geniuses:

Richard Bandler, Kenneth Grant, Maxine Hong Kingston,
Maggie Ingalls, Hayao Miyazaki.

Blessings to you all!

Other Books by Jan Fries

Visual Magick: A Handbook of Freestyle Shamanism, Mandrake, 1992 & 2001

Helrunar: Manual of Rune Magick, Mandrake, 1993 & 2002

Seidways: Shaking, Swaying and Serpent Mysteries, Mandrake, 1996

Living Midnight: Three Movements of the Tao, Mandrake, 1998

The Cauldron of the Gods: Manual of Celtic Magick, Mandrake, 2003

Disclaimer

Although both Avalonia Books and the author of this book have taken great care to ensure the authenticity of the information and the techniques contained therein, we are not responsible, in whole or in part, for any injury which may occur to the reader or readers by reading and/or following the instructions in this book. It is understood that many of the techniques, rituals and meditations are only discussed for scholarly purposes, and that there exists a potential for injury when using the techniques or practices described in this publication, especially when the full text is not carefully studied.

It is essential that before following any of the activities, physical, meditative or otherwise, herein described, the reader or readers should first consult his or her physician for advice on whether practising or using the techniques, rituals or meditations described in this publication could cause injury, physical, mental or otherwise. Since the techniques and physical activities could be too demanding or sophisticated, it is essential that a physician be consulted. Also, local, stae or federal laws may prohibit the practice of physical activities, rituals or exercises described in this publication. A thorough examination must be made of the federal, state or local laws before the reader or readers attempt to try or practice any of the exercises, techniques, rituals, meditations or any other activity described in this publication.

Neither Avalonia Books nor the author guarantees the legality or the appropriateness of the techniques, acts, rituals, exercises or meditations herein contained.

Table of Contents

Illustrations 13

Introduction 17
The Scope of this Book 19
Abbreviations of primary sources with comments 22

1: Dakṣa's Feast 25

2: Before Tantra 30
The Indus Valley 32
The Vedic Period 41
Seers on Soma 43
Vedic Religion 46
Spiritual Discipline 54
The World Soul 58
Classes of Society 61
Beyond Veda 63
New Faiths: Buddhism and Jaina 67
Elder Hinduism 71
Dharma and the Pattern of Society 74
Problems with Purity 76
Ups and Downs of the Deities 77
Vaiṣṇavas, Śaivas and Śāktas 82

3: The Texture of Tantra 88
Twilight Language 88
Śiva and Śakti 92
Sex, Gender, and Religion 97
Three and a half consciousness states 110
Skulls and Corpses 113
Animal Sacrifice 115
What have you learned? 117

4: Tantric History 119
Tantric Traditions 127
Kāpālikas and Aghoras 129
Kula and Kaula 131
Krama 135
Śrī Vidyā 139
Mahācīna 141

5: Masks of the Divine 155
The Guru Game 155
The Primal Guru 157
Guru Pūjā 159
Learning Together 160
Hymn: 161
Webs of Delusion 161
Divine Actors 163
Female Saints 167
Female Ascetics 172
Tāntrikās 174

6: Body as a Whole 181
Maps of the Body 183
Being at Ease 185
A Choice of Postures 186
Shaking, Swaying, and Primal Vibration 191
Nyāsa: a Touch of the Divine 195
Initiation and Nyāsa 196
An Armour of Protection 198
Mudrās 199
Helpful Hands 202

7: The Joy of Breath 205
Breath and suggestion. 226
Prāṇa in Antiquity 229
Classical prāṇāyāma 232

8: Mantra 236
A World of Vibration 236
Recitation 236
A Structure of Mantras 238
Svāhā 240
A Choice of Mantras 241
Śrī Vidyā's Playful Goddess 245
Bīja 251
Māyā: Waking the Mantra 259
Lakṣmī: Maintaining a Mantra 263
Kālī: Transcending a Mantra. 265
Japa Mālā 267
Using the Japa-Mālā 271
Counting digits. 274
A Chance to Wake Up 276

9: The Heart of Kula 280
The Heart in Veda 280
The Heart in Tantra 281
The Heart as an Organ 284
The Heart as a Cakra 284
Home of the Personal Deity 285

The Heart in Kashmir Tantricism ... 286
Experience of the Heart ... 288
A Note of Caution ... 292
The Heart of Dao ... 292

10: Seeing in the Heart ... 296
A World of Visions ... 296
A Question of Perspective ... 298
Coding your Perception ... 299
A Shower of Ambrosia ... 302
The Black Elixir ... 305
Yoni Mudrā ... 307
Going for Colour ... 308
Union with the Gods ... 310

11: The Path of the Serpent ... 314
Occult Anatomy ... 319
Bhūta Śuddhi: the Purification of the Principles of your Body ... 320
A Look at Tradition ... 326
Kuṇḍalinī: Consciousness, Power, and the World Glamour ... 330
Nātha Lore ... 334
A Classical Approach ... 337
Kuṇḍalinī Yoga ... 339
A Practical Approach ... 340

12: A Feast of Five ... 346
Tantric sex ... 346
Erotica ... 348
Pañcamakāra ... 352
Orgasm ... 363
Substitutes ... 367
A Day in the Life of a Neo-Kaula ... 369

13: Red and White ... 382
The Yoni Shrine ... 382
Menstruation ... 385
Mothers, Seizers, and Yoginīs ... 388
Alone with Lilith ... 397
Secret Sacraments ... 400
Science of Rasa ... 403
Fluid Gnosis ... 404
The Partner for You ... 409

14: Mahāvidyās ... 411
Ten Principles of Wisdom ... 411
The Mahāvidyās and You. ... 447
Direct Experience ... 450

15: Kālī's Kula 463
Nirṛti 463
Kālī Rising 465
Kālī Abroad 473
Masks of Kālī 478
Hymn to Kālī - Karpūrādi-Stotra 491
Rites of Kālī 500
Kālī Yantra 505
Kālī's Flowers 506
Tribute to the Jackals 507
Playing in Guyana 508

Appendix One: Language and Pronunciation 514
Vowels 516
Consonants 518

Appendix Two: A Brief Glossary of Saṅskṛt Terms .. 520
A 520
B 523
C 524
D 525
G 526
H 527
I 528
J 528
K 529
L 533
M 533
N 535
O 536
P 536
R 538
S 539
T 542
U 544
V 544
Y 545

Bibliography 547

Index 558

Illustrations

Figure 1 - Tigerblossom. 4
Figure 2 - Śiva. 16
Figure 3 - Mesolithic Rock Art. 31
Figure 4 - Indus Culture, seals. (Not to scale.) 33
Figure 5 - Proto-yantras in rock-art 38
Figure 6 - Indus Culture, seals. 39
Figure 7 - Indus Culture. Figurines from Mehrgarh. 40
Figure 8 - Buffalo-horned, three-faced deity, surrounded by wild animals. 48
Figure 9 - Agni. 49
Figure 10 - Rudra the archer. 53
Figure 11 - Early yogīs. 57
Figure 12 - Life after Life 62
Figure 13 – Unknown Goddesses 70
Figure 14 - Divine Heads 72
Figure 15 - Śiva 84
Figure 16 - Nandī at night. 86
Figure 17 - Ardhanariśvarī or Ardhanariśvara 91
Figure 18 - Bhairava 96
Figure 19 - Bhairava. 98
Figure 20 - Spotted Mouse-deer. 106
Figure 21 - Female musician (drummer). 109
Figure 22 - Lakṣmī statue 111
Figure 23 - Hyena dreaming. 118
Figure 24 - Nightside Gaṇeśa of the cremation ground. 128
Figure 25 - Chinese influence. 144
Figure 26 - From womb to womb like spiders. 164
Figure 27 - Fig tree weaving. 176
Figure 28 - Lotus. 187
Figure 29 - The Living Wasteland. 193
Figure 30 - Mudrās. 201
Figure 31 - More Mudrās. 203
Figure 32 - Yantras for Sorcery from the Saundarya Laharī. 252
Figure 33- Bījas. 256
Figure 34 - Bījas. Five phases of Krama. 258
Figure 35 - Indian Black Vulture. 279
Figure 36 - Bhairava. 282
Figure 37 - Triple Śakti 291
Figure 38 - Kāmadeva. 306
Figure 39 - Circles. 328
Figure 40 - Lovers. 350
Figure 41 - Śiva and Pārvatī. 353

Figure 42 - Gaṇapati and Siddhī.....361
Figure 43 - Lovers.....365
Figure 44 - Lovers.....379
Figure 45 - Yantra of the Kula ritual.....384
Figure 46 - Woman or Yakṣī holding her own (or a stolen) child.....390
Figure 47 - Yakṣī.....392
Figure 48 - Yogīnī with serpents.....394
Figure 49 - Skanda / Kārrtikeya.....402
Figure 50 - One way of doing Yoni-mudrā.....405
Figure 51 - Tārā.....414
Figure 52 - Tārā yantras.....415
Figure 53 - Lalitā Tripurā Sundarī.....420
Figure 54 - Lalitā Tripurā Sundarī yantras.....421
Figure 55 - Bhuvaneśvarī.....422
Figure 56 - Bhuvaneśvarī yantras.....423
Figure 57 - Bhairvī.....427
Figure 58 - Bhairavī yantras.....428
Figure 59 - Chinnamastā.....429
Figure 60 - Chinnamastā yantras.....430
Figure 61 - Dhūmāvatī.....433
Figure 62 - Dhūmāvatī yantras.....434
Figure 63 - Bagalā.....435
Figure 64- Bagalā yantras.....436
Figure 65 - Mātaṅgī.....441
Figure 66 - Mātaṅgī yantras.....442
Figure 67 - Lakṣmī yantras.....443
Figure 68 - Contemporary Lakṣmī yantras.....444
Figure 69 - Kālī & Śiva yantras.....449
Figure 70 - Siddhilakṣmī Kamalā.....461
Figure 71 - Statue of Kālī as a young woman.....464
Figure 72 - Kālī in folk religion.....466
Figure 73 - Kālī and Śiva making love.....476
Figure 74 - Bhadrā Kālī.....483
Figure 75 - Two classical Kālī yantras.....487
Figure 76 - Aranyā.....490
Figure 77 - Heads and hands for Kālī.....504
Figure 78 - Gate after Gate.....509
Figure 79 - Kālī rising.....512

Figure 2 - Śiva.

Introduction

Na-aham-asmi-naca-anyo 'sti kevalāḥ śaktayas-tv-aham
I am not, neither does another exist; I am only energies.
(Abhinavagupta, Tantrāloka, 29, 64, trans. Dupuche, 2006: 221)

This may be the beginning of the strangest journey you ever made.

The book you just bought (or are snuggling up to in the bookshop of your choice) is an invitation. Here you find Tantra way beyond the glitter and foam of New Age eroticism. Here is the hard core stuff, the real thing as it was developed in the harsh mountains of Kashmir, the scorching heat of southern India and the moist, fever infested jungles of Assam. Here is the vast and void heart of the black goddess, the secret seat of initiation and a dark doorway leading to ... you'll find out as you pass through and then, at last, beyond. Tantra.

Which isn't quite true. It's not a book about Tantra at all. There is no such thing as Tantra, at least to those who live it. The folk who invented Tantra did not call it that. It was other people, many of them way outside of the phenomenon, who coined the term, centuries after the fun and madness of the beginning. Tantra is just a word, and not a very good one. There were and are hundreds of 'Tantric' systems all over Asia, most of them in happy disagreement with each other. The more you learn about Tantra the less will you like the expression. 'Tantra' is so vast you can't pin it down, you can't define it nor need you bother to try. If you need a word for what you are doing, or a tradition to cling to, you'll never discover the essence that makes you pulse and vibrate with life. Confused? You should be. So am I, and I wrote this thing.

So it's not 'Tantra' after all, which is quite a relief, what with so many badly informed dabblers giving it a bad name. Here is something you might call Kaula, if you have to. Or which you could call Krama, if you need a name for something mysterious we can't be really sure about. It's way beyond names that the real thing happens. Beyond the labels, beyond the traditions, beyond the glamour of commercialisation or the stuffy earnestness of some academics who haven't had a good laugh in a decade. Here is the concentrated essence of experience. It's your chance to discover something new, and your invitation to make up what you can't find and manifest what you will as it suits you.

Now some of you may yearn for arcane traditions. Some may wish for 'mysterious India' - gleaming palaces, babbling mynah birds, half starved yogīs placidly baking in the sun, alluring ladies in stunningly colourful saris and, of course, the hallowed wisdom of the ancients, sticky and sweet. India, the land where everybody is spiritual. India, a culture of divine eroticism, of enchanting fables and a romantic wisdom that the poor bleary-eyed West never really had. Except for some Druids of course, who probably got it from India. Or was that Egypt? Or Atlantis? You're welcome. One huge naan bread covered with sweet and spicy things, many of them made of plastic. No, we won't have that. This is not the place for idealisation. Here is your chance to enjoy vindaloo Mahākālī and find out what it does to you. Here is your chance to think and do and discover. Because if you go for tradition you'll never get anywhere.

One reason I wrote this book is that Kālī asked me to. She is mightily fed up with all the Tantric New Age rubbish that clutters up those horrid little shops where goody-goody muzak fills the air, spirituality equates with reduced expectations, and people look as if they ate soap all day. She loathes 'Tantric Kits' filled with aromatic massage oils, scented candles, honey-dust, and ten page guidebooks offering mantras, postures, and rituals to spiritualise a boring lovelife. And she spits on those who call themselves Tantric Masters. It's true. It happens all the time. Because Kaula, Krama, Trika, Mahācīna et al are so much more. More than sex, more than religion, more than a hobby or an interest. They are all of life and go way beyond each single lifetime. They also go way beyond your personality. Beyond any personality.

You don't get it by reading books. You certainly won't get it for money. Nor is imitation enough. The one and only way to get in there and out again happily is to live the way with all the power, joy, and passion you can raise. And you can, as you will learn, when you transcend the limit. It's not enough to repeat a few mantras. It's not enough to dabble into cakras or visualise a little serpent in your spine. It's a lot more than playing gods to legitimise your lovemaking. The fun begins when you give all you've got and find that there is a lot more you never knew of. It's when you charge your body with bliss and power and take that good feeling with a huge smile and double it and fill yourself up with that joy, double it again, and double that. (Thank you, Richard!) It's when you saturate yourself and all around with sheer, mind-blowing enthusiasm. It's when you take that mantra and turn on the volume and add chorus and echo and make it blast all the way through your being so it shakes you to the core. It's here when you stop mucking around with half hearted images and serene indifference. That vision can be brighter, larger, clearer, closer, better! That experience can be a lot more impressive if you make it so! It's your brain, it's your nervous system and you can take them wherever you want. Don't just think of Kuṇḍalinī, live her, be her, know her as yourself and the whole world, and go beyond! And when you descend into the heart, go deeper and deeper, shed the forms that appear, layer after layer, until you reach the point of utter reality where form and emptiness make love. Who are you now? Who have you ever been?

Here we are way beyond mind games. If we have to call Tantra anything, let's call it a set of techniques that work; coupled with wildness, joy, daring, and the sense of going for it that shakes you out of whatever you used to be before. That's what the pioneers did. And why they got so far. That's what later generations lost when they got stuck in tradition, regulations, fancy speculation, tons of theories, chatter and dumb-headed obedience. Here is a book for those who dream and dare and do. When you wake up, you can find Kālī in here. She doesn't want tepid worship, part-time devotion, or imitation of saintliness. There are too many pretenders around as it is, in India, California, and in any occult organisation, you name it.

She wants you to put everything into the offering, Because that's the only way of getting everything out of it. Your belly for joy, lust, and good feelings. Your heart for love and laughter. Your head for learning and thinking and learning anew. When you bring these together, you are ready to surprise yourself. Do it now.

The Scope of this Book

When I was completing Cauldron of the Gods, a friend asked what I was reading. 'It's the Kaulajñāna nirṇaya', I replied, glancing happily at the little red book, with its tattered cover and the goddess-knows-what-do-they-use-instead-of-paper look so popular among Indian publishers, '...wonderful stuff on mediation and one of the most practical Tantras I've ever come upon.'

'Not Celtic stuff any more?'

'It's getting on my nerves. There is far too little practical material in surviving Celtic lore. I'm fed up with question marks, medieval myths, and idle speculation. At least the Kaula folk had a clear interest in things that work. And they had a sense of humour. That's something amazingly rare in old literature.'

'You're not going to write a book on Tantra, are you?'

'Oh no. Tantra is huge, vast, and overwhelming. You could write a hundred books on that topic. Given the amount of surviving literature, you could spend all your life researching and it still would only amount to a fragment. Sorry, a book on Tantra is impossible.'

Well, this is it.

Luckily, I did not have to write about all of Tantra. I just picked a small section of surviving (and translated) literature, combined it with a lot of daily practice, promised myself that this book wouldn't be such a monster as Cauldron and went to work. Luckily, I had been researching some of the more exciting 'Tantric' traditions for several decades. I decided to focus on these early traditions, basically Kula, Kaula, Krama, and a bit of Trika, to add whatever happens to work, some history at the beginning, and to ignore the vast majority of Tantric movements that belong to Buddhism or Right-Hand-Path-Stay-in-Line-and-do-as-you-are-told Hindu Tantra. Regrettably, I had to leave out several fascinating traditions, and even more that are so dull and boring that I won't bother you with them. As a result, the book you are reading is in no way representative for what modern Indians or Westerners deign to consider 'Tantric', for the very simple reason that only a few early, minor movements are examined, and these only in respect to practical application. Even among these lineages, a huge amount of material was not included.

Take initiation for example. For the early Kaulas, initiation refers to a complex of highly refined rituals involving a fair share of hypnosis. Here, initiation is not a formality but an experience that liberates the initiate from being a 'bound animal'. Now the Kaulas were practical people. They did not attach much importance to trust and faith. Instead, they tested their results. So should you. A student who showed the five signs of Śaktipāta, the 'descent of energy' (without being told about them previously) was encouraged to continue. For those of you who wish to know what signs they are, Abhinavagupta lists them in *Tantrāloka*, 29, 208: bliss, lightness of the body, trembling of the body, sleep of the outer sense-organs, and a certain reeling or staggering. These indicate a descent of energy (Śaktipāta), they are also signs that Rudraśakti has cleansed the various bodies of the initiate (for the time being). Which is by no means the only approach to the subject. There is a vast range of initiation formulas, many of them so obscure that it takes an amazingly competent guru to make them work. As this is a practical book, and as you obviously do your thing without such a guru (most of them seem to have died out with original Kula, Kaula, and Krama before the 14th century CE), the topic had to be left out. Nevertheless, it is an essential part of the original traditions and I apologise for not devoting much space to the subject.

Another such subject is the science of the phonemes, of the categories of existence, and the vast range of philosophical insight that appeared out of the practical experiences of those wonderfully mad seers. Here you encounter so much mind-boggling cosmology that Hebrew Qabalah, Mesopotamian astrology, and the otherworlds of the Egyptians seem like children's toys by comparison. Some systems were entirely founded on such speculations. Others focused on practical matters and when the budding Tāntrika happened to have world-shaking insights, these were acknowledged with a grin, but nobody made a big issue out of them. There are 'Tantric' systems that appear 'philosophical' but are not, as they were based on spiritual experience instead of thought and speculation. In fact, there are a lot of them and they do not agree with each other, not even in the basics. Hence, in this book 'Tantric theory' was reduced to a tiny little minimum. While you and I may prefer the practice to theories, I would not want to give the impression that all 'Tantric' gurus thought like that.

Another topic I have neglected is practical magic, sorcery, and spellcraft. Western writers tend to give the impression that 'Tantra' and 'Yoga' are disciplines meant to produce well-being, health, enlightenment, and liberation, and that their application for sorceries are perversions of the originally pure creed. Which may sound good but is simply not true. Sorcery was always there, and for most practitioners it was the main thing. You find it in the earliest texts. Rituals to create magic swords that decapitate enemies from a distance, rituals to shake cities, paralyse, stun, blind, or otherwise crush opponents and so on. Such rites appealed to sorcerers who made a profit selling spells, they were also amazingly popular among kings and politicians seeking to control other kingdoms. Far from being a low-caste perversion, such rites were cherished by well-educated folk from the highest levels of society. It may not be a popular idea, but it is true that many of the earliest yogīs and Tāntrikas did not give a damn for ethics or what modern people consider 'spiritual'.

Alchemy is another topic that had to be largely disregarded. It has been ignored by most researchers, apart from such pioneers as David Gordon White. The art of refining and ingesting mercury and cinnabar are essential to many 'Tantric' systems, such as the Siddhas, and by no means peripheral. Numerous adepts who developed Haṭhayoga and the modern seven cakra system were happily ingesting poisons, no matter the consequences. As, from the practical point of view, there is very little use in this topic - unless you want to kill yourself - I have only mentioned the matter here and there.

Last, there is an enormous range of what we may loosely call 'Folk-Tantra', based on a myriad ethnic traditions and local deities, customs, and rituals. While the word 'Tantra' essentially means 'a weaving, a text' and all we know of the earlier systems is based on their written heritage, there is an enormously complex, colourful, and mind-boggling range of non-literate traditions developed by people out on the road or leading a life as a householder in society. These topics are beautifully presented in the books of June McDaniel.

To make up for all these omissions, I can only encourage you to read as much scholarly literature on 'Tantra' as you can lay your hands on, to discover what works for you, and to improve it. 'Tantra' is not a fossil from the museum of outdated spirituality; it is an attitude that will transform your life in many ways. If you want to thank those who went before you, learn all you can, improve the lot, and take it into new dimensions.

Abbreviations of primary sources with comments

AV ***Atharvaveda*** Youngest of the four *Vedas*, the AV offers a wide range of hymns, spells and sorceries, ritual instructions, formulae and unusual material that had no place in the earlier Vedas. The Atharvaveda is remarkable for its practical-minded outlook and for its poetic refinement. The AV stands between classical Vedic thought and the more refined philosophy of the Upaniṣads.

BāUp ***Bṛhad-āraṇyaka Upaniṣad***

DM ***Devī Māhātmya*** (also known as *Śrī Durgā Saptaśatī* or as the *Caṇḍī*) A 6th-7th century CE text that survived by becoming part of the *Mārkāṇḍeya Purāṇa*. One of the earliest manifestations of the Śākta movement. A brief and poetic work in seven hundred mantras describing three episodes of the Devī's battles against demons. The contradictions indicate that this early work combines several elder traditions.

DBh ***Devī Bhāgavatam Purāṇa*** A massive work in 100,000 verses on goddess mythology and the typical Purāṇa topics, such as cosmology, genealogy, pseudo-history, geography, daily ritual, meditation, worship, one thousand names of the deity etc. Most of it was complete by the 13th century CE but a few sections seem to have been added up to the 17th century. The DBh, though professing to be a Śākta work, is strongly influenced by Vaiṣṇava philosophy and traditional Hindu ethics. Tantra is usually considered with suspicion, class remains a must, and in spite of all goddess veneration, women are not entitled to read it on their own. In spite of such shortcomings, the DBh remains an important source of unusual ideas.

GS ***Gheraṇḍa Saṁhita*** The teachings of saint Gheraṇḍa on yoga. One of the classic works on early yoga.

KP ***Kālikāpurāṇa*** c. 9th-16th century, earliest surviving manuscript 1726 CE.

KS ***Karpūrādi Stotra*** Hymn to Camphor (Kālī). Possibly the shortest summary of left-hand worship in Tantric literature.

KN ***Kaulajñāna nirṇaya*** a Tantra attributed to Matsyendranātha, c. 11th century CE, containing practices of the Yoginī and the Nātha schools. The *KJN* is remarkable for its refreshing style, its detailed instructions on meditation and visualisation and for its unorthodox, practical approach. Highly recommended.

KBUp ***Kauṣītakī Brāhmaṇa Upaniṣad***

KCT ***Kulacūḍāmaṇi Tantra*** 'The Crest-Jewel of the Kula' (i.e. menstrual blood freely given for the purpose of sādhana), an early Tantra (9th-10th century CE). A wild nigama full of ambiguous instructions for ritual and/or internal worship. Unique material on Kālī, Mahiṣamardinī and the Mātṛkā Devīs. The text often seems outspoken and down-to-earth, but this impression may be misleading. As the practical instructions are usually brief, much has to be learned from other sources (or invented). Highly recommended for advanced practitioners.

KT ***Kulārṇava Tantra*** An influential Tantra begun in the 10th century CE but modified repeatedly over the next centuries. The style is strict and unpoetic, it contains numerous contradictions due to the many contributors. Useful details on Kula and Kaula traditions of the wilder sort, such as the Five Ms, ecstatic worship, obsession, yoga etc. Occasionally very narrow-minded and given to long catalogues of prohibitions. The translation by Pandit/Woodroffe is strongly abridged, that by Rai is not quite scholarly but (except for the mantras) complete.

LT ***Lakṣmī Tantra*** A Vaiṣṇava Tantra of the Pāñcarātra tradition in the form of a nigama, c. 9th-12th century CE. A brilliant blend of refined philosophy and practical ritual, often expressed with clarity and consideration of detail.

MHB ***Mahābhārata*** An ancient epic in c. 100,000 verses. The core of the tale (the original *Bhārata*) dates around 1000 BCE, its 'modern' form accumulated up to the 4th century BCE, the textual form reached its completion in the 3rd or 4th century CE. It details the legendary war between the Pāṇḍavas and the Kauravas. The *MHB* has encyclopaedic character. It aims at recording every item of Indian lore and succeeds remarkably.

MNT ***Mahānirvāṇa Tantra*** A late (17th century CE?) but very influential Tantra containing some excellent (elder) material on Kālī and several chapters on law, inheritance and social regulations, most of them boring and conservative.

MāUp ***Māṇḍūkya Upaniṣad***

MM ***Mantramahodhadhiḥ*** 'The Ocean of Mantra', a collection of mantras, yantras and their attribution to deities and ritual, by Mahīdhara, written in 1588 CE.

Mup ***Muṇḍaka Upaniṣad*** An innovative text dating c. 500 BCE, including the earliest reference to Kālī.

PP ***Pādukā Pañcaka*** 'The Fivefold Footstool', a short, late text on Kuṇḍalinī and the cakras.

PTL ***Parātrīśikālaghuvṛttiḥ*** (also called *Anuttaratattvavimarśinī*) Abhinavagupta's short commentary on 36 verses of the *Rudrayāmala Tantra.*

PTV ***Parātrīśikā Vivaraṇa*** (also called *Tattvaviveka, Tattvavivaraṇa* and *Anuttaraprakriyā*) Abhinavagupta's long commentary on thirty-six verses of the *Rudrayāmala Tantra.* The *PTV*, written in the early 11th century CE, is remarkable for its intense clarity and its mind-blowing sophistication. Very hard to understand for those who only have theoretical knowledge but a blessing for all advanced practitioners. Good material on the heart, occult grammar, the word, phonemes, Trika lore etc.

RY ***Rāmāyaṇa*** Famous ancient epic that took written form between 200 BCE and 200 CE. It describes Rāma's search for his abducted wife Sītā.

ṚV ***Ṛgveda*** The earliest Veda, a collection of more than a thousand hymns to various deities, collected c. 1200 BCE.

ṢCN ***Ṣaṭ Cakra Nirūpaṇa*** 'Description of the Six Centres', a late text on the cakras and the raising of Kuṇḍalinī.

SL ***Saundarya Laharī*** A difficult poem in one hundred verses that hides the secrets of practical Śrī Vidyā worship under a veil of extremely cryptic symbolism. Parts of it constitute the *Ānanda Laharī*. Each verse is supposed to have sorcerous power when recited over a specific diagram.

SSP ***Siddha Siddhānta Paddhati*** A brief but very deep text attributed to Gorakṣanātha, Nātha pioneer, siddha and allegedly the founder of Haṭha yoga. Good, clear instructions on the tattvas, the internal universe, practical yoga, meditation, advanced Śaivite philosophy etc.

ŚS ***Śiva Saṁhita*** An important practical work on Śaiva yoga, visualisation and ritual with a touch of Kaula influence.

ŚLS ***Śrī Lalitā Sahasranāma*** A hymn to the goddess Lalitā consisting of one thousand names. The text aims at a synthesis of the Śrī Vidyā and the Kaula current.

TT ***Toḍala Tantra*** An important Kaula Tantra detailing the worship of the Mahāvidyās, plus short passages on yoga, mantra, Kuṇḍalinī, daily worship etc. Each of the Mahāvidyās is equipped with a partner who is a form of Śiva and Viṣṇu.

TR ***Tripurā Rahasya*** A practical work on meditation and liberation by introversion along the lines of Śrī Vidyā. Few technical instructions but many inspiring parables and tales on the cultivation of the mind. Remarkable as two major protagonists are saintly women.

VT ***Vāmakeśvara Tantra*** (also known as Vāmakeśvarīmatam) Usually only the first five chapters (the Nityāṣoḍaśikārṇava) are treated. A highly sophisticated Tantra much concerned with worship along the lines of Śrī Vidyā. Long passages on the Śrī Yantra, mantra, mudrā etc.

VBT ***Vijñana Bhairava Tantra*** A short text in 112 verses on enlightenment. Contains very little 'typical' material (such as mantras, phonemes, ritual, worship, sorcery etc.) but a lot of Zen-like thoughts. Highly inspiring.

VŚT ***Vīṇāśikhatantra*** A Śaiva Tantra that was highly influential in south-east Asia. It details the worship of Śiva as Tumburu in the centre of the world-map and the four Śaktis Jayā (east), Vijayā (south), Jayantī (west) and Aparājitā (north).

YT ***Yonitantra*** *A* short work, possibly 17th century CE, praising the yoni, its worship and the sacredness of menstrual blood. Śaivite setting but strong Vaiṣṇava undertones.

1: Dakṣa's Feast

In the time before time, the Supreme Śakti shed three forms. Meet Sarasvatī, who became wife of Brahmā; Lakṣmī, who became the mate of Viṣṇu; and Gaurī, the Golden One, lover of Śiva. Then the usual thing happened. Ever so often, there is an Asura or a Dānava who becomes too ambitious. Like the Devas, the Demon folk have a desire for liberation, and sometimes, they take spiritual discipline really seriously. This was the case with the Halāhalas, a particularity ambitious group of Dānavas. They went for extremes of tapas, they indulged in austerities, they exercised through day and night and eventually Brahmā, the Creator, had to grant spiritual powers to them. Which may not have been a very wise idea. However, Brahmā is noted for this sort of thing, no matter how often it gets the Devas into trouble. The Halāhalas said 'Thank you!' to Brahmā and left to conquer the universe. Soon they dominated the three worlds of heaven, earth, and underworld, they even stormed Mount Kailash, evicted Śiva and occupied the Vaikuṇṭha regions in the deep. In sight of such calamities, Viṣṇu and Śiva prepared for war. Brahmā would have none of this. He merely sat back and hoped the others would sort things out properly. And the gods did. Viṣṇu went to the battle accompanied by his heavenly troops and so did Śiva, whose troops are not quite as heavenly. The war lasted for 60,000 years. When the last Halāhala was sent to flight, the gods, tired, weary, and somewhat beside themselves returned to their spouses. They took off their armour, they laid aside their weapons, had a bath and a good drink and began to boast. 'We cut them down' said Viṣṇu. 'We destroyed them utterly!' declared Śiva 'In all the worlds, none could stand against us!'. 'None of you amounts to anything without us!' replied their spouses, 'Who gave you the power to fight? Who granted strength, energy, and valour to you? Who could you ever fight without Śakti'? 'Come on' said the gods, 'we did pretty well, didn't we?' The goddesses broke out laughing. 'Sure', replied the devīs, 'and now you'll learn how to get on without us.'

And without a further word, Lakṣmī and Gaurī disappeared.

The gods remained speechless. Then they began to weep. They bewailed their losses, they lost their divine radiance, they walked the world like madmen. Their power disappeared and so did their function in the universe. Seeing this, Brahmā became very worried. He knew there would be another bunch of Danāvas around before long, and he knew even better that he, on his own, had not a chance against them. In his fear he closed his eyes, introverted, and entered the sacred space of the heart. Within the all-creating cavern of truth, he learned that Paraśakti was angry with the gods, and that she had withdrawn her blessing from them. And Brahmā realised that he had to work for three. With Viṣṇu mad and Śiva deluded, he had to work as maintainer and destroyer, not that he was much good at the job. The other gods were just as shaken. Then primordial Dakṣa invited the deities, seers, and heavenly ascetics for a placation rite. They went to the slopes of the Himalaya and chanted 'Hrīṁ' for 100,000 years until the supreme goddess appeared. Paraśakti manifested in their hearts in the form of being, intelligence, and bliss. She held the noose and the elephant goad, her other two hands made the signs that dispel fear and grant boons. The gods and sages praised her, and finally she responded to their worries. 'Listen' the goddess said, who had appeared in the form of Mahāmāyā, 'the madness of the gods will soon pass away. Lakṣmī will reappear when the milk ocean is churned, she will be born together with the elixir of immortality. Gaurī is soon to be reborn, and it will be in Dakṣas family'. The assembly was delighted to hear this, most of all ancient Dakṣa, who had been a major god in Vedic times but whose importance had faded much over the years.

Now one inauspicious day the seer Durvāsā went to the river Jambū to meditate. He saw the supreme Śakti on the riverbank. Keeping his senses controlled (was the goddess nude?) he recited her bīja 'Hrīṁ' and this pleased the goddess. She approached the seer and gave him a garland of jasmine, so sweet that numerous bees hovered around the blossoms. In his bliss, the seer put the garland on his head and went to visit Dakṣa. 'What a marvellous garland this is' said Dakṣa. 'Would you like to have it?' replied Durvāsā, who was too generous for his own good. 'Everything in the three worlds may be given to a devotee of Śakti'. 'I will accept it gladly' said Dakṣa. He took the blossom and put it on the pillow of his bed. That night, the jasmine smelled so sweetly that the old god could not sleep. Desire kept him awake, heat and longing. He rolled around on his couch, sleep evaded him, and finally he arose and had intercourse. Soon, Dakṣa's wife gave birth to a daughter. The gods all showered blossoms from the skies, the sun shone brightly, and the rivers began to flow again. The girl was named Satī, she was of the nature of the supreme Brahman and truth herself.

Satī grew up and soon she was old enough to wed Śiva. The very thought made Dakṣa mad. He did not want to give up his daughter, he did not want the incarnate goddess to leave his house, and least of all did he want her married to a god who walked nude, smoked dope, and practised austerities on mountains and in jungles where no sane person would ever wish to dwell. Śiva the impure, the skull-carrier, the mad dancer at the edge of reality. Dakṣa hated Śiva, he hated the thought that his daughter would leave him, but essentially he could do nothing against it. So, in spite of much angry debate, Śiva was invited to Dakṣa's court. There, the ash-smeared god of ascetics married beautiful Satī, then the two left and made their home on the highest mountains. Some say that their lovemaking took another 100,000 years.

One day, Satī learned that her father was giving a great feast. All the gods were invited, the Gandharvas would sing, the Apsarases would dance, and there would be drinking, joy, and merrymaking. Every important deity was invited, except for Śiva and herself. Now, Satī was not at all happy about being left out. She was still angry that her father had made such an issue out of her marriage, and angrier yet that he was slighting her husband and herself. 'I shall go to that feast,' Satī declared, 'whether we are invited or not!'

'Is it worth it?' replied Śiva, who felt much happier in the jungle than in High Society.

'Why don't we just stay home and have a nice time?'

'We shall go!' shouted Satī, 'and if you won't come I'll go there on my own! I'll show my father just what I think of him!'

'You'll get into trouble' predicted Śiva, 'with your temper, there is bound to be trouble for all concerned.'

'I will go' Satī declared, 'whether you like it or not.'

And so it happened. It was a bad day indeed, when Satī came to her father's house, her face red with rage. Dakṣa had been expecting something like this. When he heard that his daughter had come, he refused to greet and honour her. It turned out to be a fatal mistake.

In her rage, Satī transformed into Kālī. She cursed her father, the feast, and the offerings, and burned herself in yogīc fire. She closed the nine gates of her body, her mind turned into fire, her body collapsed and her spirit, liberated, soared elsewhere. Then Śiva arrived on the scene. Seeing his wife dead, a flood of rage surged through him, manifesting demons, vampires, and evil spirits. Screeching with glee they came over the hallowed ground. See Śiva on the rampage! The guests scream as the offerings are ruined, burned, trampled, obliterated, defiled, and demons dance between the dishes. With one blow, Śiva decapitated the father of his bride. He took the head of a sacrificial goat and stuck it on Dakṣa's neck, so that to this day, Dakṣa is obliged to look like the goat he really was. Then the sacrifice was destroyed, destroyed utterly, and nothing remained as it was. And Śiva lifted the body of his wife. Carrying her corpse, he stumbled from the site of havoc and devastation, and returned into the solitude of the mountains.

Great evil befell the world. Like one who is mindless, speechless, and mad, Śiva walked in loneliness, the dead limbs of his mate on his shoulders. Between the frozen pinnacles of the highest mountains, along the ice-crusted rims of the greatest rivers, and in the darkness of the mountain forest, between pine and spruce and rhododendron. Wherever he walked, his tears fell, and yet he found no place to rest the body of his wife.

Soon the gods became worried. With Śiva gone, what would happen to them all? Gods have obligations, they have to listen to the prayers of their worshippers, they have to receive sacrifices and grant luck and success to those whose karman is ripe. They have to support the order of the world, and keep the demonic Asuras under control. Viṣṇu by himself was not up to the job, and Brahmā could offer little help. So the gods approached Śiva and asked him to leave the body of his wife. Alas, Śiva was so overcome by grief that he could not understand. He did not want to see that his wife was dead and rotting, he did not care about his worshippers, about the cosmic order nor did he listen to the Devas.

So the gods made a cunning plan. As Śiva walked every day, the carcass of Satī on his back, Viṣṇu sat in ambush. Whenever the god of the dance was overcome by tears, Viṣṇu hurled his cakra. The discus swept through the air faster than a speeding arrow, faster than a ray of light, and cut a limb from Satī's corpse. So Śiva walked, but every day his load became lighter. Day after day he made his circuit through India, and every day a limb of the goddess fell and was forgotten. The face of Satī fell at Kāśī, the yoni at Kāmarūpa, each part of the goddess became a place, a site of worship, a seat of power, and a place of pilgrimage where intelligence manifests. Eventually, Śiva's step became firm and his gaze cleared again. He saw the wide land of India beneath his feet, the majestic snow mountains in the north, the ochre deserts to the west, the jungles and swamps in the east and the sparkling blue ocean to the south, where islands lie like emeralds and whales sport in the waves. Śiva stopped and considered. The spell had broken, Satī was gone, but everywhere in the land, sacred places had appeared. Wherever a limb of Satī had fallen, a pīṭha was inviting pilgrims, locals, and ascetics to worship the goddess who had become all of India. It is said that 108 sacred seats were born of the limbs of Satī, but to those who have eyes to see, the goddess extends all over the land. Satī, far from being dead, had become the fullness of the world.

Eternities passed. Dynasties began and ended, great kingdoms arose and were forgotten again, Asuras and Devas fought, and life continued much as ever. Śiva, well used to loneliness, often went into the great mountains to enjoy the cold, fresh air, the sparkling diamond beauty of the snowfields and the gentle growth of swaying birches in heights where few men walk. Here, in the land of musk deer, mountain goat, and snow leopard, the god of ascetics found his peace of mind. Whenever he could, Śiva went to his beloved heights to forget the world and himself. Now the Himalayas have a king, the lord of the mountains, Himavat. He is the ruler of the heights and the generous giver of waters. From his court, the great rivers run, rivers that offer life and nourishment to the dwellers of the plains. And Himavat had a daughter. Her name was Pārvatī, She of the Mountains, and unlike most gods and goddesses, she enjoyed long walks through lonely mountain valleys and peaks. One day Pārvatī chanced upon Śiva. The lord of ascetics sat on a tiger skin, nude apart from the beads and serpents wrapped around his throat and arms, his half closed eyes unseeing and empty with the wisdom of the void. Pārvatī saw Śiva and felt her mind come apart. Long, long ago, she had been Gaurī, then Satī, and the memory of that life burst into her mind like the avalanches sweeping down the slopes in summer. Shyly, she approached Śiva, and spoke to him. Śiva, however, was way out of his mind and did not hear her. Pārvatī spoke again, she came closer, she touched the ascetic, and still she could not break his trance. Like a pillar of stone, Śiva remained unmoved, inattentive, with the far-away expression of a being who has turned inwards. Pārvatī, however, would not give up. She sent a call, a prayer to Kāma, the god of lust, love, and desire, the ancient being who had brought forth creation. Kāma appeared instantly and laughed. Here sat the lord of ascetics, in total oblivion for the fate ordained by karman. What a target! This was just the sort of fun that Kāma craved. Swiftly he lifted his bow of flowers. He aimed the arrows of the senses. He muttered a mantra and shot.

At this instant, Śiva awoke. His third eye of absolute reality opened, the eye that destroys ignorance, delusion, and glamour. The fire of truth incinerated bow and arrows. His gaze touched Kāma, and Kāma said 'Ouch!' and disintegrated. Like a fine shower of ashes, the god of desire and lust fell to the ground and was no more.

Then Śiva saw Satī, and as their eyes met, remembrance returned. They saw, and in that timeless moment, the world held its breath. Then the other gods appeared. Gods are usually curious, and when something unusual happens, they like to be around, if only for laughs. The sight of Śiva and Pārvatī embracing, yes, that was good news. But what was this? What was this miserable pile of ashes on the ground? The gods saw, and tears began to seep from their eyes. Here were the ashes of desire, of lust and love. Gone was the god whose never-ending charm had kept the universe in motion. Rati, his wife, came to her senses first. 'You killed him!' she shouted at Śiva.

'Sorry, I did not see who he was' replied the god of ascetics 'it was just an accident...'

'Well, go and resurrect him, then!' replied Rati, and so did the other gods, who were mightily scared of a dull, boring world without desire and lust. Śiva shrugged. Focusing his glance on the pile of ashes, he allowed illusion to return to the world. And Kāma arose, reborn out of the ashes of disenchantment and the gaze of the all-seeing one. From Śiva's ojas, Kāma was reborn, vibrant with life and glad to embrace the worlds again. And Kāma laughed. Of all the gods, he knew best what was to come. Śiva looked at Pārvatī, and Pārvatī at Śiva, their eyes met and desire arose between them. When the gods left, the two were still embracing. They had eternity to unite.

Note for the curious. This tale is at the core of Tantric myth. It appears in numerous versions. In this simplified version, I have blended elements from several sources, the major one being *Devī Bhāgavatam* (7, 29-31). Before you go on, read the story once again. Then tell yourself the story a few times, until it becomes a lively and vivid experience. This is a useful trance practice. Make the story vivid, add detail and put emotion into it. As you make the tale come to life, you may find that it works a magick on your mind. This is a story of initiation and you can make it yours.

2: Before Tantra

Let me invite you to a journey through time. It is also a journey through the simplified fiction that people term history, and a journey through the possibilities in belief and religious behaviour. Few countries offer such a rich field of religious development as ancient India does. Now you may be well acquainted with this topic, have read the *Vedas*, know the principal *Upaniṣads* and have a good basic knowledge of the literature of early Hinduism. If this is not the case, a little background info may help. The following chapter offers a simplified map of religious developments in ancient India before the middle of the first millenium CE when the first pieces of Tantric literature were composed. Now, Tantra did not appear from a vacuum. It did not drop from the skies ready made. Every innovator, no matter how independently minded, relies on what earlier innovators discovered. Innovation can mean creative new invention. It can mean adaptation, new interpretation, and combination with novel ingredients, and generally it involves a lot of syncretism and daring originality. There were hundreds of Tantric schools (if I may use this misleading expression) in history, most of them extinct nowadays, and each of them began when some people decided to improve matters. Even those who reject a tradition find themselves reacting to it. The history of magic and religion is not only a history of traditions but also of creative new innovation. When you plough through the next pages you will encounter the bare materials out of which Tantra was woven. You will also find the philosophies that the Tantrics did not subscribe to, for one reason or another, and emerge with a wider vision of the human quest to contact and unite with the divine. For all scholarly readers I should add that the next pages offer only a brief synopsis. I had to leave out a lot of fascinating material and to simplify the complex: in short, there are lots of half-facts and misrepresentations around. To make up for these obvious defects, let me ask you to do your own research. Generalisations are lies, and when we have to condense several thousand years of highly complex activities in a few short pages, the unique, the unusual and most exceptions to the rules tend to be overlooked. There are exceptions, keep this in mind - Indian religion is full of them. Consider this chapter an attempt at model making. Also, I cannot give sources for every little detail. In general, I have made much use of Glasenapp (1958), Gonda (1960), and Franz (1991). Unless otherwise indicated, quotations from the *Ṛg Veda (ṚV)* are in Griffith's translation, quotations from the *Atharva Veda* in Whitney's rendering. The *Upaniṣads* are quoted in Radhakrishnan's translation.

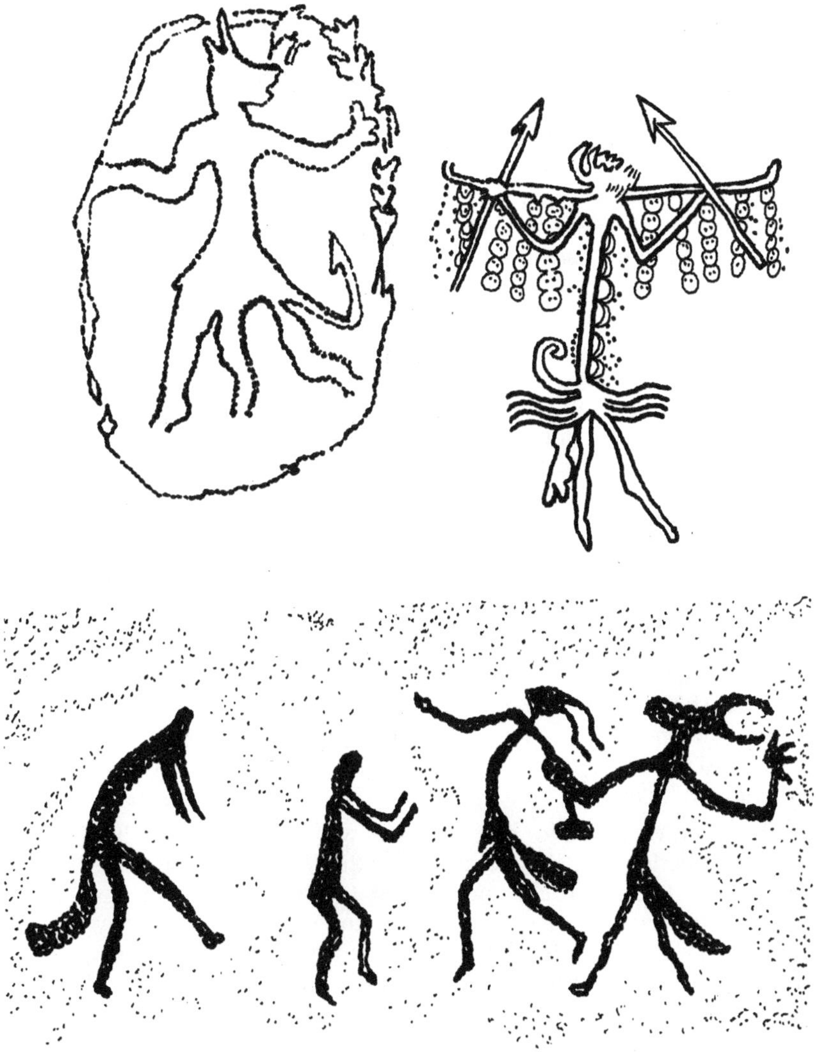

Figure 3 - Mesolithic Rock Art.
Top right and left: Two figures from Pachmarhi, Madhya Pradesh. The left figure is an animal-human dancer, perhaps a shapeshifting sorcerer, the one on the right carries an amazing contraption of skulls, and wears an animal hide loincloth, perhaps an early ancestor of skull bearing deities.
Bottom: Ritual or dance with shapeshifters, Bhimbetka, Madhya Pradesh.
After Mode and Chandra.

The Indus Valley

When the ruins of the great cities of the Indus valley culture (otherwise called Harappa culture) were discovered, they led to a creative reinterpretation of history. The long-held belief that the Aryan invaders were the first high culture of India had to be abandoned. In the Indus valley, and considerable distances beyond, a number of great cities were unearthed, each of them built of sun-dried or burned brick, and with a systematic layout of long, straight streets and buildings. These cities seemed too perfect to be the result of a local development. Consequently, their origin was suspected elsewhere. This elsewhere turned out to be Mesopotamia. The Mesopotamic Obed and Halaf cultures expanded eastwards during the sixth and fifth millennium BCE, a migration that covered most of Iran and southern Turkmenistan and reached the Indus around the fourth millennium BCE. These migrants had a well-developed agriculture and a good idea how to build settlements and towns. They did so in many places, and always used a fairly similar architecture and technology. Consequently, the scholars of the early twentieth century proposed that the Indus culture, for all its original developments, was an upshot of a Mesopotamian migration. This theory was strengthened by evidence for lively trade with Sumeria. Goods from the Indus valley were transported to modern Dilmun and then to Mesopotamia. The Sumerians mention this trade in their accounts (c. 2500 BCE), and called the Indus valley the land Meluhha. There are even finely carved Sumerian roll-seals showing ambassadors from Meluhha. Along the trade route, a number of weights, ornaments, and characteristic pottery turned up. The Indus people had excellent technical skills and produced a considerable amount of jewellery for the Mesopotamian market. They worked in gold and copper, but also in seashells, lapis lazuli, agate, and carnelian, which they cut, polished, and ornamented by etching.

However, evidence for elder cultures was also unearthed. In Mergarh some pioneering folk joined the Neolithic revolution around the 7th millennium BCE and became farmers. At the same time we have evidence for settlements made of brick, the cultivation of barley (wheat came later), and the first, extremely crude, human figurines made of unburned clay. These figures usually show sitting humans, but they are so unsophisticated that neither gender, social status, nor personal dress can be discerned. Some of them hardly look human at all. At this stage people still depended on hunting and the domestic animals looked much like their wild forms. Over the next millennium, cattle breeding became the foundation of society. So the Indus culture is nowadays considered a blend of Mesopotamian immigrants and native farmers, which explains both the similarity to many Near-Eastern cultures and the unique character of the culture. As usually, it pays to look into recent research. The first excavations focused on the famous cities Harappa and Mohenjo Daro, and produced the impression that these were the main cities of a culture that was well organised, developed, standardised and utterly boring. Several authorities proposed that the Indus valley

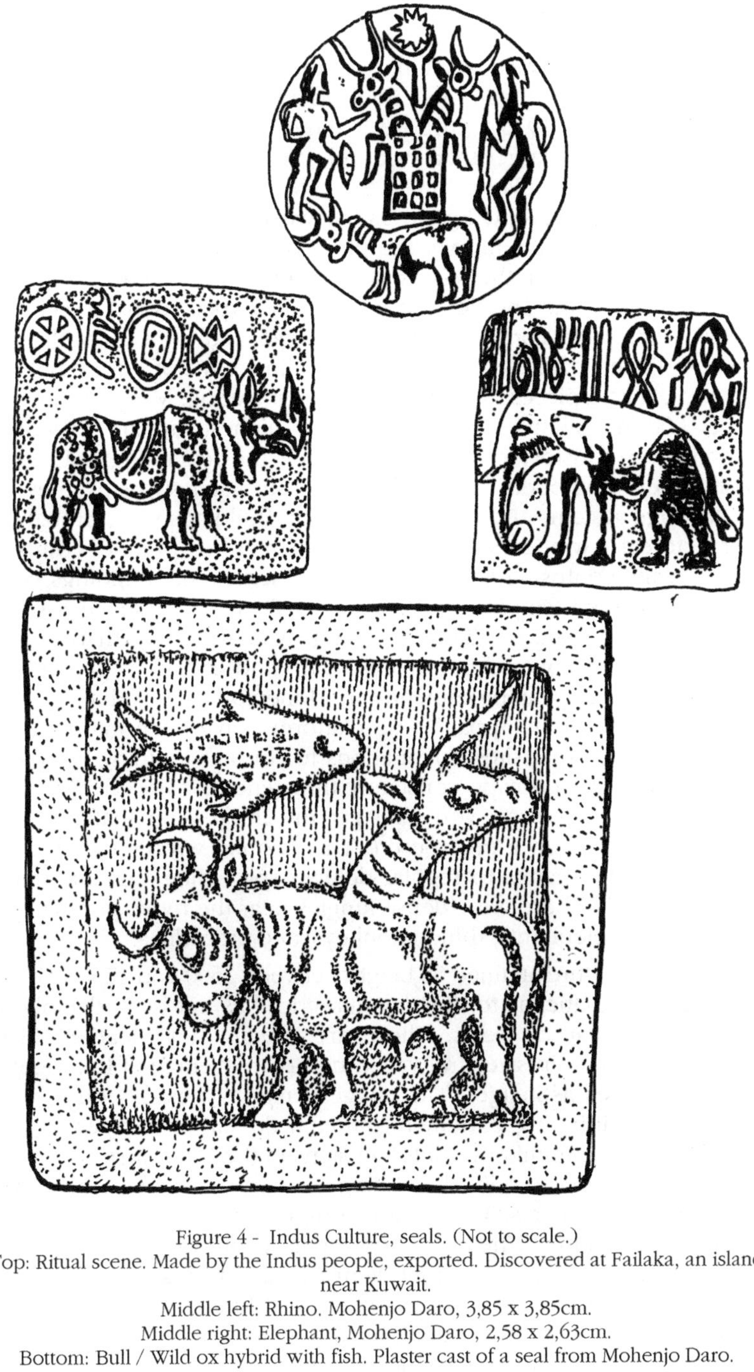

Figure 4 - Indus Culture, seals. (Not to scale.)
Top: Ritual scene. Made by the Indus people, exported. Discovered at Failaka, an island near Kuwait.
Middle left: Rhino. Mohenjo Daro, 3,85 x 3,85cm.
Middle right: Elephant, Mohenjo Daro, 2,58 x 2,63cm.
Bottom: Bull / Wild ox hybrid with fish. Plaster cast of a seal from Mohenjo Daro.

underwent great periods of stagnation in art and craft. Recent excavations have shown that the Indus culture is geographically larger than was ever suspected, and that there were a lot of unique local developments beyond the Indus valley. Very similar cities have been discovered in north-east Afghanistan, on the shores of river Oxus, between Pakistan and Iran, and north of Bombay. Estimates based on excavations in the 1970's propose a terrain of at least half a million square miles, this is larger than Pakistan. It is also larger, geographically and in terms of population, than the other two high cultures of the period, Mesopotamia and Egypt. Sadly, we have no idea whether the Indus culture extended all over the place or if it remained isolated in a number of cities. When there is a distance of up to a thousand kilometres between one city and another, it can hardly be expected that the city folk exerted a complete control over every farmer and nomad dwelling in-between. To this day, the cities form the main source of our knowledge. They were masterpieces of planning and engineering. Many of them had over 50,000 inhabitants. They also had the highest sanitary standard in the entire early history of the Near-East. Of the remaining houses, the majority were equipped with wells or a fresh water supplies, they also had drainage systems and often a bathroom. Buildings were probably in several storeys - windows did not face the street but an inner courtyard. What is really confusing is the lack of representational buildings. There are no palaces or temples in these cities. There is evidence for huge baths and public spaces. Baths (i.e. large water-tanks with no certain purpose) were discovered in Mohenjo-Daro and Lothal. Huge platforms made of bricks appear prominently in Mohenjo-Daro, Lothal, Chanhu-Daro, Kot Diji, and Harappa. These platforms have been interpreted as meeting spaces, ritual sites, foundations for further building, and as an artificial rise in a landscape constantly threatened by floods. When you look at modern pictures, you may get the impression that the Indus valley people lived in a near desert. This is quite wrong: the land was extremely fertile, thanks to regular deluges, providing vast amounts of fresh, fertile soil. There were dense jungles near the rivers populated by bovines, tigers, elephants, rhino, monkeys, and crocodiles.

The Indus culture attained its height between 2500 and 1750 BCE. It is still highly enigmatic, as to this day, its script has not been deciphered. Most texts appear on seals. These are usually tiny steatite objects, between 17-30 mm in size, and you can find an average of five signs on each seal, as well as images. This suggests names, possibly titles, which makes the deciphering extremely difficult. So far, the experts cannot even agree on the number of different signs in the Indus script, estimates range between 200 to 450, depending on how you count them. Most seals also show animals. The great favourite is a bull, shown in profile, with only one horn. Whether it represents a unicorn is unclear. It is usually shown near a mysterious item identified as a flag, a stand, a feeding-trough, and as a device to crush and filter Soma, believe what you will. Cattle, such as the aurochs and zebu, appear on many seals, also water buffalo, antelope, rhino, and tiger. A lot rarer are images of elephant and crocodile. There are several fantastic beasts, such as three-headed bulls, tigers with horns, antelopes with elephant trunks and humans with the heads of tigers. Human images are the rarest of the lot. They show people, but can we be sure it is people, and not demi-gods (such as the hero holding two tigers in a classical Sumerian design) or even deities? What shall we make of the human sitting on a tree, faced by a prowling tiger underneath? Who identified with such a picture and made it a personal seal? This leads to one of the riddles of the Indus culture: just what did these people believe in? So far, the evidence is extremely sparse. No temples, churches, shrines, or altars have been discovered. The Indus folk may have worshipped at home, or on the spacious platforms, they may have had ritual baths or sacred fires, but so far, none of this can be proved. There are no stelae or large statues of gods or humans. Only seven stone statuettes have been discovered so far; they are small and look as if they were copied from Sumerian originals. They are somewhat damaged and show kneeling men. This left the excavators with two possible sources to reconstruct religious activity. One of them is the clay figurines which have been produced, in some places, since the beginning of the Neolithic. These figurines include a large amount of women. In the early twentieth century, the scientific mainstream was still fascinated by the idea of matriarchy, and consequently, they were taken as evidence for the worship of female goddesses. Some even imagined a single great goddess. Whenever scholars came upon feminine images they were sure to propose matriarchy before starting to think. Recent researchers have become a lot more cautious. Let's take a closer look at those statuettes. Nowadays we are happy to have an idea about the different periods that produced statuettes, at least in some places.

Here is a brief synopsis by C. Jarrige, 1987, 95, in *Vergessene Städte am Indus.* The first and second periods in Mehrgarh provide the primitive images mentioned earlier; they roughly resemble sitting human beings, legs joined and extended, no arms, face, or details worth mentioning. Some show slight bulges symbolising belts or necklaces, a few are coloured with red ochre. At the same time, red ochre appears in funerals. In period 3, the human figurines disappear completely. They are replaced by clay images of bulls, some of them lovingly ornamented. Period 4, c. 4000 BCE, provides a revival of human figurines and a technical break-through: the figurines are made of separate parts. Here we have female images with bulging breasts and some attempts to show hair and clothing, mind you, they are still crude and do not look very venerable. In period 5, a new quality of clay allowed the artists to make finer figurines and to burn them at higher temperatures. There are first attempts to show arms and mask-like faces, and the hairdo becomes extremely elaborate. This process of technical refinement goes on for a while. Then in period 7 a few of the females seem to hold infants (usually blobs of clay with a face). At the same time male statuettes appear. They have a different posture and detailed genitals. This is unusual. In the female statuettes, the breasts were usually elaborated but the genitals were never detailed. Several sorts of male haircuts, such as knots and braids can be observed.

At the end of this period a new male type with a round, bald head appears, and then things become standardised. The last period of settlement in Mehrgarh provides mass-produced statuettes in large amounts, most of them very uniform and carelessly executed. Were these items objects of worship? Most figurines are crude, cheap, and fragile. Few would have survived daily handling or transport. Some female statuettes look more like budgerigars than human beings, let alone goddesses. Also, they are often broken, damaged, and occasionally burned. A lot of them did not come up in prestigious places but were discovered in rubbish pits. Statuettes, no matter whether 'Venus figures' of the Palaeolithic or clay figures from Cretan tombs, cannot always be assumed to be objects of worship. Egyptian pharaohs had images of people in their tombs as they wanted to be served by them in the otherworld. Early Chinese rulers had themselves buried with their favourite slaves, in later times statues became a cheaper substitute. Cretans had crude clay figures in their graves. These figures were not gods, they were not worshipped in daily life. Early studies on Crete over-represented the female images and proposed that they all represented some single Great Goddess. A visit to a Cretan museum will soon reveal that there were lots of male as well as female statuettes, most of them looking pretty shabby, and this is not enough evidence to reconstruct a religion. In ancient Sumeria, it used to be fashionable that better placed people had images of themselves made in clay or stone. These images (often crude and by no means supposed to show a likeness) were set up in temples and shrines. As the image represented the worshipper, the worshipper was (theoretically) worshipping at all times in the temple, even when haggling in the market place or lazing in bed dead drunk. Other cultures have statuettes to represent absent or deceased members of the family. As you can see, there can be lots of reasons to make statuettes. The ones from the Indus valley are often crude and plain, and if they were really supposed to represent gods, those gods clearly did not amount to much. So the fable of a matriarchal Indus valley worshipping one Great Goddess was dismantled. The possibility remains, but the evidence is too slim.

Then there are the steatite seals. As you'll remember, most of these have images of animals. A small number show human figures. Unlike the other great civilisations of the orient, such images are rare and have little to do with daily life. The Sumerians loved to show social events, such as court-life, work, feasting, travelling; the Indus people avoided such topics. Their human images may be people but they could also be deities. Some figures have elaborate crowns, some of them wear horns. It has been claimed that these are deities, however, the horned folk are sometimes shown worshipping trees and plants. Were the cults of the period dedicated to vegetation? Worship of fantastic trees and plants appears on several seals, and occasionally there are figures standing between the trees and receiving veneration. You might propose that the Yakṣas, the tree and plant spirits of later Hindu mythology originate in this period. It might even be true.

There are also images appearing to be gods, some of them three-headed, sitting cross-legged between animals. These have often been claimed to be early representations of the much later god Śiva, who has the title Paśupati: Lord of Domestic Animals. The animals surrounding the figure are not always domesticated, so maybe we are dealing with Śiva's ancestor Rudra, who is indeed a lord of the wild places and their beasts. However, it is hard to tell whether the figure is male or female, as all clear indications of gender are missing. This leaves us as perplexed as ever. The female images are not necessarily the (or a) Great Goddess. The sitting god is not necessarily Śiva/Rudra. How inconvenient for all those enthusiasts who took them as evidence for a 'Tantric' religion in the Indus culture.

In plain reality, we know so little about the dwellers of those cities that any attempt to define their religion amounts to speculation. And did the cities share a common religion? When you consider the enormous distances between some cities, original development is almost inevitable. The cities in the eastern part of the culture (Rājasthān, Haryana, and Guyarāt) had fewer figurines than the western ones. Were they less religious? And while it's hard to guess about the city dwellers, it is much worse among the villagers and country folk, who had neither seals nor figurines.

And how did the Indus valley civilisation end? In older studies, you can find plenty of speculation on how the violent Aryans with their well-trained warriors and their horse-driven chariots destroyed the Indus valley folk. Archaeologically, there is no evidence for such warfare, let alone the terrifying massacres imagined by some scholars. It turns out that the Indus civilisation ended four or five centuries before the Aryan migrants appeared. The great ancient metropolises were not plundered or destroyed. People left them, taking along a good many items that modern archaeologists would have been happy to find. This caused some scholarly problems. Why were the great cities abandoned? So far, there is little agreement on this topic. It seems that several influences were responsible for the decline. One was tectonic activity in the Himalayas, causing earthquakes and the drying of important rivers (Ghaggar and Hakra). There seem to have been extreme irregularities in rainfall, and some cities near the Indus may have been flooded and buried under tons of mud. In other locations, the river may have moved away from the settlements. Whatever the reasons may have been, they did not stop people from living in the country. While the vast cities were abandoned, a number of flourishing new villages and towns were founded. These soon said goodbye to their past. Gone was the age of standardised bricks, measures, and weights; each settlement developed individual ones. Gone was the time of seals, statuettes, and literacy. When the Aryans arrived, they encountered an illiterate farmer's culture showing little evidence of the sophistication of the past.

Figure 5 - Proto-yantras in rock-art
Mostly prehistoric (or hard to date).
Top left and middle left: Diagrams, Chambal valley, India.
Top right: Labyrinth, Tikla, Madhya Pradesh.
Middle right: Square diagrams, Kharwai, Raisen, Madhya Pradesh.
Bottom left: Mesolithic images including bulls, hunters, peacock, hand, fish (?) and yoni triangle. Bhimbetka, Madhya pradesh.
Bottom right: Bull heads, Chambal valley, Central India.

Figure 6 - Indus Culture, seals.
Top: One of several deities with three heads, Mohenjo Daro, 2,65 x 2,7cm.
Bottom: 'Unicorn' and strange device, Mohenjo Daro.

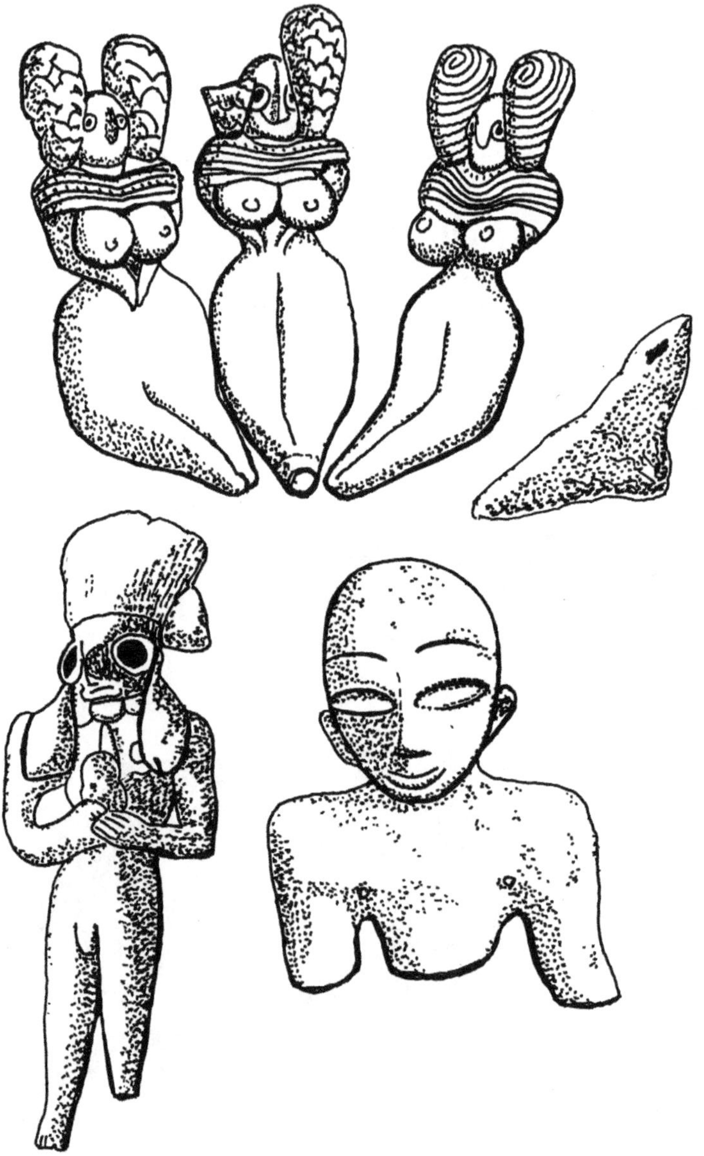

Figure 7 - Indus Culture. Figurines from Mehrgarh.
Top: Three developed female figures with characteristic headdress, abstract faces, huge breasts and no genitals. 3300 - 3000 BCE, clay, found in a rubbish pit.
Top right: The first stage of human figurines. No face, limbs or details whatsoever. If it were not for the later female figurines, we wouldn't recognise this piece of clay as a figurine at all. At this stage the item looks hardly human, let alone like a deity.
Bottom left: Male figurine, 2700 - 2600 BCE.
Bottom right: Male figurine of the bald-headed type. 2800 - 2700 BCE. At the time, male figurines amount to 30%.

The Vedic Period

Sometime between 1500 BCE and 1200 BCE, migrating tribes of Indo-European speaking nomads began to invade India. These dates are rough estimates - the chronology is far from satisfactory. The invaders called themselves Ārya (Noble Ones) and they spoke languages that share a common origin with most European tongues. Where their migration had begun is still much disputed, but we can be moderately sure that they entered India from the west, through the passes of the Suleiman Mountains, and through the Hindukush into the fertile Panjab. Their migration was not very fast. The Aryans were mainly into cattle breeding, but they paused once in a while to cultivate land. Their long journey may have taken generations. Travel transforms and shapes culture. When whole tribes are on the move for years and years, they adapt to conditions by cultivating a light sort of culture that needs less material equipment than a stationary one. The Aryans came travelling in horse and cattle drawn chariots and wagons, and the amount they could own and move was limited by their means of transport. As a result, archaeology finds little evidence for their progress. A typical sort of pottery was unearthed on several locations (usually hilltop settlements), dull stuff with grey designs, not much to teach us about the values and beliefs of an entire people. Luckily, the Aryans had a highly developed religion (or several), a wealth of poetry, and the will-power needed to memorise and pass on long texts. Here we come to the *Vedas*, our major source of information regarding the ages of conquest.

Veda, meaning sacred wisdom and lore, is a religion (or several) that was imported into India by the Aryan people. We are happy to have a few references to the conquest in the *Ṛg Veda.* A few hymns mention battles against dark skinned and flat nosed locals, the Dasyus, who are derided as worshippers of liṅgas. The word liṅga can refer to a phallus or a phallic image. It can also mean 'image' in general, so we cannot be sure just what those locals worshipped. According to the Aryans, the Dasyus had no proper religion and no real sacrifices. That they had sacrifices is implied, but they were by no means as refined and complicated as the sacrifices of the Aryans. The Dasyus occasionally lived in fortified settlements, which is why the Aryan god Indra, here called Purandara (Destroyer of Cities and Castles) was called upon to crush them. 'Cities and castles' is a bit too grand: at the time, fortified means rough wooden palisades. Stone fortifications appear at a much later date. In battle, the local armies used four-wheeled war chariots drawn by oxen. This did not help much against the Aryan warriors, who used two wheeled, horse drawn chariots, wore heavy armour, and began to make iron weapons around 1200 BCE. The Aryan warriors used their swift and mobile chariots to get close to the enemies, whom they showered with arrows. In the early period, and among those who could not afford much, the arrow-tips were made of deer-horn. Whoever could afford it made use of bronze, later iron. Often enough, the arrows were poisoned (*ṚV* 6, 75). Much later, the *Laws of Manu* prohibited poisoned missiles, but during the invasion, they were liberally used and praised. Soon there were Aryan settlements on hills and mountains. What remains a riddle is the nature of the locals. It was assumed that the Dasyus were a Dravidic people, hence related to the modern population groups of southern India, but this point is not easy to prove. So how did the Aryans get along with the aboriginal population? In some places, such as the Panjab, they almost completely expelled the locals. They could afford to do so as they were in the majority and had enough people to control and cultivate the land.

As the conquest continued, fewer and fewer Aryans were available to work the conquered territory. In these districts the locals were valuable as a work force. Aryan society was still half-nomadic then. There were minor kings who owned large herds of cattle. Wealth was counted in cattle and cattle raids were one of the priorities of warfare. Society was ordered into two classes: the kṣatra, or warrior nobility, and the viś, the free members of each tribe. A few centuries later, when Aryans conquered the Ganges plain and the Dekkan, they were not numerous enough for complete occupation. The locals remained where they were, ruled by a small upper class of Aryans. To promote separation, the Aryan nobility gradually evolved a class system. They also had a lot of wars and cattle-raids among each other. *Ṛg Veda* 7, 33 mentions a battle between ten Aryan kings, good evidence that the invaders were not very friendly to their own kin. It might have been the very battle celebrated in the much later *Mahābhārata*. But how exactly did the conquest happen? Early historians imagined a single wave of war-crazed Aryans sweeping through India. These scholars were used to thinking in terms of nations and empires, they imagined large populations on the move, and this implied large wars and devastation. As archaeology could not give evidence for such a wave of destruction, the theory was gradually toned down. The next theory proposed that the invading Aryans were not a single horde but several independent tribes entering India over a span of several centuries. Better but not good enough. A gradual conquest also leaves traces of violent destruction, and so far, such evidence is not very conclusive. Possibly some of these conquerors settled in uncultivated locations or co-existed with their local neighbours in relative peace. Mybe we ough to wait a century or two until archaeology has really made some progress. Until then, the *Vedas* remain the major body of evidence. Now the *Vedas* contain a lot of lore that is excellently suited to a war-loving, mobile culture. If we assume that the invading Aryans adhered to the *Vedas*, a violent invasion is the likeliest alternative. But did all Aryan tribes subscribe to the *Vedas*? We have no way of knowing whether the conquered population cared much for the Aryan faiths, nor do we know whether all immigrating Aryans did so. It is possible that much of Vedic lore was originally restricted to a minority of Aryan people, while natives and other Aryans worshipped in different ways. Recent research indicates that the *Vedas* are not, as has been proposed so often, a purely Aryan body of writing. There are native Indian elements in them.

Here I would like to mention another common fable. Plenty of authors pretend that we are dealing with a conflict of small, dark Indian aborigines and tall, fair-skinned, aggressive European Aryans. This picture is so simple that it hurts. Were all of the locals dark and flat-nosed or is it just a few we are lucky to know about? Did all the Aryans come from a single source? We have a good idea what some of the Aryans believed in, but what was the religion of the locals? If you trust some popular writers, any item of Indian religion that cannot be found in the Vedas is automatically a product of the local population. In recent years, a good many writers have proposed that Tantra is not a phenomena of the middle of the first millennium CE but goes back to earliest prehistory, mainly because they would like to have it so. Many new age books propose that the Great Goddess happens to be pre-Aryan. The same goes for the cakra concepts, the idea of reincarnation, even the Kuṇḍalinī is thought to predate the Vedic period. The proof for this? Such concepts do not appear in Vedic literature. This is a moot point. For one thing, the Vedas are a conglomerate of hymns, beliefs, myths, rituals, and spells that are far from homogenous. Even the earliest texts contradict themselves and others, and if there is a consensus, it derives from the editors and copyists who have kept these works in circulation for more than two thousand years. There was no script in the Vedic period, writing in India started during the third century BCE under emperor Aśoka, who made the brāhmī script popular (modern devanāgarī developed out of brāhmī). Up to that point, the Vedas, the Upaniṣads and all other texts were faithfully memorised, and we can only guess the age of a given item by estimating how archaic the language is. Thus, what we call Veda is not all of the original material. Next, consider the so called natives. At the present time, anthropology and genetic analysis come to the same conclusion as the analysis of the pre-Aryan languages: the 'natives' of India were of European origin (Wilhelm in Franz 1991: 36). The earliest settlers we know of are the Weddids, the north Indian Gondids and the middle Indian mountain dwelling Malids. All were of European origin. Next followed the Dravids, another culture of European origin. It seems that we are dealing with a conflict between several parties who were of European ancestry. The main difference between them is the date of their arrival in sunny India. But can we be sure about this? How many unknown people lived in or near India over the millenniums?

Seers on Soma

Vedic religion was shaped by drugs. The early seers celebrated a deity called Soma who was identified with the moon and with a powerful intoxicating drink. Soma, they chanted, is the tawny bull of heaven, the steer, the eagle in the sky. *On flows the potent juice, sustainer of the heavens, the strength of Gods, whom men must hail with shouts of joy.* (*ṚV* 9, 76, 1). Soma gave blessings and abundance, fertility to cattle, success in war, riches for the nobles, and gladness to the seers. The gods themselves feasted on Soma, who was their source and joy: *Soma, thundering, hath produced the Gods* (*ṚV* 9, 42, 4). Ingestion of Soma formed a vital part of the greater sacrifices and influenced the minds of those who 'saw' the proper rituals and 'heard' the true chants and sound vibrations. Indeed, Soma made the seers. The god was called Pavamāna, the Self-Purifying, and his sweet, ambrosial juice amṝta, 'death-less' (undying), the elixir of life. A good many of the early rites were received (or invented) by seers who were, we might imagine, spaced out of their minds. When we want to understand this sacrament, we encounter difficulties. The seers composed a large number of hymns to celebrate Soma, the *Ṛg Veda* contains roughly 120 of them, most of them in the 9th book, which is almost exclusively dedicated to the deity. Only Indra and Agni have more hymns, the majority of Vedic deities have to make do with half a dozen hymns or less. Soma constantly comes up when Indra the Thunderer is lauded, evidently, the rites were celebrated with his blessings. The Soma rites were the most important sacrifices of the entire Vedic period. In Soma we encounter the first panacea, the first elixir of immortality of Indian lore. This idea survived long after the secret of Soma was forgotten. Now the seers were quite aware that, no matter how much Soma they consumed, their bodies did eventually grow old and die. In Vedic lore, as in later traditions, 'immortality' is a general idea meaning 'great age', the preferred optimum being a hundred years. The only real immortality that Soma could guarantee was an immortality of consciousness, which left the body at death and departed to Indra's heaven for an eternity of joy and revelry. Reincarnation wasn't invented (or discovered) yet.

Things become complicated when we wish to work out what sort of plant Soma was and how it was prepared. The soma rites incorporated a wide range of ritual activities. They were not performed frequently, and the use of the drug was restricted to the Brahmins who performed the ceremonies. Not even the kings and nobles, the only people able to afford proper sacrifices, were permitted to taste Soma. Instead, they were offered a substitute. Each Soma ritual began with the preparation of the drug. This was an immensely complicated affair requiring days, sometimes weeks of preliminaries. Even the pressing of the Soma sap took two to twelve days of continuous ceremony, followed by another twelve days of sacrifices. Animals were slaughtered almost continuously and each stage of the rite was accompanied by the singing and recitation of hymns. The Soma rites were all-round ceremonies involving a wide range of ritual activities. They exalted the sacrificer (the noble who paid for the event) to almost divine status and provided blessings for the entire community. The greater rites involved numerous acts of dedication, purification, elaborate baths, oracles, preparations of ritual space, dances, a symbolic fight between an Aryan and a dark Śūdra, ritual arguing between a scholar and a prostitute, public coitus performed by a native couple, shooting arrows to ward off evil influences, song, music, and any amount of feasting. The priests had a strict hierarchy and there was an elaborate ritual schedule that had to be followed perfectly. Each hymn had a specific form of recitation and was divided into segments that required specific metric forms, intonation, and singers of a specific rank. Here we encounter the first bījas (seed-syllables) and 'holy words', such as Oṁ and Huṁ, useful for general purposes, and specific terms such as Hīs, to invoke rain, and Ūrj to ask for food or power. As the Soma rites are amazingly complex I can't even offer a crude outline. It would take several hundred pages to give all the references and to sum up the procedure. For a readably brief account, see *Die Religionen Indiens I* by Jan Gonda (1960: 149-162). The Soma hymns are full of riddles. We read that Soma was pressed by ten sisters clothed in gold. In plain reality, the ten sisters were the ten fingers, each of them wearing a golden ring. Such metaphors are all too common. Over the last century, many scholars have argued what sort of plant Soma may have been. Soma was born on mountains and hills. It was gathered, ritually 'bought' - the seller being ritually beaten up in the process - and driven to the ritual space on a chariot, celebrated like a king. The stalks were crushed between boards or in a mortar, pressed between sacred stones, the sap was filtered in a sieve, poured into water and strained through a woollen cloth. It was mixed with the milk and curds of several sorts of cows and consumed according to elaborate regulations. Most hymns insist that the pure juice, as it comes flowing through the sieve is brown, hence the need to pay for it (symbolically) with a brown cow. Other hymns call it tawny, yellow, gold, occasionally red and sometimes green. Soma was brilliant, clear, radiant, foamed, and tasted sweet.

One plant that may have been Soma is the fly agaric (*Amanita muscaria*), as mushroom pioneer R. Gordon Wasson proposed in 1962. Fly agarics are highly hallucinogenic when prepared properly. The mushroom has to be heated before ingestion, be it by drying in strong sunlight, over a fire, or by cooking, to transform the ibotenic acid, a slightly psychoactive but very disagreeable substance, into the five times more psychoactive muscimol. Raw fly agaric is well known to induce stomach cramps, nausea, vomiting, diarrhoea, and other unpleasant experiences, and can even be fatal (Stafford 1977, R. Schultes and A. Hofmannn 1979, Alberts and Mullen 2000). In Siberia, people on fly agaric used to collect their urine as it contained almost all of the psychoactive substances ingested earlier. Some fly agaric was recycled up to six times while losing little of its potency. There is a reference to urine-drinking in the *Ṛgveda*. The heating is strangely absent in the *Ṛg Veda*. There is just one hymn, 9, 46, 4 stating *Deft-handed men, run hither, seize the brilliant juices blent with meal, and cook with milk the gladdening draught.* What speaks against the identification of Soma with fly agaric are the varied colours of the sap, which suggest that we are not talking about any single plant or fungus, and the frequent statement that Soma tastes sweet. For more than a century, scholars have been searching for 'the' Soma plant. More than a hundred psychoactive plants have been proposed. One candidate, wild rue (*Peganum harmala*), may have been the old Persian wonder drug Haoma, a word that is related to the term Soma. Wild rue is mildly hallucinogenic, increases the effects of other drugs but produces unpleasant side effects such as vomiting, nausea and, in overdoses, paralysis of the central nervous system. The plant is usually burned as an incense, not digested, this continues to this day among the Parsian Hunza people. Other drugs that may or may not have been Soma are given by Christian Rätsch (1988), who suggests that

Soma may have been a general term for a group of psychoactive plants. Which could explain the contradictions in the hymns. That plant lore was highly developed can be seen in the *Atharva Veda*, a work that attributes the most amazing powers of healing and sorcery to a wide range of plants. Some of them were venerated much like deities. The Soma rites eventually lost importance. Wasson proposed that this happened as the Aryan tribes moved further from the cold mountain forests of the Himalayas, where fly agaric grows in the company of birch, spruce, and pine. I doubt this. The conquest of India started with the warm and flat riverlands of the Panjab. Settling in this country, seers made Soma, and proceeded to do so for several centuries while they moved across India. In the late Vedic period, the sacrifices became smaller and cheaper, and when we enter the Upaniṣadic period, around 700 BCE, the importance of drugged exhilaration had greatly declined. Instead, we observe an increase in the methods that were to become early yoga. The seers of the *Upaniṣads* cared little for sacrifices, drugs, and ritual and began to seek the divine by fasting, tapas, breathing exercises, isolation, and various forms of meditation.

Vedic Religion

Now for a brief look at the spiritual culture of the *Vedas*. As the topic is enormously complex, I shall have to restrict myself to a few generalisations, hoping not to offend too many scholars. There are basically four collections of ancient writing called *Vedas*. A *Veda* is a store of knowledge. It is also a faith and a way of life. The *Vedas* were not really written or composed, they were 'seen' by the early ṛṣi, the seers. The earliest is the *Ṛg Veda*, which was assembled between c. 1200-900 BCE. It is a collection of 1028 hymns to a wide range of deities. Some of these hymns are so old that we may wonder whether they predate the invasion of India. They are an invaluable source on early religion and mythology and offer glimpses of a culture that was just beginning to develop a common philosophy. In this period, there were no churches, no temples, and the idea of reincarnation had not been developed. Next the *Sāmaveda saṁhitā*, the Veda of songs and ways of singing was compiled. It consists of hymns from the *ṚV* plus a small amount of new material on sacrificial routines. In the *Yajurveda* you can find a compilation of sacrificial hymns and ritual, plus dedications, spells, mantras, and ritual riddles. The fourth is the *Atharvaveda (AV)*, a younger work, which is primarily concerned with the role of the house-priest. It blends elder hymns from the *ṚV* with new ideas and some really archaic items. Much of it is concerned with magic, spell craft, enchantment, plant lore, and all sorts of rituals to control the world. Unlike the first three, the *AV* was never universally accepted. It is an invaluable work for anyone interested in practical spell-work, invocation, dramatic exorcism, ritual cosmology, herb-lore, and hypnotic suggestion. Also, much of it constitutes brilliant poetry.

The main thing about religion of the early Vedic period is the role of the priest and the sacrifice. Spiritual power came from the word, song, and sound-vibration of the *Vedas*, and in a sense, the *Vedas* were thought a greater power than the gods.

At this stage there was already a wide range of deities. You can find them listed in numerous books on Indian religion, but when you enjoy the original hymns (please do so) you will discover that it is far from easy to give an adequate summary of them. Already at the earliest period, gods appear in several guises, and occasionally merge into each other. Attributes, symbols, functions, and appearances can be exchanged. This shows that the *Vedas* were by no means a homogenous system: consider them as an agglomeration of beliefs of various tribes of Aryans with additional material from the locals. Also, new gods were being made up all the time. The Brahmins were fond of turning any special power, event, or quality into a deity. Every human trait, every natural force, and everything unusual could be venerated and personified as a god or goddess. This is sound thinking: if it is strong, it must be divine. The result was a world full of major and minor deities.

Let's take a look at the major deities. The *Ṛg Veda*, with its 1028 hymns, contains roughly 250 hymns for Indra (and Indra-Varuṇa) and 206 hymns for Agni (plus 11 for Agni-Indra). These deities are the most popular of the lot. Place three in the charts is Soma with roughly 120 hymns, nearly all of them in the 9th book. If the ninth book had not survived, we would hardly be aware of his importance. In fourth place, around ninety hymns are addressed to several gods at once. Place five is held by the horse riding Aśvins (54 hymns), place six by the tempestuous, howling Maruts (37 hymns), seven is Mitra-Varuṇa (27 hymns), eight is Uṣas, Dawn in her rosy splendour (21 hymns), nine is Bṛhaspati, the priest and guru of the gods (14 hymns) and the rest celebrates a range of minor deities, some of whom became the most important gods of Hinduism later on, plus diverse subjects, such as cows, frogs, horses, weapons, pressing stones, ritual equipment, heaven and earth, and creation.

Usually, each book of the *Ṛg Veda* starts with luminous, flickering, all-devouring **Agni**. Agni is often considered a fire god, but this is misleading, unless you understand the dominant role of the sacrificial fire. Vedic religion was not a matter of churches, temples, or cults. Families employed priests, and priests performed the sacrifices. To sacrifice was the main religious practice of the period. The sacrifice nourished the gods and maintained divine harmony, the cosmic order (ṛta). There is an enormous body of texts dealing with more sacrifices than you'll ever want to know about. The main thing about these rites is that they had to be perfectly performed. The ethical qualities of the sacrificer were hardly important, compared to the precise performance of each single ritual act. Most sacrifices ended in the ritual fire and it was Agni who conducted them to the gods. In this sense Agni became the divine representative of the priest, a mediator between the human and the divine. As sacrifices were often extremely costly, it was usually the nobility who indulged in them. Through sacrifices, blessings, status, and merits could be gained.

Figure 8 - Buffalo-horned, three-faced deity, surrounded by wild animals. Considered by some to be a prototype of the much later Śiva. Mohenjo Daro, after a plaster cast.

Agni, however, is not merely the sacrificial fire or the household fire (the Lord who is always at Home). Agni also represented the solar fire and this function overlaps with such solar gods as Sūrya and Savitar. Agni also lives in wood (fire is hidden in wood) but things get more confusing as Agni was often associated with water. You find him called the child or bull of water, and when the king was inaugurated he was sprinkled with water while the Agnis of Water were called upon. This mysterious connection disappeared eventually. Similar transformations can be seen with the other gods.

Figure 9 - Agni.

Indra, for example, as a thunderbolt wielding deity of rain and storm was also related to the function of kings, and gave them their royal status. Like a king of the gods, Indra governed in might and splendour and set a shining example for his earthly representatives. Indra's net covered heaven and earth and regulated the spaces of life. He was much concerned with the order of things, battling demons and occasionally punishing evildoers. In this period there were still gods who corrected humans. He was not only a deity of the nobility but also much venerated by farmers, as his thunderstorms gave fertility to the soil.

In Indra's company you sometimes encounter a minor deity called **Viṣṇu**, who later inherited much of Indra's royal function. Today Indra is rarely worshipped, but Viṣṇu, duly transformed, is one of the most popular deities of India.

Soma is an enigmatic deity. As a god, Soma is well defined, but as a plant, or a mixture of plants, much remains to be understood. With Soma, we encounter the first references to an elixir of immortality, the production of which was occasionally likened to coitus. When a few much later Tantric movements relate their elixir of immortality to the moon and lovemaking, they are using metaphors from the earliest Vedic period.

When we look at **Varuṇa**, we encounter an all-encompassing deity closely related to the concept of divine space. Some called him a sky god, but this is only possible when we disregard a lot of his attributes. Varuṇa is a god who measured the universe, ordered its spaces, set up the mountains, regulated the rivers and so on. In one sense, Varuṇa is ever present, in another, the god disappears behind the sheer vastness of the world. He is also a god concerned with right and wrong who punishes sinners and criminals. In Vedic thought, Varuṇa came from the divine family of the **Asuras**, just like Agni, Soma, the sky deity, Uṣas, Rudra, Sarasvatī, and the Ādityas. Modern Hinduism made **Devas** (Shining Ones, i.e. gods) out of them, and turned the Asuras into a pack of dangerous demons. In the process, Varuṇa became a god of the oceans and the great deep. He is related to the Greek god Uranus. Such connections between Indo-European deities are still obvious in the early Vedic period. The Vedic wind and storm-god Vāta, who still plays a minor role in the *ṚV*, is closely related to the Germanic Wodan, Wods, Odin, Gwodan, and possibly the British Gwydyon. The Vedic Mitra has some overlap with the Persian Mithra, who influenced the famous solar Mithras, popular all over central Europe courtesy of the Roman legions. Perhaps Agni is related to the Nordic god of fire, cunning Loki, certainly both of them are associated with goats. Indra's battles against the world-compressing demon-serpent Vṛta have their counterparts in Thor's fights against the Midgardworm and in the Avestic dragon slayer Thrita. Maybe the (originally) divine family of the Asuras has some connection to the Nordic gods, the Aesir.

The *Vedas* also invoke a number of goddesses. We know most about **Uṣas**, the goddess of the red morning sky, who is related to beginnings of all sorts, and who is reborn every morning, hence, there are any amount of Uṣas, and every day a new one appears. *ṚV* 1,92 offers a brilliant description of the goddess. Uṣas is a warrior-lady who arises in splendour and radiance. She anoints herself with sunlight, spreads her web of brightness, and sings as she comes out of the dark on her ruddy, cow-drawn chariot. Uncovering her breasts, she gives light to the world. The hymn celebrates her as a giver of food, a fulfiller of ambition, and the mainspring of blessings, victory, and glory. She also has a negative side, as she makes people age and die. With every new Uṣas, life becomes shorter. She gives all beings the chance to use the day, but she is also compared to a gambler who wastes life away. Her sister, briefly mentioned in *ṚV* 10,127 is **Ūrmyā,** the goddess Night. She is briefly invoked in a single hymn to give protection from thieves and wolves. The *Atharva Veda* contains more hymns for her.

Nirṛti, black goddess of destruction and doom was widely known and feared, there are lots of texts mentioning her briefly. Her name implies the negation of ṛta, the cosmic order. Like most dangerous deities, the Aryan priests did not celebrate but placate her, and asked that she stayed far away. More on her in the chapter on Kālī.

The *ṚV* already knows a few **Mothers**, such as a Mother of the Sky, a Mother of Cattle and a forest goddess, **Aranyānī**, who is called The Mother of Game. None is described in much detail. It would be wrong to conclude that the Aryans in general did not care much about goddesses. We simply know that the compilers of the *Vedas* did not devote much time to them. In plain fact, the *ṚV* is so obsessed with lauding Indra, Agni, and Soma that little room remains for other gods.

Another obscure goddess is **Pṛthivī** (Earth) whose mate is **Dyaus**, the personified sky. The union of the two features in an early creation myth. In *ṚV* 1,160, sky and earth are two sisters, but as they are also male and female, they become the parents of the sun. The hymn invokes them to grant the sacrificer, probably a king, supremacy over the people.

A famous goddess is **Aditi**, who is related to creation, nourishment, and occasionally appears as a primeval cow. *Aditi is the heaven, Aditi is mid-air, Aditi is the Mother and the Sire and the Son. Aditi is all Gods, Aditi five-classed men, Aditi all that hath been born and shall be born.* (*ṚV* 1, 91) She may be related to the Nordic Audhumla, a goddess in cow shape who appears right at the beginning of creation, before the gods and humans come to be.

Then there are lunar goddesses, such as **Rākā**, who rules the full moon, **Sinīvalī**, who eases childbirth, and **Kuhū**, goddess of the new moon.

The *ṚV* also gives the first evidence for the goddess **Sarasvatī,** originally the river goddess of the most sacred stream of early Vedic times. In the early days this river may have been the Indus. When the Aryans began to move further east, they identified Sarasvatī with another river. *Inciter of all pleasant songs, inspirer of all gracious thought, Sarasvatī accept our rite! Sarasvatī, the mighty flood, She with her light illuminates, She brightens every pious thought.* (*ṚV* 1,3). River Sarasvatī has long since disappeared, though legend says that it is flowing underground. Sarasvatī was a giver of victory and blessings, a healer and a patroness of poetry and hymns. She mixed with another deity, **Vāc**, who is the personification of voice and speech. Their union produced the highly popular modern Sarasvatī, patroness of learning, song, poetry, and the muse of many writers.

Another prominent goddess is called **Śrī**, a term meaning well-being, good fortune, wealth, abundance. She merged with the late Vedic goddess **Lakṣmī** (for whom see the later chapter on the Mahā Vidyās). As Śrī Lakṣmī she is the most popular goddess of modern India.

The *ṚV* also has goddesses who are the female expression of male gods. *Spouses of Heroes, Goddesses, with whole wings may they come to us, with great protection and with aid. Indrānī, Varuṇānī, and Agnāyī hither I invite, for weal, to drink the Soma juice.* (*ṚV* 1,22, 12-13). This idea was the foundation of the later concept of Śakti. We are at the beginning of a tradition here that allows the gods to change into the other sex.

Last, let us take a look at the outcast among the gods, the dangerous **Rudra**. Rudra received less veneration than most gods. Only three hymns of the *ṚV* are entirely dedicated to him. He is a terrifying red god, a deadly archer and 'the Tawny Boar of Heaven', who is constantly asked to be kind and compassionate. His hymns do not invoke, they placate. The original Rudra is a dweller of the solitude and the wild places, a lonely wanderer, he is a lord of wild beasts, poisons, and diseases. An expert in herbal lore, he is also the healer of the gods. He is the creator, protector, and killer of cattle. With his bow, he takes the lives of beasts and men.

As father of the **Maruts**, Rudra is accompanied by storms and gales. The Maruts (winds) are usually Indra's warriors, but their parents are Rudra and Pṛśṇi, the colourful cow of earth. The Maruts are celebrated as workers of marvels, bards, heroes, and protectors of the divine order. They move over earth like the howling storm gales, splitting mountains, shaking forests, and releasing storm, lightning, thunder, and rain. They are the patrons of poets and singers. Their common wife is **Rodasī** (Firmament), who appears elsewhere as a wife of Rudra. Occasionally the Maruts are addressed as Rudras, i.e. as personifications of Rudra.

In the later Vedic period, we meet Rudra clad in fur, dwelling among desolate mountains, with green hair, a red face, and a blue-black throat. He is called upon by hunters and folks who have to dare the forest and by herders fearing for the health of their cattle. His sons Bhava and Śarva roam the jungles in the form of wolves. Much like the Germanic storm god Wodan, Rudra appears in a wild hunt, and is accompanied by a horde of dangerous women who are noisy and hissing, snatchers and devourers of flesh (Gonda). One of his names is Hara, meaning the Bandit, the Destroyer. Later he acquired the placating name **Śiva** (the Auspicious One), and today he is almost exclusively known by this title. As you can see, much of the Tantric Śiva is already evident in the Rudra of the *Vedas.* As an expert in poisons and diseases, Rudra became the patron of healers. He is a god of the wilderness, an eater of raw flesh, a drinker of blood, and a lord of all terrible spirits. *ṚV* 10, 136, 7 gives the

Figure 10 - Rudra the archer.

first reference to his close association with hermits, ascetics and ecstatic folk living in the wilderness. In later periods, he sometimes appears as a group, the Rudras, who were invoked in specific places. Each location has a spirit, a genius loci, and each of them is a Rudra. Thus, there was a Rudra of the cremation place, a Rudra of the crossroads, of the wind, of a river, and even a Rudra of the dung-heap. Some of this reappears in the much later Tantras.

Spiritual Discipline

The *Vedas* also provide the first glimpses at what later became Yoga and Tantra. Welcome to the concept of māyā. This word has come to mean illusion, but it can also mean creative skill. The gods use māyā for their miraculous deeds. Demons acquire māyā by austerities. Seers wield māyā when they are pure enough, and make the gods tremble. Māyā can mean magickal power, the power to create, transform, and destroy. All of this is slightly confusing, as the word māyā is a combined term that connects two streams of meaning. One of them connects with talent, knowledge, and the ability to craft and create something. The other relates to deception, glamour, lies, and illusions. As the two word streams combined, māyā became a power of creativity and deception, the magic wielded by a range of gods, demons, and seers. It was also personified and eventually became a goddess, red Māyā, creatrix of worlds, enchantress and deceiver. This māyā is a power that can be cultivated. It can be gained and used, by gods and humans, in a process that often involves tapas.

Tapas originally meant inner heat. It can also mean practices that generate heat, hence magical power, or it can be a general term referring to all sorts of austerities, such as starvation, exposure to the elements, or standing on one leg for a millennium. Tapas is used (or done) by humans who wish to cultivate special skills and powers, but it can also be performed by demons or gods. Each important event in Hindu mythology involves a measure of tapas. To become the creator (well, one of them), Brahmā had to perform austerities. When Pārvatī courted Śiva, the later was not much impressed by her. So Pārvatī performed tapas and practised spiritual exercises till the stability of the cosmos was threatened. Śiva immediately fell in love with her. Similar events abound in Hindu mythology. There are lots of tales where gods or demons do tapas to gain supernatural powers. Soma is generated by tapas, the dead gain the light by tapas (*ṚV* 10,154,2), the seers find insight and vision through tapas. In later periods, tapas became a collective term for a good many difficult and painful activities. We are at the roots of yoga here. It might be proposed that a lot of yoga consists of refined techniques of tapas, eliminating the totally painful and harmful ones.

Closely related to the meaning of 'inner heat' is the practise of shaking. The term vip-, source of our word 'vibration', means to tremble, shake, shiver, quiver, or be stirred. Vipra is to be stirred, shaken, excited, it can also mean one who is a sage, seer, ecstatic, poet, priest, or simply inspired. It can also mean the moon. In ritual, a vipra is one who uses shaking and trembling as a means of trance-induction. A vipra can be a human worshipper, a seer, priest, or forest-dwelling lunatic, but it can also be a deity busy gaining tapas. Several gods, such as Indra, the Aśvins, the Maruts (*shakers of the earth and heaven* (*ṚV* 1, 37, 6), Rudra, the sun god Savitar (the *deep quivering Asura, ṚV* 1, 35,7) and of course restless, flickering Agni are described as vipras. A vipra may 'win', may call the gods, may function as a healer, an exorcist, and a seer (Gonda 1960: 184). These trances do not appear often in Vedic literature, but they continue to our day in folk worship. Obsessed women and men still shake and tremble in their divine ecstasy and some Tantras mention tremors and shuddering during cakra visualisation or when a jolt of divine grace takes you out of your mind. Trembling is part of the worship of many fierce goddesses. For those who still have not learned trance shaking: yes, folks, it works, it's fun and a lovely way to spend an evening. You can find a practical introduction to shaking trances and how to induce and enjoy them in *Seidways.*

Apart from this we find hints on breathing exercises in the *AV*, 15,15-17. Seven breaths are named in these hymns: *AV* 15, 15: *Seven breaths, seven expirations (apāna), seven outbreathings.* 1. Fire, 2. Sun, 3. Moon, 4. Cleansing, 5. Yoni (vulva), 6. Cattle, 7. the Creatures. *AV* 15, 16 has: 1. Full moon, 2. Moon's quarter, 3. New moon, 4. Faith, 5. Consecration, 6. Sacrifice, 7. Sacrificial gifts. *AV* 15, 17 offers the following expirations: 1. Earth, 2. Atmosphere, 3. Sky, 4. Constellations, 5. Seasons, 6. They of the Seasons (?), 7. Year. What can you develop out of this? Systematic breathing exercise is hinted at in *AV* 6, 41, 1-2: *To mind, to thought, to device, to design, and to intention, to opinion, to instruction, to sight, would we pay worship with oblation. To expiration, to perspiration, to breath the much nourishing, to Sarasvatī the wide extending, would we pay worship with oblation.* While there are several sorts of breaths in Vedic literature (and not all of them are related to breathing), the idea that proper breathing increases life is already expressed. *AV* 3, 11, 5-6 is a spell to banish disease and to recover health. First, the sufferer is freed from the lap of Nirṛti (Perdition, Doom), then, life is won for him for a hundred autumns: *Enter in, O breath-and-expiration, as two draft-oxen a pen; let the other deaths go away, which they call the remaining hundred. Be ye just there, O breath-and-expiration; go ye not away from here; carry his body, his limbs, unto old age again.*

Then we have early yoga, such as sitting or standing still for long periods (*AV* 15, 3, 1: *He stood a year erect; the gods said to him: Vrātya, why now standest thou?*) and silence (*ṚV* 7, 103, 1: *They who lay quiet for a year, the Brāhmans who fulfil their vows*) to cultivate skills and magical power. And we have hymns that indicate that seers become the equals or superior to the gods: *AV* 6, 58, 3: *Glorious was Indra, glorious was Agni, glorious was Soma born; of all existence am I most glorious.*

AV 6, 86 exalts some (unknown) person: *Chief of Indra, chief of heaven, chief of earth is this man, chief of all existence; do thou be sole chief. The ocean is master of the streams; Agni is controller of the earth; the moon is master of the asterisms; do thou be sole chief. Universal ruler art thou of Asuras, summit of human beings; part-sharer of the gods art thou; do thou be sole chief.*

In *AV* 5,11, 10-11 the seer Atharvan sings: O*f us two, O Varuṇa, (there is) the same connection, the same birth. I know that which is of us two this same birth; I give that which I have not given thee; I am thy suitable companion of seven steps; - a god, bestower of vigour on a singing god; a sage (vipra), of good wisdom for a praising sage.*

And we have the first references to an identification of the body with the universe: *AV* 5, 9, 7: *The sun my eye, wind my breath, atmosphere my soul (ātman), earth my body; unequalled by name am I here; (as) such I deposit myself for heaven and earth to guard.*

What else did the ascetics do? The following hymn, *ṚV* 10,136, is the fullest account of an ecstatic in early Indian literature.

> *1. Long-hair holds fire, holds the drug, holds sky and earth.*
> *Long-hair reveals everything, so that everyone can see the sun.*
> *Long-hair declares the light.*
> *2. These ascetics, swathed in wind, put dirty red rags on.*
> *When gods enter them, they ride with the rush of the wind.*
> *3. 'Crazy with asceticism, we have mounted the wind.*
> *Our bodies are all you mere mortals can see'.*
> *4. He sails through the air, looking down on all shapes below.*
> *The ascetic is friend to this god and that god, devoted to what is well done.*
> *5. The stallion of the wind, friend of gales, lashed on by gods - the ascetic*
> *lives in the two seas, on the east and on the west.*
> *6. He moves with the motion of heavenly girls and youths, of wild beasts.*
> *Long-hair reading their minds, is their sweet, their most exciting friend.*
> *7. The wind has churned it up; Kunaṁnamā prepared it for him. Long-hair*
> *drinks from the cup, sharing the drug with Rudra.*
> (Doniger O'Flaherty, 1981: 137).

This hymn is not only remarkable for its contents. Each of the verses is associated with one of the Seven Ṛṣis, the seven stars of the Great Bear or Wain (Ursa major), one of the holiest constellations of ancient India. According to Griffith, it is also a charm to restore a sick man to life. Here we have the earliest association of shaking trances with journeys in the imagination and the manifestation of gods near or in the body. The wind in this poem is not only air in motion, it is also a term to describe the ecstatic rush of energy and excitement that accompanies shaking trances and obsession. It should be noted that our vipra is not merely a worshipper but a friend of the gods, the Apsarases and the Gandharvas .

Figure 11 - Early yogīs.
Top, stone statuette, Madhya Pradesh, 13th century, 17,5cm. If you look like this, you might be overdoing it.
Bottom: Stone statuette, yogī using a sash for prolonged trancing. Tamil Nadu, 16th century.

This is worth considering. In Hinduism, the Apsarases are a class of heavenly nymphs who dwell in Indra's heaven. Occasionally they visit earth to tempt a seer or to marry a king or hero. Gandharvas are heavenly youths and celestial musicians. In Vedic times, both were a lot more sinister. The *Atharva Veda* contains several spells and hymns to exorcise them. In *AV* 4, 37 the Apsarases are banished into a stream while the Gandharvas are castrated by Indra's missiles. Both are told to remain among themselves, married to each other, and to leave humans well alone. *AV* 4,38 gives a spell that can be used to evoke an Apsaras who promotes gambling: *She who delights in the dice, bringing pain and anger - the rejoicing, the delighting one: that Apsaras I call on here.* In *AV* 8, 6 we learn that the Gandharvas are devourers of infants and slayers of embryos. The situation is ambiguous. In some hymns of the *AV*, the Apsarases and Gandharvas are celebrated and praised as divine beings, in others they appear as demons, haunters of humans, bringers of disease. What sort of friendship did our long-haired seer cultivate with them?

We also have a reference to an unspecified drug our shaking ecstatic received from a goddess called Kunaṁnamā. Her name may mean witch or, more precisely, hunchback. There is an entire Tantric tradition devoted to a goddess called Kubjikā, the Curved, Crooked, or Coiled One. Maybe Kunaṁnamā is her prototype. What sort of drink did our seer share with Rudra? It probably wasn't Soma, as Rudra was excluded from the Soma sacrifices. Spirituality in Vedic times was not only conducted by serious-minded sacrificial priests but also by crazy ascetics dwelling happily at the fringes of society.

The World Soul

In the early Vedic period we encounter the first roots of a phenomenon that was to become one of the essentials of Indian thought. There were always a lot of deities around, both among the Aryans and the local populations, but this was not to everyone's satisfaction. Some seers sought for a unifying principle. Here we encounter Prajāpati, Puruṣa and, a little later, the ātman concept (Gonda 1960, 180-198). Prajāpati began as a god of creation. The *Ṛg Veda* offers several differing accounts of creation, without much enthusiasm, as in the early Vedic period creation myths did not matter much. The main issue was proper conduct during sacrifice. Prajāpati starts as a god who is associated with creation, fertitlity, and the genitals. He is called the Lord of Descendants and All Creatures and is called upon to grant children. This was a bit too simple, so other seers elaborated on the theme. We enter the time of the *Brāhmaṇas* here, which celebrate him almost as the highest deity. In the before-the-beginning, Prajāpati was bodiless consciousness. It felt lonely and desired (kāma) to become many. This makes the god Kāma one of the earliest deities in evidence. It is, first of all, Desire who motivates creation. Prajāpati assumed form and created the world out of himself by speech. Naming things made them be. This job was possible thanks to the goddess Vāc/Vāk (Voice, speech), who is his mate and Śakti. Well, this is just one of the variations that can be found in our early sources. The tale of Prajāpati was retold and transformed numerous times. Usually Prajāpati is creator by making things appear out of himself. These emanations include sun, moon, stars, earth, the primal oceans, the gods, Asuras, humans, the Brahmins, and even the rituals and metric forms. The order of the seasons, the times of the day, the whole ritual year are the body of Prajāpati. Like all great artists, Prajāpati does not only create, he also does tapas to gain power and suffers great fits of exhaustion after creation. He 'saw' the Soma sacrifice and performed it, thereby creating it. Afterwards he felt exhausted. So he saw the sautrāmaṇī rite, which restored him to health again. Prajāpati does not get everything right from the start. He occasionally makes mistakes. The first creatures he made out of himself devoured each other. I should add that the activity of Prajāpati is not something vague and obscure happening at the beginning of time. In Indian thought, creation is never finished. Every new thing that appears is creation at work. And Prajāpati is the sacrificer and the sacrifice. One myth tells us that his head became heaven, his feet earth and his chest the atmosphere. As in real life, creation and its creator are never completely separate.

Prajāpati, however, was not the only candidate for being an all-encompassing deity. Here's a figure with a similar function: Puruṣa. This deity is a close relation of the primal giant Ymir whom you can find in the *Eddas*, the primal being Pan Gu and the creatrix Nü Wa of early Chinese myth, and a few similar Eurasian proto-deities. We are on the track of something really old. Puruṣa is usually a huge giant who is sometimes simply called 'the man'. 'Man' sounds human but isn't. *ṚV* 10.90 tells us that Puruṣa extended all through the earth. It had a thousand eyes, heads, and feet. It was all that has been and all that was to be. The gods laid out Puruṣa as the primal sacrifice. They dismembered the primal unity and created the seasons out of it. Its fat became the animals of forest, air, and village. Its body became the poetic metres, the verses and chants. The moon was made out of mind, the sun out of the eye, the wind out of living breath, while the mouth brought forth Indra and Agni. The head became the sky, the navel the middle realm, the feet turned into earth, the ears divided the quarters of space. The limbs were separated to create the varṇas (classes) of society. Good evidence that we are dealing with a fairly late hymn: in the earliest Vedic period, the classes are still unknown. The Brāhmaṇa (priests, teachers, scholars) were created out of the mouth, they recite the sacred texts and maintain a tradition of learning and ritual. The arms became the Kṣatriya (warriors, aristocracy), whose duty is to fight, to protect, and to govern. The thighs became the Vaiṣya (farmers, merchants, traders, money-lenders), i.e. those who produce food and distribute it. The feet became the Śūdra (craftspeople, servants, artisans, menial labourers, hired hands), who are literally at the bottom of the social system. Everybody else, such as foreigners, tribal people, aborigines, and those handling unclean substances do not even appear in this model. Puruṣa, though cut up and divided, did not die. *Gods, sacrificing, sacrificed the victim: these were the earliest holy ordinances* (*ṚV*, 10, 90, 16). Puruṣa became the origin, but also the wholeness of the Vedic world. The spirit of Puruṣa was the all-pervading sentience, the body, the substance of all that exists.

This is not the only creation myth of the *ṚV*, there are others, who attribute everything to a golden embryo (10, 121), to cosmic heat (10, 190), to an All-Maker (10, 81-82), and to the cosmic cow Aditi: *In the first age of the gods, existence was born from non-existence. After this, the quarters of the sky were born from her who crouched with legs spread.* (10, 72, 3, trans. Doniger O'Flaherty). Aditi brought forth Dakṣa, Dakṣa brought forth Aditi, who brought forth eight sons, and the gods made the worlds swell.

A third concept is ātman. Originally, the ātman is the self-principle, the consciousness behind the senses and the mind. In the *ṚV*, the word means breath, vitality, life. Ātman resides in all living beings but disappears into the winds upon death. Later periods transformed this simple concept. In the *Upaniṣads* the ātman becomes an undying, eternal 'soul'. It is the essence behind all consciousness but it dwells in the primal voidness of deep, dreamless sleep. Call it the subtle essence of all that lives and breathes. Before long, the *Upaniṣads* equipped every being with the essential quality of ātman. It is only a small step to the concept of ātman as the world-soul and the all-consciousness. The *Bṛhad-āraṇyaka Upaniṣad* identifies ātman with Brahman and proposes that to behold ātman is to unite with it.

Puruṣa and Prajāpati are not very well defined, as their primary function is to produce everything else. This role was developed in the *Brāhmaṇas*, but by the time of the early *Upaniṣads* (c. 8th century BCE) they fade. In their place arose the concept of Brahman as an all-self, a world-soul, and a nameless, formless, all inclusive consciousness, source of the gods, the demons, humans, beasts, plants, and the elements. This concept has remained popular to this day and is one of the essentials of Hindu philosophy. It is precisely as all beings take their awareness from Brahman that gods and humans can become one another, beings change their shape and awareness and the attainment of cosmic consciousness is possible. Of course these ideas were developed over the centuries. Puruṣa was not completely forgotten but became a metaphor for spirit and consciousness; in some Tantras you can find Śiva or even Viśṇu called the Puruṣa, occasionally the term simply means 'the self'. Brahman was personified by some and turned into a deity called Brahmā. As the earlier Brahman remained such an important concept, it was not replaced by the personified Brahmā. Indeed, Brahmā always appears as a relatively minor god. He is associated with the act of creation but receives fairly little veneration. Even this function is not his proper right. You find Brahmā saying 'But I am the creator!' and Viṣṇu replies 'Sure, and I made you'. Once, when Brahmā boasted too much, Śiva cut off one of his heads with a swipe of his fingernail. This was not very polite and Śiva had to make up for the deed, but still, Brahmā lost a head and never got it back again. Obviously, if you personify the un-personifiable, a lot must be lost.

Classes of Society

The class-concept is one of the most restrictive inventions of the late Vedic period. You are probably used to the word 'castes'. It's not a useful term. 'Caste' comes from 'casta', a term used by the Portuguese when they attempted to colonise India to designate different ethnic groups. It was later applied to social classes. As you recall, there are basically three upper classes who are entitled to a superior spiritual status. Every boy of these classes receives spiritual education from one or more gurus and is invested with a sacred thread to show that he is twice-born. The lower classes and all women are not entitled to this initiation; they never reach spiritual maturity. The upper three classes are expected to devote some of their time to learning and sacrifice, the lower classes are lucky when they are allowed to listen to a Brahmin. From the beginning, classes were rigidly defined. It was believed that it is better to be a failure in one's class profession than a genius in the profession of another. Knowledge was a monopoly of the Brahmins, who did much to keep it that way. Now the *Vedas* were obviously composed by people belonging to the Brahmin class, who had a strong interest in keeping themselves at the head of society. Brahmins were not only priests but also incarnate deities, or so they taught. To feed a Brahmin is to sacrifice to the gods, hence the importance of dakṣiṇās. A dakṣiṇā is a part of the sacrifice that is not offered to the gods by means of fire but given to the Brahmins. If the offering is food, it is eaten by the officiating priests, who conduct it to the gods. There is an amazing amount of literature extolling the virtues of the dakṣiṇā (see *Devī Bhāgavatam*, 9, 45). A lot of priests insisted that the choice morsels (originally, the minimum was one cow) they personally received were the very part of the sacrifice that is most auspicious and sure to get good results. While the Brahmins were certain that they were the heads of society, the warrior class (Kṣatriya) disagreed. The Kṣatriya were fighters, warriors, and aristocrats, and consequently the wielders of power. Each king came from this class, and kings are not the sort of folk who like to be ordered around by priests. As a result, there was a lot of quarrelling between Brahmins and Kṣatriyas, and it might be proposed that the hostility between these classes became so strong that the entire Vedic world-view was threatened. Perhaps the amazing speculations of the *Upaniṣads* are grounded in a social situation that cast doubt on traditional theology. The hostilities did not end then, of course. They are still alive in modern India.

Figure 12 - Life after Life

Beyond Veda

The early Vedic period, incorporating much lore and ritual that may have been imported by the Aryans, gave way to the later Vedic period, which did much to develop the rituals and sacrifices. Here we can observe a change from imported concepts to beliefs developed in India. Much of what we know about practical worship comes from a class of writings called the *Brāhmaṇas*, most of them composed between the tenth and seventh century BCE. The *Brāhmaṇas* are often commentaries to the *Vedas*, but they also show major new developments. One of these was the class structure discussed in the last section. As this idea came to be generally accepted, it caused considerable friction and unease in society. Another is a wealth of original mythology, much of it based on earlier beliefs. Younger are the *Śrautasūtras*, specifying the do's and don'ts of sacrifice, the *Gṛhyasūtras* on household sacrifices and finally the *Āraṇyakas*, the Forest-books, discussing material deemed too dangerous for village communities. All of these works elaborated and developed Vedic ideas. Gradually, they also came to transform them. This is a matter you should keep in mind when studying Indian thought. Most philosophers shied away from declaring that they had invented anything new. Old stuff is good stuff in Hindu philosophy. So when some seer wished to propose something new, it was politely claimed that this was just a new interpretation of a much older (and usually Vedic) tradition. Several Tantras propose that Śiva gave the *Vedas*, then the *Upaniṣads* (when people were ripe for a new understanding), and eventually the *Tantras*. Of course these texts are in wide disagreement. However, it is not very polite to say so. Old stuff was rarely disagreed with. It was simply laid aside as an elder wisdom and ignored.

With the early *Upaniṣads*, we are entering a new period of Indian thought. In the eighth and seventh centuries BCE, several new philosophies were being defined. These found their first manifestation in the early *Upaniṣads*, namely *Aitareya, Kauṣītakī, Chāndogya, Kena, Taittirīya, Īśa, Kaṭha* and *Bṛhadāraṇyaka*. Next, possibly between the seventh and fifth century BCE, followed *Praśna, Muṇḍaka, Māṇḍūkya, Śvetāśvatara, Maitrī, Subāla, Jābāla, Paiṅgala, Kaivalya*, and *Vajrasūcikā*. There are a lot of other *Upaniṣads*, as the name refers not only to a class of literature but also to a way of thinking. Some *Upaniṣads* were composed only a few hundred years ago. These, the so called '*minor Upaniṣads*' are roughly divided into three groups: Śaiva, Vaiṣṇava, and Śākta. Such concepts did not exist in the time of the early *Upaniṣads*; we can roughly date the minor *Upaniṣads* as beginning in the first century BCE and continuing to the 15th century CE. (Sharma 1972).

Outwardly, the *Vedas* were still the backbone of religious activity, but on a more subtle level, the later commentaries brought about a flourishing growth of innovative interpretations. There were so many changes that I shall restrict myself to a few basic ones. Starting c. 1000 BCE the sacrificial priests began assembling and elaborating creation myths. You have already heard a few of them, there are even a few in the *ṚV*, but the topic was only of minor importance at the time. Now it assumed a greater importance, as more and more minds began to speculate about the nature of the world. In the wake of these speculations we observe the growth of different philosophical schools. There had always been a lot of variation in worship, but now the variation began to engulf the entire world-view. With it we encounter an increase of doubt. Gradually the gods began to lose importance. The rites, developed to extremes of complication, were thought to be so important that the gods, if the sacrifice was well-performed, were obliged to offer their blessings. This is almost an automatic process: proper sacrifice equals predictable results. With this sort of belief a god can be expected to perform just as the priests desire. In consequence, much of the original vitality of the deities began to disappear, while the power and authority of the ritual specialists was ever increasing. This produced tensions between the Brahmins and the warrior-aristocracy. We also observe the increase of 'all-self' concepts, such as Puruśa, ātman, Prajāpati, and finally, Brahman. Here Indian thought left polytheism and began to explore pantheism. With the *Upaniṣads*, Brahman became the most important spiritual concept. This implied a new estimation of the human role in reality. Earlier periods had insisted that cosmic order (ṛta) is upheld by regular and precise sacrifices. Now, the main connection of humans to the divine was the all-soul. As each being is endowed with a self (ātman) it may remember its connection to the all-self, Brahman, and eventually return to it. We are at the roots of the quest for liberation. The early Vedic priests sought to uphold cosmic order, they were not interested in dissolving in an all-self. The priests of the *Upaniṣads* began to see sacrifices as secondary priorities; the object of their quest was freedom from limited human existence by becoming one with the all. In the wake of this enterprise appears a dramatic re-evaluation of the meaning of existence. This appears in two radical new ideas: rebirth and karman.

How rebirth was discovered (or invented) remains one of those riddles. In Vedic times, there were a few otherworlds, some paradises of the gods and some vague hells that people could go to after death. These were not very defined at first, but the *Brāhmaṇas* certainly developed the theme. At some point this began to change. The otherworlds remained, but they became mere points of transition. For example the *Kauṣītaki Brāhmaṇa Upaniṣad*, 1, 2 proposes that after death, souls go to the moon. Those who understand the moon as the door of heaven and know 'how to answer it' may ascend to the higher realms. Those who do not return to earth as rain and find rebirth as animals or humans. Just when the change from afterlife to reincarnation took place is unknown. The *Upaniṣads* were still developing the theme, they had not reached the consensus that appears in early Hinduism. However the idea of rebirth came up, it was certainly useful. In a society which was steadily becoming more rigid some must have worried how to make sense of it all. A firm division into classes is just the thing that strikes some as jolly unfair. Perhaps the idea that things can get better in the next life is a small comfort to those who are down at the bottom. The same may be said about the idea that your present misery is not fated but your own fault. In this sense, reincarnation became a convenient explanation for those who felt unhappy within the class-system. It proved a philosophy that kept people more or less where they were supposed to be. This sort of thinking reduces social unrest and is generally encouraged by the government.

The elder *Upaniṣads* introduced the idea that all doing produces effects. The same goes for not-doing: whatever you happen to do or avoid doing influences the world. As beings go through life, they produce karman. Karman means action, doing, and the results of the deeds. This simple observation had a radical character. In the early Vedic period, human fate was believed to depend on proper ritual, sacrifice, magic spells, and being on good terms with gods and priests. People could do something to avert an evil fate, they could find release from bad luck and past sins by doing the proper rituals. Even a horrible fate after death, the dreaded second death (punarmṛtyu), could be avoided by proper sacrifices. Karman put a stop to this. In the earliest rendering of the karman philosophy, we learn that people are responsible for themselves. What happens after death depends on proper conduct while living. Karman was considered a subtle influence that attaches itself to the individual soul (ātman) during life and influences the next birth. If you are enjoying a good life right now, this is due to the karman you developed in your last lives, as well as your conduct in this. Karman was not only an abstract quality, the law of causality, it also became a moral principle. Good deeds and bad deeds both produce karman, and karman, no matter whether good or bad, implies bondage. This is not quite what modern Hindus, let alone New-Agers or Theosophists, consider karman. In many people's beliefs, karman is like a bank account. Good deeds increase the value of the account, bad deeds reduce it, and when you have collected enough bonus points you may become holy or pop out of existence entirely. The flaw in this social philosophy is distinguishing between good and bad deeds. Good and bad are categories of evaluation, they depend on the individual point of view and have no existence as such. Good deeds do not necessarily have good results, bad deeds and sins are not necessarily harmful for everyone. And just because your intentions are good does not mean that your deeds have good results. *Muṇḍaka Upaniṣad* 1,2,7-11 derides such activities as proper social conduct, doing good deeds, cultivating knowledge, performing rituals, sacrifices, and acquiring merit as useless. Instead it proposes the life of the forest dwelling mendicant as a road to liberation.

In the philosophy of the *Upaniṣads*, the karman idea was just being developed, and our sources are not in agreement with each other. Some saw karman as an abstract principle (the law of causality, if you like) while others made it primarily a moral principle. We even encounter the notion that a father's karman is inherited by the son (*Kauṣītaki Brāhmaṇa Upaniṣad*, 2, 15), but it never really became popular. What is important for the Upaniṣadic period is the idea that all karman, no matter whether good or bad, causes attachment to the world. Liberation from this attachment was possible for those who managed to merge their human self (ātman) in the all-self, Brahman. This notion transformed the entire religious landscape.

All beings produce karman at all times, whether they like it or not, and this includes the gods. If the gods are held in bondage of karman, just as humans are, they are no longer free to wield their divine powers as they used to. This put a stop to the Vedic belief that gods punish evildoers. The all-seeing Varuṇa, the club-throwing Indra, the deities of law and order simply lost their function. If a person did evil, the karman of the deed was just punishment. The gods had nothing to do with it, unless it was their karman to enact a punishment which had been decreed by the karman of the evildoer. Divine rewards were likewise only possible when allowed by karman. In short, with the introduction of karman and rebirth, the gods lost much of their importance. Indeed, some texts, such as the *Bṛhadāraṇyaka Upaniṣad* 1,4,10 propose *Whoever knows thus, 'I am Brahman,' becomes this all. Even the gods cannot prevent his becoming thus, for he becomes their self. So whoever worships another divinity (than his self) thinking that he is one and (Brahman) another, he knows not. He is like an animal to the gods.* Just as humans feed on animals, the gods feed on ignorant worshippers. The ritual sacrifices, while still being celebrated, were despised by many philosopher saints. Instead of ritualism, they proposed that liberation can be found by direct experience of Brahman. This is the knowledge that frees from evil, that liberates from all bondage, this is way superior to all ethics. The authors of the early *Upaniṣads* had a good word for ethics once in a while, but they repeatedly emphasised that liberation is something beyond ethical values altogether. It's not doing good or doing bad, the trick is to leave the whole game - and everything else. Now the idea of karman does seem a little pessimistic. This was not so at the beginning. The *Īśa Upaniṣad*, proposes that, while bondage is the norm, liberation is possible to all who sever their attachment to the world. We are at the beginning of a new movement here: at the time, there is evidence for growing communities of forest dwelling ascetics, nude drop-outs, and wandering mendicants of all descriptions, folks who have said goodbye to the values of society. While some texts praise the life of the forest ascetics (*Chāndogya Upaniṣad* 5, 10) others plead for a spiritual life within society. At the same time, the *Maitrī Upaniṣad* introduces a totally pessimistic vision of karman. Here we can find the bitter and hopeless mood that became so typical for early Buddhism. To begin with, the body is foul-smelling, insubstantial, full of faeces, phlegm, urine, and disease, bound by desire, anger, delusion, covetousness, a *'cart without intelligence'*. The gods themselves may be worshipped, as expressions of Brahman, but their benefits are temporary and should be discarded. Unity is attainable when all is destroyed. The best methods to attain peace are yoga and austerities, by shaking off all good and evil the sage becomes self-less, empty, absent. The text contains some useful new concepts, such as the suṣumṇā, meditation on sound, meditation of the thumb-sized seer within the cave of the heart, voiding thoughts, plus some odd elements of ritual, but on the whole it is certainly no happy message. This attitude became one of the prevailing elements in Indian thought. When modern people hear of reincarnation, they generally see this as good news. To the people of old India it was something rather to be avoided.

New Faiths: Buddhism and Jaina

The *Upaniṣads* proved to be a breakthrough in Indian philosophy. Though they did not attempt to invalidate the earlier *Vedas*, they had a liberating effect on many thinkers. The Brahman concept reduced the importance of personified gods and allowed the development of an abstract and sophisticated spirituality that could do without many of the earlier rites and sacrifices. This change came subtly, not in a clear break from earlier traditions. In the centuries after the early *Upaniṣads* a host of new philosophical schools appeared. Many of these were highly dissatisfied with stratified society and rigid adherence to class-duties. Two innovative systems survive to this day. They were founded by contemporaries, but the actual date of this event is highly disputed. Buddha's death (at the age of eighty) was thought to be one of the few reliable dates in Indian prehistory, and many sources agreed that it happened around 486 or 480 BCE. Recent research has thrown doubt on this and shown that the demise of the Enlightened One could just as well have happened around 350 BCE. If this is the case, the *Upaniṣads*, the *Vedas*, and indeed the Aryan invasion have to be re-dated (Wilhelm in Franz 1990: 99).

Enough has been written about the Buddha and his teachings, so you'll forgive me for not repeating material that can be studied better in any library. For the present, it should suffice that Buddha built on the foundation of the *Upaniṣads* in that he accepted the concept of reincarnation. Early Buddhism is full of Upaniṣadic ideas. The evils of the body, the snares of bondage and attachment, the futility of human effort and the like were taught for centuries before Buddha incorporated them in his lore. He also made use of a good many practices, such as meditation, voiding of thoughts, cultivation of poverty, and so on, which had been developed in the early *Upaniṣads*. In his time a growing number of mad sages had begun to dwell in forest communities. Many of these went their own ways; good evidence that loneliness, isolation, absence of social pressure, and plain lack can lead to interesting states of mind. One strong school proposed that the soul, and its fate after death, are not only unknown but also unknowable. What is unknown and unknowable does not exist. Buddha combined the idea of reincarnation with the non-existing soul, and proposed that there is no enduring or lasting thing whatsoever. Unlike earlier sages, Buddha claimed that karman is not dependant on a personal soul, an ātman, to continue its influence. Causality continues, no matter whether there is a soul or not. Instead of a soul there is a group of illusionary and painful states ('self') that continue life after life. These states are what people consider themselves to be. Eventually the dance comes to an end: the last remnant of personal identity disappears and the 'self' fades into nothingness. This is liberation in the primal Buddhistic sense: the disappearance of all illusions together with anyone who could perceive them. End of form, end of awareness, end of the show. This essentially pessimistic philosophy held a lot of attraction for folk fed up with life and its limitations. (A friend suggested that I shouldn't call it 'pessimistic'; in his opinion, 'realistic' is more accurate. I call that cynical). Buddha's teachings turned out to be highly attractive to the rulers of the time, who liked their subjects to sit back and resignate. Unlike many other philosophers of the time, Buddha did not call for a change in society but expected his followers to leave or endure it. We are a long way from the *Vedas* here. The hope of celestial paradise has given way to the longing for total disappearance. Buddha made much use of the elder term nirvāṇa for the goal of all spiritual effort. This word, often understood as 'liberation' means literally expiration, cessation, and was frequently applied in Buddha's favourite metaphor, that of the extinguished flame of an oil-lamp. When the oil is burned up, the flame disappears without trace. Likewise, when karman is consumed, the self disappears. We have a polarity here: nirvāṇa (cessation) against saṁsāra (the cycle of rebirth). Together with the self a number of other fancies were abolished, mainly those that make people form bonds of attachment to life. This included emotions, such as greed, hate, desire, craving, ignorance, love, duty, friendship, and so on. When all bonds are severed, the soul attains liberation (i.e. disappears) though body may continue living until it drops dead. The whole thing was packaged as four noble truths, starting with the idea that all life is suffering and the root of all suffering is desire. Kāma again, the deity of desire, had become the epitome of evil. In a world where no such thing as a self exists there is obviously little need for deities. The historical Buddha considered them as unhappy and bound by illusion as his fellow humans. In this sense Buddhism was never a religion, and to this day many Indians consider Buddhism a form of atheism.

The faith, thoroughly serious and grim in its early stages, underwent a lot of changes over the centuries. It split into two basic movements and developed into many degrees of subtlety as it spread throughout Asia. It also underwent a lot of reinterpretation. Buddhism had to become a lot more tolerant to become really popular. When you hear a modern Buddhist say that nirvāṇa is identical with saṁsāra you are witnessing an insight that is centuries away from the early Buddhists and their escapist efforts. In India, Buddhism began to decline around the seventh century CE. While the cult was still expanding into China, Japan, Korea, south-east Asia, and, a few centuries later, into the Himalayas, its original country was beginning to transform the core teachings of the Enlightened One. The seventh century saw the development of a new Buddhistic school in northern India, the Vajrayāna (diamond vehicle), which was highly influenced by Hindu Śākta doctrines. What we call Tantra today (the people of the time did not) may be a fusion of several Hindu and Buddhist traditions. Tantric Buddhism is a long way from the pure and stern asceticism of the historical Buddha. For a start, it is not as negative and pessimistic. Also, it began to refine yoga, visualisation, ritual, drama, trance-practice, obsession, divination, music, and, in some traditions, ritual lovemaking. When the Muslims came to conquer northern India in the 13th century, Tantric Buddhism was so thoroughly interwoven with Hindu Tantra that they were hard to distinguish. Many worshippers felt at home in both systems. The Muslims did not approve of either. As the Buddhists were dependant on temples, monasteries, and libraries, it was an easy matter for the invaders to crush the cult. It continued to thrive outside of its home country.

The faith of the Jaina developed in the same period as Buddhism. Its founder was called Mahāvīra (Great Hero) or Jina (Victor), his original name was Vardhamāna. These martial titles do not imply that their bearer was a violent man. In Jaina, the real fight is against the demons within, and the road to victory is total asceticism. Like Buddhism, Jaina was in strong opposition to the Vedic class-bound society and to the sacrificial excesses of the Brahmins. Unlike Buddha, Mahāvīra believed in reincarnation and the reality of the soul. In his faith, all souls keep reincarnating and all beings and things are endowed with a soul. Thus, the first principle of the Jainas is to cultivate ahiṁsa (non-injury): if you hurt even the smallest creature you hurt yourself, and the all-self, and suffer a lot of bad karman. Ahiṁsa became the prime law of the faith. No other religion in the world has been so careful to avoid hurting fellow life-forms. You can recognise strict Jainas as they brush the ground to avoid stepping on insects and wear a cloth before the mouth to avoid inhaling them. In their practice, the Jainas had to cultivate strict asceticism. Desires were ignored or negated and basic comforts were denied. The question of whether clothes might be worn split the religion into two quarrelling factions, one in white, the other sky-clad (nude). Not all followers of the cult went to such extremes. The lay followers were allowed to lead a worldly life, provided they adhered to the important regulations. As ahiṁsa remained the summit of perfection, a lot of professions were unattractive. Even a farmer kills life when he ploughs the ground. As a result, the majority became traders and gained considerable economic influence. Many made more money than their faith allowed them to spend. Their cult was never a mass-movement, as it demanded too much discipline and ascetic idealism (plus the rigorous adherence to hundreds of rules), on the other hand it never became decadent or lost its early ideals. Ahiṁsa influenced many Hindu religions and several Tantric movements. I should add that Buddha and Mahāvīra were by no means the only original philosophers of the time. As long as forest communities existed, far from the influence of city-bound Brahmanism, there were new schools of salvation available. Thanks to Buddhist historians we know of three other schools. We know of gloomy Gośāla who proposed a fierce pre-determined fatalism. In his lore, all beings are as they are and cannot change one bit. Fate, nature, and chance are inexorable, free will is an illusion and karman functions like a blind machine. His followers, called Ājīvikas had an initiation and spent most of their lives cultivating an extreme asceticism. This cult seems to have survived in southern India up to the 14th century, it influenced the Vaiṣṇnavas (Gonda 1960: 286).

Figure 13 – Unknown Goddesses
Top: Unknown Goddess, terracotta, second century BCE, Bangarh, Bengal, 15cm height.
Bottom: Unknown goddess, terracotta, c. 150 BCE, Mathura.

A more indifferent attitude was taught by Pūraṇa Kāśyapa, who believed that no activity, no matter how bad or good influences karman. The very ideas of sin and merit are meaningless in his system. By contrast Ajita Keśakambalin proposed a materialistic interpretation: beings consist of the four elements. After death, the body dissolves into the elements. A soul does not exist, hence, death is final and absolute.

If you want to treat yourself to some interesting experiences, explore such philosophies for a while. Spend a day as a raging fatalist or become a materialist. Find out how your behaviour changes when you change the parameters of your beliefs. You'll be surprised!

Elder Hinduism

After these preliminaries you will no doubt be happy to come to a topic that is even more complicated. What is Hinduism? The Indian government defined Hinduism as all of the religions that were developed in India. This includes Veda, Buddhism, Jaina, worshippers of Śiva, Viṣṇu, Brahmā, Śakti, tribal religions, village cults, and the Sikhs, who vehemently protested against this classification. The word Hindu comes from Persia, it means a native of the land of the Indus. The term began to have a religious connotation when Muslims began to settle in the Indus valley in the eight century, it became popular when they occupied northern India in the 13th century. The English formed the modern term 'Hinduism' under the mistaken impression that all India would adhere to a single religion. In their eyes, there was a main religion divided into numerous sects. Like many Europeans, they could not imagine that so many distinct religions could exist in relative tolerance. Indians tend to speak of their religion as dharma, i.e. the eternal law, duty, rightness, truth, order that defines each person's place and spiritual development.

When we come to early Hinduism we encounter such a vast field of study that I can only recommend that you do some on your own. There were so many developments between, say, 500 BCE and 500 CE that a single lifetime would not suffice to explore all of them. I shall restrict myself to a brief summary of some of the major trends and hope that the gods of learning and scholarly precision will forgive the over-simplification.

As you have seen, Hinduism is not a very specific term, nor was it a concept the people of the time were aware of. That something new was developing escaped their attention. The evolution of spiritual concepts took place gradually and without radical cuts. The teachings of the past were never denied, they were simply superseded by new interpretations and customs. The holy writ of antiquity remained holy, as it remains holy to this day, even if it had to be reinterpreted as an elder vision of the truth.

Figure 14 - Divine Heads
Top: head of Pārvatī or Umā, terracotta in Gupta style, 5th century. Śiva temple of Ahicchattrā.
Bottom: Head of Śiva, terracotta in Gupta style, 5th century. Śiva temple of Ahicchattrā.

The thousand years treated in this section saw a lot of political changes on the subcontinent. In this place I should only mention the rise of new large kingdoms, the introduction of writing under emperor Aśoka (himself a Buddhist), the invasion of India under Alexander the Great (an event of such minor importance that Indian historians hardly bothered to mention it), and the rise of Greek-Indian dynasties, which had such an enormous influence on art and sculpture. During this period, India became a concept that fascinated Europeans. Greek and Roman historians began to record weird tales from the east where giant ants collect gold, unicorns thrive, and elderly men set fire to themselves. Trade began, and India was soon connected with the economic networks of the Roman empire. By 25 BCE there were 120 ships a year voyaging to India from Myos-Hornmos alone. The journey was partly overland through Egypt and Arabia by caravan and partly by sea, it was long, dangerous, and demanding, but it was certainly profitable and led to the establishment of Egyptian and European sailor communities in north west India. Under the first Caesars, Indian trade produced enormous profits. The Indian market was highly interested in metals, in purple colour, chemicals, and wine, whereas the European markets were so hungry for Indian spices, incenses, ivory, rare woods, and luxury goods that every year a lot of Roman money went to India, where it remained. In some districts it became the most valuable currency. Soon enough, ideas were being exchanged and so was religion: just look at the introduction of the Egyptian goddess Isis, patroness of sailors in the Roman Empire, to India where she became the only veiled deity of the pantheon (Mogg Morgan discusses this fascinating topic in his currently unpublished work *Isis in India*). In a similar fashion, India acquired Mesopotamian astrology, if in a Grecian form, and adapted it to its own needs. A similar amount of trade and cultural exchange took place with the countries east of India, mainly with China. Hindu religions were also exported into the countries of south-east Asia between the second century BCE and the sixth century CE. Within India, writers began to produce not only about 200 new *Upaniṣads* but also a flood of law texts, poetry, and finally two massive epic poems, the *Mahābhārata* in 100,000 double verses and the slightly shorter *Rāmāyaṇa.* On the surface, both epics are concerned with heroism. The first is the extensive account of the battles and disputes of two branches of a royal family, many of whose members happen to be incarnate deities. The second, younger and shorter, piece expounds the life of Rāma (an incarnation of Viṣṇu), his marriage with Sīta, her abduction by a demon, and the rescue mission. These works developed over several centuries and eventually reached encyclopaedic dimensions. No other works had such a deep influence on the development of Indian thought. To this day, priests and storytellers recite episodes of these epics, and though this happens in archaic saṅskṛt, and most of the audience understands little but the names and a few odd words here and there, these events are not only popular but sacred. When the *Mahābhārata* was shown on TV, pious Hindus decorated their TV sets with flowers and burned incense. Partaking of these tales means winning merit and finding release from past sins. Another such field of literary evolution were the (basic) eighteen *Purāṇas*, which set down an enormous amount of mythology, rituals, hymns, scientific discourses, geography, cosmology, genealogies, and anything that fascinated their authors. These works can be considered encyclopaedias. Some were dedicated to single deities, others attempted to reduce the tension between the growing cults of Śiva and Viṣṇu by being nice to everybody. All of this literature is complex, stylistically refined, and full of contradictions. This has never bothered Indian people much: there has never been a single dogma about anything.

Dharma and the Pattern of Society

With the advent of early Hinduism we observe an increasing importance of dharma. Dharma is a term that used to refer to cosmic order in the elder days. This order was reflected in society and in the life of each living being. A lot of concepts went into this package. Dharma can mean harmony, truth, rightness, it can be the laws of nature, and when applied to human behaviour it is the force that binds people to stations of society. By following class duties, each Hindu supports dharma, by violating social laws, cosmic dharma is threatened. Dharma permeated the entire body of Hindu religion. It allows for connections that do not exist in other philosophies. A sin or crime, though they violate human dharma, is apt to have repercussions in the natural world. A sinful king, a ruler who disregards the rites or breaks some religious taboo, violates dharma, and this can lead to terrible weather, plague, or invasion by enemies. Corrupt priests, kings, and ministers can be a threat to order on all levels. The social world, the natural world, and the divine are not separate, they are one dharma, and a damage of dharma can upset them all. Of course dharma was more than just a principle, it was also a force and a deity. The most important aspect of dharma in daily life was the duty of each being to follow its natural obligations. Plants follow dharma, animals follow dharma, gods follow dharma, and humans are obliged to do the same. In the process, the class system became ever more complex. Where the late *Vedas* were satisfied with three upper classes and one lower (plus a lot of class-less folk), early Hinduism developed more and more classes. Likewise, distinctions between classes became stronger. Late Vedic texts still mention a fair share of class-changing by merit, achievement, and marriage (especially between Brahmins and warriors). Early Hindu literature does not approve of this sort of thing. We observe a proliferation of class distinctions. This was due to the integration of more segments of society, the need to account for new professions and ethnic groups, and so on. To this day, scholars are debating why the class system became so exaggerated and oppressive. Here it should suffice that by the time of Manu (well, one of them) there were already more than fifty classes. The class system worked by giving each person her or his dharma and hence a duty in the world. It also worked as it allowed all newcomers a niche in society. This is important: each new influence could be integrated. In one package with classes and dharma came karman, reincarnation, and purity laws.

Now the status of the individual in society does not only depend on varṇa (class) but also on jati. Jati is an extremely difficult concept for non-Indians. It is not a Vedic idea but one that developed together with early Hinduism. Jati describes, roughly speaking, what specific groups in society a person belongs to. Jati can be birth, origin, kinship, clan, or family relationship. It can also be connection to specific religious groups, provinces, country, profession, ethnic background, and so on. These are the fine details that specify the personal status within a given varṇa. Jati can also transcend varṇa. People with high income may well achieve a status that is much higher than their varṇa. Brahmins, though theoretically the heads of society, often have a tiny income and are happy to get a job as a teacher, an accountant, or a cook. Warriors and Brahmins often depend on money-lenders to keep up their place in society, and merchants occasionally make more money than both. Doctors were often considered unclean, as they came in contact with secretions, blood, corpses, and other dirty substances. Nowadays their status has improved amazingly, thanks to high wages. Add to this the widespread habit of improving the past. There are lots of low-class people in India who stoutly insist that they were originally of Brahmin stock, but had to change names and professions to evade persecution. As a result, many people try to improve on their varṇa, and few believe in what their neighbours claim about theirs. Hindu society, nowadays divided into more than 3000 classes, looks like a well-ordered hierarchy, but things are less rigid than they seem. This makes marriage a really complicated matter. In theory, the classes are supposed to marry within themselves, or preferably with their superiors. In practice, there are a lot of considerations involved, such as property and power, and finding a proper mate provides entertainment for the entire clan. If possible, families try to marry their daughters into a class of higher status, and usually the husband's family demands a lot for this honour. When there are many daughters, too much marrying can ruin the family. Marriages of men into higher classes are frowned upon and rarely happen. This makes it hard for top-class women to find a mate. I have to add that there is still a lot of persecution going on. While class-discrimination was theoretically abolished by the British and is frowned upon by the modern Indian government, in the real world it goes on as ever. To deny the existence of classes is to deny the structure of dharma in the human world. Where do the people come from who dive into the sewers of Indian cities without any protective gear to unclog drains? Who do you guess gets beaten up for showing self esteem? Who builds houses and tills the fields of the landowners for free? Every year class-less folk get stoned by their social betters. In the cities, this trend is gradually weakening, but out in the country everything is as bad as ever. Sometimes people are killed just because their shadows touched an upper-class fanatic.

Problems with Purity

Every person is contaminated every day. You only have to go out of doors and the purity of your class is threatened. There are millions of unclean and forbidden things in the wide world, and each Hindu has to do a lot to remain clean and pure. A daily bath and worship ceremony are the basics to keep up one's spiritual and social status. Company is the next issue: even talking with an inferior equals contamination. Public transport was not an issue in early Hinduism but nowadays it is. Few innovations have endangered class-separation as much as taking a ride in a train or bus. Food is especially difficult. Hindu theology is so obsessed with food as it can only be accepted from people of one's own class or superior ones. Everyone is supposed to eat and drink with people of the same varṇa. While travelling this obviously becomes a problem. To make up for inevitable contamination a host of minor rites were invented. If you buy food from a lowly trader, you have to clean it by ritual or by contact with sacred substances, such as the five jewels of the cow. *Vasiṣṭha 6,27* insists that if a Brahmin dies with food accepted from a Śudra in his belly, his next life will be as a pig. Study of Veda and scripture won't help one bit. Poor Brahmins often become cooks. Their varṇa is so high that everybody in society can accept food from them. The result is an amazingly complex set of feeding rules. You find a major obsession with food in many *Upaniṣads*, and things did not get better over the centuries.

Keep this in mind as you read Tantric texts. When the Kaulas propose that there are no rules to feeding, that ritual food can come from any source, that adepts can eat what they like and with whom they like, this is an enormous break from social norms. The same appears in certain forms of clandestine group worship where social classes are abolished. Kaula rituals involving worship with or of women is another break with Vedic tradition. To venerate a low-class woman as a goddess or to make love with her is unthinkable to traditionalists. It's even worse when unclean substances, such as body secretions, are treasured and ingested. To foreigners such things may not matter much, but to strict minded traditionalists they constitute anarchy and mind blowing heresy. Such acts threatened social stability, one more reason why certain Tantric cults were not popular.

Purity was also threatened by contact with dead humans and animals, hides, excrement, body secretions, and a wide range of unlucky people. The list includes criminals, murderers, classless folk, illegitimate children, and women, especially when they are nude. Some early texts recommend that men should protect themselves with amulets when they approach women, on some days (and many nights) women should not be approached at all. Menstruation is one such time, more detail about this will be found further on. Pregnancy is another dangerous time, birth is worse, but marriages and deaths in the family also require special rituals and purification. The range of purification rites is extensive. There are simple rites to clean food by repeating the Gāyatrī mantra 108 to 1008 times, more serious contamination can necessitate weeks of ritual bathing, prayer, extensive sacrifices, making gifts to Brahmins, ascetic exercises, fasting, and doing good deeds. Some sins, such as travelling over the ocean, leaving India, having a child from a Śudra woman, murder, or stealing from a Brahmin were so dreadful that a Hindu lost his class and had to reacquire it at great cost and effort. Indian troops, employed by the English outside of India had one hell of a time when they came home to their relations, who refused to speak with them. Purity aside, dharma dictated the role of each person in life. The early Hindus believed that life should be ordered in stages, and that each male should go through a specific set of functions in life. This began with the age of initiation (differing for each class) and continued through maturity. Theoretically, each upper class male was supposed to fulfil three obligations: the gods demand sacrifice, the ancestors demand sons, and the seers demand study of the *Vedas*. Those who did not fulfil their obligations could expect a long time in hell, followed by some nasty reincarnation as a beast. Part of these obligations was the idea that life should end by withdrawing from society. This took several forms. In some cases, elderly householders left their families and clans and became pilgrims or hermits. In other cases, the aged couple left the family and began to live in a crude hut in some secluded forest, dedicating their lives to extreme asceticism and saintliness. It was considered good form to find eventual death by starvation. Still others claimed that it is a waste of time to delay holiness to the end of life and proposed that the earlier one becomes a recluse, the better. Here we have the same old conflict as in the early *Upaniṣads*: should people bother to become householders or should they drop out straightaway?

Ups and Downs of the Deities

Gods do not die, but eventually they may fade out of common awareness. Divine powers and attributes can shift from one deity to another, the same goes for myths and functions. Some Vedic gods remained in business, but their relative importance changed a lot. Another innovation was a system of attributes, such as divine animals, colours, weapons, and so on. Possibly this attempt connects with the introduction of divine images. We know that the Aryans originally did not worship using images (or at least those Aryans we know about) but that some of their dark skinned opponents venerated liṅgas, images, possibly phallic. Images did not matter much in the religions before early Hinduism, but in the centuries before the common era they begin to multiply. Soon enough, the gods were equipped with more or less permanent attributes. A good many of these had been around since the early *Vedas*, you'll find them changing now. I should add that the gods, after they had lost so much of their fear-inspiring qualities now became a popular topic for poets and storytellers. Some of them had a strong, even bizarre, sense of humour. As a result, most gods began to develop highly human qualities, characteristics, and shortcomings. Here we observe a pantheon that is not really feared any more. The gods, just like humans and all other beings, are subject to karman. They are no longer rulers but fellow actors in a divine play. By contrast, the dangerous power of seers and ascetics turned into a popular topic. The *Mahābhārata* contains several tales of seers who did their tapas so fiercely that they became a threat to the gods. Good reason to distract them by sending a few alluring Apsarases to earth.

The **Asuras**, once a respectable family of gods, were turned into a bunch of terrifying demons. This happened during the period when the *Atharva Veda* was compiled - before 500 BCE. With the advent of early Hinduism, gods who had been Asuras in earlier times were considered members of the Deva clan, their past history was conveniently ignored. Much of early Hindu mythology is based on the theme of good Devas fighting evil Asuras, a topic that can become a trifle boring after a few hundred repetitions.

Several Vedic deities almost disappeared. They were not forgotten, as the *Vedas* remained sacred literature, but they ceased to receive much veneration. Among them were the Maruts, the horse-riding Aśvins, Uṣas, Nirṛti and a host of minor deities.

Agni lost some importance as the great sacrifices of the Vedic period were being downsized or abandoned. He has remained popular to this day due to his connection with the household fire. This fire was and is the sacred focus of domestic life - it is the centre of home, family, and daily ritual. His earlier connections with water disappeared. In the new interpretation, Agni can also be like a hungry demon and an untrustworthy companion who is apt to go away from time to time. He also appears as a greedy old man and as a sex-hungry goat. In goat form, he could also appear as a favourite sacrifice and as the entire universe.

Varuṇa, once the god who ordered the universe, became a god of the oceans. As his power extended over the waters and water was a prominent part of the healing sciences, he also assumed the role of the divine healer. In general his importance declined.

Indra remained popular as the king of the gods. In actual worship, his importance gradually faded and most of his divine functions, especially with regard to kingship, were assimilated by the cult of Viṣṇu. Gradually, Indra assumed the form of a heroic young man who lives in a happy otherworld with hundreds of youths. In this form (and others, as he is a competent shape-shifter) he appears in lore and legend. His supreme status faded, by the end of the period he is a god who makes mistakes, needs help of others and occasionally shows fear and cowardice. This makes him immensely human, possibly likeable, but goes much against his earlier Vedic status as the summit of divine authority. Eventually, he needs 60,000 years of yoga and tapas plus the help of Śiva and Viṣṇu to fight the world serpent Vṛta, now in human form, who appears as a regent and even a Brahmin (hence Indra's reputation as a killer of Brahmins).

Sūrya, god of the sun, is equipped with a family. He is not of general importance any more, but remains popular with a group of worshippers called Sauras (after his name) and as the patron deity of astrologers. His old crony **Mitra** is now also a deity of the sun, provided he is mentioned at all. His cult had a revival in north-west India in the first century CE, thanks to Persians who introduced their own solar, fiery Mithras.

Yama remains lord of the desolate realm of the dead. He is made more darksome and terrifying than before: the great epics make him a god of war, doom, and disease. He becomes lord of all hells, judge of the dead, and is occasionally identified with Kāla, time, as the devourer of all. Whether he received much veneration or remained as a popular literary figure is one of those questions.

Vāyu, god of wind and storms splits into several Vāyus, who are in charge of various phenomena. He appears occasionally as Indra's messenger, then again he is independent and receives worship as a god of speech, freedom, poetry, and even the soul. Some praise him as the essence of life and identify him with prāṇa. He swiftly gobbles up the functions of the **Maruts**.

The goddess of wealth and prosperity, **Śrī**, merges with the goddess of beauty and rural fertility, **Lakṣmī**, together they become Śrī Lakṣmī, to this day the most popular goddess in India. The river goddess **Sarasvatī** unites with the goddess Vāc/Vāk (Voice, Speech). Together they become the goddess of learning, music, poetry, and knowledge. The river Sarasvatī remained one of the sacred rivers of India, even after changes in climate made it dry up. You can still find it invoked in blessings and water rituals. Sarasvatī had much popularity in literature, mainly as the poets and writers saw her as a patron deity of their craft and regularly invoked her blessings at the beginning of a book.

Kāma, Vedic god of desire, had become the epitome of vice and temptation among the early Buddhists, who occasionally equated him with Māra, god of evil and death, and opponent of the Buddha. In Hinduism, he was not such a negative figure. Equipped with a bow of flowers he shoots arrows of desire and love, this made him a popular deity for lovers and a useful figure for literature. He is equipped with a wife called Rati (Lust), together the two appear in Tantric art. He develops a connection to Śiva, who once incinerates him by mistake, and refashions him on popular request.

Viṣṇu is one of the two winners in early Hinduism. In the early *Vedas*, Viṣṇu was a minor god in the company of Indra, whose prime function was to make space for Indras Vṛta fight by walking three steps. This produced the three realms of heaven, earth, and underworld, and allowed Indra to wield his thunderbolt. Starting from these humble beginnings, Viṣṇu became so popular that with the advent of early Hinduism, Indra had become a pale shadow and Viṣṇu is the installer of kings, ruler of the cosmos, and supreme sovereign of the spiritual world. He is married to Bhūmi, goddess of the divine earth and all prosperity. By the time of the *Mahābhārata*, the kings rule in Viṣṇu's name, and Viṣṇu, in one form or another, is the most celebrated deity of that monumental epic. The early Viṣṇu is still equipped with a few characteristics of the Vedic original. He is omnipresent, pervades everything, and contains the universe. As such, the god is of such a universal nature that we cannot discern much of a personality in him.

This changed when Viṣṇu was blended with two non-Vedic gods. One of them is a deity of herders and farmers called Kṛṣṇa (Black) who appears in popular mythology as a warrior deity and as a happy flute player who spends his days at the edge of the wilderness flirting with the cow girls. The other is Vāsudeva, who has such an active part in the *Mahābhārata.* Vāsudeva and Kṛṣṇa may have blended by the fourth century BCE, and only a few hundred years later both were considered incarnations of Viṣṇu. Kṛṣṇa did not begin as a god. Early Hinduism was highly interested in the figure of the half-god, the incarnate deity and the human who becomes deified (generally after death). Many of the heroic figures of the great epics are incarnate deities. As such, they have human nature and are inferior to the non-incarnate gods, but they still amount to much more than mere humans and return to their divine status after death. When a deity incarnates, it tends to become subject to human traits. It may err, be subject to emotion, delusion, and desire, and is often in need to pray to other gods. In the *Mahābhārata,* Kṛṣṇa is one of the crucial figures. He is not the hero, he is the person who helps the heroes to win supremacy and uses the opportunity to dictate a new approach to religion. This is the theme of the *Bhagavadgītā,* one of the later additions to the *Mahābhārata.* Kṛṣṇa is an innovative deity. He is not very fond of the old Brahmanic order of things and has frequent conflicts with Indra. Kṛṣṇa is also the god who praises a new approach to salvation: bhakti (devotional love). The main innovation of the *Bhagavadgītā* is the idea that ritual and sacrifice are not as important as right action and total devotion to the deity. Action and participation in dharma were promoted, instead of resignation and withdrawal. This devotion was originally simply love and affection, but as the bhakti movement gained popularity, it developed into a whole series of sentiments and emotions. Of course loving devotion to a deity is not a thing that began with the cult of Kṛṣṇa or Viṣṇu. Throughout history there have been seers, drop-outs, and lunatics who came to love the divine in one form or another. The great innovation of bhakti is the idea that loving devotion can be used systematically and that it is superior to the earlier forms of worship, ritual, sacrifice, and asceticism. Kṛṣṇa of the *Mahābhārata* is both a human hero (who dies after receiving an arrow in his foot) and an incarnate god. He appears under several names, each of them possibly another human or deity who got assimilated in the cult, such as Janārdana (The Oppressor of Enemies), Govinda (related to go-, meaning 'cow'), and he is even called an incarnation of Nārāyana. Originally, Nārāyana used to be an ecstatic sage and a son of the god Dharma who lived near the Ganges. He was occasionally identified with Brahman and appears in company of Indra. Fairly early, Viṣṇu was identified with Nārāyana, of whom the *Mbh* 12,334 states that he was born in the first world age as Nara, Nārāyana, Hari (Lion), and Kṛṣṇa. The basic teachings of bhakti are attributed to him. Sometime between the early *Mahābhārata* - around 200 BCE - and its late version, Kṛṣṇa became an incarnation of Viṣṇu. He was not to be the only one. As Viṣṇu is such a pervasive god, he is in charge of cosmic order and balance, and as such a maintainer of the universe. It's not an easy job. To ensure the continuity of the world, Viṣṇu tends to reincarnate from time to time. The idea of regular divine incarnation came to form the avatāra succession. This is fundamental to the cult of Viṣṇu; it is not very important in other Indian religions. Over the centuries, worshippers of Viṣṇu selected a series of ten heroic or divine figures, who were thought to be incarnations of their god. The selection took quite a while, and not all texts are in agreement on the range of divine impersonations. Some invented more than twenty. Nowadays the basic ten are:

First world-age

1. The divine fish (Matsya) who saved the first human, Manu, from the great flood.

2. The tortoise (Kūrma) who was the support of the world mountain when the gods stirred the milk-ocean and won the elixir of immortality.

3. The monstrous boar (Varāha) who lifted the submerged earth from the depths of the ocean.

4. The man-lion (Narasiṁha) who destroyed the demon Hiraṇyākṣa.

Second world-age

5. The dwarf (Vāmana) who defeated the demon Bali by measuring the three worlds in three steps.

6. Rāma with the Axe (Paraśurāma), destroyer of the warriors who had killed his father.

7. Rāma, son of Daśaratha, husband of Sītā, destroyer of the demon Rāvaṇa, hero of the *Rāmāyaṇa*.

Third world-age

8. Kṛṣṇa, slayer of the demon Kaṁsa.

Fourth world-age

9. Buddha, the Enlightened One (an idea that made a lot of Buddhists angry).

10. Kalkin, the white horse (or rider of the white horse) who will come at the end of the present age to begin a new era.

Out of this complex of myths and divine personages arose the thriving cult of Viṣṇu whose followers are generally called Vaiṣṇavas. They form the majority of worshippers in wide parts of modern India. Over the last centuries, they had an enormous influence on Indian thought. When it comes to rewriting history, taming wild deities and turning raging goddesses into obedient housewives, Vaiṣṇavas cannot be equalled.

The other winner of early Hinduism is **Śiva**. He began as Rudra, the fierce god of the wilderness, lord of ascetics, hermits, healers, and all who live at the fringes of society. The name Śiva (Auspicious) is one of the many titles the god acquired in the late Vedic period. Unlike such names as Hara (Destroyer), Bhīma (Terrible), or Kāla (Time, i.e. the great destroyer) the term Śiva attempts to placate the deity with a respectful and friendly title. Being nice to terrifying gods is something you can find in many cultures, just think of the term 'the Good Neighbours' for the dreaded fairy folk of Celtic countries. The Vedic Rudra was a dreaded and terrifying god who received placation, not praise. As Śiva, he became more popular. In character, Śiva has a function that is diametrically opposite to Viṣṇu. Where Viṣṇu maintains cosmic order, Śiva tends to disregard or avoid it. Śiva is a wild god, an outcast from divine society, and his followers were often dreaded as they tended to be as wild, mad, and anti-social as their deity. Rudra became popular in some of the early *Upaniṣads*. We encounter him as Śiva in early Hinduism. By that time the god has changed a great deal. He has become identified with the liṅga, a phallic image well known from folk-worship, and with the true liṅga, the unmeasurable, eternal column of sheer energy that gives direction to the cosmos. This pillar is not a phallus. It comes closer to such concepts as the tree of life, the pole reaching to the north star, the cosmic axis, allowing seers and shamans to travel to the height and depth. Also, he has gained the bull Nandī as his vehicle. Rudra is called a bull in one of the hymns of the *Ṛg Veda*, but this is an exception, as in Vedic times, the bull was the vehicle and symbol of Indra. Nevertheless, we find Rudra closely associated with cattle in the *Atharva Veda*. When Śiva acquired liṅga and bull, he also acquired a vital function in rural life. As god of the phallus, Śiva was identified with fertility, lust, and general procreation. This is not very much in tune with the ascetic Śiva, the half starved mendicant dwelling alone in mountains and jungles. Early Hinduism made Śiva a god full of paradox and extreme contrasts. Śiva gives life and fertility, but his children are diseases, poison is his elixir, and the battlefield is his playing ground. He gives life and death, and is the liberator from both. Such notions seem to conflict, but to devotees of the deity the conflict is a dance of equipoise, and the extremes balance. This enigmatic figure is much more clearly defined than the vague and omnipresent Viṣṇu. Like Viṣṇu, Śiva inspired several devotional systems. Unlike the simple method of bhakti, which can be adopted by any person, no matter the age, class, or level of intelligence, the teachings of Śiva demands a lot of learning, training, and discipline. You can find these expressed in many of the Āgamas and Tantras, where Śiva, or some form of Śiva, teaches complicated rituals, visualisations, and sorceries.

An important part of the cult of Śiva was the integration of female deities. The cult embraced sexuality, and this made the partner of the god an important and active figure. The followers of Śiva equipped their god with a wide range of partners, all of them former local goddesses.

Vaiṣṇavas, Śaivas and Śāktas

By the time we reach the end of early Hinduism, the main cults were those of Viṣṇu, Śiva, and local deities, most of whom were female.

Hence modern Hinduism developed the basic religious movements called Śaivas (worshippers of Śiva) and Vaiṣṇavas (worshippers of Viṣṇu). These movements were by no means clearly defined and there were no hard boundaries between them. Think of them as temperamental preferences, not as churches: no religion of India has ever managed (or bothered) to evolve a single dogma. A good many worshippers delighted in both movements, or made up their own personal version of them. One of the new ideas of these systems is that Viṣṇu can be a personification of Brahman, and that worship of Viṣṇu equals union with the all-self that had been of such importance since the *Upaniṣads*. Thus, to Vaiṣṇavas, Viṣṇu became Brahman, the supreme principle. The Śaivas saw things in the same light, only that they proposed that Brahman is really to be found in Śiva, who happens to be the supreme principle. This idea was first proposed in the *Kaivalya Upaniṣad*, 16-18, but it took some centuries before it became popular:

> *He is the supreme Brahman, the self of all, the chief foundation of this world, subtler than the subtle, eternal. That thou art; Thou art that. The world which shines in the states of waking, dream and dreamless sleep, knowing that it is Brahman who I am, one is freed from all fetters. In the three states of consciousness whatever appears as the object of enjoyment, or the enjoyer, or the enjoyment, I am different from them, the witness (thereof), pure consciousness, the eternal Śiva.*

Viṣṇu and Śiva assumed function and characteristics of the all-self, they became the vast consciousness that extends throughout all being. Here we have religions that were interpreted in many ways. In folk religion, Viṣṇu and Śiva remained gods with tales, personality, and temperament who could be called upon to get things done. In more intellectual circles, the anthropomorphic representations of the gods were seen as conveniences. Thus, the gods could be understood in many ways, and every single one of them is true.

With the advent of Śaiva worship, the role of the local goddesses, village goddesses, and goddesses of the land began to gain importance. These goddesses had been popular for a long time before we encounter them in literature. Literature is usually written by learned people, often city-dwellers, who have little interest in the customs of the countryside. Few Brahmins bothered to record the beliefs of the common population, and, for this reason, our knowledge of goddess worship in early times is tantalisingly incomplete. With the advent of the Śaiva movement, some of these goddesses began to be mentioned in literature. At first they are only partners of Śiva, who functions as their superior and often as their teacher.

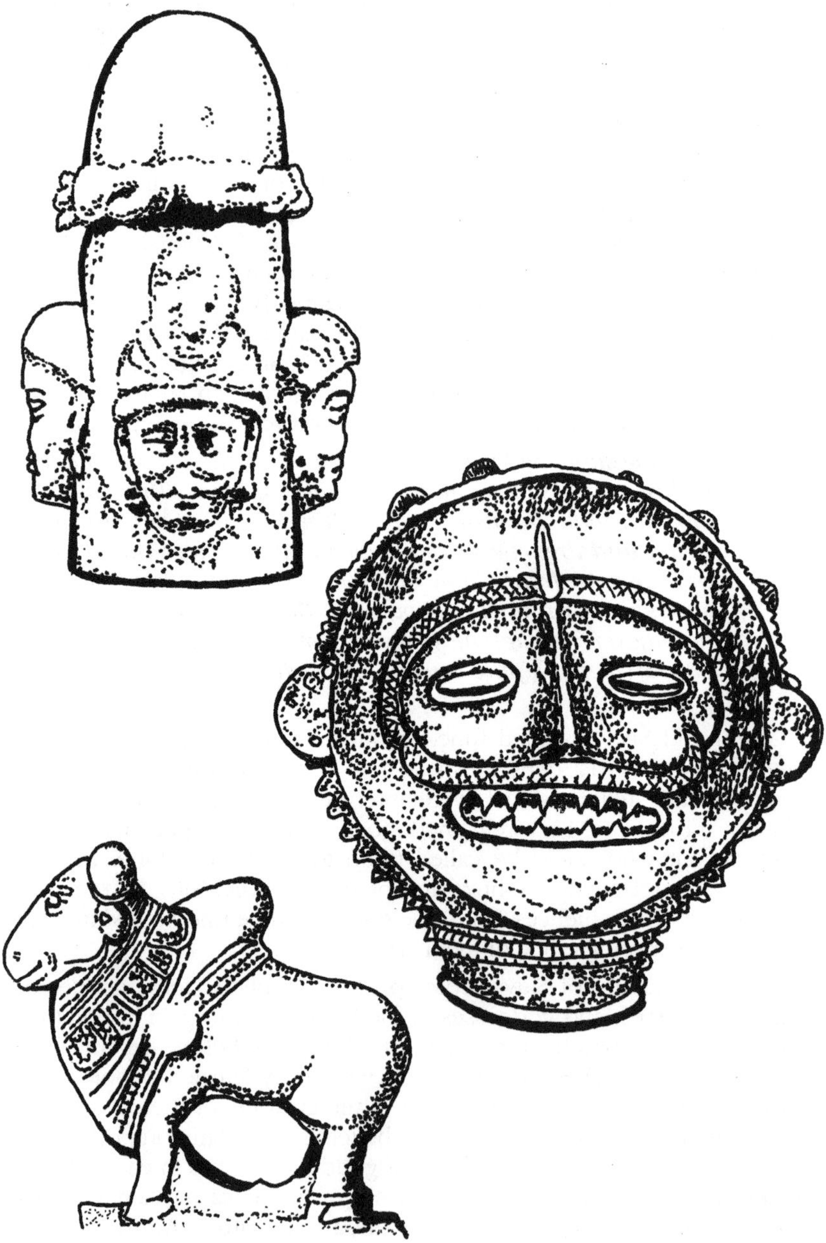

Figure 15 - Śiva.
Top: Śiva liṅga with four heads, stone, 2nd century BCE.
Middle: A terrifying Śiva, brass, Rajasthan, 17th century, 32,5cm.
Bottom: Śiva's bull Nandī (The Happy One), terracotta, 2nd century BCE.

When you see images of large Śivas with tiny women sitting on their knees, you are witnessing this sort of attitude. The goddesses were the personal Śakti (power, energy, might) of their male partner. Evidently some people thought the goddesses were more important than that. Two passages in the *Mahābhārata* show that goddesses like Kālī, Durgā, and Jayā were not only worshipped but also considered to share a common essence (see the later chapter on Kālī). A few centuries later, around the year 500 CE, this situation changed completely. A new group of worshippers surfaced who are nowadays called Śāktas. These accepted Viṣṇu and Śiva, but they insisted that the highest road to liberation can only be found through the worship and experience of the goddesses, i.e. Śakti. Śakti means energy and power, a term that includes form and matter in Indian thought.

This power can be understood in many ways. To the Śaivas, Śakti is power but Śiva is the power-holder. As Śiva could be equated with the formless, undefinable Brahman, the all-pervasive consciousness of the worlds, Śakti could be understood as the totality of all form, being, manifestation. This forms a divine couple composed of consciousness (Śiva) and form, energy (Śakti). Or we have Śiva as formless consciousness and Śakti as consciousness in form. In the basic Śaiva model, Śiva is the supreme awareness and Śakti is his expression. Now Śakti rarely appears as such. Generally she manifests as one of the thousands of goddesses of popular folk religion. The Śāktas insisted that Śakti is not just energy/matter but also consciousness. In their world-view, Śakti is the supreme principle. It is Śakti who leads to liberation, and it is Śakti who creates Brahman plus all gods, spirits, and living beings. You find Parāśakti as the absolute consciousness, sometimes but not always coupled with Sadaśiva. Parāśakti gives birth to everything, her fist child being Śiva as formless consciousness. Śiva in turn creates Śakti as consciousness-reflected-in-form-and-energy. Out of this Śakti appears the entire universe. Such matters were developed to amazing degrees of enlightened complication. In southern India we have an emphasis on benevolent and well behaved goddesses while northern and eastern India developed the cults of dangerous and destructive goddesses. Their cults show some radical differences with regard to how you approach the deity and what she does with you. But things are more complex than this. As June McDaniel (2004: 5) summarises so neatly:

> *Some Shakta traditions say that all goddesses are manifestations of the same great goddess, Adi Shakti or Parama Shakti, while others say that that the many goddesses are separate and unique, or sometimes that they are manifestations of one or more gods. There is Shakta monism, in which all phenomena are the parts of the goddess, whose deepest nature is brahman or universal consciousness. There is Shakta monotheism, in which all other deities are aspects of a single goddess, who has created the universe. There is Shakta dualism, in which the divine couple Shiva and Shakti are the primordial deities, and Shakti is the more important figure, the mother of the universe. There is Shakta polytheism, in*

Figure 16 - Nandī at night.

which many goddesses hold great power, and sometimes compete for power and devotees with other goddesses or with male gods. And there is Shakta henotheism, where many goddesses are recognized as legitimate, but one is most powerful.

The Śāktas emerge as a cult that venerates the divine female. In their world-view, the gods are static and passive while the goddesses are dynamic, active, and alive. This could mean a local goddess or a group of them. Śākta worship became especially popular in Orissa, Kashmir, Gujarāt, north east India, Bengal, Assam, and the southern Himalayas. By the sixth or seventh century it began to seek a unifying principle, i.e. a goddess who could incorporate the many local goddesses. One such goddess was simply called Devī, a term meaning literally Goddess, from dev- shining one. Her first appearance is in the sixth or seventh century *Devīmāhātmyam*. The Devī attracted worshippers from all classes of society. Many Westerners assume that The Devī is the hidden essence of all the other goddesses, a single goddess who manifests in a myriad of forms. This is to say, the unifying principle is the essence of all the particular forms. Historically, it was the other way around. For thousands of years a wide range of goddesses had been worshipped. Each of them has been praised as the great goddess by her devotees, just as each god has been celebrated as the greatest god of all. To each devotee, the personal deity was and is the greatest of them all. In this sense the Devī was the sum of all goddesses, but on the other hand the Devī was just the manifestation of the personal goddess. Each village deity is The Great Goddess to the villagers, who manifests as all other goddesses and of course as the Devī. I emphasise this point as there are still writers who claim that there may have been a single great goddess (monotheism) in unknown prehistory who became thousands of separate goddesses (polytheism). The goddesses are not simply aspects of one great goddess. Some Śāktas called her Devī. Others had a similar idea and sought to install Lalitā as the great goddess. Or they went for Kālī, Lakṣmī, or Durgā. There is no single great goddess in Indian thought, though you may encounter many Indians who insist that their personal deity is the greatest of them all. Then there is worship. Śākta worship can take several highly distinct forms. It can be intellectual or illiterate. It can be silent and serene, as in calming meditation, or ecstatic and mad, as in shamanic cults of divine possession. It can be based on obscure Tantras or widely known Purāṇas. It can be folk worship in ritual and sacrifice, it can be the highly refined rites of inner (meditative) alchemy or it can be bhakti, involving extreme emotionality and loving devotion. Or it can be a mixture of these. As you can see, Śākta is a very loose term that may be understood in many ways. And with the emergence of the Śāktas we are happily at the beginning of the Tantric period.

3: The Texture of Tantra

Twilight Language

If you have read a few original Tantric texts, you will be aware that their contents are usually veiled in a highly metaphoric form. Unlike most books, they do not convey their messages as an author speaking to a reader. The frame of most Tantras is a dialogue between a form of Śiva and some form of Śakti. The reader is invited to witness this dialogue, the author remains in the background. The question of the author's human persona becomes irrelevant; the text is basically what you make out of it. Most Tantric works make use of a number of key concepts, but as you will soon become aware these concepts are not always interpreted in the same way. There was never a consensus regarding terminology in the Tantric lineages. Each metaphor has several meanings, and is coded in a way to suggest rather than define. In this respect, Tantra is not unlike the coded gnosis of the *Eddas*, the Qabalah, the alchemical writings of the Daoists, or the bizarre ravings of the Celtic bards. In each case, the meaning is not obvious, and if it does seem obvious for a brief and surprising interval, you will soon find another secret lurking behind it. 'What the hell is this all about?' is a good question, no matter whether it is asked of mystic writings or of works of art.

In Tantric literature we frequently come upon examples of the sandhyā bāṣyā, the so-called 'Twilight Language'. This term is not without difficulties. Early translators considered the sandhyā bāṣyā a language of riddles and mysteries. Haraprasād Shāstri (1916, cited in Eliade 1960) proposed that the term means twilight-language, mainly as sandhyā means twilight. In 1928, Vidushekar Shāstri proposed that the term is a corruption of sandhāyā, meaning 'intentional'. In his interpretation the secret language is not twilighty and diffuse but on the contrary aims at something specific with full intent. There is some truth to both interpretations. On one hand, the metaphors are full of a secret and hidden intent, on the other, they are twilighty in that they half suggest and half define, and leave a lot open to your interpretation. Eliade preferred the *'Intentional Language'*, as do others who believe that there is something specific hidden behind each odd piece of symbolism. However, this is not always the case. In many instances a metaphor turns out to be a code for another metaphor, meaning something else in turn which is equally perplexing. The hidden meaning is an entire series of hidden meanings and there is no end in sight. Good! An open system is just the thing to keep you alert and awake. The body itself can be a metaphor and any thing can represent something else. Now there are some scholars who believe that the sandhyā bāṣyā was employed to hide a true meaning from uninitiates. I have my doubts regarding this interpretation. Here is a passage from a poem by Rāmprasād Sen, translation by Rachel Fell McDermott, highly recommended (2001: 106-7)

All her modesty gone,
she plays with him
overturning sexual custom
by being on top.
Choked up,
waves of bliss sweeping over Her,
She hangs her head and smiles-
Love incarnate!
The Yamuna, the heavenly Ganges, and between them
the honourable Sarasvati-
bathing at their confluence
confers great merit.

What is the meaning of the passage? Our poet alludes to the raising of the Kuṇḍalinī. The three rivers are the subtle channels within body; here, river Sarasvatī corresponds to the suṣuṁnā. Their confluence is the ājñācakra in the brain. Now why would anyone bother to keep the technique of Kuṇḍalinī waking secret? It's hardly worth the effort. There are millions of people on this planet today who have read something regarding the Kuṇḍalinī at one time or another. What was it good for? How many have any practical experience? When we speak of Kuṇḍalinī, of the fire snake or the supreme Śakti we are still deep within the realm of twilight language. Kuṇḍalinī is not a serpent, the serpent is not on fire, and the supreme Śakti is such an enigmatic concept that getting to understand her can take years of dedicated spiritual exercise. The rivers are a metaphor (i.e. a useful lie), but so are the energy channels of your body, and indeed so is your body. Everything that has form is a metaphor. Mere talk, and explaining one symbol with another, has never made anybody happy. If you think that you can find the real thing hiding behind a cryptic term, you are forgetting that in Indian thought real things do not exist. So what if we leave the concept of a language of codes and ciphers and replace it by a language of suggestion and stimulation?

Let's look at some examples of sandhyā bāṣyā, the Twilight Language.

Kālī, as you can see in countless images and statues, wears a garland of human heads. What is the meaning of this gory image? On the crudest level it could be an image of human sacrifice. Humans were occasionally sacrificed for religious reasons in ancient India, though in later periods only the kings retained the right to make this offering and rarely made use of it. Here is a goddess, say the severed heads, for whom people died, a goddess used to consume humans and beasts, a deity with the power of life and death. On a more subtle level the heads are symbols for the phonemes of the Saṅskṛt alphabet. Each head signifies one of the primal sounds that make up the world-glamour, a current, a path, a form of energy and sentience. As the heads can be sounds, so the sounds can be heads. Each sound has a consciousness, has organs of sensual perception, and each of them has a subtle personality. Assembling the syllables of Kālī's necklace is to create words, dreams, images, is to combine streams of fluid vibration that form, maintain, and dissolve realities. In this sense each word is alive and the purer its vibration the more powerful its efficiency. A third interpretation is more personal: the heads are the lifetimes you have given to the Great Work, the many, many reincarnations dedicated to the refinement of yourself. A fourth interpretation could cite the heads as the personalities you assembled and shed during this lifetime. How many persons have you been? How many of them were built up, worn, and discarded in your dance through the spirals of time? You change, as you have ever changed, and all that you were, are, and will be are the jewels adorning the throat of the dark goddess. How precious are those gems? What have you offered and what will you offer next? Here we meet Kālī as sheer liberation. The head you are wearing now will be the next one to drip its quintessence into the polished bone cup, and so will be the next. Who feeds on the essence?

Which interpretation do you prefer? You just won 52 bonus karma points if you chose all. The true meaning is all of them, and a good many besides which you or I have never even thought of. This is the time to be creative. What else do the severed heads mean to you? Think up at least five before you decide that you understand anything.

Śiva's ash-smeared body is another good example. The lord of ascetics appears white due to the ashes on his naked body. What are the ashes? On a material level, ashes can be used to repel some insects and parasites, which may be useful when one is living on mountains, roadsides, and cremation places. Some ashes make good disinfectants, their astringents being useful to draw wounded tissue and insect bitten sores together. On a more subtle level, the ashes are the metaphorical ashes of the world consumed by fire. Having burned up all desire and bondage of and to the world, the god of adepts goes naked, clothed only in a thin and dusty layer of soot, the purified memories of past attachments. A third level is more specific, here the ashes are the ashes of the dead, collected at the cremation place, and worn on body to show the death of the personal or human identity. A fourth interpretation, more pastoral in its outer form, appears in the numerous rituals telling in long detail how the manure of a cow should be collected - caught in mid-flight - consecrated with various gestures and mantras, and burned on a sacred fire till only the ashes remain. These are applied to body as a heal-all, they are also use to whitewash houses. The manure is considered one of the five jewels of the cow and appears prominently in Āyurvedic medicine. These rituals were carried to amazing extremes of pointless complication. See, for instance, the *Devī Bhāgavatam*, 9, 9-15. On a much rarer and more obscure level, there are a few Tantric sects that hold the term cow as an euphemism for the sacred human female, the five jewels being bodily excretions of the inspired and entranced priestess. These systems evolved a science of refining psychosexual

Figure 17 - Ardhanariśvarī or Ardhanariśvara
The divine hermaphrodite, the Lady or Lord made of two parts. Stone, central India, 12th century.

sacraments. One of these is the incinerated excrement of the priestess who has refined it in her state of raging ecstasy. Is this all there is to them? Of course not. Pause and think up at least another five meanings if you want to plumb the deep for further insight.

Whatever level of meaning you obtain in your contemplation, you can be sure it is not the final one. One true purpose of twilight language is not to veil a single and obscure 'real meaning' but to open the mind for fresh inspiration. The Tantrics had no need to be secretive about the 'real thing', there are lots of 'real things' around for anyone to comprehend, and most of them go by unnoticed. By avoiding defining their terminology precisely, those adepts created texts of such depth that you can spend all of your life seeking and finding meaning in them without ever coming to an end.

Śiva and Śakti

Well, you know about this. Everybody does. There's Śiva and Śakti, male and female, penis and vulva, and the whole thing can be packaged as divine sexuality. We owe so much rubbish to New Age Tantra. In the real world things are a lot more complicated. They also make much more sense and are not quite as sexistic. Ready to open your mind?

One of the basic concepts that people assume to be Tantric is a polarity. Before we go into polarity, we should start out at the beginning. Most Indian religions postulate an ultimate Brahman, an un-defined, nameless, all-enclosing consciousness. As Brahman is everywhere and nowhere, it is also everything and nothing. What you, I, and every other living entity perceives as its self is essentially Brahman in the form of jīva (the incarnate all-self, i.e. 'soul') plus a lot of misconceptions. These are called personality, personal history, ego, or identity. To be conscious of everything, Brahman has to be No Thing. Out of Brahman arises the divine game. Numerous Indian religions started out from this point and decided that out of Brahman arises a polarity. This polarity is sometimes (not always) personified as Śiva and Śakti. And here things begin to get complicated. Śiva, as you know, is a much older deity than the Tantric movement. In popular folk belief, he is a god of ascetics, dancers, philosophers, saints, and yogīs who walks the earth nude, or only clad in a leopard loincloth, smeared with white ashes, hair long and tangled, wearing serpents around his neck, a moon on his head, and a trident in his hand. It's an image of the ascetic who has left society to seek liberation. To make things more complicated, his sign is a liṅga, usually a phallic image, carved out of wood, stone, or made from clay or other materials. This has lead a lot of Western writers, especially disapproving ones, to identify him as a god of fertility and sexual indulgence. While there is some truth to this identification, you might consider that liṅga has several meanings. In the Purāṇas, the liṅga appears as a radiant pillar of flame and sheer energy. It has no beginning or end, is attached to nothing and crosses all the heavens, earths, and underworlds. The primal liṅga is a column of vibration much like the countless trees of life, world pillars, world mountains that appear in Eurasian Shamanism. It is the axis of the world and the way by which a shaman may travel into other realities. The primal liṅga is not a penis at all. The word liṅga has more meanings. 1. characteristic; 2. sign, symbol, emblem; 3. Śiva's emblem; 4. penis; in twilight language it can also be a metaphor for the human spine, or for the entire human form sitting erect in meditation and yoga. Some texts, such as the *Kaulajñāna nirṇaya*, describe a liṅga within body which is adorned with various flowers: an image of the energetic counterpart of the human spine and the various cakras. Here, the worship of outer liṅgas, no what material, is considered a grave misunderstanding. Other systems propose that one should meditate on liṅgas in head, breast, and belly, here the word means signs or characteristics. The *Tirumantiram*, verse 1726 (D. J. Smith, 1996) states:

The human form is like the Śiva liṅga
The human form is like Cidambaram
The human form is like Sadāśiva
The human form is like the Holy Dance.

Now Śiva is not only a god of folk-religion, he is also a god with numerous faces. There are hundreds of gods in India which have been identified, at one time or another, as aspects of Śiva. When you read original texts (which I dearly hope you will) you will notice that the usual frame of the text is a dialogue between Śiva and Śakti. This does not necessarily mean that these names appear anywhere. Often you can find the two calling each other by dozens of names within a single text.

Folk religion often misleads when its imagery is too simple. When Śiva's image is a penis (liṅga), the image of Śakti is a vulva (yoni). The two forms often appear in temples and shrines, much to the disgust of conquering Muslims, Christian missionaries, and Indian reformers, and have produced the mistaken idea that their cult is primarily one of lovemaking. To this day, and possibly today more than ever, people assume that Tantra is a form of sanctified eroticism, and that its devotees are obsessed with sexuality. Some of them may be, but just as many are living in chastity, in fact most of the surviving schools of Tantra recommend celibacy.

While Śiva is easy to recognise due to his highly specialised iconography, Śakti remains universal. There are few representations of Śakti as such. Śakti, meaning force, power, energy (this includes form and matter in Indian thought) is rarely shown as herself in popular iconography. Instead, she appears as one of many hundreds of goddesses. Depending on the mood of their interaction, Śakti and Śiva assume various forms and personalities. In folk-religion, the two are a divine couple whose lovemaking creates, maintains, and destroys the multiverse. This is a very simple idea as it implies human gender and sexual dynamics. It also implies a male and a female participant. Well and good for the simple minded, or for the people who go to 'Tantric workshops' to get a bit of basic sexual education. In the more refined systems of Tantra, especially among the traditions of Kashmir, the polarity of Śakti and Śiva is a lot more refined.

Tantric lore is complex when it comes to the question of gender and divinity. Some Tantric texts proposed that males manifest Śiva while females manifest Śakti. In the influential *Kulārṇava Tantra 8, 103*, Śiva states: *O Kuleśvarī! Why to speak much. In the midst of a Cakra all men become like Me and all women like You.* Maybe a step in the right direction, as it acknowledges a divine element in all human beings. However, as Śmaśāna Kālī insists, to believe that people are divine according to their genital shape and social role is daft beyond comprehension. It may violate the sensibilities of a good many simple minded Śāktas, but it takes much more than a simple set of genitals, costumes, and mannerisms to manifest Śakti or Śiva. People who invest humans in roles of deified sexuality simply do not go far enough. Being Śakti or Śiva according to gender roles and anatomy is not good enough. We have had millennia of sexual discrimination without anybody being significantly happier or wiser. Bodies may appear female or male, incarnate souls are both and neither. In most human beings divinity resides only in potential, and possession of a vagina or penis is hardly enough to claim holiness. In fact, the more 'male' or 'female' people pretend to be, the less divine they usually are. Spirituality should aim at wholeness and understanding, sexism aims at keeping people different and separate. It hardly matters whether a given gender is damned or deified: to insist on fundamental differences is to further apartheid. What happens when you forget about gender definitions (biological and social) and begin to see each being as unique?

Think about it. In a few generations, the biological sciences will have developed to such a point that there will be dozens of genders in body and mind. People of the future will chose what they want to be. They will look back at the past and wonder how incredibly primitive we were.

Luckily, there is a deeper stratum to Kaula which transcends the limits of body and social conditioning. Above, you read how the *Kulārṇava Tantra* deifies gender roles. The good book is a compilation that has been meddled with for at least three centuries. Hence, it is hardly surprising to find contradictions. *Kulārṇava Tantra, 8, 97*, trans. Rai:

> *Whether a woman or man, a Cāṇḍala or a high-born Dvija, there is absolutely no discrimination in the cakra (ritual circle). Everyone here is considered like Śiva.*
>
> *9, 41. O Devī! Body itself is the temple. The Jīva (incarnate soul) itself is god Sadāśiva (Eternal Auspiciousness). Do away with the faded flowers of ignorance and worship with the consciousness of 'He am I' (So'haṁ).*
>
> *42. Jīva is Śiva, Śiva is Jīva, the Jīva is only Śiva. When in bondage it is called Jīva; when freed from bondage it is called Sadāśiva.*

In advanced Kaula, Krama, Trika, Śiva is not a male god but pure consciousness. Śiva could be described as pure, passive awareness, as a watcher and witness, as the formless self that delights in the ceaseless play of images, entities, and realities that constitute the world. As such, the supreme consciousness is literally nothing. Abhinavagupta wrote:

> *"That thought, viz 'nothing is mine' by which the senseless creatures are reduced to wretchedness incessantly, that very thought viz 'nothing is mine' means to me 'I am everything'" (PTV, 2002:57)*

Śakti, by contrast, is force, power, energy, and as all things that exist are energy, Śakti is literally every thing. We are a long way from gender here. Let's have a look at kula and akula. Kula means family, group, cluster, clan, and refers to Śakti. As Śakti is form and power, she is also all things, and things, as we all know, relate to each other, create, maintain, and destroy each other, in short, you cannot even perceive a single thing without being in relation with a lot of others. Thus, the way of kula is from the monad to the multiple, everything that exists is a Śakti and every Śakti creates more Śaktis. Akula means without family, group, cluster, or clan and refers to Śiva. Here Śiva is the sentience that, free of relation and attachment, exists within the play but is not part of it. In meditation, kula is a form of trance where you disappear into everything, and akula a trance where you withdraw from everything to nothing. Both of them are pretty much the same regarding the outcome, but the way of trance-formation differs. When kula and akula unite, we attain Kaula. In this model, there are no male or female participants. Every being is consciousness (Śiva) and form/energy (Śakti). Awareness is Śiva, body is Śakti. This means that every single thing this wide world consists of is Śakti. The body of every person, animal, plant, mineral, element, spirit, or god is Śakti. This goes for males as well as females. *The male form, the female form, any form - all forms are undoubtedly Her Supreme Form.* (*Gandharva Tantra*). And where it comes to ritual worship, whoever YOU are, you are Śiva consciousness in Śakti body. When you unite with your partner, you are always Śiva, no matter whether you happen to inhabit a male or female body, and your partner, no matter the gender, is always Śakti. By the same mouth you are Śakti to every other living being. In a very important way Śakti is what Austin Spare referred to as All-Otherness, while Śiva might be considered all Thisness, if the Thisness were anything at all (which it isn't). As most Tantric traditions proclaim, Śakti and Śiva are two in principle, but in reality they are one (or none). It's impossible to tell the difference. Without awareness, form does not exist. Without form, there is nothing to be aware of. Hence the famous saying that Śiva is Śava (a corpse) without Śakti. Nor is this all there is to it. Another interpretation goes beyond this and proposes that both are consciousness, Śiva being formless consciousness and Śakti being consciousness-in-form. A third interpretation proposes that both of them arise out of the Supreme Śakti, who happens to be pure consciousness.

Figure 18 - Bhairava
Bhairava in Chola style, bronze, 10th - 11th century. Today in Paris.

Sex, Gender, and Religion

In traditional Indian thought, women seem a necessary evil. This was not always the case, if only barely so. In Vedic times (1500-800 BCE), as W. F. Menski (in Leslie 1992) shows, women still had a few rights and a measure of respect. The *Vedas* honour women for fertility and compare them with the fields which nourish all. This may not seem much, but it is better than in classical times (800 BCE-200 CE), when they were considered mere vessels to receive sperm and bring forth sons. In the Vedic period, girls were considered ripe for marriage when they were physically old enough to bear children. In the classical period, child marriages became the norm. In Vedic times, women could play an important, though secondary part in the great śrauta sacrifices. Like everybody else, they had to employ a host of Brahmins to do the ritual for them. It did not happen often, but we do have evidence for high-ranking ladies sponsoring sacrifices and gaining the spiritual benefits. In the classical period their role was much reduced. Those women who used to participate in ritual were replaced by priests who assumed some of their roles, and their presence could be substituted by items of gold or female figures made from sacred kuśa grass. As a result, female ritualism shifted from the public śrauta rites to the private, domestic gṛhya rites. These rituals were not as standardised as the official ones, in fact, they developed into a wide range of individual varieties. In certain circumstances, such as marriage, the women's contribution to ritual remains essential.

Now what sort of life could a woman expect in ancient India? The birth of a girl is not generally a happy occasion. To this day, there are families who are driven into bankruptcy by having too many daughters. Sons remain in the family and often provide the old age support for their parents. Daughters leave the house after marriage, and indeed the dowry, marriage celebration, and the feeding of the guests can throw the family clan into debt for decades, if not generations. So in spite of human instinct, a good many families saw the birth of a daughter as yet another step towards starvation. When a girl married, she was supposed to forget her old family (not that this ever worked). She was literally expected to venerate her husband as a deity, to obey all commands, to satisfy all of his whims, and to give up any individuality she had possessed earlier. In a traditional Hindu marriage, the woman becomes *'half of her husband'*, but her husband doesn't become half of his wife. Hindu women had very few choices. When they were young, their parents ordered them around, when they were married the new family continued the job. Look at the *Varnāśrama Dharma* (Glasenapp 1958), where you can read that the girl is protected by the father, the wife is protected by her husband, the sons protect her in old age, and never shall she be independent. The *Laws of Manu* have a very similar passage, only that Manu did not care about protection. In his version, the issue is 'being obedient to'. The laws of Manu also state: 'animals, drums, illiterates, low classes and women are worthy of being beaten.' This trend began

Figure 19 - Bhairava.
Wooden sculpture, southern India, 19th century.

fairly early. In the Soma rites, Soma is occasionally identified with sperm. In the great Soma rite, women were not allowed to draw the sacred fluid.

As a legend relates (F. Smith in Leslie 1992) the Vedic goddesses tried to draw Soma with a cup, but the Soma was weak and 'could not stand'. *Taittirīyasaṁhitā* 6.5.8 states: *Therefore women, who are powerless, inherit nothing and speak more humbly than an evil man.* For the same reason, we learn, they have no identity. Finally, the gods fashioned a vajra (thunderbolt) out of ghī. It strengthened the Soma, but it smote and emasculated the goddesses.

Old Indian literature is full of nasty remarks on women and the laws based on these teachings are just as merciless. A traditionally minded Hindu woman spends all of her life serving the males in her family. Even women of high caste do not have the right to undergo the ritual of the second birth, when Brāhmaṇa (priests, teachers, scholars), Kṣatriya (warriors, aristocracy), and Vaiṣya (merchants) acquire their spiritual maturity and are invested with the sacred thread. Śūdra (farmers, servants, artisans), tribal folk, untouchables, and outcasts are not admitted to this ritual and neither are women. Officially, women are not allowed to study the *Vedas*, to sacrifice for themselves, to lead religious ceremonies, or to leave society as an ascetic. The situation may be a bit easier for women of high castes and good family, and a lot better in the city than in the country, but on the whole there is an amazing amount of cruelty to women that continues to this day. Just as an example, in 2001 more than seven thousand newly married Indian women were killed by their husbands or husband's families because their dowry was considered too small.

Now the general opinion of society is not quite what the fringes believe. Hindu scripture is thoroughly Brahmanical, i.e. it reflects the way the Brahmin class would have liked to order the world. They never really managed to get so much control, so when you find regulations in the holy writ, you should remember that the vast majority of Indians did not quite live up to scriptural law. In India, just as everywhere in the world, you find parents who dearly love their daughters, and husbands who have the good sense to listen to their wives. Nor should we project Western notions of liberation and equality on a culture where a good many people believe that liberation can only come to people who endure and suffer anything and everything the universe can throw at them.

The value of women depends very much on the society they live in. The Vaiṣṇavas generally accept strict Brahmanical lore, meaning that women are to serve their husbands as ever. Nevertheless, there are small groups of Tantric Vaiṣṇavas who worship women in general as embodiments of the goddess Śrī Lakṣmī. This idea is elaborated at some length in the *Lakṣmī Tantra* 43, 59-72, where the goddess herself explains that all women are her manifestation. To abuse a woman is to abuse the goddess, to think badly of a woman is to disrespect the goddess. *O Śakra, just as there is sin neither in Nārāyaṇa nor in myself, nor in a cow, nor in a brahmin, nor in a scholar of Vedānta, so, O Śakra, there can be no evil in a woman ... Those who aspire to the attainment (of fulfilment) in yoga should always act so as to please a woman barring to commit a sin. One should regard her as one's mother, as god and as myself.* (trans. Sanjukta Gupta). This sort of ideology must have galled the traditionalists a lot. It was also much against the belief of those Vaiṣṇavas (the vast majority) who did not embrace Tantra. The *Lakṣmī Tantra* (*LT*) is an almost revolutionary work in the eyes of the fundamentalists. Nevertheless, it contains elements of traditional restriction, such as the notion that a woman may receive initiation only if she respects her husband, never neglects her religious and social duties, has a clear idea of truth, and when her husband allows it (*LT 21, 40-41*). There were several ladies who were acknowledged Tantric saints and who had to keep their spiritual activity private as their husband's families were against it (Gupta in Leslie 1992). This sort of thing is typical for Vaiṣṇavas, you don't find it so often among Śaivas and Śāktas. To Tantric Vaiṣṇavas, the identification went even further. In the worship of Viṣṇu, the most popular form of the deity is charming, cheerful Kṛṣṇa. Consequently, worshippers attempt to unite with him. To do so, they imitate the loving yearning felt for Kṛṣṇa by his Śakti Rādhā. In this system, Rādhā is not only in love with Kṛṣṇa, she also goes through a detailed and systematic range of emotions that range from mild affection to raging passion and involve a lot of special performances, such as jealousy, obsessive brooding, spite, mad rapture, delirious scatterbrainedness, and whatnot. The entire spectrum of human longing and fulfilment is her art, and as she loves not a human but a deity, she is a role model for the worshipper. Easy enough for the women in the congregation and mind-expanding for the men. Some of the more devout male worshippers identify so intensely with Rādhā that they dress as women and live in the women's quarters. A good example is Bengal's mad saint Rāmakṛṣṇa, who went into Rādhā-consciousness to such an extent that the women in his company completely forgot that the bearded guy in a sari was physically a man. Rāmakṛṣṇa usually did things to extremes, so no-one was really surprised when, a while later, he decided to worship Rama as Hanuman, the monkey-god, tied up his cloth so that a long tail dangled between his legs and spent some weeks living in a tree.

Among the Śaivas, Śakti became the perfect role model for the partner of the god. Here the bias was still towards Śiva, who was often assumed to be the source, guru, and lover of Śakti. Women had their place in this system, even if it was a slightly inferior one. Among the Śaiva Tantrics, women are sacred in that they embody a goddess. However, Śiva remains the supreme principle. Here Śakti is the supreme power, but Śiva is the power holder. It is only among the top level mystics of Śaivism that you encounter the realisation that Śiva and Śakti are not only the same, they can't even be told apart. At this level of no-difference, it does not matter whether you speak of Śiva or Śakti, as all you are saying is merely words.

Then there are the Śāktas, worshippers who believe that Śakti is the highest principle and that the male gods are mere expressions of her will. *Therefore, O king! Know this that this whole universe is under the control of Yoga Māyā; The Devas, men, birds, what more everything from Brahmā down to a blade of grass are all under the control of Yoga Māyā. Brahmā, Viṣṇu and Hara all are bound by the rope of Her Māyā. So they roam easily by Her Māyā from womb to womb like a spider.* (*DB*, 5, 1). There are several distinct movements among the Śāktas, but most of them propose some goddess, or group of goddesses, as the gate to Brahman. The more extreme sects even propose that Brahman is an expression of Śakti, and teach that the polarity of Śakti/Śiva is really a unity, which is Śakti. You would think that such cults tend to have a high opinion of women, but this is not always the case. It is one thing to worship a goddess and quite another to treat the little housewife well. Even the most massive work of Śākta theology, the *Devī Bhāgavatam*,(1, 5) has a nasty little episode where the goddess Lakṣmī declares that the natural qualities of women are falsehood, vain boldness, craftiness, stupidity, impatience, over-greediness, impurity, and harshness. Quite a contrast to hundreds of pages celebrating the absolute sovereignty of goddesses! Casual sexism can also be observed in the very last chapter of the work (*DBh* 12, 16) where we learn that at navarātrī, all can read the book, no matter what caste or which goddess is worshipped as the personal deity. *Never any woman nor any Śudra is to read this herself or himself, even out of ignorance; rather they should hear this from the mouth of a Brāhmaṇa.* Very considerate, especially as the Brahmin deletes anything he doesn't like and wants to be paid for the job. Thus, being a Śākta means that a goddess is worshipped but does not always imply that women have rights. The existence of powerful goddesses says nothing regarding the rights of living women. Just think of ancient Greece. Athena, goddess of war, crafts, and wisdom (an uneasy mixture) was venerated by a good many respectable men. Nevertheless, the women of Athens had hardly any rights. They could not leave the house without male company, they had to wear heavy veils in public, could not own property, and were generally treated with contempt. Most grew up without any education and the sole respect they received was for fertility. The only women who were cherished in classical Greek society were the better sort of prostitutes, who were often skilled in the arts, learned in literature, and able to converse on all manner of subjects. The respectable Greek housewife had fewer rights than most women in the classical world. In ancient Rome, by contrast, where Athena was venerated as Minerva, women owned property, went where they liked, worshipped any god of their choice, and divorced their husbands when they felt like it. So when we think of Śāktas, we should keep in mind that this is a general term for a wide range of religious movements. A few of these accepted the idea that women embody a goddess, and some of the worshippers certainly made an effort to live according to this teaching. However, a religion is not the same thing as a system of self-cultivation. A good many Śāktas simply imagined their god in female form without attempting to do something regarding woman's place in society.

It is only among movements of the left-hand path, such as the Kaula, Krama the Yoginī Kula, and some minor schools of Tantric Buddhism that anyone tried to do something for women as such. Several important source texts explicitly insist on the rights of women. The *Kaulajñāna nirṇaya* declares that worshippers should never speak harshly to maidens or women. It also advises that girls and women should be worshipped as they are Śakti. The same mood can be found in several Kaula texts. *One should make obeisance on seeing a young woman of a Kaula family. One should bow to any female, be she a young girl, or flushed with youth, or be she old, be she beautiful or ugly, good or wicked. One should never deceive, speak ill of, or do ill to a woman and one should never strike her. All such acts prevent the attainment of Siddhi.* (*Kaulāvali Tantra*).

The *Mantra Mahodhadhiḥ* 1 states: *The devotee of Kālī should refrain from killing or beating women or misbehaving with them, or indulging into unpleasant dialogues with them if he is desirous of welfare.*

Likewise, the *Mahānirvāṇa Tantra* contains several chapters in which Śiva advises kings on matters of law. These legal chapters, while full of the dullest middle-class morality, contain very clear instructions regarding the protection of women. Men who commit incest or seduce Brahmin women are to be castrated, and *a man who ravishes a woman, even if she be the wife of a Chandala, should be punished by death, and should never be pardoned.* The laws are also very strict with regard to adultery and generally punish the man harder than the woman. This may be because in old India a woman who lost her reputation also lost her husband, her home, her status, her children, and often her life. What a price to pay for a bit of fun! Among Kaulas, harming a woman was a major offence, and for this reason, some Kaula Tantras favour a monogamous lifestyle and propose that the worshippers should be married. I should add that in ancient India, there were several forms and types of marriage ranging from the very serious and traditional involving ritual participation of both family clans to the more informal rites performed by lovers who have run away from their families (and who could blame them?). The Vaiṣṇava Tantrics do not always concur with this opinion. As their favourite incarnation of Viṣṇu, the black, flute playing god Kṛṣṇa is not very faithful to his consort Rādhā and spends lots of time flirting and making love with the cow-girls of the countryside, the worshippers of some cults consider adultery a form of worship and attempt to imitate their deity by doing likewise.

The topic of adultery is one of the most enigmatic in Tantric literature. Many Tantras propose that the worshipper should have congress with the Paraśakti. Now 'para' has two meanings. It can mean the supreme or ultimate, in which case the Paraśakti is the absolute goddess, the supreme reality which creates Śiva (consciousness) and Śakti (form/energy) plus everything else. This supreme Śakti is not a human being. However, in the preparation for ritual intercourse the human partner is identified with the Paraśakti. The partner is adored as the deity and the image of the deity is superimposed over the body of the partner. When the deity and the partner fuse, obsession begins. The other meaning of 'para' is 'of another'. In this reading, the Paraśakti is the Śakti (here, mate, or woman) of another (man). A text proposing that the worshipper should unite with the Supreme Śakti may be misunderstood as adulterous union with the wife of another man. The first interpretation is often taken by adepts, the second is very common in anti-tantric propaganda. There are, after all, Tāntrikas who take everything as of symbolic value while others insist on taking everything literally. To confuse things further, there were some Kaula teachers who believed in transgressing any social norm on principle. These people went for adultery simply as it was forbidden, but they also identified the partner with the supreme Śakti. Finally, we should keep in mind that a large number of worshippers chose an ascetic lifestyle on the road. Some of them married other ascetics, but others lived primarily alone and had very few opportunities for making love with anyone, except married women and prostitutes. One of the reasons that several Tantras eulogise barber girls, washerwomen, and prostitutes is that these low-class women were more easily available than women from the higher classes.

In the teachings of the left-hand-path, gender distinctions are not always of importance. To quote Vimalānanda (commentary to the *Karpūrādi Stotra,* 1837 in Woodroffe 2001): *He who is Śiva is also Śakti and She who is Śakti is also Śiva. Fatherhood and Motherhood are mere distinctions of name. In reality they stand for one and the same thing. The Tantra Śāstra again says that Śakti, Maheśvara, Brahman all denote the same Being. Male, female, neuter are verbal and not real distinctions... We may meditate on Mahādevī as either female or male, for these terms may be attributed to any gross body.*

A similar sentiment is expressed in the *Devī Bhāgavatam*, 9, 1: *... those that are foremost and the highest of the Yogīs do not recognise any difference between a male and a female. All is Brahman.*

The same appears in Tantric Buddhism. Padmasaṁbhava allegedly said: *The basic condition for enlightenment is a human body. Male or female makes no great difference. But when the spirit turns towards enlightenment, a female body is better.*

Or take this highly revolutionary statement attributed to the goddess Tārā: *As there is no such thing as a male or female, bondage to the 'male' or 'female' is hollow.* (Trimondi 1999: 381, 373)

When it comes to divine conduct, we encounter gods who are apt to change their gender as they will. Each male deity has a female form. In each case, the Śakti form is the active and powerful one. In a certain sense, Śaivī is the Śakti of Śiva, but so are a number of goddesses, such as Durgā, Kālī, or Pārvatī, who appear as independent entities and not simply as Śiva in feminine form. This may sound paradoxical but isn't: in Hindu religion, gods are not sharply defined separate beings but tend to change appearance and merge into one another whenever they (or the worshippers) feel like it. In mythology, cases of sex-changing are not unusual. In the *Cidambara Māhātyma* the gods Śiva and Viṣṇu go to the pine forest to tempt the ascetics. Śiva assumes the form of an unusually good looking young beggar while Viṣṇu appears as his beautiful wife. They successfully seduce all the younger ascetics and their wives but fail with a few elder sages, who try to destroy them by magical weapons projected from the sacrificial fire. Out of the raging flames tiger, deer, axe, mantra, and dwarf appear and assault the deities. Śiva subdues them all and takes each of them as his attribute. Then he dances the world destroying, liberating tāṇḍava dance for the very first time.

Śiva also appears in female form. Mookerjee (1988) gives an episode from the *Purāṇas* (no source specified): ... King Īla, while hunting, came upon a grove where Śiva was making love with Pārvatī and had taken the form of a woman to please her. Everything in the woods, even trees, had become female, and as he approached, King Īla was turned into a woman. Śiva. laughing, told him he could 'ask any boon except masculinity'.

It should not be assumed that the invention of such Śaktis is merely a philosophic device to produce a female form of a usually male god. Some texts, such as the *Mahānirvāṇa Tantra* (5, 56) include such Śaktīs in their daily ritual routine. In the morning, the worshipper meditates on Brahmī, who is a reddish maiden, clad in black antelope pelt, adorned with a crystal mālā, holding a gourd of sacred water and riding on a swan. At midday, the worshipper meditates on Vaiṣṇavī, who is a golden lady within a solar disk wearing a garland of wild flowers. She has full breasts, her four hands hold conch, mace, discus, and lotus, and she rides a Garuḍa bird. The evening meditation is on Śaivī, who appears as an ancient crone, white and clad in white, friendly and generous, whose four hands hold trident, noose, spear, and skull. She rides a bull.

Here we encounter Brahmā, Viṣṇnu and Śiva in female form. The Śaktīs, however, are more than just copies of the male gods. There are individual developments to the devīs (such as the three times of the day) which do not occur in their male form. Some male deities were modelled on female goddesses. The terrible Mahākāla (Great Devourer, i.e. time), black, nude, with bulging eyes, terrifying teeth and snakes, is modelled on Mahākālī. He is Mahākālī's spouse and officially a form of Śiva, but on close examination he is clearly a male personification of the dark goddess herself.

Three Temperaments

Indo-Europeans in general were crazy about trinities. If anything could be ordered in groups of three, it usually was. You find this foible among Celts and Germans just as in Greek myth and Indian cosmology. One of the best known and least understood trinity is the guṇas. The word guṇa has several meanings, two of which are: 1. Thread 2. Quality or characteristic. The three qualities are one of the fundamental ideas in Hindu philosophy. Śakti as Prakṛti (nature, matter) is thought to consist of three guṇas: sattva, rajas, and tamas. Tamas is easiest to understand: the word means 'darkness' (related to English 'dim' from the IE. *demu-, darkness, twilight, gloom) and is used to describe heaviness, inertia, stability, and, in the range of human emotions, ignorance, sloth, routine-mindedness, worldliness, and materialism. Rajas is hot, energetic, active, restless, and the only changeable guṇa. In human experience, rajas is expressed as excitement, passion, outbursts, obsessions, drives, restlessness, sadness. Sattva, the saguṇa, is called 'good' in the sense of 'goodness'. Sattva is the most delicate of the three guṇas. It appears as refined, calm and subtle, hard to define, and not always comprehensible.

The three qualities are often identified by colour. Tamas is dark, black, or brown, rajas is red and fiery, and sattva is of a pale, moonlike whiteness. These colour codes are often found in Hindu literature, where they sometimes yield a deeper meaning and just as often produce confusion. An example. To some people, the popular trinity of gods follows the pattern of creator, maintainer, and destroyer. These functions are filled with several deities, and as many believe, the proper order is Brahmā for creation, Viṣṇu for maintenance, and Śiva or Rudra for destruction. This is a popular idea that looks good in books but has little to do with what the worshippers of these deities believe. To devotees of Śiva, Śiva is not only in charge of destruction but of all three functions, and the same is believed by all devotees of Viṣṇu and the few who still worship Brahmā. Śiva is often coupled with Kālī, who also appears dark and destructive to the uninitiated, and consequently a lot of folks believe that Śiva and Kālī have a tamasic nature and are dark gods. To the worshippers of these gods, things look a lot different. Kālī's all-devouring mouth, for instance, is said to contain all three qualities: the lips are dark (tamas), the gums are red (rajas), and the pointed teeth are white (sattva). When the goddess devours the worshipper, the latter goes through all three guṇas before finding liberation in the central void.

From the guṇas arose a triple structure that is vital for the understanding of Tantra. Worshippers are classed according to the qualities that dominate in their character. We are talking of qualities here, not of people as such. Keep in mind that this is a very fluid model of the world and that people change all the time. Imagine a string spun of three fibres, one black, one red, and one white, and imagine the weaving in the texture of the world. Each living being is composed of all three guṇas and all three are needed for liberation. It is only when one guṇa dominates the others that things tend to become extreme.

Paśu. First are the paśus, a word that can mean a layperson, a person lacking spiritual education, or a domestic animal. Depending on the tone of the Tantra, a paśu can be a simple and ignorant fellow-human or, more often, a beast of burden, bound by the chains of attachment, involvement, and sensuality. Some texts portray the paśu as a stupid beast, a crude and unspiritual person. This is not quite true. The paśu is already a Tantric worshipper. The word paśu evolved from paś, meaning to bind, a pāśa is a noose. The *Kulārṇava Tantra* lists eight basic forms of bondage:

1. Pity, 2. Ignorance and Delusion, 3. Fear, 4. Shame, 5. Disgust, 6. Family, 7. Custom, and 8. Station in Society, Caste.

Anyone bound by these snares is still, technically speaking, in the realm of the paśu. You may notice that this goes for almost everyone on this bonny earth. Paśus suffer of three inpurities: 1. Lack of or wrong knowledge of self, 2. Belief in separate identities, and 3. Bondage to activity, doing, and its results. To be free of all these is to be Śiva. In the

Figure 20 - Spotted Mouse-deer.
You know those tusks!

paśu, rajas acts on tamas and this tends to produce worldliness, ignorance, and sloth. Lots has been written about this type, suffice it here to say that paśu lives in a dualistic reality where s/he is apart from the gods, the gods are apart from each other, society has its ordained distinctions, and so have cultures, religions, and countries. The paśu leads a worldly life and likes it. S/he is religious to some extent, in practice or in principle but there is often a wide gap between what is believed in general and done in particular. Paśu worship has its time and place, it is not usually extended into daily life or allowed to interfere with a good meal. Regarding deities, paśus are often inclined to install them in parent roles. *'Hey dad, these boys were nasty to me! Go and hit them! Hey mum, can I have some sweets?'* In this sense, a good many worshippers chose to curl up in the lap of Mother Kālī, not because Kālī's mythology is particularly motherly, but as appealing to her as a mother expresses the hope that she'll be nice to her child-like devotee. With regard to Tantric ritual, paśus are not allowed to do night-time ritual; this excludes them from personal Kālī-worship. They do not usually make use of yantra or practice night-time japa of mantra. Instead, their worship often follows Vedic lines, involving external sacrifices, lots of ritual baths and abstention from eating meat, fish, or having sexual intercourse except for procreation. When a paśu wants to practice the pañcamakāras, meat, wine, fish, parched grains and ritual intercourse are prohibited. Instead, a number of symbolic alternatives are used. It should be added that a paśu is such due to her/his spiritual competence. There are rituals forbidden to paśus because they simply couldn't comprehend, let alone participate in them. A paśu attempting to enjoy the five sacraments in their vīratic form is not likely to do much worship, because of getting too excited.

Vīra. A vīra is literally a hero. Here rajas dominates and acts on sattva. The vira exhibits a 'heroic temperament' . S/he tends to be active (if not over-active), ambitious, and is rarely satisfied with any achievement. Vīras are excitable and often have a sense of the dramatic. Vīratic worship can involve rituals that make use of skulls, bones, and even corpses, it can be practised in bed-chambers, jungles, deserts, crossroads at night, and at the cremation place. In encountering the goddesses and gods, the vīra stands upright and heroically integrates all fears and desires. Vīratic meditations usually include fierce, terrifying, and revolting deities. In coming to terms and eventually uniting with them, the vīra transcends the limits of the human personality. When their temperament is more sattvic, they chose the path of liberation, but when their temperament shows strong tamasic influences, the vīra may prefer to cultivate siddhis (magical powers, skills, accomplishments) to achieve something in the world. There are also vīras who think, pragmatically, that liberation alone may be well and good, but a few magical skills may make things easier. This is true enough, but the difficulty is in doing it. The classical rite of the pañcamakāras is expressed in vīratic terms. The greatest problems of vīras is that they often act faster than they think. As they go in for drama and excitement, they naturally produce lots of it. Being involved in the world and acting with so much energy, they tend to make loads of mistakes and generally suffer from them. Indian literature associates sadness and sorrow with vīras, as they so often fall flat on their face.

Divya. Here we encounter what is sometimes considered the 'highest class of worshippers', i.e. those in whom the divine quality is strongest and a sattvic nature dominates. This sort of person is very hard to describe as the divine quality, whether in humans or the world at large, often tends to appear paradoxical. Some texts have attempted to define the divya. The *Kubjikā Tantra*, quoted by Sir John Woodroffe in his introduction to the *Mahānirvāṇa Tantra*, gives such a description. To mention just a few points, we learn that the divya spend most of the day with worship (at least thrice daily) and most of the night doing japa of mantra, is clean, well-read, educated, tolerant of other faiths, gives charity, makes no difference between friends and foes, eats only food blessed by the guru, always speaks truth, avoids godless company and talk, bows to the feet of women (whom he regards as his guru), worships all deities, offers everything to the supreme goddess, perceives Śiva in all people, and so on. This sounds like holiness, and like holiness it can be misunderstood and imitated. Plenty of people err when they try to play the divya. Mere imitation of outward holiness may impress fools, but not the gods, and certainly not the all-consciousness. If being a divya takes effort, it is obviously not natural. The more refined divyas transcend all this, they even transcend the notion of holiness, and where they practice ritual it is often veiled as profane acts in daily life or happens completely in the mind. Their big problem is that the people around them are not quite as holy. Divyas tend to see the deity in everyone. They forget that people are run by their egos, and that a potential deity is not the same thing as a manifest one. In short, they often assume the best and encounter disappointment. Also, divyas have problems in coping with every-bloody-day reality, with power politics, hierarchies, and a wide range of very typical human games.

Of course you have already wondered what class you belong to. This is a useful thought but also a misleading one. The three temperaments are not arranged in a linear progression from ignorant to active to divine. Think of a triangle. Each of the points is one of the temperaments; each has its strong points and its weaknesses. The temperaments in themselves are not role models but extremes. In between the points is where you encounter life. Invent at least two stages between paśu and vīra, two stages between vīra and divya, and (here we enter new lands) two stages between divya and paśu. You will soon learn that each temperament has advantages and shortcomings. A paśu may be more steady, reliable, and patient in devotion than a vīra, for example, and a vīra may get things done when paśu and divya are still sitting around waiting for something to happen. Of course the vīra is also likely to make mistakes when being busy, the price of doing is always misdeeds, and the price of interference is bondage. Vīras are so excitable and hasty, they often begin things without considering their outcome. Divyas, by comparison, may be calm and holy, but they do have problems in comprehending ordinary humans. A divya may be inclined to forget

Figure 21 - Female musician (drummer).
Surya temple, Konarak, Orissa, 13th century. To gladden oneself by making music, as the KCT advises after the morning purification and before beginning worship, is probably the most neglected part of Tantric worship nowadays. This is your chance for something new. Get an instrument and make yourself feel good!

about material necessities. Divyas in general often require help, if only to survive, as few of them manage to hold steady jobs. Often enough they damage their bodies when their ritual ecstasy is stronger than common sense (drinking Ganges water for instance or staying in cold or heat for too long). Occasionally the 'vision of no-difference' can destroy their physical vehicles or waste away their property.

Several Tantras point out that in our day and age, vīras are rare and divyas are a lot rarer. They find it hard to exist in a world that is run by materialistic idiots, war-mongers, profit-seekers, and exploiters of the innocent. Perhaps this is the chance to introduce some innovations. Make a pause now and think of yourself as all three characters. What are you like when you act the paśu, the vīra, and the divya? At what times do you play these parts? On what occasions? In which company? What mask is useful for which activities? When do you move from one consciousness to the other? What marks the moment of change? When could you do with a change for another role?

Three and a half consciousness states

In the *Upaniṣads* you can find attempts to order the way people experience the multiverse. This is called model making. In the classical model, there are three basic states of experience. These states are roughly known as deep sleep, waking, and dreaming. In **deep sleep** you are unaware of body, mind, and yourself. All definitions of what you consider yourself to be cease to operate, all sense of identity disappears, as does all awareness and attention. In this sense, dreamless sleep is pretty close to perfection. **Waking consciousness** is what you can perceive with your senses. Now the senses do not show the world as it is. What they offer is a suitably abridged summary of sensual experience, edited and adapted to your belief of what reality is like. No matter how good you hear, observe, feel, or otherwise sense the world, what your mind is showing you is still a representation. No matter where you are and what you do, you are living in an artificial representation, and this goes for all of us. **Dreaming**, in Indian thought, covers all internal experiences. These include dreams you have asleep and dreams you dream when awake. Each time you think something, some of your attention goes away from the outside world and into an inner world of your own making. Some call this thinking, planning, speculating, remembering, or imagining. The seers of the *Upaniṣads* called it dreaming. These three states, so the seers thought, are the basic material of the divine play that we consider of our reality. Beyond or within them is a secret core. This is the fourth state, **turīya**, which is considered to cause and transcend the other three. Turīya is hard to define as it transcends definition. It is not even a fourth state but a mysterious in-between sentience, hence it is usually not counted as a full state but as a half one. This gives us three and a half states, which correspond to the three and a half coils of the Kuṇḍalinī. In literature, turīya is usually defined by telling us what it is not. Just look at the definition given in the mantra chapter (under Oṁ). It is very hard to approach something that

Figure 22 - Lakṣmī statue
Stone, probably Kajuraho.

does not exist as a positive value. You cannot do, obtain, reach, or control turīya. As long as there is effort and intent, there is still thinking, doing, and dreaming, and a person who is involved in such things. How about not-doing? This implies that the way to turīya is an inward way, a return to the source of the three other states. Some authors compare turīya to dreamless sleep, in that it is not waking nor dreaming, not in the outside nor inside world. Unlike dreamless sleep, turīya is very much awake.

To understand these three and a half states it can be useful to devote some days to observe your activities. Whenever you remember, consider what you are doing. Are you awake right now? Or are you dreaming? Or are you somewhere in between? Here it can be helpful to consider the states as 'worlds'. The world of waking consciousness is what you can sense with your sensual organs. It is, as others propose, the material world. It can be seen, touched, heard, smelled, and tasted. It can be measured, it can be shared (to an extent) with others. Some, usually folks who have lived in a hole in the ground for the last few centuries, assume this to be the objective world and consider it 'real'. Others, who have bothered to torture their minds with philosophy and brain research, propose that it may be relatively sort-of-objective, not that we'll ever be sure about this, but for the time being it will do. The material world is real to the instruments that can perceive and measure it. The dream-world is a different matter, as it is much more subjective and suited to your body/mind system. Unless it has a material carrier, such as a painting, a statue, a poem or a movie, it is very hard to communicate or share with others. I would propose that we speak of two worlds here: the world of sleep-dreams and of waking dreams. The dream-worlds are real in their own way, in that they provide the ideas, emotions, and inspirations which shape the material world. Every item in your environment which did not get there naturally is a manifestation of the dream world. Houses, streets, cars, books were all ideas and dreams before they manifested in material shape. Lots of people confuse the reality of these two worlds. Indeed there is a lot of overlap between them. You can see, feel, taste, smell, and sometimes hear a tree, this makes it part of the material world and waking consciousness. You can visualise a tree and sense it with your imagination. If you do it well, that tree will impress you, move you, cause a reaction; a test for the reality of imagination is that it moves you and causes a reaction. Both experiences will become memory; a memory of a tree you experienced with your outer and with your inner senses. Both trees were real in their own world, both trees are representations. What remains is a memory of a representation of your outer and inner senses. Both trees are real, but each is only real in its own world. A monster hiding under your bed is not real or measurable with the outer senses (waking consciousness), it is part of the dream world. It is not real in the material world, but it sure is real in the imagination. Hidden monsters have kept a lot of kids scared in the middle of the night, and any idea that can do that is pretty real. The same goes for the trances that people have when they are in love, afraid, paranoid, greedy, angry, ambitious, sad, inspired, and so on. You cannot measure love in the waking world, but it is certainly strong enough to affect people. You cannot measure fear, and yet fear is so strong that it causes wars, social obligations, hierarchies, traditions, and regular working hours. Each of the states has a lot of reality in itself. The reality of waking consciousness is absent when you sleep and dream, it is meaningless when your mind day-dreams and you experience strong inner sensations such as longing or worry. Sleep-dream experience is utterly real when you are in dreamland, it fades into memory when you wake up in the morning. In magic, ritual, and religion, the worlds tend to overlap. A material object can have a strong imaginal reality, a dreaming can be projected on the world of waking experience. When the worlds coincide, we get transformation. It is only from in-between and outside, i.e. turīya, that the other states are accessible to change under will.

Skulls and Corpses

Over the last decades, a host of ill-informed would-be gurus have popularised the idea that Tantra is simply spiritual eroticism. It proved to be an idea that sells. Countless new-age prophets are selling costly 'Tantric Workshops' where people receive a bit of much needed basic sexual education. What sells as 'Tantra' in this market has very little to do with the original. Massage, overcoming shyness, sensuality, odd postures, retaining ejaculation, producing an erotic atmosphere, Reichian body therapy, bio-energetic exercises, and the like are well and good, but they are certainly not what the Tāntrikas had in mind. In fact, if you accept the new-age vision of Tantra as the real thing you may arrive in a mind space that promotes hedonism, sensuality, and worship of the body as an end to itself. I suspect that those Tantric lineages that actually promote lovemaking in their program knew what happens when people see the erotic as the only road to liberation. If you worship body too intensely you may end up in total attachment to it. If you cultivate only the beautiful, the alluring, and the desirable, what will you do when you and your partner grow old? Buddha had his own radical ideas regarding the beauty of youth. To help his followers overcome the temptations of the flesh, he recommended meditation on age, death, and decay. The same idea appears in numerous Tantras, especially of the northern tradition. Here we encounter Tāntrikas, Hindu and Buddhist, who made a point of seeking out sites of danger, horror, fear, revulsion, and pollution. Most prominent among these were cremation grounds. In orthodox Hinduism, corpses are among the most polluting objects conceivable. A strict Hindu may not touch corpses, and visits to cremation places require considerable re-purification. At this point it may be useful to understand that cremation places are not only sites where corpses are burned. Poor people often did not receive much of a funeral, corpses were not always thoroughly incinerated, and in some famous cremation grounds, burial is common. Kinsley (1998: 153) mentions the famous Tārāpīṭh in Bengal, where up to 60% of the corpses are buried. The regular addition of new corpses shifts elder ones, and consequently it is an easy matter to acquire skulls and bones. Several resident ascetics collect skulls which they use for begging bowls, ritual decoration, or for the erection of the classic corpse-seats. Such a seat may be freshly arranged, but it can also be made by burying a number of skulls in the earth floor of a hut or ritual space. Traditionally, under the seat should be the skulls of a Śūdra, jackal, tiger, snake, and a kumārī (virgin girl). These five skulls form the seat of the adept, they constitute a focus of power and a link to the otherworld. Then there is corpse-sitting, another topic you'll never hear about in a 'Tantric Workshop'. It features prominently in the rites of Kālī, Tārā, Bhairavī, and is often associated with the Mahāvidyās. Usually, corpse sitting was part of the basic initiation, sometimes it was practised for specific rites of sorcery to gain special powers or to attain liberation. Some worshippers were initiated on a corpse at night. Traditionally, Tantric adepts used fresh corpses. Usually those of low class men or women who had died suddenly, be it from suicide, poison, snakebite, accident, drowning, murder, or killed on the battlefield. Corpses of immoral, famous, starved, or diseased people were not recommended. Nor those of the upper classes, if only because their relations kept them guarded at night. In general, the corpse was specially laid out, decorated, identified with a deity, and worshipped. Incidentally, such worship was thought to benefit the soul of the deceased. At some point the corpse was laid on its belly. A yantra was drawn on the back, a mat placed on top, and the worshipper straddled the corpse much like riding a horse. During the night the initiate worshipped the corpse, and the deity within it (often Śiva), recited mantra, did prāṇāyāma, and made offerings. At some point, the corpse moved, made weird sounds, or even began to speak. You have to be pretty spaced out to get this effect. Others placed a board on the corpse and sat on that. Then there are those who buried the corpse of an infant, baby, or foetus to sit on. Such rituals, revolting as they may seem, were not rare perversions of a spiritual tradition. They appear in earliest Tantric literature and for all I know they are still practised secretly. Think deeply about the symbolism. The corpse, a thoroughly polluting thing, becomes a vehicle that carries its rider out of acceptable social reality and conditioning. It destroys all class-connections. A Hindu who touches a corpse loses class and literally drops out of the social and divine order. Moreover, the freedom enjoyed by the freshly initiated adept is based on acceptance and integration of death. While the rite may produce karmic benefits for the soul of the deceased, it certainly reminds the initiate of her or his own mortality. In a certain sense the corpse is not just a corpse. It is your own corpse. When you can sit on your own dead body you'll understand what liberation is all about.

Starting with such rites, numerous Tantric adepts introduced emblems of death in their worship. Several schools of Tantric Buddhism use thighbone trumpets and bone ornaments for ritual. Yoginīs, both Hindu and Buddhist, frequently wore aprons made of human bones. Skulls feature prominently in several Tantric systems of Bengal. They were often placed on altars or buried beneath them, just as they were buried underneath buildings and shrines. It might remind you of the skull worship in Celto-Germanic religions. Skulls could represent deities, they could also represent deceased worshippers. Some assembled skulls, painted bright red to represent energy, in their shrines as a source of power. Others accepted the skulls as students and taught them to achieve liberation, just as human disciples are educated. A guru gains power and merit by liberating others, no matter whether they are alive or dead. It was assumed that the souls that used to inhabit the skulls obtain blessing and karmic benefits in the process. For a vivid account of the use of skulls in Kālī worship see June MacDaniel in White, 2000: 77, and her full presentation of the subject *Offering Flowers, Feeding Skulls* (2004). All of which may suggest that a well organised Tāntrika needs good connections to the Untouchables who collect and burn the dead. Finding corpses is not very difficult in a country where every new plague provides dead bodies at the roadside. The problem lies in collecting them. In old India, folks who handled the dead and the dying had an extremely unpopular place in society. Those who touched corpses in their worship did so as secretly as possible. The alternative to using real corpses is meditation. Numerous Tantric adepts repeatedly imagined their own death in trance states. They visualised their dying cramps, the final spasms, the release of excrement and urine, the cooling of the flesh. Many imagined how scavengers devour them, beasts like jackals, hyenas, ravens and crows, all of them vehicles of the goddess. They imagined decay, putrefaction, and the final dissolution of all body. Then they rebuilt their body-vehicle from mantras, energies, coloured lights, and returned to daily life full of enthusiasm.

Animal Sacrifice

Killing beasts for religious reasons is one of the earliest expressions of human worship. Whenever we observe humans sacrificing, we find the sacrifice is something valuable. The sacrifice is a means of saying 'Thank You!' for favours received or an appeal for favours to come. Humans are gift-making animals. We give to each other and when we approach the spiritual world the giving and taking continue. No matter the period, an animal was always a highly valued gift. Think of the Ārya who invaded India around maybe 1500 BCE. These migrants were breeders of cattle, sheep, and horse, and to them, the sacrifice of a horse amounted to the greatest gift that could be given. The horse sacrifice, often elaborated and sometimes used as an easy excuse to wage war against other countries, was turned into a more philosophical matter in the Upaniṣadic period. The horse ceased to be a simple, if admirable and expensive, gift to the deities and became a complicated philosophical concept. This drift appears with a lot of regularity in Indian religion; a material gift is reinterpreted as a spiritual one. The trend is from the crude to the refined. In Brahmin society, eventually all killing of animals became unfashionable and to this day the better sort of Brahmin is supposed to live a strictly vegetarian life and to abstain from drinking alcohol. Humans being what they are, these rigid religious demands were never adhered to by everyone. Though religious laws are strict in these matters, a good many Brahmins preferred to ignore them, and as their caste is (theoretically) the highest in society, it was often the Brahmins who could most easily afford such luxuries as meat and alcohol, and sneer at those who dared to criticise them. On the other hand, there was always a large number of low caste people, allowed by religious law to feed on any unclean substance that came their way, who preferred to become vegetarian, as this was sure to improve their karman.

In India, most of the carnivorous deities are female. These deities are often dangerous. Where religion was controlled by Brahmins, i.e. in the civilised parts of the country, near cities and governmental institutions, these blood hungry divinities were often set on a highly symbolical vegetarian diet. I've seen pumpkins sacrificed to Durgā, instead of her traditional bull-offering. In the outskirts of the Brahmanical world, among tribal people and outcasts, such replacements were not always acceptable. A lot of blood-hungry goddesses were equipped with a little sister. While the acceptable goddess in her temple gets a lavish offering of vegetables and flowers from the local Brahmin, the little sister in her secluded shrine receives the blood offering from an unofficial priest of lower class.

At this point I have to add that a blood sacrifice in India is not as brutal as most Westerners tend to believe. Unless things are totally debased, or the temple wants to set up a record for mass-destruction, animals are not slaughtered wholesale. Usually, only male goats are sacrificed. They are brought to the altar with care and consideration, they are treated with kindness and calmed with prayers and mantras. To sacrifice an unwilling animal is to commit a crime. The goat is watched closely, if it exhibits fear or struggles it is unsuitable for the sacrifice. Behind this is the belief that an animal can gain a better station in its next life when it allows itself to be sacrificed to a deity. The killing is actually a kind act that reforms and improves the beast's soul and perchance allows it to incarnate as a human being. When the curved knife falls, it falls swiftly and the animal dies fast. Death comes with a single, clean stroke. The offering does not stop here. The deity receives the goat, usually through the service of some priest. In the process the goddess devours the spiritual energy of the offering and imbues the carcass with divine power. The dead body of the animal becomes prasāda (purity, grace). Most of it is returned to the worshippers who are now free to eat it. The goat is often grilled over an open fire next to the shrine and the worship ends with a happy meal for the whole family. Given that India is a poor country, this meal is often a lot better than what people have to survive on the rest of the time. It's strange that so many Western people feel revolted at the thought of such sacrifices. Nowhere in the world are animals raised, kept, and slaughtered under such insane conditions as in the flesh hungry industrial world. The Indian goat has lived a real life and is gently dispatched from one world to the next. The pig, cow, or chicken of the industrial world has never seen the light of day and spent its sorry existence narrowly confined in concrete and metal, feeding on waste, hormones, and antibiotics, before it is slaughtered with all the indifference of an assembly line.

Here is a little meditation on animal sacrifice. Imagine a rite where a goat is sacrificed. Use a dissociated perspective, i.e. see it as if you were an outside observer. Now go in. See the ritual through the eyes of the worshipper. See it through the eyes of the goat. And finally, see it through the eyes of the deity.

What have you learned?

We have at least three levels of meaning in animal offerings: the actual animal sacrifice, the symbolic animal sacrifice (think of the pumpkin), and the spiritual sacrifice, which makes use of the symbols of animal sacrifice to convey an altogether deeper layer of meaning. When Tantric texts speak of animal sacrifices, they often have the third variety in mind. In their language of animal symbolism, we encounter the Six Enemies or Vices that have to be offered to the deity: the cat is greed, the camel is envy, the sheep is delusion and stupidity, the buffalo is anger, the goat is crude lust, and man is pride and arrogance. All six are well known sacrifices to the dark goddess, which have to be made again and again.

Figure 23 - Hyena dreaming.

4: Tantric History

What is Tantra? Let us begin with one of the most enigmatic questions. Since early in the 20th century, when Sir John Woodroffe began to translate Tantric texts (much against the resistance of established Indology), scholars have been debating what exactly constitutes Tantra. Then, the question was almost impossible to answer. Today, we are much better informed but we still don't know. Tantra is such a vast subject that all definitions tend to become invalidated by the sheer amount of exceptions to each rule. However, as you have been kind enough to read to this point, you may hope to find out just what Tantra is all about. So do I.

Tantra is a word that means literally 'an extension', 'a weft', a 'piece of woven material', 'a textile'. Textile is a brilliant word, as it is so closely related to our word 'text'. A Tantra is just that: a piece of writing and a literary tradition. In this sense, 'the Tantras' is a loose term for a wide range of texts. As you recall, there were any amounts of texts in Indian history. So just what is so special to the Tantras that they came to be identified with a cluster of spiritual movements?

We have our first evidence for what became Tantra around the fourth or fifth century of the common era. Some scholars doubt this, and prefer to locate the beginning of the movement in the first centuries of the common era. Others argue for the sixth or seventh century, or point out that the phenomenon became most popular after the tenth century. The first appearance of a Tantric adept is in a seventh century satire describing a south Indian ascetic who managed the temple of the goddess Caṇḍīkā. Our Tāntrika is described in unsympathetic terms. He has a tumor on his brow (knocking the head against the floor can do this to you), is blind on one eye (invisibility salve destroyed it), and has ruined his health by ingesting a mercurial elixir of doubtful quality. Apart from this he is a collector of manuscripts on Tantra and mantra, and babbles all day about alchemy and hidden treasure (White 1996: 49).

The very term 'Tantra' is artificial. None of the early practitioners of what we choose to see as a 'movement' nowadays called themselves 'Tantrics'. They called themselves by their lineage, by their particular tradition, if they called themselves anything at all. Just as often, it was the disapproving outsiders who coined descriptive terms. Vedic traditionalists, Hindu reformers, missionaries, and disapproving scholars made the term 'Tantric' popular during the last centuries. They also produced the misleading impression that Tantra is something like a movement, a religion, or a world-view, and that it can be divided into various schools. Outsiders think like this. They make up a name to specify something that goes beyond their comprehension. By contrast, a good many of the people we call 'Tantrics' today did not bother to muck about with formalities, traditions, and the need to keep themselves distinct from other people. Practitioners went for direct experience, and this leads to the cultivation of subjectivity and original new insights. They also learned from other folk. Many important teachers had several gurus from several traditions, and there are texts that recommend guru-hopping as it widens the mind. The key word is syncretism. As our Tantric practitioners wanted practical experience instead of second-hand revelations, they, like you and me, went for anything that works. Keep in mind that even the established Indian traditions had no single dogma nor did they have a centralised control. There were no churches in our sense, people did not subscribe to any single piece of holy writ, nor to a specific set of rules and regulations. This went for the main religions but it went even further for the minority of drop-outs and crazed ascetics living at the fringes of society. The beginnings of Tantra were developed by people who did not belong to the mainstream. We know that there were early 'Tantric cults' around the middle of the first millennium CE, but as next to none of their literature has survived we are very much in the dark regarding their origin and nature. With so little evidence almost anything can be argued (and generally is). What we do know is that there was a growing body of revelations called 'Tantras' in those days. As a Tantra is primarily a text, you may wonder what it is about. We know that there were lots of Tantras in those days, as later Tantras occasionally list them, or quote from them. Sadly, most did not survive.

Now a Tantra is not just a text, it is often a text that aims at spiritual development. In some contexts, the word 'Tantra' can mean a text on ritual. Here our difficulties continue, as not all Tantras are like this. The most popular 'Tantra' is undoubtedly the *Pañcatantra*. It was composed fairly early, was widely read by all sorts of classes, translated into Arabic, and before long it found its way to medieval Europe where it was translated into several languages and became highly popular. Tough luck that it is not a 'proper' Tantra at all: the book is a collection of moral tales and animal fables that has very little relation to spiritual activity. Not all texts called 'Tantric' belong to the Tantric movement, whatever that may be. On the other hand, there are a wide range of texts that were highly popular among 'Tantrics' which do not call themselves by the name. Some are called *Āgamas*: texts on spiritual discipline, mythology, and ritual as revealed by Śiva. Others were called *Nigamas*: much like the *Āgamas*, only that they were revealed by a goddess. In the *Āgamas*, we find a goddess questioning Śiva, in the *Nigamas*, we have a form of Śiva (often Bhairava) questioning a goddess. The question of superiority does not occur in this frame. As so many texts make clear, both goddess and god are quite aware of the hidden truth. They merely assume the roles of questioner and answerer to provide a new revelation for initiates. The format has some similarity to the popular question and answer contests favoured by Hindus and Buddhists as a spiritual discipline. It may be a contest, but it can also be a game. Then there were *Yāmalas*, *Śaiva*, and *Śākta Upaniṣads*, plus a wide range of *Stotras* (hymns) often with a distinctive 'Tantric' content. Some well known Tantras (such as the *Vāmakeśvara Tantra*) received the name 'Tantra' several centuries after their composition. Last, there is a distinction between original works ascribed to a divine author and the later 'Tantric digests' (*Nibandhas*) which have a known, human author who compiled elder texts. In between are a range of semi-mythical authors who revealed and compiled. What is generally classed as Tantric is a body of texts which relate to spiritual activities as practised by a general movement. This may sound as if it means something but actually it doesn't. Just what movement are we talking about? To begin with, there is no way to define this movement with any degree of precision. So let me frame the matter as a series of questions.

Who started Tantra? We simply don't know. The earliest Tantric cults were so thoroughly unpopular that none of their literature survives. We know of several sects, cults, and lineages from the works of other people. Several Purāṇas contain references (usually unfriendly) to such systems. Even the best known of these cults, the Kāpālikas, has to be reconstructed from a tiny body of unfriendly references. However Tantra began, it certainly found no approval from the Vedic establishment. We shall examine the early systems further on. Here it should suffice that our knowledge is so fragmentary that we cannot even be sure whether Tantra began as a Hindu system or as a Buddhist innovation. The matter has been discussed for decades but, in the absence of so much early material, I wonder whether it can ever be decided.

Let's take a brief look at the matter. The Buddhists were good at a number of refined meditations but their dogma was, at best, indifferent regarding women. The historical Buddha did not want to admit women to his system. Tough luck that he depended on the donations of a number of aristocratic ladies to keep the community alive. One fine day, his favourite disciple Ānanda said that it might be a good idea to allow women to participate. The Buddha would not have this. So Ānanda remarked that the great Enlightened One himself had stated that even worms and plants can attain to Buddhahood, so why not women, too? Reluctantly, old Grumpy gave in. Nevertheless he stated that due to the admittance of women the system would become extinct several centuries before its due time. He also ordered that men should not look at women, or speak with them, unless forced to. Better, he declared, for a man to insert his penis in the mouth of a serpent or in a furnace than in the yoni of a woman. This mood continued through early Buddhism. Theravāda/Hīnayāna Buddhism recommended celibacy and taught its adepts to flee women. Its ideal was the Arhat, a saint who had passed through temptation, delusion, and material bondage to find release, and obliteration, in total cessation. Women were tolerated, but even the highest-ranking woman remained inferior to the youngest and least intelligent male. Then came the time of Mahāyāna Buddhism, with its keyword 'compassion'. The ideal of Mahāyāna is the Bodhisattva, who does not seek liberation (cessation) for himself but remains in the world of illusions to help others find release. It was accepted that women could be spiritually competent, but regarding their ability to attain Buddhahood, they would need to be reborn as a male first. The very notion that a woman can be a ritual partner, let alone an initiatrix or a guru, is alien to original Buddhism. This changed when certain Buddhist adepts encountered Hindu adepts belonging to the proto-Śākta movement. (The term Śākta only became popular around the tenth or eleventh century, long after the fusion we are discussing here). Soon enough, the Buddhists noticed that they were missing something vital. By the seventh century CE there were 'Tantric' Buddhists whose rites included worship of women, lovemaking, and ingestion of sexual secretions. They travelled extensively and often encountered their Hindu colleagues at the places both favoured for worship and meditation: cremations grounds, forests, and mountains. It produced a number of new Buddhist movements, such as Vajrayāna, Tantrayāna, and Mantrayāna. By the fusion of Buddhist and Hindu methods, what we call 'Tantra' was born. Plus some techniques from Daoism and elsewhere, often introduced by Buddhists who had been to the east. When we explore the Yoginī cults, we find Buddhists and Hindus embracing very similar ideas, rituals, and meditations. They also worshipped very similar women. So let us leave the question 'Is Tantra a Buddhist or Hindu invention?' to scholars who like to squabble about words. Considering that so much early literature has been lost, and that the people of the time did not call themselves 'Tantrics' anyway, it may well remain an unsolved problem of Indology.

Is Tantra a religion? Most of the Tantric systems we know of function within a religious context. The theme is often a dialogue of two deities. Also, many Hindu Tantras incorporate references to gods and goddesses, sometimes as a literary convention, usually as symbols for states of energy and consciousness. However, Tantra is not simply a faith. Most religions demand faith and sacrifices from their worshippers to maintain the status quo (dharma) or to improve it in times of need and danger. What we may loosely class as Tantric are a number of systems that go a long way beyond these simple demands. Many Tantras emphasise experience, direct experience, and faith in a couple of deities is simply not enough. In this sense, much of Tantric literature is concerned with practices that aim at the attainment of various goals. These goals are widely different. Some want liberation, or union with the gods, or aim at becoming identical or superior to the gods. Others cultivate magical powers (siddhis) for worldly purposes. Some systems are highly devotional, others tend towards intellectual contemplation or deny the existence of deities (plus everything else). Some wish to join enjoyment and liberation simultaneously, others seek total release from rebirth or aim at becoming immortals. A few cultivate sexual worship, the majority practice lovemaking in the imagination or symbolic form, or demand total chastity in order to conserve vitality. What is common to the lot is the idea that you have to do something to be successful. Various sects developed techniques of spiritual practice to achieve the stated goals of the movement. These techniques proved more enduring than the lore that came with them. We find a wide range of Tantric techniques in all sorts of Asian religions. The two major realms of Tantric practice are in Hinduism and in Buddhism. Hinduism is a religious affair while Buddhism, strictly speaking, does not accept the existence (or reality) of gods at all. Both traditions happily incorporated a lot of Tantric activity in their program. It gets more complicated when we extend our field of vision. Tantra had a strong influence on a wide range of Asian cultures. You find Tantric elements in the Bön religion of old, pre-Buddhist Tibet, in the wide diaspora of Buddhist cults in China, Japan, Korea, and south-east Asia. There is Tantric lore in Nepalese shamanism and in cults of Mongolia. Some Jaina sects are largely Tantric, and there are even a few Tantric cults in Islam. There is also a fascinating core of similar practices in Daoism and Tantra that ought to be explored more fully. More on this later on. In Hinduism, Tantra can appear anywhere. There is a majority of Śaiva and Śākta worshippers in Hindu Tantra today, but there are also Tantric Vaiṣṇavas, not to mention worshippers of Gaṇeśa and many obscure cults. And Tantra is not a world to itself. Some 'Tantric' practices have their roots in the *Upaniṣads* and in early yoga. If anything, this is good evidence that Tantra is a practical approach that can transcend ideology and faith whenever people feel like it. Good news for all enterprising mind explorers: Tantric practice can be adapted to pretty much any religion or world-view you chose to entertain. This has been going on for a long time. You can find Tantric elements in Arabian alchemy, in medieval European sorcery, and even in such recent cults as The Hermetic Order of the Golden Dawn, Crowley's Cult of Thelema, the original OTO, and in modern Wicca (which incorporates elements of all the former). All of which boils down to the insight that Tantra may be religion, atheism, polytheism, pantheism, or monotheism, but it is certainly practical.

Is Tantra yoga? There are numerous similarities between the approaches. When we examine them more closely a few crucial differences appear. For a start, what we call yoga is not a single thing, school, practice, or method to while away the time. Yoga means union, and union is something that appeals to many spiritually minded persons. Some find their yoga by fasting, pilgrimage, isolation, physical exercise, breathing, meditation, recitation, art, music, devotional love, or sensory deprivation, to name just a few options. We have our first evidence for practices that were later termed 'yogīc' in the *Vedas* and the *Upaniṣads.* At that time, they were generally classed as tapas, i.e. austerities. Tapas were practised by recluses living in isolated jungle communities, or by gods and semi-divine heroes when they needed a bit of extra power. Later on, the tapas-practices underwent a certain refinement and came to be systematically applied. At this point we notice the emergence of several distinct systems emphasising different means to attain union. Some of these systems predate Tantra. However, they did not develop in isolation. A good many early Tantrics learned from yogīs, and likewise a good many adherents of yoga came to incorporate Tantric methods and symbols in their craft. This does not make the terms interchangeable, but it does indicate that cross-fertilisation happened frequently. Several influential Tantrics were also accomplished yogīs, such as the famous Nepalese adept Gorakṣanāth, who blended Kaula and Nātha methods with his favourite, Haṭhayoga. Some Tantrics were yogīs, but this certainly did not apply to all of them. Many yogīc and Tantric systems emphasise the importance of body for joy and liberation, but the way to accomplish this aim differed widely. Allow me to utter a few dreadfully oversimplified generalisations. Yoga evolved from tapas, and tapas is usually an unpleasant occupation. Consequently, there were yogīs who went for austerities, and carried fasting, self-mortification, and doing-without to extremes. Sorry folks, the idea that yoga is good for your health is a recent innovation. Some of the elder sorts of yoga were so keen on union with the divine that they simply did not care what happened to body. Many prominent yogīs, sages, and hermits were celebrated renouncers. In these schools, a yogī (one who aims at union with the absolute) could not be a bhogī (an enjoyer of worldly pleasures) and vice versa. The Kaula lineages, always good at opposition, went against this attitude and proposed that a Kaula should be both (*Kulārṇava Tantra*, 2, 23-24). This revolutionary step demands more discipline, as it aims at reaching liberation by any means, including desires and pleasures, in fact by the very things that are deemed dangerous, sinful, and delusive by the religious orthodoxy. Many Tantras aim at making enlightenment enjoyable. While several Tantras declare a basic amount of physical training essential for advanced practice (or simply do not mention the matter at all) they do not make such an issue of it. Competent yogīs may devote hours every day to the cultivation and purification of the body, in Tantric literature the emphasis is often on ritual, visualisation and inner alchemy. The Krama system, and a number of Tantric Buddhist systems, reduced the classical eight-limbed yoga to a six-limbed variety by deleting three disciplines and adding a new one: spiritual discrimination. Some Tantras ridicule elements of standard yoga, such as vegetarism, nudity, isolation, self-denial, recitation of sacred words, and sacred baths (*KṇT* 1, 79-86). Others claim that the yogī is so proud of physical skills that the result is vanity and attachment to body. *Lakṣmī Tantra* 44, 54-56 praises mantra sādhana. It points out that recitation of mantras requires no hardship, no tiresome sitting in postures, no painful breathing exercises. You can simply assume a pleasant posture, calm the mind, focus on the mantra and attain the objective. Nevertheless, we can observe a lot of overlap between Tantra and yoga. However, comparing the 'two' may be a wrong idea from the start, as yoga is a wide range of systems and methods, and the same goes for Tantra.

Is Tantra rebellious? A lot of activities that were called 'Tantric' over the last centuries tend to upset social norms. Worship with and of women, drugs, alcohol, meat, disregard of social convention, class-less assemblies, breaches of Vedic purity rules, cultivation of magical powers, necrophilic symbolism, veneration of 'unclean substances', and a healthy appreciation of body are just what you need to make a lot of people go hopping mad. There is something to upset most orthodox Hindus in Tantra, and consequently, a lot of folk have been trying to put a stop to it. So much for one half of the picture. On the other hand, many issues, often considered typical for Tantra, are not so typical at all. The well known rite of the Five Ms, for instance, involves a feast that includes eating meat and fish (abhorred by Vedic traditionalists and Jainas), drinking wine (forbidden to Hindus, Jainas and Muslims) and ritual lovemaking (forbidden since the late Vedic period). This well-known format is only one version. The heroic worshipper is supposed to practice such rites, while the beast-like worshipper has to use harmless substitutes, and the divine worshipper transcends the physical enactment by feasting in the mind or in symbolic form. So only one of three classes of worshippers were supposed to practice in this form, and only with the guru's permission, after several years of strict training and spiritual refinement. The rite of the Five Ms is not as popular as some would have it. While badly informed books make it the sum and total of all Tantra, many sects of Hindu Tantra do not practice it at all. A few enact it in symbolic or imaginary form. And when we look at Buddhist, Jaina, or Islamic Tantra, even less of it appears. Several Tantric traditions go to great lengths to deny its validity. In short, what characterises Tantra in the eyes of most Westerners is an exception practised by a section of a minority. To these, however, the rite involves the breech of many taboos. Should we call it a ritual of rebellion then? Again, this is not necessarily the case. The rite, as we know it today was not always such an upsetting activity. Meat and alcohol were not always forbidden, and ritual intercourse can be traced to a few rites in the early Vedic period. As to rebellion, it may come as a surprise that Tantric movements were not always unpopular. The common notion that 'Tantrics' were shy folks who had to hide their activities to avoid persecution has a foundation in historical fact. Many early Tantras demand secrecy and advise the worshippers to pretend that they are Vaiṣṇavas, fools, imbeciles, or madmen. Many 'Tantrics' had to live in hostile environments. Nevertheless, this did not apply to all Tantric movements. Scattered throughout Indian history you can find kingdoms that chose to include Tantric rituals and philosophy in their state religions. Between the eighth and eleventh centuries, a number of kings embraced Kaula lore, mainly as it promised power, success (in war), possibly even physical immortality. The regents of the time became the centre of the cult of the yoginīs and built numerous temples for them, usually round and roofless, so the yoginī spirits could arrive from heaven. Among their ministers were gurus who trained generation after generation of kings to take the central place in the world-maṇḍala. Under such kings a good many 'secret' rituals were performed more or less openly, including rites to generate and ingest sexual fluids. In these periods, Kaula ritual was the religious mainstream while the Vedic traditionalists found themselves out of favour (White 2003: 12) These parts of Indian history are rarely discussed. It seems that the Hindu scholars of the last centuries went to considerable lengths to Vaiṣṇavise history and to delete Tantric influences wherever possible. What we loosely call 'Tantra' today has not always been a fringe phenomenon. For a few centuries it was the state religion in several parts of India. A few of these traditions continue to this day. Many 'Tantric' monarchies were destroyed by Brahmanic monarchies, the Moguls, by invaders from Afghanistan, Holland, and Britain. However, the regents of Bhutan, Nepal, and Tibet were and are Tantric monarchs and occupy the central space in the socio-religious mind/world maṇḍala. Their priesthood has just as much right to the term 'Tantric' as the obscure worshippers who celebrated unspeakable rites at cremation places. Tantra is not always a movement of spiritual non-conformists. In some cases kings were installed with Tantric rites and government was formed along Tantric principles. Architecture was based on Tantric cosmology and art followed Tantric conventions. Much of this was the sort of Tantra where people do not assemble for nocturnal orgies, ignore class-distinctions, purity laws, and become free to do what they will. Whenever a movement becomes a state religion we can be sure that its wilder elements are either reduced or restricted to the aristocracy. It may not be the Tantra that appeals to you, but it was just as Tantric as anything enjoyed by obscure worshippers in clandestine rituals.

An attempt at synopsis. So just what have the many Tantric cults, sects, linages, and movements in common? This is the toughest question of the lot and can only be answered with extreme caution. Let us narrow the scope to Hindu Tantra to make things easier. In my ignorance I would propose the following points:

-Tantra tends to emphasise practical means to attain direct experience. These means vary enormously. Practitioners use what works for them; in this sense, Tantra involves enlightened subjectivity.

-Tantra projects one or several mind/world maps on experience which appear in diverse forms that include yantra, maṇḍala, mantra, mudrā, numerology, obscure language, symbolism of phonemes, cakra-systems, and sacred anatomy. All of these unite the outer and the inner, the human and divine, the seer and the seen. This can be an act of projection, but it can also be an act of remembrance and recognition, a return to a lost unity and wholeness.

-Tantra is often (not always) highly critical of orthodox faith and religion, established dogma, social norms, and common morality. Lore is often communicated by initiation, ritual, and regular lessons by one or more gurus (human and/or divine) as suits the individual disposition of the student. The main thing is practice, not talk. The system aims at transcendence: the capable student surpasses the guru, the tradition, and possibly the gods when all goes well.

-Tantra is usually a revealed system given by various deities or semi-divine teachers.

-Tantra is theoretically open to all, regardless of gender, age, nationality, or class, provided the guru is willing and the aspirant has a lot of desirable character traits to begin with. In this sense, Tantra is practised and developed by an elite. The basic idea is integration, be it physically, symbolically, ritually, or in the imagination.

-Tantra incorporates body in spiritual activity instead of denying it. Body, awareness, and the multiverse are closely related and form an experience-whole-totality (piṇḍa). Most, though not all, Tantras I have read had a positive, benevolent attitude towards body.

-Tantra usually seeks to unite pleasure and liberation. The mood is generally optimistic and the ideal state is freedom to do your true will.

-Most Tantras emphasise the interaction of consciousness and energy/form in some way, often characterised as Śiva and Śakti, Bhairava and Bhairavī, Viṣṇu and Lakṣmī, Prakṛti and Puruṣa, Brahman and Māyā or some similar polarity.

Tantric Traditions.

Now for a bit of confusion. When we look at the history of the 'Tantric schools' we run into a number of difficulties. For one thing, the 'schools' are not schools at all, nor can they be compared to cults or churches. Practitioners identified themselves by their lineage, and by the sacred texts and mantras they were initiated into. As most gurus had several students, each generation produced several lineages. These interacted, cross-fertilised each other, and when a student learned from several gurus, we find separate strands coming together again. All of which produced an amazing 'weaving' of lines and links, and prohibited the formation of exclusive systems. As a result, the 'traditions' of Tantra are not really distinct or sharply defined. Gurus interpreted the lore according to their own understanding and the comprehension of each student. As there was no fixed dogma anyway, we encounter any amount of individual development. To make things more complicated, you should remember that the Hindus were by no means as good as the Buddhists at keeping records. The Buddhists favoured monasteries, and built up huge libraries, while many Hindu teachers worked in a badly organised way as they travelled through India. They relied on literature, just like the Buddhists did, but their collections were private and usually much smaller, unless the Tāntrika happened to come from a noble family with an extensive library, like Abhinavagupta. Over the centuries, the Hindu gurus kept few records, and this is bad news when you rely on an unbroken tradition for your pedigree. Consequently, by the eleventh century a number of Tantric linages began to make up their own past, and invented gurus wherever there was a gap in the transmission. They got entangled in lore and myth, confused preceptors with similar names and generally made a mess of their own history. When we try to work out how the different Tantric systems evolved we find ourselves in a quagmire, which may be the main reason why there is not a single satisfactory history of Tantra to this day. In the following section I shall supply a very brief introduction to some of the movements that are mentioned in this book. I had to ignore several fascinating traditions, such as the Western Transmission of Kubjikā, the Nātha schools, the Siddha alchemists, and the refined Trika of Kashmir. This book is by no means complete, please do not confuse my rough sketches with proper definitions.

Figure 24 - Nightside Gaṇeśa of the cremation ground.

Kāpālikas and Aghoras

One fine day the gods were sitting in heaven quaffing Soma. As it so happened, Brahmā, the Creator, began to boast about the wonderful job he was doing. Śiva disagreed, there were words, and punches, and then Śiva got really cross and chopped off one of Brahmā's heads with a fingernail. This left Brahmā with four heads and a pain in his neck, while Śiva had to do penance to make up for the deed. He had to carry the skull of Brahmā, or perhaps only a bowl made of that skull, and make a living by begging for alms for twelve years. It didn't make Brahmā very happy, as he never got his fifth head back, but it started Śiva on a career as the divine skull carrier. This myth is at the roots of one of the earliest recorded Tantric systems. The Kāpālikas seem to have been well known by the sixth century and their cult flourished till the 13th or 14th century. Of course, in the beginning nobody thought of any activity as 'Tantric'. The concept hadn't been invented yet. Each Kāpālika (female form: Kāpālinī) made a living by carrying a skull bowl, preferably made of the cranium of a Brahmin. It served to collect alms, food, or share drink, which often (and preferably) happened to be alcoholic. The Kāpālikas were pioneers. Before the advent of the infamous Kaula tradition they were already exploring the limits of Hindu religion and often transgressed the social and ethical taboos. As a result, few of their contemporaries had a kind word for them. Nor did anybody bother to record (or copy) their scripture. Not a single text composed by a Kāpālika has survived. What we know, or believe to know about them, comes from the writings of unfriendly outsiders. You can find a good synopsis of such material in Mircea Eliade's *Yoga* (1960). Sadly, Eliade presents his material as if it were genuine evidence, not slander, and hardly hints that things may have been otherwise. To summarise those fables, the Kāpālikas worshipped Śiva in his terrible form as Mahākāla, meaning Great Time or Great Devourer, as it is time which devours everything. They considered the killing of animals and humans 'heroic', wore ornaments of human bone, practised human sacrifice (by throat slashing) for Mahā Bhairava (the Great Terrible One, a form of Śiva), and generally worshipped on cremation places. This took the form of drunken orgies involving public coitus and cannibalism, with crazed worshippers feeding on charred corpse-flesh. For sexual rites, prostitutes were highly esteemed and generally assumed the role of the goddess. They considered incest a sacred act and twice a year, in spring and autumn, they assembled for group-sex orgies to which a number of other religious and philosophical groups were admitted.

So much for the negative, and highly questionable, reputation of the cult. An entirely different picture emerges from the researches of David Lorenzen (in White 2000). In his essay, Lorenzen offers a short satirical play (*Mattavilāsa*), allegedly composed by Mahendra Varman, a south Indian king who reigned from 600-630 CE. The story revolves about a Kāpālika and his beautiful companion. The former, completely drunk and tottering, loses his skull-cup and accuses a passing Buddhist of having stolen the item. The two quarrel, then a Pāśupata ascetic mediates, and finally a madman turns up who had abducted the bowl in the first place. Fine amusement for better society and as fresh and entertaining today as it was during its composition (please read it, will you?). Anyway, what concerns us here is the way the Kāpālikas are described. To begin with, the couple are parodied, but they remain sympathetic. There is not a single hint at human sacrifice, group-sex, or cannibalism. The Kāpālika is drunk and certainly blasphemes, when he identifies the drinking stall with the Vedic altar, but apart from this he is not stupid, evil, or threatening. He simply drinks, eats meat, and enjoys lovemaking. Even more interesting is his female companion Devasomā. As the daughter of a barber, she comes from a very low class (contact with hair is polluting). The two share alms, meat, and drink from the same skull-bowl. He addresses her as 'my beloved' while she calls him 'lord', but apart from that, their behaviour is by no means typical for Hindu couples. Devasomā is not an inferior. She says what she likes, speaks with outsiders without any sense of shame, looks after her drunken companion, and even fights with the Buddhist after her mate has collapsed. In one scene they both go happily mad and dance around, drumming on their cheeks, thereby copying the famous cheek-drumming of Śiva and Kālī. It comes as no surprise that she is oath-bound (an initiate) and a 'female devotee'. As she is strikingly beautiful, both the Buddhist and the Pāśupata ascetic (unsuccessfully) lust after her. What makes this episode so interesting is that we encounter a proto-Tantric couple which lives pretty much as equals. There have been too many scholars (usually Western and male) who proposed that women had little say in Tantra, apart from being worshipped and 'used' for ritual reasons. Devasomā does not fit this theory at all. More so, as the play is from the early seventh century, it predates most surviving Tantric literature, and gives good evidence that spiritual women of the time did not automatically assume the 'little housewife' role expected by Hindu orthodoxy.

What else do we know about the Kāpālikas? Lorenzen gives a few points worth considering. The Kāpālikas undertook a Great Vow (mahāvrata), specifying that the adept must beg, drink, and feed from the skull bowl. The cult had a doctrine (nowadays lost) called Soma-Siddhānta, the Doctrine of Soma. Unlike the Vedic Soma, the Kāpālikas identified Soma as the union of Śiva and Umā (Parvatī). Here, Śiva is the sound Sa plus Umā yields Soma. It may be an early identification of the elixir of immortality, the divine drug of the Vedic seers, with the fluids generated by lovemaking. The Kāpālikas were not always dangerous nutters dwelling at the fringes of society. One account mentions a vipra called Somi-Bhaṭṭaraka who was an expert in Soma-Siddhānta and happened to be the abbot of a Śiva temple. He walked covered in ashes, equipped with a club-staff, a skull, a rotation drum (ḍamaru), a two-faced drum (the mṛdaṅga), and a (thigh bone?) trumpet, plus six insignia. These are given in another source, they consist of two sorts of earrings, a necklace, a jewelled (?) crest, ashes, and a sacred thread. If we follow a hint in the *Mattavilāsa* the 'sacred thread' may have been snakeskin.

Eliade proposes that the Aghori or Aghorapanthi developed out of the Kāpālikas. Aghora means 'not terrifying' (or should that be 'not terrified'?) and is usually used to denote a group of friendly goddesses, i.e. those who seem nice to the ignorant. Again we encounter a lot of vicious rumours. The Aghori were associated with the same sorts of fun activities as the Kāpālikas, with an emphasis on eating forbidden things. Allegedly they ate all sorts of polluting things, including any form of meat (except, for some inexplicable reason, horse) to destroy their basic social conditioning and to make the devotees realise that good and bad, clean and polluted, and so on, are mere categories of thought. They did not believe in class, saw the function of parents as a coincidence, and respected only the guru and Śiva, plus some goddesses such as Sītalā, Parṇagīrī, and Kālī. Unlike the Kāpālikas, they devoted themselves to absolute chastity. How true is this account? As before, Eliade did not bother to question his sources. He was so keen on discovering head-hunting religions in Tantra that he took any odd rumour for gospel. Including tales of cremation place cannibalism practised to the end of the 19th century under British rule.

Kula and Kaula

The term Kula is one of the most important and thoroughly perplexing in the wide field of Tantric movements. There are more than twenty different explanations for it, and for the closely related term Kaula. Briefly, because we'll get to the deeper meaning of this symbolism further on, Kula means family, group, clan, cluster, and organisation. All of these imply form, and form is energy, and vice versa, hence they are Śaktis. Indeed, Kula can be a name of the Clan-goddess. Form produces more form and Śaktis generate more Śaktis. In this philosophy, anything that has form is Śakti. This goes for constellations, planets, continents, countries, districts, communities, biospheres, landscapes, people, groups, organisms, individuals, animals, plants, elements, molecules, atoms, and smaller particles. We are not talking about personalised gods here, nor are we discussing the divine feminine. Women, men, gynanders, androgynes, gods, spirits, plants, beasts - as long as they have name, form, shape, duration, and body they are Śakti and belong to the category of Kula. By contrast, Akula means without clusters, family, group, or suchlike. This is a term for Śiva/Bhairava, provided we understand that Śiva is not a male god who walks around as a stoned nudist. Here Śiva is formless, nameless, undefined pure consciousness. What the Kaulas term Śiva was called Brahman in earlier periods. It has no name, no form, no energy. If you could name it, it would immediately become form, i.e. Śakti. This Śiva is in the core of every being and every thing.

For each being, all other beings are Śaktis, each of them containing a Śiva within. When Śiva (Akula) and Śakti (Kula) unite, we arrive at Kaula. This is one explanation for the name of the Kaula movement, and it is not the only one.

Another aspect of the term Kula is simply the family or clan structure. Those who joined 'the group' became Kulas. Men received an initiation by the kulamṛta, they imbibed the elixir of the clan i.e. the elixir of the goddess, and became sons of Kula. Women shared the drink. They usually manifested yoginīs or fierce goddesses by direct obsession. As sources of the sacred juice, they were the central focus of the cult. Relationship within the Kula was modelled on families. A guru was known as 'father' or 'mother', fellow students as 'sisters' and 'brothers' and disciples as 'daughters' and 'sons'.

In history, Kula and Kaula are by no means a single phenomenon. Some traditions, such as the Yoginī-Kaula, can be ascribed to historical founders (here: Matsyendranāth). Others, and White lists eleven of them (2003:25-26), are listed in the *KJN* but remain tantalisingly obscure: the Kaula of Emission, the Great Kaula, The Darkness-Kaula, the Mother Kaula, the Serpent-Kaula, and so on. All of these are very early branches listed in an early Tantra. As their literature is lost, we may never know what they were all about. In later periods the term Kaula became even more enigmatic. It seems that around the 13th to 14th century CE, most of the elder Kaula traditions disappeared. The reasons are unknown. However, I would guess that the Muslim occupation of northern India plus several devastating plagues contributed to the situation. This did not stop people from using the name. Kaula revivals of all sorts, with widely different teachings, continued up to the 18th century. Several of them are so tame and law-abiding that the earlier Kaulas wouldn't have recognised them.

There have been numerous Kula movements, as the texts that call themselves 'Kaula' show wide divergence, especially regarding deities, mantras, and rituals. A good study on this subject is long overdue. In general opinion, the Kaulas are practitioners of the left hand path who indulge in all those rites that are considered unclean, heretical, heterodox, and dangerous by orthodox Hindus. For most of Indian history the Kaulas were not popular at all. For good reason, most Kaula Tantras insist on strict secrecy and hide their teachings behind a veil of metaphors. This is not always the case, some late Kaula texts, such as the *Yoni Tantra*, can be astonishingly outspoken. Not that they are easy to understand. All Kaula texts I have seen, no matter whether in plain or secretive language, convey several levels of meaning where the ignorant only sees one. All of them leave things hidden, unsaid, or vague on purpose, and woe to the reader who takes everything at face value. A single interpretation is never enough. Now what exactly constitutes Kaula depends very much on what Tantra you are reading. Let's have a brief look at a few.

One of the earliest surviving Kaula Tantras is the remarkable *Kaulajñāna nirṇaya*, attributed to Matsyendranāth (also called Macchendrapada, Macchindrapada, Matsyodara, or Macchagna) who is today worshipped in two shapes (red and white) as the guardian deity of Nepal. He is sometimes credited with founding the Kaula tradition, but on closer examination it is only one branch, the Yoginīkaula, which can be attributed to him. The 9th to 10th century *KJN* is one of the most lucid Tantras ever written. The emphasis is on meditative practice, mantra, extensive visualisation and a wide range of internal forms of worship.

The text has a few references to the worship of women, who generally represent or happen to be yoginīs, and the ingestion of sexual elixirs. Apart from this, the emphasis is meditative visualisation, inner alchemy, 'cheating death', and cakra stimulation to obtain siddhis. As you will read later on, it describes a wide range of distinct cakra systems. An interesting detail is the definition of the yoginīs, who are incarnate women (who practice yoga), mantric formulas, and a wide range of dangerous nature spirits who move and play in the world in the shape of (mostly) female animals. The text is much concerned with the three Śaktis Kriyā, Jñāna, and Icchā, while the usual Hindu deities are rarely mentioned.

The *Kulacūḍāmaṇi Tantra* (9th to 10th century) offers Kaula worship with all the elements of heroic drama. It is a mysterious, highly metaphorical account of worship, sorcery, and ritual involving plenty of darksome cemetery celebration, sexual mysteries, refinement of secretions, rites for Kālī, Tripurā, Araṇyā, Mahiṣāsuramardinī, and the Mothers. Much of it looks darker than it really is and often behind the frenzied language lurks a refined ritual of internal meditation. When lovemaking is intended, it is usually on a small scale, i.e. internal with the Paraśakti/Kulakuṇḍalinī, in the imagination, with a spirit, deity, or a single partner. Those passages that seem to pertain to group orgies tend to happen in the imagination, when you consider them with a bit of common sense (see the chapter on the secretions). Likewise drinking is encouraged, but the text makes a point that the real wine is the elixir generated in the cakras of the head, i.e. the yogī's internal brain-secretions. The Kaula rites of this Tantra seem wild and heroic, but they are often spiritual and internal.

By contrast, Kaula teachings, as formulated by Abhinavagupta (10th to 11th century CE), show a degree of spiritual refinement and a sophisticated philosophy that is amazing in its depth and abstraction. Abhinavagupta wrote on a level that pertains very much to the divya, the divine temperament. Abhinava was something like a universal genius. He joined several distinct traditions, learned from a wide range of gurus, wrote the most refined works on Tantra imaginable, turned dualistic Kashmir traditions into monistic ones, and in-between composed a wide range of books on art, architecture, grammar, aesthetics, and similar matters. It may be claimed that he not only recorded the lore of numerous Tantric systems, he also refined it to a point where only well-educated intellectuals with practical experience were able to digest what he was talking about. Here and there some of the hard-core Kaula stuff appears in his works, but most of it disappears under a flood of mind-blowing speculation. It's one of those questions whether he 'cerebralised' Kaula beyond recognition, making it inaccessible for most, or whether he simply recorded a refined Kaula philosophy which is rarely apparent in Kaula Tantras. Without his contribution the full depth of many Tantric systems would have remained unknown.

Now for the well-known *Kulārṇava Tantra*. This complex work was begun in the 11th century, but it was edited and elaborated over several centuries and is consequently full of contradictions. Some of it is of the highest quality and offers brilliant insights and great freedom of experience, other sections praise dull-minded obedience, guru-worship, and offer far too many rules and regulations. Long passages give a definition of the Kaula yogī who fits the common image of the wild and orgiastic celebrant. Heroic drinking coupled with spiritual practice and lovemaking are encouraged to the point of delirium and seem to happen in clandestine group orgies. Celebrants are intoxicated to the point at which when they forget who and where they are (more on that in the later chapter on the Five Ms), it's goodbye to feeding rules, purity laws, marital relations, gender, and rules of conduct. Instead, the party is loud, exhilarated, and a long way from the hidden rituals promoted in earlier works. Of course secrecy remains a must, but then, how do you keep a bunch of drunken revellers secret when the entire neighbourhood can hear the noise? All of this might be metaphorical, but it certainly does not read like symbolism. In the 9th ullāsa the Kula or Kaula yogī is defined as one who lives in the divine truth, always in the ecstasy of wine and meat, completely free from doubts. The Kulamārga (Kula path) is treasuring what is rejected by the world and rejecting what the world cherishes.

> *9, 56,* trans. Rai: *O Kuleśvari! Improper conduct is proper conduct. What should not be done is to be done. Even falsehood is Truth for the Kaulikas.*
> *57. O Kuleśvari! For a Kaulika non-drink is a drink, not to be eaten is worth eating, and that which should not be resorted to is worth resorting.*
> *58. O Kuleśvari! For a Kaulika there is neither injunction nor rejection, neither merit or demerit, neither heaven nor hell.*

Likewise bad qualities become good, enemies become friendly, kings become servants, and lack of dharma becomes dharma, death becomes a helping healer, and the Kaula's home becomes heaven. All of this utilises the law of reversal and contains a much stronger spirit of revolt than earlier sources. Indeed, unwanted and inappropriate conduct becomes a key to hidden power and doing-things-contrariwise a virtue. Such a spirit of rebellion looks as if the authors of the work had to stomach a lot of suppression. Where earlier Tantras prescribed ritual for its own sake, these sections of the *KṇT* are much in opposition to the establishment. In the next passages, we learn about the need to hide and disguise Kaula practice. The Kulas may dwell anywhere and do anything, may wear any disguise and behave like the ignorant, the uncultured, the mad, and lowly. They may seem drunk, like children, dullards, or idiots. They must never reveal their lore, to avoid people flocking to them (as if they ever would), and yet they must act only for the good of the world and never for their own desires.

> *73. Such a Yogī lives in a way that the men of the world may laugh, feel disgust, revile and seeing bypass him from a distance leaving him alone.*
> *74. He would go about in different guises, at times like one worthy, at time like one fallen, and at times like a ghost or a demon.*

In spite of such a dismal appearance, the yogī is ever pure, ever full of compassion, and never tainted by any sin. The superior Kulika plays with the serpent of the senses but is never stung, lives free of duality, without misery, released from ego, jealousy, arrogance, anger, pretence, and desire. The Kulika who is beloved by Śiva is truthful in speech, peaceful, and when the Kula is lauded, his hair stands on end, his voice quakes with emotion, and tears of joy pour down his face. What better thing can happen than to have a Kaula yogī in the neighbourhood? Śiva goes on to elaborate the great blessings granted to people who show generosity and respect to Kaulas, to places and communities where Kaulas dwell, and to families who offer their girls and women for worship. We are getting into the wishful thinking department here, it continues over several pages, and the admonitions to be nice to a Kaula become increasingly strained. What a tough job, you play the loony all day, being a boon to the universe, and still nobody loves you. This mood is entirely absent in earlier texts. Last, a brief look into the *Mahānirvāṇa Tantra*. This late work - some parts were composed under British rule - also claims to offer Kaula teachings. However, its general style is miles away from earlier works. We encounter so-called Kaulas who are well settled in society, who try to blend Vedic and Tantric lore, who worry about middle-class virtues, and with regard to lovemaking, the text is so shy that it hurts. Ingestion of secretions, the main focus of the early Kaula traditions, is hardly hinted at, the rite of the 5M's is so complicated that it takes years to master the ritual schedule and what really excites the author are several long chapters on laws, property rights, inheritance, and similar issues. If it did not include a few useful sections on Kālī I would wonder just what it has to do with Kaula at all.

Krama

The word Krama in general can mean a succession, tradition, or lineage. Applied specifically to Kashmirian monism, it is the name of a Tantric tradition which started around the 7th century and had its peak between the 9th and 12th centuries, when Kashmir became a place of great spirituality and scholarship thanks to the patronage of several Tantric kings. Then the tradition gradually lost importance. There were a few brilliant revivalists but by the 18th century, Krama had faded into oblivion. Unlike the other monistic systems of Tantra, Krama originated in Kashmir. According to the earliest sources, the system was founded by a woman who appears under the names of Mangalā Devī or Makāra Devī. Sadly, we know next to nothing about her, and the same goes for the first generations of participants. Nowadays, Krama is one of the most enigmatic systems. In an attempt to become popular and easy to understand, the majority of Krama authors chose to use the local language instead of saṅskṛt, which turned out to be a good idea for the time being, but a bad strategy in the long run. As a result, much of Krama literature developed outside of the scholarly elite, who did not take much notice of its teachings. Today only a small amount of Krama texts survive, most of them remaining untranslated. Add to this the difficulty that Krama appears under a wide range of names, such as Mahānaya (Great System/Way), Mahārtha (Great Principle of Meaning/Reality/ Truth), Devatānaya and Devīnaya (System/Way of the Goddess), Kālīnaya (System/Way of Kālī), plus several others which may or may not be names for Krama or Kula, if only we knew. According to Navjivan Rastogi, whose brilliant study of Krama is my main source on this topic, Krama started out as a philosophical system and became more 'Tantric' and practical as it developed. Our knowledge of Krama is far from satisfactory, as so much has been lost. However, a few points emerge which might be worth considering. Krama, like Kula, is very concerned about practice. It aims at direct experience of the unity of the individual self and the universal all-self. This is not a process of attainment but of remembrance and recognition. The experience of the world and oneself is not something distinct from the universal self, but an expression of reality. The Krama adepts shared the Buddhist idea that 'all is void', but unlike the Buddhists, they did not see this as a negative thing. To the Buddhists of the time, the realisation of voidness implied that life is meaningless and futile, while the Krama folk saw the voidness (sūnyatā) as a positive and beneficial state. Now Krama starts, just like the other schools of Kashmir Śaivism, with the idea that there are four or five Acts of the Absolute.

1. Sṛṣṭi - emergence, emanation, appearance.
2. Sthiti - sustenance, maintenance.
3. Saṁhāra - withdrawal, submergence, disappearance, retraction.
4. Tirodhāna - concealment, potential existence, resting.

This phase appears in Krama as Anākhya or Kālīkrama and refers to the nameless, unknown state of being and becoming. So far our system has four phases, and for many practitioners this was good enough. I hope you noticed that the first three stages are very close to the general Hindu model of creation, maintenance, and destruction. Some worshippers went beyond the fourfold symbolism and proposed that there is a fifth stage, Anugraha (dispensing grace). In Krama, an alternative term for the fifth stage is Bhāsakrama, meaning Pure Light. There was a lot of theological quarrelling about the question of whether the fifth stage is included in the fourth or not, which happily does not concern us here. To the Krama Tāntrikas, the important thing about the succession of phases is not the phases themselves but the mystery that combines them, and makes them cyclic. It is saṁvit (Awareness Reality) which continues through the cycle, in fact saṁvit is the absolute and Krama (succession) itself. In Krama lore, saṁvit is the hidden unity that continues through the cycle. To realise saṁvit as oneself and the all-self is to attain liberation within one's lifetime. But Krama went beyond this. As a philosophical system, it is much concerned with sequences. Each of the four phases of the system were subdivided into three stages (beginning, maintenance, and dissolution), resulting in twelve phases, which were identified with twelve Kālīs. Some went beyond this and proposed that the ultimate cycle of development consists of thirteen Kālīs, and so the system split again. These Kālīs are important for the sequence in which they appear. Krama means sequence, succession, and the like, consequently it appears as time in the phenomenal universe. In the realm of the absolute truth it appears as the potential that lies hidden as a substratum of all apparent changes, a timeless awareness termed Akrama (not-succession). Krama and Akrama are one phenomenon, their relative existence depending on the point of view.

As a practical system, Krama is said to have been revealed (or invented) by a number of yoginīs. In this context, yoginīs are not necessarily spiritual entities but women who practice a form of yoga, or who manifest the presence of a divine yoginī through their being. Things may have started with the mysterious Mangalā Devī or Makāra Devī. Then followed Niṣkriyānanda and his wife Jñānadīpti, Vidyānanda and Raktā, Śaktyānanda and Mahānandā, and finally the earliest preceptors of whom we have some data, Śivānanda and Samayā. It seems remarkable that the first four 'generations' of Krama teachers are remembered together with their wives. While the guru's wife represents the incarnate goddess and receives respect, if not veneration from the Tantric student, it is by no means common that the names of these women are recorded in history. That Krama starts with the transmission of these couples may say something about the importance of these women in the system. Sadly, there is no information regarding the lives or teachings of any of these persons. With Śivānanda, otherwise known as Avatārakanātha (c. 800 – 850 CE), a widely travelled guru, scholar, and innovator, we arrive at the first traceable preceptor of the tradition. As his immediate students he had three female ascetics, Keyūravatī, Madanikā, and Kalyāṇikā, plus approximately twenty other students who remain obscure. Each of the three became the guardian deity of a pīṭha (seat, sacred place) and had a number of capable students. The wide range of different Krama lineages began with these brilliant ladies. Keyūravatī seems to have been the most influential of them. Her disciple Eraka eulogised her in a poem as one who has attained the state of khecarī, a goddess in constant unity with absolute reality. In early Tantra, khecarī means 'She who moves in the Void' and refers to a class of yoginīs who have attained supreme siddhis, such as the power to fly through the air. In contrast to her is the bhūcarī (She who moves on Earth). Khecarīs were considered eminently powerful beings who may do considerable harm to anyone who is afraid of them. Later, Abhinavagupta proposed a four-fold flow of cosmic energy going through the phases of khecarī, gocarī, dikcarī, and bhūcarī, i.e. from the most sublime to the firmly manifest, which may well have its roots in Krama thought. Anyway, after our three illustrious initiatrixes, Krama history becomes rather silent about female participation. Many of the early proponents chose to live in chastity, hence there are few guru's wives in evidence, and regarding a good many others we have no details of their private lives. Rastogi has done an excellent job in researching the (small) range of known Krama exponents, but his account suffers from the fact that most of them are writers and innovators, while the vast majority of practitioners did not write books and were not remembered. Does this mean that Krama became more male-oriented? Or do we simply remain ignorant of it's female worshippers? I would not like to give any judgement on this issue. In medieval India, it was a lot easier for men than for women to break out of the cage of conventions and become travelling ascetics. Likewise, men were usually more literate than women. Consequently they left more traces of their activities in history. However, Krama is a tradition of which so little material survives that, before Rastogi's pioneering study, scholars were inclined to disregard it as a minor deviation form the Kula tradition. How many illiterate practitioners, female and male, contributed to Krama is something we will never know for certain. With regard to its general orientation, Krama split into two distinct (and quarrelling) schools, one of them favouring the idea that Kālī is the absolute reality while the other insisted, in conformity with the other schools of Śaiva monism, in an absolute reality as Śiva. As the followers of Kālī were in the majority, and often more influential than the Śiva worshippers, Krama is generally considered to be a Śākta system, or at least more Śāktic than Kula, Trika, Pratjabijña, and the philosophical Spanda system. Provided such distinctions make sense at all.

This leaves us with the question just what sort of practices the Krama folk believed in. According to a beautiful model, Krama is equated with the northern face of Śiva, i.e. the Northern Seat (uttara pīṭha) tradition. Śiva's northern face corresponds to the left (vāma) side, hence Krama overlaps with certain aspects of the Vāmamārga, the left-hand path. How far this similarity goes is far from certain. Krama ritual involved the three sacraments: wine, meat and love-making, with regard to the other two M's very little is recorded. We do not know how widespread these rites were nor whether they were performed physically or in the imagination. What differentiates Krama from other systems is its general attitude of indifference. As it expresses unity in duality, it generally tends towards an ambiguous attitude. Krama perceives realisation as a gradual process which follows certain stages. Pratjabijña (a general term for Kashmir Śaivism) and Kula disagree. In their lore things appear in clusters (Kula) and enlightenment is an instantaneous event. With regard to orthodox ritual practices, Siddhānta Śaivism insists that they are a must, while Kula and Kaula either condemn them or propose their own rites often in direct opposition to the mainstream. The 'forbidden and impure' is a major obsession of many Kula works. There are Kula Tantras that make a point of taking a non-conformist attitude at any cost, and aim at liberating the practitioner by making her/him break as many taboos as possible. Where it comes to reversing the common order, several prominent Kula Tantras are just as dogmatic and narrow-minded as traditional Hindu lore. Krama, by contrast, accepts all and does not insist. Likewise, the matter of freedom versus bondage, always something that gets the Kulas excited, is largely ignored by Krama and Trika, which refuse to see the world in such narrow categories. The very distinction between freedom and bondage seems irrelevant to the Krama writers, and the same goes for the concepts of duality and non-duality. In daily practice, Krama does not care about such matters as religious vows, pilgrimage, wearing matted hair, smearing ashes on body, worship of liṅgas, and disregards a lot of orthodox regulations. It is even indifferent towards the question whether the gods should be worshipped. With regard to yoga, Krama replaced the classical eight-fold yoga by a six-fold yoga which is similar to the yoga of Tantric Buddhism. It eliminates the three stages yama, niyama, and āsana (recommended forms of living, prohibitions, and posture) and adds tarka: the pure knowledge that discriminates between the spiritually relevant and the spurious. In other words, a certain amount of critical thinking was cultivated. In the eyes of the spiritual mainstream, such distinctions did not matter much. Krama was often confused with Kula. Over the centuries Krama ceased to be a separate system. It became so thoroughly mixed up with Kula that few could tell the difference.

Śrī Vidyā

Corresponding to the southern face of Śiva is the Śrī Vidyā tradition, a term which might be translated as Auspicious Wisdom, as Douglas Brooks put it. His study is one of my main sources for this section. Śrī Vidyā began sometime between the fourth and sixth century, but it made its major emergence around the eleventh century. As a Tantric system, Śrī Vidyā is characterised by three elements around which the system revolves.

One of them is the well known Śrīcakra, also known as the Śrī Yantra, which appears prominently in most popular books on Tantra as a diagram of 'the Devī'. This symbol is more than a meditational device and a focus of attention. It is also a map of the body/mind system and of the ritual circle. When projected in three dimensions the diagram appears as the sacred Mount Meru, home of the gods, and so does the worshipper. In worship, the yantra is carefully measured, drawn, and a wide number of deities are installed at the various points. This arrangement is extremely complex. Within Śrī Vidyā, there is some controversy regarding the way the diagram is drawn. Early sources, from the time when Śrī Vidyā was still linked with the Kaula tradition, prefer the version where the central triangle points downward. In this form, the deities are installed from the rim to the centre, where absolute, formless consciousness resides. It's the way from the material world to absolute reality, and, as you can see, it is a way of simplification and dissolution. After the 16th century, the school of Lakṣmīdhara turned the diagram upside down, reinterpreted the design, and proposed that worship should begin with the absolute at the centre and proceed to the outside, into the manifest world.

The second element of Śrī Vidyā is the worship of an all-inclusive goddess called Lalitā or, in full form, Lalitā Mahātripurasundarī. The goddess is also worshipped under a wide range of names, such as Ṣoḍaśī, Tripurā, Kāmeśvarī and Rājarājeśvarī. Indeed the term Śrī Vidyā itself is a name of the goddess. More on her nature and appearance in the chapter on the Mahāvidyās.

The third element is a mantra that was supposed to be secret, but can be found in numerous works, such as the *Vāmakeśvara Tantra* and the

Saundaryalaharī. The mantra has fifteen or sixteen syllables, corresponding to the lunar stations, and is divided into three 'peaks' which correspond to stages of initiation and realms of the body/mind complex. More on it in the chapter on mantra.

These three elements form the foundation of Śrī Vidyā. All of them are highly esoteric in that there is an enormous amount of theology associated with them, most of it incomprehensible to outsiders. Where it comes to defining the system we have to consider two very distinct phases. In the earlier period, up to the 16th century, parts of Śrī Vidyā seem to have overlapped with Kaula. Adepts of the time had no problems in calling themselves Kaulas, though what exactly they meant when they used this vague term remains open to speculation. After all, kula means 'the group' and there are plenty of groups one can belong to.

Śrī Vidyā is a tradition that can be found all over India, though its two main centres were Kashmir and southern India. Today the Kashmirian branch is extinct, but the south Indian form thrives and constitutes the most popular Tantric system in existence. In fact it is the only Tantric system that finds any approval in modern India. Typical for Śrī Vidyā is its closeness to the Vedic tradition. Where other Tantric systems saw themselves in opposition to the Brahmanic mainstream (Kaula), or simply didn't care (Krama), Śrī Vidyā made a point of uniting Tantra and Vedic practice. Many of its adherents consider themselves members of both traditions. To make this unlikely mixture work, a wide range of basic rituals and meditations were abolished. It produced a system that could be mentioned in public, mainly as all wild elements had been excluded. Of course practitioners do not agree. In their opinion Śrī Vidyā is the 'original secret' of the *Vedas*, and their sādhana is conveniently considered the oldest that exists. Śrī Vidyā Tāntrikas are often intellectual types. Most come from the upper classes, are educated, literate in saṇskṛt, well acquainted with Vedic lore, and often belong to the class of smārta Brahmins. Though Śrī Vidyā is basically a textual tradition, it relies on the guru to interpret the texts. As in other branches of Tantra, there is no special canon of sacred literature. However, the adherents tend to read what their gurus recommend and show little interest in other systems. In consequence, Śrī Vidyā became a narrow little world to itself. This is especially visible in such works as the *Saundaryalaharī*, which looks like a bizarre hymn to praise the goddess but contains, deep under the surface, instructions for practical worship. To find these you have to understand the idiom, which may take several decades, and depends much on what the guru tells you. The language of Śrī Vidyā is so specialised that it remains incomprehensible to outsiders, including initiates of other Tantric traditions. As Brooks points out, Śrī Vidyā adepts show little interest in other traditions and lineages, even to those belonging to their own system. To read sacred texts remains a must, but studying their commentaries, let alone textual analysis, remains unpopular. Who needs a commentary when, after all, the guru is the final word on everything?

In Śrī Vidyā you can observe a system that contains very little internal conflict. Goddesses are mostly adored in their benevolent (saumya or aghora) form, while those with terrifying (ghora) characteristics are largely excluded. Śiva and Lalitā appear as a happy couple. In actual worship, Śrī Vidyā contained Kaula elements of the softer type (known as the Śrī Kula tradition) up to the time of Lakṣmīdhara (16th century), who transformed the system by eliminating a lot of Kaula festivity. In Lakṣmīdhara's opinion, the supreme pinnacle of Śrī Vidyā consists of internal worship. This approach, termed Samaya Śrī Vidyā, prohibits all outer rituals. It is vehemently opposed to the Five Ms, to meditation on genitals, to group worship, and especially to activities that threaten class-purity. Such practices, he proposed, are to be abhorred as 'Kaula' Tantra. We owe Lakṣmīdhara the emphasis on differences between the right and left-hand path, together with the notion that internal worship is the most superior form of spiritual evolution. Now Lakṣmīdhara had by no means invented internal worship. You find it praised in Kaula literature well before the tenth century. However, the early Tāntrikas considered inner worship, using imagination, visualisation and deep meditation, as one option among several. Several esteemed it highly, but they did not prohibit the outer, physical forms. It is typical for Lakṣmīdhara's narrow-minded attitude that he simply damned outer ritual, group worship, and anything remotely resembling lovemaking. After his time, very few Śrī Vidyā adepts dared to call themselves Kaulas any more. Nevertheless, Lakṣmīdhara was not completely successful. Modern Śrī Vidyā practitioners still perform minor rites of outer worship, but they draw the line at matters involving unclean substances, violations of Vedic taboos, and physical congress. Lovemaking is allowed for procreation if the participants are married, but it is not considered a valid form of worship. Even during internal worship a host of abstract symbols keep the matter of sex conspicuously in the background. Consequently, numerous members of India's most popular Tantric system prefer to live in chastity.

Mahācīna

The Mahācīna (or Cīnācara) tradition is one of the most notorious in Tantric literature, both Hindu and Buddhist. It is closely associated with all the prohibited practices that orthodox worshippers condemn as dangerous, morally corrupt, and contaminating. Bharati quotes the following account from one of the *Rudryāmala*s. In it the saint Vasiṣṭha (more on him in the section on Tārā) complains to Buddha about the Mahācīna tradition: *How is it that wine, meat, women are drunk, eaten, and enjoyed by heaven-clad siddhas who are excellent and trained in the drinking of blood? They drink constantly and enjoy beautiful women. With red eyes they are always exhilarated and replete with flesh and wine.* (Bharati 1983: 68). Luckily, Buddha assures him that this is quite as it should be, and that with a bit of worship of the goddess, everything will be all right.

Where do the left-hand path rituals originate? From where did the Tāntrikas derive those infamous rites involving coitus, ingestion of body elixirs, and worship involving corpses? To this day, such questions are not entirely cleared up. To respectable Hindu scholars of the past centuries the question was easy to answer. Such rites, they assumed, could not really be an invention of the locals. Like all bad, corrupt, and contaminating things, they must originate in foreign parts. For an orthodox Hindu, all foreign countries are dangerous territory. A strict Hindu may not leave India, neither by ship nor over land, and consequently few bothered to travel and even fewer brought back reliable information. So, when we read that the rite of the Five Ms originated in Mahācīna what shall we make of this proposition? Just where is Mahācīna on the map? Here we encounter difficulties. The term Mahācīna means literally 'Great China'. It sounds like geography, but isn't. Various authors have identified Mahācīna with a wide range of countries. You find the term used with total carelessness for any country north or east of India. In most cases it is applied to Tibet, China, and Mongolia. As Indian geographers had only the vaguest of ideas about the lands to the north, this does not get us much further. For this reason, a good many Tantric scholars take the term Mahācīna to mean 'foreign' with no specific geographical location in mind. While this may be accurate in many instances, I would argue that occasionally, Mahācīna may have been a real reference to China.

Mahācīna is closely related to the cult of the goddess Tārā, who is often called Mahācīnatārā, and who is typically invoked by ecstatic rites involving meat, wine, and congress (Bharati, 1983: 58-79). There are two basic forms of Tārā; one of them Buddhist, the other Hindu. The two are so distinct that I wonder whether they were really developments of each other. Just as possibly, two different goddesses became popular under the same 'name'. Or maybe a single foreign goddess was reformed in two widely different ways. Today the Buddhist Tārā is the patron goddess of Tibet, but her cult did not originate there. The Tibetan King Songsten Gampo (617-650 CE) had two queens. One of them hailed from China, the other from Nepal. The latter introduced the King to Buddhism and imported a statue of Tārā to Tibet, where she sought to establish the cult. Her efforts, and indeed the King's attempts, to introduce Buddhism to the Tibetans did not prosper. The new faith had a slow start and didn't get very far. While King Songsten was later identified with Avalokiteśvara and his wives with a green and a white Tārā, the locals cared very little. It took several centuries before the Tibetans were ready to accept Buddhism. So much for the legendary account. Presently, only the Chinese Queen can be considered historical. She was definitely a Buddhist and came to Tibet in the company of numerous scholars, artisans and skilled labourers, who did much to improve Tibetan culture and technology. So Tārā allegedly came from Nepal. Not that she originated there, we can find her earlier in India, where the Buddhists wrote about her. Yet to the Indians, Tārā was a foreign goddess. How did she come to India? One option is the journey by sea. Tārā is often called the saviouress who helps believers to cross the ocean of life. In this function she is represented by a boat, which might imply that her cult had come from overseas. Another option is the journey overland. One Buddhist tradition claims that Tārā, and the knowledge of using mercury for alchemy, were introduced into India by Nāgārjuna. This famous saint is very hard to identify as there were quite a few ascetics of that name. Anyway, we find Tārā and mercury connected, and both of them were said to come to India from Mahācīna. There is almost no mercury in India; the siddha alchemists had to import their favourite minerals. Most of the mercury and cinnabar came, along with the basic ideas on alchemy, from China, where the Daoists had been experimenting with them since at least the second century BCE. A text on life extension from 133 BCE (Eichhorn 1973: 119) proposes that by sacrificing to the oven (deity) one can reach the spirit beings. When this has succeeded cinnabar can be turned into gold. By eating from cups and dishes made of such gold, life is extended and one may visit the Xian ('immortals') on the triple peaks of P'êng Lai island in the eastern ocean. The oven goddess, by the way, is a beautiful girl dressed in red. It might remind you of a lot of red yoginīs, semi-naked, smeared with blood, who aid the Tāntrika during the rites of inner alchemy (*KJN*, 19, 2-5 & 24, 4-12).

While we cannot estimate whether Tārā and mercury arrived in India by land or sea, we do have evidence for quite a bit of travelling between India and China. Most of it was done by Buddhists, who didn't have to fear contamination when leaving Indian soil (White, 1996: 61-66). If Tārā was originally a Chinese or Mongolian goddess, we might wonder about her original name. Tārā means 'saviour, protector', and is a title, not a name or a description. Her Hindu iconography is so close to Kālī that the two can hardly be told from each other. Both are dark and terrifying deities with wild hair and wilder manners.

Tārā's connection with mercury and alchemy is worth considering. In ancient China the most famous goddess in charge of alchemy, the elixir of life and immortality, was Xiwangmu (Hsi Wang Mu), whose name used to mean 'Queen of the Western Land of Mu'. Before the common era, she was venerated as a dangerous goddess dwelling in the mythical Kun Lun mountain (usually a metaphor for the human spine) in the west (the land of the dead) with a range of immortals. She is the guardian of the elixir of immortality and, as this elixir is produced by rites of alchemy (meditative, sexual or using chemistry), she is also known as Jin Mu, 'Mother of Metals' or 'Mother of Gold'. Her first appearance may be on the oracle bones of the Shang dynasty (c. 1600-1045 BCE), where we find reference to a Mother of the West who is associated with tigers and counterpart of an unknown Eastern Mother. Sometime between the fourth and third century BCE Zhuangzi (Chuang Tse), chapter 6, recorded: *The Queen Mother of the West got it (the Dao) and took her seat on Shao-Kuang - nobody knows her beginning, nobody knows her end.* Another work of the fourth to second century BCE, the *Classic of Mountains and Seas* (trans. Anne Birrel, 1999: 24) gives the first detailed description: *Three hundred and fifty leagues further west is a mountain called Mount Jade. This is where Queen Mother of the West lives. In appearance, Queen Mother of the West looks like a human, but she has a leopard's tail and the fangs of a tigress, and she is good at whistling. She wears a victory crown on her tangled hair. She presides over the*

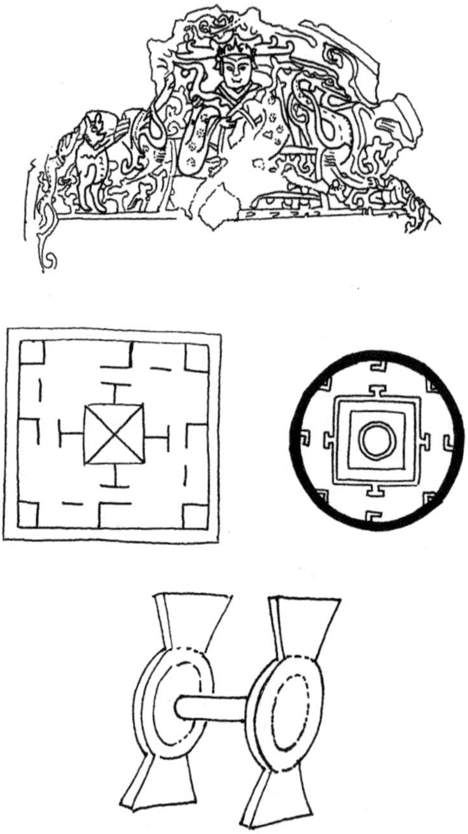

Figure 25 - Chinese influence.

Top: Upper half of a gilded bronze disk that graced a coffin from Wushan, late second to early third century, after Kaogu 1998 in Bagley 2001:54. The design, partly damaged, shows Xiwangmu seated on a throne in the centre. She holds two sceptres and wears a leopard-skin robe. She is flanked by dragons. To the left is a hare holding an object which might contain the classical medicine of immortality. To the right a toad is kneeling. It's hard to see as the head is missing.

Middle left: the basic design of the gameboard used for Liubo. The earliest such board possibly dates from the middle Shang dynasty, maybe around 1400 BCE. The central design shows a square, possibly symbolising the world mountain, from which four T shapes emerge. In Shang oracle bone script, the T signifies both 'deity' and 'altar'. The four T shapes signify the four directions of the (mythological) map of Shang religion, the four gods of the quarters, the four winds, clouds, sacred mountains and so on. Several royal tombs of the late Shang capital Yin (near modern Anyang) show a similar groundplan: a central squarish or rectangular chamber flanked by a smaller square in each direction. The same image appears in the centre of early Chinese astronomical maps.

Middle right: Around 200 CE, the basic symbols of the Liubo 'map' had become a popular design on the back of round bronze mirrors, which were often elaborated with writing, mythical animals, gods, plants etc. The centre became a hub. These items are generally called 'TLV mirrors' due to their basic symbols. Mirrors were more than household articles. They were among the most popular tools of Wu shamans, sorcerers and exorcists. Could this design be the ancestor of the basic shape of so many yantras?

Bottom: The special Sheng headdress occasionally associated with Xiwangmu (drawing based on Cahill, 1993: 24).

Catastrophes from the Skies and the Five Destructive Forces. (2, 3) Mount Jade is just one of the many peaks associated with the goddess, who enjoyed a thriving mountain cult and is intimately associated with the Xian, the so- called 'immortals', a word that combines the ideograms of 'mountain' and 'human'. The 'Catastrophes' and the 'Five' are two constellations otherwise known as 'Grindstone' and 'Five Shards'. Here the goddess appears as a shaman's deity. Partly human and partly beast, she represents the powers of the West, of metal (gold), tigers, autumn, harvest, and death. Tigers might remind you of the Hindu Tārā, who is often worshipped as a blood-drinking, semi-nude, laughing, madwoman with tangled hair, clad in a tiger skin. The 'victory crown' is a sheng head-dress (see illustration), possibly a symbol for the brake mechanism of a loom. She is also related to the Weaver girl star. Another passage associates her with the north and with Mount Snake-shaman (12): *Queen Mother of the West leans against her raised seat. She wears her victory headdress and holds her staff. To her south, there are three green birds which gather food for Queen Mother of the West. The place where Queen Mother of the West resides lies north of the Waste of Offspringline.* Offspring is something many early Daoists were not overly keen on. As a goddess of death and immortality Xiwangmu makes and guards the golden elixir. It is her job to devour those who come and ask for it. All part of the initiation and you are welcome to it. As Laozi (33) had it: *He who dies without perishing, will have long life.* Later generations did a lot to tame this wild goddess. Where earlier generations had invoked her as a goddess of death and immortality (at plague times the population was encouraged to play the board game liubo in her honour), the post-Han Chinese transformed the spelling of her name, and with it her nature and function. Xiwangmu ceased to be the Queen of mysterious Mu (which nobody could find on the map anyway) and became the Queen Mother of the West. Today she is venerated as a mother goddess and she is not very happy about it. She had a strong revival during the T'ang dynasty (618-907), when the ruling emperors all belonged to the Li family. The family's supreme ancestor is said to be Li Erh, or Li Tang, otherwise known as Laozi (Lao Tse), and Daoism became the state religion. In this period, the cult of Xiwangmu reached unequalled popularity. The goddess was identified with the Dark Female (chapter 6 of the *Daodejing*) and became the supreme Daoist goddess. Even Chinese Buddhists felt obliged to worship her. Some of them travelled to India searching for scripture. For a mind blowing study of the goddess in the T'ang dynasty see Suzanne Cahill, 1993. After the end of the T'ang things changed radically. Daoism fell from favour and Neo-Confucianism became the supreme (and suffocating) dogma. Xiwangmu remained as an important, but rather boring, goddess with an emphasis on her 'motherly role' that had little to do with the raging shaman's goddess of earlier times. Art usually represents her as a stately matron who dwells in an all-purpose paradise and entertains guests with banquets of immortal peaches every couple of thousand years. Only poets, Daoists, or mad folk like you and me seem to remember her dramatic past. It is quite possible that Xiwangmu contributed to the cult of Tārā.

With regard to rites involving congress, Chinese history is not very helpful. After all, most Chinese scholars were Confucians, and Confucius was strictly against any sort of lewd living. His followers even proposed that husband and wife should never touch or come close to each other in daily life. Just what were they afraid of? In spite of the Confucian influence a touch of the erotic remains in the myths of Xiwangmu. One legend, quoted by Blofeld, proposes that she used to be a human woman. She collected the sexual elixir of a thousand young men and became a goddess. Now did she actually collect it or did she receive offerings? A similar story, attributed to a woman called Nü Ji, appears in the *Liexian Zhuan* (Eskildsen 1998: 16-17). Nü Ji used to brew and sell wine. One jolly day an immortal had a drink at her place and left a number of scrolls in lieu of payment. Heavy drinking, I should add, is an activity frequently favoured by Daoist immortals. The scrolls contained instructions on gaining immortality by 'nurturing the vital principle by copulation'. Nü Ji was impressed. She invited young men into a specially prepared room, gave them a drink, and enjoyed them overnight. Soon she had regained her youth. When the immortal came for a visit, he was delighted by her transformation and accepted her as a student. Likewise, the jade girls and jade boys dwelling in the gardens of Mount Kun Lun have a sexual connotation, as indeed does pretty much everything related to jade. They are frequently invoked in rites of Jia Daoism, the dangerous Dao of the Left and in rites of inner alchemy, where they become helpers and mates of the practitioners.

When we look for early evidence of sexual alchemy in China, the manuscripts of Mawangdui (written before 165 BCE) come to mind (in Cleary 1994). They include several treatises recommending retention of sperm, special diet, lots of sleep, gentle and leisurely lovemaking, and the importance of female orgasms. The last point is emphasised. Though the Mawangdui texts generally address themselves to male readers, those readers, called 'knights of heaven' were concerned that their partners had one or several good orgasms. Such ideas appear in the Huang Lao school of Daoism before the common era; you won't find much of them in later literature.

The *Liexian Zhuan* (Lives of the Immortals), attributed to Liu Xiang (77 BCE-6 CE), claims that Lao Tse (Laozi) attained immortality by nurturing his jing (vital essence, here: sperm) and by copulating without ejaculation. His teacher Rongchengong used the same methods and consumed the jing of the Dark Female (Eskildsen 1998: 16-17).

Regarding the cultivation of inner energy, Daoism and Tantra are very close. Both considered the sexual secretions as something magical and special. The actual meaning of this varies a lot. Some Daoist schools, just like some Tantric schools, believed that the sexual secretions should be conserved by all means, and that any form of orgasm or ejaculation should be avoided. This meant total abstinence for some. Others indulged in lovemaking (without orgasm) to make the body produce a maximum of secretion, which could be refined and circulated through body in rites of inner alchemy. A few became exceedingly obsessed by the matter. It may be a late development; in the Mawangdui manuscripts, orgasm is still allowed occasionally to release overmuch pressure. Others believed that the secretions attain their full potency when they are mingled in the vulva and recycled by ingestion afterwards. These people enjoyed orgasm, and took great care to feed on the secretions, directly or diluted in water or wine. Modern ritual Daoism, I should add, frowns on sexual disciplines, and men who practice sperm retention are barred from the higher ranks.

This brings us to the *Daodejing (Tao Te Ching)* attributed to Laozi and dating from around the fourth or third century BCE. The standard Wang Bi version (3rd century CE) refers to the mysterious Dark Female in verse 6 (trans. Duyvendak*): 'The valley spirit never dies'; this refers to the dark female. 'The gate of the dark female'; this refers to the root of heaven and earth. In fibrous ramifications it is ever present; its activity never ceases.*

The two Mawangdui versions, c. five-hundred years earlier, state: *The valley spirit does not die - this means: hidden femininity. The gate to hidden femininity - this means: root of heaven and earth. How continuous! Ever present. Untiringly active.* (after the German trans. By Möller). Likewise, verse 20 has Laozi exclaiming: I *alone am different from others because I prize feeding on 'the Mother'.* An alternative rendering is to eat of the mother. Such lines remain a mystery to most Sinologists, but they do make sense in a Tantric interpretation. Here Chinese and Tantric alchemy meet on a very similar terrain. Both of them link immortality with the cultivation and/or ingestion of sexual fluids.

They also exchanged ideas in historical times. White (1996: 62) mentions that during the T'ang dynasty, around 664 CE, a group of Chinese alchemists travelled to India. They presented a saṅkṛt version of the *Daodejing* to the king of Assam in exchange for information on elixir- and transmutational alchemy. So there were people in Assam, one of the hottest places for yoginī Tantra, who had access to Daoist lore. When they read of the Dark Female it must have brought Kālī to their minds. In Hindu iconography, Tārā, the Chinese goddess, looks exactly like Kālī.

Next, let us take a look at another Chinese tradition The earliest form of (known) Chinese spirituality may be loosely classed as 'shamanistic'. Some scholars don't like this term at all, so perhaps we should prefer the Chinese word Wu. The Wu had a colourful history. First traces of their activity appear in Neolithic burials and in masked faces painted on pottery. But the evidence remains slim until we come to the Shang dynasty. This is China's earliest traceable 'dynasty', though, as you'll read in my next book, the term 'dynasty 'is woefully wrong. Let's call it period instead. The Shang period lasted from c. 1600 to 1045 BCE, a date chosen by a number of leading historians by common consent. The Shang were a well developed, literate bronze age culture thriving around Anyang, Henan not far from where the Yellow River ran. Their culture was extremely religious, so that we find the kings, queens and aristocrats conducting a wide range of rituals which would have been the domain of priests and shamans in other countries. But they also had a group of professional ritualists, the Wu. Their activities are recorded on a number of oracle bones. The Wu sacrificed to the high god (or gods) Di. Usually small sacrifices, as Di wasn't much into offerings, such as a dog, or maybe a dog and a pig, or a dog and a sheep. They calmed the howling tempests (the storm bird Peng), and soothed the rage of the deities of the holy Yue mountain, the Yellow River and the earth god. It's not much information, but enough to tell us that a group of people called Wu were ritual specialists. The only such ritualists apart from the diviners and the highest aristocracy. Sadly, we have no idea who belonged to the group.

Wu is also a place name, and a family or clan name, as T. T. Chang pointed out, and if we assume that professions were inherited, it might be that the Wu clan, from place Wu, supplied these early sacrificers. 'Place' Wu comes from a reading of oracle bone inscriptions, saying things like 'Yi-Chou (day 2) crack making (divination) / pour wine/ sacrifice human/ on Xin-Wei (day 8)/ at / Wu?' (Hu, 1, 4, 1). The tricky bit is the word 'at'. The Shang had a rather careless approach to grammar and 'at' could also mean 'for'. In which case it might be a sacrifice for Wu. Which lead scholars like David Keightley to propose that Wu might be a deity. A deity of the directions in fact. The original ideogram shows a cross composed of four equal-sized 'T' shapes. In oracle bone writing, the radical 'T' often appears in words relating to the divine. And when we have four T shapes extending in the four directions, we have a sacred glyph indeed. Now perhaps Wu in this reading was really a deity of the directions. The Shang had plenty of them. In fact they had so many that I wonder if they would have needed yet another one. Or it could be a shaman/ess well balanced in the centre of the magical universe. Or the Wu (shamans) were considered something like incarnate deities. Or they became divine when they were obsessed by deities. It's all possible. We just can't be sure.

And we read in Sima Qian's history that two persons called Wu Xian served under Shang regents. One governed the royal household and advised the prime minister under king Tai Wu. Another appears four kings later, under the reign of Zu Yi, and is likewise entrusted with high office. One Wu Xian used to sacrifice at mountains and streams, as the *Bamboo Annals* have it. Wu Xian became something like the ancestor of the profession and appeared in numerous later works, such as the *Chuci* (Lisao) and the *Shanhaijing*, where he resided on a holy mountain, holding a blue and a red snake in his hands.

Animals were highly important in Shang religion. Numerous people and families had animal names or animal clan-totems, and on two remarkable Shang vessels we can see Wu clinging to huge tigers. Mind you, these tigers are highly abstract. The Shang were fond of blending numerous animals. And so the tigers incorporated other beasts such as goat, bats, snakes and dragon (on the bottom of the vessel). This passion for animal totems has been a reason why many scholars perceived something like animal-spirit shamanism among the Shang.

The Shang period ended when the House of Zhou killed the last Shang king and set themselves up as regents. In their time the scholars began to record and invent proper history, and so the data on Wu increased a lot. In the venerable *Shujing* (Book of Documents), the Shang time minister Yi Yin admonishes a young regent not to have constant drunken dancing and singing in his palace, as this would be Wu fashion. It is just one reference which connects the Wu with ecstatic activities. Wu of either sex (a large number of them was female) were famous for conjuring spirits with song, dance, drumming or by strumming lutes. And as this is not the place for a detailed account (sorry), let me just summarise that Wu excelled at several occult discipline. They sacrificed, conjured, banished, exorcised evil influences, participated at demon-dispelling processions, recalled souls from the otherworlds, prophesied and divined. Some Wu had a remarkably high reputation for spiritual attainment. A passage in the *Guoyu*, relating to King Zhao (c. 500BCE) states that in early times, the Wu were perceptive, focused and dedicated people, which allowed them to understand what was occurring far away and beyond. For this reason, the spirits descended into them. When they were women, they were called Wu while men were called xi. They regulated the rituals, sacrifices and ceremonies. The spirits were pleased and natural disasters did not occur. But at some point, the world fell into disorder and every family began to have their own amateurish Wu and xi. The people lost their respect for the spirits and vice versa, and life became chaotic. At that point, the connection between heaven and earth had to be severed, so that only skilled professionals could be in touch with the spirit world. It's a neat story, but has its weak points. Only very few sources bother to give a special term (xi) for male Wu. Before and after the *Guoyu* was composed, most authors simply said Wu, regardless of gender, and some, such as Zhuangzi and Liezi, did not specify gender at all.

Another early Wu, Wu Peng ('peng' is the word for drum) was credited for inventing the yarrow stalk oracle. The very thing that later became the Yijing (I Ching). They also got involved in politics. During the Shang, they already had a very high status, and were possibly recruited among the semi-divine aristocracy, just like the few diviners whose family connections we can reconstruct. And in the Zhou period, a group of Wu accompanied the king at several state occasions. Especially dangerous visits of condolence, when the king was required to visit the family of a deceased minister. They carried white reeds and staffs of peach wood to exorcise demons (Liji). On other occasions, there were even two groups of Wu, female and male, in the company of the regent. Ranking as officials, they had a fixed number of attendants and servants. They advised kings, but they also were involved in plots. Some served as spies for King Li of Wei (878 BCE), who employed them to oppress the population (Guoyu). According to the *Zhouli*, male Wu performed the court sacrifices of wintertime, the dangerous, dark yin-season, when they exorcised innumerable spirits. In spring, they invoked the gods and expelled the demons of disease. The female Wu exorcised at fixed periods of the year and made offerings with aromatic herbs. When drought prevailed, they performed dances and rituals to exorcise the drought demoness and to invoke rain. Some regents, believing that the Wu were especially beloved by heaven, used them as drought sacrifices. At such occasions, the Wu were exposed to the glaring sun, in the vague hope heaven might be compassionate with them and send rain. On other occasions, the Wu themselves performed human sacrifices. One well known tale (Sima Qian writing about King Wen of Wei, who ruled around 400 BCE) relates how an old Wu lady, accompanied by a whole troop of young initiates, toured the countryside to select the annual bride for the river god. The rich families all offered bribes to the sorceress to avoid the honour of having their daughters chosen. For after a lot of worship and public festivity the river-bride floated away on a sinking boat. Such marriages to deities were widely celebrated, but they did not always have a fatal end. Usually brides and husbands for rivers and mountains lead a chaste life and took no human mate. For the simple reason that no-one dared to marry them. The custom seemed offensive to strict minded officials, who eventually passed a law that only the offspring of the Wu might be married to a nature deity. In consequence, most of these marriages ceased (*Books of the Late Han Dynasty* on the year 57 BCE). They did not stop entirely, however. Gan Bao, writing in the fourth century, recorded several cases where people married spirits or deities and acted much like mediums for them. Otherworldly marriages happened all through Chinese history and were by no means limited to professional Wu. From time to time the odd visionary fell in love with a spirit lady, maybe one of the many daughters of Xiwangmu, and lived a spiritual life recording the wisdom of his bride. You might call it automatic writing, if you prefer a modern expression. Quite a few mystical books were dictated by spirits. Even Xiwangmu occasionally visited earth to grant such a heavenly document to a select emperor.

Wu were also the first who experimented with herbal and mineral medicine, and indeed the early form of the character 'healer' (Wu yi) was written with the character 'Wu'. And they were the pioneers of longevity. *Lü Bu Wei*, writing shortly before the so-called first emperor united China (for a brief fifteen years of sheer terror) mentions adepts of life extension, drinkers of dew and exhalers of stale energy, sitting at the feet of Wu Xian. The Wu developed the first breathing exercises of Chinese history and fed on a wide range of unusual items to improve their health and life expectation. It killed lots of them. In all likeliness they were also influential in the development of qigong exercises and early gongfu. The *Zhuangzi*, assembled between the fourth and first century BCE, contains a passing reference to those who do breathing exercises to prolong life and imitate the motions of animals, such as bears and birds, for physical exercise. It was the dawn of the first recorded form of qigong, the 'play of the five animals'. Much earlier, there used to be a class of Wu exorcists with the grand title Rescuer of the Country who participated at demon expelling processions and funerals. They wore four-eyed masks, bear skins, and wielded spear and shield. And like so many animal-related shamans world wide, we might assume they imitated the motions of their helping animals.

The Wu were a varied lot, ranging from highly educated advisors of the highest regents to mad inspired mediums living in the outskirts of the cities. And with the advent of Confucianism they began to encounter massive opposition. Kongzi (Confucius) himself avoided to comment on religious matters. His aim was the reform of society by moral behaviour, strict rules of behaviour and a generous amount of law and order. Ecstatic rituals or drunken singing and dancing were not his idea of proper conduct. His followers went beyond this, and deliberately sought to destroy what they considered superstition. Instead, they promoted serene and calm sacrificial rites which upheld the due order and hierarchy of society. People were to worship the ancestors, not to become obsessed with them. In consequence, whenever they influenced a king, that court would become a bad place for the Wu. But the descendantf the Wu went a lot further than this. King Wudi of the Han dynasty, himself passionately interested in magic, spells, divination and longevity recipes, became highly paranoid in old age. Several times during his reign he had the court purged of wugu sorcery. The first of these witchhunts (130 BCE) is badly documented, while the second (91 BCE) got the full attention of grand historian Sima Qian, who narrowly escaped with his life. When a human figure was allegedly discovered buried in the innermost chambers of the palace, a number of high ranking aristocrats were sentenced to death and armed troops slaughtered suspicious folk among the citizens. Finally, the crown prince himself, under threat of execution, sent his troops against the king's army. They fought it ought in hand-to-hand combat, right within the capital. The fighting took five days and ended with several ten thousand people dead. It was not the only such incident. Another Wu-hunt happened in 89 BCE, when judges, equipped with 12000 armed followers were sent to arrest any person suspected of Wu sorcery or sedition. And when King Wu was finally dead, one of his five sons employed a talented Wu lady who performed sorcery on the Wushan (Wu-mountain) to help him win the throne. When his plan was discovered, he had her and her attendants poisoned and committed suicide with his favourite concubines. The emperor approved of the suicide and granted a pardon to his eight sons, who were merely reduced to the rank of commoners. (Books of the Early Han Dynasty).

Wu were frequently blamed for supporting ambitious aristocrats with gu sorcery or dangerous prophecies, and a good many came to a painful end. Gu sorcery, by the way, is one of the more obscure arts associated with the Wu. In one version, which remained popular until the end of the Qing dynasty in the twentieth century, a vessel is used as the home of a spirit. A number of venomous animals, such as toads, snakes, centipedes and scorpions are thrown onto the pot, which is carefully sealed. In the narrow, dark enclosure they fight it out with each other. The surviving animal becomes a spirit who has acquired all the lethal powers of its companions. It can be sent out to kill people and steal their wealth. Another form of gu sorcery involves making human images of wood or cloth for spell casting. Usually such figures were buried at prominent places or near public roads. A third type of sorcery involved the killing of a person by charms, poison or violence. Then the soul was attracted, caught and bound and became a slave of the sorcerer. Such forms of magic were heavily punished. They were generally only taught to close family members. And they were by no means only practised by the Wu.

But the Wu were not only opposed by no-funny-business Confucians and paranoid kings. They also lost prestige when a new class of sorcerers, the fang shi or method masters, occupied their position at court. These spell casters used sigils and writing for much of their art, and were usually skilled diviners, historians and scholars. In short, they were better behaved than ecstatic spirit mediums and exorcists. And finally, the Daoist movement, getting on the way around the third century BCE, began to intrude on the occupation of the Wu. The early Daoists made use of a wide range of Wu techniques. They experimented with weird drugs, plants and minerals in their quest for longevity. Yijing divination passed from the Wu into Daoist control, and many of the trances that were usually Wu sorcery, such as spirit journeys to the other worlds, became typical Daoist activities. The very mountains, so popular for Wu ritual, now came to house Daoist hermits fleeing uncaring society. Where in earlier ages, the Wu had been flying up and down Mount Kunlun, it now became the skill of highly trained Daoists to ascend to heaven and come back with remarkable tales. In short, most of the Wu found their functions distinctly reduced. Finally, healing became the job of professional physicians. The Wu remained at the fringes, performing as exorcists and spirit mediums, and suffered the scorn of all who profited from the Wu tradition. Sometimes they made a brief comeback, when a gifted Wu performed for a warlord or when a Hunnish or Mongol regent usurped the throne, and introduced shamanic Wu from his homeland, but on the whole, they never regained their former rank. And how could they, what with Confucian scholars writing the history books. But no matter how bad things became, they never disappeared either. To this day there are a handful of Wu performing as spirit mediums for poor people in Taiwan. And there are shamans of all sorts among the minorities of Yunnan, Guangxi and Sichuan, many of whom believe that their clans originate from sacred animals, plants, sacred locations or even objects. A few shamanic traditions survive in China's rural Wild West, among the Uighurs, Tartars, Turks and the descendants of the Mongols. A few elderly shamans, many of them female, make a living in the Amur region between China and Siberia. They still recall what tiger spirits are all about, and believe that to initiate a healing, a patient should make the shaman laugh. And the Wu's close relations in Japan (the miko) and Korea (the mudang) also manage to make a living. They are by no means popular, and often suffer from anti-superstition campaigns and political oppression, but when it comes to placating an angry spirit or removing bad luck from a sufferer, they do their job much as they ever have. When medicine and psychotherapy fail, the Wu are often successful.

As you can see from this much simplified account, some Wu rites have similarities to Tantric activities. For a start, all through history a large number of Wu were and are women. It must have been one of those surprises for any travelling yogī or Buddhist from India. That women can be spiritually competent had largely been forgotten by Indian philosophers. Another common element is excited and even ecstatic ritual, involving a wide range of offerings, drinking, dancing, gesture and music. Singing, music and dancing appear in some Tantras as part of the solitary morning worship (see KCT. 2, 13). It's excellent magic. Play some music and change your feelings. And as some of the more refined Wu used string instruments, so did their Tantric colleagues in India. Indeed the Indian lutes were often identified with the human body, the frets corresponding to the power zones. It works much like suggestion, but it doesn't rely on words.

Then there is alchemy, be it by ingesting drugs, plants and minerals or inner alchemy making use of breathing, posture, visualisation, animal imitation and so on. Some early Daoists made much of ingesting sexual fluids (jing). Was it a Daoist innovation or an earlier Wu tradition? Journeys to the otherworlds are also worth considering. Then there are sacred spaces within body, and the trances of introversion. You find them popular in early meditative Daoism and alchemy. Again, were they an inheritance from the much derided Wu? What about talisman drawing and weird sigils? We will never know for sure. And finally, there is a special relationship to the spirits and deities. Remember how people married gods?

Now let me introduce you to the magnificent *Nine Songs* (see *Altchinesische Hymnen* trans. Weber-Schäfer 1967, *The Songs of the South* trans. Hawkes 1985, *Teachings of the Tao* trans. Wong 1997) These songs are among the earliest evidence of Wu shamanism. Regretfully we do not have their original text as it was sung during invocations, but an edited and paraphrased version. They were sung by female Wu when the deity was male and by male Wu for goddesses. Not that it is easy to tell the difference. With regard to several of those gods the gender is not altogether clear. Generally each song consist of two parts. In effect, the first part of each song consists of the invocation. Then follows a pause during which the ritualist celebrated union with the deity, whatever that may mean. Each song ends with a lamentation for the deity who came so briefly, united with the Wu, and departed to its own realm. What makes these early songs unique is not only the brilliant poetic style. The Wu shamans approached their deities as lovers. The songs express longing, love, erotic symbolism, and the sadness that comes when one's beloved has departed. In a sense, the shamanesses and shamans of ancient China were spouses of their deities. You can find a similar mood in several early Tantras. Lovemaking with a partner who manifests a deity (or the Paraśakti) is not very far from this attitude.

Another interesting ritual of the period is mentioned briefly by Marcel Granet (1963: 56-57). Again we encounter a group of high ranking women who seem to be aristocrats, shamans, or both. In this ritual the assembly was divided into two groups. One group consisted of witnesses and musicians who crowded into a small, closed room with thin walls and played on drums and flutes. The other group consisted solely of women who were nude, wore perfume, and danced in a circle. As they danced they passed a flower to each other. The flower was the moving focus of the rite. It was used to attract the soul of a deceased human, spirit, or deity, to gain magical power or life-extension. To the Chinese, a human soul is not far from a god or spirit. Most Chinese gods began as human beings and became deified after death. Or they began as gods, were turned into mythical ancestors, and then became deified again! Anyway, the flower moved from woman to woman. Once the soul arrived it was trapped by the blossom. The woman holding the flower began to look insane (obsession?), passed the flower to the next in line, and collapsed (tranced off). The rite was accompanied by a 'ghostwind' and the terrifying voices of the otherworldly ones.

So far, we have encountered alchemy, sexual rejuvenation, dark and red goddesses, obsession, ecstatic rites, union with deities, heavy drinking, and an assembly of nude shamanesses in Chinese ritual. Others points where Chinese traditions share close similarities with Tantra, including the Heart, the Rain of Elixir, and the cakras will be discussed in other chapters. While I would not claim that Mahācīna is simply a term for elder Wu shamanism or early Daoism, it may well be that these systems contributed to the concept.

5: Masks of the Divine

The Guru Game

The Guru is oneself. The Siddha is oneself. The pupil is oneself. Śiva is oneself. Those fettered by ignorance know not of this, whilst he who does know is already free.
(*KJN*, 11, 26, trans. Mike Magee)

First, last, and in between, the aim of many Indian religions is union with Brahman. As Brahman is formless, undivided, total consciousness beyond all names and definitions, it cannot be perceived directly. Brahman can be sensed in all the forms it sheds, all the masks it wears, all the gods, spirits, humans and beings and shapes it casts off in its manifestation. To attain the consciousness, union with and ultimate merging in Brahman, a variety of forms are employed. Here you encounter the gurus. The primary guru of each practitioner is her or his iṣṭadevatā (personal deity). For Śaivas, the personal deity is some form of Śiva, and Śiva is the supreme guru. To Vaiṣṇavas, Viṣṇu or, more often, Viṣṇu's incarnation as Kṛṣṇa is the supreme guru. The Śāktas encounter the supreme guru as a Devī (goddess) of their choice, or as several. Then there are the followers of Gaṇeśa and a few who worship the sun. Other traditions add tribal deities, family deities, deities of professions, classes, or even the deity of the (incarnate) guru to this list. Even ancestors can be venerated as deities, or as representatives of deities. Each of these deities can be the supreme deity to its worshippers, the Gate to Brahman, and whoever it may be to you, it is your primary guru.

If you acknowledge your deity as your guru, you stand a good chance of learning much that is hidden to your everyday human personality. As few are able to speak with the gods from the start we have to bridge a gap and human teachers may be convenient. The human guru is considered an incarnation of the divine guru. This is the ideal state: you have a student hungry to learn and an experienced teacher who has "been there and done it". If the two are well attuned, willing to learn, and open to all sorts of feedback, you get the ideal teaching situation. The guru is not only an enlightened being, to the student (śiṣya) s/he is the deity itself.

Most Indian traditions place great emphasis on the role of the guru. This is especially the case in the Tantras, where you can find lengthy hymns that praise the guru and emphasize the importance of total submission to the guru's instructions. Again and again you can read that the guru is the jewel of wisdom, the incarnate deity, and the one and only solution to the countless problems of the aspiring sādhaka. The guru initiates, the guru teaches, the guru enlightens, and in order to enjoy these wonderful feats the pupil has to offer total and absolute submission. Theoretically, the student bows to the guru, washes the guru, houses the guru, feeds the guru, and clothes the guru. The slightest whim of the guru is a divine command for the pupil. To break the ego of the student, a good many gurus demand servitude of the hardest sort, including austerities, penance, and doing a lot of dirty work. This topic is elaborated to some length in several Tantras. *Kulārṇava Tantra* devotes several (slightly boring) chapters to the interplay of guru and śiṣya. It demands so much sanctitiy from the aspiring śiṣya that I wonder why a guru is needed at all. Then again, it goes to the topic 'what can be expected from a true guru' and the requirements are just as superlative. The process does not demand faith. Instead, the śiṣya and guru are supposed to test each other. Again and again the śiṣya is warned of false gurus, of pretenders and charlatans, and is asked to discriminate cautiously between the fake and the living reality. This is something of a joke, for if you can recognize the real thing you are hardly a student any more. A guru who is truly inspired can appear crazy, childish, or demonic to the uninitiated. Who says that divine madness and enlightenment have to conform to conservative middle-class notions of ethical behaviour? So let me ask a difficult question. By what sign can you tell the presence of true holiness? Pause now and think about this before you go on. Write it down in your diary and read it again after a few years, so you know how far you have come.

If you wish to explore Tantra, the scriptures say that you need a guru. Such scriptures were generally written by gurus, many of whom had a strong interest in getting food, shelter, clothes, and twenty-four-hours of free room-service. As it turns out, not all acknowledged saints had a guru. Some simply learned from fellow ascetics, some naturally developed states of intense awareness, and some only started to learn properly once they had left the guru and retired into the wilderness. Others, like Abhinavagupta, learned from a wide range of gurus and sought initiation into anything. A guru may be well and good, but sometimes the incarnate teacher gets in the way of the real guru within.

Do you need a human guru? The answer to this one depends on what you wish to learn. If you wish to master the more complicated forms of classical ritual, or if your will drives you to explore the more athletic forms of yoga, a guru is essential. Classical ritual involves a good many deeds, gestures, moods, and atmospheres, which written texts cannot communicate. If you have no guru, you may practice classical rituals, but they will be very much of your own interpretation. This is something abhorred by traditionalists, while I for one encourage it. It's much more efficient to suit a tradition to a practitioner than to force a practitioner to conform with a tradition. When you invest an old ritual with new meaning, new passion, and new inspiration, it may well turn out to work a lot better than any dull routine sanctified by tradition. Not for the world at large but for specifically you. With yoga things are less simple. While Haṭha yoga in general should be a gentle process of growth and development, there have been an amazing number of traditions that attempted to force results. Not all ancient forms of yoga are actually good for your health. Prolonged staring into the sun may seem spiritual, but it will certainly destroy eyesight eventually. Pressing the neck's arteries to reduce the oxygen supply won't make your brain very happy. Many advanced breathing exercise are only suitable for a fully trained and absolutely healthy yogī under the observation of an experienced teacher with a good knowledge of medicine. Some systems of yoga train the body/mind complex for decades to make it a fit vehicle of the divine current. If you attempted to use their techniques without a rigorous training, your body would get hurt.

This, however, does not mean that you cannot progress without a guru. Lots of exercises can be learned from books and even more can be discovered by learning from yourself, the gods, the spirits, your partner, your friends, and whoever else participates in your magickal multiverse. An old adage says that when the student is ready, the guru appears. This saying is absolutely true, even if you live in the slums of Calcutta, Glasgow, or Washington DC, provided you extend the term guru to its full meaning.

The Primal Guru

Who was your first Guru? And who was the guru before that? Who taught the first lessons? Just after you came out of your mother's womb somebody gave you a slap. It triggered a reflex and you began to breathe. Your breath guru did the job well and so you are alive to read this book. You don't even have to think about breathing, it happens naturally. Next someone else held you. It felt strange enough and then a huge nipple appeared. This triggered another reflex, and you began to suck. Your first nourishment was white and fluid, and if you were lucky it came from your feeding guru, your mother, and not from a bottle. As the mother is usually the first guru, she is called the ādyāguru, the primordial teacher. Note that the very first lessons were taught by triggering reflexes. You learned something radically new by awaking a potential skill that had always been there. These genetic programs are another ādyāguru: the coded wisdom of all ancestral flesh, the memories of past bodies, the serpentine wisdom spiraling in each cell.

They made you twist around, made you move your limbs, made you wriggle fingers, and explore muscles. The first thing you learned was yourself. You did not know that the hands were your hands. When you looked, they were amazing things with many wriggly ends that somehow moved when you did something within yourself. You put them into your mouth and, wow! You felt both ends of the sensation. The baby has to learn its own body, and body is guru, who teaches the possibilities of motion and rest, of pleasure and pain. Well you moved around for a bit and twisted this way and that and somehow you rolled over. This was great; all of a sudden the world looked totally different. How had you done this? Welcome to another guru for life: gravity is beginning its lessons. You learn to wriggle like a maggot, to crawl on all fours (usually backwards for a start, another weird surprise), and when you rise up, gravity shows you the way down again. It's a tough game learning how to pull yourself up, how to stand holding on to things, and how to take the first steps. Here you were pretty much alone. Parents may lend a helpful hand on occasion, but most of the work in learning to get along with gravity is something you did on your own. Whatever you did, you got instant feedback from the gravity guru. You fell on your bum and you got up again. You learned, you learned, and you learned anew. The gravity guru was not always kind to you, as you learned soon enough, but it could also provide a lot of fun. Do you remember the joy of being tossed in the air and caught again? This is playing with gravity, it made you squeak with delight. At this time you had already learned that there were lots of incarnate gurus around. Practically everybody in your world was busy with incomprehensible things. This didn't surprise you much, for when you were really young the entire world was an amazing and often overwhelming multi-sensual experience. Luckily, you had a guru within yourself who helped you sort it out: this was the guru of interest. This is one of the tricky gurus who likes to stay in the background. Other gurus may teach this and that, but without the guru of interest, they are simply backgound noise. The guru of interest made a pact with the guru of pleasure, then the two set out through the jungle of experience, the swamp of the unknown, and the mountains of great events. On the way they met the guru of unpleasantness, who is in charge of teaching the nastier parts of reality, and the guru called memory who likes to predict stuff by looking at things that may have happened. His friend, the guru of imagination joined the fun, and just look at what became of you!

Or let me mention some other gurus who were vital to you. Can you remember the trees, stones, cliffs and buildings who were your gurus of climbing? The animal gurus who taught you how to deal with non-human consciousness? Children like to play with animals, some of them love to pretend being animals, the same goes for a good many shamans and sorcerers, and all of them get a great kick plus un-human abilities and wisdom from the experience. So you had gurus wherever you went. Inside and outside. Most of them before you even went to school. It was your will to learn that allowed them to do their job.

Before we go on, here is a little meditation to remind you of your evolution.

Close your eyes now and think of all the persons, animals, natural forces, spirits, deities, artists, authors, events, and so on. who were guru to you. Think of those from whom you learned valuable skills, and give your thanks to them.

Next, think of all the people and entities from whom you learned what to avoid. An idiot can be an excellent teacher if you wish to avoid that particular idiocy. You can learn a lot from errors, and if you are wise you leave committing the worse errors to other people, and simply learn from them what to avoid. Think of these teachers, and give your thanks to them.

Then think of those gurus who showed both characteristics: you learned some fantastic stuff from them, but you also drew a line and refrained from copying their shortcomings. How many can you think of? Give your thanks to them.

Now reverse the game. Think of those for whom you were or are a guru, whether you knew this or not. Recall what has been useful to others and thank them and yourself for having participated in this learning.

Then think of all the errors you made, and how you can help others to avoid them.

Last, think of what others are learning from you and what you can learn from their learning. What are you missing? What could be better? And what should you be glad and happy about?

You can do these exercises as a discipline and an offering right up there in your mind. You can also make it more impressive and touching by making a ritual of thanksgiving out of it. When you have meditated on the various gurus from whom you profited, and all those who profited from you, bring the whole thought structure into ritual form.

Guru Pūjā

Here are a few ideas on how you can proceed. Feel free to improve on them as you will and enjoy, this is your life, your will, your magick, and your self expressing themselves.

You could close your doors and windows for a start, turn off the light and sit in the dark for a while, breathing deeply but gently. Go easy and aim for smooth breath, if you get dizzy or find your head throbbing you are overdoing it. Let silence reign, then ring a bell or clap your hands, light a candle and some incense, and offer these to your gurus and all other players in the learning game. Then name the gurus who have influenced you most and thank them in a friendly voice. Do this audibly, not only in the imagination; some things have to happen on the physical plane. You could start by thanking the spiritual gurus, such as the spirits and deities of your reality cluster. Then thank the human gurus, all the persons in the wonderful game of life from whom you learned, for good or ill, what was beneficial for you. This can turn out to be a formidably long list, so it might be a good idea to give detailed thanks to the persons from whom you learned most, and to mention the others only briefly. Last thank the animal and plant gurus, the places of power, and finally the abstract gurus, such as the sun, moon, stars, gravity, time, weather. When you are well prepared, a lot will come to mind, and you may find yourself busy for an hour or more. Good! The primary offering is emotion; put feeling into your words, speak from the heart, and fully sense what you are talking about. It does not have to be well-worded or precise, simply open your mind and heart, and unseal your mouth. If you allow your words to speed up you may well become excited and ecstatic. Don't worry if you repeat yourself or if things don't seem poetic enough; the important thing is deeply felt love and passion. You are giving your thanks for a lifetime of support. You are doing well when you are getting carried away. This is an ecstatic feast, go ahead and enjoy.

As to the words, give attention to the tenses: past, present, and future. Give thanks for what you learned, what you are learning, and what you will learn. This is an ongoing process, if you remember only past experience, you may forget the present and future. You can offer passionate words, you can offer sheer honesty, you can offer song and dance and music. On the physical plane, you can offer good food and drink to the gurus and add whatever you feel is fitting. Dare to be creative! You have lots of unique gurus and I hope you are a unique guru yourself. If you invoke and thank your gurus in three groups (gods, humans, nature) you might give three offerings, one for each group. No, I won't burden you with classical formalities here. You will know what works when you find out what turns you on. Thank those from whom you learned and learn, thank those who learn from you, and thank all for participating in the learning game. This is intelligence multiplying with intelligence. Finally, affirm that the world is guru to you as you are guru to the world. Give your thanks to all, give your thanks to yourself. Then confirm your unity with the gurus of the universe, eat the offerings and drink the blessed fluid. Last, end the rite, extinguish the flame, pour the excess energies out of your body into the earth, and sit in silence and darkness for a while before you get up and enjoy life.

Learning Together

In the Indian traditions, much has been done to give firm rules for the conduct of guru and student. Formality, as you will remember, was already a major obsession in Vedic times and for many Indian traditions it still is. When we see the communion of guru and pupil as a divine game, or as a very rigid ritual of interaction, several behavior forms become apparent. The student is supposed to get various powers, skills, and ultimately enlightenment and liberation, but for this treasure a price has to be paid. S/he has to give up ego and make servitude to the guru, as the incarnate deity or divine principle, the central act of worship. Now, if the guru is really a fully enlightened being, this may work. A good guru teaches, but the teaching may have unusual forms. Discourse and answering questions are part of this program, but they are certainly not the most important elements. Words often veil more than they disclose. An answer may disclose an intellectual truth, but this is only a very limited experience. If you want the full experience, you have to go beyond the simple answer and use your own brain. Just look at yourself! Here you are reading this book! How fast are you? Are you reading faster than you think? Have you thought about the things you want to learn, and thought deeply? Do you think about a topic or do you want me to do the thinking for you? Words are miles away from direct experience. Too many people know the words and understand them rationally. They think they understand what they can define, explain, and prattle about. All of this is a diversion from true knowledge. You can study Kālī, you can speak about Kālī, you can define the forms of Kālī, but when you meet Kālī, you will know the difference.

Sometimes a guru can be a diversion from thinking and experiencing for oneself. When information becomes too easily attainable, people consume more and contemplate less. So how can you think, contemplate, and understand more deeply?

Give yourself time.

Pause frequently.

Think NOW.

Go for long and silent walks.

Think and think again before you ask or look things up in a book.

Ask inward before you ask outward.

Invoke and assemble a specific thought-cluster, then open your mind and experience.

Assume unusual points-of-view.

Connect the unexpected.

Cultivate many interpretations.

Be insider, outsider, and in-between.

Trust jackals and hyenas to have the last laugh.

Hymn:

Hrīṁ, Śrīṁ, Krīṁ. And as you do this and enjoy your Tantric awareness meditation of today you can sense that you have always known wake up a lot more than you ever knew before you learned that it has always been there and what effects it has on you and your reality to understand that living it is the full knowledge of yourself which is coming from you for you as you advance and realize it's here and now body mind spirit secretes secrets to enjoy when you see what is without you are looking through the eyes of within, who knows and you can turn to. Welcome back home and there's knowbody there. Thank you. **Svāhā**.

Webs of Delusion

Sadly, human gurus tend to bring out not only the best but also the worst parts of a person. Addiction to words instead of experience is one such pitfall. Then there is lack of initiative. When the guru is traditionally minded, or stuck in the formalities of Vedic ritual, the best students will turn out to be the least original ones. It's dangerous to follow a person who does your thinking for you. Another danger is copying the guru too closely. When the student looks like a copy of the guru, something went wrong. People can't help being unique. We all grow up differently, have distinct experiences, and by the time we are old enough to consider spiritual evolution, we do not need spiritual practice in general but specifically the practice that suits our talents and hang-ups. So a good guru seeks to develop the connection between the student and the divine, and when a student begins to behave exactly like the guru, does everybody a favour by tactics of chaos and confusion. Seemingly mad behaviour has its place here, weird humour and spontaneous disruption of belief patterns. Luckily this happens pretty naturally, as no real guru can be expected to accord with the silly views that students have regarding holiness.

It is not only the student, however, who is in danger of delusion. Being the guru is just as dangerous a trap. If you are the person who is supposed to be the ultimate authority, you may find yourself in the trap labelled 'perfection'. Not even your own perfection but the idea of perfection that other people entertain. When one plays the guru game round the clock one may get totally out of touch with the divine game of the world. After all, it's an easy job to play 'holy, holy' when everyone around you plays the same game and supports your belief in yourself. The true test and the real guru for all spiritual enclaves is the dreaded outside world. A guru is supposed to be free from bondage, but when s/he has to think, act, and decide for a student, it's goodbye to freedom for all concerned. Worst of all, the guru may begin to entertain the delusion that s/he really knows best. When you know best you are not learning any more. This has happened to many people in guru functions, including therapists, priests, and scholars. If you get paid for being right you may forget how to be wrong. So the guru has to break out of the trap of the guru profession. Some gurus embrace mad behaviour for this purpose. Others, like Bengal's mad saint Rāmakṛṣṇa, refuse to be called guru or father. In Rāmakṛṣṇa's view there are thousands of gurus, but the only real one, and the only one he ever had, is Sat, Chit, Ānanda (Being, Consciousness, and Bliss). Think about it. A good guru learns at least as much from the student as the student from the guru. A good guru does not claim saintliness, all-knowledge, or perfection, and thereby remains in contact with the divine. The whole thing reaches its summit when the student decides to devote all to spiritual development, and becomes a sannyāsin or sannyāsinī. This used to be an extremely solemn and important ritual (see the *Mahānirvāṇa Tantra*). A sannyāsin gives up everything, including family ties, religious belief, faith in gods, ownership of property, relation to the guru, and station in society, and conducts her or his own funeral rites, thereby breaking all social bonds forever. During the ritual, the guru reverses the roles and worships the sannyāsin as guru. After this rite, there is no student and no guru any more.

The same sort of thing can happen with the divine guru. One of the countless legends in the *Devī Bhāgavatam* describes how Manasā worshipped Kṛṣṇa with such fervour that Kṛṣṇa in turn worshipped her. She became a serpent goddess in the process.

Nowadays it is mightily hard to find good gurus of the more interesting Tantric currents. This even goes for India, where devotees are persecuted by militant atheists, narrow-minded traditionalists, totally unspiritual folk, and, worst of the lot, fluffy-minded New-Age tourists. A lot of lineages have become extinct over the last three centuries. You can make up for it by getting really close to your iṣṭadevatā / s. And you can decide that learning never stops and that everyone can be a guru for everybody else.

Dhyāna:

Every person whom you meet is better than you at something.

Everybody you meet can learn something from you.

Pause now to think of various friends, acquaintances, relations, and even totally fictional characters. All of them are good at something. This could be something you admire. It could be something you would like to learn from them. Or it could be something that you would much rather avoid. Some people are perfectly good at perfectly horrid things. This is also an achievement and ought to be appreciated. All behaviour, when well done, is an achievement if not a work of art. Study them really well so that you can learn their strengths and avoid their errors. How precisely do they do their thing? What do they have to think, believe, and imagine in order to do it? What skills go into the process? What do they do, in body and mind, and in what order? Imagine a situation where those horrible things might be really useful. Can you imagine how perfectly horrid behaviour may be applied usefully? Change the setting of the behaviour. Or keep the setting and change the behaviour. Learn from those who are good at things. Think of at least twenty persons and work out what they are really good at. Make a list and write it down if you like. Meet them, ask them, find out HOW it's done. And how can you use it?

Next, reverse roles and think of the same people. What skills do you have which might be of use to them? Think deeply. Learning is everywhere.

Divine Actors

What is there beyond the game of guru and śiṣya? Here we leave the realm of strict learning relationships and come to the wider world of anything-can-happen. Who are you in this world, what parts do you play in the līlā, what is the motion, direction, and purpose of your life?

One of the transformations that come up in any sort of magick, Tantra, or shamanism is the development of a magickal personality, or a divine one, if you like. The word 'person' literally means 'mask'. The personality of the aspirant is always artificial. All personalities are, all persona you have been, in this and other lifetimes, are convenient masks assumed to allow you to do your thing. When you grow up, a name is attached to you, a family, a location, a time, and a lot of other matters that shape your early childhood. You grow into a mask, a stage, a play, and though there are minor changes possible, you have to assume these forms before you can decide what you really are and what you want to do with it. Thus, you developed childhood personalities. You developed adolescent personalities, you developed personalities that seemed more

Figure 26 - From womb to womb like spiders.

adult and mature to you (in your innocence), and later in life you changed them again. When you were young, you probably sought to be older, riper, wiser; when you are getting old you may be busy becoming younger again. Some folks get so serious minded in the 'adult world' that they need to have children, or to get drunk, to rediscover spontaneity and playing.In most societies, the first things you learn are the ones relating to your survival. Next come the rules that define good behaviour, socially acceptable norms, and though these norms differ from culture to culture, there are always some norms, no matter where you grow up. This is the worst part of reincarnation: you have to learn a lot of rubbish before you become old enough to question whether it is worth it.

In this sense, growing up equals getting really involved in the world of appearances (some call this bondage). You have to get attached to the world to learn to handle it. And you have to get out of it at some point if you wish to discover your primordial self-nature and live the life that is natural for you. In between these two states comes the dream of religion and spiritual refinement. If people have any brains at all, at some point they become dissatisfied with consensual reality. This happens easier to minorities, to outcasts, to folks who are not in the sugar coated top level of the American dream. It is often those who are socially unacceptable who resign first from the usual rat-race of ambition and achievement, and search for other spaces to enjoy. So they get into student roles, and with a bit of luck they also find teachers, within and outside of themselves. Yet life is more than being in a teacher-student relationship. The student who is not having lessons is just a human being. The guru who has no student is just a practitioner. Both of them coexist only in company. So what happens when they get along on their own? More precisely, what happens to YOU as you travel through life? How do you achieve the consciousness you will, how do you manifest your experience in word and deed and action? What do you do when you are neither beginner nor expert, neither teacher nor student, neither innocent nor experienced?

When you discard the role definitions of spiritual maturity, you come to something very simple. And you begin to develop your own expression of living a whole life, a magickal life, a life that is precisely what you will to live. You require a personality to make this easy.

Here we have to get rid of a lot of rubbish. What does holiness look like (to you) ? How can you recognize divine awareness when it appears in human form? What will you be like when you come to yourself?

Most people in the industrial world cherish a dream of holiness that has very little to do with the real thing. Generally, the dream tends to take two forms. One of them is the glamour of the silent, motionless adept who sits in serene meditation. This person is usually imagined self-sufficient, often a recluse, who moves like a shadow through the world of illusions without being part of it. If that person speaks, it is slowly, and each word drips enormous importance. If this person walks, it is lightly and with dignity. If this person encounters others, it radiates love and understanding. Alone or in company, our perfect adept is always serene, joyous, blissful, competent, wise, and free of any problems or confusion. Such a dream has its attractions. Many desperate seekers look for the outward manifestations of this sort of holiness and fall for any actor good enough to mime them. This has always been a nuisance, nowadays it is a whole industry. Many entertain the opinion that the perfect saint is permanently blissful, dignified, slow, understanding, tolerant, radiating a general I-love-anything spirituality, no matter whether in ritual or everyday life. In short, this wondrous creature is permanently stuck. If you have to be in a single consciousness at all times and in all places, this can only be done by getting rid of a lot of other states. If you wish to be an example, you need those who need such examples. In short, the saint depends on the not-so-saintly to exist at all.

The other form of holiness that sells well on the spiritual market is the extroverted shaman figure. Here we have dancing, singing, chanting, drumming, animal imitations, wild playacting, dramatic gestures, and a lot of fancy fetishes, symbols, talismans, and knickknacks. You find people playing at being 'spiritual warriors' who have never considered what war is all about.

Popular opinion in the Western world generally attributes serene, silent stillness to Oriental saints while Native Americans and African fetish priests are the favourites for extroverted, loud, and passionate spirituality. So are we to imagine the practitioners of yoga and Tantra as blissful, introverted, withdrawn recluses? Even a brief look at elder literature shows that the Indians themselves rarely entertained such beliefs. The *Mahābhārata* is full of episodes describing enclaves of saintly seers and yogīs. These are usually set in paradise landscapes where sacred waters flow, enchanted birds sing, and age-old trees offer shelter from the elements. Gentle breezes waft through lush growth, the scent of a thousand blossoms bedazzles the mind, animals play innocently in the sunlight glades, and all nature is generous, beautiful, and divine. Unlike the setting, the saints themselves are rarely beautiful or enchanting. Many of them are given to amazing fits of rage and anger. They are proud, arrogant, and take offence at the least provocation. True, in principle the yogī is supposed to be above such sentiments. However, why are the most powerful saints, whose power is feared by highest gods, so given to aggression, pettiness, and a total lack of tolerance? Why is it that Indra, fearing that a given saint may acquire world control, has to ask a heavenly Apsaras to seduce and distract? And why are even the Apsarases mistreated and abused with depressing regularity? Similar events occur in many venerable works of Indian literature. A lot of top-notch saints of the Purāṇas may be admired for their discipline, their austerities, and their uncompromising efforts. Still they remain an unfriendly bunch you wouldn't like to spend an hour with. So we arrive at the first insight regarding human saintliness: it does not mean being nice to everyone.

Female Saints

Let's take a closer look at a few saints. Some of the most famous saints of Indian lore were historical persons, and though their histories are cluttered with legends of all sorts, you may find it useful to see a few examples of what you can expect from the thoroughly inspired. Usually people discuss male saints. You find loads and loads of them in Hindu literature. Here's something different. Here are a few women who became saints, one way or another, and profoundly influenced Indian belief.

Kāraikkāl Ammaiyār was of Tamil origin. She lived in the sixth century and is one of the earliest known practitioners of bhakti (devotional love). Unlike most devotees of bhakti, Kāraikkāl came form a Śaivite background. In her time the loving dedication of bhakti was not yet expressed in erotic terms. Devotees assumed filial roles to the deities of their choice. Kāraikkāl must have shown signs of her spiritual powers early on. Freshly married, she was abandoned by her husband, who was scared of her spiritual powers. He moved away, married elsewhere, and named his first child, a daughter, after her. Kāraikkāl was not too upset about the episode. She retired to the nearest forest and became an ascetic. Living in isolation she worshipped Śiva and asked two gifts from him. The first was to become as ugly as a ghost, thus ensuring that she could remain alone and unmolested. It sounds like a woman who is scared of bandits, rapists, and the like. But Kāraikkāl made it a magickal personality. She literally became the ghost of her former self. This is more than appearance, it is the complete identification with one who has lived, died, and become a member of the spiritual world. The other boon was to witness the legendary dance contest of Śiva and Kālī. When the great event happened, Kāraikkāl participated as her own ghost amongst Kālī's retinue. She herself became part of the mind-blowing savagery when hordes of skeletons, demons, ghosts, seizers, and body-snatchers, accompanying the deities entered the most ferocious dance contests of all times. Her vision survived. She saw Kālī defeated by Śiva's supreme dancing skills (he could stand on one leg and lift the other to the sky while Kālī allegedly could not) and wrote two famed poems on the event which survive to this day. In art, Kāraikkāl is usually shown as a nude, emaciated woman, skinny, with thin, hanging breasts, and enormously tangled hair. As Sanjukta Gupta (in Leslie, 1992: 196) points out, as she adored Śiva, she may have copied the appearance of Śiva's mate Kālī. However, her poems describe her as Śiva's servant, not as his spouse. Her life is largely undocumented. She became a Kāpālinī (skull-bearer) and composed a number of poems (four survive) for which she was highly praised by several famous Śaivite ascetic poets.

Āṇṭāḷ, otherwise called Godā (Cow-giver), lived in south India of the early ninth century. She came from an exceptionally devout Brahmin family and dedicated all her life to the worship of Kṛṣṇa. She was so mad for her god that she married him in an extended ceremony. Her primary aim in life was the practice of Tantric Vaiṣṇava rites. She was an adept of visualisation and successfully superimposed the primitive rural village of

Kṛṣṇa over the town where she lived, all the way to the point where she couldn't keep the two apart (or didn't want to). In spite of her high birth, she chose to live in a cow stable, or so it is said. Her poetry is full of erotic elements testifying to her lifelong yearning. She certainly achieved a high degree of enlightenment and left us a wide range of magnificent poems. Nevertheless, she did not quit city life as so many female worshippers of Kālī and Śiva did. Doing duty at a temple, she spent her life in isolation and died young. Her pilgrimages remained all in the imagination. Today she is acknowledged and worshipped as a wife of Viṣṇu. (Hudson in White 2000: 206-227, and Gupta in Leslie 1992: 202)

Akkā Mahādevī lived in the twelfth century. She came from an upper-class family in Karnataka and was famed for her beauty and her unusually long hair. A local king proposed to marry her. Akkā came from a Śaiva family and was intensely devoted to her *Lord, white as jasmine.* The king happened to be a Jaina. As the story goes (and you don't have to believe this, kings being kings), he promised to become a Śaiva if only she would marry him. They married but, as could have been expected, the royal house did not abandon Jainism. This made Akkā raging mad. She left the palace and threw away all of her ornaments, possessions, and clothes. Clad only in her long hair, and looking much like raging Kālī, she disappeared into the forest and took up the life of an ascetic. Akkā eventually travelled to an ascetic community of viraśaiva ascetics in Kalyani. Coming from an upper class family, I wonder whether she was very good at living on the road and in the wilderness. Apparently she looked so mad and wasted by the time she arrived that the adepts wondered whether she might be a dangerous lunatic. Non-Indians sometimes assume that in India any devout madman is venerated as a saint. This is not the case. Indian ascetics draw a line between those who are touched by the gods and those possessed by demons, and there are strict examinations to determine whether a given person is inspired or simply insane. In Akkā's case, a verbal examination sufficed. The ascetics asked all sorts of highly critical questions, and Akkā, in spite of her looks, gave the right sort of answers. She was accepted and found a guru, Allammā Prabhu, who gave her the name Akkā (Elder Sister). Gupta remarks that in Saṅskṛt, the word Akkā would be Jyeṣṭhā, who is a complex goddess. She became an honoured member of the community and wrote a lot of devotional poems. People occasionally commented on her habitual nudeness, but Akkā replied with poetry stating that shame cannot exist in a world where the eye of the lord (Śiva) sees everything. When one ascetic remarked that her densely matted hair would also constitute a form of clothing, she answered with a poem asking his pardon. She gracefully acknowledged that she had not yet become completely free of her personal shame, but then, neither had the ascetics around her. Later in life she travelled to a hill-top temple in Kalyani, where she ritually married Śiva in his form as Mallikātjuna (White as Jasmine). Allegedly, she merged into the statue of Śiva and disappeared.

Lallā Ded was born into a Brahmin family in Kashmir in the fourteenth century. She married (or was married) early, but as her biography indicates, her husband was very much a under the control of his mother, who hated the young and highly devoted wife. Lallā did not have any children and before long she was kicked out and told to go back to her family. She didn't. Instead, she went for the forest and became a yoginī. Practising her worship in isolation, she favoured Tantric practices that would have disgusted most Brahmins. Lallā wore very little or no clothes, ate meat, drank alcohol, worshipped Śiva in devotional poems, and proceeded to raise Kuṇḍalinī. Her poems hint at deep meditation and breath-retention, making truth arise and a light radiate through her body into the outer world. She was highly critical of contemporary worship and derided the renouncers as folk who are just as bound as worldly people: *Those who win a kingdom find no rest. Those who give it up will not find peace. Free of desire, the soul will never die. The soul who knows, dies while it is alive.* (after Glasenapp's German translation, 1958: 236). She also derided conventional sacrifices and those who make a difference between one deity and another. It is uncertain whether she ever had a proper guru. She may have learned from ascetics, and discovered a lot in her trances, but if there ever was a human teacher she fails to mention it. In her poems, she gives good evidence that her guru and lover was simply Śiva. Some of her songs show radical views. She was against the worship of images, just as she didn't approve of temples, and called both mere lumps of stone. In worship and behaviour she took the uncompromising attitude of an avadhūta, i.e. an advanced Tantric practitioner who simply goes where s/he wills and does what s/he wills. She met some harsh criticism from the establishment but gained the respect of her fellow ascetics, of the common population, and (allegedly) even of several Sufis. Her poems survive.

Bhairavī Brahmaṇī was a scholar and a Tantric saint of the 19th century. She came from a high class family and combined a number of hard core Tantric practices with Vaiṣṇava-style devotion (bhakti). She is chiefly remembered in connection with her most famous student, the celebrated Rāmakṛṣṇa Paramahaṁsa (1836-1886). Rāmakṛṣṇa was a natural. As a child he used to develop natural trance states which blew his mind but which he could not control. Driven by an amazing hunger for the divine he served Kālī and Śiva (plus, later on, an astonishing range of other deities) but he was still given to fits of swooning, obsession, and mad behaviour. Bhairavī, so the story goes, arrived by boat. Allegedly, she greeted him by saying: *'My son, everyone in this world is mad. Some are mad for money, some for creature comforts, some for name and fame; and you are mad for god.'* (McDaniel 1989: 96). She had dreamed of Rāmakṛṣṇa, her third student, and soon proceeded to train him. All in all, she lived about three years with Rāmakṛṣṇa. She also arranged a conference of scholars and seers and introduced Rāmakṛṣṇa to them. Arguing fiercely and quoting wide ranges of scripture, she convinced the experts that Rāmakṛṣṇa was neither mad nor possessed by demons, but an avatāra, an incarnation of the divine. Bhairavī did not leave it at that. June McDaniel gives a brief summary of practices which are not usually found in biographies of Rāmakṛṣṇa: *She had him sit on skull-seats, chant mantras, eat fish and human flesh from a skull and* *perform the practices described in the major Tantras. She brought him women with whom Rāmakṛṣṇa could perform some of the rituals, but the biographies are unclear about his practice with them - Rāmakṛṣṇa claimed to have fallen into trance, and been unaware of performing anything.* (McDaniel 2004: 114) He often did that. There are several episodes in his life where close proximity to women made him lose consciousness or prompted fits of devotional worship. Bhairavī taught him a range of Tantric techniques, including the raising of the Kuṇḍalinī, and two important techniques of Vaiṣṇava bhakti. In the first, vātsalya, Rāmakṛṣṇa transformed into a woman to serve the goddess. He dressed as one, spoke as one, wore artificial hair, and lived among the women of the house, completely forgetting his male conditioning. Doing mādhurya bhāva, the sentiment of erotic love, he became Rādhā, lover and mate of Kṛṣṇa. Rādhā loves Kṛṣṇa, but as her mate is often absent, or dallying with pretty cow-girls at the fringes of the jungle, she is frequently alone, unhappy, and jealous. Rāmakṛṣṇa had fits of anguish, wept for days, and refused to take food. At one point, he became paralysed, then unconscious for three days. Coming to his senses again, Bhairavī dragged him to the river for a bath. He was in such a state of hyper-sensitivity that he could not bear the touch of her hand. As it turned out, Bhairavī was only the first among numerous teachers. Rāmakṛṣṇa joined a wide range of religions and discovered the divine again and again. He became the most famous Indian saint of the 19th century and founded a movement that is alive and well to this day. Considered from the Tantric point of view he was a bit of a failure. In spite of being trained by an exceptional female guru, and becoming a woman for more than six months of his life, he never managed to come to terms with women. Rāmakṛṣṇa married Śāradā Devī (1853-1920) when she was six. The two began to live together when she was nineteen and led a devout but singularly unerotic life. They never had children. She acted more like a mother to him and to the thousands of followers flocking to Dakṣhiṇeśwar, and when his trances and ecstasies became overly intense, it was she who muttered mantras into his ears to bring him back to sense. Rāmakṛṣṇa appreciated her support, he identified her with Tripura Sundarī, and told others to worship her. But he did not make much of an effort for women in general. To the end of his life he insisted that women and money are the two prime obstacles to spiritual progress.

Phoolan Devi (Flower Goddess) was born into a poor Mallah family (a low class of śūdras) in a tiny village in Uttar Pradesh on the day of the flower-feast in 1962 or 3. Her childhood was characterised by continuous harassment, violence, and exploitation. Mallahs frequently have to do the worst jobs in any rural district and they rarely get any payment apart from blows. At the age of eleven she was (illegally) married to a widower of thirty-five who turned out to be a crazy sadist. Phoolan was raped, abused, and tortured, each attempt to flee ending in being sent back. In rural India, women have very few rights, and are supposed to obey their husbands at all costs. A woman without a husband has no honour or protection whatsoever. When she finally managed to escape, her family, and indeed her entire village, considered her defiled, leading to ever increasing abuse, exploitation, and repeated rape by the police and by members of the superior classes. Unlike so many poor women in India, Phoolan refused to submit and fought back as well as she could. She had no education but a lot of determination. Finally, a mixed gang of bandits was hired to abduct and kill her. One of their leaders, Vickram Singh, an educated and religious outcast with a strong sense of ethics, married her and made her his partner. Whether they had a love-life remains an open question. Whatever may have been the case, he certainly adored her. Eventually Vickram was assassinated by his former teacher, a bandit called Shri Ram, and Phoolan fell into the hands of that gang. More torture and rape followed. Finally, a village Brahmin helped her escape (and was burned alive by Shri Ram). Phoolan founded her own gang and began a successful career as a 'bandit queen'. Driven by a tremendous hunger for revenge and justice, she specialised in robbing rich people. Low class villagers, especially women, were asked about the ethics of the rich of their district. Phoolan, identifying with her personal deity Durgā, sought the exploiters and rapists. She punished, castrated, and killed. Her gang was so successful that major police operations were launched against her; one chief minister had to retire from office as he couldn't handle the situation. Eventually, most of her gang were exterminated. In February 1983, after lengthy negotiations, she capitulated under her terms in a public ceremony. She went to prison without trial, where she lived like a minor celebrity. In February 1994 she was released. Soon she began a political career. In 1996 she became a member of parliament. She was among the nominees for the Nobel peace prize and was so popular among the lower classes that she became a candidate for the office of prime minister. She was expected to get around 70% of the votes. A few days before the election three professional, and well-informed, assassins gunned her down. The case was never cleared up but the government set up a grandiose memorial. Now you may ask what exactly makes Phoolan Devi a saint. To the common people Phoolan was not just a saint, she was an incarnate deity. This identification goes back to the first days of her abduction, when a saintly ascetic declared that she was an incarnation of Kālī. It was Vickram who told Phoolan that she should have a personal deity, and Phoolan chose Durgā. She never seems to have practised any classical sādhana, apart from informal prayer and the odd offering at Kālī's and Durgā's shrines, as was common custom among the more ethical bandits. However, she certainly got her share of extreme consciousness states. As a bandit leader, and for several months on her own in the jungle, she frequently suffered from hunger, thirst, lack of sleep, and the paranoia that comes naturally when hordes of police are out to shoot you. During these states she developed very close ties to wild animals. Frequently, Durgā appeared to her in the shape of a young girl, telling her when to avoid drinking water, which road to take, where the police was waiting in ambush, or where to hide during bombardment. These visions seem to have occurred in half-sleep, during dreams or in states of extreme exhaustion. Sometimes she saw the goddess, more usually she heard her voice in her head. Phoolan's life became an example for many of the poor and low of India. Numerous movements tried to make her a symbol of their creeds and turned her into a socialist revolutionary, a feminist, or a freedom fighter. Others saw her as a romantic figure and made movies of her life. None of these designations are strictly true, as Phoolan spent most of her life being simply an uneducated, abused girl without any greater aims than simply staying alive. It was Durgā, not socialism, who made her become a scourge of the mighty. Her life turned out to be highly embarrassing for many cultivated Indians who found the international press becoming interested in the social conditions of the countryside. If you think that slavery is a thing of the past, that India is a holy land, or that the class-system is abolished, let me recommend Phoolan's autobiography.

Female Ascetics

Female ascetics, as Lynn Denton has shown in her study *Varieties of Female Hindu Asceticism*, tend to come in three basic forms. Doing her field work in Varanasi (Benares), the most popular site for pilgrimage in India, she found some 1300 ascetics in the city. Of these, roughly ten percent were women. Some of them were old, some were acknowledged gurus, but the majority were, at the time, in their twenties. These women can be classed in three types.

First we have **sannyāssinīs**, renouncer ascetics who have cut all ties to the world. Initiation ceremonies differ widely, but they do contain a few typical elements. One of them is an extended ritual (often several days long) during which the woman renounces her place, name, and past in human society. Usually she fasts, does the funeral rites (śraddha) for herself, and sometimes she burns a straw effigy representing herself. She vows to forget her past, family ties, place in society, assumes a new name, and proceeds to live an entirely new life under very harsh conditions.

Nowadays the word sannyāsa (renunciation) has lost a lot of the meaning it used to have. A number of would-be gurus, the best known being the incomparable 'Osho' Rajneesh, have felt free to give this title to their devotees, most of whom did not even know the status it used to have, nor what it really entails. To the traditional renouncers, the journey into asceticism is not a fancy game but the complete dedication of all their being, nature, identity, and property to a spiritual idea. During the initiation ceremony, the guru asks the initiate whether she chooses to follow the path of the householder or to renounce it for spiritual liberation. The contrast is crucial. To most of the women interviewed by Lynn Denton, being an ascetic renouncer defined itself exactly by not being a householder. To these women, the wheel of phenomenal existence (saṁsāra) is precisely the sort of lives they left behind: work, household duties, raising the kids, venerating the ancestors, being obedient to almost everybody. While ordinary Hindu women are expected to do a wide range of religious acts for the sake of their husbands and children, they gain little spiritual benefit for themselves. At best, they can hope to be reborn as a man. The sannyāssinīs, by contrast, seek to leave the entire cycle of rebirths. Apart from this, the actual activities of sannyāssinīs differ enormously. Most meditate frequently and practice mantra-japa. Some devote themselves to rituals of worship (if they still have any relation to the gods), others practice yoga, visualisations or devote themselves to extended pilgrimages. Others seem less religious. Some run spiritual schools or make a living by conducting hymn-singing sessions or tell legends. Some advise their neighbourhood regarding worldly matters, a few were running fashionable private schools. As it turned out, not all sannyāssinīs believed that they have to make real efforts to reach liberation. For many, liberation is guaranteed by the initiation ritual, ensuring that, if they stay away from worldly life and duties, they will automatically find liberation when they die.

Brahmacārya is celibate asceticism. The women (brahmacāriṇī) who chose this path make much of the earliest stage in life, that of studentship, and remain at this level indefinitely. As a result, they simply do not enter the life of a householder. Studentship is the first stage in life. It involves celibacy, study of sacred writ, a strictly vegetarian diet, obedience, and service to a teacher and great care not to breech any of the purity laws. Being a brahmacāriṇī is not an easy path, as there are so many rules and regulations for proper purity. Nevertheless, almost two thirds of the ascetic women studied by Lynn Denton fall into this class. Denton describes several distinct forms of celibate studentship. One consists of living under monastic conditions until the woman is old enough to become a renouncer. Another field for chaste ascetics appears in several new Hindu movements, where groups of celibate women accumulate around teachers. There they tend the sacred fires, make offerings, recite ancient texts, and often acquire a respectable amount of learning. Brahmacāriṇīs often live in communities led by elder women. Their daily life is rigorously scheduled. They tend to wear white and have their hair cropped short. Most of their lives are confined within their small monastic communities. They only dare the outside world in groups.

The third category of ascetic women studied by Lynn Denton is the group of **tāntrikās**. These women were less easy to class than the others, as they show more individual development. They were also smaller in number, Denton could only find a dozen of them. Generally, tāntrikās can rarely be classed by specific traditions or schools. They often have close ties to their gurus, and to the lineages of those gurus but, all in all, they tend to favour whatever practices suit them. Tāntrikās have a certain disposition towards fierce and dangerous asceticism. Their rituals involve a number of terrifying elements, and meditation on or near cremation places are still encouraged - unlike corpse-sitting, which may have become a thing of the past (or isn't discussed openly). The Tantric ascetics generally seek to attain and cultivate siddhis, but unlike some major Tantric movements, they do not believe that the acquisition of magical powers (siddhis) and liberation are mutually exclusive. Our tāntrikās of Varanasi go for both. Sexual rites may be practised freely, that is, each tāntrikā may have intercourse with her father (guru), brother (fellow aspirant), or son (her own student). In a similar way, a male practitioner may have congress with his mother (guru), sister (fellow aspirant), or his daughter (his own student). In tantric circles, such family (kula) titles are used to indicate the closeness within the group-community. To outsiders they look like incestuous relationships, which is certainly not the case. Such rites, however, are not of major importance. More essential are daily discipline (sādhana), difficult and dangerous practices, and good interaction with the guru. Denton loosely classed the tāntrikās in three groups. The first consists of yogīnīs, i.e. women who practice yoga or tapas in some way. Such women often favour a very strict discipline and cultivate will-power by performing difficult and painful austerities. The second call themselves Perfected (siddhā) and prefer rituals of the left-hand-path. The siddhās aim at getting rid of worldly ties and do rituals to ensure their liberation. Some practise yoga, but this is not a must. As the main object of their asceticism is the cultivation of magical skills, they are ready to perform a number of acts that seem disgusting to purity minded traditionalists. Here sexual rites have their place, just like the morbid rites, and the many 'rebellious' acts that aim at the deconditioning of the mind. The third class of tāntrikās may be considered professional sorceresses. These women have cultivated siddhis, one way or another, and put them to use. Some make a living near shrines or temples by selling amulets, good luck, or protection. It may be interesting to consider that the tāntrikās in general do not simply aim at liberation. In their world-view, humans can go much further. Liberation is well and good, but it does not have to wait till death. It can be experienced while alive, and the same goes for divinity. Many tāntrikās seek to become divine, equal or superior to the gods, within their lifetime. Quite a few succeed.

Tāntrikās

More on this important topic appears in June McDaniel's *Offering Flowers, Feeding Skulls*, the best study on Śākta folk religion and obsession in modern India which I have ever come upon (highly recommended). McDaniel classes several types of Tantrikās. Of course, the situation of modern Tāntrikās differs from those a thousand years ago, hence I would ask your caution in projecting the status quo on periods about which we know far too little. Nowadays, several types of women are involved in Tantra. First, there are the **female gurus**. Like male gurus, these women are professionals who have dedicated themselves completely to the spiritual life. Most of them have undergone decades of training. Especially the ones who were never married and remain celibate have a high status in the eyes of the population. However, celibacy is not a must.

Then there are **holy women** and **widows** who lived a married life, had children, but received a religious call. These Tāntrikās left their families, went on pilgrimage, associated themselves with some temple or institution, and generally only visit their husbands and kids on occasion. Such women often live on the road. They make a living by begging, making talismans, telling fortunes, and some of them gain followers or students. Obsession by deities is an important part of their spiritual discipline.

Then there are the **Tantric wives**. Here we encounter women who are living in marriage with their husbands. In many cases, it is the husband who is devoted to Tantric discipline, while the wife sees it her spiritual duty to participate. Orthodox Indian thought demands absolute obedience from housewives, hence, even if the woman participates in hard core ritual she still remains dutiful to traditional Dharma. Such women generally receive training from a guru. Some of them achieve a high degree of spiritual and magical competence. Others only do the rites as this is expected of them. In either case, the married Tāntrikā is usually reluctant in talking about her activities. She does not seek fame, wealth, or contact to outsiders.

An early form of the 'Tantric wife' may be the **veśya**, who appears in elder literature. The term veśya literally means a prostitute, but the actual meaning is that of a sexually active and independently minded Tāntrikā. Unlike a prostitute, the veśya is married to her partner. She practices ritual, has training in mantra and visualisation and seeks union with the divine. Within the relationship she can be quite demanding. Nevertheless, she is expected to remain true to her husband. Should she have congress with other men, she is sure to suffer divine punishment, and so will the men who bed her.

Then there are **celibate wives**. Usually they receive a divine call, or simply become obsessed or visionary. Such women remain living in the household, but they dedicate themselves completely to a religious life. Some achieve a high status as holy women, organise public ceremonies, or run religious communities. Their husbands can say goodbye to any sort of lovelife, but they do gain a high status in the eyes of the community. They often profit from the money made by their spouses and generally believe that their karman improves.

Last there is a group of **professional Tantric ritual assistants**. These women often follow a hereditary tradition, you might almost call it a class. Such women receive training from one or several gurus. The program includes breathing exercises, meditation, mantras, and a lot of yoga aimed at controlling sexual passion and inner energy flow. Such women hire their services to Tāntrikas who have no competent ritual partners. The greatest danger to their profession is to become pregnant. In this sort of ritual format, men are expected to retain their sperm. A pregnancy is not desirable at all, in fact, a male orgasm means that the rite has failed. McDaniels cites a study by Bholanath Bhattacharjee, who interviewed forty-eight professional ritual consorts. In one case story, the worshipper impregnated the woman and then abandoned her. *However, he later came back, saying that if his guru liked practicing with her, he would take her back and also pay her rent and support the baby.* The woman agreed, mainly as poverty forced her to. Eventually she met the guru and became his ritual partner (bhairavī).

Figure 27 - Fig tree weaving.

It has become a fashion to claim that Tantra was basically a male affair where women participated as ritual aides. In the opinion of several experts (it's a nice day and I won't bother to name names) women were simply used by the male adepts.

They were a part of the rites, but the rites were performed for the spiritual and magical aims of the males. Women, so it is claimed, got some food, presents, got drunk, and got fucked for the sake of male spirituality or sorcery. They may have had a bit of fun when they were venerated as the goddess and perhaps an orgasm or two, but that's it.

This picture is so incomplete that it hurts. What of the women who founded Tantric lineages, such as Krama? What of the women who initiated men? What of the women who were gurus? True enough, Hindu Tantric literature cites few instances of female leadership. For all their Śāktic preferences, many texts seem aimed at male readers, if only as it was highly uncommon that women could read. Then there are the conventions of language. In Saṅskṛt, just as in many European languages, it is common usage to use the male form, all the while implying that female readers (readeresses) are also addressed. Such conventions make it difficult to discern female elements. Likewise, Tantras are usually attributed to gods. There are Tantras around which may well have been written, edited, or amended by highly initiated women, but as the text is of divine origin, we have no idea who composed it. And there are further signs for those who look closely. What of the Yoginīs mentioned in the *KJN*, dwelling at the Yoni shrine, eager to initiate devout men? No, this is not a reference to temple prostitution, which became a fashion a few centuries later, and had no Tantric meaning whatsoever. Shared ritual in Tantra is by no means confined to sexual activity. Indeed, lovemaking constitutes only a small section of possible activities and it is usually not the most important one. After all, Tantra aims at liberation, and if you go for that, you will find daily discipline, meditation, ritual, devotion, and the transformation of your own demons, fears, cravings, and hang-ups to be more essential than an occasional feast of the Five Ms. Only New Age Tantra is totally obsessed with sex and hedonism. While most Hindu Tantrics seek to transcend or transform the world, Western Tantrics wallow in it. McDaniels spoke to numerous Bengali Tāntrikās who considered sexual rites to be of peripheral importance. In general, so she was told, it is the men who need sexual ritual to learn to control their passions and desires. From this perspective, men are weaker than women. As she points out, *Indian sons are indulged and petted, while Indian daughters are taught to give the best food and toys to their brothers. Indian women thus learn to sacrifice their desires at an early age. Sexual ritual is basically for people who are weak rather than strong - and weak people do not belong at the burning ground.* (McDaniels 2004: 121)

The same may be said regarding larger ritual assemblies or cakras. In some Tantras (such as the *KNT*) the ritual circle is described like a mad, drugged group-sex orgy. However, we have no way of estimating what they were like in real life. Some of the accounts are so over-the-top that I suspect that they happened in the imagination. In modern Bengal, cakras are prohibited. Even so, thy do happen on rare occasions. However, as June McDaniel explains, they are not opportunities for sexual indulgence or wife swapping. The main goal of a cakra is to attain union with the gods or to become temporarily obsessed by them. When sex is involved, it is simply to copy the behaviour of the deities. There exists, however, a new sort of ritual cakra in modern Bengal. It is called the paśu cakra and promotes all sorts of indulgence, sexual and otherwise. The aim of the paśu cakra is pleasure by all means. Its participants lack all spiritual training and discipline, their sole ritual being a parody of the genuine rites. As it turns out, the paśu cakra celebrates exactly the sort of loose living that Westerners, in particular New Age Tantrics, mistake for real Tantra.

What of female gurus (stri guru)? One of the *Rudrayāmalas* (Goudriaan & Gupta, 1981: 48) quotes her specifications. She must be righteous, of good conduct, devoted to her guru (i.e. in a line of spiritual succession), she must be in command of her senses, know the essential meaning of all mantras (this is much like taking a university degree), enjoy worship, be of good character, with lotus-like eyes, good at recitation, she must possess jewels and ornaments (a reference to her cakras?), peaceful, of kula-family, with a moon like (cool and serene) face, able to explain Śiva's wisdom (you can do that only if you are Śiva), and able to grant final release. Well, a woman like this wasn't born enlightened. To become a guru you need training.

The *Tripurā Rahasya*, a beautiful work on inner worship of the Śrī Vidyā tradition, gives a lengthy account of one such guru. One day prince Hemacūḍa was out in the forest hunting. He lost his companions, as royals always seem to do when faced with the real world, but eventually he came upon a singularly beautiful hermitage. There he encountered Hemalekhā, the adopted daughter of the jungle dwelling Śaiva saint Vyāghrapāda. The two fell in love and before long they were married. Instead of being a well-behaved queen, however, Hemalekhā proceeded to initiate her husband, mainly by telling him wonderfully complex stories and sending him to a lonely room for months of meditation. In due course, Hemacūda became an enlightened sovereign, fiercely devoted to the inner worship of the goddess Tripurā. Thanks to Hemalekhās teaching, all inhabitants of the city became enlightened and even the birds chanted mantras through the lazy, sunny day. If you like trance-stories closely resembling the style of Milton H. Erickson, this is the book for you. And while we are at it, another interesting woman sage, clad in saffron robes, with long, tangled hair and a youthful appearance thanks to rejuvenating yoga appears in chapter 15. She instructs the court of king Janaka and defeats the hot-headed Aṣṭāvakra in philosophical argument.

KJN 20, 13-19 gives a list of the qualities a ritual Śakti should have. Among them are beauty, white eyes, dishevelled hair, eloquence, fearlessness, devotion to Kulāgama, calmness, a lovely nature, freedom from doubts, truthfulness, freedom from cruelty and being grounded in her own body. The good book calls her a heroine and 'the ultimate one'. Again, a partner with so many good qualities does not fall from heaven.

Such a character needs years of training and meditation, possibly over several lifetimes.

The *KCT* goes beyond this. Chapter 4, 21-34 describes a form of courtship. The well-advanced sādhaka arrives in a village, town, marketplace, or square where he is seen by a young woman. On seeing him, she is freed of her sins. Looking at him sideways, longing enters her mind. She is jolted out of her everyday behaviour, her mind is troubled, she allows her sari to slip, revealing a nipple, and hastily covers herself again. At the junction of her feet (i.e. at the yoni) the sexual urge arises. She speaks with her friends, makes enquiries, and learns who the sādhaka is, from what family he comes, what he is doing, and so on. About five minutes later the two are in bed together and he is moving his penis just like the god Kāma. The episode is striking as it tells of the entire affair from her point of view. She picks the worshipper, she gives him a sign of invitation, she enquires about his qualifications, and allows him to approach. All of it in highly poetical language. It is her desire that makes the union possible, without her consent he stands no chance at all. Later on she addresses him as 'my son', and indeed, the relationship between them is much like that between a goddess and her worshipper. Was this passage of the *KCT* composed by a woman?

In Tantric literature women (just like gurus and students) suffer from idealisation. You read of their exalted qualities and their closeness to the divine. Often they are called young, beautiful, tender, wise, un-worldly, polite, well behaved, highly spiritual, quiet, peaceful, and so on. How about elder Tāntrikās? How about Tāntrikās who despise fancy dress and submissive behaviour? What of those resolute ladies who have survived years on the road, who have shaved their hair, slept on cremation places, and run their own spiritual communities? In some texts, the ritual partner is described in the same poetic metaphors as a goddess. Which makes it hard to tell the difference. Are we talking of flesh & blood women living real lives, of idealised consorts worshipped from a distance, or is the perfect ritual partner a spiritual entity, a manifestation of the Paraśakti in the imagination?

Tāntrikās are easier to trace when we look at Tantric Buddhism. Buddhism itself was not very favourably disposed towards women (apart from pitying them), but when Indian Buddhists encountered Tantric Śāktas, usually while having a picnic at a cremation place, the systems fused and created something entirely new and practical. Indeed there are some systems, such as the Yoginī-kula, which can be found in Hindu and Buddhist Tantra. Anyway, it seems that the Buddhists learned to worship women, and with women, when they encountered Hindu Śāktas. Unlike the Hindus, the Buddhists were organised and they collected books in libraries. Now once the Muslims invaded northern India, they crushed what remained of Indian Buddhism and destroyed all the monasteries and libraries they could find. This meant the end of Indian Buddhism but, of course, the libraries in other countries survived. For this reason we find some of the most important Indian Buddhist scriptures in Nepal, Tibet, China, and other countries. Not that the Yoginī cults were popular. The Buddhists may have been better at documenting history than their Hindu colleagues, but nevertheless a good many frowned at spiritually dominant women. As a result, a lot of female gurus were turned into male gurus by the simple method of misspelling their names. It often takes only a single letter to change the gender of a name. Last, there is plain dumb sexism. Tibet, for instance, had a wide range of pioneering female saints (see Miranda Shaw's ground-breaking *Passionate Enlightenment* and read it!). These women composed scripture, sang songs of enlightenment, gave Tantric feasts, initiated males (including most of the founding fathers of Tibetan Buddhism), founded lineages, taught, educated, trained, and shaped much of what remains best in Tantric Buddhism. Many were sorceresses, ran Tantric organisations, performed miracles, healed, cursed, and brought enlightenment. Today, with regard to women, Tibet has the most retarded sort of Buddhism anywhere. The brilliant ladies of the early days are happily forgotten. For several decades, the present Dalai Lama has been sharply criticised by feminists. In his branch of Buddhism, unlike all the others, women cannot attain the highest degrees. Will this ever be changed? Sadly, as he claims, he is stuck within the system and cannot alter it. Which strikes me as a dumb excuse. If Avalokiteśvara incarnate cannot change this sorry little system, who can? Anyway, there is a lot missing in Hindu scripture that appears with glaring directness in Tantric Buddhism. Where most Hindu Tantras barely hint at lovemaking, secretions, and the role of the Śakti, some Buddhist texts of the Yoginī school are more than explicit. Ingestion of fluids, veneration of women, men who fail in their liberation as they cannot transcend their sexism... all of it appears, boldly outspoken, in works composed by brilliant female gurus. And as it just so happened, these masterpieces of spiritual literature happen to be thoroughly unpopular in modern Tibetan Buddhism.

6: Body as a Whole

Most of the sages who composed the *Upaniṣads* were not very keen on body. To the renouncers of the post-vedic age, body was a means for incarnation but not anything to identify with. When we read of body we occasionally come upon the most negative descriptions. To identify body with self, for example, was frowned upon. *Chāndogya Upaniṣad*, 8, 8, 1-5 mentions two ascetics, divine Indra and demonic Virocana, who performed austerities under the tutelage of Prajāpati. Seeing their reflection in water, they assumed the image of the body to be an image of the self and went away deluded. Sighing, Prajāpati declared that anyone following this doctrine, no matter whether god or demon, is bound to perish. Nevertheless, Virocana, returning to the demons, declared that body is the self and should be satisfied, served, and made happy. Indra had second thoughts, went back to Prajāpati, and learned that body is not identical with the self. *Maitrī Upaniṣad* 1,2-3 goes beyond this point. We read of king Bṛhadratha, who, disappointed that body is not enduring, went into the jungle to perform austerities. For a thousand days he stood with uplifted arms, staring into the sun. Such practices are not unusual. To this day there are worshippers who believe that holding up an arm, day and night, is a sure way to transcendence. In the process, the limb withers and decays. A great example of how will-power can be abused to mutilate oneself. This sort of thing is not far from the austerities practised by Christian mystics of the past, many of whom made a high art out of the mortification of the flesh. When king Bṛhadratha met the ascetic Śākāyanya, he declared that body is foul-smelling, insubstantial, a mixture of bone, skin, muscle, marrow, fat, sperm, blood, mucus, tears, rheum, excrement, urine, flatulence, bile, and phlegm, subject to fear, desire, greed, delusion, envy, hunger, thirst, disease, and sorrow etc. etc. - so what good is the enjoyment of desire?

By contrast, some of the classical works on yoga and Tantra assume a different attitude. Please note that I wrote *some*. There are Tantric texts that echo exactly the same mood, such as the *Tripurā Rahasya*, 4, 85-88, where we learn that the components of the body are full of decaying elements and hopelessly disgusting. Who thinks of the parts of the body feels revulsion, and who enjoys the pleasures of the body is like an animal. Thank you. In 20, 103-5 the goddess Tripurā declares: *Perfection means considering the body to be non-self and centring one's awareness in the self.* Whoever wrote this certainly favoured worship in the mind, and only in the mind. Luckily, there are also Tantras that get along without abusing or disrespecting the body. *Kulārṇava Tantra* 9, 41 states that body itself is the temple. The jiva (incarnate 'soul'/divinity) is the eternal

Śiva. The *Śiva Saṁhita*, 2, 1-5 also sees body as something divine, but goes a long way beyond the 'temple' metaphor.

> *In this body, the mount Meru - i.e., the vertebral column - is surrounded by seven islands; there are rivers, seas, mountains, fields; and lords of the fields, too. There are in it seers and sages; all the stars and planets as well. There are sacred pilgrimages, shrines; and presiding deities of the shrines. The sun and moon, agents of creation and destruction, also move in it. Ether, air, fire, water and earth are also there. All beings that exist in the three worlds are also to be found in the body; surrounding the Meru they are engaged in their respective functions. (But ordinary men do not know it). He who knows all this is a Yogī; there is no doubt about it.*

Let's have some details. Gorakṣanātha's *Siddha Siddhānta Paddhati*, 3,1-5 offers an amazingly complex system identifying all worlds with the human form. He describes a wide range of cakras, energy points, energy connections, and much more. *Who knows all moving and unmoving beings and all things in the body is a yogīn, and to know these is to know the body.* The tortoise (foundation of the universe) is in the soles of the feet, Pātāla in the big toes, Talātalam in the tip of the big toe, Mahātalam on the back of the foot, Rasātalam in the ankle, Sutalam in the lower legs, Vitalam in the knees, and Atalam in the upper legs. The seven underworlds are governed by Rudra in his angry form as the fire of destruction (Kālāgnirudra). The world Bhū is near the anus, the world Bhuva near the genitals, the world Svar near the navel. All three are governed by Indra, who is the lord of all senses. Brahmā rules the four worlds Mahar (at the root of the spine), Jana (near the 'cave of the spine'), Tapas (within the spine), and Satya (at the root cakra). These worlds exist in body in their self-form of manifold egoism and will. Viṣṇu's world is in the belly, causing manifold doing. Rudra governs the heart in his fierce self-form. Īśvara governs the world of the self-form of satisfaction in the chest, Nīlakaṇṭha's (blue throated Śiva) world is in the throat, existing eternally. In his incomparable self-form, Śiva resides in a world at the opening of the palate. Bhairava dwells in the world at the root of the tongue in his all-transcending self-form. The world of Anādi (without beginning) is in the centre of the brow, in it, the self-form of the highest self of bliss resides. The Śṛṅgāṭa point contains the Kula world, where Kuleśvara resides in body, in the self-form of bliss. The opening of Brahman contains the world Parabrahma. Here, Brahman resides in body as infinite perfection. The upper lotus contains the world Parāpara, where the supreme lord Parameśvara exists in body as the state of the all-including highest. The place of the three peaks within the sahasrāra is the world of Śakti, inhabited by the supreme Śakti who resides in the state of being the all-creatrix of all deities. Such is Gorakṣanātha's account of the twenty-one places of the cosmos, plus the seven underworlds, within the body. He continues at great length (*SSP* 3, 6-14). There are seven continents in marrow, bone, head, skin, hair, nails, and flesh, and there are seven oceans in urine (the salt-ocean), spittle (the milk-ocean), slime (ocean-of-sour-milk), fat (the ghī-ocean), brain (ocean-of-honey), blood (sugar-ocean), and semen (ocean-of-immortality-nectar). The nine apertures of the body are identified with India, Kashmir, the Land of Potters, Sandalwoodland, Shell-land, Land of the one-legged, Land around Kandahar, Land of Fishers, and the Land of Mount Meru. The major eight mountains are Meru in the spine, Kailāsa (aperture of Brahman), Himālaya (back), Malaya (left side of the neck), Mandara (right side of the neck), Vindhya (right ear), Maināka (left ear), and Mount Śrī on the brow, plus lesser mountains in fingers and toes. The major nine subtle nerves are identified with nine great rivers. The inside of body houses twenty-seven constellations, twelve signs of the zodiac, nine planets, fifteen lunar days, while the great amount of stars and asterisms reside in the 'waves' (hair?). 330 million gods dwell in the hair on the arms. Gods, spirits of nature, demons, and ghosts dwell in the bones. The supreme lord of the serpents resides in the chest. Seers and wise ascetics dwell in the hair of the armpit, the mountains in the hair on the belly, Gandharvas, Apsarasas, Kinnaras, and their kind in the belly, Śaktis and fierce deities in the swift body-winds. The places of pilgrimage are in the joints, the infinite perfection in the illumination of the mind, sun and moon in the eyes, trees, plants and flowers in the hair of the legs, worms, insects, and birds in excrement. *What is joy is heaven. What is suffering is hell. What is doing is attachment. What is free from differentiation of thought is liberation... in this way, the highest lord, the highest self, who has the all as his own form, dwells in all bodies... such is the knowledge of the body.* (3, 14) You may observe that this account does not even hint at decay, corruption, and disgusting organs. Similar systems can be found in several Tantras, especially among the Nāthas, Siddhas, and Kaulas. When the *Hymn to Kālī* speaks of the worship of the *greatly satisfying flesh* this is a long way from the mind-space of adepts who got a kick from abusing their physical form.

Maps of the Body

Indian philosophy produced several models to describe what happen within body. Alas, this is already an oversimplification. There are several distinct schools of Indian philosophy and, as you know, they are not always in accord with each other. Just look at the cakra systems (discussed in full later on). Early proponents of the cakra theory agreed more or less that there are foci of energy and sentience along the subtle equivalent of the spine, but they could not agree on the actual amount of cakras, let alone on their appearance, function, and characteristics. This may be confusing from the scholarly point of view. For practical minded people it constitutes a blessing. Where so many models contradict each other anything is possible. Welcome to individual subjectivity.

Take the model of the five kośa (sheaths). The human body, so several philosophies propose, appears on several planes of being. The coarsest form is the **annamaya kośa**, the 'sheath of food' which might be called the material human being. Food, in this context, is thought to be the essence out of which the material body takes its existence. This is the body of differentiation. It has age, form, gender, and a lot of genetic characteristics. It is similar to other human bodies but is not the same as any of them. Some parts, such as bone, muscles and marrow are thought to come from the father, while hair, blood, and flesh were thought to come from the mother. Here you can find the organs of sense and the organs of action (mouth, arms, legs, anus, genitals). In an attempt to unite this model with the cakra models it was proposed that the physical body connects with the three lower cakras. The next kośa is the **prāṇamaya kośa**, the sheath of vitality, breath, and life-energy. This sheath consists of the 'winds' that move within body. Breathing is one function of these winds, another is the metabolism. It is the energy body that feels hunger and thirst, that feeds, digests, excretes, wakes, and sleeps, is powerful or feels exhausted. Your energy body is the mediator between spirit and matter. More refined is the **manomaya kośa**, the sheath of thought. This sheath has four aspects (in some systems), namely: doubt/certainty, determination, I-sense (ego, identity), and evaluation of sense impressions. Without the sheath of thought, the sense organs may do their job but there is nobody there to be aware of it. The thought sheath is something you develop while you grow up. How healthy this body is depends on your use or abuse of the sense organs, the importance you attach to your ego, or the way you decide what to believe and what to doubt. The thought sheath is also the origin of desire, which in turn influences the sense organs. The **Vijnānamaya kośa** is a lot more subtle. Here you can find the faculties of understanding, contemplation, and the ability to imagine and to create. The sheath of understanding is usually associated with the higher cakras in the mouth or third eye region, meaning that when your attention dwells up there, you are literally thinking with your body of understanding. I shan't bother to comment on this refined body, mainly as I mistrust models that define very subtle processes in a flood of vague nominalizations. For a thorough, but somewhat confusing, treatment of these issues look into the introductions of the *Mahānirvāna Tantra* and into *The Serpent Power* by Sir John Woodroffe, which can at times be even more perplexing. Last we have the **ānandamaya kośa**, which is the sheath or body of bliss. This may be alluded to as the immortal self, the seat of the divine intelligence. This body is so subtle that it does not die. It experiences reincarnation time and time again until it finally cuts all bonds of attachment and finds liberation in dissolution. In the cakra system it is usually localised above the brow, sometimes above the head. In this model each body is more subtle than the former. The degree of subtlety connects with the cakras, hence when your awareness rises from cakra to cakra, you are also moving from kośa to kośa. This idea is vital for your understanding of such rites as raising Kuṇḍalinī or the purification of the elements (bhūtaśuddhi). Whether such models are relevant for your actual practice is another matter. In general, I find it more useful to experience and observe what happens than to force experience into a model from the start.

Being at Ease

Tantric practice begins and ends in body, flesh, and living reality. Body is the primary temple of each practitioner, and this is not a poetic metaphor but a sober statement of fact. The form you inhabit is Śakti, and as Śakti is consciousness-in-energy/form, you are living in the manifestation of the divine. In magickal rituals, the identification of body with the Multiverse constitutes the key to causing changes in the phenomenal world. By identifying your body and your reality with the entire macrocosm - and vice versa - both can influence each other. This is the background for numerous trances and things you can do to surprise yourself. So how do we integrate body in our meditation?

As you know, there are lots of postures in yoga. Some of them are supposed to improve health. Some refine the sensitivity of your system. A few are recommended for meditation. Most non-Indians assume that āsana (seat, posture) is always something exotic, cramped, and complicated. This may be the case for beginners, and it may be the case with postures which regulate health, but when we want a posture for meditation we need something that is moderately relaxed and can be enjoyed for a while. This is in tune with some of the earliest traditions. Patañjali's famous textbook on yoga makes a point that:

> *2,46. Āsana implies steadiness and comfort.*
> *2,47. It requires relaxation and meditation on the Immovable.*
> *2,48. Then opposing sensations cease to torment.*

Before we move on, consider. The seated posture is steady and comfortable, Patañjali said. Sounds like a contradiction? It may seem that way before you get used to it. A good sitting posture has a straight spine, neck, and head. To do this properly you need a certain amount of tension. Unless some muscles in your back and shoulders stay tense and alert, your body will lean in one direction or another, and before long you'll be out of balance. So we need a certain amount of tautness. On the other hand, we are not trying to fulfil a military ideal. Tense muscles inhabit the circulation of blood, hence the oxygen supply to the cells, one of the reasons why tense people look pale. Tension is also a great inhibitor of pulsation, joy, laughter, and well-being. We should keep the amount of tension at a necessary minimum.

Then there is relaxation. For long trances, I prefer to lie on the ground with a small pillow under my head and a piece of cloth over my eyes. In this posture, I can relax very deeply and remain content for an hour or two. As the hard ground supports body, I can ignore physical sensations. Soon I forget the periphery and body seems to lose shape and is forgotten. When you can forget your body, you can focus on your mind. All of this is easiest when you rest.

It is more difficult when you wish to meditate or trance in a seated posture. When you sit, you need some tension. Complete relaxation while sitting means that you collapse. So what we need is a sort of balance between tension and relaxation. Learning to find this is already a meditation which will teach you a lot about body, breathing, balance, and your attention span. In general, the idea is to relax into each posture. So you learn to sit. But how do you meditate? As you'll soon discover, watching your posture is a job that requires attention. This is not a good start if you want to trance. Many trances require forgetfulness of your body, and you'll never get there when you keep watching it. At this point, two forces can be helpful. One is habit. When you persist in sitting in a specific posture for a while every day, some aspects of the posture will become 'natural' as you grow accustomed to them. You will begin to enjoy the tautness of your back, and will find that you can relax into it. The other force is attention. Did you notice that Patañjali recommended relaxation and meditation on the immovable? Some may think that you have to get the posture right before you begin to meditate. However, when you meditate, you may find that your posture stabilises. This is especially the case when your attention moves. An old rule of yoga and Chinese martial arts is that when your attention goes up, your body tends to become unstable or top-heavy. When your attention moves down, so does your weight. In consequence, if your attention stays up there in your head and you glance down to check if your body is erect, you are already out of balance. If you allow your awareness and the senses to go inward, and descend into the vast cavity of the heart, or deeper still into the 'golden pavilion' of the belly, your posture will stabilise naturally. Meditation can be one of those activities that make good posture possible.

A Choice of Postures

In the *Gheraṇḍa Saṁhita*, we learn that there are as many āsanas as there are life-forms. 84,000 have been explained by Śiva. Of these, eighty-four are exceptional, and of these thirty-two are auspicious in the realm of the living. This means that lots of postures are available. Though some treatises attempt to classify the thirty-two auspicious postures, there are also some, such as dear Abhinavagupta, who claim that any posture assumed in moments of ecstasy and enlightenment automatically becomes an expression of these states and hence, holy. As this is a book on left-hand Tantra, and not on yoga, we shall limit ourselves to a very few postures here and discuss them for their relevance in meditation and breathing.

A straight spine is essential for good and natural breathing. This is easiest in five postures:

1. **Lying** on the ground. Use a blanket or a warm quilt if you live in a cold climate. A bed is not recommended as it is too soft and may invite dozing or sleep. Lie on your back, keep the feet together and the hands at the sides. This is a form of śavāsana, the posture of the corpse. A small pillow under the head may be useful and a piece of cloth over the eyes if you want to improve inner vision. Note that this is a matter of preference; some people visualise and imagine easier against a dark background, others against a bright one.

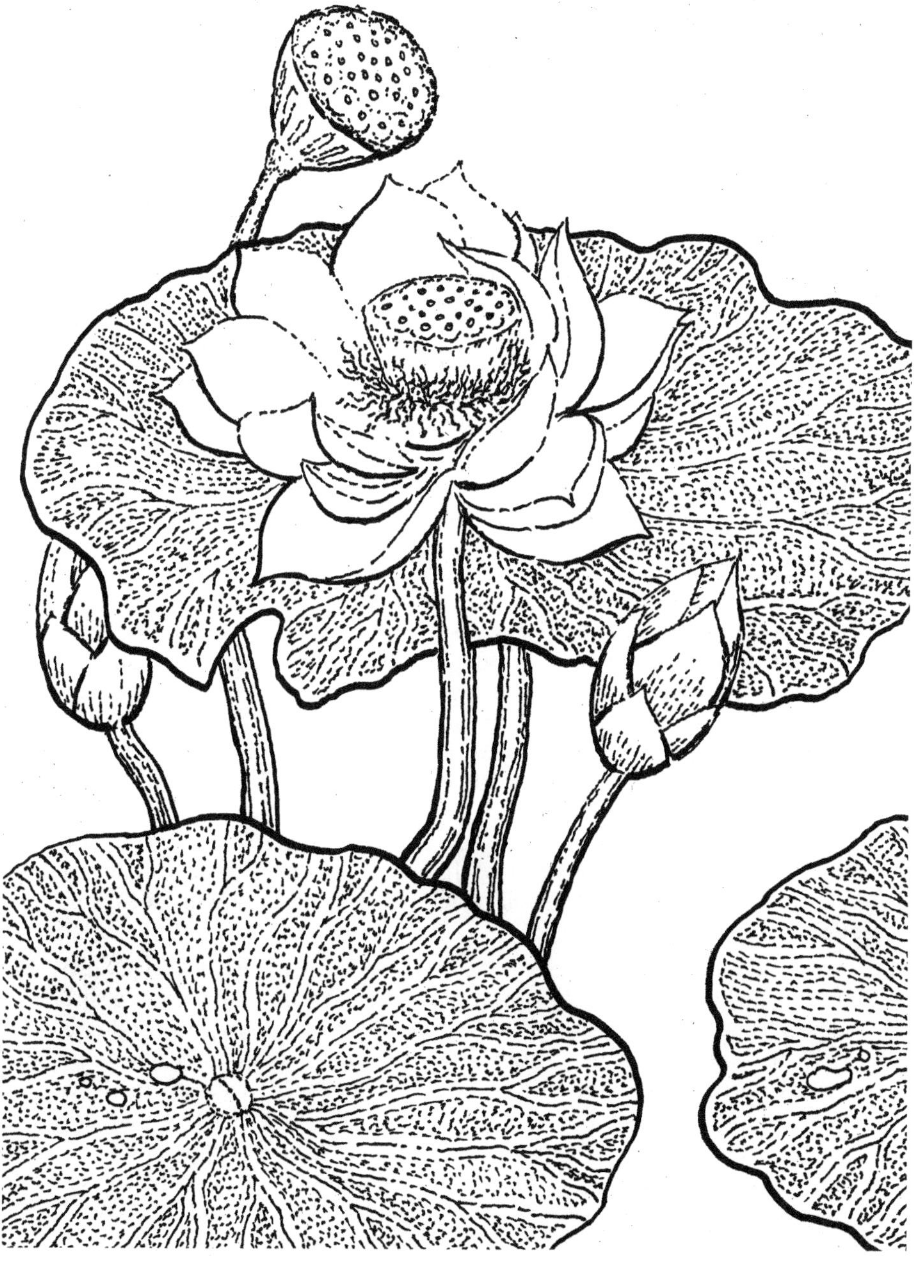

Figure 28 - Lotus.

Śavāsana is a nice way of relaxing for long periods. It can also be a trance state when you identify with Śiva as a corpse and play dead. The advantage of śavāsana is that the posture is almost completely relaxed. You can let go and trust gravity to support you. At first you may find that body needs a few minor adjustments. Relaxing begins with becoming aware of your body. Make yourself comfortable. Adjust your limbs, wriggle around a little, then let go and forget.

2. **Seated** on the ground. In many Tantric and Yogīc traditions, the recommended position is the Lotus-posture (padmāsana), where you have the legs crossed, each foot lying on top of the opposite thigh. The spine is kept erect and the head bends down slightly at the junction of the skull and the spine, the hands rest in your lap, on the thighs or soles of the feet or are crossed behind the back. Personally, I would counsel that you are very careful with such postures or simply avoid them. Much depends on where you come from. People in Asia generally have more compact and durable knees than Caucasians, whose limbs are generally longer and whose joints connect more loosely. This is not racism but the outcome of a study made by *Black Belt magazine* around the late seventies or early eighties. Studying advanced Taekwon Do practitioners, it turned out that knee injuries are a lot more common among Caucasians than among Asians. Hard and high kicks can really wear out the meniscus, the same goes for the wonderfully twisted postures used by some Wu Shu styles and for a good many meditational āsanas. This does not mean that Westerners can't practice such things. They should be aware, however, that after some years, they may get a heavy bill for their pursuit. Generally, knee injuries do not appear instantly, but when they do they may result in swollen knees, stiff legs, and a lot of pain whenever one tries to walk up or down a slope. They do not only happen to yogīs, martial artists, dancers, or soccer players. Half of the people who undergo knee surgery are housewifes, gardeners, tile-layers, archaeologists, and anybody who happens to kneel a lot. Meniscus surgery, by the way, is not a well developed art and frequently results in long-term damage.

I should add that people who practise Crowley style Yoga also feature on this list. Crowley wrote about an obscure form of yoga he claimed to have learned in Ceylon. To master posture, he proposed one has to assume one of the more advanced and straining positions of classical yoga and remain in it without any motion. This soon leads to cramp, then to pain, and if you persist, so the old trickster proposed, eventually the pain disappears and you obtain a wonderfully relaxed and blissful posture that can be held for hours with no problems whatsoever. So much for the theory. Of course I tried this and spent months of daily practice in sheer agony. Instead of becoming pleasant the posture only became unbearable, and the only relief happened when the blood circulation stopped and the limbs went 'to sleep'. Not even this was satisfactory and the result was totally useless for meditation. Over the years I met a few people who had been through the same torture. None of us had achieved any good results, but some had severely damaged their knees. I wonder whether Crowley actually practised what he wrote about. Pain is a warning signal. If you ignore it out of sheer stupid thick-headed persistence, you may hurt yourself more than you notice.

Other kneeling postures, such as the diamond-posture (vajrāsana) i.e. kneeling on your shins, sitting on your feet or between them, can also eventually lead to knee troubles. This is a great shame as the posture is so good for absolutely centred resting. Sitting with crossed legs, especially when these are sort of loosely crossed, may be a little easier on the joints but tends to produce a slumped posture, which may interfere with breathing. This can be reduced to some extent by sitting on a hard and high cushion.

Some yogīs use a variant of the cross-legged seat. They tie a broad belt or sash in a loop. Sitting cross-legged within the loop, they gain some support for their back by putting pressure on the legs. This makes the knees rise to some extent. Of course this posture is not very upright and does not invite deep breathing. It can be useful for minimal breathing and prolonged visualisation, however.

Last, there is a posture for meditation that does not involve sitting with a straight back. It is called yonimudrā in the *Toḍala Tantra*, 2, 17c-22 ab (see Sanjukta Gupta in White 2000), but you shouldn't let the term confuse you. There is a wide range of different postures, acts, and gestures that have been called yonimudrā at one time or another. Sit on the floor, facing east or north. Stretch your legs before you. Now pull up the knees and cross your arms on top of them. Lean forward and rest your head on the knees. This is easiest when you do not keep your feet side by side but cross them at the ankles. This posture requires a lot of relaxation. It is useful for trancing and seeing visions. When your head rests on the hands/knees, you will find that your breathing is restricted. It's very hard to take deep full breaths when there simply is no space for them. Instead, the posture promotes shallow and reduced breathing. This makes it eminently useful for visions, oracles, or when you simply want to refresh your system. Note that shallow breathing can be enforced if you want to do this the stupid way. Its much easier when you introvert and go into the heart-cave within yourself. When you turn inward, you may find that breathing becomes shallow and faint naturally.

3. **Sitting on a chair** is a useful alternative. Sure, it does not look very yogīc, holy, or even moderately exotic. Nevertheless it has a lot of advantages and quite a long tradition in the East. If you sit on a hard chair, your bum almost on the edge, and the legs about one shoulder width apart, hands on thighs or knees (depending on the length of your arms), you can enjoy an erect spine, full lung motion, and avoid all strain on the knees. Men should take care that their testicles hang freely, that's one of the reasons to sit on the edge. Watch out for a few minor details. Make sure your chair is really level. Keep your lower legs vertical and the feet at the same distance and angle - it's amazing how easy it is to get out of balance by even the slightest difference in leg position. And keep the upper arms hanging vertically too, otherwise your torso might bend

slightly forward or backwards. The proper position of the hands on the thighs is easy to find. Sit erect and allow your arms to hang at your flanks. Take a few deep breaths. Then lift up your hands and lower arms while keeping the upper arms exactly as they are hanging, and place the hands on the thighs. The shoulders should be set back a little. Keep them down as you breathe. You'll know when you sit straight as it feels good. The proper sensation is firm, relaxed, and pleasant.

4. **Standing** is easiest but also a bit tricky. Most people do not stand very erect, and when you learn (or remember) to do so you may find that there are more joints where posture can be a tiny little bit off centre, out of balance, or away from the centre line than you ever imagined. Keep your feet shoulder width apart. The knees may be slightly bent, as stiff legs tend to freeze the pelvis (Wilhelm Reich's expression). You will soon learn that body tends to slump from time to time, unless you happen to experience an all-body energy flow that keeps you vertical. This means awareness, watchfulness, and regular adaptation. Hold your head high! Tilt it forward so that you look slightly down. This tilting is traditionally recommended for most postures, it is done by bending the head at the junction of the spine and skull, like drawing your chin towards the throat. If you simply allow your head and neck to slump forward this may obstruct the flow of energy. Keep the shoulders down and back, the arms hang relaxed at the sides. Some like to cross their arms behind the back, or to clasp their hands behind the back. All of this sounds not only difficult, it may also overload the beginner with so many points to watch that breathing becomes strained and posture is cramped. Relax and smile. You are journeying, and learn as you proceed. Things take a while to develop. Learning upright posture can be quite an achievement. Every posture has a lot of advantages and shortcomings, especially when kept for longer periods. Occasionally it is useful to move a little. Especially when you practice full breathing you may find that you have to move your arms from time to time, to stretch, or to walk a few steps. Do so!

5. **Walking**. This is hardest to learn, as you need to stay in motion while keeping very much erect. On the other hand it is most fun, as it allows you to combine a gentle and slow (or slower) walk through nature with a lot of highly enjoyable breathing. If you do breathing exercises while walking, stop from time to time to check your posture and to make sure the energy is steadily aligned and your weight is centred in the belly.

6. Any **relaxed posture**. Yogīs do not always sit straight like a pillar. Apart from some loonies who get a kick from suffering, a yogī likes to recline just as everybody else does. One way to ease the back is a small crutch. You can see it on some pictures of Śiva. The god sits wonderfully upright, but one of his arms in set in the crutch so he can relax and lean a little. Others sit with their back against a wall. Chose a warm one,

leaning against a cold wall in a cold climate is not very good for your health. Another option is to recline on some easy chair or sofa. You won't find this in the elder textbooks on yoga, but it is certainly recommended by more recent teachers, such as Swami Śivananda (1982: 187). Insisting on any special posture is a form of rigidity. As a species humans have evolved sufficiently to leave trees and move on ground. We have adapted to upright posture, but we are not properly developed for it. Every posture, no matter how tense of loose, becomes unbearable when assumed for too long. As mobile animals we should move from time to time, and enjoy it.

Shaking, Swaying, and Primal Vibration

As you discovered earlier, there used to be a class of seers in ancient Vedic India who were called vipra, as they used to vibrate when in states of ecstasy. These seers came from many levels of society. Some were Brahmins by birth, others came from less exalted classes. Some were seers, sages, recluses, yogīs, or simply dropouts living on the fringes of society. Even the gods became vipras when a bit of magic was required, and shook merrily while they projected glamours. With the advent of early Hinduism, such events seem to have become less common. The class of vipras continued, you can find a fair share in the *Mahābhārata*, but the act of shaking is suspiciously absent in many texts on yoga. Did people cease to shake, just as they ceased to ingest soma? Or did they cease to mention it in literature? Is shaking something that appeals to Brahmins, or is it restricted to folk religion?

Here are some sources that show how shaking, trembling, and swaying continued. Not necessarily in straight yoga. A good many yogīns attempted to become completely still, if not rigid, and succeeded remarkably. They formed the common impression that in Indian yoga trance and meditation require a body as inert and stiff as a corpse. What most overlook is that a vast amount of spirituality happens without any sort of yogīc discipline.

Consider bhakti. Bhakti means partaking. In the bhakti movement, you can see fervent believers who go to extremes of god-loving, settle down, and live there. You do not need much training for bhakti, nor do you need a keen intellect, self-knowledge, education, or any special merit. All you need is love. Maybe this sounds simple, but love, as a pure emotion, is also a world-shaking experience and a complex trance-state. Love can be woken, purified, refined, and applied with devastating results. In bhakti, love for the divine mingles with dedication and sacrifice. Devotees offer themselves to their deity, just as they are, and give their all. Some attain great states of longing, yearning, and craving, others float off into a bliss of sheer, unsophisticated unity and the deity manifests through them. In bhakti, the main thing is not technical skill or intellectual knowledge. Bhakti works with strong emotions and total abandon. It is based on simplicity and produces the greatest effects when the worshippers are simple, unpretentious, and humble. Such events are common enough at public festivity, during group rituals, or an holy days, especially among members of the 'lower' classes. Some sway while they sing, others stagger around like they are drunk, or shake all over. All of which works excellently, but rarely makes it into serious treatises on yoga or Tantra, which are generally written and read by intellectuals, i.e. folks who are naturally challenged by simple, humble emotionality. But even among studied folk there are occasions when the old excitement wells up and body begins to shake. The *Kaulajñāna nirṇaya*, 14, mentions trembling of hands, limbs, head, voice, and the entire body during the activation of the cakras. When June McDaniel interviewed Tapan Goswami, a priest of Kālī (in White, 2000: 74), he related that possession by Kālī or his grandfather (an ancestral spirit) usually begins with a cold wind in his back. Then follows shivering, his hair seems to stand on end, and then the deity or spirit takes over. Unlike many possessed people, Tapan Goswami does not suffer amnesia but remains fully conscious and is able to recall the entire event. More on shaking Kālī worshippers further on.

In the *Caitanya Caritāmṛta*, 2,2,63 by Kṛṣṇadāsa Kavirāja, (in June McDaniel, 1989: 36). We read of the famous Caitanya, devotee of Kṛṣṇa: *Caitanya's body was paralyzed, trembled, perspired, paled, wept and choked. He was thrilled. He would laugh, cry, dance and sing, running here and there, and sometimes he would fall unconscious on the ground.*

The *Caitanya Bhāgavata*, 2, 8, 157 by Vṛndāvana Dāsa (McDaniel, 1989: 37) states: *From time to time all of his limbs shake violently and his teeth chatter like a child who is freezing*. Such behaviour is not unusual for the mad saints of India. Indeed, Indian medicine draws no firm distinction between behaviour exhibited by ordinary lunatics and the spiritually excited. The behaviour of both may look similar, but the internal experience differs. An ecstatic seer goes into the 'fit' voluntarily and may also leave it at will. No matter how odd the symptoms, the genuine saint rides the flow of divine ecstasy and returns with a vision of integration. S/he is spiritually nourished by the experience, while the ordinary lunatic is not. June McDaniel describes Kālī priests and worshippers who sway while they sing hymns to the goddess, and adds: *The Śākta states of divine madness are characterized by confusion, passion, and loss of self-control: trembling, laughing, weeping and crying out before the goddess, rolling on the ground.* (1989: 117).

Swaying may be considered a slower form of shaking. Body easily begins to sway in rhythm with mantra and song, and when this is encouraged, the mind may become excited, inspired, and accelerate the pulsation. Slow swaying can lead to calm and soothing trances, vigorous and enthusiastic swaying may naturally give way to full shaking. Before long, you may find yourself happily trembling. The frequency of the shudders can be influenced by your mind, just as your awareness is influenced by the ecstatic pulsation. Your mind's excitement can make body shake, your body's shaking can make your mind excited. Done properly, body and mind form a feed-back loop and reinforce each other. Add the presence of the divine and you'll find yourself exploring states of awareness you've never known before.

Figure 29 - The Living Wasteland.

The *Kulārṇava Tantra*, 14, 64-65 (trans. Rai) cites the symptoms of vedha, the 'piercing' that happens during a special form of initiation. The impact of the guru and the deity produce six symptoms: *64. Ānanda (joy), Kampa (tremor), Udbhava (new birth), Ghūrṇā (reeling), Nidrā (sleep), Mūrchā (swooning) these, O Kuleśvarī, are said to be the six conditions of Vedha. 65. O Kuleśvarī! These six characteristics are seen at the time of the impact of Vedha. Wherever be the person so struck he is liberated, there is no doubt about it.*

Do the Tantric gods shake? Mike Magee's translation of the *Kulacūḍāmaṇi Tantra,* 4 seems to suggest so, as it shows Kālī shaking. In Louise Finn's more scholarly translation, it is not Kālī but the earth beneath the goddess who shakes. In our correspondence (spring 2005), she admitted that it might be conceivable that the earth, seen as a goddess (Medinī), trembles, but the original text does not allow for Kālī's trembling. However, from practical experience I can add that when the seer shakes, both goddess and the earth beneath her take on a certain vibrating appearance. The optic system in eyes and brain tends to reduce the visual effects of the jolts, but even when vision is perfectly smoothed, a certain vibration remains.

Louise Finn kindly supplied me with two quotations (thank you!) from a text she is translating, the *Prapañcasara Tantra,* 34, 74: It describes the goddess as 'the daughter of the mountain' (i.e.Pārvatī) with *'three eyes... and a quivering slender body.'* The word used for quivering is 'sphurita' from the root 'sphur'. It can mean 'to dart, tremble, throb, quiver, palpitate, flash, gleam, sparkle'! However, as the goddess is also (unusually) riding a horse, the context does not suggest ritual shaking behaviour. Also 34,28: *'There will approach a submissive woman enfeebled by the arrows of the god of love and swaying/stumbling with desire'.* She added that the more usual verb to indicate 'shaking, excitement and agitation' would be kṣubh.

Here is another one: **kampa** (see *Tāntrikābhidhānakośa,* 2, p. 49). Kampa can mean shaking, trembling, but it can also mean a column (good news for all who know the world tree, earth axis, Mount Meru, or Mahāliṅga within them). In shaking, it can easily happen that you feel like a pillar of sheer energy, oscillating, vibrating, and pulsating between the height and depth. In Siddhānta literature, kampa is part of the Śaktipāta, a moment of grace when the power of Śakti shoots through the body of the worshipper. Śaktipāta can be granted by the touch of a guru, but it is a blessing given only to selected, rare disciples who have exhausted all their resources and still find themselves stuck. What modern systems call Śaktipāta, namely a ritual when entire groups are blessed, has no relation to the elder custom. More frequently, Śaktipāta is spontaneously granted by the gods. Kampa can also occur during dikṣā, when a mantra wakes or during the ascent of Kuṇḍalinī. Abhinavagupta related kampa (like everything else) to the heart, and classed it as the third (of five) visible signs of divine possession. It may be interesting to note the importance of sphur in Abhinavagupta's lore (Muller-Ortega, 1989: 118). Here, the self-consciousness within the heart is characterised by a certain vibration (spanda) that turns out to be the sub-stratum of all manifest experience. The whole world, and our experience of it, is based on vibration. If you are an experienced trancer, you may be aware that good shaking is not done by conscious effort, it happens by inspiration and release. You do not enter the world of vibration, you return to it. When you allow your body and mind to participate in the all-inclusive sphurita you may realise that all things vibrate all of the time.

The fifth sign is called **ghūrṇi**, staggering. According to Abhinavagupta (*Tantrāloka*, 5, 104b-105a and 107b-108), staggering happens when a yogī has united with the universe, be it by experiencing divine bliss or by possession by a deity. *Then, having attained the plane of the supreme Reality, experiencing (his own) consciousness as the universe, he staggers, for staggering is 'the great pervasion'.* (*Tāntrikābhidhānakośa*, 2: 217). He adds that the five signs show when five cakras are pierced, staggering appearing when the Kuṇḍalinī reaches the highest sphere (above your head). It can also happen when the yogī, immersed in Kula/Śakti, has drunk the supreme wine of Bhairava. In this state, any posture assumed by the adept automatically becomes a sacred mudrā. He goes on to describe Śiva as *staggering, intoxicated by his absolute freedom.* Staggering is well attested from devotional ritual. When Rāmakṛṣṇa became ecstatic, he staggered and stumbled, and had to be supported by his students. The same went for Rāmprasād Sen, who staggered when the bliss of Kālī came over him. Both seers were often thought drunk by the uninitiated. Drunk on the divine, they both tended to assume that real drunkards are enflamed by divine grace.

For a practical introduction of swaying and shaking trances and how to enjoy them, read *Seidways.*

Nyāsa: a Touch of the Divine

Nyāsa means 'placing'. This ritual act can happen at several points of ritual. How does the Tantric start the day? In many texts, we begin with a ritual bath involving immersions in a river and some mantra recitation. After the bath, the worshipper collects water in a vessel for further ritual and goes home. S/he prepares a ritual space, a place to sit, and usually performs a little purification ceremony. One such method is briefly alluded to in the *Kulacūḍāmaṇi Tantra* 2, 15.

First, the **Purification of the Self (ātmāśuddhi)**. This may be done by intoning your favourite mantras while 'placing' (nyāsa) them on a number of cakras. Placing means touching. The actual technique is of little importance. Some spots will be fine when you apply your fingertips, others, such as the belly and heart, may be stimulated when you use the whole palm. You can touch, but you can also use a Daoist technique and gently rub the location in circles. In some systems, it is enough to touch navel, heart, and head. In others, you begin by touching the heart and then move upward, touching various cakras. Every cakra system is a convenience. There are as many cakras as you chose to discover and develop. Body is full of sacred spaces. Find those that make sense to you and develop them. In addition, the palms of the hands are anointed. As you recite the proper mantras, you circle the palm of one hand with index and middle fingers of the other and strike it sharply. Incidentally, this mudrā (index and middle fingers extended upward, the other fingers curled) appears prominently in practical Daoism and in Chinese martial arts, where it can symbolise a sword, and in the esoteric rites of Tantric Buddhism of China and Japan, where it is frequently used to bless, invoke, place, move, banish, anoint, or draw sigils. The amount (and nature) of mantras placed at various locations varies widely. Some systems carried the rite to extremes of complication, others preferred the fast and simple style. May I suggest that you explore both possibilities to become really flexible?

Bhūmiśuddhi, the Purification of the Earth, is the next step. This simply involves striking the ground with your heel while reciting mantra. Usually the practitioner turns around and stamps on the ground in all (four or eight) directions. This act is a banishing, especially when it is accompanied by clapping hands and vibrating the fierce mantra 'Phat!' (the Ph sounds like an aspirated, explosive P, not like an F). It scares away evil spirits, to be sure, but it also has the advantage that it wakes attention, puts out a clear signal, and gives a certain shock to the body. It is very useful to shake the mind out of routine thinking and lethargy.

Last follows **dehaśuddhi, the Purification of the Body**. For this rite, you call upon your personal deity by intoning its seed mantra. Visualise and feel the seed mantra vibrating in your palms. Then smear it over your body from head downwards to the toes seven times, vibrating it all the time. Well done! With these preliminaries you have purified your consciousness, ritual space, and body and are ready and prepared for further meditation.

Initiation and Nyāsa

These simple ritual acts are not the only forms of nyāsa. Something very similar takes place during initiation rites. In traditional Kaula worship, it was good form to make love only among initiates. To practice ritual love-making with an un-initiate was strongly forbidden. Good thinking. When you integrate someone else in your ritual, you have to be certain that this person is competent for the job. Most Tantras are very strict on this point, and for good reason. If you want to energise your magic with the participation of a partner and her/his elixirs, you have to be sure the partner is competent to handle the ritual and its energies. In many rituals, the partner assumes the role of the deity, in some cases s/he is obsessed by that deity. You can't get such a level of magical competence by simply falling into bed with anyone who strikes your fancy. To make sure that a certain standard of skill was achieved, several Tantras give catalogues of virtues that a ritual partners should exhibit. Being very devoted to the gods, inward of nature, peaceful, of good character, and of pure thinking are just the beginnings of the requirements. And even with the best character in the world, the ritual partner still required some form of initiation. This might be a safety mechanism, as it ensured that rites involving congress were only performed among people who knew what was going on. Compare this with Crowley's sexual magick. The old crow was not very considerate of other people and frequently engaged prostitutes for his purposes. Unlike most Tāntrikas, he did not bother to initiate them, or even to inform them that they were participating in a ritual. Of course finding a partner for sexual rites is a lot easier when that person simply assumes that you want to make love. It's not very honest, though, and can put a lot of pressure on the partner, who probably is not very competent in dealing with it. Such things are apt to recoil.

In left-hand Tantra, initiation of the partner is a must. The simplest way of doing it is to whisper a seed mantra into her/his left ear. This is usually the mantra Hrīṁ, useful for beginnings of all sorts and one of the basic vibrations of the goddess in her creative phase. This act starts the initiation, which is completed only when the deity is fully brought into the body of the partner. Anything below this standard is not good enough.

In the *Kulacūḍāmaṇi Tantra*, 4, 56-58, a basic initiation by nyāsa appears. As usual, the description is very brief, meaning that you either need a guru to fill in the gaps or an inspired creative mind to develop something really good. If you know your inner guru, you can have both. By touch, the sādhaka places cakras on a number of places and worships them with devotion. According to Louise Finn's commentary, these spots are 1. Devīkuta (the top surface of the feet), 2. Uḍḍīna (legs?), 3. Kāmarūpa (the genitals), 4. Sloping Ground (thighs), 5. Jālandhara (breasts), 6. Pūrṇa (belly, stomach?), and 7. Sacrificial Ground (inner genitals). After reciting mantra eight times, ten times, a hundred, or a thousand times at these places of worship, the sādhaka finally moves his pītha (seat, sacred place, here: penis) into *the abode of the pot.* This does not end the ritual, indeed the worship continues all the time. You may notice that there are faster and simpler ways of making love. Initiation by nyāsa is a complex and extended affair that takes a while. This is typical for lovemaking or adoration of genitals in the left-hand path. Usually, the preparations involve a formidable amount of mantra repetition, giving even an inexperienced partner time to tune in to the divine consciousness. More so, the process was not a formality. When you go to a Catholic mass, nobody is going to check whether the sacrament had any effect on you. In many cults, people are initiated as the initiator says so. Some experience a change of awareness and others do not. The convenient excuse is that these were initiated unconsciously, and that the effect will (hopefully) appear sometime in the future. For Tantric explorers, such acts of wishful thinking are not good enough. As the *Lakṣmī Tantra* 43, 78 makes absolutely clear, there are signs that show when Lakṣmī has entered the body of a Śakti. S/he experiences stillness, complete relaxation, and a blissful state of samādhi. The text cautions the sādhaka that the Śakti will love this state so much that the rite should better be performed only with one's own spouse. Doing it with the partner, mate, or wife of another can lead to problems. Initiation is more than just making a show according to ritual formulas and hoping for the best. When it works, there are specific symptoms that the divine presence has entered the body/mind of your partner. Many schools of Tantra were eminently pragmatic. They did not simply assume that things work, they observed closely and tested their results.

An Armour of Protection

Placing of mantras equals placing of deities: a mantra is usually a deity in its body of sound. Using touch, you can localise deities, spirits, power-beasts, energies, elements, and numerous other uplifting experiences in your body and thereby earthe them in your world. One such form of nyāsa is to install a number of deities all over your body, so that wherever you walk or rest, you are effectively within a complex temple and well protected from dangerous influences. Such a rite was considered the creation of an armour. It is especially popular among worshippers of the heroic sort, who are expected to do their rituals and meditations in dangerous, dramatic, morbid, or unclean locations. Let's just look at one variation of the rite. It comes from the *Mahānirvāṇa Tantra*, 7, 55-64 and is called: The Protective mantra Trailokya-Vijaya (Three-Worlds-Conqueror) of Ādyā Kālikā. I have used and adapted Woodroffe's 1913 translation.

Its seer is Śiva, the metre is anuṣṭup (thirty-two syllables in each verse), the deity is the primordial Kālī, the seed is Hrīṁ, the Śakti is Kāma bīja (Klīṁ or Śrīṁ), and its kīlaka (bolt, i.e. ending) is Krīṁ.

Hrīṁ, may the Ādyā (Primordial One) protect my head;
Śrīṁ, may Kālī (Black) protect my face;
Krīṁ, may Paraśakti (Supreme Energy/Form) protect my heart;
May Parātparā (the Supreme of the Supreme) protect my throat;
May Jagaddhātrī (the Universe-Supporting Mother) protect my two eyes;
May Śaṅkarī (She who grants Prosperity) protect my two ears;
May Mahāmāyā (Great Illusion/Creation) protect my power of smell;
May Sarvva-Maṅgalā (All-Auspicious) protect my sense of taste;
May Kaumārī (fem. of Kaumāra/Kārttikeya, god of war) protect my teeth;
May Kamalālaya (Lotus-Dweller, i.e. Lakṣmī) protect my cheeks;
May Kṣamā (Benevolence or Forgiveness) protect my upper and lower lips;
May Cāru-Hāsinī (Sweetly Smiling) protect my chin;
May Kuleśānī (Sovereign Mistress of the Kulas) protect my neck;
May Kṛpā-Mayī (Merciful One) protect the nape of my neck;
May Bāhu-Da (Arm-Giver) protect my two arms;
May Kaivalya-Dāyinī (Giver of Emancipation) protect my two hands;
May Karpadinī (Wearer of Tangled Hair) protect my shoulders;

May Trailokya-Tāriṇī (Saviour of the Three Worlds) protect my back;
May Aparṇā (She who had not even Leaves for Food) protect my two sides;
May Kamaṭhāsanā (She who sits/dwells in the kamaṭa vessel, i.e. gourd, coconut etc.) protect my hips;
May Viśālākṣī (Large-Eyed) protect my navel;
May Prabhā-Vatī (Radiant One) protect my genitals;
May Kalyāṇī (Propitious One) protect my thighs;
May Pārvatī (Daughter of the Himalayas) protect my feet;
May Jaya-Durgā (Victorious Durgā) protect my vital breaths;
And Sarvva-Siddhi-Dā (Giver of Perfection) protect all parts of my body.
As to those parts as have not been mentioned in this Kavacha (armour), and are unprotected, may the Eternal Primeval Kālī protect all such.

As you may have noticed, this sort of protective nyāsa is by no means unique to the Tantrics. Very similar consecrations of the body by naming divine entities and touching various parts of anatomy abound in worship worldwide. Just consider how Catholics cross themselves, how the devil is officially exorcised from each limb, or think of the Island-Celtic Loricas (Lorica: armour) of the late Middle Ages. I wonder whether these are imported Tantric techniques. Anyway, I am sure you need no further illustration. Just go ahead and compose a similar spell that incorporates the gods and spirits of your world - in *your* body. Find, discover, make up, or invent what you need. You need not worry if this takes a while. The gods like to be integrated in body, but they may also like to move around a bit. Don't worry about getting everything perfectly right. Magick requires flexibility. When you have invented a useful system, ask the gods if they like it and put it to practice. You may need a bit of experience. After a few weeks of daily application you will know whether things are fine. Maybe some of your gods, spirits, power animals, or whatever will shift around or find a better place. Maybe you'll have to integrate a few more, or find that similar ones move into the same spot. Whatever you cook up will be a working solution. It will work when you imbue the rite with passion and joy, and put a great big ecstatic smile into each centre that you touch. Go for feeling! Mere imagination and speech are not enough. You will sense when the proper connections are made. The presence of the gods should make your body feel joyous, ecstatic, powerful. And don't you simply sit there waiting for it to happen! When you want joy and bliss in your body you can jolly well put it there!

Mudrās

Fingers have power. Gestures have power. You only have to find and wake it. Look at a baby. At a very early stage, it will begin to explore its hands. Hands are weird things. They are attached to your body in a distant sort of way. They come out of your wrists and end in five wriggly things that move independently. It takes a baby a while to discover how this works. At this stage it often rests in deep concentration and stares at its fingers in awe.

Mudrās! Each position of the hands is a miracle. And each of them can mean a lot to you.

When we get older, we get used to this, and forget the miracle. You can put the magick back in your fingers. Simply go into trance, return to baby consciousness, remember, and discover anew.

Now that you have done this you might like to explore the matter further. Think of the Tāntrikas who used to roam India up to a few centuries ago. Many worshippers, male and female, went travelling and visited sacred places, teachers, and sites of learning. On the long, dusty road, all excess baggage is too much. So the religious equipment was reduced to a few basic items that could be carried easily. Tantra includes many minimalist elements. Why shrines, temples, and images of gods when you can locate the deities in your body and wake them with a bit of mantra and inspired imagination? Why carry a huge diagram of the cosmos when you can scratch a yantra into the ground? Why use all sorts of ceremonial daggers, swords, wands, fly whisks, flowers, blossoms, sacrificial animals, and whatnot when you can represent these phenomena, and involve them in ritual, simply by shaping your fingers in an odd way?

Mudrā is one of the most enigmatic concepts of Tantra. In most books the term is simply translated as an unusual position of the hands. Mudrās can be complicated alignments of fingers and hands, but the term has a much wider range of meanings. The root 'mud' may come from 'to please' (yourself, a deity, your partner, or whoever).

A mudrā can be a seal or a bolt. It can be a posture of the body, sealing the apertures. It can be a gesture of hands and arms, but it may also be a posture of the entire body. Occasionally, the terms mudrā and āsana (seat, posture) are synonyms.

Here is a good one. Karālā, Karālī (She with the Terrifying Gaping Mouth) is a fear-inspiring Tantric goddess (or a whole group of yoginīs) who exhibits awful teeth and has the power to attract anybody. To do her mudrā, pull the corners of your mouth apart with ring and little fingers, look fiercely, wriggle your tongue, and shout 'hāhā'. This scares demons and improves your mood. Try it first thing in the morning before your bathroom mirror.

In the rite of the Five Ms, mudrā may mean 'parched grain', which may be real grains or a spicy dish made of kidney beans (an aphrodisiac). It can also, as some scholars hypothesise, be a code term for some unknown drug. Or it could be a reference to bījas, i.e. seed mantras parched by the fire of desire. Or to the seed (sperm) of a yogī after its parching in the yoni of the yoginī. Among the north Indian Nāthas, mudrās were heavy wooden ear-rings, a sign of their spiritual tradition. Not that this is all. In ritual, a mudrā can also be a reference to some trance state, or to the technical means of obsession. And to round

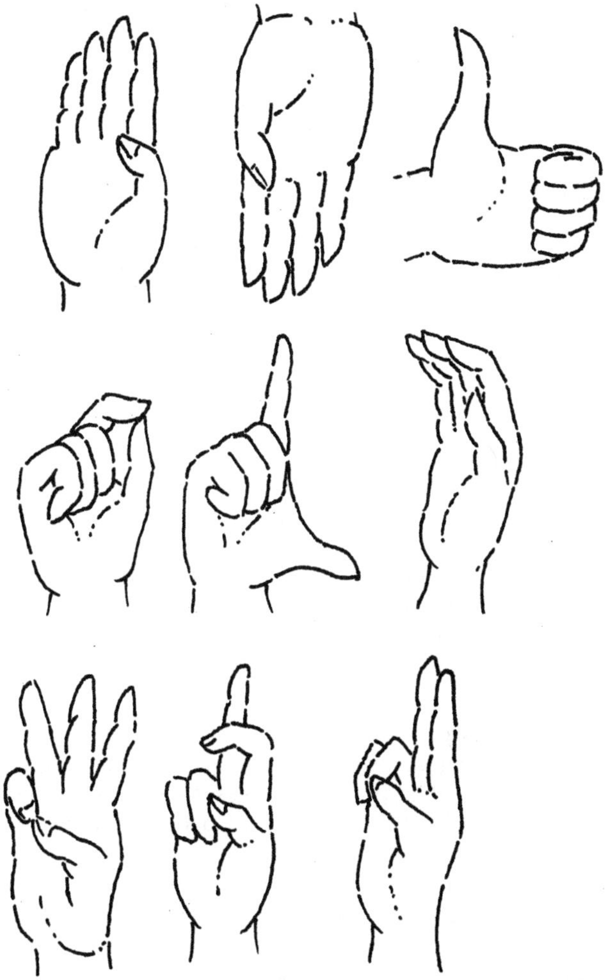

Figure 30 - Mudrās.
Top left: Abhaya. Top centre: Vara. Top right: Sikhara.
Middle left: Kapittha. Middle centre: Candrakalā. Middle right: Sarpasirsam.
Bottom left: Trisula. Bottom centre: Aṅkusa. Bottom right: Khaḍga.

things off, in early Hindu and Buddhist Tantra a mudrā is the term for a female ritual partner. Or for the juices created by making love.

As this book makes things nice and simple (I'm sure you noticed this), we'll focus on mudrā as hand gestures here. No doubt you have seen a lot of mudrās in Indian books or dance performances. They look elegant and exotic and carry their very own glamour and enchantment. Some find it enough to look up a few in some trashy book. They knot their fingers and believe that all sorts of powers and blessings transform their lives. Well and good. For some people, a simple placebo seems to be enough. For the more sceptical, things are less easy. They do not experience massive changes of consciousness just because their fingers are twisted in a meaningful way. Pretence is one thing, but when you want effects, you may have to be more thorough.

Helpful Hands

Let's look at a few mudrās of the Tantric traditions. Some may be useful for you, others too strained or specialised. No matter. Any mudrā will work when you associate it properly to the states you wish to experience. If you find nothing suitable, invent a new one. Some mudrās simply happen. You may find yourself in some extreme trance state and use the postures and gestures of that state as a link to access it another day. Just like āsanas, mudrās may happen naturally. Body tends to invent mudrās, given half a chance.

Abhaya Mudrā. This gesture appears prominently in divine images. It liberates from fear and assures safety. The thumb position can be varied. As you can see, the hand is open, signifying emptiness, and the fingers point upwards. This symbolises the upward path of Kuṇḍalinī, i.e. the process of dissolution that frees the jīva from the limitations of body, identity, and form. Fear is only possible when there is somebody to be afraid. When body/identity dissolve, fear cannot exist. This is the path of liberation,

Vara Mudrā. This gesture is the opposite of abhaya. It symbolises generosity, the granting of boons, and the fulfilment of wishes. On a simple level it means that the deity gives to you. In a more mystic interpretation it symbolises the downward path of Kuṇḍalinī, or of the shower of elixir, which creates the worlds as it descends from the height. As consciousness returns to earth, it becomes ever more dense and material, and induces changes in the world. This is the path of magical manifestation.

Sikhara is a popular mudrā from the sacred dance traditions of India. It symbolises, among other things, Śiva and the Śivaliṅga, but it can also mean holding a bow or sounding a bell, a pillar, asking a question, and embracing another.

Kapittha is another dance mudrā. First of all it can represent the goddesses Lakṣmī and Sarasvatī. It can mean an offering of incense and camphor, denote the act of milking cows, and represent pulling and holding things.

Candrakalā is the unit of the moon, hence a symbol of the elixir. It means the moon, a face, Śiva's crown (Kālī and Śiva have moon-sickles in their hair), and a cudgel.

Sarpasirsam signifies serpents in general and cobras in particular. It can also mean 'to sprinkle water' in a context of benediction, the ears of an elephant, or the broad arms of a wrestler.

Trisula mudrā represents the trinity. Well, you know that are quite a few trinities in Indian lore, so go ahead and make your choice. It also represents the trident carried by Śiva and Durgā.

Aṅkusa is an elephant hook. This is a useful utensil to prod and pull any big beast (such as your ego) and to direct its course. The sign has its relevance in learning and teaching, but it can also be used to pull something to you or to make it move away. Good for invocations and consecrations!

Khadga means sword or sabre. This mudrā is one of the most popular in east Asian Tantra, and can be found among Hindus, Buddhists, and Daoists, including Chinese martial artists. In general, the sword is the force of the intellect to differentiate, to separate, to divide, to cut complex things into smaller elements. A highly useful but also a very delusive tool. You can wield a sword to banish an undesirable or hostile influence, but you could also understand that separation is only possible on the plane of phenomenal existence. Good exorcists don't banish so much, they integrate. However, in the realm of difference, the sword is a tool that makes a difference. Hence the gesture is often used for banishing and purification. It can also be used to project energy and consciousness, especially when a few mantras have been muttered over the fingertips. In the hand of Kālī, the sword liberates.

Lelihāna means 'to stick out'. The little finger sticks out of the fist and represents the ONE, Brahman, the single unifying principle, your personal deity, and who- or whatever occupies the central spot of your mind/world maṇḍala. Use it to anoint objects (or your brow) with fluids, red colour, or what you so will.

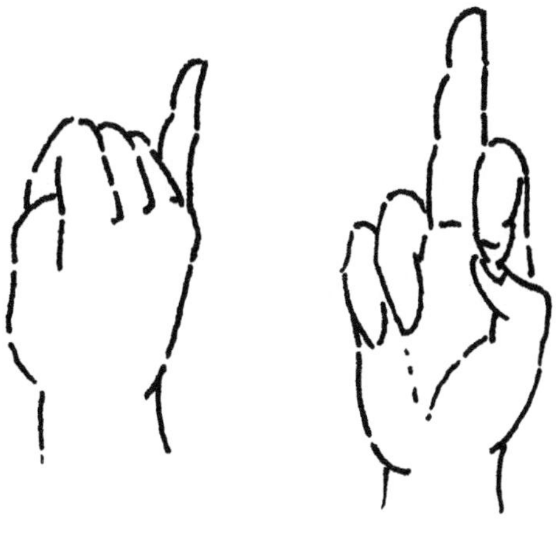

Figure 31 - More Mudrās.
Left: Lelihāna. Right: Paramī.

Paramī is a useful mudrā for consecrations. Generally, you look at the object or person you wish to bless and draw a circle around it with the middle finger. You can use paramī to consecrate food, offerings, ritual tools, but you can also do the gesture in the air to consecrate from a distance.

While these mudrās appear very occult and exotic, I can assure you that they won't amount to much unless you activate them first. If you want to use the sword mudrā, learn the sword first. Have a few meditations on swords and all they mean to you. Wake up to the nasty side of swords and also understand their beneficial use. A good fighter is not angry, a noble soul does not delight in violence. The sword, properly used, separates what does not belong together. Go into this consciousness. Understand that analytical thinking is the sword of the mind. It can cut apart illusions but it cannot join. Meditate on the sword in your magical universe. What is its purpose, what is its nature, how is it wielded wisely? When you have sorted all these matters out, make the mudrā. Allow all the sword power and awareness of your meditations to flow into the form of your fingers. Put emotion into the act, and determination, and responsibility. A sword is not a toy - great power requires responsible use. When you can allow all of these to unite in the mudrā, you have begun to create a gesture of power. Use it for a few months in your meditations and rituals and it will begin to work properly. The same goes for all mudrās. Twisting fingers and hoping is not enough. Each hand-sign has to be identified and connected with whatever it is supposed to convey. The association should be so direct that making the gesture almost automatically wakes the relevant power and sentience.

7: The Joy of Breath

Breath is rhythm. Breath is flow. Breath is pulsation. Above all, breath is bliss. In daily life, breath is nourishment. There is energy in breathing, which may be refined, stored, and moved through body. This energy is called prāṇā and its application is called prāṇāyāma. Prāṇāyāma is one of the eight limbs of yoga and has been used for several millennia to transform consciousness, to instil the body of the yogī with a lot of extra energy, and ultimately to achieve union with the divine. As breath is shared by all living entities, it is also a unifying principle. Consider it a way of sharing life.

I would like to emphasise that breathing is a not a technique, it's a communion. There are people who believe that, using the right technique, any state of awareness may be produced in anyone. This is a very materialistic attitude. If simple technique were enough, yogīs would not bother to clean and simplify their minds. Who cares for refinement when a simple cycle of out- and in-breaths, or maybe just an overdose or lack of oxygen could produce enlightenment? Yoga is a lot more than technique, and Tantra even more so. No single technique is ever guaranteed to produce a desirable result. This is the reason why there are hundreds of techniques in Tantra. Even with the best of them, you need an element of spiritual grace and personal magick to get results. Enlightenment, absorption, insight, and inspiration can happen anytime. They may appear after you have learned and practised something really difficult for years, or they may happen when you return to something so simple and basic that you hardly think about it. Remember. Technique is a tool, it is not the solution.

Prāṇāyāma may be translated in various ways. Prāṇā can mean breath, wind, life, energy, power, and refers to vital energy, the life-force. This concept is very close to the Chinese Qi (Ch'i) and the Greek pneuma. The concept of prāṇā goes back to the Vedic period. In the *Atharva Veda* and the *Upaniṣads* references to prāṇā abound. The concept of breath, however, is not limited to our modern idea of breathing. Prāṇā is closely related to ātman, the soul principle, which resides within body. At death, the ātman escapes upwards towards the heavenly regions. One hymn that invokes the power of breath is *AV* 2, 15, 1-2: *As both the heaven and the earth do not fear, are not harmed, so, my breath, fear not. As both the day and the night do not fear, are not harmed, so, my breath, fear not.* The formula is repeated with sun and moon, sacrament and dominion, truth and untruth, what is and what is to be. In each case, breath is connected with freedom from fear. Good psychology; when people are afraid they tend to tense up, which makes proper breathing difficult. Emotional upset generally restricts breathing, one of the reasons why people who want to avoid or repress emotions often tense and breathe badly. In *AV* 2, 16,1 we read: *O breath-and-expiration, protect me from death, svāhā.* *AV* 3, 31, 6-9, a healing chant, gives a good example that the seers considered breath a cosmic force: *Agni puts together the breaths; the moon is put together with breath: I away from all evil have turned, away from yakṣma, to union with life-time. By breath did the gods set in motion the sun, of universal heroism, I away from etc. By the breath of the long lived, of the life-makers, do thou live, do not die: I away from etc. With the breath of the breathing do thou breathe; be just here, do not die: I away from etc.*(trans. Whitney 1987).

These examples show that breath was a lot more than a simple activity of the lungs. Breath was a cosmic force shared by all beings, an energy that gave motion and life to the universe. Similar ideas abound in the early *Upaniṣads.* Here, breath is often coupled with the senses. The *Bṛhad-āraṇyaka Upaniṣad* offers some good examples for the miracles of breath. In 1,5,9-10 mind, the form of what is known, is contrasted with breath which is the form of what is unknown. In 1,5,20 we hear of the divine breath, born from water and the moon, which, whether moving or non-moving, cannot be injured or upset. Who knows this becomes the self of all beings. Another popular topic are rivalries between the senses, faculties, and breath. It usually turns out that beings can survive without hearing, sight, smell, taste, feeling, or cognition, but when breath ceases the system dies. Breath is also a divine energy. It infuses the chants with vitality, thereby making them magically potent. Breath is a force giving success in the struggle between Devas and Asuras, breath produces nourishment and food. Breath is formless, 2,3,5 identifies it with the sacred space within the self. This breath is so much more than mere inhalation and exhalation that I can only ask you to think of it as a mystery.

In many texts, prāṇāyāma is used primarily as a synonym for breathing exercises. There are, however, a few texts that use the term prāṇā for a range of vital energies that have little to do with breathing. Gorakṣanāth speaks of ten breaths or winds within the body (*Siddha Siddhānta Paddhati,* 1,68). The prāṇa-wind dwells in the heart, regulating in-breath and out-breath, consisting of Ha and Sa. The apāna-wind dwells in the anus, its nature is to hold and empty. You can find the samāna-wind in the navel, regulating the fires that digest food. The vyāna-wind is everywhere within body, regulating drying and nourishment (i.e. distributing the food-essences). Udāna-wind is in the palate, controlling feeding, speech, and vomiting. The nāga-wind penetrates all limbs, invigorating and liberating. Kūrma-wind opens and shuts the eyes. Kṛkala-wind causes the sensation of hunger and releases gas from the stomach. Devadatta-wind causes yawning. Dhanañjaya is tone, this, the tenth wind, produces sounds. Other sources give fewer details. Often, the prāṇa-wind is only contrasted to the apāna-wind, prāṇa being the upwards moving breath, vitalising and inspiring, while apāna-wind is the downward moving energy, manifesting as excrement, urine, and sexual fluids. Some exercises require that the yogī pulls up the muscles of perineum and genitals, thereby preventing the apāna-wind from descending, while allowing the prāṇa-wind to rise. When you study elder texts on breath and winds, find out what the author is talking about first.

The idea that breathing influences consciousness and vitality is shared by many ancient cultures. Prāṇāyāma is not just a science of energy generation and management, it is also an art of refining consciousness. Prāṇā is more than force (Śakti), it is also sentience (Śiva), and prāṇāyāma is the pulsation of both. The *Kauṣītakī Brāhmaṇa Upaniṣad* (see below) tells us that the breathing (living) spirit is Brahman, the mind is the messenger, the eye the protector, ear the announcer, and speech the house-keeper (2, 1). Breath is the hidden force behind the functions of the senses and the operations of the mind. Indra declares (3, 2-3) that he is the breathing spirit, life, the intelligent spirit, and immortality. *Life is breath and breath is life... or indeed with the breathing spirit one obtains immortality in this world, by intelligence true conception ... What is the breathing spirit, that is the intelligence self.* Here we are at the beginning of a spiritual tradition that equates awareness with breath. (More on classical prāṇāyāma below.) There is practical value in such words; breathing changes consciousness and consciousness changes breathing. I hope that you are perplexed enough to open your mind really wide. Prāṇāyāma is a lot more than simple breathing exercises.

Āyāma means to extend, stretch, lengthen, control. Thus, prāṇāyāma means to extend, refine and control breath. This is a tricky concept as the very idea of control is misleading. Control is not something achieved by the conscious mind, nor is it done by force. Good breathing is not learned by force, it is achieved by allowing things to develop naturally. An Indian proverb compares prāṇāyāma with the taming of dangerous beasts like lions and tigers. You need a certain amount of force for this job, but you need even more love, respect, caution, attention, and the wisdom to allow the beasts to follow their own true nature. A lion trainer can 'force' a lion only by setting up a situation where the lion likes to do what is expected of it. This looks as if there were control, but it is really a way of making will manifest naturally.

Another etymology of the word prāṇāyāma proposes that it consists of the words prāṇā and Yama. Yama is the god of death, the ruler of several hells and otherworlds. Thus, prāṇāyāma means the cessation of breathing. It implies a practice cultivated by those who think that minimal breathing is still too much.

According to the *Devī Bhāgavatam* (11, 1), there are six basic forms of prāṇāyāma.

1. When the breaths are not steady.
2. Better than the former.
3. When united with one's mantra.
4. When without thought of any mantra.
5. When the heart (attention) is fixed on one's deity.

6. When the heart is not fixed on one's deity. This may sound confusing but is worth thinking about. Are we dealing with a linear progression?

Last, a thought on prāṇā. If you consider prāṇā as a sort of energy you may not be thinking deeply enough. In Indian cosmology, all that exists is alive (to some extent) and all that is alive is sentient. Prāṇā is not only alive, it is the essence of life and consciousness, and as a form of energy it is obviously a Śakti. Volume 11, chapter 8 of the *DB* gives an account of her:

> *There is a red lotus on a wide boat in a vast ocean of a red colour; on this lotus is seated the Prânâ Shakti. She has six hands holding, in due order, the trident, the arrows made of sugarcane, noose, goad, five arrows and a skull filled with blood. She is three-eyed. Her high breasts are decorated; the colour of Her body is like the Rising Sun. May she grant us happiness. Thus meditating on the Prânâ Shakti, Who is of the nature of the Highest Self, one ought to apply ashes on his body in order to attain success in all actions.*

Invoke her as you explore the joy of breath.

General Considerations. Prāṇāyāma is a loose term that can refer to a wide range of exercises and meditations, many of them related to breathing. Some of the basics can be learned and explored on your own, provided you are careful, cautious, and refrain from overdoing them. For the more refined types of prāṇāyāma, a teacher, incarnate or within you, is essential. Not all of the techniques in this chapter are suitable for everyone. Much depends on your health, your fitness, and the wisdom you need to observe what happens and to know when you have had enough. For those who wish to explore prāṇāyāma, let me give a general outline. Keep in mind that prāṇāyāma is much more than simple exercises. Prāṇāyāma influences the motion of vitality within body and the state of awareness of your mind. Be gentle and cautious with yourself, proceed with patience, and use your brain to observe the results.

Breathing exercises should be done gently. Breath should flow through the nose in most exercises, the flow should be smooth and gentle. The nose is the ideal organ of breath as it has a system of filters that clean the air and temperate it.

If you have a clogged nose, you can try cleaning it with a solution of lukewarm water and a tiny amount of salt. Most yogīs take a little of this mixture from a cup or the hollow of the hand and hold it right under the nostrils. To pull it up, they make a pumping motion by allowing the jaw to drop while keeping the mouth shut. This pumps up a small amount of fluid and is a lot nicer than trying to breathe it in. Some use their own urine for this purpose, urine is both salty and has body temperature, it also contains a mild disinfectant.

Nose breathing is especially important when the air is cold. If you have to breathe through the mouth, keep the lips almost shut and the tongue fixed to the palate (not the teeth or gums). The tongue should also be at the palate when you breathe through the nose. Keep it there without pressure, experience will teach the right location. Saliva generated during exercise is traditionally supposed to contain beneficial substances and swallowed. In general, breath should be smooth, uninterrupted, and pleasant. You will find that you have more time when you use your lungs with more efficiency. Hasty breathing and panting are only acceptable when they happen naturally for brief exercises or short periods in trance states of extreme excitement. Prolonged hasty breathing is harmful and can lead to bad health. The same goes for forcing air into your lungs and indeed for any activity that causes strain, unease, or pain. Be nice to yourself. Belly breathing is a natural thing, when done gently and unconsciously it can go on all day. Full breathing is intentional and has the character of an exercise, the same goes for all the special variations developed by Indian yogīs. These forms of breathing should be learned patiently and the length of the exercise should be built up slowly. You will progress faster when you go slowly. If you can, begin the day with a cup of warm water and a bit of breathing. This should be done gently. Have an open window if the climate permits it and chose a style of breathing that gradually supplies a lot of fresh air. Never force your breathing. Be nice and gentle to yourself, in the morning body is still stiff and waking up should happen gradually. When you want to take deeper breaths make sure that you exhale properly. The trick is to use what you have instead of cramming more air in. When you exhale properly more fresh air will flow in naturally. May I repeat this? Exhale, exhale, exhale.

Troubles. When your health is weak, when you have breathing problems or are recovering from an illness, be extra gentle with yourself. It is better to stop doing exhausting exercises than to make the disease worse. This is especially the case with diseases of the respiratory system and the heart. Gentle belly breathing lying on the ground is less strain than doing complicated exercises sitting or standing up. Great care should be taken when you have just had a cold (or are almost having one). When you breathe too much cold air, you will cool your nose, mouth, the cavities, the bronchial system, and the lungs. For similar reasons, deep breathing should be avoided when the air is moist.

Food. Breathing exercises on a full stomach are a remarkably unpleasant experience which doesn't make anyone really happy. Likewise, hunger can distort posture and reduce the calming or exhilarating effects of breathing by causing edginess and unease. The golden mean is a state between fullness and hunger. Traditionally, opinions on this subject vary a lot. One authority, B.K.S. Iyengar (1981) proposes that one should not practise breathing exercises for four or six hours after a meal. After breathing exercise another half hour should pass before you eat again. This is an eminently unpractical solution, unless you happen to be independently rich (or on welfare) and able to organise your whole day around your yogīc training. It does make sense when you practise the Iyengar type of yoga, which is much like the training of a world-class athlete and involves plenty of painful episodes. Other sources, speaking of Kuṇḍalinī yoga, propose that the yogī should never be entirely hungry and never fully stuffed. They propose a light meal every three hours. One good solution is breathing exercises (of the more gentle sort) before breakfast.

Ground ozone and other sorts of **air pollution**. Exhaust fumes of cars (without a catalyser), lorries, tractors, and lawnmowers produce fumes that interact with strong sunlight and heat to produce ground ozone. They also produce substances that bind ground ozone, but they are in the minority. A few sunny, windless days in the city can produce formidable amounts of this irritating gas. Ground ozone has a lot of negative effects. It can make people weak, edgy, ill-tempered, and tense. It irritates the muscuous membranes, makes the eyes burn, and may lead to headaches, nervous disorders, and sudden breakdowns of blood pressure. During the long, sunny day, the concentration of ground ozone builds up in the city and along highways. In the process it is pushed out into the country. By night traffic continues within the city. Lacking sunlight, the ozone production stops and other ingredients of the exhaust fumes begin to bind the stuff. This clears the air to some extent. Out in the country, traffic is reduced by night and the ozone is not bound. It is often in the periphery of cities, far out in the country where everything looks green and natural that the highest concentrations of ground ozone accumulate. Some governments are sensitive to this and warn farmers, lumberjacks, and athletes to avoid physical activity. Ground ozone may also increase when meadows or fields are cut, not to mention indoors ozone pollution from printers and photocopy machines. When you've had a few windless sunny days and find the air tasting horrible and notice that even small activities seem to exhaust, you can be sure that the ground ozone level is high. Breathing exercises should be avoided at such times or done extremely cautiously, preferably very late at night or in the early morning. In some places, such as Los Angeles, Mexico City, or Beijing, it might be a good idea to consider moving.

The yogīs of old did not have to consider ozone pollution. However, they had to worry about other things. Dust storms are very common in Northern India, where the country is much like a desert. Any yogī doing prāṇāyāma under such circumstances has to get rid of a lot of colourful phlegm through the day.

Smoke is another such problem. Air pollution has been around since our ancestors learned how to handle fire. Wherever people depend on burning of wood, coal, animal manure, and so on for heating or cooking, they are doing damage to their lungs. Most of history took place in small buildings with bad ventilation and a lot of smoke pollution. To this day, a spittoon is one of the few objects that a yogī may own. If you do prāṇāyāma, you'll find that some of the exercises will clear your throat and nostrils. It's useful to have a vessel nearby which can be reached with a minimum of motion.

Preliminary exploration. The lungs are not a muscle, they are two spongy bags, which are protected by the ribs and moved by muscles from outside. You cannot feel with your lungs, but you do have nerves around them. Try this. Lie down on the floor and take a few breaths. Sense how you do this. Which muscles are moving? Where do they pull, where do they push, where are they attached to your spine? Then try a few variations. The muscles needed for belly breathing are not the same as you use when you breathe with chest or shoulders. Explore!

Breathing has several variables. Each breath has a certain speed, length, pressure, rhythm. How fast do you breathe? Please take a watch now and find out how often you breathe in a minute. This is great fun - you will notice how your awareness tends to influence the score. Do this a few time so you'll know your average for resting, walking, and during exercise. Make notes. It can be useful to time how long you keep tea stewing. Next use the opportunity of timing breathing during unusual circumstances. How fast do you breathe when you are calm or excited, tired or awake? How do you breathe when you are really happy? How do you breathe when you wake up, are working, moving about, or going to sleep? What is your breathing like when you read or watch a movie? How do you breathe when you are overworked, have serious emotional problems, or feel sick and miserable? And just how are your lungs moving in these states? Any chance your belly is still moving or is it just the shoulders that go up and down? Does you breath change when you are in company and when you are alone? How do you breathe when you make love? How do you breathe before you come, as you come, and afterwards?

Do you like the way you breathe? Will you enjoy the changes that you're going to experience?

Watching breath. This is the beginning of your journey, it is also a point to which you will return again and again. What is the sound of your breath as you inhale and exhale? Please listen carefully. Indian tradition has it that the in-breath sounds like the letter Sa and the out-breath like the letter Ha. This is the usual form, a few sources give it the other way round. Generally, the letter Ha is assigned to Śiva and the letter Sa to Śakti. Each complete breath cycle is the union of Śiva and Śakti and forms the Śri Parāprāsāda mantra (the auspicious mantra of the highest sacrifice) called variously Haṁsa (a title of Śiva, occasionally of Viṣṇu or Brahmā), Sa'haṁ (I am She) and So'haṁ (I am He). The letter ṁ is the nada-bindu (vibration-point), introduced for grammatical reasons between the Ha and the Sa, and pronounced nasally between M and NG. The mantra Haṁsa is one of the most celebrated in the whole body of Tantric literature. It is repeated by every living creature, it is inherent in every being and thing, mobile and immobile, from the smallest particles to the greatest galaxies. Humans are said to recite it 21600 times within one day and night. There is an immense amount of theology behind it, which will be explored further on. Right now it should suffice that the mantra is called ajapā, it takes no effort to do japa (repeated recitation) of it. This means quite simply that you shouldn't make a fuss about it. Don't interfere, don't attempt to control. Breath takes its own way, breath makes its own rhythms. Relax, calm down, and observe. How smooth is it? How long does it take? How does it move your body? Be aware of the flow. Hear it, feel it, enjoy. If you listen carefully, your inner speech will become silent. With a bit of practise you will get into calm and tranquil trance states using this method. How about ten minutes of practice every day?

Watching pauses. There are four distinct phases in each breath. For convenience's sake we might consider that in-breath is creation, holding (full) is maintenance, out-breath is destruction, and resting (empty) is transcendence. No doubt a lot of deities will come to mind now who are more or less associated with these functions. When you identify the breath-phases with seed mantras and visualisation of colours or figures you can make this an entire meditation. Breath consists of at least four phases, but it is generally only the two active ones, in-breath and out-breath, that appear in awareness. This is doing, and people usually define themselves by their doing. Change now! Just as important (and often even more so) is not-doing. Not-doing (Wu wei) was developed into a fine art by the Daoists, but you can also find it lurking in the hidden corners of Tantric yoga. Before doing is not-doing. After doing comes not-doing. After repeating mantras, Haṁsa allows you to be silent and listen. The highest mantra is no word at all. When images and words have exhausted themselves, silence reigns supreme. The equivalent to silence is the pause between breaths. This is the gap, the interval, the timeless space in-between. This is the gate of insight and the moment of absentminded tranquillity. It is the śmaśāna (cremation place) where desire is burned up and self is freed from thinking. It is the cross-roads between realities. As you read this, pause now. Focus attention on the gap. You can observe the pause between in-breath and out-breath, when your lungs are full and the energy pulses in your body. This is nourishment. You can observe the pause between out-breath and in-breath. This is transcendence. Do this often. As you go about your daily business, as you sit down to a cup of tea, as you wait and as you do. Pause now. Open your mind and embrace the silence.

Warm up. Breathing is easiest when your body is flexible, limber, and warm. This is not always the case, especially among modern folk, who generally tend to spend too much time sitting. For a start, you should begin your breathing practise by a bit of physical exercise. The easiest way is to join a yoga group or a martial arts class. A few months of regular exercise will teach you a wide range of warming, stretching, and limbering-up exercises. If no group is available, you might proceed as follows.

PLEASE BE CAREFUL WHILE YOU DO THE EXERCISES. This is not a contest, it is not a sport nor a form of muscle building or toughening up.

Everything should be done with care, caution, and consideration. Never force results. Go gently, rather do too little than too much. Be friendly with yourself. Body is easily hurt, especially in times of ill health, cold temperature, when too hungry, or too stuffed with food or drink. You alone are responsible for the well-being of your body. You are the student, but you have to be the teacher too. So put a lot of awareness into your exercise and listen, watch out, and feel how your body responds to the motions.

Good breathing is easier when your body is limber and relaxed. A few short minutes of exercise may be just the thing to prepare you. Here are some suggestions.

Warm up by shaking your limbs. Run and jump on the spot, forwards, sideways, on one foot, with both feet at once, with crossed legs, dance with swinging feet, and when you are thoroughly warmed up, move on to the hips. Move the pelvis forward and backwards, in small and large circles, make motions as if you wanted to scoop up water with your pelvis, try oval motions, fast and slow, experiment and keep moving. This sort of thing works wonders in unfreezing the hips. Imbue the motions with lust and passion. What you are enjoying here will improve your lovemaking. Try obscene motions. After doing hip and belly motions for a good while, do something for the flanks and back. Stretch upwards, stretch sideways, reach for the sky. Bend forward and down, then reach up again. Gently turn around to the left and right. Be careful with your spine! Stretch your arms and let them move in large, slow circles along your sides. Make the circles smaller, then big again. Move the elbows in circles, stretch your hands in the eight directions (up, down, right, left, and four in between) while you exhale, draw them in as you inhale. Moving up and out you exhale, moving in and down you inhale. Rotate your shoulders gently. Move your head in slow and gentle circular motions. Careful! Look after yourself. There is no need to hurry, if you go slowly you will progress faster. If you exercise in haste the result could be a torn or strained sinew, a dislocated vertebra, or a torn muscle. The risk of such accidents is greater when the climate is cold and when your body is stiff, especially after resting or sleeping. You are exercising with body, not against it.

Good breathing can be done in many positions. Read the section on posture before you start. It's useful to have a straight spine when you breathe.

Belly breathing. As you breathe in, your belly comes out, as you breathe out your belly goes in. Remember. As a child it was natural for you. Belly breathing is a more efficient form of breathing than the usual adult-person chest breathing, it utilises more of the lung volume, so you can take deeper breaths. Anatomically, you may observe that it is not actually the belly that breathes. Your lungs are up there in the chest, protected by the ribs, which is quite as it should be. How do you expand them? In chest breathing, the ribs expand and allow the fresh inflow of air. As the ribs can't move much, the amount of air you process is not very large. In belly breathing, the lungs expand downwards and press against the diaphragm. This is the horizontal membrane that divides the upper cavity of your body, containing heart and lungs, from the lower cavity where the liver, spleen, intestines, and the enteral nervous system do their job. As you breathe in, the pressure massages the intestines and the belly bulges out. Good for the digestion and it also centres your balance.

There is a spot approximately five centimetres below your navel which is the centre of your body and one of the most important energy sites. In Hindu yoga and Tantra, it is occasionally called the maṇipūra cakra. The exact location of this point differs from system to system, some place it on the navel, others below it, and still others propose both to provide for all possibilities. In Chinese Daoism, which also makes use of this power site, it is called the lower Dantian (Tan Tien) and symbolised by such metaphors as the 'Lowest Cinnabar Field', 'the Palace of the Golden Pearl', the 'Oven of Immortality', 'the Gold Pavilion', and so on. The very place to meet Xiwangmu and to relax within the swirling golden vapours. Many Chinese arts, such as drawing, painting, calligraphy, singing, and martial arts make use of this point to centre the body and to concentrate the life energy. The place can be used to store excess energy, which is especially important in states of high-power functioning, rituals of obsession, Kuṇḍalinī Yoga, spontaneous rapture, and overwhelming emotions. When you are emotionally upset, you may find that a few minutes of belly breathing, focusing your attention near the navel, will calm your mind and energy.

In learning to do belly breathing, the easiest approach is to lie on the floor on your back with the hands at your sides or on your chest. Place a small weight on your belly so you can feel it more distinctly. Simply breathe in (the weight rises) and out (the weight sinks) and observe all sensations. Once you can do this without too much consideration, try it in a seated posture. This is easiest to learn when kneeling, sitting on the feet or between them, but it can also be done sitting on the edge of a chair. Keep your spine straight and focus your attention below the navel. As you breathe in, the belly comes out, make sure it is ONLY the belly, and that the chest remains immobile. Breathe slowly and in calm, even waves through the nose. As you breathe out, the belly comes in again, and at the very end of the exhalation, you bow forward a little. Do this the way it is done in Asia. Europeans tend to bow from the shoulders or mid torso, Asians tend to bow from the hips. This keeps your spine straight as you bend forward very gently. Hold a tiny instant, raise your spine again until you are quite erect and allow the next breath to flow in. In this exercise, the main thing is that you go gently, slowly, and peacefully. Stay relaxed as you sit and breathe quietly through the nose. Your awareness should emphasise the outflow of breath, and you will notice how you calm and slow down, how your body becomes really centred, and how your attention focuses in the power zone of the belly. This is a meditation in itself, it is also a fine art. It will take a while before you develop the proper feeling in the belly. Practice this technique for a few months, at least twice a day, if only for five minutes. Beginners should do this often, but only for short periods. Practitioners report that they feel calmed and soothed, that their body becomes stable within itself, that they have more energy and better health than before. They may also report that all sorts of suppressed feelings come up, this is especially the case with people who have spent years tensing their bellies in order to reduce feeling, lust, and emotion. Go gently as you practice, never force your breathing and give yourself time. All breathing exercises should begin and end with a bit of belly breathing to ensure your physical, emotional, and spiritual stability.

Rubbing the Belly. This should be the finale of your daily exercises. Place your palms on the belly and feel the warmth of your hands. Imagine the rich power zone within you. Now circle your palms on your maṇipūra cakra and imagine how the energy of your whole being comes to this point and spirals inward to the belly cauldron, where it can be refined and stored. As you feel this, imagine that the energy expands again. Radiating from the centre, it spreads in a delightful golden hue through your belly, your torso, through limbs, legs, and head. The trick lies in putting a great big smile into it. Smile into the belly, smile into the energy that comes out of your belly, smile into your whole body as the energy saturates you. Can you feel the joy? This should be stronger. Take that small little smile and make it bigger. Expand it. Make the joy stronger, fill yourself with joy, have the joy drench every cell of your body and lighten up the aura beyond. When you begin to smile an unbearably crazy Timothy Leary smile you are doing just fine. Life should be more full of joy anyway, so help yourself to a good amount several times a day. Wherever the joy flows, there is also an increased flow of energy, and where the energy goes, body heals and refreshes itself.

Some modern Daoist schools make a lot of fuss about the direction of the circling hands. In their opinion, rubbing in a clockwise direction is yang and counter-clockwise yin (imagine a watch lying on your belly). Men who circle counter-clockwise and women who circle clockwise are supposed to be in grave danger to mess up their sexual energies. These schools recommend that each gender should circle in its proper direction plus a little bit of the other direction, as there should be a little yin in yang, and a little yang in yin. Indians are different, in their belief clockwise is usually a lucky direction. Going anti-clockwise also has its uses, it appears in dangerous nightside rituals, exorcisms, and acts of destructive magic. Anatomically, I can only add that if you circle clockwise you are following the direction that food takes. Prolonged counter-clockwise circling goes against the intestines and may upset the belly.

Reverse belly breathing. Your belly comes out as you breathe out and moves in as you breathe in. This is not the natural way of breathing but can happen occasionally to beginners when they get confused. The technique is used for short, therapeutic treatments in Chinese hospitals to provide a strong massage of the intestines in order to prevent constipation, and in some more powerful Daoist exercises.

Chest breathing is a very common matter in our society. As you breathe in your chest expands, and as you breathe out it compresses again. Chest breathing utilises less of the lung volume than belly breathing and is less efficient, a reason why professional singers, players of wind instruments, and actors who have to speak in a loud and clear voice avoid it. It also makes the body top heavy and upsets balance, which is why martial artists and many dancers do not like it either. However, it conforms to the military ideal and produces a posture that allows people to repress their deeper feelings more easily. In exclusive chest breathing, you can keep your belly cramped all of the time, this reduces emotional sensibility, inhibits sexual pulsation, and produces what Wilhelm Reich called muscular and character armour (please read his classic book *The Function of Orgasm* for full details). Much of our culture is based on this terrible ideal.

Shoulder breathing is when your whole body stays inert as you breathe, only the shoulders move up and down as the lungs expand and constrict. This is the least efficient way of breathing. You can occasionally observe it in sick people, very old people, and those suffering from extreme anxiety.

In-breath and out-breath. As you breathe you can emphasise the inhalation and the exhalation. To emphasise may mean putting attention into it. It may also mean extending it. One way to relax is to emphasise the out-breath. Be aware how breath gently flows out of you and how it becomes slow and slower as you reach the end of the exhalation. Go with the flow. It is easy to relax into the exhalation. Body naturally tends to relax on the out-breath (this means you feel a slightly heavier) and to tense a little on the in-breath (meaning that you feel a little lighter). If you put attention into the slowing down and the sensation of heaviness, you can reach states of deep relaxation and tranquillity. Amplify this! Imagine that you sink deeper and deeper with each exhalation.

For some mysterious reason most people tend to associate the direction DOWN with calming, soothing, and relaxing sensations (parasympathetic nervous system) while thy react to the direction UP with excitement, passion, and wakefulness (sympathetic nervous system). Just compare what it means when I tell you to 'slow down' or 'speed up'. These metaphors tell us something about direction and tempo, and though they make little sense to the rational mind they do work. How come people 'sink' into 'deep trance' and 'get up' or feel their 'spirits rise'? Think about it. How many 'ups and downs' can you find in everyday metaphors? Several modern schools use the slow out-breath, combined with the visualisation of sinking down, and a soothing mantra to allow their students to drift gently into a calm and peaceful trance state. Others replace the mantra with counting. You can count one number with each exhalation, going from nine to one (repeat this cycle as long as you like), and find yourself getting slower and more tranquil with each breath. All of this is well and good to calm and refresh your mind. After a while you will arrive in a pleasant and calm trance state. This is assumed to be meditation. I disagree. Meditation is not going into trance, it's what happens when you are in trance. So what will you do now you are deeply in trance?

No matter whether you want to relax or wake up, much depends on congruence. The out-breath relaxes providing you do it in a relaxed fashion. If you blow it out sharply or strain to force the last bit of air out of your lungs it won't relax you at all. In a similar manner, emphasising the in-breath can lead to energetic and dynamic states. If you breathe in visualising all the extra energy that rushes into your lungs and belly, this may provide a powerful boost. It gets even stronger when you imagine (or realise) that the pores breathe and that fresh air goes into all pores at once and saturates your whole being with fresh energy. Your whole being can breathe this universe in! Pore breathing is another idea of early (Huang.Lao) Daoism. It is recommended by some works found in the grave library of Mawangdui (before 165 BCE).

There has been some research on the effects of inhalation and exhalation. Hu Bin (1982) mentions Chinese clinics where animal experiments were conducted. Stimulating the brain at the centres of exhalation extended to the parasympathetic nervous system while stimulation of the inhalation centres excited the sympathetic nervous system. Considering that our culture obsessively overemphasises the sympathetic nervous system (which makes you active, fast, dynamic, and restless, just like your employers crave), most of us could do with a bit of calming to appreciate the joy of life.

Physical power. Most martial artists are aware that the exhalation can be used to increase the physical power of the body. When you have to lift or move something heavy, you will find that this is easier when you exhale a little as you apply force. The same goes for vigorous hitting and kicking. If you add a sharp, short exhalation (or a shout) to your punch, the impact will be stronger. Likewise, when you receive a blow to the belly, you can take some of the force out of it by exhaling a little. All of this needs practise.

Full Breathing. This is the method of breathing that permits maximal use of the lung volume. Great care should be taken as you learn it. Be gentle with yourself, train your lungs carefully, avoid strain and tension and be nice to yourself. Full breathing takes months to learn properly, and you will progress faster when you avoid overdoing it. **Should you suffer from diseases of heart, lungs, or any other organ, consult**

your doctor before you experiment. This is a very powerful technique and should be approached with caution and respect.

Begin with a straight spine. Exhale properly. Now breathe deeply into your belly so it bulges out. Then take in more air as the chest expands. Keep the belly out as you do this. These are two distinct motions: belly bulges forward and the ribs expands sideways. Keep your shoulders down as you do it and your posture straight. This results in a peculiar and pleasant feeling of light tension under the arms. Now the important thing is that you do not force results. Whatever you do, be gentle with yourself. Regular practise will make this complex motion easy and natural. It will also teach you how to keep an erect posture in the process. Hold the breath for a moment, then slowly empty your chest (ribs move inward) and afterwards the belly (belly moves inward.) Rest a moment. Then breathe into the belly again.

Thus, the pattern is as follows:

belly moves out as you inhale, chest moves out as you inhale, pause, chest moves in as you exhale, belly moves in as you exhale, pause.

A common error in this routine is to move the belly out and when the chest moves out to allow belly to go in again. Belly should stay out when the chest expands.

With a bit of practice the various movements will blend into one elegant and extended motion like a surging wave.

This is the basic form, but of course variations are possible. If you like to make the exhalation as complete as possible, bow forward a little. This is not obligatory and only recommended for those with good posture, should they like to introduce a slightly swaying motion. Another option is to allow the pelvis to tilt forwards at the end of the exhalation. Still another is to lift the muscles around the perineum, the genitals and the anus, i.e. the entire pelvic floor, as you exhale, this sort of thing may happen naturally in certain trances. Don't worry too much about these special forms, doing it in a simple and immobile straight posture without any bending is absolutely fine.

Full breathing produces a wonderful energy and oxygen high which can be combined with visualisation and mantra practice. It is really useful for ecstatic trance states, euphoria, and inspired madness. It is not a good way to go through the day and should not be done for prolonged periods or using force. If you overdo it, your energy will be disrupted, you may become dizzy, or suffer a black out: this is called hyperventilation, for which see below. Too much oxygen at once is not a good idea. If you encounter any sort of pain, pressure in the head, tingling limbs, or find sparkles dancing before your eyes you are overdoing it. Go gently. For the beginner, five minutes are quite sufficient. If you want to do more, do it twice a day but not for twice as long. Prolonged deep breathing has to be built up.

When you practice full breathing while sitting, standing, resting, or walking (slowly) you supply body with more air than it actually needs. There is a great difference to deep breathing as it happens during physical work or sport. Athletes usually breathe pretty fast and deep when they train but they need the increased amount of air to make up for the physical motion. When you breathe deep and swiftly without physical motion, the excess has to go somewhere. One of its effects is a change of consciousness. A light excess can lead to states of exhilaration, especially when you combine it with mantra, prayer, visualisation or the assumption of god forms. A strong excess also exhilarates, it can also make you dizzy and produce headaches, hyperventilation, and over-emotionality. People who like to breathe deep and fast get a kick which might be compared to some drugs. It's an extreme and dramatic experience, sometimes pleasant, sometimes utterly draining and exhausting. The important effect, however, does not happen during the intense breathing itself but sets in afterwards. I suspect that full breathing releases endorphins, as it can produce a sensation of joy, happiness, and bliss that may last for hours. You can get this effect simply by breathing deep and hard for ten or fifteen minutes if you want to do it the rough, stupid, and damaging way. You can also do it by gentle full breathing at a moderate speed. A little more air over a while works just as well as a lot more air in a short period. It takes longer than the extreme method, but it produces a smooth consciousness of higher quality and is less straining on your health. If you love to breathe, you will sooner or later go for the moderate form, as frequent hard and fast breathing tends to be so demanding. I know that moderation is not easy for the more ecstatic among my readers (it's not easy for me either). Keep in mind that maximum efficiency is not simply breathing as hard and fast as possible. If you pump your lungs like mad you don't give them enough time to make efficient use of the excess air. There is a limit to the amount of air your lungs can process at a given time, and breathing harder and more forceful is not going to improve things one bit. The trick is learning to breathe at a rate that permits your lungs to process the air properly. This means efficient posture to make best use of the lung volume without strain and tension, and a breathing rate that is not fast but only a little faster than usual. If you use the lung volume properly, even your normal breathing speed will produce an excess of air intake. Really good full breathing is a high art form that needs lots of practise and watchfulness. Be gentle and careful with yourself! When you are doing it really well, it comes easy and naturally, with very little effort, no strain, and is pure joy. Another trick is to do it briefly, but often. I like to do it on forest walks. First five minutes full breathing, then a little slow walking, then another pause for breathing and so on. In between I stretch a lot and loosen up the body. This gets me much further than doing it for half an hour at once. Also, remember that full breathing is a strong stimulant. Don't do it before going to bed, unless you like being wide-awake and sleepless.

After you have done full breathing for a while, end the practise with a few minutes of belly breathing and belly rubbing. Give yourself a great smile. It will ensure that your energy is centred and your body-mind is in balance.

Kapāla bhāti. This exercise means skull-shining, it is supposed to clean and clear up the head (i.e. the nose cavities). It simply consists of rapid full breathing without pauses. The exhalation in particular is done by contracting the belly muscles. Done properly, it can clear up a lot of phlegm from mouth, throat, and nose, so keep a spittoon handy. Beginners generally start by doing twenty rapid full breaths to clear up the head prior to less violent exercises. With practice, one can gradually build this up to more than a hundred breaths. This should be done gradually and over several months. Keep in mind that the respiratory tract needs training. This is a short exercise, if you overdo it you'll get hyperventilation.

Hyperventilation is what you get when you breathe too much, too fast, or both. It sometimes happens when people are under shock or suffering from extreme stress or emotional turmoil, and can also be a regular disease requiring the attention of a physician. Hyperventilation can be caused by too fast and too deep breathing. Some people like this state as it produces a remarkable kick. It is also extremely exhausting for body and mind and may well result in damage of the respiratory tract and other parts of your anatomy.

Several modern cults and forms of therapy make use of what comes dangerously close to hyperventilation. They like to do ecstatic breathing and lots of oxygen (so do I) but they take it to the point where you have to ride a wave of dizziness, tingling limbs, head pressure, and be really careful not to suffer a blackout. This can damage the respiratory organs, it can also produce numbness, paralysis of the limbs, and a lot of cramps. Seated hyperventilation, followed by getting up suddenly can even knock you out. How much is too much?

Gentle Breathing. This is one of the methods of calming the mind by smooth breathing. It is quite easy and some, such as Swami Śivananda, claim that it is a preliminary exercise prior to real prāṇāyāma (which, as you can imagine, is supposed to be complicated breathing using various forms of rhythm and counting). Gentle breathing means that you breathe in without a sound. Excellent, when you listen closely to yourself being very silent, you'll gradually become more silent. Exhalation is as slow as possible (without straining yourself). You'll have a slow in-breath (inaudible breathing is never hasty) and a much slower out-breath. The latter, especially if you use full-breathing, will involve a steady tightening of your muscles as breath smoothly leaves your lungs. When you have fully exhaled, you just have to allow your abdominal muscles to relax slowly, and the in-breath will fill you naturally. In doing gentle breathing you do not hold your breath at any time. This practise is very useful to clear mind of emotional worries, it produces a smooth consciousness that has an almost ophidian quality. As you'll spend each in-breath listening to silence, inner voice activity will be reduced. You'll soon learn how slowly you may exhale in order to keep up an adequate supply of air. Too slow and your body will show strain. All in all, gentle breathing is not just a preliminary but something you can enjoy and come back to all through your life. It can induce interesting trance states and occasionally leads to light swaying and nodding. Allow it.

Minimal breathing. Some early Daoists, and a lot of early yogīs practised techniques that reduce the amount of breathing to a minimum. This was usually done while resting on the ground or a hard bed. The early Daoists called it 'foetal breathing' and assumed it might lead to an immortality of consciousness - what happened to their physical body was not always important to them. Foetal breathing is so soft that it can hardly be detected by an outside observer. The same thing was aimed for by a good many yogīs, who noticed that their meditation took on a special depth and clarity when breath was very shallow. There were attempts to produce this breathing by technique, but on the whole, technique tends to interfere with it. Light and shallow breathing happens naturally when you rest in a deep trance and your mind is busy elsewhere. I find it happening naturally when I introvert and descend into the cave of the heart, the void centre of all being. The same happens when I do astral projection and my body rests for an hour or two. It also happens in moments of deep insight, when the mind is really fascinated by something important. This does not mean that shallow and light breathing itself goes on for hours and hours, just as a resting body is not necessarily totally immobile. When you sleep, you move your body occasionally, and this is good for your health. People who do not move in their sleep, like alcoholics, tend to get problems with their blood circulation and may develop a characteristic paralysis of the limbs they sleep on. Shallow breathing is nice for a while. Body wants some fresh air from time to time, so allow it to take a few deep breaths on occasion to freshen up the lungs. Minimal breathing, when it happens naturally, has a calming and soothing effect. When you are tired it might send you to sleep. This is why the early Daoists did this in company. One person held watch while the other went trancing.

A pause in breathing. Whenever a rhythm shows a gap, you can discover something new. It happens in meditation, when you become aware of the pause between two thoughts, and expand it. It also happens in breathing practice. In yoga, the pause between breaths is termed kumbhaka. Kumbhaka is usually translated as holding breath, but the word really means 'vessel', such as a clay pot. Kumbhaka can occur at two times. You can pause after you have taken a breath, with your lungs full. This stimulates the sympathetic nervous system and may improve dynamic power and wakefulness. Or you can pause after exhaling, which stimulates the parasympathetic nervous system and tends to soothe and calm. In each case, the effect only happens when the pause is not forced but occurs gently and naturally. In practice, kumbhaka happens easiest when you practice full breathing. If you use your full lung capacity at the speed of your normal breathing, you will get an excess of air. This may be exciting, but it does not make for long trances or for a calm and tranquil state of mind. To make up for the excess of air, you will notice that body slows the breathing. One good way to do this is to pause a little between each breath. This is a natural and gentle thing. To quote Akashanath (1995): *...the yogī becomes aware of a slowing down towards the end of the out-breath, and a slow acceleration of the breathing during the first part of the in-breath. Eventually, a complete pause naturally occurs at the end of the out-breath, during which the body is completely still for the first time since birth, and when the mind and body are coherent. After this point is reached, the techniques tend to focus on various ways of extending this moment (through muscular control, use of drugs, mantra and sexual intercourse). This is pranayama proper. What many people, including Crowley, completely fail to grasp was that this can only be achieved by complete relaxation and total concentration, and cannot be forced in any way.* The pause in breathing is there to be enjoyed. It is a delicate moment of great peace and clarity. It can also last for a surprisingly long time, provided you simply enjoy the silence and wide minded wonder that happen naturally. Allowing such pauses to happen, you can turn full breathing (essentially a stimulating, dynamic activity) into a tranquil and calm trance of great intensity. Kumbhaka is not holding breath, it is allowing breath to pause effortlessly, a moment when time stops and mind returns to simplicity.

Let me mention something from an entirely different cultural setting. When you do kumbhaka, emptying the lungs well and holding for a while, the next breath will rush in naturally. This requires really good posture so breath can come in smoothly. It also requires care, as it should be done without forcing results. Now look at these lines by one of the Taliesins:

Which are the four elements.
Their end is not known.
What pigs, or what wandering of stags.
I salute thee, Bard of the border.
May he increase thee, (whose) bones (are of) mist.
(Where) two cataracts of wind fall.
(*Book of Taliesin* 7, trans. Skene)

I suspect that this might a reference to breathing exercise. There are several references to breathing in the songs of Taliesin, such as the line when the inspired seer inquires when the breath is black (*BoT*, 7), and even more material can be found in Irish lore. Regarding the meaning of this passage here are some of my intuitions. Of all the animals popular in Celtic lore, pigs and stags are most closely connected with the otherworlds. Both are well known to pass from this world to the other/s. The bard of the border stands between mundane reality and the otherworld (the Land of the Living). A common metaphor for the translation of consciousness between the worlds is the hedge of mists, well known from Irish Druidic sorceries and European folk lore. The bones are the trans-personal essence of a person, they feature prominently in Celtic burial rites; in *Cauldron of the Gods* I included material on phased burials involving corpses decaying in the open until some bones could be extracted and used for ritual exposure or burial. Bones are what remains when the person and the flesh have disappeared. The two cataracts of wind fall through the nostrils and through the windpipe where they divide again and go into the two lungs. The *falling* breath is important. You do not suck it in using strain and force but allow it to come naturally. Curiously, a text of the Huang Lao school found in the tomb of Mawangdui uses almost the same metaphor. The text *Ten Questions*, 4, proposes that during the morning meditation, exhalation should follow nature (i.e. without any effort or meddling of your conscious mind). The inhalation should fill the lungs as if the air was stored in a deep abyss (Cleary 1994). How much did the bards know about going to the otherworld using unusual forms of breathing?

Breathing in fixed intervals. This is part of the routine of many yogīc schools and constitutes what many believe to be prāṇāyāma. The idea behind classical prāṇāyāma is that you regularise the time of in-breath, holding, out-breath, and holding. Usually a steady rhythm was sought. Various traditions invented numerous rhythms and attributed a wide range of effects to them (B. K. S. Iyengar 1981). The timing was done by repeating mantras, usually the short bīja (seed) mantras, and by counting them with the help of a japamālā (rosary for the counting and offering of mantra). This combined japa (repetition of mantra) with breathing and produced interesting states of mind. Sadly, it is also a technique that can lead to a lot of unpleasant side effects. One common method to increase vital energy is given by the Devī in the *Devī Bhāgavatam*, 8, 35:

> *Taking in the breath by the Idâ (the left nostril) so long as we count 'Om' sixteen, retaining it in the Susumnâ as long as we count 'Om' sixty-four times and then exhaling it slowly by the Pingalâ nâdi (the right nostril) as long as we count 'Om' thirty-two times. This is called one Prânâyâma by those versed in the Yogas. Thus one should go on again and again with his Prânânâyâma. At the very beginning, try with the number twelve, i.e. as we count 'Om' twelve times and then increase the number gradually to sixteen and so on. (...) When this Prânâyâma is practised repeatedly, perspiration comes first when it is called of the lowest order; when the body begins to tremble, it is called middling; and when one rises up in the air, leaving the ground, it is called the best Prânâyâma.*

A very similar technique is recommended by Śiva in the *Mahānirvāṇa Tantra*. Here the count is on the Māyā bīja Hrīṁ, the only difference being the remark: *The doing of this thrice through the right and left nostrils alternately is called Prânâyâma.*

The *Kulacūḍāmaṇi Tantra* (trans. Louise Finn), a much older work, offers another version. 5, 47 gives the classical Kālī bīja Krīṁ, the most secret of secret. The bīja may be faulty (mantras can have numerous faults, see the chapter on mantra), i.e. it appears *asleep, drowsy, intoxicated, delusive and inclined away.* 48 suggests that these can be remedied by combining the bīja with the breath mantra (pallavam/Haṁsa). When reaching the end of the exhalation, known as *night worship, day worship and twilight worship* the bīja is recited. In real life, night worship is taking a breath through the left nostril (the īḍā, or moon channel), day worship is breathing through the right (piṅgalā or sun channel), and twilight worship is breathing through both nostrils at one. Note that this form of breathing is not identical with the method treated above. Night, day, and twilight worship are one breath each, ending with the mental recitation of Krīṁ.

Another technique from the *DB* (11, 1) identifies the mantra Oṁ (spelled AUM) with the three phases of inhalation (through the left nostril counting A thirty-two units for Viṣṇu), holding (count U sixty-four units for Śiva), and exhalation (M sixteen units through the right nostril for Brahmā). This practice is used as a preliminary to the raising of Kuṇḍalinī.

Breathing in intervals may sound nice and easy. This impression is misleading. Anyone who forces breath into a rigid rhythm, especially when it involves holding breath for such a formidable interval, is in grave danger of exploding. It is easier when the rhythm does not involve holding breath (one of my favourites is two units inhalation to eight units slow exhalation) but even this requires training if you want it to happen elegantly and without strain. Holding breath can make things a lot more difficult. Even when the units of time are reduced to a shorter rhythm, (the formula being 1:4:2 or 2:4:1) the whole thing is not without danger. Any sort of forced breathing can damage the body. If you have breathed deeply for a while, your body will be so saturated with oxygen that it may naturally get into long intervals of resting breath. Likewise, some trances naturally involve a cessation of breath from time to time. Making yourself do so on purpose and without preparation is a very different matter. In exercises that regulate breath according to fixed patterns, a guru well versed in emergency medicine is essential. Just remember the case of Victor Neuburg who was ordered to do complicated breathing at fixed intervals by Aleister Crowley, who was a brilliant magician but an inexperienced yogī. During the process Neuburg found his mouth filling with blood and, as his sister remarked, his health never fully recovered.

Dog-like panting. Not an exercise but a technique to raise body temperature. For this I am indebted to Dieter who learned it from Lama Anagarika Govinda. It can be very useful up in the mountains in winter. Pant as fast and shallow as a dog in summer. Use rapid belly breathing for it. Your belly should go in and out really fast, this heats the belly muscles which in turn generates heat for the whole system. Do it for a minute, then go easy and relax again. Rub your belly if you like and spread the joy and glow and happiness. Resume in a few minutes till you feel comfy and warm. Remember to do it only for very brief periods. This is one of the practices that makes use of mouth-breathing as the rate of exhalation and inhalation is too fast for the nose. To guard against the cold air, keep the mouth almost shut and the tongue against the palate. Visualise fire spreading out of your belly and through your body for amplification. Note: do not breathe through the mouth for long periods when the climate is cold and wet, as this may lead to bronchitis and other afflictions.

The Crow Beak. One of the favourite methods of Abhinavagupta. Discussing the vital breath that penetrates the entire being and merges in the form of the heart, Abhinavagupta introduces a form of breathing called the crow beak (Muller-Ortega 1989: 216). The idea is that you pursue your meditation in the heart with your lips pursed as if you wanted to kiss the entire manifest world. The position of the lips resembles the beak of the crow, hence the name, and produces *the enjoyment of an extremely cold taste, whose nature is the soma-moon and whose form is the condition of 'being' - and, 'being sealed in the navel', that is, having as limit the site of the navel by the practice of the absorption into the 'full pot', then the entire assemblage of mantra-s and mudrā-s are manifested in his body, which is then as if ruled by them.* Not easy to understand but worth contemplating in depth, that's Abhinavagupta for you.

The *Śiva Saṁhita* 69-83 has an easier explanation:

> *69. When the skilful Yogī, by placing the tongue at the root of the palate, can drink the Prâṇa vâyu, then there occurs complete dissolution of all Yogas (I.e., he is no longer in need of Yoga).*
> *70. When the skilful Yogī, knowing the laws of the action of Prâṇa and Apâna, can drink the cold air through the contraction of the mouth, in the form of a crow-bill, then he becomes entitled to liberation. Verse 71 recommends the crow bill in order to destroy fatigue, heat, fever, decay, and old age.*
> *72. Pointing the tongue upwards, when the Yogī can drink the nectar flowing from the moon (situated between the two eye-brows), within a month he certainly would conquer death.*
> *74. When he drinks the air through the crow-bill, both in the morning and evening twilight, contemplating that it goes to the mouth of the Kuṇḍalini, consumption of the lungs (phthisis) is cured. To continue, the crow beak destroys diseases, produces clairvoyance and clairaudience, frees from sins, makes the yogī a Bhairava, Kāmadeva frees from obstacles, hunger, thirst, and so on.*

Viloma. This technique, meaning literally 'against the hair' (against the natural flow), is based on interruption. Breath does not flow continuously but is interrupted repeatedly. There are several forms. In the basic form, the yogī relaxes in a comfortable posture, preferably lying on the back. In-breath happens slowly and gently, and is interrupted by a brief pause every two or three seconds. During these pauses, the belly remains still. The exhalation is slow and steady. The second type is to inhale in a smooth, slow flow and to interrupt the exhalation several times. The third variety is to interrupt both inhalation and exhalation. Each method should only be performed for five to ten minutes. Viloma should be gentle and pleasant. If you feel strained or uneasy something is wrong. After the exercise, rest for a few minutes and relax without interfering with breath in any way. In the fourth form, for well advanced yogīs, the method is coupled with prolonged kumbhaka and done sitting.

Breath and suggestion.

Let me tell you a story. As I mentioned in *Seidways*, I used to be an overexcited kid. When drawing exciting pictures (which I did lots of times, who cares about unexciting ones?) I used to get into states that set my body trembling, my imagination was often as vivid as 'real life', and at night I had plenty of nightmares. Then, one summer holiday with my grandmother Nena on the island Sylt, things changed enormously. One of my granny's friends was Dr. Gisela Eberlein, who had studied hypnosis under Dr. Schulz, the inventor of Autogenic Training. AT is one of the early forms of self-hypnosis and, like so many early things, it was full of crude and inelegant elements. Being such a nervous and wild-minded kid, the adults decided that some relaxation would do me good. So I became the first child she ever taught. I had to lie on a table, a rolled up blanket under my head, and she began suggesting. The first thing I learned was to speak to the parts of the body. She suggested I should imagine telephoning my arm, but this was not too efficient, as my arm was so close that speaking into it was much easier. Well, Autogenic Training makes use of some very simple suggestions which are repeated with a lot of monotony. Those were the days when hypnosis was based on endless, dull repetition. So, as I was breathing out, she slowly repeated 'your right arm is very heavy. Your hand is very heavy. Your muscles are heavy as lead. Very heavy. Everything is heavy...' This was done with all parts of the body. Sometimes she repeated the suggestions, then again she had me say them to myself in my inner voice. Nowadays few practitioners of autogenic training use Dr. Schulz's 'heavy like lead' any more. Thanks to pollution, lead has become a very negative concept, so it was replaced by 'heavy like stone'. Not too elegant either, isn't 'heavy' enough? Metaphors are tricky things. Lead is heavy but it is also toxic, stone is heavy but it is also hard. Good trancing shouldn't make you hard, hardness interferes with good relaxation. When you introduce metaphors, consider what they suggest apart from what you want.

The next stage, when body is really heavy and relaxed, was to suggest that the blood circulation and blood pressure are steady. 'Heart beats slow and steadily', 'blood pressure is even and steady', 'body is pleasantly warm' were typical suggestions. Then followed 'The solar plexus is radiantly warm' until I felt a wonderful glow saturating my torso. Then it was 'breath flows slow and steady', 'breath flows steady as the waves on the sea', 'it breathes me'. This was a good one, every day I sat on the beach and stared at the white foaming waves come thundering, surging, hissing, and licking over sand, shells, and tangled seaweed. It's not easy to breathe in the same rhythm. If you want a bit of extra fun at the seaside, give it a try. Some wave rhythms can be paced by a good breather, others cannot (depending on the weather). The basic training ended with the suggestion 'the brow is pleasantly cool'. By then I had become so wonderfully relaxed and warm that I felt totally at home. She left me in this state for a while. Luckily I did not get a treatment of Dr. Schulz's suggestions 'to build character' ('duty is pleasure', 'order is pleasure', 'my desk is tidy' etc.). Coming out of the trance consisted of speeding up the inner voice, making it sound interested and exciting. 'I come out of trance now. Body is lightweight, my breath goes faster, my body wakes up, my limbs move, I feel refreshed and wide awake.' This was accompanied by stretching the limbs and speeding up the breathing. Finally I was allowed to open my eyes, taking in an amazingly fresh and impressive new world, and getting up very slowly. We had these sessions over several weeks, coupled with other exercises, such as vowel song and deep breathing. By then I was using the method several times day, whenever I had a pause, did not know what to do, and while going to sleep, and she was beginning to teach other kids. Of course I was very curious about what else could be done. I kept asking her to hypnotise me, as I had read that hypnosis is something really exciting, she always said no, and then did it anyway. Of course I never noticed, as I expected hypnosis to be dramatic and to involve blackouts, loss of memory, and doing things against my will. Instead, I felt very much aware and in touch with myself in these trances. At home I read up on Dr. Schulz and began to invent my own suggestions.

The art of suggestion has come a really long way since then. In the old days, it was believed that 'the subconscious mind does not understand negations'. Studies over the last decades have clearly shown that this is not the case. It simply needs more time to process negations, and when suggestions are fast and involve a lot of negations, it can get confused about them.

Or it may get annoyed when suggestions are too boring. People who repeat the same dull suggestion to themselves hundreds of times may end up with a really annoyed deep mind.

Also, suggestions should remain in the range of possibilities. If you tell yourself 'my headache is gone' when this is plainly not true, it won't work. Instead, you will keep the headache on your mind and it will hurt more than ever. It's easier to suggest that body feels better with each breath (most of it actually does), that you relax, that muscles loosen, and to send a lot of attention into all those parts which do not suffer from a headache. It's amazing how well your feet and legs can feel while your head throbs. Send your attention there and spread this feeling upward to all other parts that do not hurt until the headache is confined to a tiny area. Or ignore the sense of feeling altogether and put attention into inner sound (voice or music) or images. Doze off and if you are lucky you will feel better when you come round again. This is even more important when you use suggestion for 'positive thinking'. Telling yourself that you are successful, popular, and sexy when this is simply not true will only produce delusion or frustration. Suggesting that you are LEARNING will get you a lot further. Avoid suggesting impossible states (I am X) and go for process (I am learning to X).

The old belief had it that suggestions should be short, direct, and brisk, many of them actually sounding like commands. Modern hypnotherapy uses more organic forms of speaking, meaning long sentences made up of short suggestions connected elegantly 'so as you listen you may notice that your body relaxes and your limbs feel warm and loose as you lie there and notice that while I speak you feel rested and enjoy the good feelings of your body as you let go and calm down and slow down and feel deeply refreshed as this is good and it is coming home to yourself...'. The old school believed in constant repetition of the same few suggestions, the new methods involve dozens of really artful forms of suggestion, direct, indirect, subconscious signalling, hidden emphasis, story telling, journeys in the imagination, and a lot of other joys. People differ, circumstances differ, and suggestions have to be adapted to the person who listens to them. Monotonous repetition of the same stuff may work occasionally with some people, but in the long run you will get a lot further when you introduce variation and play. If you wish to learn something really valuable, read and practice the brilliant *Tranceformations* by Bandler and Grinder, Richard Bandler's *Guide to Trance-formation* or study the works of Milton H. Erickson. I also recommend that you watch Richard doing hypnosis on DVD. It is a miraculous experience and a wonderful work of art.

What remained similar in old and new hypnosis is the use of breath. Ms. Eberlein used to give calming suggestions using a calm and soothing voice while I was exhaling. This is sound practice: while exhaling, the body tends to relax, while inhaling it tenses a little. If you wish to suggest something soothing, emphasise the outflow, if you suggest something exciting, use the inflow. The same thing applies to yoga: emphasising exhalation tends to soothe and sedate, emphasising inhalation tonifies and excites. To emphasise can mean that you put more attention into it, or that you prolong it, or make it congruent. To relax, put a sensation of 'letting go' into the out-breath; to excite, make the in-breath dynamic. Body becomes naturally heavier while you exhale and lighter as you inhale. Thus, when you suggest that your body feels heavy and relaxed on the exhalation, you are confirming what happens anyway. Of course this pattern needs not to be followed slavishly. It's inconvenient to suggest exclusively on the exhalation. A natural speech flow in a calm and soothing, slow voice that merely emphasises the exhalation is a lot more efficient. Nor does it always have to be slow and calm. Good trancing has its ups and downs like the motions of the waves. Trances can and should involve interesting, fascinating and exciting stuff from time to time, and on these occasions, you are wise to use an exciting and swift voice. Nor do suggestions have to remain on the level of spoken words.

A Chinese system of soothing breathing found in *The Method of Reading Silently* (Hu Bin 1982) has the practitioner write the characters of words such as 'silent and loose' in their minds while they exhale. Advanced practitioners can become extremely relaxed simply by thinking 'relax' while exhaling, and when I feel bored by suggestions I simply focus on the out-breath and enjoy to let go. When you use a mantra or vidyā instead of spoken suggestions, consider whether you wish to soothe or excite yourself and adapt it to the flow of your breath.

Finally, I should mention the little known fact that Autogenic Training is Dr. Schulz's adaptation of a Tantric system of meditation. Schulz developed his process over a decade and was not very clear about his sources. He did mention the Indian background and the fact that he had eliminated the religious elements of the practice. In some of his more scholarly works, there are references to yoga, śavāsana (the corpse posture), prāṇāyāma, the Kāpālika sect, and even attempts to introduce shamanism to the medical establishment. The combination of breath and suggestion has a long history in yoga. You can find the idea in the *Bṛhadāraṇyaka Upaniṣad* 1,5,23 where we learn that only one observance should be performed. *He should breathe in and breathe out wishing, 'Let not the evil of death get me.'* This process wins complete union with the deity. You may argue that the suggestion is formulated in a very negative way, i.e. you have to imagine what you do not want to happen, and then cancel it. This is too complicated. 'May the goodness of my life continue' is easier to imagine. Well, we are at the beginning of hypnotherapy here, maybe 800 BCE, and shouldn't blame the early pioneers for not getting everything right from the start. In Autogenic Training, the monotonous and unchanging repetition of the same suggestions has its roots in mantra-yoga. The suggestions of heaviness correspond to pṛthvī (earth); the blood flow to āp (water); the warm solar plexus to agni (fire); the sensation of 'it breathes me' to vāyu (air); and the slightly cool brow to ākāśa (spirit/space). The sequence of suggestions follows an Indian system of occult anatomy, which places earth in legs and perineum, water in the belly, fire in the chest, air in shoulders and throat, and spirit in the head. The cool brow was originally supposed to activate the third eye but Dr. Schulz eliminated that. I should add that the brow should be only slightly cool. My grandfather used to be very interested in oriental philosophy. Once he experimented with Autogenic Training on my mother who was still a child. He got it wrong and suggested 'your brow is cold', which made her faint. Sometimes good intentions are simply not enough.

Prāṇa in Antiquity

The early Upaniṣadic period, around the eighth and seventh century BCE, provides us with the first attempts to define the role of prāṇa in religion, consciousness, and meditation. It was a magnificent time for really complicated cosmology and subtle texts alluding cautiously to ritual practices and meditations with hardly a clear word among them. What is lacking in conciseness, however, was made up by repetition of lines and by creative interpretation expected from students and sages. After all, the prime function of an obscure text is to make you think for yourself. At this early age, prāṇa had become a central concept of philosophy and life. The idea of prāṇa goes a long way beyond 'breath' or 'life energy'. The prāṇa of the *Upaniṣads* is also the force behind the senses, and the senses, as I'm sure you already guessed, happen to be deities. It is prāṇa which gives life to the senses, and these in turn make body and intelligence possible. A bit of practical experience with various breathing techniques will soon reveal that breathing does indeed alter sensual perception. The senses, however, do not entirely correspond to the five senses that Aristotle defined. Some flexible thinking is required here. As you are by now hopefully delighting in breathing exercises every day I would like to add some of the fascinating ideas that may get you beyond the realms of mere breathing and vitality into magickal and philosophical spaces really worth exploring. Let me sum up some ideas from the *Kauṣītakī Upaniṣad* 2, 1-3, 4 (trans. Radhakrishna, 1953).

The breathing spirit is Brahmā. Brahmā's messenger is the mind, the protector is the eye, the ear is the announcer, and speech is the keeper of the house. It is possible to become obsessed by any of these. The breathing spirit, Brahmā, receives offerings from his servants, the deities mind, eye, ear, and speech, though he never begs for them, thus, the prime lesson is 'Do not beg' for there are always those good enough to give without being asked. The divinities come in a certain order, which leads gradually to refinement. First comes speech, behind speech the eye, behind the eye the ear, and behind the ear the mind and behind the mind the breath (prāṇa). The text gives a multipurpose rite to obtain results: the highest treasure can be obtained in the night of a full or new moon or in any night of the bright fortnight provided there is an auspicious constellation. The ritualist sweeps the ground, strews sacred grass, sprinkles water, builds a fire, and bends a knee while offering oblations of ghī (melted butter), saying : '*The divinity named speech is the attainer. May it obtain this for me from him. Hail to it.*' These lines are repeated inserting the names 'breath', 'eye', 'ear', 'mind' and finally 'wisdom'. Then the ritualist smears the limbs with the ointment of melted butter, inhales the smoke, declare the wish, and goes forth in silence. As you can see the order of the divinities does not agree with their earlier appearance, can you detect or invent a reason? The same ritual is used to become dear to any woman or man. The phrase to repeat is: '*Your speech I sacrifice in me, hail to you.*' Speech is replaced by breath in the next repetition and so on. Then one only has to stand close to the person, preferably from windward, and success is ensured. Our text goes on to explain that when you speak, you cannot breathe (properly), thus you are sacrificing breath. When you breathe (properly) you are unable to speak, this means sacrificing speech. One or the other are always being sacrificed at any moment of your life, they are the unending immortal oblations which are always offered, whether you are waking or sleeping. Unlike other sacrifices, which have a beginning and ending, these two are continuous.

Brahman, we learn, lives when the fire burns and dies when it is extinguished, then its light goes to the sun, and its breath to the vital breath. The same goes for the sun, which returns its light to the moon, the moon dies and its light goes to lightning, and the light of lightning, in its dying, returns to the regions of space. Though all this speaks of Brahman's dying, all these things do not really die when they enter the vital wind, but come forth again. Next, Brahman shines forth when one speaks, when one speaks not, Brahman dies and its light goes to the eye and its vital breath to the wind. When the eye sees, Brahman shines forth, but dies when one sees not, thus the light of the eye returns to the ear and its vital breath to the wind. Hearing makes Brahman shine forth, not-hearing makes the light go to the mind and its vital breath to the wind. Brahman thrives when the mind is thinking but dies when thought ceases and its light goes to the vital breath, like its vital breath goes to the vital breath. And though they all die in the process, they are not really dead but come forth again. Confused? This is clearly a process of meditation, there is a progression towards simplicity until consciousness returns to the non-defined vital breath. The next discipline is a little obscure. If I interpret it properly, it has the ritualist lying un-breathing like a rotten log of wood. A process akin to astral projection (travelling in the imagination) seems to be implied: First, breath disappeared (or seemed to, a case of minimal breathing) from body, next mind went, then the ear, the eye, and finally speech. This is the pattern of dissolution, it resembles the process of death. In its reversed form the text tells us how to come to life again: first, speech enters into body, and body lies speaking with speech (hypnotic suggestion?). Next the eye comes along, and body speaks and sees. Then follows the ear, body speaks, sees, and hears. Mind follows, so body speaks, sees, hears, and thinks. Finally, the vital breath comes in and body arises at once. In between the two phases comes the actual journey:

> *All the divinities, verily, having recognised the superior excellence of the vital breath, having comprehended the vital breath alone as the seat of intelligence, went forth from this body, all these together. They, having entered into the air, having the nature of space went to the heavenly world. The sage who knows this can travel on the vital breath. He goes to the place where the gods are. Having reached that, he who knows this becomes immortal as the gods are immortal.*

Another rite follows during which the dying or seriously disabled father invests his son with speech, vital breath, eye, ear, food, pleasure, pain, wisdom, mind, and a lot of other blessings to transmit the tradition. Should death ensue, a good funeral is assured, if not the father has to live under the authority of the son or leave the house to become a wandering ascetic. No doubt this rite was only performed when death was really imminent. To confuse things a little, the next sections disagrees with the beginning by telling us that it is Indra, not Brahman, who is actually the breathing spirit. This can only come as a surprise to those who believe in specific gods with sharply defined functions, anybody acquainted with Indian thought will only give a brief sigh and read on. Indra said:

> *I am the breathing spirit, meditate on me as the intelligent self, as life, as immortality. Life is breath and breath is life... with the breathing spirit one obtains immortality in this world, by intelligence true conception... the vital breaths, verily, go into a oneness, (otherwise) no one would be able, at once, to make known a name by speech, a form by the eye, a sound by the ear, a thought by the mind... while speech speaks, all the vital breaths speak after it. While the eye sees all, the vital breaths see after it. While the ear hears, all the vital breaths hear after it. When the breath breathes, all the vital breaths breathe after it.*
> (3, 2 Radhakrishna 1953)

This doctrine is developed at some length and I am sure you are happy to read it for yourself. Suffice it to say that speech produces all names, breath all odours, the eye all forms, the ear all sounds, and the mind all thoughts. These constitute the totality of experience, and the driving sentience and force between these divinities of the senses is prāṇa, vital breath. The *Chāndogya Upanishad* (3, 13, 1-6) expands this scope of concepts by aligning the breaths with the directions. At the time, the concept of the heart as a hollow space within the centre, seat of the soul, was well developed. The heart has five openings for the gods:

In the **east** is the up-breath (prāṇa), the eye and the sun, which should be meditated upon as glow and health.

In the **south** is the diffused breath (vyāna), the ear and the moon, meditate on them as prosperity and fame.

In the **west** is the downward breath (apāna), speech and fire, meditate on them as the lustre of sacred wisdom and health.

In the **north** there is equalised breath (samāna), the mind and rain, meditate on them as fame and beauty.

Above is the out-breath (udāna), air and space. Meditate on them as strength and greatness.

These are known as the Five Brahma-persons, the doorkeepers of the world of heaven. By meditating on the five, their qualities are attained. And so they should be. Even reading such complicated stuff should improve your karman no end.

Classical prāṇāyāma

When we explore the early teachings of yoga, we encounter a wide range of breathing techniques. Sadly, most of the early pioneers of Yoga did not bother to give many details. Thus, we find only a few bare bones in Patañjali's famous treatise. His comments on prāṇāyāma are so brief that you have to know what he knows to understand what he's talking about:

1,33. Mind attains peace by associating with the happy, pitying the miserable, appreciating the virtuous, and avoiding the vicious.

1,34. Also by expulsion and retention of breath.

2,49. The next step is prāṇāyāma, the cessation of exhalation and inhalation.

2,50. Exhalation, inhalation, cessation of breath, may be short or long, according to length, duration and number of breaths.

2,51. A fourth method of breathing is that which is determined by a uniform external or internal measure.

This is not exactly helpful. Luckily, other authors supplied more details. To give you an idea of what these techniques include I shall give a brief summary of the eight basic methods of kumbhaka listed in the *Gheraṇḍa Saṁhita*. These are classical techniques which appear with some regularity in a good many Tantric and yogīc treatises. Of course there are also plenty of variations. The texts are not always very clear, quite understandable as the author/s assumed that any reader would practice with the help of an experienced guru. Please understand that the technical descriptions are not complete and that such exhausting techniques require the presence of a skilled teacher. Do not practice these methods on your own!

1. **Sahita** (with in-and out-breath). Seated towards the north or east, the image of Brahmā full of bright red rajas is visualised in the shape of the letter A. Inhalation is through the left nostril while sixteen A-bījas are repeated. At the end of in-breath, the uḍḍīyana-Bandha is performed. Then Hari (Viṣṇu) is visualised full of sattva in the shape of letter U while the U-bīja is repeated sixty-four times. While exhaling through the right nostril, Śiva full of tamas but of white colour is visualised as the letter ṁ, the ṁ-bīja is repeated thirty-two times. The nostrils are traditionally closed by using thumb and ring- or little finger. The exercise can also be done without counting bījas by circling the palm of the left hand around the knee the required number of times. The result of this method is first sweating, then trembling, and finally levitation.

2. **Sūryabheda** (penetration of the sun). In-breath through the right (solar) nostril, assume jālandhara mudra, and hold until sweat runs down your hair and hands. This is supposed to excite the vāyus (winds) and to wake body. The vāyus are focused around the root of the navel. Hard and uninterrupted exhalation through the left nostril follows.

3. **Ujjāyī** (conquering). Breath is inhaled through both nostrils into the mouth, where it is compressed. This description is hardly clear, but the *Yogabīja* adds that a sound should be made while inhaling (in between snoring, buzzing, and singing) which prolongs inhalation. The

technique is supposed to clear the phlegm out of the lungs and to conquer death.

4. **Sītalī** (cooling). Inhale through the rolled up tongue, fill the lungs slowly (use belly-breathing), hold for a while and exhale through both nostrils. This is supposed to cool the yogī. Note that the ability to roll the tongue is a genetic gift, part of the population cannot do it.

5. **Bhastrikā** (bellows). Gently but swiftly breathe in and out through both nostrils without pause. After twenty repetitions hold breath. Repeat three times, this is supposed to destroy all diseases.

6. **Bhrāhmarī** (like bees). Practice at night in silence (not very likely in India). Close the ears and hold breath. Listen for the following sounds in your right ear: crickets, flute, thunder, drum, bee, bell, gong, trumpet, horn, various drums, and the like. All of these are expressions of the heart sound, the sound that is not produced by striking. In their sound is light and consciousness dissolves in it. This practice eventually reduces breathing to a minimum, as it is very hard to listen to fine internal sounds when the lungs are doing their job.

7. **Mūrcchā** (to faint). Consciousness is centred between the eyebrows and breath is held effortlessly and without strain (sukhena). According to some, this is done until one is really close to fainting. The other interpretation points out that holding breath gently is not the sort of thing that leads to loss of consciousness. Patañjali (1,34) hints that the real thing is to exhale very thoroughly and to hold breath.

8. **Kevalī** (exclusively holding). Inhalation is through both nostrils. Mind is focused on the ajapā mantra Haṁsa. The force of breathing is reduced. Force is measured as distance at which the exhalation is still perceivable. When resting, breath is supposed to extend twelve fingers, while making love thirty-six fingers, during physical work even more. The idea behind these measures is that life-energy is lost when the breath extends far, and conserved when it extends very little. To keep breath within body is to conquer death. In a very difficult passage, we learn that the amount of ajapā mantras (i.e. breaths) is doubled. The yogī practices to hold breath for sixty-four units of time. This is repeated every three hours until the kumbhaka lasts for 5 x 64 units. This is supposed to produce the unmanī state, i.e. exaltation of consciousness. The text is very difficult and the technique has seen several widely different interpretations. One interpretation proposes that the amount of breaths is doubled, leading to very fast breathing. Maybe this comes from the meaning of unmanā in modern Hindi, where it is primarily used for restless, scatterbrained, and absentminded states. In older texts, unmanī is considered a synonym for samādhi, i.e. for the highest trances possible. This interpretation proposes that breathing is slowed so much

that in-breath and out-breath practically become kumbhaka, as there is always air within the lungs which does not move very much. For a detailed treatment of these methods see Sacharow 1954.

8: Mantra

A World of Vibration

Mantra yoga is the art and science of using sound, vibration, rhythm, breath, melody, and words to effect changes in consciousness. The word mantra means *liberation by thought.* According to the etymology chapter in the *Kulārṇava Tantra* (Pandit 1984), the word consists of Ma from manana (thinking, meditation) *on the luminous deity who is the form of Truth* and tra from trāyate (to save), meaning liberation from bondage to the world of phenomena. Thus, a mantra is something thought to attain liberation. This is not very reliable etymology, but it makes a lot of sense. The *Gāyatrī Tantra*, quoted by Woodroffe (1979) tells us: *...that is called Mantra, by the meditation on which the Jīva acquires freedom from sin, enjoyment of heaven and Liberation and by the aid of which he attains in full the four-fold fruit.* A mantra can be a word, a meaningful phrase, a magic spell, a sound-pattern, a name of a deity, and the deity itself. Mantra is all of these, and much more. It can be a tool to invoke, to calm, to excite, to banish, to focus, to offer, to manifest, and to purify. This does not mean that mantra is only a tool. It is one of the essentials in mantra yoga that the mantra is very much alive. As primal sound (śabda) arises from Brahman, all mantras are manifestations of consciousness itself. Think of them as a forms of Kuṇḍalinī-Śakti, the force and sentience that manifests the worlds. Each mantra has a Śakti, which is the deity who manifest in the vibration. In this sense, mantra is not only a device to contact a given deity but a manifestation of that deity in its body-of-sound.

In general, a mantra is practised in three ways.

Recitation

Vācika Japa: loud recitation. This can be useful in the beginning of a ritual, especially when the sound vibration is refined by over- or undertone singing. Vibrating a mantra aloud can be useful to clear the mind and to induce a new consciousness. It can also be a great start when you want to learn a new mantra. This is especially the case when you happen to feel shy about it. Loud vibration affects the physical universe. It can be heard by others, including neighbours, and so the wise know when and where to do it. To sing a mantra aloud needs determination, any sort of 'foolish' behaviour in public does. Are you up to it? Do you really care about the deities your mantra is to evoke? Do you dare to experience them in the flesh, the world, the manifest universe?

It can also happen that mantra becomes loud during a trance. Here the sound-body of the deity wishes to emerge, to release, and to earth itself. It manifests the sentience of a deity (your sentience) and releases all the fierce energy into the wonderful wide world. Vibrating a mantra aloud a few minutes to sense its vibration on the physical plane is a lot more efficient than singing it for hours. If you keep vibrating it physically, a lot of your awareness will be tied up in the physical act of chanting, which may make it harder to turn inward and realise. For this reason many gurus frown on extended loud recitation. And for reasons of secrecy, of course.

Upāṁsu Japa: whispered recitation. Whispering is considered more refined than loud chanting, especially when the whispering gradually goes silent and only the lips move. This sort of practice has a remarkable in-between quality, it is partly physical and partly in the imagination. As you whisper, watch your tonality. Does it sound exciting? Whispering often does. Quite early in life, you learned to associate whispering with secrets, hidden communication, and the dangers of being discovered. A whispered mantra can be very exciting when it is whispered in precisely the right way. Give yourself a treat and do it. Then try an unexciting tonality. What makes the crucial difference? What turns you on? Make it sound alluring. Make it sound dramatic. How can you whisper your mantra so that it sounds soothing? There are many ways to whisper. Experiment!

Mānasa Japa: mental recitation. The subtle form is to vibrate a mantra entirely in the imagination. This is favoured for prolonged repetition, especially when you move among people and want to avoid being locked up. In many Tantric traditions it is also preferred as a lot of mantras are thought to be highly secret. This involves a curious paradox. Traditionally, worshippers used to receive a mantra from a guru or directly from a deity, if they were among the more inspired sort, and this mantra was assumed to be extremely powerful. If it were to become known, it would be liable to be abused by anybody who chanced to hear it. Other schools claim that revealing a mantra exhausts its power; a worshipper who reveals the mantra necessarily needs a new one, please consult your local guru. Learning a mantra from a book is damned by some Tantras, such as the *Kulārṇava Tantra*: using a mantra heard by chance leads to disaster, while getting it from a book is to commit a sin tantamount to Brahmanicide.

Nevertheless, the good book gives numerous mantras in code. It specially emphasises the importance of one mantra, the famous Haṁsa, which is not really a mantra but the sound of out-breath and in-breath. Other sources reveal mantras in plain language on every page, just look into the magnificent *Mantramahodadhiḥ*. How secret should a mantra be? I wouldn't recommend that you tell your favourite mantras to anyone who comes your way, but insisting on absolute secrecy, when all the secrets have been revealed time and time again, seems totally absurd.

Just consider how paradoxical it is. The belief that only mantras given by gods or gurus work contrasts sharply with the idea that any chance hearer could make use of them. It also disagrees with those practitioners who found their mantras in elder texts. The earlier Tantric texts, and it should be kept in mind that what survives of Tantra is first of all a literary tradition, gave mantras in full. Perhaps their authors were aware that a mantra, and the deity it manifests, are not liable to be abused by any power-hungry loony. Perhaps they were not paranoid enough to make such a fuss. Later texts are usually more secretive and give mantras in complicated codes and ciphers. This ensured that only well-read clever folk, or worshippers with a well-informed guru, have a chance to decipher them. All of this sounds as if a mantra were power ready for use. This, however, is not the case. An image of a deity is not the deity, and the mantra is exactly an image. When used by the uninspired, it is a form resembling something which it evidently isn't. A statue, an image, and a mantra have to be woken. Unless you happens to be in a very inspired state, shaking in the joy of Śaktipāta or deep within the trance/awareness of the heart, such a process may take days, weeks, or months. Merely repeating a phrase is not enough. A mantra is neither a 'word of power' nor a bit of mental chewing-gum. It has to be filled with ojas, with vibrant vitality, with joy, meaning, and your very own life essence before it can work its magic on your mind and world.

A Structure of Mantras

The choice of a mantra used to be an extremely important occasion. As could have been expected, a good many traditions made a great fuss about the matter. This starts with the attempt to impose a pattern on the various varieties. In general, mantras are divided into several categories. Technically speaking, when a mantra is considered masculine or neuter, it usually ends with the exclamation hūṁ or 'phat!' Neutral mantra end with namah. The female and lunar mantras are called vidyā (science, magical knowledge, wisdom), you can recognise them as many of them end with the word svāhā (*Kulārṇava Tantra* 16, 40-41). As vidyās are incarnate goddesses, they are sometimes called Śaktis or young women. *Kulacūḍāmaṇi Tantra*, 5, 51 states that by meditation on young women, siddhis arise, an ambiguous reference to the recitation of a vidyā, to meditation on a young woman, goddess, or spirit, or both.

So we read of male, female, and neutral mantras. Of course there are lots of exceptions to these rules, there always are, especially when it comes to something as stupid as attributing gender to deities. Mantras are further classed according to their length (according to the *Nityā Tantra*), a one syllable mantra is called a 'pinda' or 'bīja' (seed), those with three syllables 'kartarī', four to nine syllables 'bīja', ten to twenty syllables 'mantra', and more than twenty syllables 'mālā' (garland). Traditionally, there are several methods how a guru selects a mantra for the disciple. The easiest is to pick the mantra of the personal deity of the devotee. If that deity is unknown, popular choices are the deities of the guru's tradition, or deities associated with the worshippers family, clan, social class, occupation, village, or district. Last there were several highly esoteric methods. There are diagrams that order the phonemes according to the zodiac, to the tattvas (principles), 'elements', and similar models. You start by finding the first letter of the disciples name. The group of sounds it appears in is usually beneficial. Other groups are considered friendly, neutral, or hostile. Mantras starting with a friendly phoneme were preferred. Such systems are elaborated in the *Kulārṇava Tantra* and in the *Mantramahodhadhiḥ*. Personally I think that a guru who has to resort to such devices isn't very competent or is simply ignorant of the nature of the student. Nowadays, with all the mass-marked spirituality sold by charismatic gurus to bedazzled Westerners, such tactics are more popular than ever. In earlier periods gurus were happy to have only a few, selected, and capable students. Modern gurus often have so many students that they can't know them all personally.

How do you integrate the mantra vibration in your body? Some sects take the easy way. When you vibrate the mantra of a deity, you merge yourself in its vibration, which forms a sphere of energy/sentience around you. Those who worship in a dualist context feel themselves pervaded by the divine vibration. Those who prefer a non-dual approach become the deity of the mantra. They superimpose the divine shape on their own body and reinforce the union with nyāsa. Using touch, sound and visualisation, the deity is brought to dwell within the living flesh. Some experience a shift in awareness, others begin to sway slightly. There are also folks who 'get vibration' and start to tremble and shake, this usually leads to obsession and all sorts of fun activities.

The complicated approach is favoured by some sects who make a whole science of mantra yoga. In their teaching, it is not enough to know the deity and the mantra to get going. You also have to know a number of divine personages who are related to the mantra and who are placed in various spots of the body by nyāsa. Usually, a mantra comes together with viniyoga. Viniyoga looks like another mantra, but it is really a set of instructions about how to handle the mantra. Each mantra has a ṛṣi (seer), a chanda (metre), a devatā (deity), a bīja (seed-phoneme), and a Śakti (energy/form). The ṛṣi is the seer who received the mantra from the deity (usually Śiva). As the ṛṣi is the guru of the mantra s/he is placed on your head. The metre is the pronunciation, rhythm, vibration pattern, and melody of the phonemes. It is placed on your mouth. The devatā is the deity of the mantra and its life-principle. It is placed on the heart, in the centre of your being. Theoretically this means that you pronounce the deity's name and touch your heart. If you want a really thorough experience, wake the deity when your awareness has withdrawn from the world and your body, and comes to rest as pure consciousness in the empty core of yourself. This is not the heart as the physical organ nor is it a cakra. The heart of your reality-cluster is a cave where your true self (pure consciousness) engages in loveplay with all body, form, and energy. Within the heart, the deity comes to life and the mantra awakes. You wake the mantra by being inside the cave of the heart with it. More on this in the next chapter. The bīja is the seed that makes the mantra efficient. It is usually a 'meaningless' sound pattern that speaks directly to the deep within. It is placed on the genitals. The Śakti is the energy/form of the mantra. It empowers the mantra and manifests its effects. It is placed on the feet. As this book aims at making complicated things simple, I have omitted these aspects of mantra lore. You can find them, with all the flowery elaboration of many long traditions, in the *Mantramahodhadhiḥ* and similar works.

Viniyoga also tells you what the mantra is good for. Much of the art of mantra yoga aims at specific goals. There is a vast body of literature relating how to recite mantras, using gestures, diagrams (yantras), special offerings, ritual acts etc. to achieve very specific results. Such texts are rarely concerned with pure love, devotion, or a desire for liberation. Much more common is the desire to gain magical powers (siddhi), wealth, health, and absolution of sins, or to effect specific sorceries. Such rites are not only performed with proper mantras. Vedic hymns, verses from holy books, and the like can be recited a specific number of times for purposes of result magic. The japa (recitation) is a highly complex ritual. The yogī has to withdraw from society, friends, family, and acquaintances. Only sacred food may be eaten, three baths a day are a must, and internal purity (of manners, mind, emotions, thoughts) must be observed. Any lapse into ordinary behaviour or thinking results in the abortion of the entire ritual. Usually rites for the fulfilment of desires or the acquisition of siddhis take several days, sometimes weeks or months, and involve the daily recitation of a hundred thousand mantras. As you can see, mantra yoga is a lot more than simply repeating a few exotic words.

Svāhā

A mantra or vidyā is the subtle manifestation of a deity or abstract force in the realm of vibration. An example: The goddess Svāhā appears early in Vedic literature, she is the wife of the sacrificial fire (Agni) and the force that conducts the sacrifice to the gods. The vidyā 'svāhā' is called the 'two Thas' (two moons. The letter Tha, sounding like an aspirated t, is the moon letter). Much later, the *Devī Bhāgavatam* makes a long story out of this. Once the gods went to Brahmā's council to decide about the food-question and the offerings they wanted to receive. As they complained, none of the ghī (clarified butter) poured into the sacrificial fire reached them. Brahmā meditated on this and took refuge in Kṛṣṇa. Kṛṣṇa advised that Brahmā should worship Mūla Prakṛti (Root-Primal-Nature), and as Brahmā did so, a beautiful blue goddess arose from Prakṛti whose name was Svāhā. She asked Brahmā his desire, and Brahmā replied:

> *O Devī! Let Thou be the burning power of Fire, without Thee Fire would not be able to burn anything. At the conclusion of any Mantra, whoever taking Thy name, will pour oblations in the Fire to the Gods, will cause those oblations to go to the Gods and reach them. And then they will be very glad. O Mother! Let Thou be the wealth of Fire, the beauty and housewife of Fire; let Thou*

be incessantly worshipped in the regions of the Gods and among men and beings. (9, 43)

Now Svāhā, once born, decided to worship Kṛṣṇa, and performed extreme austerities, such as standing on one leg for ages, until Kṛṣṇa appeared and told her that she should marry Fire (Agni). Brahmā ordered Fire to go and worship her on a Salagrāma stone (a petrified ammonite) or on an earthenware jar, and though Fire was a doubtful worshipper at first, things soon improved and the new couple enjoyed a fit of one hundred divine years of lovemaking. By then she was about to give birth and her vidyā had acquired so much power that all the other mantras became as feeble as snakes without poison unless her name was joined to them. Her vidyā had become the very epitome of success and was uttered at the end of ceremonies *with the expectation of getting the desired fruits.* Her mūla (root) mantra is

Oṁ Hrīṁ Srīṁ Vahnijāyāyai Devyai Svāhā

and her sixteen names are: 1. Svāhā, 2. Beloved of Fire, 3. Wife of Fire, 4. All-Pleasing, 5. Śaktî, 6. Action, 7. Bestower of Kāla (time), 8. Digester of Food, 9. Dhruvā, 10. Resort of Men, 11. Burning Power, 12. Burner of Everything, 13. Essence of this World, 14. Deliverer from the Terrible World, 15. Life of the Gods, 16. Nourisher of the Gods. Who reads (recites) these names with devotion gets success in this world and the next. I wonder whether the sixteen names of the 'two moons' relate to the sixteen kalās of the moon. Think about it.

A Choice of Mantras

What follows is a selection of mantras from the *Mantramahodhadhiḥ* :

Agni mantra: **Vaiśvānara Jātaveda ihāvaha lohitākṣa sarva-karmāṇi sādhaya svāhā.**

Mantras of Brahmā the creator: **Oṁ Brahmaṇe namaḥ**. **Oṁ namo Brahmaṇe**.

Mantra of Bṛhaspati, guru and priest of the gods: **Bṛṁ Bṛhaspataye namaḥ.**

Mantra of the river Gaṅgā stationed in the head of Śiva**: Oṁ namaḥ Śivāyai Nārāyaṇyai daśaharāyai gaṇgāyai svāhā**.

Gaṅgā mantra: **Aiṁ hili hili mili mili gaṅge māṁ pāvaya pāvaya svāhā.**

Mantras of Gaṇeśa, the elephant-headed destroyer of obstacles :

Oṁ śrīṁ hrīṁ klīṁ glauṁ gaṁ Gaṇapataye vara varada sarvajane mevaśa mānaya svāhā. Vakratuṇḍāya huṁ. Medholkāya svāhā. Hasti piśāci-likhe-svāhā. Gaṁ hasti-piśāci-likhe-svāhā.

Oṁ namaḥ ucchiṣṭa gaṇeśāya hasti-piśāci-likhe-svāhā. Oṁ hrīṁ grīṁ hrīṁ.

A mantra of Hanumān, the monkey god, son of the wind god, agitator of the three worlds:

Hauṁ hsphreṁ khphreṁ hsrauṁ hskhphreṁ hsauṁ hanumate namah.

Kālī mantras: see the chapter titled 'Kālī's Kula' later on in this book.

Mantra of Kulasundarī, the sweet one of the Kulas: **Aiṁ klīṁ sauḥ**.

Kubera mantra bestowing wealth and prosperity: **Yakṣāya kuberāya vaiśravaṇāya dhana dhānyādhipataye dhana dhānya saṁṛddhiṁ me dehi dāpaya svāhā.**

Mantra of Lakṣmī: **Oṁ śrīṁ hrīṁ śrīṁ kamale kamalālaye prasidā prasidā śrīṁ hrīṁ śrīṁ oṁ Mahālakṣmyai namaḥ.**

Mantras of the Mahāvidyās: see the later chapter on the topic.

Eight Mātṛkās:

Oṁ braṁ Brahmāṇyai namaḥ. Oṁ māṁ Māheśvaryai namaḥ. Oṁ kauṁ Kaumāryai namaḥ. Oṁ vaiṁ Vaiṣṇavyai namaḥ. Oṁ vāṁ Vārāhyai namaḥ. Oṁ nāṁ Nārasiṁhyai namaḥ. Oṁ aiṁ Aindrayai namaḥ. Oṁ cāṁ Cāmuṇḍayai namaḥ.

Mantra of Pārvatī, the daughter of the mountains: **Hrīṁ Pārvatyai namaḥ**.

Pārvatī about to marry Śiva: **Oṁ hrīṁ yogīni yogīni yogeśvari yogeśvari yogabhyaṁkari sakala sthāvara-jaṅgamasya mukhaṁ hṛdayaṁ mama vaśamākarṣayā-karṣaya svāhā.**

Mantras of Prāṇa Śakti: **Oṁ āṁ hrīṁ krauṁ yaṁ raṁ laṁ vaṁ śaṁ ṣaṁ saṁ hoṁ oṁ kṣaṁ saṁ haṁsaḥ hrīṁ oṁ haṁsaḥ mama prāṇā iha prāṇāḥ.**

Oṁ kṣaṁ saṁ haṁsaḥ hrīṁ oṁ.

The three Śaktis Iccha (will), Jñāna (wisdom) and Kriyā (action): **Oṁ hāṁ Icchāśaktiyai namaḥ, Oṁ hīṁ Jñānaśaktiyai namaḥ, Oṁ hūṁ Kriyāśaktiyai namaḥ.**

Śiva mantras:

Death-conquering Mṛtyuñjaya mantra: **Oṁ jūṁ saḥ**.

To assume the form of Rudra: **Oṁ namo bhagavate Rudrāya. Oṁ Rudrāya namaḥ.**

Kumāra mantra for the worship of liṅga: **Aīṁ hūṁ kṣuṁ klīṁ Kumārāya namaḥ**.

Sadāśiva (Eternal Śiva) mantra: **Oṁ namaḥ Śivāya**.

Mahādeva (Great God) mantra: **Oṁ namo Mahādevāya**.

Hara (Destroyer) mantra: **Oṁ namo Harāya**.

Mantra of red Sumukhī-Devī who sits on a corpse, holding a skull: **Ucchiṣṭa cāṇḍālini Sumukhi Devi mahāpiśācini hrīṁ ṭhaḥ ṭhaḥ ṭhaḥ**.

Mantras of sun-god Sūrya: **Oṁ hrīṁ ghṛṇih sūrya ādityaḥ śrīṁ. Oṁ Sūryāya namaḥ.**

Mantra of white Svapneśvarī, the devī who gives dream-oracles: **Oṁ śrīṁ svapneśvari kāryaṁ me vada svāhā**.

Mantras of Viṣṇu, maintainer of the worlds:

Hriṁ Kṣrauṁ Hrīṁ.

Oṁ Kṣrauṁ Oṁ.

Nṛsiṁha (Lion-Man) mantra which destroys all fears: **Jaya Jaya Śrīnṛsiṁha**.

Gopāla mantra for worldly happiness and emancipation: (**Klīṁ**) **Gopījanavallabāaya svāhā**.

The wish-fulfilling Govinda mantra: **Klīṁ hṛṣīkeśāya namaḥ**.

Kṛṣṇa mantras: **Śrīṁ hrīṁ klīṁ Kṛṣṇāya svāhā.**

Klīṁ govallabhāya svāhā. Klīṁ Kṛṣṇa klīṁ.

The poison-destroying Garuḍa mantra: **Kṣipa oṁ svāhā**.

Mantras of the wish-fulfilling Vaṭa-Yakṣiṇī abiding in the depth of the forest:

Ehyehi yakṣi yakṣi mahāyakṣi vaṭa vṛkṣanivāsini śighraṁ me sarvasukhyaṁ kuru kuru svāhā.

Śrīṁ śrīṁ Yakṣiṇī haṁ haṁ haṁ svāhā.

Yama Dharmarāja mantra which destroys misery, saves from hell and dissolves the fear of enemies**: Oṁ kroṁ hrīṁ āṁ vaiṁ vaivasvatāya dharmarājāya bhaktānugraha kṛte namaḥ**.

Next, some mantras from the *Devī Bhāgavatam:*

Śrīṁ, Hrīṁ, Klīṁ, Aiṁ Kamalavāsinyai Svāhā. The root-mantra of Mahā Lakṣmī, likened to the wish-fulfilling tree in Indra's garden. By means of this vidyā, Kubera gained his wealth.

Oṁ, Śrīṁ, Klīṁ, Hrīṁ, Dākṣiṇāyai Svāhā. The root-mantra of the Dakṣiṇā Devī, which is recited when offerings are made, libation is poured or mantras are recited to make them fruitful and efficient. Dakṣiṇā grants the fruits of all deeds.

And from the *Kaulajñāna nirṇaya*:

Hrīṁ Ā Hrīṁ Hrīṁ Iṁ Hrīṁ Hrīṁ Ūṁ Hrīṁ Hrīṁ Ṛṁ Hrīṁ Hrīṁ Lṛṁ Hrīṁ Hrīṁ Aiṁ Hrīṁ Hrīṁ Oṁ Hrīṁ Hrīṁ Hrīṁ Aḥ Hrīṁ

The mantra of the first devī. A wonderful example how bījas can be arranged to establish rhythm and melody. Try this aloud to get a feeling for the ringing and chiming vibrations. There are eight bījas between the Hrīṁs: **Ā Iṁ Ūṁ Ṛṁ Lṛṁ Aiṁ Oṁ Aḥ.** These are combined with another set of eight syllables, which have an anatomical attribution to eight cakras:

Kṣa: Brahmarandhra (top of the head), **La**: forehead, **Ha**: between the eyes, **Sa**: mouth, **Ṣa**: throat, **Śa**: heart, **Va**: navel and **Hla**: genitals (Bagchi proposes the root centre instead).

This yields a number of mantras such as **Lāṁ Līṁ Lūṁ Lṛṁ Luṁ Laiṁ Lauṁ Laḥ**; **Hāṁ Hīṁ Hūṁ Hṛṁ Huṁ Haiṁ Hauṁ Haḥ, Sāṁ Sīṁ Sūṁ Sṛṁ Suṁ Saiṁ Sauṁ Saḥ** and so on, all the way down the spine to the genitals.

These mantras should suffice to provide you with a range of choices. When you decide to wake a mantra, stick to it for a while. Explore it in the consciousness of the heart before you invoke it in ritual, and give it time to come to life and get used to you. A mantra is a bit like a person.

You have to get used to it, and it to you, before you know if you will be friends.

Mantras can also function like suggestions or magical spells. In this case they are not recited hundreds or thousands of times but accompany ritual acts. Here is an example from the *Mahānirvāṇa Tantra*. It is part of the morning rites of the celebrated Five Ms, an exceedingly complicated ritual that can easily last all day, on which more details further on.

Oṁ Hrīṁ. Amṛte amṛtodbhave amṛta-varṣiniamṛtam ākarṣayā-karṣaya:

siddhim dehi: Kālikām me vasham ānaya

'Oṁ Hrīṁ. *Ambrosia, that springest from ambrosia, Thou that showereth ambrosia, draw ambrosia for me again and again. Bring Kālikā within my control. Give siddhi;* **svāhā.'**

Ambrosia is amṛta: without death. The elixir of immortality. In this case it is not wine nor a secretion but Vijayā, (hashish) usually cooked in milk and ghī, sometimes adding honey and spices. The mantra is used to consecrate the drug before it is offered to the guru in the sahasrāra, the goddess in the heart and the mouth of the Kuṇḍalinī (i.e. the mouth of the worshipper). Woodroffe notes that in Bengal, the term siddhi (usually: perfection, magical power, skill) means hemp. The worshipper then recites:

Aiṁ vada vada Vāgvādini mama jivhāgre sthirībhava sarvva-sattva-vaśangkari: Svāhā

> *'Aiṁ, Thou who art the Ruler of all the essences, do Thou inspire me, and remain ever on the tip of my tongue; svāhā.'*

After reciting this mantra, the worshipper drinks the vijayā, salutes the guru, Gaṇeśa, and the Eternal Ādyā Devī, and meditates on the goddess.

Śrī Vidyā's Playful Goddess

One of the most impressive collections of mantras is the *Śrī Lalitā Sahasranāma*. Its anonymous author did the incredible and wrote a hymn listing the thousand names of the goddess Lalitā. It is not the only effort of this sort. The *Kurma Purāṇa* lists the Thousand Names of Umā/Pārvatī, elsewhere you can find the thousand names of Viṣṇu, the thousand names of the Devī, the thousand (or only a hundred) names of Kālī, the hundred names of Durgā, the hundred names of Gaṇeśa, and so on. For obvious reasons, the lists show some similarity and tend to overlap.

Lalitā can mean the Playful One. It can also be interpreted as Lovely or Beautiful, and Bhāskararāya tells us: *The word lalitā has eight meanings, namely brilliancy, manifestation, sweetness, depth, fixity, energy, grace and generosity, these are the eight human qualities*. He adds that the *Kāma-śastra* says: *Lalitā means erotic actions and also tenderness*. (Brooks 1992) This may give a wrong impression, as neither source bothered to mention the dangerous, destructive, and demon slaying qualities of the goddess. In the *Śrī Lalitā Sahasranāma* she is imagined as a vermilion-red goddess seated on a lotus. She wears a crown of rubies and holds a noose, a goad, an arrow of flowers, and a sugarcane bow. Occasionally she also holds a jewelled cup full of elixir and a red lotus. Lalitā is an early attempt at assembling an all-inclusive goddess. Like The Devī, who includes all goddesses (and gods), Lalitā was to be a goddess of whom all other deities are but partial aspects. Both of them seem to have been discovered or invented pretty much at the same time. Unlike the cult of the Devī, which has a fairly orthodox attitude and remains largely within the range of mainstream worship, the cult of Lalitā belongs primarily to the Śrī Vidyā and secondarily (before the 16th century) the Kaula tradition. It seems to have been a goal of her cult to blend several traditions. 923. **Oṁ dakṣiṇ' ādakṣiṇ' ārādhyāyai namaḥ**: *Salutations to Her who is worshipped according to both Dakṣiṇācāra and its opposite, by the learned and unlearned.* The right hand path and the left hand path, the city people and the folk traditions. Now the *Śrī Lalitā Sahasranāma* is an amazingly complex work. If you had to invent one thousand titles of your personal deity, you might eventually come to a point where repetitions are inevitable and your brain turns to cheese. Even all-inclusive goddesses have to dwell in a state of balance between the mind-blowing totality of all that is and the specific vision that enflames the heart of the worshipper. There are lots of references to various deities and their attributes scattered through the texts. The *Śrī Lalitā Sahasranāma* offers such a wealth of praiseful titles that anybody can find good mantras among them. These range from the physically descriptive to the spiritual, the mythical, and the abstract realm. Here are a few examples. I quote them with the translation by Swami Tapsyananda.

1.**Oṁ Śrī - mātre namaḥ**

Salutations to the Divine Mother, who is the mother of all.

2. **Oṁ Śrī - mahā - rājñyai namaḥ**

Salutations to the Great Empress of the whole Universe.

3. **Oṁ Śrīmat - siṁhāsan' eśvaryai namaḥ**

Salutations to the Great Sovereign enthroned on the lion's back.

4. **Oṁ cid - agni - kunda - sambhūtāyai namaḥ**

Salutations to Her who came out of the fire of Pure Consciousness.

5. **Oṁ deva - kārya - samudyatāyai namaḥ**

Salutations to Her who ever promotes the cause of Divine forces.

6. **Oṁ udyad - bhānu - sahasrābhāyai namaḥ**

Salutations to Her who is as radiant as a thousand suns rising together.

Some of Lalitā's names are poetic descriptions of the deity and, in essence, instructions on how to visualise her form. In this matter, form is not random but highly symbolic. The shape has meaning, and the aspirant meditates on the shape in order to comprehend the hidden reality behind it. Praise of the body of the goddess is such an extensive topic that we are rather over-informed concerning her appearance. She holds a noose representing love, a goad of anger to restrain evil, a sugarcane bow that represents mind, and five arrows (the subtle elements, also the senses). Her hair is full of fragrance, her crown shines with gems, her forehead radiates with the crescent of the moon (on the eight night, actually), her face is the home of Kāma (Desire), her eyebrows resemble archways leading to the abode of beauty, her eyes move like fish, her nose looks like a campaka blossom, her nose-ring exceeds the brilliance of planet Venus, her ear pendants are sun and moon, her cheeks are fairer than a mirror of ruby, her teeth resemble the sprouting of true knowledge (Śrī Vidyā), her smile inundates the mind of Śiva, there is gold on her arms, gems around her neck, her full breasts are the offering to her consort, Śiva, in return for the gem of love he bestows on her, her back almost breaks under the weight of the breasts (indicating that the goddess offers nourishment to the whole universe), her girdle is of chiming bells, her calf muscles look like the quiver of Kāma, the arch of her feet is like the back of a tortoise, her gait is like the waddle of a swan (haṁsa), and so on. There is a great deal more, so far we are still in the range of the first fifty names, I hope you'll excuse the lack of further details (and get yourself a copy of the text for in-depth study). Some of the names may sound a bit overdone, but then, such is the language of mystical love and devotion. Other favourite texts of Śrī Vidyā are a lot less restrained in their imagery. The descriptions also go beyond the personal. There are more than sixty verses identifying her with the various cakras and the spirits within them.

Mythology provides further names: Lalitā is identified with Sadāśiva, Bhairavī, Brahmā, Bhagavatī, Viṣṇu, Rudra, Kubera, Ambikā, Kāma-Kalā (the hexagram), Māyā, Mahākālī, Candikā, Cāmuṇḍa, Prāṇa, Bhairava, Tripurā, and more. She is those deities, but also the source of their creation, she is worshipped by them, she is the female deities, the male deities, the male and female deities transformed into the other sex, the union of the deities, the bliss of this union and ultimately all that goes beyond them. She is the creator of all beings, from Brahmā to the lowest worms, reclines on a couch made out of the corpses (passive consciousness) of the greatest gods, has thousands of faces, eyes, hands and feet... the list goes on indefinitely, and the wider her description becomes, so does the mind of the worshipper.

Further on, the goddess is described in abstract terms. Some examples:

251. **Oṁ cinmayyai namaḥ**

Salutations to Her who is pure consciousness.

254. **Oṁ dhyāna - dhyātṛ - dhyeya - rūpāyai namaḥ**

Salutations to Her who is meditation, the person meditating and the object meditated upon.

255. **Oṁ dharm' ādharma - vivarjitāyai namaḥ**

Salutations to Her who transcends both good and evil.

257. **Oṁ jāgariṇyai namaḥ**

Salutations to Her who is the waking state.

258. **Oṁ svapantyai namaḥ**

Salutations to Her who is the Dream state.

260. **Oṁ suptāyai namaḥ**

Salutations to Her who is the state of Deep Sleep.

262. **Oṁ turyāyai namaḥ**

Salutations to Her who is the Turīya which transcends all states.

263. **Oṁ sarv'āvasthā - vivarjitāyai namaḥ**

Salutations to Her who is devoid of all states.

Regarding the Kaula rites and the worship of the left-hand-path, there are several references, sometimes in veiled form, in the hymn:

37. **Oṁ aruṇ' aruṇa - kausumbha - vastra - bhāsvat - kaṭī - taṭyai namaḥ**

Salutations to Her who wears a garment of deep red around Her hip.

12. **Oṁ nij' āruṇa - prabhā - pūra - majjad - brahmāṇḍa - maṇḍalāyai namaḥ**

Salutations to Her in the rosy splendour of whose form the whole universe is bathed.

52. **Oṁ śiva - kāmeśvar'āṅkasthāyai namaḥ**

Salutations to Her who is seated on the lap of Śiva, the conqueror of desire (Kāmeśvara).

376. **Oṁ śṛṅgāra - rasa - sampūrṇāyai namaḥ**

Salutations to Her who is the essence of Love (or who lives where love in fullness is found).

382. **Oṁ rahas - tarpaṇa - tarpitāyai namaḥ**

Salutations to Her who is gratified by secret libations.

440. **Oṁ kula-kuṇḍ' ālayāyai namaḥ**

Salutations to Her who is the deity in the Kulakuṇḍa (the Mūlādhāra).

441. **Oṁ kaula - mārga - tatpara - sevitāyai namaḥ**

Salutations to Her who is worshipped by those who are devoted to the Kaula tradition.

945. **Oṁ vāmakeśvaryai namaḥ**

Salutations to Her who is the deity of the leftward path.

950. **Oṁ pañca - saṅkhyo' pacāriṇyai namaḥ**

Salutations to Her who is worshipped with the fivefold offering.

This should easily suffice to provide some interesting experiences for you. If you want more (which I hope you do) get yourself a copy of the hymn and devote a ritual to Lalitā by reciting her thousand names in a single day.

Let us now take a brief look at the Pañcadaśākṣarī (the basic fifteen syllable form) and the Ṣoḍaśākṣarī (fifteen syllable form), of the supreme mantra of the Śrī Vidyā tradition. It is usually given in code, as in verse 32 of the *Saundarya Laharī* (trans. Sastri and Ayyangar, 1937, with my additions):

O Mother! Śiva (ka), Śakti (e), Kāma (ī) and Kṣiti (la);

and then, Ravi (ha), Śitakirana (sa), Smara (ka), Haṁsa (ha) and Śakra (la);

and thereafter, Parā (sa), Māra (ka) and Hari (la);

these (three sets of) syllables,

when conjoined severally at their ends with the three Hṛllekhā-s (hrīṁ),

become the components of Thy name.

The mantra consists of three lines, which are considered peaks (kūṭas). These peaks have a lot of symbolism to them, as numerous adepts have tried to associate them with every conceivable trinity of Hindu philosophy. They can be Brahmā, Viṣṇu, Śiva; Iccha, Jñāna, and Kriyā Śakti; waking, dreaming, and deep sleep; sattva, rajas, and tamas; heaven, earth, and underworlds; and so on. These lists are long, and the more meaning is crammed into them, the more do they contradict themselves.

ka e ī la hrīṁ
ha sa ka ha la hrīṁ
sa ka la hrīṁ

The top line is the peak of Vāk (Voice), the goddess of speech, who is usually identified with Sarasvatī. The middle line is called Kāmarājakūṭa, i.e. Peak of the King of Desire, or simply Kāma-bīja. The King of Desire could be Kāma, or it might be Śiva as the slayer and re-creator of Kāma. The bottom line is the Peak of Śakti. The whole vidyā consists of fifteen syllables, which connects it with the kalās (digits, units) of the moon. Combine the first and last syllables: ka and la, and you get kalā. In advanced practice, the 16th syllable **śrīṁ** is added. The sixteenth syllable is so terribly secret that its very existence is rarely mentioned. It is only added by adepts of high attainment who have realised that it constitutes the fourth peak of the mantra.

A later form of the mantra is the so-called sixteen syllable Mahāṣoḍaśī, it also relates to the lunar mysteries:

oṁ śrīṁ hrīṁ klīṁ aīṁ sauḥ
oṁ hrīṁ śrīṁ
ka e ī la hrīṁ
ha sa ka ha la hrīṁ
sa ka la hrīṁ
sauḥ aīṁ klīṁ hrīṁ śrīṁ

Of course this extremely secret mantra (highly popular in southern India) only adds up to sixteen syllables when the three new lines are considered one syllable. When we get to the meaning of these mantras things become extremely complicated. When a tradition only offers one supreme mantra, that mantra is apt to be filled with more meaning than anyone can digest. Some of its adepts, like Bhāskararāya, propose that its efficiency relies on knowing its exact meaning. He supplies an attempt at explanation, but of course others disagree widely. According to Bhāskararāya, **ka** and **ha** can be tat, that which is, and Brahman. He also attributes **ka** to Śiva the Enlightener, from the syllable kan, to shine, and to women in general, who are supposed to be attracted by the mantra (kam means to desire). **E** is Śakti, but it also relates to buddhi, and learning. **Ī** stands for Śiva and means 'to pervade', it also stands for radiance, shining, and the cause of creation and maintenance. **La** signifies earth as the manifest goddess. **Sa** refers mysteriously to savitur (three syllables) and is connected with the words so, to enjoy, and su, to procreate. **Hrīṁ** refers to Māyā. This is just a simple account, as the meaning of the syllables also depend on their combination and position within the three peaks (see Brooks' *Auspicious Wisdom* 1992 for a full account). If you look at the bījas given in the next section, you will recognise a number of them in the supreme mantra. **Ha** can be Śiva, **sa** can be Śakti. **ka** can be Kālī or Kāma and **la** refers to earth (manifestation) and the root cakra. All of this may give the impression that the mantra's efficiency rely on a thorough study of dodgy etymology. This is not the case. In mantra yoga, there are adepts who invest every single letter with several cryptic meanings, while others prefer to enjoy sound as such. From their point of view, a mantra is supposed to stop thinking, hence the more meaningless it is, the closer it comes to silence, pure awareness, and the full manifestation of the divine.

The three peaks also appear in a shorter form. Here the vidyā goes: (**Oṁ**) **Aīṁ Klīṁ Strīṁ**. The *Śiva Saṁhita*, 5:

189. By knowing this highest of the mantras, the Yogī certainly attains siddhi: this gives all power and pleasure to the one-pointed Yogī.

190. In the four-petalled Mulādhār lotus is the bīja of speech, brilliant as lightning (Aīṁ).

191. In the heart is the bīja of love, beautiful as the bandhuh flower (Klīṁ). In the space between the two eyebrows is the bīja of Śakti (Strīṁ), brilliant as ten of millions of moons. These three seeds should be kept secret - they give enjoyment and emancipation. Let the Yogī repeat these three mantras and try to attain success.

192. Let him learn this mantra from his Guru, let him repeat it neither too fast or too slowly, keeping the mind free from all doubts, and understanding the mystic relation between the letters of the mantra.

193. The wise Yogī, intently fixing his attention on this mantra, performing all duties peculiar to his caste, should perform one hundred thousand homs (fire sacrifices) and then repeat this mantra three hundred thousand times in the presence of the Goddess Tripurā.

194. At the end of the sacred repetition (japa), let the wise Yogī again perform hom, in a triangular hollow, with sugar, milk, butter and the flower of karavi (oleander).

195. By this performance of Homa-Japa-Homa, the Goddess Tripurā Bhairavī, who has been propitiated by the above mantra, becomes pleased, and grants all desires to the Yogī.

Bīja

Vīja or Bīja means *seed.* A seed mantra is the shortest possible type of mantra, it usually consists of one syllable. Anything shorter than a syllable falls under the category of pure and primal sound. It is not a letter in the old Indian Devanāgarī script, each letter is already a syllable (or better, phoneme). Seeds are not on the level of words any more. They sound and vibrate, but they are not semantic symbols or parts of a language. This does not mean that they are totally without meaning. Like so many other cultures, the Hindus attributed a range of specific meanings to each phoneme of their script. These meanings, however, vary in each tradition, cult, or lineage. As you will see in the following collection, even within a single textual source the letters can have different meanings.

According to the *Tantra Kalpadruma*, the bīja Krīṁ, manifesting the essential vibration of the goddess Kālī, is composed of the letters K (meaning citkalā: the unit of pure consciousness and jñāna, divine knowledge, gnosis), R (the fire letter, attributed to Agni-Vahni), Ī (Mahāmāyā; Ratī, wife of Kāma), and Ṁ, the nāda-bindu (focus of vibration).

Another interpretation, found in the *Varadā Tantra*, has K for Kālī, R for Brahmā, Î for Mahāmāyā and nāda (vibration) as the matrix of the universe, while the bindu (point) is the Dispeller of Sorrow.

According to the *Toḍala Tantra*, K grants dharma (eternal law, truth, duty), R grants kāma (desire, love), Î grants artha (wealth, prosperity), and Ṁ grants mokṣa(liberation).

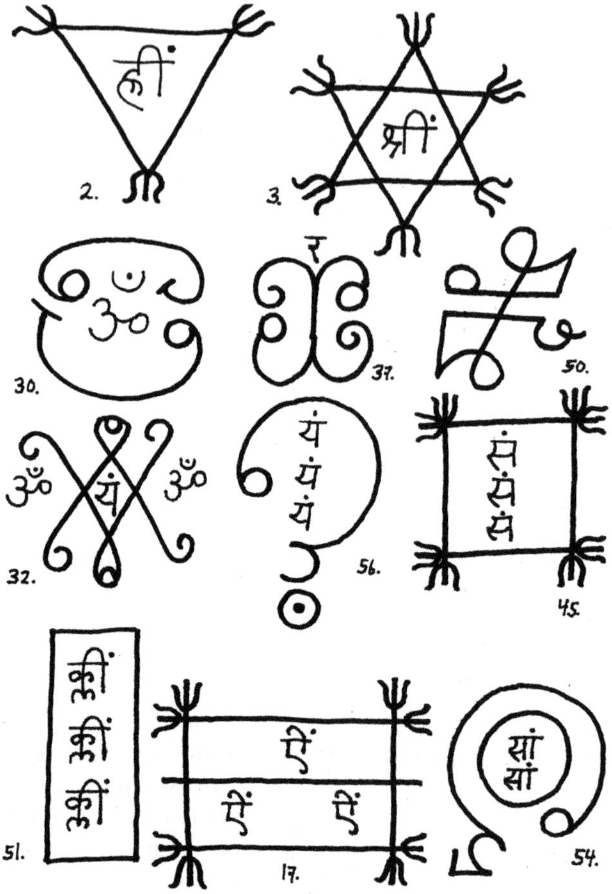

Figure 32 - Yantras for Sorcery from the Saundarya Laharī.
The numbers refer to the verse of the poem, which is recited as a mantra.
2. To conquer matter and nature. 1000 repetitions on 55 days. Engrave on gold and face north.
3. To gain knowledge of the Vedas. 2000 repetitions, 54 days, gold plate, face north east. Or to gain wealth, 1000 repetitions, 15 days.
30. To gain magical power. 1000 repetitions for 96 days, gold plate.
37. Protection from obsession by demons. 5000 repetitions, 45 days, gold.
50. Immunity from smallpox. 1000 repetitions, 5 days, engraved on gold or written with water.
32. Knowledge of alchemy and science. 1000 repetitions, 45 days, gold. Or success in business, same as above.
56. To break locks, open shackles and make guards run away. 20 000 repetitions, 45 days, engrave on gold plate, crocodile tooth or crocodile skullbone.
45. To be eloquent and tell fortunes. 1000 repetitions, 45 days, gold plate.
51. To enchant people and gain all desires. 1000 repetitions, 45 days, engraved on gold plate or drawn with sandal paste.
17. Mastery of sacred literature. 1000 repetitions, 45 days, gold plate.
54. To cure genital diseases or gynaecological afflictions. 1000 repetitions, 45 days, engraved on gold plate, laid out in medical herbs or ink dissolved in water in a vessel.
That such sorceries are associated with their most sacred poem is a source of annoyance for strict-minded followers of Śrī Vidyā. Unless they happen to need them.

Quite a lot of meaning for a simple syllable. When meditating with this seed, it can be useful to go into each separate sound from time to time, and to taste, savour, and extend it fully. There are no rules saying that seeds should be vibrated fast, so if you want to experience them for a few hours, it is sound practice to introduce variation. A mantra, no matter how long or short, is something very much alive. The life is not in it automatically, you will have to put it into the seed to make it wake and work. It is your life which gives life to the bīja. If you repeat it monotonously you will produce a monotonous consciousness and eventually fall asleep or get a headache.

There are a long list of seeds in evidence. The earliest appear long before Tantra in the Vedic period. They range from very abstract sound patterns, usually associated with the more important deities, to simpler ones, which are made by intoning the first syllable of the name of a deity. Here I would like to offer a brief list of some of the more popular bīja. The last sound of each is the nāda-bindu, spelled in transcription as ṁ, the root-vibration which can be expressed as a nasal NG sound. It is sounded high up in the nose to stimulate the third eye, but can be extended into a wide range of dark vibrations when practised aloud. To get the ṁ right, try it loud for a while. Sing something like angangang or ongongong (try the other vowels as well) and explore the vibration. Move and wriggle your tongue, widen and narrow the mouth cavity, chew it, taste it, sense how it buzzes in your head and move the vibration through your body. When you can do it properly aloud, move it into the barely audible and then into the imaginary sound range. Now for the bījas. The analysis of letters generally follows the *Varadā Tantra,* 6 (Woodroffe 1979: 262-265) unless otherwise stated.

Aṁ. Used in the worship of the circle of the sun with its twelve kalās.

Aiṁ. Ai is Sarasvatī:, goddess of literature and art, bindu dispells sorrow. The bīja invokes Sarasvatī, but it is also known as the guru-bīja. Sometimes it's called the yoni-bīja and used to awake, stimulate, and worship the vulva.

Bhaṁ or **Yaṁ.** Seed of Vijayā Śakti. She is a fear inspiring red goddess, riding an owl, bearing arrows, bow, and sacrificial fish, meat, and wine.

Bruṁ. Seed of Bṛhaspati, Lord of the Brahmins, sacrificer and guru of the gods.

Duṁ. Da is Durgā, U is to save, nāda is the Mother of the Universe, bindu is to do. This is the classical seed of Durgā, the alluring and terrifying goddess who rides a lion or tiger and rids the world of demons.

Gaṁ. Ga, I speak to thee, is Gaṇeśa, the elephant-headed-god, the destroyer of obstacles. Bindu dispells sorrow.

Glauṁ. Ga is Gaṇeśa. La is that which pervades, Au is tejas (fire). Bindu dispels sorrow.

Haṁ. Seed of Śiva and of the element of spirit (ākāśa). Also seed of Aparājitā Śakti. She is black, wears black clothes, rides a chariot, and roars.

Hauṁ. Ha is Śiva, Au is Sadāśiva. Bindu is that which dispels sorrow.

Hing. *Atharva Veda* 9,6, 45-48 calls it the sound of dawn, of the rising sun, of the forming clouds, and the sound uttered when greeting guests. In 9, 10, 6 it is the sound of the cow lowing for its calf. In 11, 7, 5 Hing is in the remnant of the sacrifice.

Hrīṁ. The seed of Mahāmāyā, the creatrix of the play of illusions, the manifest world. Ha is Śiva, Ra is Prakṛti, Î is Mahāmāyā, nāda is the Mother of the Universe, bindu dispells sorrow. Also, Ha (Vyoma) is manifestation, Ra (Vahni) is involution, Î is the maintenance of the worlds. (*Svatantra-Tantra*). According to the *Devīgītā*, quoted by Woodroffe, the Mahādevī states*: H is the gross body, R is the subtle body, Ī is the causal body. I am Hrīṁ the Turīya.* Hrīṁ is called the Māyā Bīja or the Mū Bīja. In the *Devī Bhāgavatam* (10, 13) the sound Hrīṁ is droned by the myriad of black bees and hornets that adorn the costume of the Devī; in 11,1 it is the seed of Kuṇḍalinī-Śakti. In the *Lakṣmī Tantra* 44, 6-8, the bīja of Tārikā. Perhaps the most popular mantra in Tantric initiations, worship of Śaktis, initiation of women, etc.

Hsau. The bīja of the Mahāpreta (great corpses) i.e. Devī's couch made of five corpses (Sadāśiva, Īśāna, Rudra, Viṣṇu, Brahmā).

Hūṁ. One of the oldest seed-mantras, an enormous amount of literature has been written about it. Ha is Śiva, Ū is Bhairava (Śiva as the Fear-inspiring One). Nāda is para, i.e. supreme, bindu dispells sorrow. Hūṁ is also called the *causal aspect*; also *that which awakes Śabda* (sound, a form of Śakti), the Armour-Bīja. Its deep droning vibration can be used to stimulate and awake Kuṇḍalinī-Śakti. In sorcery, it is occasionally used to cause death. The *Viśvasāra Tantra* states that *He who makes japa of Hūṁ is more praiseworthy than Deva or Asura.* Hūṁ is also a personal bīja of Chinnamastā, the self-decapitated goddess of wisdom, and the sound of terror that surrounds Kālī when she destroys demons on the battlefield. It is also a bīja of turīya consciousness.

Jaṁ or **Yaṁ**: seed of Jayā Śakti. She is white, holds club and shield, and rides a corpse or a ghost.

Klhrīṁ. The seed of Bhairavī, the Fear-Inspiring Goddess.

Klīṁ. Ka is usually Kāmadeva, the god of desire. Occasionally the Ka is said to mean Kṛṣṇa. La is Indra, the wielder of thunder and lightning. Î is contentment, Am grants happiness and sorrow. Used in combination with 'Phat' to purify the mat in the Bhairavī Cakra. Also a bīja of Kālī, who is its creatrix.

Krīṁ. Primary bīja of Kālī, called the Ādyā bīja (primordial seed), associated with dissolution, transcendence, liberation, and enlightenment. See comments above.

Kṣaṁ. Seed of Tumburu, the white, four faced, eight armed, bull-riding Śiva, of the *Vīṇāśikhatantra*. He sits in the centre, on a four-petaled lotus, surrounded by Jayā (east), Vijayā (south), Jayantī (west), and Aparājitā (north).

Kṣrauṁ. Kṣa is Nṛsimha, Ra is Brahmā, Au is teeth pointing upwards, bindu dispells sorrow. Used to worship Nṛsimha (Viṣṇu as lion-man). In the *Vīṇāśikhatantra*, the seed appears as **Kṣroṁ** or **Kṣmroṁ**. It is used in prāṇāyāma during a visualisation of the body-of-sin being burned up.

Laṁ. Seed of the earth element and of the thunderbolt wielding storm- and rain-god Indra.

Maṁ. Used in the worship of the circle of fire with its ten kalās.

Oṁ. The perfect root mantra, the sound of all creation, the embodiment of Brahman, the All-Consciousness. It is composed of the letters AUM which are said to represent the Trimurti (usually Brahmā as Creator, Viṣṇu as Maintainer, and Śiva/Rudra as Destroyer) as well as a lot of other concepts. Oṁ, the praṇava, has its first written appearance in the *Taittirīya Saṁhitā* of the *Black Yajur Veda*. It is the greatest mantra of the *Upaniṣads* and celebrated in countless texts and traditions. Here are some examples:

This sound (AUM) is that syllable, the immortal, the fearless. Having entered this, the gods became immortal, fearless. He who knowing it thus, praises this syllable, in the immortal, fearless sound, and having entered it, he becomes immortal, even as the gods become immortal. (*Chāndogya Upaniṣad*, 1, 4, 4-5)

As all leaves are held together by a stalk, so is all speech held together by AUM. (*Chāndogya Upaniṣad* 2, 23,3)

According to the *Kaṭha Upaniṣad* (1, 2, 15) the word Aum is the essence of all *Vedas*, it is proclaimed by all austerities. Aum is the everlasting Brahman, the support of all, the highest end and the fulfiller of all desires. The *Māṇḍūkya Upaniṣad*, a brief text of twelve verses dedicated entirely to the meaning of Aum, gives a lot more detail. It proclaims that Aum is everything. Aum is past, present, and future, and that which is beyond time. It is Brahman and self, and appears in four divisions. These correspond to the four consciousness states: waking consciousness, where attention is fixed on external phenomena; dreaming consciousness, where attention is involved with internal phenomena; deep dreamless sleep, which is pure bliss; and turīya, the fourth consciousness state. Turīya is described as *not that which cognizes the internal (objects), not that which cognizes the external (objects), not what cognizes both of them, not a mass of cognition, not cognitive, not non-cognitive. (It is) unseen, incapable of being spoken of, ungraspable, without any distinctive marks, unthinkable, unnameable, the essence of the knowledge of the one self, that into which the world is resolved, the peaceful, the benign, the non-dual... this is the self, which is of the nature of the syllable aum, in regard to its elements.* To waking, active consciousness the syllable ā is assigned, to dreaming, inner consciousness the syllable u, to dreamless sleep the syllable m. Turīya goes beyond this: it includes all three and transcends them. *He who knows this enters the self with the self.*

Figure 33- Bījas.
Top left: Oṁ. Top right: Aiṁ.
Middle left: Klīṁ. Middle right: Strīṁ.
Bottom left: Sauḥ. Bottom right: Phaṭ.

In Tantric literature, Oṁ is often called the Tārā bīja, as it saves the worshipper and helps to cross the ocean of illusions. In spite of being the mantra of Brahman, the all-self, women and Śudra are not allowed to recite Oṁ. That's not very kind. May I suggest 'bollocks!' instead?

Phat. This is the Weapon bīja, it sounds explosive and fierce. The PH is not pronounced as 'F' but as a forceful, aspirated P. It is often used to banish malignant influences, exorcise demons, and dispel wrong thinking. For this purpose it is sounded loud and accompanied by clapping the hands and stamping on the ground with one heel. The four or eight directions are thus exorcised. It is also used to exorcise the ego-demons and purify oneself. Also called Astra (missile) bīja and the Fierce Mantra.

Raṁ is the seed of fire. It is associated with fire god Agni and occasionally with Rama.

Sauḥ. A general bīja for Śakti. Highly popular in Kashmir Śaivism, explored at length by Abhinavagupta as the Heart Mantra. Here, S is Śakti as Bhairavī, ḥ is Śiva as Bhairava, and between them, au, is the essence of the sixteen vowels, the union of consciousness-as-form and consciousness-without-form and so much theology that I leave it to you to read it up (Muller-Ortega 1989). According to Abhinavagupta, you pronounce it sa-au-ahhh.

Śrīṁ. The Kamalā Bīja, or seed of Lakṣmī, nourishing the world and bestowing prosperity. Śa is Mahālakṣmī, R is wealth, Î is satisfaction, nāda is Īśvara (the lord), and bindu the Dispeller of Sorrow.

Strīṁ. Sa is deliverance from difficulties, Ta the Saviour, Ra is salvation or liberation. Î is Mahāmāyā, nāda the Mother of the Universe, bindu dispells sorrow. This is the Vadhū (Bride-like) Bīja of Tārā. Also a general bīja of Śakti.

Trīṁ. An elder form of Tārā's bīja.

Uṁ. Used in the worship of the circle of the moon with its sixteen kalās.

Vaṁ. Seed of Varuṇa, here associated with the element of water and the great deep.

Yaṁ. Seed of Vāyu, god of air, and of Vāta, the vedic storm god.

Figure 34 - Bījas. Five phases of Krama.
Top left: Hrīṁ. Top right: Śrīṁ.
Centre: Krīṁ.
Bottom left: Hūṁ. Bottom right: Svāhā.

Māyā: Waking the Mantra

To experience a mantra fully, it is essential to wake it up. Without proper attention and intonation, the mantra stays asleep. The mantra is not just a word. It is also a sound pattern that gets you going. And it is the vibration-body of a deity. Unless you are very lucky and get everything unconsciously just right, repeating a mantra is usually not enough. The easiest way to wake a mantra is in the consciousness of the heart, which we'll look at in the next chapter. The heart awareness provides the necessary clarity. Once a mantra is awake in the central void, it easily transforms awareness in waking and dreaming consciousness.

But how do you bring the mantras into life in your everyday awareness, into all those moments when you do not have the leisure to introvert and sink into the depth within? How can you wake a mantra? What can you do with your inner voice?

Here we enter the wonderful world of submodalities. This is a term for a phenomenon that was first explicitly applied by Richard Bandler, who wrote a lot of books on Things that Work which you should really read. A brilliant introduction to the submodalities and how you can enjoy them is given in his *Using Your Brain for a Change* and in *Time for a Change.* Essential books for every daring mind explorer. Before we get into the sub-modalities we might give a thought to the sense-modalities themselves. In Bandler's NLP-related writings, the sense-modalities (sight, hearing, touch, taste, scent) are the ways we experience the world (and ourselves), i.e. through the outer sense organs and the inner senses (imagination). Each of these senses can be used to explore the outside universe and the universe within. The submodalities are the finer differences within each sense-modality. In the visual sense, you could consider how large something is, how close, how colourful, where it is, its brightness, clarity, motion, contrast, and so on. We'll play with the visual system in the chapter on the personal deities. In mantra magic, as in daily life, the auditive system may be worth exploring. Your inner (and outer) voice(s) have lots of specific qualities. Listen to yourself now. Say something in your inner voice and listen really well. The voice within your very own mind has a lot of unique characteristics. Let me ask some questions:

How loud is it? How fast is it? How forceful is it ? How much bass is there and how high is the pitch? Where does it come from? How clear is it? How steady is the sound? Is there an echo or a hall? Are there pauses or is it continuous? Can you discern rhythmic elements? Are any sounds emphasised? Is there distortion? Does it move?

Anything you can say has a lot of extras. Hey! It's time to have some fun now!

Say something to yourself in your inner voice. Chose something neutral, not material with emotional content. Or pick a few lines from a newspaper or a book.

Repeat it, but change the volume. Make it loud and louder. Observe your emotional response. Does volume affect your experience? How loud can it get? Is there a threshold at the very loud end of the scale, and what happens beyond it? Then turn the volume down, let the words go towards silence. What effect do you get from inner whispering? Or listening to really faint sounds? Make a few notes on your emotional response.

Then try the next one. Repeat your words but speed them up. Make the inner voice faster and faster. What do you experience? What effect does it have on your state of mind? Then go the other way. Slow down the inner voice. Let the words come out with ever greater intervals, let the letters form one after the other each by itself and enjoy the pauses. What happens to your consciousness? Speed is a variable that is used by many people. How often in life have you been speeding yourself up by accelerating your inner voice? Sometimes this is fun and sometimes it is just stressful. And isn't it nice and comfy to slow the inner voice gently and gradually as you calm down and enter a slow trance state?

What's next on our list? Try all variations, each one by itself, play around with all possibilities and discover new ones I would never have imagined. Everybody does the most wonderful things up there in the head, and many of them are pretty much unique. Some people get a kick from hearing the inner voice from specific positions. Try this! Hear it from above, from belly level, from below, from behind you to the right and left, from the sides, and from within your body in all sorts of places. Make the inner voice come out of various centres along your spine. And explore voice quality! Make it clear, then try diffuse, add bass or turn up the high sounds. Explore a voice that moves, comes from several places at once, or surrounds you entirely. What happens when you add hall, distortion, or an echo?

What happens when you add background music? Try something soft or something fast and furious. What else can you do to enjoy yourself?

You can go beyond this. Identify some of the submodalities that really make a difference to your experience. What happens when you combine them? Turn up the volume, speed up the words, add a hall, make it come from above your head and surround you entirely. Some people get a real kick from this sort of thing. Others need a different combination of effects. As you are unique, part of your fun is learning how to turn yourself on.

Or approach the subject the other way. Speak or read the text in a restful voice, a loving voice, a happy voice, a lazy voice, a sleepy voice, and angry voice, an exciting voice, a bored voice, a shy voice, a confident voice, a doubtful voice, a dramatic voice, a holy voice, a crazy voice, a sexy voice, a friendly voice, a hopeful voice. By now you'll be aware that a sleepy voice requires a specific speed, intonation, energy tonus, and a number of other qualities. The same goes for the sexy voice, the dramatic voice, and all the others on our list. Each of them has one or more specific effects on your consciousness. A fast and dramatic inner voice, for example, can be just the thing to wake you up. What voices do you use when you are having a good time? And how do you sound when you are miserable? Are you aware that the qualities of your inner voice are parts of the behaviour you need to maintain your states of mind? So what do you do? Are you happy with your inner voice right now? Will you enjoy to listen more closely when you sound better to yourself?

These submodalities form the body of your experience. As you explore how you sound to yourself you'll become more aware how other people use their (outer) voice to keep up their specific reality tunnel. A happy voice can increase the happiness of life, and a miserable voice take the joy out of living. All of this is part of the greater magick, the magick of how you use your senses and your mind to world-weave a reality of your choice.

Mantra intonation means applying the skills you have just developed. Take a given mantra. Make it sound soothing, and you have a device to bring you into states of deep calm and relaxation. Make it sound exciting and you're in for a passionate experience of being very much alive. It is possible to take pretty much any word or mantra and to say it so you can get any effect you like. You only have to know which way of speaking really influences you.

Playing around with tonality was certainly known to the ancient seers. In the *Chāndogya Upaniṣad* 2, 22, 1 you can find some hints on intonation and chanting. *Of the Sāman, I chose the high sounding one as good for cattle, this is the song sacred to Fire. The undefined one belongs to Prajā-pati, the defined one to Soma; the soft and the smooth to Vāyu, the smooth and strong to Indra; the heron-like to Bṛhaspati, the ill-sounding to Varuṇa. Let one practice all these but one should avoid that belonging to Varuṇa.* The same considerations apply to mantra-yoga. When you wish to invoke a deity by saturating your being with its mantra, the important thing is **CONGRUENCE**. This matter can hardly be over-emphasised, it is one of the most essential keys to all shape-shifting, obsession, and trans-personal experience.

If you wish to unite with a deity, be congruent with it. Kālī reacts (manifests) to a Kālīnian mood and Lakṣmī to quite another (unless you really annoy her). Each god has a specific range of emotional and temperamental preferences. By becoming congruent with the deity of your choice you can tune in and identify with it. Each mantra is a means to this identification. By becoming the mantra in its specific mood, mind, and flavour, you can be one with its presiding deity.

Another point worth considering is **breath**. As the *Kulārṇava Tantra* tells us, japa (recitation of mantra) should be joined with dhyāna (visualisation) and prāṇāyāma ('control' of breath/energy), which produces *'drying up of the body', 'burning of the body' and 'bathing the entire body' in the nectar of union of Kundalini and Shiva.* Align each mantra with the supreme mantra Haṁsa, the sound of out-breath and in-breath: *Mantras that are not conjoined with this great Mantra do not yield fruit.*

Another useful approach to waking a new mantra is to take it for a **walk**. Not very traditional but it works. As you join the rhythm of your steps to the rhythm of your breath and the rhythm of your mantra, you may be in for a lot of fascinating experiences. It is sound practice to do this while walking slowly or at a moderate pace. Unless you are careful, you will find that walking to a mantra tends to speed up both the pace and the mantra. This can lead to very tense states of consciousness when pursued for too long. People who walk too fast tend to miss a lot.

Finally, a word on **repetition**. A good many people believe that a mantra works when it is repeated often enough. This approach has a general sort of truth to it, but no amount of repetition will make a mantra wake unless you imbue it with awareness for a start. More so, repetition on its own is not a key to success. Some Tantras urge that you put so much awareness into the mantra that a single utterance (loud or in the imagination) is enough to produce complete rapture. This is not easy, especially for beginners, but it is something useful to go for. Finally, a word on **duality**. Most Indian systems make a big issue out of this. There are sects which hold that the gods and humans are separate, but can commune via ritual, meditation, and sacrifice. Others hold it that the gods, while not quite the same as humans, can make humans almost like gods. Then there are cults that propose that we are the gods already, and the gods are us, the important issue being how to remember and realise. This usually means purification, waking oneself up to divine consciousness, identification, and enactment (or possession). Mantra yoga usually aims at union with gods, or some abstract definition of 'higher consciousness'. Now the important thing is that as you wake the mantra, you also wake the deity. This may mean waking it around you (dualism) or waking it within (non-dualism) or both. We are dealing with a classical case of invocation here.

Now the thing that gets the gods, spirits, and ancient ones going is **emotion**. Sheer emotion produces the initial energy burst needed to break down the barriers between the human and the divine. This emotional energy can assume many forms. It can be joy, longing, love, but it can also be the sort of emotional energy that comes from crisis, despair, exhaustion, and madness. A terrible deity may scare you out of your head, producing a rich emission of emotional energy. Well-behaved and benevolent deities take longer. To wake the mantra, and to wake the deity, a good surge of energy is essential. In the initial phases, the worshipper puts as much emotion into the mantra as possible. If you begin to laugh or weep in the process, you are doing fine. Later on, when you have come really close to the deity and the distinctions between the human and the divine cease to matter, such outbursts of passion are not always required. Once you and the deity are awake, and understand each other as one consciousness expressed on different planes of meaning, there is hardly a reason to sob or despair. It may even go the other way, and you may become emotional and unhappy when you have to leave the divine consciousness and return to the world of humans. Emotional outbursts are only needed when you have been so entangled in human affairs that your divine side is forgotten, or so vibrantly divine that the everyday world of people abusing each other seems unbearable.

Lakşmī: Maintaining a Mantra

Traditional Tantric practice not only makes much of proper japa (recitation, repetition), it is also very concerned with doing it for long periods. Ten minutes once or twice a day to calm and bless you may be well and good, but what many adepts prescribed was a schedule of 100,000 repetitions each day, followed by another 100,000 by night. If you go for this, you'll be reciting regardless what you do. This is in contrast to the selective practice prescribed by standard Hindu teachings. In the orthodox form, you'll say your mantra only for a few periods of the day, just as each Brahmin is supposed to say the Gāyatrī Mantra once a day. Orthodox Tantric practice requires that the practitioner is clean, in a purified environment, and only interested in the divine. The *Kulārṇava Tantra* lists forbidden situations, such as when one is unwashed, has uncombed hair, is nude, wears dirty clothes, has been in contact with excrement and other secretions, feels tired, angry, lazy, and so on. Likewise, excessive food, bad company, chatter, idleness, yearning, attachment to others and the like ought to be avoided. It also lists favourable sites and conditions. *The holy centre of pilgrimage, the bank of a river, the cave, the summit of a hill, the place of holy bath, the confluence of rivers, the holy forest, the vacant garden, the root of the Bilva tree, the slope of the hill, the temple, the coast of the sea, one's own house-these are the places lauded for the sadhana of Mantra Japa. Choose any of these or live where your mind is contented. Japa is praised when done in the proximity of the sun or the fire, Guru moon, lamp, water, cow, a brahmana family or tree. For the purpose of the Japa, the enclosed space of a house is good; better is the dwelling of a cow; still better is a temple and the best is in the immediate presence of Shiva.* The text also lists unfavourable conditions, such as ruined temples and houses, dead trees, polluted rivers, and the presence of wicked people, wild beasts, and politicians: *The knower of Mantra shall not stay where move kings, ministers, officers, nobles.* This is eminently good thinking, especially for beginners. It is a lot easier to focus on the divine when you are dwelling in a beautiful natural place, in silence and loneliness, far from the corruption and stupidity of basic humanity. On the other hand, if you rely on such conditions to experience the divine, you are still miles away from living it.

A lot of traditions, especially those of the left-hand path, insist that the holy and the corrupt ought to be treated without making a difference. To these worshippers all is a manifestation of the divine, no matter how ugly or evil it seems, and in these cults, worship is not confined to special locations and occasions but continuous. If you want to repeat your mantra all day through you can't only to do so when you are ritually pure and doing holy things; instead, you'll soon find that every activity had better become pure, no matter how dirty or profane it seems. Purity, profanity, and dirt do not exist in the real world, after all. They are evaluations made up in your mind. The grand recitation is a way of saturating yourself and the whole world with the energy-sentience of the mantra. You'll find yourself reciting as you walk, eat, rest, make love, or do the dishes. This is easier than most people think. Reciting a mantra can be an obsessive activity, and humans are good at obsessing themselves. Recitation soon becomes a habit, and once a habit is formed, it may continue almost continuously. There are a few activities, however, which are a bit difficult during recitation. When your attention is with your inner voice, it can be difficult to listen properly, be it to music or other people talking. Thus, if you wish to go dancing, either chose a mantra that has the same rhythm as the song or stop reciting for a while. The same goes for making music. Reading books while reciting is useless. Having a good chat is also problematic. If you want to understand what the people around you are saying, rest the mantra a while.

The next issue is repetition. If you repeat a given stimulus in exactly the same way for a while, the sensation becomes dulled and the whole thing slips out of awareness. It happens when you repeat a mantra for hours or days. Your attention lapses, the pronunciation changes, and before long you are not living a vibration but recycling empty chatter. Some Tantric adepts approve of this. In their opinion, most bījas are meaningless arrangements of sound anyway. If you forget the meaning they are supposed to have, you come close to empty-mindedness. Most writers do not agree with this. They insist that a mantra has to be filled with awareness. If you find your mantra has become dull and pointless, say welcome to change. How are you repeating the mantra when it seems dull? How loud, how fast, how clear does it sound? Find out how you are maintaining this dull consciousness state. Every consciousness state is an achievement that requires a lot of specific behaviour and constant maintenance. You are not just experiencing it, most of it is your own doing. Play around with the variables. You can change the way you think and do it now. This way, a mantra can be kept awake and fresh for long periods. Try variation. Speed it up, slow it down, change pronunciation and inflection. Change the mood of how you are saying it. Experience it letter by letter. Enjoy a pause after each recitation and extend the silence. Or change the mantra from time to time. As you saw in the list above, it is possible to use several mantras for very similar phenomena or deities. If a three syllable rhythm becomes boring, change it to another rhythm. Bījas can be combined in all sorts of variations and orders. Explore them! You'll get much further when you assume a playful and interested attitude than if you grit your teeth, knot your brows, and will yourself to persist. I find it useful to enjoy several mantra patterns relating to my personal deities. Depending on how the deities respond and the mood we are in, I change from mantra to mantra.

Some traditions associate complex visualisations with mantra yoga. In simple cases, these are the personified deities of the mantra. More abstract forms tend to colours and letters. An example from the *Mantramahodhadhiḥ*, 4:

First meditate on the Māyā bīja (hrīṁ), red like the chinarose in your navel. Let flames flare from this centre, burn up your body and your sins. Imagine the Tārā bīja (trīṁ or strīṁ) glowing yellow and gold in your heart. A wind arises from the brightness, it blows away the ashes of your being. Last, visualise the turīya bīja in your forehead (hūṁ), white like a kunda flower or the moon. When the white nectar pours from this centre you can reconstruct your body like that of gods.

Mantra practice can go wrong. A mantra, no matter how holy, is not a guarantee for good results, siddhis, or liberation. A mantra can develop faults. The *Kulārṇava Tantra*, 15, 65-69 lists sixty defects (trans. Rai). A mantra can become *obstructed, cunningly worded, bewildered, tied, angry, pierced, infant, adolescent, young, mature, old, proud, immobilised, swooning, intoxicated, impaled, broken, malignant, slow, reverse-faced, scattered, deaf, blind, unconscious, servant, hungry, paralysed, fallen from its place, afflicted, without affection, maimed, destroyed, lifeless, controverted, asleep, reviled, low, faded, dangerous to be approached, without essence, conquered, burnt, cunning, horrible, overthrown (?), censured, cruel, fruitless, torn assunder, deluded, cursed, diseased, troubled, devoid of some limb, torpid, enemy, apathetic, ashamed, enchanted and indolent.* To erase these defects, mantras have to be purified from time to time. *KT* 15, 71-72 proposes that with the ten rituals of purification the mantras can be kept potent. The rites are summed up as *giving birth, giving life, striking, making aware, consecration, cleansing of impurity, satisfying, libation, lighting and covering in protection.* To revive a worn-out mantra I can only recommend that you go into the trance-awareness of the heart. When you have become very silent, formless and clear, make friends with the mantra once again. Experience it in full, as the Śakti-body of sound awareness. Refresh the meaning, wake up to the intricacies of sound, remember that the mantra is not a sedative or a meaningless jumble of letters. When you have exhausted or abused a mantra, make up for the damage, imbue fresh awareness in it, and come to understand that it is always new and original. If nothing else helps, apologise to its deity for repeating it so thoughtlessly. Listen to what the deity replies. Then take the mantra into everyday life and associate it with an experience of joy and inspiration.

Kālī: Transcending a Mantra.

What is the use of mantra? In some contexts, such as when you repeat a mantra to calm down or wake up, the mantra is a tool and your mind, using tempo, pronunciation and inflection, crafts the desired consciousness. For this purpose you don't have to use any specific mantra. You might as well pick any word from your language and repeat it. If you chose the proper acoustic submodalities, that word will calm you or excite you, just as you will. Please try this.

Things are a little different when you make use of a proper mantra or the name of a deity. A mantra is the body of its deity. It is also a means to embrace this body and to unite with the deity. This union is the purpose of mantra yoga. Well, if you repeat a mantra to invoke, contact, and become a deity, the process comes to a natural stop when the deity is there and your consciousness has merged with it. You call a person by name to get her/his attention. You don't have to repeat that name all the time once s/he listens. Likewise, a mantra should unite the deity and yourself in full awareness. After that point, you are the deity and the deity is you. As you are the deity, there is no reason to continue invoking it. Thus, you go into full samādhi or into full obsession, as you like, and only return to mantra recitation when you slip out of this consciousness again.

The same applies when you have recited a mantra for a few hours and find that it begins to run dry. Every trance has a limit: your attention span and the energy you can put into it. Humans are not made to exist in exactly the same awareness all the time (though many idiots try), and changes are not only inevitable but also beneficial. So when you have been busy reciting for too long, you have the choice of either returning to mundane consciousness or to go on into silence. Recitation may be well and good, but it is not something that should go on indefinitely. You can repeat mantras for a while, be it for ten minutes or a few hours, or maybe for a day or three if you want something substantial, but ultimately, there comes a time when it is wise to go beyond words altogether. Some people do this naturally; Crowley, for instance, saw mantra as a means leading ultimately to silence. Nema proposes something similar in *Maat Magick*, to her it is a natural process that mantra, after a bit of repetition, fades out of consciousness leaving only silence. This is not the case with everyone. When I get a mantra going, it does not fade naturally but continues indefinitely. It is the last thing going in the acoustic channel as I fall asleep and the first thing I recognise when I wake in the morning. Even when I have to interrupt recitation as I want to speak, listen, or write I find the recitation going on, a little muted, in the background. Some days when I am going about my everyday business, a mantra just wakes up and starts going on its own accord. So when I want to go from mantra to silence, I have to do this actively. One way to do this is to slow the mantra. You can make a mantra, or even a bīja so slow that it takes several breaths to recite it even once. Likewise, you can extend the pause that follows. How long can you make this pause before other thoughts intrude? With a bit of practice, the pauses will get longer and longer. Enjoy it. After so much acoustic thinking, a bit of silence can be quite a relief.

Another way is to switch to the celebrated Prāsāda-mantra Haṁsa. The *Kulārṇava Tantra* devotes pages simply on this mantra, and promises that it frees from sins, purifies the soul, gives capacity, wisdom, insight, happiness, liberty, and a lot more. By the recitation of this mantra, the paśu (domestic beast, lay worshipper) becomes Paśupati (Śiva as the Lord of Domestic Beasts), gains the skill to awake deities in images, realises the truth of Śiva and Śakti and ultimately transcends the gods. As I already mentioned in the chapter on breathing, Haṁsa is not just a mantra. It is the only mantra shared by all breathing creatures and also the only one that needs no effort. You learned it directly after you were born. Your lungs filled, you screamed, and from that point onward you have been reciting Haṁsa all your life. The mantra Haṁsa is not a mantra as such. It is the sound of breathing itself. According to various Tantras, Ha is the sound of Śiva, the Puruṣa (primal spirit) and Sa is the sound of Śakti, the Prakṛti (primal nature). This produces HaSa, and for grammatical reasons, the sound ṁ is inserted between them. Haṁsa is considered by some to be a title of Śiva as the absolute. Others reverse the order and give the mantra as So' Haṁ (I am He, usually a reference to Śiva or Viṣṇu) or as Sa' Haṁ (I am She, a reference to any goddess of your choice). Some chose one or the other, some alternate the two forms. But Haṁsa can also be a divine swan, gander, or waterbird, a symbol for free breath and pure consciousness. Listen to your breath now! What does your inhalation sound like? What is the difference to the exhalation? In the *Kulārṇava Tantra*, the exhalation is identified with Ha and Śiva, the inhalation with Sa and Śakti. Not all texts agree with this. However, it hardly matters which part of the mantra is identified with what deity. Haṁsa is not recited like any other word. You don't speak it: you listen to it happening naturally. As you listen, you can calm and smooth your breath until it becomes almost inaudible. You can listen to what you can hear and listen to what you cannot hear. This is what silence is all about.

Japa Mālā

The recitation and repetition of a mantra is called japa and a magical tool for this purpose is a special sort of necklace, a rosary, called the japa-mālā. The japa-mālā is one of the most brilliant magickal inventions ever. To begin with, the item is absolutely useless. It has no practical function whatsoever, and the activity associated with it can be done quite as easily without it. As the japa-mālā is totally free of all practical uses, it can be used for a number of highly irrational activities. This is one of its strongest points and a reason that mālās did not only become popular in India but were soon integrated in Islam and Christianity. The japa-mālā can be found, in one form or another, all over Eurasia. Now there are some differences between the various sorts of rosaries. Indian mālās tend to have 108 beads. This has numerological reasons: 1 x (2x2) x (3x3x3) is 108, which sounds as if it means something. In actual practice, the number 108, while being especially holy and all the rest of it, was chosen to make sure that each round of recitation involves at least one hundred repetitions. The extra eight beads are there in case you count sloppily, miss some beads during repetition or in case some beads break over the years. Another type popular in India has larger beads. Here the usual number is fifty, fifty-one, or fifty-two, depending on how many phonemes you attribute to the devānagarī script. Islamic rosaries have different numbers of beads, nowadays, the most popular numbers are ninety-nine (for the ninety-nine names of Allah), sixty-six, or thirty-three. European Christianity embraced the use of the rosary during the medieval period under the name paternoster, as it was used to count repetitions of the 'Our Father' prayer. This was of importance as the priests regularly ordered sinners (i. e. everybody) to do penance by repeating a given prayer a specific number of times. The paternoster thus functioned as an instrument of punishment and purification. They soon became so popular that some writers remarked that no Christian could be seen who wasn't carrying a paternoster.

The japa-mālā is not only a simple string with beads. Beginning and end of the cycle are clearly marked by one, two or three beads, sometimes of different shape than the rest, which stand out from the circle. These beads represent the guru, the personal deity of the worshipper, or ideally both. When they are reached, there is time for a pause, for silence or for prayer. Then the japa resumes and the beads are counted in the other direction. Traditionally, one is not supposed to go "over the guru bead".

There are some japa-mālās, especially in northern India and the Himalayas, which have two short strings as extra counters dangling from the main loop. Usually each of them has ten beads, which are pulled up before recitation. One of them counts the cycles, i.e. you pull down one bead after each whole cycle. When you have done ten cycles, you pull down one bead on the other counter and start anew. In this way, it is possible to keep count of more than 10,000 mantras, which is really important when you have more faith in numbers than in quality. A lot of cults have. It is, after all, easy for anyone, no matter how simple or stupid, to repeat a given word or phrase for lengthy periods. Making the mantra come to life and experiencing union with the deity is a lot more difficult. So instead of teaching people visualisation and proper mind management, the plain repetition of sacred words was declared to produce 'merit' which could be saved up to make up for a million minor sins. People in many countries invested their energy in brainless repetition while the leaders of their religions, who might have known better, looked on and smiled. The japa-mālā, primarily a tool for liberation, can become a shackle when it is misapplied. Like any other obsessive activity, japa can become a habit or an addiction when its true purpose is forgotten. Also, as in all cultures that made use of the japa-mālā, the material of the item soon became eminently important. Nobility often had mālās made of precious stones, costly metals, amber, coral, and rare pearls; poorer people had to make do with wood, bone, horn, or even nuts and seeds. Some carried mālās made of large metal beads for self-defence. Wherever people made use of mālās, they invested them with talismanic virtues or symbolic meaning. Tantric literature often makes much of these matters, so let us have a brief look into the wide scope of possible materials. The *Mantramahodhadhiḥ* gives the famous ṣaṭkarmāṇī, the six rites of sorcery. These are the rites to appease, subjugate, immobilise, divide, banish, and destroy. The worshipper uses a mālā of conch shells, held by middle finger and thumb, to appease, pacify, unite, and heal. A mālā of lotus seeds is used to subjugate, command, and control, it is held by middle finger and thumb. This posture is also used for rites that aim at worldly enjoyment, acquisition and liberation. To immobilise, to paralyse and render inactive, a mālā of tree-fruit is held between ring finger and thumb. To cause discord, enmity, or to division, a mālā is made of the teeth of the dead. It is held by index finger and thumb. The same posture is used for eradication, banishment, and exorcism, here, the mālā is made of horse teeth. For acts of destruction and liquidation, a donkey-teeth mālā is held between little finger and thumb. For auspicious rites, mālās of 108, 54 and 27 beads are preferred. Destructive rites can be done with fifteen beads.

The *Lakṣmī Tantra*, 39, 36-47 gives the following preferences: Best are rudrākṣa seeds (see below), dhātrīphala and badara nuts are of medium excellence. Gold is useful for rites of prosperity, ancestral worship, and to attain some object. Silver and copper are used in rites to acquire intelligence, valour, and victory. Tin is used in rites to conjure alluring and dangerous female tree spirits (Yakṣiṇīs), often the only girls available to forest dwelling mendicants. Lead is used to master the man-eating Rakṣas and the ghoulish Piśācas. Bell metal (a blend of 7-11 metals) is used to control the Vetāla spirits who enter into corpses and animate them. Brass gives mastery of reptiles and snakes. Iron is used for minor rites. Jewels are esteemed for rites of longevity, health, and prosperity. Crystal gives peace of mind and liberation, coral beads give good luck and plain string (with knots?) is used for liberation. Beads from the roots of the tulasī plant are good for wealth, tranquility and liberation, beads made of lotus give success, shell offers prosperity. Pearls provide a long life, offspring, and fame.

Rudrākṣa seeds are red, gnarled seeds of the tree Eloecarpus Janitrus. In India, they are called rudrākṣa, meaning Rudrā's eyes, and are a special attribute of the Vedic god Rudrā, the healer and destroyer, who transformed into Śiva in early Hinduism. According to the *Devī Bhāgavatam*, Śiva had to spend a thousand divine years in meditation to produce the wonder-weapon aghora to fight the demon Tripura or Tripurāsura, the regent of the three cities. During this time, he could not close his eyes for an instant, and so tears fell, which struck the earth and brought forth rudrākṣa beads. Twelve yellow seeds fell from the solar right eye, sixteen white seeds fell from the lunar left eye, and from the fiery third eye between the eyebrows fell ten black seeds. In the Tantric Buddhism of Tibet, the name rudrākṣa was shortened to some extent, making them rākṣa beads. Rakṣas are usually fierce, blood-thirsty, homicidal demons, who appear disguised as friendly men and seductive women and assault lonely travellers. Occasionally they also appear as guardian spirits and helpers of yogīs and saints, and they do receive offerings in certain rituals. Rudrākṣa seeds are often composed of five segments. These are usually sacred to Śiva. Then there is also a variety of six segments, which is much rarer, and even less common varieties ranging from one to fourteen segments. The *Devī Bhāgavatam* makes a great issue out of the rudrākṣa beads: it devotes a large section of volume 11, chapters 4-7 entirely to the praise of their virtues. The beads are classed according to an interesting numerology:

1 segment: Śiva made manifest. It reveals the highest tattva (principle) and makes Brahman visible.

2 segments: the Deva and the Devī. Ardhanārīśvara, a form of Śiva who is half woman, half man.

3 segments: fire, Agni, the Vedic god of fire and life.

4 segments: Brahmā.

5 segments: Rudra.

6 segments: Kārtikeya or Gaṇapati / Gaṇeśa.

7 segments: Ananga. Also the seven Mātrikās (mothers, matrixes), the sun and the seven ṛṣis (the constellation ursa major, the wain).

8 segments: Vināyaka. Also Brāhmi, the eight Mātrikās, the eight Vasus, the river Ganges. Makes the jīvas truthful.

9 segments: Bhairava, the Fear-inspiring One. Also Yama, who frees from the fear of death.

10 segments: Janārdana, the Deva of the Devas.

11 segments: the eleven Rudras and Indra. It enhances happiness.

12 segments: Ādityas. Also Viṣṇu made manifest.

13 segments: becoming Kārtikeya himself. Also Kāma-Deva, the deity of desire.

14 segments: becoming Śiva. Destroys all diseases and grants eternal health.

There is also a lot of material on which particular sin is destroyed by what type of rudrākṣa bead but this is hardly relevant here. The beads, so the text has it, are of such a sacred nature that owning even a single one is sufficient to free one from all sorts of evils. There was one donkey, for instance, who used to carry loads of rudrākṣas to the market. On some fatal day the poor beast collapsed under the weight and died. Though it wasn't especially wise or saintly, the presence of the beads was enough to liberate its soul. It soon showed up in Śiva's abode, in a human body but with the head of an ass, smeared with ashes and holding a trident. Chapter 6 gives the following anecdote. Once there was this youth studying the *Vedas* at the house off his guru. As he looked just like the god of love himself, the guru's wife became attracted to him and before long the two were secretly making love. To get the guru out of the way, they poisoned him to death. When his father and mother came to know this and complained he poisoned them as well. Then he became addicted to all sorts of bad habits, wasted his wealth and property away, and began to roam wherever he liked. He drank heavily, broke into Brahmin's houses to steal, and was cast out of the family clan by a number of upset relations. He was banished from his home town and settled in a wild forest with the guru's widow. To make a living he killed Brahmins and robbed the corpses. So he lived a short and eventful life doing just about everything prohibited in Indian society. Finally, when he died, the gates of the underworlds opened and thousands of messengers of Yama came out of the deep to carry him to his just punishment. Imagine their surprise when they encountered thousands of Śiva's messengers, who had just arrived from Śiva-loka (Śiva's world). Both parties protested that the soul belonged to them. Yama's gang insisted that sinners belong to the deep, but Śiva's troupe pointed out that the dying man, though a terrible sinner, had died on a spot where a single rudrākṣa bead was buried fifteen feet below the ground. As rudrākṣas destroy all sins, he obtained liberation. This story is well worth considering. From the orthodox point of view, it is the story of an evildoer who gets salvation by sheer good luck. Seen from a left-hand path perspective the story reveals a lot of deeper meanings. Here the killing of the guru can be symbolism for transcending the teacher, or for Kuṇḍalinī surpassing the third eye (site of the true guru) on her ascent to the absolute. Making love with the guru's wife makes sense when the guru's wife is the goddess. Killing the parents may symbolise destroying all family ties; being banished from society is to go beyond humanity altogether. Loss of property equals transcending worldly desires. Drinking is prohibited to orthodox Brahmins, in left-hand Tantra it is part of the worship, and wine can be a synonym for intoxication, rapture, divine bliss, and a number of bodily secretions. Living in the forest is what ascetics used to do and robbing Brahmins is to live without a leader, making use of their treasures (teachings) without an authority. The fifteen feet depth are also meaningful, just think of the fifteen angled yantra of Kālī and the rite of the supreme elixir on the 15th night. All in all, the great sinner can also be a great saint, depending on how the symbols are interpreted.

Using the Japa-Mālā

One useful text is the *Mahānirvāna Tantra.* It contains dozens of mantras for all events in daily ritual and routine, and the mālā features frequently in them. In a rite for the consecration of the japa-mālā, the worshipper recites:

> *O rosary, O rosary, O great rosary, Thou art the image of all Shaktis. Thou art the repository of the fourfold blessings (dharma, artha, Kāma and mokṣa). Do thou therefore be the giver to me of all success. (6, 171)*

It is, perhaps, typical of the Tantric philosophy that the mālā is not an instrument to do penance for past and future sins but an instrument to attain success. A mālā can be a device to focus the mind, to offer attention and love to a deity, and a means to refine oneself. It can also be used to invoke, to banish, to cast spells, and a good many other activities, some of which you'll hopefully discover for yourself.

In the *Mahānirvāna Tantra,* japa is a vital part of the offerings. Having visualised the deity, the devotee offers a variety of flowers, such as absence of egotism, absence of anger, absence of pride, etc.:

> *Let him offer (to the Devī) the ocean of ambrosia, a mountain of meat and fried fish, a heap of parched food, grain cooked in milk with sugar and ghee, the Kula nectar, the Kula flower, and the water which has been used for the washing of the Shakti. Then, having sacrificed all lust and anger, the cause of all impediments, let him do japa. The mālā (rosary) prescribed consists of the letters of the alphabet, strung on Kundalinī as the thread. After reciting the letters of the alphabet from Ā to Ḷa, with the Vindu superposed*

upon each, the Mūla-mantra should be recited. This is known as Anuloma (ordinary order). Again, beginning with Ḷa and ending with Ā, let the sādhaka make japa of the mantra. This is known as Viloma (reversed order), Ksha-kāra is called the Meru. The last letters of the eight groups should be added to the Mūla-mantra, and having made japa of this mantra of one hundred and eight letters the japa should be offered (to the Devī) with the following Mantra: "O Ādyā Kālī, who abidest in the innermost soul of all, Who art the innermost light, O Mother! Accept this japa of my heart. I bow to Thee."

Having finished the japa, he should mentally prostrate himself, touching the ground with the eight parts of his body. Having concluded the mental worship, let him commence the outer worship. (5, 150-157)

A few explanations might be useful here. Remember that they are not the only ones; please think for yourself. The offerings are based on the celebrated five-M offerings. Kula nectar is, as Woodroffe remarked so shyly, *Nectar produced by means of the Shakti*, and Kula flower refers to 'the opening of the flower', which means menstruation. The motion of the beads parallels the motion of Kuṇḍalinī. In Kuṇḍalinī Yoga, the parts of the body are associated with the syllables of the alphabet. Vindu is usually spelled bindu, and refers to the nasal ṁ drone, which is added to each syllable. From Ā to Ḷa means to go through the entire alphabet from beginning to end (the letter Ḷ only occurs in ancient Indian and the Marāṭhī script). The mūla (root) mantra in this ritual is:

Āṁ, Hrīṁ, Śrīṁ, Krīṁ, Parameśvari, Svāhā.

The Ksha-kāra is the prominent central bead, which here represents mount Meru, the seat of Śakti and Śiva. The eight groups are the groups into which the alphabet is divided. The first letters of each group are **A, Ka, Ca, Ṭa, Ta, Pa, Ya, Śa**, which is a time honoured mantra of Mahāmāyā. The last letters, employed in the worship of Kālī, are **Au, Ṅa, Ña, Ña, Na, Ma, Va, Ḷa**. Each of them is pronounced with the ṁ at the end. Prostration of the eight parts of the body means touching the ground with feet, hands, knees, breast, head, eyes, mind, and words. You could call it prostration but earthing comes closer to the mark.

Some authorities favour the use of the mālā as they want the motion of the mind to be connected with the motion of the body. People who find it hard to focus their thoughts may find prolonged repetition easier when there is body to remind them of the job. This is especially useful when you aim at doing a given number of repetitions and find yourself daydreaming or falling asleep. Personally I disagree with this attitude; if body is tired, it is better to sleep and resume the practice with a fresh mind. Likewise, when you are really deep into the mantra, it can be a distraction to keep up a motion of the hand simultaneously. The mālā is a tool for meditation, it is not the end and summit of it. There are occasions when it is wise to forget body, motion, and mālā. When you merge with the gods, stop fiddling with beads. As with all things, it is useful to know when you have had enough.

Well, so much for a few examples how the mālā can be integrated in daily ritual. You don't have to imitate them, it is much more rewarding to experiment and develop forms of trance and worship that are suited to you. Just as you can use the name of any deity, no matter the culture, age, or tradition as a mantra, or make up your own mantras when suitably inspired, it is possible to use the mālā in entirely original ways. Over the years I have tried quite a few of them. I have found it useful to anchor the use of the mālā to specific states of mind. I use the right hand to do active, energetic japa with full attention on the deities, the sounds, and the breathing. This japa, blessed by will, wisdom and action, has the quality of prasāda. The left hand is used for japa without mantra or intent; as I move the beads, gently and slowly, I become quiet, calm, open, receptive. Often, the experience has a rapturous, intoxicating, and stimulating quality. The different effects of each hand were established in the heart-consciousness trance with the blessings of the personal deities. I usually do a routine of at least one cycle with the right hand to invoke and energise, followed by several cycles with the left hand to receive and enjoy. For these purposes, I often use a small mālā of 18-25 beads or a simple loop of red string. It generally lives around my wrist and may be used in public without getting too much attention.

Have you ever wondered how moving the beads makes a difference? One traditional way is to begin the mantra while holding the bead between index and thumb. Then the mantra continues, and on its last vibrations, the bead is allowed to slip into the hand. This is not the only way. It makes a difference when you move the bead during recitation, or when you move it after recitation. Holding the bead while reciting seems to generate a certain tension, moving it after each recitation is more relaxed but can lead to faster and faster recitation, as the motion seems to accelerate the words. How fast are you moving the beads? How does speed influence your experience? What happens when you slow down and become ever slower? What if you move the beads in a faltering fashion and occasionally slip them forward and backwards? Does your experience change when you move several beads at once? As you go along, observe what you are doing. Are you moving the bead to the rhythm of the mantra or are you forcing the mantra to accord with the rhythm of your fingers? What difference does it make for you? What are the differences that make a real difference? Which sort of recitation gets you energetic and powerful? Which sort calms, settles, and soothes your mind? What do you want your mālā to do for you?

If you want to stabilise a soothing trance, here is one way to do it. Go into a deep trance for a start. When you have reached a suitable level, gently reach for your mālā and hold it. Now move the beads very slowly. As you do so, suggest to yourself that the mālā will always be a gate into gentle and relaxed trance states whenever you use it. You could also use it for other states of mind. Go into a consciousness that seems attractive. Then ask your deep mind to produce exactly this state whenever you use the mālā in a specific way. Practice a bit. And suggest that the experience becomes stronger as you explore it. This sort of thing is easy to combine with all the varieties of moving the mālā between odd combinations of fingers. It is also in all likeliness what the Tantric sorcerers did to make the odd combinations functional. Just because you move the beads between an unusual configuration of fingers is, after all, no reason that you automatically have the power to make friends or slay enemies. Each of the postures, and indeed any mudrā, is only powerful when you have associated its form with the required state of mind. Using such methods and keeping an open mind, you can invent a dozen new applications of the mālā which go far beyond the traditional routine. The mālā has no purpose as such. It has no effect at all. You can give it a purpose and an effect, and make it come true.

Counting digits

Most cultures began to count using fingers. One hand for five numbers, two hands to count up to ten. This is the start of the decimal system. Others continued with the toes, here we find maths based on a count of twenty, very popular among Mayas, Aztecs, Inuit, Ainu, and Celts. And this was just the beginning. Some cultures simply counted fingers, toes, and a wide range of anatomical places, others narrowed down on the hands and attached more and more numbers to the digits. Elaborating things a lot, the Chinese developed a method of counting to 100,000 on a single hand. For this purpose, each joint provides three numbers (right, middle, and left side of the finger), the little finger counting the numbers 1-9, the ring finger the tens, the middle finger the hundreds, index the thousands, and thumb the ten-thousands. Some even invented methods of doing calculations on the hands. There is a method to multiply numbers between five and ten using the fingers, and another system for numbers between ten and fifteen (Ifrah 1993: 96-98).

Occasionally you can read of yogīs counting the repetition of mantras on their fingers. This tradition may predate doing japa with a mālā. Islamic religion, as mentioned earlier, attaches great importance to the recitation of the ninety-nine names of Allah, or really the hundred names (the last name remains a mystery). The Prophet once informed some women that beads or small stones should not be used to count the repetitions of the sacred names. Instead they should count using their fingers. As a result, the Muslim rosary, which began to become popular in the ninth century, was not accepted by a number of important Islamic authorities until the 15th century CE (Ifrah 1993: 89-90). Counting with fingers was preferred.

In India the same seems to have been the case. There are several approaches to finger-counting. One method is to assign a specific hand-posture to each number. For example, you could start with an open hand and indicate numbers by closing specific fingers. Bending the little finger of the left hand gives one; folding little and ring finger two; little, ring and index finger three; ring and middle finger four; middle finger five; ring finger six; and so on. Using all sorts of finger-positions and physical gestures (such as touching the groin for 90,000 and folding the hands for a million) a wide range of numbers can be communicated. Not very easy, as each number is a gesture, but useful for signalling. The Romans had such signals, the same goes for the Greeks and the Persians. They may have derived their versions from the ancient Egyptians. There are paintings of fifth dynasty Egyptians haggling by pointing fingers at each other. The venerable Bede described this method in the seventh century, his account is almost identical to a Persian system.

Another possibility is to assign numbers to the joints or digits of one or two hands. This method is neater as it involves less motion and gesticulation. One system, especially popular in east India, Bengal, and Bangladesh, counts the joints of the fingers. Number one is at the base of the little finger, two in the middle of the little finger, three at the top joint of the little finger. Four at the root of the ring finger, five in its centre, six at the top joint. Seven is at the base of the middle finger, and so on. After twelve (top joint of the index) follows thirteen at the base of the thumb, fourteen at its middle joint, and fifteen at the top joint. This allows you to count to fifteen on one hand, using both hands you can count to thirty. Useful for calculations based on the old Indian half-month, where you have fifteen units (kalās) for the bright (waxing moon) and fifteen for the dark (waning moon) fortnight. Halhed (1778 in Ifrah 1993: 88) saw it in use. It was not only popular for counting. Traders used it for bargaining. Customer and trader would stand before a small desk. Putting their hands under a piece of cloth, they haggled by touching the finger-joints of each other. With such a silent form of negotiation, bystanders and competing traders remained ignorant of the prices offered and, finally, accepted. A very similar method of counting became popular in wide parts of the Islamic world. To count the ninety-nine names of Allah, both hands were counted thrice, starting at the base of the little finger of the left hand. For the last three units (to make up a total of thirty-three), the tips of the fingers of the right hand were added; thirty-one is the tip of the little finger, thirty-two of the ring finger, thirty-three the tip of the middle finger.

Another system was based on the number twelve, useful for calculations as twelve can be divided by two, three, four, and six. Here the digits of the fingers (not the joints) are touched by the thumb. Counting started with the top digit of the little finger, then followed the middle digit, then the bottom. Next the top of the ring finger and so on. The thumb has no numbers, it points at the digits of the other fingers. This system was (and probably is) popular in India, Indo-China, Pakistan, Afghanistan, Iran, Iraq, Turkey, Syria, and Egypt. Possibly it is based on ancient Egyptian mathematics. The Egyptians had days consisting of twelve bright and twelve dark hours (with varying length according to the season). On the other hand, the Sumerians also made much of the number twelve. We owe them the twelve signs of the zodiac and the calculation of time in units of sixty. Sixty was a sacred number to the Sumerians, who based their maths on a sexagesimal system, i.e. a complete cycle involves sixty numbers. To count to sixty, you count to twelve on the right hand, using the thumb of the left. When twelve are complete, you fold the little finger of your left hand and count from thirteen to twenty-four using the thumb. For twenty-five, fold little finger and ring finger of the left hand, and so on. As there are five fingers on the counting hand, you can use this system to count to sixty. These are by no means the only possibilities. Should you care to count mantras or breaths make up any system that suits you.

A Chance to Wake Up

A good mantra is a lot more than a device to change awareness. It can be used for trances, but it also has its use when it comes to getting out of the deep trance that constitutes 'everyday awareness' in most people. Better still, it can be used to fuse inner and outer reality. When do you recognise that the world is speaking to you? When do you become aware that the divine is not only near, but surrounds you in all shape and form, including your own? There are moments when unusual sights, sounds, and events take you out of your routine. Nothing is as dull as everyday awareness. No matter just what constitutes this consciousness, as long as it works on habit and routine you may believe that you are awake, but your Kuṇḍalinī certainly isn't. There are so many chances to wake up. There are so many opportunities to change what you are doing and thinking. You have to recognise them. Then you recite a mantra, make a gesture, and realise that everything is here.

Kulacūḍāmaṇi Tantra, 4, 5-20 offers a great opportunity to wake up. The mantras are quoted from the translation of Louise Finn (highly recommended).

When you see a vulture, say hello to Mahākālī.

When you see a female jackal, worship Kṣemaṅkarī. Remember that female jackals can be messengers of Yama (death), they can also be incarnations of Pārvatī (who has the name Śivā: Jackal), they can be attendants of Kālī and shapes chosen by Yoginīs as they play on earth.

When you observe an osprey, eagle, crow or a black cat, greet the black goddess by reciting:

> *Pūrṇodarī, Mahācaṇḍā, Muktakeśī, Balipriyā. You whose look is kindly disposed to Kula worship! Homage to you, beloved of Śaṅkara (Śiva).*

Pūrṇodarī means the one with a full stomach or belly, she is the all-devouring, all-including, perfectly centred goddess. Mahācaṇḍā is the Great Fury, the Great Wild One, Muktakeśī is the goddess of wild, tangled hair (a reference to spider magic?), and Balipriyā the goddess who is fond of (bloody) offerings. In a general Śākta context, this means usually a goat slaughtered in the temple and grilled on the lawn, in the initiated tradition it is the offering of the secretions that fashion the world, in physical or abstract form. These four names form a magnificent mantra that should be experienced in the vastness of your heart.

Should you come upon a graveyard or a corpse, two of the most inauspicious things in traditional Hinduism, do something even more inauspicious and circumambulate in counter-clockwise direction (good for rites of sorcery) and cheer yourself up by reciting:

> *Oh you with the terrible tusks! With the cruel (sharp) eyes! Who shouts with the cry of the wild boar! O mother who yells most dreadfully! Homage to you who dwell in funeral pyres!*

When you see a black (dark) flower or a red dress, stretch out on the ground like a rod (use your imagination. It's the emotion and intent that count.), and worship Tripurā:

> *To you who have the appearance of the Bandhuka flower! O Tripurā! Destroyer of all fear! Who have appeared for (my) good fortune! Homage! O lovely lady*

When you see a dark flower, a king, a prince, an elephant, a horse, a shield, a hero, a buffalo, an image of a Kula deity or Mahiṣamardinī (the Slayer of Mahiṣasura), dangers and troubles can be averted by worshipping Jayadurgā (Victorious Durgā) and reciting:

> *Oh Jayadevī! Upholder of the world! Tripurā! Ambā you who are the triple form deity!*

When you chance upon a vessel of wine, fish, flesh, or a Kula woman, worship the goddess Bhairavī (the Fear-Inspiring One) by reciting:

> *Oh you who make the Kula ritual prosper in order to destroy the terrible obstacles! I bow to you oh goddess! Bestower of favours! Adorned with a garland of skulls! You whose mouth is smeared with streams of blood! I bow to you: (Oh goddess! Remover of all obstacles! Homage to you who are the beloved of Hara!)*

Doing these acts makes the siddhis prosper, forgetting them is said to cause loss of siddhi. This should make a walk in country or city an exciting opportunity to liven up everyday experience with a bit of drama. As you can see, most of the mantras are not the sort that are recited for hundreds or thousands of times. They are more like spells (or suggestions) connecting events in the outer world with power and awareness in the inner. Learning to respond to such sights you respond to the Supreme Śakti who is the whole world and all-consciousness. And I hope that you extend the practice. Several items on the list might be a bit rare in your country, so maybe you could replace them with similar beings or things that do exist in your world. A fox can replace a jackal, a raven can be a substitute for a vulture, be creative and find alternatives. It's no use to salute elephants with a mantra when you have to go to the zoo just to see one. Not that elephants should be kept in zoos, for that matter, they are far too intelligent. If you adapt the rite to your environment, you will find the environment waking you from your everyday awareness. But the *Kulacūḍāmaṇi Tantra* goes beyond this point. In verse 18, the goddess declares that if you kill, hurt, or trap any of these beings, no amount of initiation will make your siddhis arise.

All of them are beloved of the goddess and the Kula worshippers, and appear out of the universal essence. What was that? Should we consider the Kaulas conservationists, animal lovers, and nature worshippers? I should hope so. In the *Kaulajñāna nirṇaya,* 23, 1-11 these ideas are elaborated. Devi asks how the Yoginīs move on earth and Bhairava replies that all the deities move on earth, assuming the shape of female animals, such as doves, vultures, swans, hens, birds, dogs, wolves, owls, hawks, bees, beetles, jackals, goats, cows/buffaloes, cats, camels, mongooses, tigers, elephants, peacocks, cuckoos. They also appear as horses, cocks, serpents, stags, scorpions, bulls, mice, frogs, and certain human beings. All of them should be revered and when they die, they are not to be eaten. The Yoginīs move on earth in the shape of diverse animals: *One should never show anger of speech and mind to them, nor should one ever speak harshly to maidens or women.*

In this sort of world-view you can encounter the gods in all sorts of shapes and walk in their midst as their companion.

Figure 35 - Indian Black Vulture.

9: The Heart of Kula

The Heart in Veda

The heart of Kula is the experience of the heart. Before we get there, it might be useful to consider the heart in Indian symbolism. Our first references to the heart (hṛdaya) are as old as Indian literature. You can discover them in the *Vedas.* Now the heart is a tricky thing. If you are not an Indian you are likely to get the wrong ideas. Europeans generally tend to associate a lot of concepts with the heart that are a long way from Asian thought. In medieval Europe the heart was the seat of the soul. It was also the seat of the emotions, hence the idea that love, longing, and desire arise from the heart. People had an open heart when they were honest and frank, they had a heart for those who suffer, and those who were without compassion had a cold heart, or even a heart of stone. Some lost their hearts when they fell in love, others broke theirs, and died of it. This is just the start, for a bit of fun stop now and consider the meaning of the heart in your culture, your language, and your period. In ancient India, the heart was a different matter. As in European thought, Indians accept that the heart is the source of emotions. However, it is also the source of every other experience. From the heart arise knowledge, thought, belief, doubt, awareness, and every other faculty of mind and senses. Visions arise in the heart, sound and revelation are heard in the heart. In worship and meditation the heart is the meeting-place of gods and humans. The *Vedas* are full of allusions to the heart that go beyond the European symbolism. Here are just a few examples from the *Ṛg Veda* (trans. Griffith):

> *ṚV 10, 183,2 I saw thee pondering in thine heart, and praying that in due time thy body might be fruitful...*
>
> *ṚV 10, 129, 4 Thereafter rose Desire (Kāma) in the beginning, Desire, the primal seed and germ of Spirit. Sages who searched with their heart's thought discovered the existent's kinship in the non-existent.*
>
> *ṚV 8, 89, 5 Then spake my spirit to the heart within me...*

The heart had an important place in the Vedic period, even though it was not the most important religious symbol.

In the *Upaniṣads* the theme continues. *BāUp* 3,19-27 proposes that the forms perceived by the agency of sun and eye are supported by the heart. The offerings are supported by faith and faith is only supported by the heart. Likewise, water is supported by semen and semen arises from the heart. This is meant to say that lust is a function of the heart, which manifests in sexual elixirs. Initiation rests on truth, and truth is supported by the heart. Fire rests on speech, and speech arises out of the heart. Ultimately, body and heart rest on breath (prāṇa), which rests on apāna (here: outbreath), which rests on vyāna (diffuse breath), which rests on samāna (balanced or middle breath). This is the self, and it is described much like Austin Spare did: *That self is not this, not this.* Further on, *BāUp* 4,3,7 states that the self is the person here, who consists of knowledge gained from the senses, *the light within the heart.* Similar references abound. We learn that the self of all beings is located in the heart. In humans this self is thumb sized or even smaller. But there is more than just the self concept within the heart. *BāUp* 4,4,22 speaks of the unborn self. You can find this self, the controller of all, the lord of all, the ruler of all, within the heart. You may note that at this early stage, the heart was already used as a term that went a long way beyond the physical organ. When people die, for instance, they do not leave their bodies directly. Instead, they gather their breaths, all particles of light, and descend into the heart (*BāUp* 4,4,1-2). Then the point of the heart lights up, and by this light the self departs through eye, head, or one of the body's apertures. Keep this in mind as you explore the trance awareness of the heart; the way into the depth of yourself closely resembles the way you'll go when dying. In Upaniṣadic thought the entire core of each being is empty, and this emptiness, alive, aware, and full of self, is the true heart.

The Heart in Tantra

The primary meaning of the heart in Tantric lore is the conjunction of consciousness and form. This makes the heart the locus of cognition, thinking, and awareness. It is not the only place. Several Tantric schools proposed that the true seat of awareness (or the jīva) is in the head. Others preferred the heart. The former had this thing about head-worship, not a bad idea after all. Now it is not the intent of this chapter to argue about the true location of the self. The point is that introversion into the heart is a practical experience. If you withdraw all of your awareness into your head, you will find that your body gets top-heavy, making it harder to sit in a relaxed and upright posture. Also, too much head and you might get tangled in thinking. When you locate your awareness in your heart, by contrast, you will sit deeper and find yourself relaxing. It will be easier for you to withdraw from the outside world and you will have less distraction.

Figure 36 - Bhairava.

In Tantric lore, unlike Indian religion in general, the heart became one of the most essential symbols. You find the metaphor used in a wide range of arcane texts. In the *Kulacūḍāmaṇi Tantra* 4,49 Kālī is established and dismissed *in the crossroads of the heart.*

Kṣemarāja stated: *Hṛdaya means the light of consciousness inasmuch as it is the foundation of the entire universe.*

The *Śiva-sūtra-s,* 1,15 have: *Due to the union of the mind with the Heart, objects, and also the void, appear (as ... a form of consciousness).*

Utpaladeva declares: *This consciousness is vibratory light (sphurattā). It is absolute reality (mahāsattā) which is beyond spatial and temporal distinctions. This consciousness being the universal essence is called the Heart of the Lord.* These quotations are from Paul Eduardo Muller-Ortega's excellent *The Triadic Heart of Śiva,* where the matter is treated in great detail. The work focuses on the experience of the heart in the non-dual Kaula Śaivism of Kashmir, as expressed by Abhinavagupta. The latter developed a deep and highly complex doctrine of the heart that makes sense as soon as you know the heart from direct experience. Here 'philosophy' arises out of practice, as it should. In *The Short Gloss on the Supreme / The Queen of the Three* (Parātrīśikālaghuvṛttiḥ), Abhinavagupta wrote: *The power which arises in the Heart of consciousness is freedom itself. The purpose of its creative activity is the 'group' (kula), the entire range of perceiving subject, perceived object, and process of perception. Thus it is called kaulinī-having to do with the group. She is the noble lady of that constructed group, she rules over it. By knowing it, she causes its manifestation, as well as reabsorbing it in herself.* (commentary to 2b-3a) . In his long commentary on the *Rudrayāmala* (PTV), Abhinavagupta extends the meaning of the heart into several new dimensions. It is one thing to learn that the heart is the core of all reality, which unfolds from the vibrating, pulsing, and shimmering self-nature within. On the other hand, he also saw the heart as a useful locus/state for specific meditations. In his system, mantras awake in the heart, and indeed the heart is the manifestation of all mantras. Likewise, the powers inherent in the sixteen vowels are explored and applied in the consciousness of the heart. And within the heart specific meditations happen (commentary to verse 35-36). The yogī should meditate on the female genitals and the yoginī on the male genitals within the heart lotus. Lest this location be confused with the usual heart cakra, Abhinavagupta hastens to add that the term 'lotus' is only used as a figure of speech, for the two organs are characterised, just as the heart and indeed awareness is, by contraction and expansion. He links these two processes to the pulsation of in-breath and out-breath, and incidentally to the upward rising prāṇa and the descending apāna current, to the drinking of nectar and the incomparable heart mantra, Sauḥ, which is at the core of so much of Abhinavagupta's writing. Heart can mean awareness, it can be Bhairava and Bhairavī, it can even be the sexual secretions. Indeed, what you perceive of the world has its origin, maintenance, and dissolution in the heart. Yes, this sounds confusing, and it won't get any better when I continue writing about it. Words don't make it. You'll learn about the real heart as soon as you turn inwards and experience the central void.

The Heart as an Organ

In Indian thought, the heart (hṛdaya) has at least four different levels of meaning. The first is the most obvious one. Think of the heart as the physical organ. You may consider it a muscle that pumps your blood. This is a modern idea. In ancient India, medicine was not as developed as today. Old Indian medicine is a brilliant science when it comes to principles of disease, cure, and healthy living. However, it has its shortcomings regarding anatomy and the functions of the organs. Indian physicians usually had a philosophic idea of the activity of the organs. In their society, contact with dead people was frowned upon. Dissecting corpses was a violation of religious law. There was a vague general knowledge of what you can find inside the body, but few ideas what it is good for. They invented beautiful theories, however. The general idea was that body consisted of seven basic elements (Glasenapp 1958, vol. 2, 226). 1. The rasa (sap, juice, fluid) is digested food and moves through the body thanks to the 24 channels that emerge from the heart. Thus, the heart is the first and central distributor of foodstuff. 2. Blood. The rasa receives its red colour when it moves through the liver, where it is heated by the gall-bladder. 3. Flesh consists of digested and congealed blood. 4. Fat is digested flesh. 5. Bones are built from digested and dried fat. 6. Marrow consists of digested bone. 7. Sperm and menstrual blood develop out of digested marrow. The essence of all these elements forms ojas, the life energy. Disease results naturally when any single element increases or decreases too much. In this system the digestive process is the primal power of transformation. The whole process, from digestion of food to its appearance in its most refined form (the sexual secretions) takes twenty-eight days. It is a slow, alchemical process ranging from crude, material nourishment to the production of the very essence that goes to create new human beings.

The Heart as a Cakra

The second meaning of the heart can be found in various cakra systems. Here the heart had a variety of meanings and received various descriptions which have very little to do with anatomy. In later periods, the heart was usually considered the site of the anāhata cakra. Anāhata means a sound that is produced without two objects striking each other. Now most forms of sound require two objects to emerge. A drum and gong needs a hand, mallet, or voice to sound, a string resonates when it is moved by fingers, mallets, plectrum, bow, or wind, a flute and whistle reacts to the friction of the air. The heart, so it was assumed, sounds without being struck, touched, or otherwise influenced, hence its sound has a cosmic quality closely related to the sound-nature of Brahman. Listening to the anāhata sounds became a major practice of nāda yoga. The identification of the heart as the source of the anāhata sounds is a majority decision. Some authors localised the sounds elsewhere. More on the cakras further on.

Home of the Personal Deity

The third meaning of the heart is the residence of the personal deity. This location, a little below the anāhata cakra, is called the ānanda kanda. You won't find it on the usual cakra pictures as it exists on a different sort of map. The same body can be described in many ways. Each description is a model of reality, and each of them is incomplete when examined on its own. The ānanda kanda is not part of the well-known seven cakra model. However, it is an important locus for the centring of yourself in your vision of the divine. Are you ready for some practical dreaming? Here is a good one.

Traditionally, the iṣṭadevatā (personal deity) is supposed to be located and worshipped in the heart. Now the cakra housing the iṣṭadevatā is also a place, a state of awareness, and a location to visit on your journeys in the imagination. Several texts describe the place in more or less detail. A brief description appears in the *Gheraṇḍa Saṁhita*, where it is proposed for a sthūla dhyāna (coarse meditation). See a vast ocean of nectar in your heart. In the centre of the ocean, imagine an island of gems. The sand on the shore is sparkling jewels. To all four sides of the island kadamba trees are growing, they are in full blossom and breathtakingly beautiful. There is a garden in this grove, where all sorts of trees flower, mālati (*cocculos cordifolius*), mallikā (*jasminum samboc.*), macis, kesara (*rattleria tinctoria*), campaka (*michelia champaka*), pārijāta (*erythrina indica*), and lotus blossoms, their scent pervading everywhere. In the centre of the island imagine a kalpa tree, enchanting the senses, with four Veda branches, ever full of blossoms and fruit. Bees buzz and cuckoos call. The air is warm and the colours bright. Imagine a pavilion made of ruby and other priceless jewels. Imagine a throne within it. Imagine your iṣṭadevatā seated on the throne, observe its ornaments, its attributes, its animal companion. Contemplating the iṣṭadevatā in this fashion is called sthūla dhyāna. I suggest you don't just stand there worshipping like an imbecile. Get closer to your deity. You two share a common essence. When you touch, embrace and become your deity, you will understand.

This sort of meditation is considered gross as it relies on images and things rather than abstractions. It is fairly typical for a good many similar meditations, all of them based on the principle that it is easier to imagine a deity when you provide it with a proper setting and take your time to develop the dream. There is so much you can imagine and get excited about in this visualisation that it will be easy for you to spend some time establishing it in full detail. No doubt your deep mind will provide a lot of other items to beautify your heart island. This is called creativity and should be encouraged. The more surprises you discover on your island, the more will the visit teach you. Look for the unexpected!

There are numerous descriptions of the jewel island in Indian literature. It is not always located in the heart, but it is always a place of joy and beauty. You can go there whenever you need a bit of warmth and relaxation. Some accounts are so extensive that it would take months to memorise all the details. Here the island is brimming full of buildings, palaces, courts, shrines, pools, gardens, and the like. It is peopled by all sorts of spiritual beings, and as you know, there are more spiritual beings around in Indian lore than anybody could ever need. This sounds like complication, but it isn't. When you visualise, you will soon learn that imagining a simple symbol or object for a minute can be a real challenge. Getting into a voluptuous dream full of vivid details and overwhelming beauty is a lot easier. If you take your time and develop your journey so that it becomes a tale, it can take off on its own account and carry you to entirely new realities. Human minds like to make up stories, and when a story is begun it may well continue under its own volition. Are you ready for action? This is something to do and experience for yourself. Go there and develop an island that really suits your nature. If you merely try to imagine an Indian setting you may be missing something vital. It's your heart island, so make it an island after your own heart. Make it a sacred space where you feel happily at home. This is one test for your meditation: if you feel your heart open, you are doing fine. An open heart, I should add, is not necessarily a heart that is constantly full of love and bliss. An open heart is a heart that is able to perceive fully. This can mean a wide range of possible experiences. The heart island of Tantra is very similar to the islands of the immortals in Daoist lore, and maybe we have a bit of cultural exchange here. Other sources describe the location as a yantra. In the *Mahānirvāṇa Tantra* (5, 133-135) the ānanda kanda is visualised as a red, eight petaled lotus. In the petals are the eight nāyikās (attendants) of the pīṭhas (seats, sacred places), whose names are: Mangalā, Vijayā, Bhadrā, Jayantī, Aparājita, Nandinī, Nārasinghī, and Vaiṣṇavī. In the tips of the petals are the eight Bhairavas: Asitānga (He of the Black Body), Caṇḍa (The fierce One), Kapālī (The Skull-Wearer), Krodha (The Angry One), Bhīṣaṇa (The Terrific One), Unmatta (The Mad One), Ruru (?), and Sanghārī (The Destroyer). In the centre of the red lotus abides Ādyā Kālī, who is black-blue like the dark rain clouds and clad in a crimson raiment. The devotee offers the elixir that cascades from the peak of the head to wash her feet (yoni). Your mind and all your thinking is her sacrificial food. This is true bali. I'll spare you the details: go there and find out for yourself.

The Heart in Kashmir Tantricism

The fourth meaning of the heart is a lot harder to comprehend. While many religious people went to the jewel island in their trances, only a few managed to embrace the central void. We are approaching an interpretation that is popular among the Kulas, Kaulas, Krama, and Trika lineages, especially those who are influenced by Abhinavagupta's teaching (late 10th century CE).

In Kula lore the heart is a lot vaster than you read earlier. Physically, the term can refer to any location between your shoulders and hips. Some even used the term 'heart' for the bowels. In this interpretation the word heart does not refer to any organ or limited space. Neither does it refer to a cakra. It comes closer to the meaning of middle or centre. Of course this is not a new idea. You find the foundation of the metaphor in the *Upaniṣads* and in the earliest texts on yoga. Let's have some examples from one of the most practical texts, the *Śvetāśvatara Upaniṣad.* As a fairly late *Upaniṣad* (5th century BCE?) it contains elements of what became early Hinduism, such as the worship of the highest self under the names of Rudra and Śiva, the notion that the self within each being is neither male, female, or neuter, and the emphasis on meditation and realisation (instead of sacrifice and duty). The text was and is a favourite of the much later Tantric schools:

> *2,8. Holding the body steady with the three (upper parts, chest, neck and head) erect, causing the senses and the mind to enter the heart, the wise man should cross by the boat of Brahman (AUM) all the streams which cause fear.*
>
> *2,9. Repressing his breathings here (in the body), let him who has controlled all movements, breathe through his nostrils, with diminished breath; let the wise man restrain his mind vigilantly as (he would) a chariot yoked with vicious horses.*
>
> *3,11. He who is in the faces, heads and necks of all, who dwells in the cave (of the heart) of all beings, who is all-pervading, He is the lord and therefore the omnipresent Śiva.*
>
> *3,13. A person of the measure of a thumb is the inner self, ever dwelling in the heart of men. He is the lord of the knowledge framed by the heart and the mind. They who know that become immortal.*
>
> *3,20. Subtler than the subtle, greater than the great is the self that is set in the cave of the (heart) of the creature. One beholds Him as being actionless and becomes freed from sorrow, when through the grace of the Creator he sees the Lord and His majesty.*
>
> *4, 17. That god, the maker of all things, the great self, ever seated in the heart of creatures is framed by the heart, by the thought, by the mind, they who know that become immortal.*
>
> *4, 20. His form is not to be seen; no one sees Him with the eye. Those who through heart and mind know Him as abiding in the heart become immortal.*

In these lines you can find the basics of the heart metaphor that became so important to the mad saints of Kashmir. Here the heart is a vast cave or hollow within the body (any body, all-body, the entire manifest world) and the self enters this cave, its natural dwelling space, by a process of introversion. The nature of this heart is emptiness, but from it, all forms of consciousness arise. In Kaula lore, these basic ideas were elaborated and refined. Let me give a brief summary, and remind you that the words you are reading are but a pale shadow of the living experience.

There is a heart at the centre of each Kula. As you remember, the word Kula may mean a group, clan, tribe, family, or cluster, be it of things, matter, events, or experience. Cakras are Kula, for example. Kula may also mean a self-contained system or organism. An atom is a Kula, a molecule is a Kula, each plant, beast, or person is a Kula, and the same goes for biotopes, habitats, planet earth, and indeed our universe.

Let me add that this idea, simple as it is, does have its complications. You, as a living organism, are self sufficient enough to be a Kula in a world of Kulas. However, you cannot reproduce on your own. Human organisms reproduce by sexuality, and in this sense, the true Kula is not you on your own but you with your partner. For this reason, some see the individual as the Kula while others consider the couple, or the divine couple, as the true Kula. This Kula consists of two who become one. They both believe themselves to be a self, and each has a heart, but as the nature of the heart is emptiness, this is a shared, undifferentiated, and non-dual emptiness.

But let us continue exploring Kulas as such. As all Kulas consist of matter and energy, each Kula is a Śakti, and one of the general names for Śakti is Kula. Use this moment to consider yourself as Kula. Your body is Kula, as it consists of organs, fluids, functions, molecules, energy particles, and odd squishy things that do jobs you don't really want to know about. Your identity is Kula. Try to define yourself! Who are you? Who have you been and who will you become? What is your place in the world? What is your character, your nature, what constitutes your mind space? All of these, whatever and however you name it, are part of the Kula that encloses your awareness. Each Kula has a centre, and this centre is the heart. The centre of the Kula is awareness. Abhinavagupta identified Bhairava/Śiva with pure, formless awareness. We are a long way from personified deities here. Consciousness is not a deity, consciousness is the faculty that makes the deities and indeed all beings and things appear. Awareness is not a thing. Unlike the Kulas, which define themselves by relations to other Kulas, awareness is Akula, i.e. without clusters. Your awareness is not your awareness at all. It is just awareness. Awareness exists wherever being is, and as awareness is indivisible, it is continuous. Here you have a clue why Śiva (awareness) exists in every living entity and in all that exists. Not your Śiva or my Śiva or any other Śiva that can be defined. Consciousness is not a thing. Things have shapes, forms, power, meaning; they appear, transform and disappear again. Consciousness is unlimited, undefinable, ever-present and never known. It is not a thing but an absence, and an absence of an absence, and an absence of that. This absence never was but always is.

If you agree you may be wrong.

What we need is not philosophical speculation but direct experience. The heart can be experienced anytime you like. The heart is here, wherever you are.

Experience of the Heart

The experience of the heart is the secret core of a lot of Tantra. The actual practice is surprisingly simple. You can experience the heart today, you can do it now. However, you may need a bit of practice it get used to it, to explore the creative, pulsing, vibrating void, and to understand what it is all about. For a start, it may be useful to find a quiet place where you will not be disturbed. Lie down on your back and put a piece of cloth over your eyes if you like. Some imagine more easily against a dark background, others against a bright one. What do you prefer? Are you more imaginative in a dark or bright space? Or do this sitting on a chair. Sit erect, allow your body to settle into the posture, take some deep breaths and look around before you close your eyes. You might start by being aware of the Kula around you: what do you sense of the outer world? Then move inward to the periphery of your body, where the sense organs are. You can feel the ground (or the chair), you can sense the clothes you are wearing, the presence (or absence) of light before your closed eyes, the sound and feel of your breath as it moves out and in smoothly. Take a while to explore the sensations, give yourself time to slow down and turn inwards. I prefer not to recite mantra or speak suggestions as I go inward to the heart. The heart experience is simplicity, so I keep the process of introversion simple. The next step is in the imagination. Step back from the periphery of your body. Withdraw from your skin, your sense organs, your face. Leave your limbs out there. As you move inwards, your shape becomes diffuse. The outer shell of experience defines so much of what we sense of ourselves. As you go inwards, your body and your self-definition dissolve. Become smaller. Then sink down into the cavity of your heart. Do this leisurely, peacefully, slowly. How big are you? In the *Śvetāśvatara Upaniṣad* your self is as big as a thumb. It can be atomic if you will, or virtually non-existing. As you descend within yourself, you enter the vast cave of the heart. This is the entire centre of your manifest experience (Śakti). We are not talking about the physical organ. We are talking about the voidness of the pre-create. What is the nature of your heart? As it is void, it can take on any form. What is the nature of yourself? As it is void, it can take on any form. Both heart and self are undefined, diffuse, pulsating. The void may be empty of form and definition, but it is not static or inert. There is vibration, there is pulsation, there is contraction and expansion. From this womb all realities arise. Any thought can manifest in the heart. You can explore the play of consciousness and matter/energy in this vastness.

The heart is the experience of the central void. Your world is Kula, your body is Kula, and your definitions of yourself are Kula: clusters of form and energy, of organs and functions, Śaktis arising from the play of consciousness. When awareness leaves the periphery of experiences and turns inward, the limits of body dissolve. By turning inward, you are entering the City of Brahman. Penetrating layers and layers of outward manifestation, you reach the core, the heart, the central void. This is not something you imagine. For one thing, you do not exist in any specific form within this void. Instead, it is the diffuse, unspecific you as awareness that projects form and matter on the Śakti-Matrix of the outer shell. There is a hollow within yourself and this hollow is you. It has no fixed boundaries, its limits cannot be defined. It is as minute as the smallest thing and as vast as the entire pulsating multiverse. Within it, forms appear and disappear in the interplay of awareness and shape, the loveplay of Śiva and Śakti. The heart is wider than the world. By withdrawing inwards you are entering the infinite. The true heart is not a heart. It is not your heart, as the you is absent, and it is not within body, as body is a projection of consciousness. Within the central void, the awareness of your self can assume and transform, dance and play with all forms. Here all things begin and end. Thinking a bīja even once produces echoes in spatial dimensions. The sound instantly becomes shape and colour, it casts off reflexes of suggestion and materialisation, and disappears into the realm of the undefined as soon as the vibration ends. Within the heart, each mantra assumes form and works its magick. Within the heart, symbols crystallise the energy flow and deities appear and disappear in visions of personification. The heart cavity, the greatest cave in the world, can contain everything. The heart expands, the heart contracts. Out of it, all appears, in it, all is maintained by the act of awareness, and disappears when awareness ceases to operate. You encounter yourself in this non-state; a self that is formless, shapeless, and without specification (Brahman) and that produces glamours (form, matter) by sheer awareness of them. When the forms appear, consciousness becomes aware of itself, it becomes self referential, as Abhinavagupta proposed. When form disappears in the undefined, consciousness returns to clarity. The virtue of the heart is that it is not a place, not a state, not a thing. In it, there is a constant play of light and dark, it pulses, vibrates, and moves by its own essence: you. As a potential, it can become a place. It can be full of ideas, personifications, images, and sounds. Then it empties again and becomes the primal purity of the pre-conceptual. This is the true nature of Śiva/Śakti, of Bhairava/Bhairavī, the truth within the Kula of the body. During the experience of the heart, much of the outer world, such as your body and the surroundings, cease to matter or are simply forgotten. Going into the formless purity of the heart cavity means that you stop paying attention to the way you sit or rest, to the way you breathe, and to the conditions of your trance. Perhaps your body, out there, begins to pulse or sway. Perhaps it rests quietly, perhaps you simply do not notice. Literally Every Thing is somewhere out there. Śakti as breathing breathes you, Śakti as body supports you, everything works on its own accord and follows its true nature. Within the heart, you cannot control or interfere what happens 'out there', and if you do, you will find that awareness moves into the periphery again and that the central void disappears. In this sense, whatever happens in the heart is not done or not done, it is not controlled or without control, it is not known or unknown. Heart awareness transcends these conditions and definitions, it transcends proper definition, and trying to express its essence produces ecstatic raving (sorry!).

When you wish to return to manifestation, reverse the process. Move up, become bigger, fill the body, breathe deeply, stretch your arms and legs, open your eyes, and get up very slowly. Nyāsa is useful here, it helps to stabilise you in the world of matter and sensation. Enjoy. After a good trance within the fullness of emptiness, you are sensitive and very open to new impressions. Take your time, go slowly. After a while you

Figure 37 - Triple Śakti.

can return to daily life. Shifting awareness from the heart to daily life is not the end of the union. Introversion is the first part of the experience, the experience within is the second, and returning to the outside world is the third. The heart experience would be sheer escapism if it did not involve the transference of the great discharge into the outer universe.

A Note of Caution

After I wrote these passages, Anad remarked that I should mention that heart-exploration takes practice. Unless you have a good deal of experience in accessing inner trance-states, it is likely that you'll encounter all sorts of mental images, thoughts, memories, and whatnot before you come to enjoy the inner emptiness. When beginners turn inward, they usually get access to repressed material, which may be upsetting, boring, or simply beside the point. On your way within and down, any sort of thought may come your way. Should you find yourself thinking about what happened the other day, what you'll do after the trance, or the rubbish you saw on TV, you are plainly a long way from the heart awareness in its pure form. However, you are already within the heart consciousness, only that your heart is cluttered with a lot of unneeded mind-stuff. Clearing the heart may be a useful operation before you explore what you can do in there. So, when you go inward and find all sorts of disconnected ideas welling up, allow them to pass by unhindered. Whether you like it or not, each thought is a form/energy, hence Śakti. Go further inwards, become smaller, withdraw into the core of nothingness. If you still have form, dissolve it. Become ever more minute, insubstantial, undefined. Thoughts disappear on their own accord when you practice non-attachment. Don't interfere, don't struggle, don't make a scene. Just allow the material to pass you by, allow it to float past you and disappear. When you have found a measure of peace and quiet, explore this. Or focus awareness on a mantra, a deity, an image, or a simple sound. When you get good access to these, everyday thinking may disappear naturally. Sorry that I can't express this any more clearly. The heart is very sensitive, it reacts to the slightest stimulation. In many cases, you will find your way inward by practising not-doing and allowing the mind to come to rest naturally. Let's hear Abhinavagupta (*PTV*, trans. Jaideva Singh, 2002: 206): *This penetration into the core is not like a literal statement as in: 'I have entered the heart, it is the supreme goddess', rather it is the search inside the heart.*

The Heart of Dao

Very similar concepts abound in early Daoism. After all, the material of the *Upaniṣads* is close to the earlier Daoist writings, and the question 'who influenced whom?' is still far from settled. The Daoists understood the term 'heart' much like the Kaulas did: the heart is the centre of consciousness and awareness. In many Daoist texts, the word 'heart' can be a term for what we call 'mind'. 'Voiding the Heart' is an essential of

Daoist refinement. Like so much Tantra, Daoism is basically a reversion of natural evolution. Where in the world at large, simple things develop into more complex structures, the Daoist is primarily interested in returning to the nameless, incomprehensible source of all being. This is achieved by a process of meditative simplification. 'Voiding the Heart' was first alluded to by Zhuangzi (Chuang Tse), later generations developed several complex meditations of that name. The ten-thousand things are reduced to the eight signs (bagua, pa kua), then to the five 'movers' (earth, water, fire, metal/gold, wind/wood), the movers are simplified into yin and yang, which becomes the primal unity, and culminates in the nameless simplicity of the original chaos. 'To empty the heart' can be a general term for any trance that gradually empties awareness and identity. It can also be a specific term for a number of highly complex ritual meditations, during which the faculties of sense and awareness are first evoked as spirits, and then expelled out of the body. In this process, the Daoist becomes ever simpler and emptier. All of this is complex nowadays, there being such a wealth of refined meditations and mind-knotting rites of inner alchemy. In the old days, things were a lot simpler. There is a famous line by Laozi (Lao Tse), *Daodejing,(Tao Te Ching)* standard version of Wang Bi, 3rd century CE: *3. Therefore, the Saint, in the exercise of government, empties their* (the peoples) *hearts and fills their bellies, weakens their wills and strengthens their bones, thus constantly ensuring that the people are without knowledge and without desires and that those who have knowledge dare not act. He practices Non-action and consequently there is nothing that is not well governed.* On the surface, this seems like an appeal to keep the population simple, stupid, and docile. I am sure a good many regents liked it that way. Read as an instruction on inner alchemy, the people are the elements that make up the state, i.e. the body/mind complex of the adept. To empty the heart is to empty awareness, to fill the belly is to store the vital energy, Qi,(Ch'i) in it. The idea is to go beyond reasoning and planning, and to revert to simplicity and natural vitality. In the Mawangdui versions of the text, verse 47, (165 BCE) we read: *He empties the hearts. He fills the bellies. He weakens desire, he strengthens the bones.* This makes more sense than the weakening of the wills invented by later generations.

In Daoist lore the body/mind complex is not only symbolised as a state. It is also compared to a house:

> *47. To know All-under-heaven without going out of doors! Without peeping out of the window, to see the way of heaven! The further one goes out, the less one knows. Therefore: the Saint knows without travelling, names (things) without seeing them, achieves without acting.*

The same process appears in 56. *He stops his apertures, he closes his doors. 'He blunts sharpness, he unravels tangles, he dims brightness, he levels tracks.'* This is called the mystic equality. Under such conditions, the house may be cleaned and emptied. When there is nobody and nothing within, the numinous spirit of primal awareness arises naturally.

Finally, there is the journey to the Golden Pavilion in the belly. Daoist lore is more concerned with the belly than the heart. One basic meditation of Daoism, which became the foundation of the Highest Pure School, founded by Lady Wei Huacun in the fourth century, begins by developing belly breathing and learning to focus attention on the belly and the lower Dantien, a little below the navel and inward. This is the centre of your body and weight, it is also the site where Xiwangmu distils the sacred elixir. Once this place/awareness is well established, the adept learns to become a small point of awareness or a flame and sinks downward, past the heart and into the belly. Arriving in the centre of the body, within the golden cauldron of vital qi energy, s/he explores slow breathing and observes how the qi sinks with each in-breath and rises with each out-breath. Daoist alchemy makes much of the 'Method of Turning the Waterwheel'. Actually there are several of them. There is a small circle, confined to the torso, and a large circle, going all the way from head to heels. More so, there are variations. Some reversed the motion of the waterwheel, some installed a double waterwheel (going both ways simultaneously) and some proposed that there should be three waterwheels. Let's ignore these developments, you'll read more about them in my next book. The basic set is a small and a large waterwheel. There is the small circuit which leads from the mouth down the front of the body past heart, belly, genitals, to the perineum. Next the qi rises from the perineum, up the back, past shoulders, to the top of the head and down the face to the mouth. The tongue, touching the palate, connects these two channels.

The large circuit goes beyond this. First the qi goes down the front of the body, past the perineum, thighs, knees and to the front of your feet. Then it rises past the heels (hence the ancient Daoist idea that the true immortals breathe with their heels), goes up along the back of your legs, to the perineum, and along your spine up to the head and mouth. Again, breathing should be slow and silent.

Now there are two basic ways to breathe. You can use the Tiger method, which moves qi actively. This means that the qi goes down on the inhalation and rises up the back during the exhalation. This technique often uses reversed belly breathing and very long breaths. It can be somewhat intense, and is often preferred by advanced martial artists.Or you can use the Dragon method. This means that you move your spirit (attention) which makes the qi move automatically, without strainor effort. Here, the qi sinks as you relax into the exhalation and rises as you inhale again. Natural belly breathing without tension, effort or control is required. In essence, both eventually lead to a similar awareness. Dragon corresponds to spirit, Tiger to qi. As one moves, the other automatically follows.

Some accompany the process by moving their eyes up and down. When the qi is circulating properly, attention goes back to the centre in the belly. You become empty, formless, silent, and void. All thoughts, fears, hopes, and emotions are somewhere up there, in your head and chest, far, far away. In this state, without interference or attention, the qi circulates naturally and the Dao manifests on its own accord. Without doing, attention, or interference, you dissolve in pre-create harmony. This relatively simple process was elaborated by Wei Huacun. In her ritual format, the spirit of the heart is a red robed warrior. Once the qi circles on its own accord, the red warrior descends from the heart and enters the golden pavilion in the belly. In the process, he becomes a ruddy child, laughing and bursting with vitality. Then follows a journey through the organs and further alchemy with the spirits abiding in each. The process is not that easy to describe but it is certainly worth exploring in detail. A good introduction is Michael Saso's *The Gold Pavilion.*

10: Seeing in the Heart

A World of Visions

Visualisation is one of the fun parts of Tantric devotion. Like all the other senses, the visual sense can be improved, amplified, and enjoyed. We explored sound and vibration in the section on mantra, let us now take a good look into the meditations. Meditation is occasionally described as 'seeing in the heart', which may be a literal description, as any communion with the gods, insight, or realisation appears in the heart. No need to repeat this, you did read the last chapter, did you? Gods, visions, transformations. Well and good. Before we get to that topic it might be useful to consider the art of visualisation itself. If you are a total beginner and find it difficult to become aware of your inner vision, it might be a good thing to read *Visual Magick* for the basics. As you may recall from the mantra chapter, changing the acoustic submodalities does produce changes in awareness. Some of them can be intense. The same applies to the visual system. This is hardly new. Lots of people do the most amazing things in their minds, but few of them are aware of what and how they are doing them. The following practice is something you can find in full detail in Richard Bandler's incomparable *Using your Brain for a Change*.

Think of some event you really enjoyed. Pick a good visual memory and explore it. How big is it, how close, how colourful? Lets go into the details now and find out what happens to your emotional response. Make that image come closer. Does this change your emotional reaction? Now let it go away. What happens? Bring it to its original position again. Try size. Make it big, and bigger, and *even bigger...* what happens to your experience? Is there a size where it becomes really impressive? And is there a size where it stops being impressive because it becomes too big? There are thresholds in your perception. Some things are impressive when they are too big, but if you make them still bigger, you pass a certain threshold and suddenly they only seem silly, or incomprehensible, and the emotional impact disappears. Try a nasty memory. Imagine someone shouting at you. If you make that image bigger it will become more upsetting. If you make it as big as a mountain, a planet, or the entire solar system, it will only look ridiculous and out of place. Don't just take my word for it. Try it, do it, find out what happens in your mind! And just what happens when you make it smaller? Take a nasty memory and reduce its size. So when we play around with submodalities, we have to be aware that impressive experiences are only possible within a certain range. Go back to the nice memory you started with. What about brightness? How bright is the memory? Make it brighter. What happens? Now make it dimmer. How does your experience change? Lots of folk find bright images more attractive than dim ones. When they go out in the bright sunshine they feel elated while a few days of gloomy weather bring them down. Of course you have to be careful about exceptions. If your memory is of a night you spent watching stars making it brighter will ruin the mood. And discover the thresholds. When does a memory become too bright for comfort? When does it become too dark to make sense? Let's try something else. Is your memory colourful? Increase the colour. Does this change anything? Then gradually reduce the colour again. Make it pale, and fade, until you reach the black and white end of the scale. What happens to your emotional perception? Some of you will get a strong effect from this. Many people find black and white images a lot less emotional than colourful ones, which is one of the reasons that 'serious' newspapers use black and white to suggest a certain rational and serious minded attitude. Seeing bad news (most news is bad news, and bad news sells) such as shot-up soldiers, polluted countryside, and sheer poverty in black and white is easier to stomach than in full colour. It also has the advantage that the big, colourful advertisements, with their good news (buy this and be happy!) come out more impressive. This works for a lot of people, but not for all. A colourful picture is only more impressive when the bright colours fit the message. Think of pictures that are more impressive in pale colours, or in black and white. If you remember the beauty of a foggy dawn among the megaliths, bright colour might completely ruin the mood. Let's try some more visual submodalities. Take your nice memory again and try this. Where do you see it? Is it before you, above, below, sideways? What happens when you shift it to another position – that is, change your point of view? Lots of people get responses from this. A lot of vertebrates are used to playing the top dog and underdog game. Things that are above you, starting with your parents and most people when you were really young, are impressive, dominant, and sometimes threatening. For this reason many churches have the congregation look up to the preacher, sacred images, and, incidentally, to god. What about looking down? Lots of folk find it really hard to take small people seriously. However, they may get a sort of responsible feeling for them. And what when the memory shifts to the side? How many people put something 'to the side' when they wish to ignore it for a while? Position is a crazy submodality. Some people use position to organise hierarchies. Important ideas are located 'further up' while less important stuff is 'down there' somewhere. When you shift the ideas they have carefully sorted by height you can really upset their values. What happens when you change the format of your memory? When you make the picture larger than your field of vision? When you wrap the image around you so that you can only see those parts that are straight before you? Some use this to get a good worry going. When you take an unpleasant image (such as 'what could go wrong?') and make it so big that it surrounds you, you will find it impossible to sort it out. This is a brilliant way of getting totally upset, it gets even stronger when you make that image spin around you. What happens when you step back to a safe distance and take a new look? All of this is happening all the time.

People don't simply imagine something; they imagine it in a specific configuration. Every image you can think up has a certain size, distance, colour-intensity, position, clarity, density, stability, and so on. If you change the configuration, you change the experience. The way these changes happen, however, is not identical for each person. Most people get a stronger response from a bright than a dim image, but not all of us do so. For this reason I am not simply telling you to imagine something in a specific way. It's much more rewarding that you discover specifically which submodalities turn you on and off. Your mind is unique and we shall celebrate this uniqueness by finding exactly what works wonders for you.

Well, we have had several submodalities already. We explored distance (close to/far away), size (big/small), brightness (bright/dark), colour intensity (colourful to pale to black/white), and position. I am sure you made notes as you played around with your brain, good! - here are some more things to play around with. Here is a list of some visual submodalities which you should explore before you go on. The better you do this, the better will you understand how your mind processes visual information and the easier will your progress in visualisation be. Explore the following: Clarity (clear/diffuse); texture (detailed/uniform); contrast (sharp/diffuse); motion (fast/slow/static); solidity (solid/transparent); endurance (short glimpse/extended vision); alignment (upright/tilted). There are many other visual submodalities, but for a start these may do. What else can you think of? As you will soon notice, some submodality changes will make great differences to your perception and others will not. The submodalities that really make a change are the ones you'll use for your magick. Make a list of submodality changes that make a real difference to your experience. Combine them with each other. Add the better acoustic and kinaesthetic submodalities for a real kick. And go beyond the magick. You can change your life very thoroughly when you change the way you are thinking.

A Question of Perspective

Here's another useful experience. Again, we had this in *Visual Magick*, but for all those who are new to it (or would like a refresher) let's move. Think of a given memory. Can you see what happened? Well, do you see it from out of your own eyes (and hear with your own ears, feel with your own body)? This is technically called associated perception as you are fully within yourself, within the scene, and experience it as if it would happen to you. Now try the same memory from a dissociated, or dis-associated perspective. Go out and see yourself in the memory. Watch yourself engaged in the event. What do you look and sound like when seen from an outside point of view? What difference does it make? Try this with several memories. Make notes. You will soon find that associated memories (or visions, dreams, and the like) provide full emotional access to the event. This is excellent for all the memories and visions that are enjoyable. It is not as useful when you have horrible or traumatic memories or visions. The dissociated vision, by contrast, reduces the original emotion. You may have emotions *about* the event, but this is not the same as the emotions you originally felt. Dissociated perception can really take the pleasure out of memories (a lot of people use this tactic to make themselves depressive). It can also take the horror out of memories, which makes dissociated perception so useful when you have to recall unpleasant or traumatic events. I would not want to give the impression that dissociated perception is something that only reduces emotion. It allows you to cultivate emotions that have nothing to do with the original event. Sometimes a dissociated vision is more attractive than the real event. Imagine that you are seeing yourself having fun at the seaside. Imagine what you might feel there. Attractive, isn't it? Well, your vision may have left out a lot of little details. When you get there in reality, maybe the sun is too hot, the wind too brisk; the water cold, and screaming kids get on your nerves. Seeing yourself haunting the nightside forests doing wild and shamanic things may look really attractive (from the outside). Being there you may find that it is dark, cold, and nobody told you about bloodthirsty insects, or sudden rain-showers in the middle of the night. People often motivate themselves by making up an attractive dissociated vision. They see themselves with the partner of their dreams, they make up conversations and nice events, and from time to time they step into the vision and get access to good feelings. Then they make up an even nicer (dissociated) dream and go into that. Its one method of maintaining the trance called 'being in love'. Or they do it the other way around. You can bedazzle yourself with attractive dissociated visions and you can annoy yourself with unpleasant ones. The trick about associated and dissociated perception is knowing when to use them wisely. Finally, here is an example of dissociation from Maxine Hong Kingston's *Fifth Book of Peace*:

> *'Wittman looked down at his own house and the scene of his party. A trick that always makes him happy: detach yourself and view things from overhead. Get an overview. See from this perspective, and be happy.'* (2004:180)

Coding your Perception

Let's use these methods to change your inner experience. Bothered by a nasty image? Find out how you are doing it. Change the representation, change the way you are thinking. Is that image of a deity, symbol, sigil, or astral environment not impressive enough? How do you do it? Change it! The mind is there to enjoy. The brain is there to play with. While most of you are now in a hurry to get on to the meditations, I would like to add a few comments on the submodalities. What we are exploring in the visual system is essentially a system to order and sort information. Think of a filing system. In the days before computers, people filed their information using various sorting systems. They used filing cabinets with various drawers, colour-coded cards, numbers, headings, alphabetic order, and assigned priorities. This is pretty much what the brain is doing anyway. Modern brain research, using all sorts of scanning mechanisms, is beginning to realise that visual information, be it perception or memory, is not stored like pictures or movies in a storeroom. A given picture is processed by several parts the brain. One location processes size, another colour, another clarity, another motion, and so on. Each image is split up into the submodalities that make up its representation. The code for the combination is stored in some mysterious way, and when you recall that picture, the parts of the visual system reconstruct the whole out of many separate items. Memories are not 'things', they are *constructs*. Recall is not just reconstruction, it is also construction, and this always involves a measure of creativity. Memories are not static. They change with each remembrance. When you change the submodalities of your memory, you are changing the instructions on how a given image is to be stored, evaluated, and accessed. Imagine a filing cabinet. Take a card with 'top priority' classification and put it into the file marked 'who cares?' Once it is in its new file it will be treated like all items in that file. You might still get excited about it, but chances are you won't even look at it again. Possibly the brain uses similar tactics in sorting data. It has its way of marking important and unimportant data, of distinguishing between matters that are vital and optional. It knows that when it takes a given idea and makes it really large, bright, colourful, and so on, it will get a specific response from your mind. So some of the ideas you are having seem impressive and others do not. Not because they are really important or not. Something that seems impressive does not really have to be important; it is quite enough when it *seems* so. People make use of this for their motivation strategies. They use it to be excited, to be creative, enthusiastic, and obsessed. Or they use it to ruin their lives and to be really miserable. So when you think you are thinking, find out how you are thinking it.

Think of something that makes you really enthusiastic. How do you represent it? What submodalities do you use? Now pick something you would like to be enthusiastic about but aren't. Represent it using the same modalities. What happens? Or find something that is really irrelevant to you. What submodalities express 'irrelevance' in your mind? How do you know that a given visual idea is irrelevant? Is there something you would like to find irrelevant? Change the submodalities to irrelevant and be rid of it.

Submodalities are essential when you want to change the beliefs that constitute your personal reality. 'Belief' is a specific configuration of visual, acoustic, and kinaesthetic submodalities in your mind, just as 'doubt' and 'ignorance' are. Whatever you believe will appear in a certain configuration of submodalities. So will whatever you doubt, or are uncertain about. This topic is developed at length in Richard Bandler's books, where you will learn how to transform stagnant belief into uncertainty, and hence create new beliefs to change your life.

The mind is built to allow re-programming. This is essential, as most of us begin to program the mind at such an early age that errors in classification and evaluation are unavoidable. Most people have a lot of coincidence in their programming. Take a baby who is scared by the sudden bark of a dog. The mind, storing this information, might use submodalities spelling shock, danger, and high priority. When in later life a dog suddenly barks the experience may be processed exactly on those lines. If the child was lucky, the bark was only stored as potentially dangerous. In this case the adult may be a little uneasy when surprised by a sudden bark but that's all there is to it. What if the baby stores the sudden bark under the heading 'extreme danger, survival threat'? Old-school psychologists might be tempted to call this experience an 'imprint' (whatever that may mean) and to pretend that very little can be done about it, apart from having three sessions of therapy a week for fifteen years. Like a phobia, it is an example of learning something horrible really fast. If you change the way the dog's bark is coded, you will also change the response. Thoughts in themselves are simply information, they have no value by themselves. It is your mind that decides what value a given thought has, and uses its very own system of classification to sort and order it. This system produces a representation, and the form of the representation makes sure that you respond to specific thoughts in a specific manner. Much of magick is learning how to represent given thoughts in order to produce specific responses. This is something you can find in all magickal systems. As an example, take the 'Vibration of Divine Names' as taught by the Hermetic Order of the Golden Dawn. The adept stands in a prescribed posture and takes a deep breath. Breath is held while the name is pronounced in the heart. Then name and breath are pushed down, so they pass the sphere of yesod (the genitals) and descend to the feet. The name is formulated in the feet, *then, bringing it rushing upwards into the lungs, thence shall he breathe it forth strongly, while vibrating that Divine Name. He will send his breath steadily forward into the Universe so as to awake the corresponding forces of the Name in the Outer World* (commentary on the symbolism of the Opening of the Grade of the Neophyte in Regardie 1971 vol. 3). This is accompanied by the gesture of the Enterer, symbolising the Egyptian war-god Horus radiating a flood of sheer energy with outstretched hands. What submodalities can you recognise? Position within body is one of them. Another is size; the breath/name expands into something really big (the universe) and awakes forces in the outer world. This also involves distance; where are you and where are the 'corresponding forces'? Think of the kinaesthetic aspect; as you hold breath the urge to release the name (and get some fresh air) adds a dramatic element. Submodality changes also appear in Golden Dawn ritual when the mage transforms into a deity larger than her- or himself. As MacGregor Mathers, who composed the bulk of the Golden Dawn rituals, wrote: *And thus let Him or Her judge the question as apart from his ordinary human personality; and to this end let him be sure to formulate himself in the figure of the God as colossal; and not simply as an ordinary sized figure. And though this may be at first difficult, it will gradually become easier of performance.* (*Theoricus Adeptus Notice*, 1. Nov. 1894, in Howe, 1978). Size again. Most people will get a strong reaction from a big voice, or a big deity. Some won't react so strongly, and will get a better response from some other submodality. The old magi were not aware of the fact that all sensual experience can be sorted and influenced by submodalities. Occasionally they discovered a submodality that gave them a real kick and passed that to similar minded students. Students requiring a different submodality change were considered failures. Nowadays this seems pretty superficial. Every person uses submodalities that really produce an emotional effect. You don't have to suit yourself to the system; you can get a much better effect when you learn what really works for you. In the following pages we will explore some of the visual meditations of a few Tantric systems. Please use the knowledge you have gained regarding your very own submodalities to make the visions really impressive. Blend the visual submodalities that work best for you with your favourite acoustic and kinaesthetic submodalities, and add scent and taste for a really detailed experience. Most people find visions more impressive when they involve many senses. So when you visualise a deity, give that deity a setting, and add sound, feeling, scent, and taste till the vision becomes as real as you will. Go for something impressive! No half-hearted fiddling around with vague images. Your imagination is there to be enjoyed!

A Shower of Ambrosia

One of the ideas involved in Kuṇḍalinī yoga (more detail in the next chapter) is that the fire serpent, after her ascent from the perineum to the top of your head, releases a shower of ambrosia which pours down, rejuvenating and immortalising the body/mind system. This idea appears in several forms in Tantric lore. It has an even older origin. You can find it in the writings of some early Daoists, such as the *Cantong Qi* attributed to Wei Boyang, dated c. 142 CE. In Daoist alchemy, the life energy, Qi (Ch'i), is imagined to rise from the perineum up the spine, along the back, past the shoulders, and into the head, where enlightenment occurs. This phase is symbolised by rising fire (and several dozen other metaphors). From the crown of the head it moves down along the front of the body. It goes to the palate, passes the mouth via the tongue (which is fixed to the palate), descends through the throat, sinks through the lungs, passes the solar plexus, the centre below the navel, the genitals, and finally arrives at the perineum, from where it rises up again. While you circulate the energy, you move your awareness into the empty space in the centre. This is much like descending into the heart. Within the central void, your mind returns to simplicity and the energy circles on its own accord. It is typical for this trance that the initial effort gives way to natural circulation and that breathing becomes minimal. In its perfect form there is no effort at all. Thus, the Daoist method has much in common with Kuṇḍalinī yoga, only that the passage of the Qi is considered a circuit. When the Qi descends from the head, it is often visualised as falling water. In Wei Boyang's writing, translation by Eva Wong, you can find the passage:

> *Cultivate without stopping,*
> *And the mass of energy will move like clouds and rain.*
> *Flowing like spring showers,*
> *Dripping like melting ice,*

From the head falling down to the feet,
And from there rising up again,
Coming and going, swirling the limitless,
And stirring everything throughout.
Those on the path of return know the Dao.

This is a remarkably clear description by Daoist standards. At the time when Wei Boyang wrote, Tantra and the Kuṇḍalinī concept had not been developed. It seems likely that the Daoist idea of falling water influenced the shower of ambrosia so vital in Tantric meditation. Here we have evidence that Daoism influenced Tantra. And vice versa. At a much later time, the Daoist adept Zhang Boduan (983-1082) gave detailed instructions on meditation (Cleary 1991). These involve withdrawing from the world, closing the avenues of the senses, visualising the golden elixir of immortality near the navel, and refining the True Breath until it becomes so subtle that it is hardly detectable. To open the secret passages in the body, Zhang Boduan recommended visualising the Qi rising from the soles of the feet. It ascends the legs, meets at the genitals, and unites at the perineum, where it assumes the form of a small serpent. The serpent is an innovation. Maybe Zhang invented it but more likely he had access to Tantric literature. Well, our serpent penetrates the base of the spine (the first pass), rises along the spine past the ribs (the second pass) and ascends the neck where, at the base of the skull (the Jade Pillow), it penetrates the third pass. It enters the centre of the skull (the nirvāṇa palace), moves to the heavenly eye between the eyebrows, and descends like cooling water. It saturates and vitalises the body, washes out impurities, collects at the genitals, moves to the perineum, and ascends the spine again. As you can see, the traditional method of 'Turning the Waterwheel' has been improved by the visualisation of a serpent and the introduction of three passes, which correspond to a degree with the three 'knots' the Kuṇḍalinī yogī has to penetrate in some systems. The 'knots' are a confusing topic that appears in numerous different varieties. It seems possible that Zhang Boduan, his teacher Liu Cao, or maybe even his teacher, the immortal Lü Dongbin, have been reading early Tantric literature.

While the shower of elixir has its place in Kuṇḍalinī yoga, it also appears independently of it in a number of texts. One of the most rewarding is the refreshing *Kaulajñāna nirṇaya.* In the fifth chapter, Devī asks Mahādeva Bhairava (Śiva) about the conquering of death. This is a topic that has excited countless Tantrics, Daoists, and free-style alchemists over the ages, most of whom did not agree with each other regarding method, terminology, or even the basic idea about what immortality consists of, and whether it applied to body or consciousness. Luckily, Śiva has a few tested methods to attain immortality. They also produce the siddhis as a side effect. The first method is to meditate on a cooling, white, lunar fluid that comes from heaven and drenches all tissues of the body. This fluid goes through all the subtle nerves of the body, vitalises the organs, and is sure to produce immortality. The second method is somewhat similar. Begin by visualising the milk ocean.

This is the primordial ocean composed of poison and elixir out of which Lakṣmī arose. Imagine a huge, white lotus of 100,000,000,000 petals in the centre of the milk ocean. Imagine yourself wearing white clothes and ornaments in the centre of this lotus. The white radiation moistens your mind and destroys disease. Another method is to visualise three full moons. They are established in your head, your heart, and your navel. Meditate on the milk-white fluid of the upper moon cooling and moistening your mind. In chapter seven this matter is alluded to again, here we learn that the upper full moon is situated at the back of the head, at the place where spine and skull join. Yet another variation is that the Devī manifests the cakras in your body. Focus your attention on the thousand petaled lotus at the crown of your head and imagine the pale moon-juice pouring downwards, soaking all the cakras in its flow. Or imagine a snow-white lotus of sixteen petals, each petal the sphere of Śiva's love-play, and how the flood of pure white milky nectar soaks your body. This technique promises the adept to become the equivalent of Śiva, free of illness, affliction, or mortality, walking the earth in freedom, doing one's true will, and being worshipped by more gods and heavenly maidens than anyone can cope with. As you noticed, all of these techniques can be seen as variations of a single theme. Matsyendranāth, the author of the work, was clearly aware that different people need different visualisations to get a good effect. His techniques are varied so the reader can experiment. Each technique is supposed to be practised daily for at least a year before results are assured. Think of the submodalities that really turn you on. How can you make such meditations really impressive? Did you notice that the crescent moons gracing the heads of Śiva and Kālī may be related to this meditation? Have you ever found a white light shining from behind your head? Some people have this experience. It takes a dark setting to notice. I sometimes find it happening when I play a frame-drum in the twilight or walk in the forest at night. It happens naturally in absent-minded states.

What I find especially interesting is the pale white, milky fluid. Pale white gets a different effect from pure white, radiant white, or even glaring white, which might be too bright for the curative effect. The whole thing may remind you of the Simonton method of cancer therapy. Put simply, the Simontons developed a series of visualisations of white blood particles destroying cancer cells. To wrap this up in a more exciting form, the patients imagine the white antibodies as polar bears, white wolves, or policemen in white uniforms. This works pretty well, especially when children do the visualisations. In his book *Beliefs*, Robert Dilts pointed out that the flaw of such visualisations is the fact that they are modelled on war. He developed a milder form, where you visualise white sheep leisurely eating up the cancerous growth. When you flood your body with sacred white moon-fluid, you might be stimulating your white blood-particles to eliminate disease. Think about it - and better still - do it.

The Black Elixir

Up to now, the suggested visualisation may have reminded you of the 'white light' meditation often favoured by the esoteric scene. The white of our visualisation, however, is not a bright light but a pale, milky, moon-like glow. It cools, refreshes, and illuminates gently. This point of view is expressed in chapter seven of the *Kaulajñāna nirṇaya*, where the reader is asked to consider the moon friendly and the sun hostile. Chapter seven begins with Devī asking how ageing and wearing-out may be avoided. Bhairava responds by giving a very similar meditation as the previous one. The first method is to start meditation at the first day of the lunar half-month. You visualise yourself within the cakra of the Devī. To begin with, the top of the head is visualised pure, pale white. This whiteness saturates the body. Now, at the crown of the head, a black fluid begins to appear. It flows downward, regenerating the skin and refreshing the cells.

The second method is to visualise the black elixir overflowing from the Brahmarandhra. This is the topmost point of your head, the place where your incarnate consciousness stops and your extra-terrestrial awareness begins. Usually it is imagined as a tiny hole. If you meditate in a lonely place, imagining yourself black, wearing black clothes, you are promised to gain freedom from the turmoil of life and all disease. If this meditation is done for six months in a beautiful, desolate location, accompanied by offerings of rice and incense, by an adept adorned with various flowers, the result is becoming equal of Kāmadeva, the god of desire, lust, and love. Another, somewhat unspecified, instruction is that the three cakras (?) are located in the Brahma-granthi (the knot of Brahman), each of them being dissolved in Brahman, who is likened to a piece of collyrium. This black substance heals the body and, after six months of visualisation, it rejuvenates. To become like Kāmadeva you can also visualise the following:

Imagine the piṇḍa with its sixteen petals, each of them attributed to a vowel. Each petal has a certain amount of blackness. The piṇḍa is a complex idea. Generally it means mass, but in a Kaula setting it can mean body; your body, the body of your world, and indeed your entire reality. When this lotus is dissolved in the Brahmarandhra (practised daily for six months) youth returns. *One becomes like Kāmadeva, the God of Love, by becoming one in the place of the Yoginīs whilst meditating on them as black and oneself as being of black colour.* Given so many options, I am sure you can work out a visualisation that works perfectly for you.

Figure 38 - Kāmadeva.

Yoni Mudrā

Now for a related practise from the *Śiva Saṁhita*, 4, 1-9. It is called Yoni Mudrā. This may be a bit confusing. Tantric lore contains a lot of references to something called yoni mudrā. As usual, the authorities disagree and there are a wide range of techniques classed under this innocent name. You read one in the chapter on body. Here is another.

Yoni mudrā may mean folding the hands over the face. You put your thumbs in your ears, place the index fingers over your closed eyelids, and place the other fingers loosely over nose and mouth (to allow for reduced breathing). Sit on the ground with your elbows resting on your knees. Yogīs use it to listen to the anāhata sound, and all the bizarre sounds within body. The roaring of your blood circulation was considered the thundering of the Kuṇḍalinī. Adepts practice listening to finer and finer levels of sound, until they discern flutes, drums, bells, gongs, crickets, string instruments, and suchlike. This is part of the science of Nāda yoga, which introverts awareness into pure sound and vibration. The posture also heats the face and can be remarkably refreshing.

In the language of gesture, yoni mudrā can mean a position of the hands, which are formed into a triangular shape that represent the female genitals. Others saw yoni mudrā as a posture where the sādhaka lies flat on the ground, licking the Śakti's genitals; here, the term mudrā means 'to please'. In the *Śiva Saṁhita*, the term refers to a meditation that releases a shower of inner elixir. It is similar to Kuṇḍalinī yoga, but a good deal less complicated. Here is the full text in the translation of Rai Bahadur Srisa Chandra Vasu, my comments are in brackets. The text uses the term yoni, usually vulva, as a synonym for 'source'. As such, the yoni is simply a cakra.

1. *First with a strong inspiration fix the mind on the adhar lotus* (sink consciousness to the mūlādhāra, the perineum, during inhalation. Several breaths may be required, give yourself time). *Then engage in contracting the Yoni* (cakra), *which is situated in the perineal space.* (contract the muscles of the perineum and pull them up).

2. *There let him contemplate that the God of Love* (Kāmadeva) *resides in that Brahma Yoni* (the source of creation. Brahmā is four-faced, the root cakra has four petals) *and that he is beautiful like Bandhuk flower - brilliant as tens of millions of suns, and cool as tens of millions of moons* (avoid over-heating). *Above this* (centre) *is a very small and subtle flame, whose form is intelligence. Then let him imagine that a union takes place there between himself and that flame* (you are consciousness/Śiva, the flame is Śakti/energy).

3. *There go up* (attention and energy rise together) *through the Sushumnâ vessel* (the etheric counterpart of the spine), *the three bodies* (corresponding to belly, heart, and head and three degrees of subtlety) *in their due order. There is emitted in every chakra the nectar, the characteristic of which is great bliss. Its colour is whitish rosy* (like the

mixture of sperm and menstrual blood), *full of splendour, showering down in jets the immortal fluid. Let him drink this wine of immortality which is divine* (the true wine of the sacrament. All other wine is mere booze), *and then again enter the Kulâ* (return consciousness and energy to the cluster at the perineum).

4. *Then let him go again to the Kulâ through the practice of mátrá yoga* (earthing awareness in the root cakra by steady prāṇāyāma). *This yoni* (source) *has been called by me in the Tantras as equal to life.*

5. *Again let him be absorbed in that Yoni, where dwells the fire of death - the nature of Shiva, &c.* (dissolve form and return to pure consciousness) *Thus has been described by me the method of practising the great Yoni-Mudrā. From success in its practice, there is nothing which cannot be accomplished.*

In the next verses, Śiva goes on declaring that yoni mudrā is the heal-all for deformed, paralysed, scorched, evil, or otherwise unfruitful mantras, that it absolves from any sort of sin and other minor offences, such as gurucide, murder of a thousand Brahmins, alcoholism, theft, seduction of the guru's wife, and killing all inhabitants of the three worlds (oh really?).

9. *Therefore, those who wish for emancipation should practise this daily. Through practise, success is obtained; through practise one gains liberation.*

Going for Colour

We had white, black, and pink so far, and from what our texts tells us, the results of them are pretty similar. They heal, intoxicate, enlighten, and rejuvenate. Good news, as this allows you to play around with other colours too. Indian religion makes much of the three guṇas, and so the next colour to explore is red. Red is a favourite colour in many Tantric sects, no matter whether they actually use the red fluid in their rites or prefer symbolic worship and visualisation. Before we start, you might find out what sort of red really stimulates you. Red may be red to most of the population; to the artist, the mage, and the Tantric explorer the word is unspecified. Which sorts of red excite you? What shade of red would you like to embrace, to eat, drink, and saturate yourself with? Go out into nature, to a botanical garden or a shop stocking artists supplies. I have no idea what red will work for you. For me, a useful red is the hue of poppy on the last day before the petals drop, when the blossom radiates a rich, ripe red, seen against the light of the sun on a bright day with a blue sky. What do you prefer? To cultivate Yoginī-Siddhi, so chapter 19 of the *Kaulajñāna nirṇaya* tells us, the devotee should visualise the sixteen yoginīs as *black skinned, youthful, maidenly, wearing red clothes, smeared with blood, red ornaments, adorned with red flowers and red garlands. One should worship them as being one with oneself.* Chapter 22 alludes to the same meditation, pointing out that a vīra should always meditate on them inwardly. Chapter 23 gives the same meditation of the sixteen red yoginīs, sweet faced, drunk on madira blossom wine, like the icchā (will) Śakti, granting gifts and longevity. Please consider the connection between the sixteen red yoginīs and the sixteen kalās of the moon. To obtain liberation, the same meditation is done replacing red with white. While red is a very basic colour - it is the first colour a baby learns to see - it does not produce the same responses in all people. Some do get very little effect when they surround themselves with a sphere of red, no matter how much they play around with various shades of the colour, and some may even get negative effects, should they happen to dislike red. Some folks are a lot happier with other colours. Good! It does not matter whether some authorities of Tantra prescribe red, white, pink, and black, just because it happened to work for them. The essential issue is that you find a colour that produces a specific excitement in your mind. You need an energetic colour, a cooling and purifying colour, and a restful and liberating colour for a start. If these functions are fulfilled by red, white, and black, fine. If not, chose colours that really mean a lot to you. Go after the function and effect, this is real magick - everything else is only tradition. When you've studied the colour symbolism of a few distinct cultures you'll soon realise that any colour can mean just about anything. The question is simply: what works best for you?

Obviously, a few Tantric gurus played around with colours. This shows not only in the confusing colour attributions of the various cakra systems, it also appears in Tantric sorcery. Chapter 5 of the *Kaulajñāna nirṇaya* mentions twelve cakras, of which nine are named and seven are detailed regarding the number of petals. We learn that colour visualisation in these sites produces various effects. Red gives subjugation and great pleasure. Yellow paralyses, purple banishes, white heals and gives peace. Milky white gives victory over death. Fluid gold allows the worshipper to shake cities.

A similar system of colour and magickal skill is known as the ṣaṭkarmāṇi, the Six Rites. These rites appear in several forms in literature, such as the famous *Mantramahodhadhiḥ* (*The Ocean of Mantra*). The six rites are a group of magical practices: to appease, to subjugate, to paralyse, to cause enmity, to eradicate, and to liquidate. Each of the rites has specific guiding deities, colours, mantras, sacred directions, seasonal attributes, suitable days, postures of the body, mudrās, symbols, yantras, and so on. It would be a bit too much to go into all the details here, the interested reader can find them in the good book or in Gudrun Bühnemann's essay (in White 2000). Of the five rites, appeasement cures diseases and is supposed to be beneficial. The other five rites effect changes in the behaviour of other people. White is used to appease and heal, its goddess is Rati, who is imagined in white. Red is used for subjugation, command, and control, its goddess is a red Vānī/Sarasvatī. Paralysis, immobilisation and inactivity are caused by a yellow Ramā. Enmity, dislike, and discord show variegated colours, and so does the goddess Jyeṣṭhā. Eradication, banishment, and exorcism are done by Durgā, whose colour is dark. Liquidation and total destruction are in the domain of Kālī, who is visualised (unusually) in grey. The rite is further refined (or complicated) by the introduction of various mantras, the observation of the motion of breath, oil-smeared fire sticks made of various woods, special mālās combined with unusual positions of the fingers (you've read about them earlier), various shaped fire-pits, vessels, foodstuff, writing equipment for yantras, and so on. The worshipper is warned of attaching too much importance to the achievement of worldly desire, of the danger of becoming ensnared by certain mantras, the need to be attentive to auspicious and inauspicious dreams, and the importance of realising Brahman. This is sound advice, as there are few things as deluding, ensnaring, and bedazzling as mucking around with obsessive spellcraft. Sorcery can be habit-forming.

Union with the Gods

Personal deities are the ones that appeal to you. Hindu religion has the concept of the 'chosen deity', the iṣṭadevatā. In Hindu lore, all beings may have chosen deities. *Kūrma Purāṇa*, 1, 22, 40-47 gives a good introduction. Verse 40 states: *Whatever deity appeals to a man is his deity.* In case anyone finds this too easy or difficult, our text elaborates that specific professions, classes, and even classes of being should have specific iṣṭadevatās. Kings should worship Viṣṇu, Iśa, or Indra; Brahmins should worship Agni, Āditya (the sun), Brahmā, or Śiva, and so on. Women worship Umā, Viṣṇu, Śiva and the sun. The gods themselves should worship Viṣṇu; the Dānavas should worship Śiva; Gandharvas and Yakṣas should worship Soma; the man-eating Rākṣasas should devote themselves to Śiva. In other words, if you are up to it, choose what you will. If not, pick a deity for your class, profession, or gender. It's not the only way. Some chose a deity, others are chosen by a deity, whether they like it or not. Some choose a family deity, a local deity, or have one selected for them by the guru.

Whatever it may be, iṣṭadevatās tend to come in certain forms. One of them is similarity. Here the deity is much like you are, or rather, much like the better parts of you. Think of ash smeared ascetics who look like Śiva, act like Śiva, and venerate Śiva as themselves. Think of motherly women celebrating the Great Goddess. Call it union by similarity. The other choice is union by difference. When a woman worships Śiva as her personal deity and a man some form of Śakti, much of the union depends on integrating what seems different. Austin Spare called it 'all-otherness'. When your chosen deity is of the other sex you have a chance to learn a lot of new things. You will also discover a ritual partner in yourself with whom you can share life, company, friendship, love, and spiritual evolution. When your god is much the same as you are already, it will make you stronger, but possibly also a bit narrow-minded.

Another interesting variable is number. Some go for a single deity. Others prefer a deity who appears in several forms. Or they prefer several deities who share a common element, a mutual essence. In these matters, it is good sense to ask the gods what they want. Don't ask your reason, don't think so much. The gods are quite capable of sorting themselves out. You, as a human being, are simply not qualified to decide whether a god is a single entity, or a cluster, or a single being appearing in different guises in different cultures. This is not the place for ideology or theology. Ask your god/s, they know much better than you do, and don't expect your rules to apply to other people or other deities.

Next, you may wonder how to decide on an iṣṭadevatā. Well, you don't have to. It's not your conscious mind that makes the choice. The ego is far too daft for such a decision. The easy way is to explore gods in general. Chose a deity, invoke, worship, integrate, communicate, earth the current, and understand. Then pick another, preferably one that is not too similar. If you do this for a few months or years, you will gradually evolve a circle of gods. Sooner or later you will learn who is your iṣṭadevatā. It will tell you.

In general, coming really close to a deity is a fairly simple process. I can tell you a basic structure, but from that point, you'll be in for a lot of individual developments. The process of becoming a deity, of 'being obsessed', or of 'assuming a god-form' is easy. First you learn as much about the deity as you can. This means weeks and months of persistent study. It means a lot of reading, many visits to museums and hours spent leafing through pictures and images. If the deity is not from your culture, you will have to learn at least as much as a native of that culture would know about it. This may sound like hard work, and so it is. Deities do not come from shelves in shops, they develop within cultures. Each deity has form, structure, functions, a history of development, and appears within a cultural, historical, social, and ecological context. If you do not understand the context, your understanding of the deity will be limited. Should you think that Kālī is the same as Kālīka, Mahākālī, Durgā, or Pārvatī, you are missing a lot of vital details. Each form of a deity was developed as this specific form was needed. On one level, there are differences and individuality, on another level, all deities, spirits, demons, and other entities are manifestations of the supreme Brahman. The same is true for you, me, and all living beings.

Luckily, your research is not only work but also play. To study and contemplate is part of the invocation. The more you get into the mind-space of that deity, the easier will you come to know each other. You should also make a point of being critical of what you read. Much of what we know about elder deities is extremely distorted. Maybe it never was just like what you read. Or maybe the deity would prefer a new form or function in the present time. Don't take things for granted - learn from the living reality. Before you have lived with a deity for years, you are in no position to judge and evaluate. Next, change from input to output. After you have crammed so much into your head, allow your creativity to manifest. A classical method, much favoured by the Golden Dawn and its various offspring, is to draw or paint a picture of that deity, or possibly several. Now this picture need not be perfect. The important thing is that it touches you deeply, that it combines the essential aspects of the deity and that the deity likes it. This image, sculpture, or picture is the focus of your invocation. It is a body for the deity, but it is not the deity itself. The deity is what you contact using this focus. Most cultures do not worship idols, but see them as the mind-focus connecting with the real divinity. Hindus clap their hands to wake a deity in an image, and clap them after the ritual to de-activate the contact. When you have a material carrier, such as a picture, effigy, or fetish, you can put energy (ojas) into it. Gods are a life-form that thrive on the energy of emotion, attention, lust, and love. They can also be fed using fear and terror, or with the emotions raised by extreme austerities, but these energy sources are not very reliable and apt to produce a lot of trouble as a side effect. If you pray before that image (put emotion into it!), make offerings, dance before it, make music for it's entertainment, speak with it, live with it, and so on, you will charge the image with ojas. If you pray often and passionately you'll get along fine. The next step is to go for inner worship. Visualise your deity. Do this often, during the day, in trance, when going to sleep, and so on. The image will stabilise before long. If you find it hard to imagine the deity (creative construction), simply remember what your painting looks like. Whatever you do, the image is a link. It does not have to be perfect. Sooner or later the deity will transform it anyway. By then you will learn a lot from the deity, and probably you will get indirect messages from it in daily life. Look out for funny coincidences, synchronicity, omina, and presents from the universe. If you are getting close to a deity who has many worshippers, your progress may be fairly swift. Deities who have very few worshippers, or deities who have been almost forgotten over the millennia, are harder to contact and require a lot more ojas to provide them with a body. They may also need a few updates. I've met a few who were really confused about the present period (well, so am I), and some who did not take kindly to being woken. Anyway, before long you'll become very familiar with the deity, and the deity with you. If you like each other, you may come closer still.

The next step is to become the deity. One way is to imagine the deity as large or larger than yourself. Then step into it and associate. See through its eyes, move with its body, assume its characteristic form and mood. In the process, you will enjoy a new consciousness, and the deity will delight in your body. The first tries can be unpredictable. Some get mind-blowing effects for a start, others get more subtle changes. Some encounter sheer fear and terror, others find themselves switching fast and erratically between human and divine awareness. Some feel so blissful that they find it hard to return to the everyday world. Body may join the fun, and shake or sway as the trance sets in, and maybe you'll stagger around a bit as the deity has yet to learn how to move you. What happens in this stage is very much your own affair. You will to be a god, a god wills to be you, and both have to come to terms to realise their mutual self-hood. It may take months to come to a workable balance. During this time, the human being is apt to undergo a lot of crisis states, surprising revelations, and sudden changes of belief. This is part of the fun. Initiation is something that changes you. Some gods may be gentle in this, others subtle, tricky, or drastic. It depends on the god of your choice and on the you of the god's choice. All in all, you will eventually come to terms. In the process the upheaval is reduced and the transformation of consciousness is less pronounced. Life is not all fireworks. The closer you get to a deity the more you'll become like it. This makes it easier to change from one awareness to the other, but it will also reduce the drama. The closer you get the less pronounced will the change be. One of the reasons why people ought to explore several deities before settling for a personal one is that each god is habit-forming. When you explore your first deity, you may be so overwhelmed that you think it the most important deity in the world. Fresh converts are always a bit narrow-minded and out-of-balance. The thing about magick, Tantra, and all the rest is that it should make your mind wider and more flexible. Why limit yourself? How about more choices? If you get along with one deity, find another deity who is not like the first one and learn something new. Before we leave this section it might be useful to consider a safety check. If you feel proud of your iṣṭadevatā, if you consider it superior to any other spiritual entity, or if you assume that it is there to do your bidding there is something seriously wrong. It's you.

11: The Path of the Serpent

Tantric lore is well known for its mapping and charting of power zones in body and the world at large. Sometimes these zones are called kulas, meaning clusters, groups, clans, families. Each kula is a bundle of experience, awareness, power, and intelligence. Kula can also refer to the whole group of cakras at once. And to the goddess who combines them and shifts awareness in her motion. More common is the term cakra, meaning wheels, disks, and circles. A cakra can also be a magical circle or a ritual assembly, as in the rites of the Bhairava cakra. Cakras exist in living beings, but as in Indian lore, just like the real world, everything has some degree of life and awareness, cakras exist pretty much everywhere. Here we are concerned with the cakras within the body. In the occult anatomy of humans, animals, and plants, a number of cakras are said to exist. Each of them is a specific focus of energy and sentience, i.e. a place of union for Śiva and Śakti. Up to this point most people agree. When we get down to the little details, however, things get a lot more confusing. I am sure you'll love this as much as I do. Nowadays, it is generally assumed that there are six cakras in the human spine, plus a seventh one on top of the head. Life can be so simple, as long as we avoid real research. Let us take a close look at some remarkable assumptions.

Do people have cakras? The answer is yes in theory, as every living being has cakras in potential. They are not functional, however, unless they are carefully woken, refined, developed, purified, maintained, and cared for. This process implies years of spiritual evolution. In spite of the claims of result-hungry new age cults, it is not enough that a guru presses a thumb against the brow, or knocks the eager student over the head with a big stick (not a bad idea, really). When someone claims to open, align, or wake the cakras of another, this is basically a suggestion accompanied by gesture to make things happen. The gesture shapes belief. It works brilliantly when the guru is believed to be a representative of the divine and the student absolutely submits to the guru's way of life. More prosaically, we could argue that the initial opening of a cakra is a placebo. The same goes for most initiation ceremonies. The devout follower believes that the guru's touch can initiate, and indeed it does. When the guru is in a state of bliss, the touch can produce an amazing effect on a suitable person. This, however, is just the start of the game. It's not enough to have a cakra activated for an hour or two, the important issue is to refine a cakra that remains awake for days, weeks, months, and years. The guru, though maybe helpful in getting a good start, is hardly able to accompany you through life to keep your cakras spinning. Every state of mind is not only an achievement; it is also something that needs maintenance. Feeling whole or holy for a few minutes in the company of fellow aspirants may be well and good, but much more important is the ability to take that awareness with you as you leave the holy enclave and embrace every-bloody-day-reality with all its snags and difficulties.

Where are the cakras? Nowadays, most people assume that the cakras are situated in or near the human spine. This fits numerous Indian paintings. But how can the spine and the cakras interact? The spine is a physical part of anatomy that can be felt, touched, dissected, and so on. The cakras cannot be discovered by surgery. In short, the spine and the cakras exist on different maps. The spine is part of the dense, material map and the cakras are part of the subtle, energetic map. They coincide roughly with one another, but the link between them is subtle. A number of occult authors have proposed that the cakras correspond with the glands. This is a very materialistic way of interpreting ancient lore. Some of the cakras are indeed located close to glands, but others are not. Some of them are on top or above the head. The cakras influence the function of the glands, but they are not the occult counterparts of them, as Sir John Woodroffe, who wrote as Arthur Avalon, explains at considerable length in *The Serpent Power.* Nor do the cakras exactly follow the spine. The third eye between and behind the brows is not very close to the spine, nor is the sexual centre, the solar plexus, or the root cakra at the perineum. In Indian lore, the cakras are not located on the physical spine but in a much more refined concept, the suṣuṁnā, a subtle nāḍī (energy connection, nerve, channel). The suṣuṁnā is roughly equivalent to the spine on a subtle and not quite defined level, but it is not identical in position or function. Indeed, the suṣuṁnā can be considered a model of vertical awareness of which the spine is but a crude manifestation. Nor do all Tantric cults follow this model. Some works, like the *Kaulajñāna nirṇaya* prefer to speak of a liṅga within body, adorned with many-coloured flowers. Here the liṅga is a pillar or tree connecting heaven and earth. The liṅga has its ups and downs, but as it is a more metaphorical concept than the suṣuṁnā it is not as easily mistaken for the spine. Others use of Mount Meru as a metaphor. If we want to understand the cakras we have to get away from purely physical explanations. Suṣuṁnā, Mount Meru, and the body liṅga may be metaphors, but so is the physical spine. Everything that you perceive, think, and communicate is metaphor.

A word on models, maps, and metaphors: A cakra, for instance, is an incomprehensible reality. None of them can be seen, heard, or touched except in the imagination. It is the trained imagination that activates the cakras, moves Kuṇḍalinī, and drenches body/mind/world in the nectar juice of immortality. All of these are metaphors, all of them are parts of models, and like all models and stuff that people make up to handle the incomprehensible, they are lies. A model is a description, it does not have to be true as long as its useful. Each branch of yoga and Tantra developed models and metaphors to handle the mystery. These models are useful. They are not the real thing, as none of us is equipped to perceive or comprehend the real thing, but they are convenient to contact and activate the living reality. Thus, ideas like cakras, Kuṇḍalinī, the liṅga are all attempts to describe and handle a mystery that lies at the very core of the play of reality. Don't mistake the words for the living truth. You will read of several widely different models in these pages, and each of them is valid and useful in some way.

What are the cakras? Here we get into deeper waters. In classic literature, the cakras are rarely defined. Concepts like disks, wheels, lotuses, blossoms, flames, precious stones, palaces, islands, heavens, or worlds suggest possibilities but they do not attempt to describe what really goes on. This is a good thing because a metaphor is sometimes more efficient than a prosaic definition. As the cakras are never quite limited to a specific meaning, they allow for any amount of direct experience and wholesome subjectivity. What people see as cakras when they allow themselves to have visions or dreams is not the real thing. Every item that you see with your mind's eye is not a thing as such but a representation. Now, some people have wonderfully detailed and vivid visions. This tells us that their visual imagination is well developed, but it does not mean that any of their visions is particularly true. In the same way, a hazy vision may seem less convincing, but it is not necessarily unreal. We talk about representations, not about reality. Reality is behind the representation and we make up images to handle it. Well, a vision is never the reality, just as a word is not the thing it represents. Whatever the cakras are, they remain safely incomprehensible. Metaphors, while misleading, may turn out to be useful when it comes to dealing with them practically. Think of the lotus. Lots of pictures show people with lotus blossoms in their bodies. What few realise is that the lotus flowers horizontally. In Indian art, the lotuses are generally shown upright, which comes from mixing two perspectives. What else is there to the lotus? Its petals have fine hairs that prevent dirt or water clinging to them. Thus, the lotus, no matter what life throws at it, remains pure and clean. Then there is the growth of the plant. The roots of the lotus are firm within the darkness of the underworld. Like you and me the plant grows through mud and slime and rises through the murky water until it reaches light and air. Above the surface of the lake the petals open and the blossom flowers. Take it as a metaphor for the evolution of humans through earth, water, fire, and air. And there is more to follow. When the blossom at the surface dies, the next bud rises from the deep to unfold its beauty. A lotus is not a single plant, it is a plant with numerous rebirths. This suggests motion.

In theory, the amount of petals of each lotus is determined by a conjunction of energy channels, the subtle nāḍīs that criss-cross the entire body. A lotus of four petals is a junction of two nāḍīs, a lotus of twelve the meeting place of six . The lotus is not fixed to a specific direction. Woodroffe (1974: 338-9) quotes from the *Māyā Tantra*: *Mahādeva said: The Lotuses, O Devī, have their heads in different directions. In the life of action they should be thought of as having their heads downward, but in the path of renunciation they are always meditated upon as having their heads upward turned.* This is a general rule, descriptions of the cakras do not always follow it. A lotus can point in any direction. Consider the similarity of the lotus on its stalk to the numerous world trees that appear in Eurasian shamanism. Shamans climb their trees - or forks, ladders, pillars, mountains. The way up is always a dissociation of the material world, the ordinary personality, the world of human effort and terrestrial experience. The way down is the path of manifestation, the way of incarnation, the eventual return to the material world. In the process, the shaman changes. You can find the same idea in Kuṇḍalinī yoga. The way up is a way of release. This is called laya yoga, the yoga of dissolution. Raising the serpent-self is not just climbing a ladder having an enchanting experience on each step. The further you climb, the more dissolves behind you. Each cakra that you pass loses meaning, shape, purpose. And so do you. When you arrive at the top, all that had occurred earlier has lost its meaning. The upward path is the way towards formless, primal simplicity, a way of freeing yourself from attachments. It may come as a surprise that the cakras are not something the adept is proud of. Instead, laya yoga means finding release from the clusters of experience, joy, and bondage expressed by each of the lotuses. The opposite applies on the return path. Eventually, the serpent returns down the central channel. Eventually, the bright moonlike elixir cascades from the height, pouring down the body, drenching the entire system and rejuvenating it. Eventually, you come back to earth. As you return to the world you make your whole body/mind system a vehicle for the great work. During the downward passage, the centres are brought to the perfection required for your true will and, as a side effect, the siddhis come into being. In the language of European occultism the upward path (dissolution) is mysticism, the burning up of body, belief, personality in order to unite with the supreme (whatever form it may take). The downward path (manifestation) is magick, bringing the fire from heaven to earth (in a hollow tube, as Prometheus did), transforming the world with a new consciousness. Remember how we started out with the simple lotus image? All of these ideas, and more, have gone into the metaphor. All of them are meaningful, and all are easier to contemplate than abstract junctions of energy and sentience. Now think of the other metaphors used for the cakras. What can be communicated by images of crystals, flames, wheels, palaces, heavens, temples, worlds, and the like?

How many cakras exist? This depends a lot on the age of a given system. Early Tantric texts tend to be really confusing with regard to number and location of cakras. It is not that a brilliant seer had a sudden vision of hidden reality and convinced all the world what things are really like. Seers rarely agree with each other (it's part of the job description) and, as you know, the initial act of each new faith is rebellion. Even within single texts there is often confusion. Here is one of my favourites.

In the pioneering *Kaulajñāna nirṇaya*, chapter two alludes to three zones, representing the three manifestations of Śakti: Kriyā (right activity), Jñāna (right knowledge, gnosis), and Icchā (true will), and introduces the idea that liberation depends on dissolving one into the other (see below). Chapter three mentions cakras of five lines, sixteen lines, sixty-four petals, plus lotuses of 100, 1,000, 10,000,000, and 30,000,000 petals above each other, each of them resembling flames. Plus an indescribable, eternal one above the lot. Chapter 5 has a meditation on an unlocalised lotus of 100,000,000,000 petals in white. It also mentions one of one thousand petals and one of sixteen. Further on it refers to eleven cakras, of which nine are localised in genitals, navel, heart, throat, mouth, brow, peak, skull joints, and in the Tridaṇḍa. They have five, eight, ten, twelve, sixteen, one hundred, and ten million petals (?). Chapter 6 refers to oral lore, which is localised in navel, heart, throat, mouth, and nostrils. Chapter 7 alludes to the 'bone cakra' on the peak of the skull, from whence the life-renewing black elixir flows. Chapter 8 gives some details regarding the qualities and functions of eight cakras without localising or naming them. Chapter 10 lists eight cakras with the syllables they are associated with (Brahmarandhra, forehead, between the eyes, mouth, throat, heart, navel, genitals), each of them having eight petals (provided a number is mentioned). Each of the cakras is visualised as a bright flame, the text also informs us that imagining the cakras in various colours produces subjugation (red), paralysis (yellow), liberation (crystal clear), death (black), and the power to uproot (smoky). Chapter 13 lists seed mantras attributed to the cakras in anus, penis, navel, mouth, right nostril, left cavity, right cavity, right ear, left ear, brow, forehead, left ear, right ear, left eye, right eye, left nostril, right nostril, mouth, navel, penis, anus.

This is more than a series of power zones, it is a pilgrimage through the sacred body. Chapter 14 proposes that one should become free of time and the cakras, sadly, it doesn't say how. Instead, we learn that the root cakra is the source of ecstatic trembling and shaking, which give rise, as everything else in this yoga, to various miraculous siddhis. Four fingers above the root cakra is localised the Devī's cakra, which produces more trembling, plus siddhis relating to speech and sound. Next, the Brahma Granthi is described, then follows a flaming cakra revolving above the head, also associated with tremors and trembling. Meditation on the heart cakra appears next, inducing trembling and vibration and more powers than anyone has ever use of, plus the ability to cause sexual excitement in a host of other- and underworldly beings. Then the throat cakra is discussed (more of the same), the refreshing of the subtle body by the white elixir (here called celestial semen), and the act of placing awareness in a given cakra by taking in the scent of a flower (now really!) and directing the breath. A bit further on the forehead is activated by imagining the phonemes there, leading to more trembling and eloquence. Then follow the fissures of the skull, a secret place within the skull, meditations on being everything and nothing, meditation on the heart-lotus (of the nature of nothingness), plus the Mātṛkā cakra, the Khecarī cakra, a cakra blossoming in spontaneity in the navel and the yoni nādī. Chapter 15 discusses a meditation on three cakras. Here the emphasis is on dissolving one cakra after another on the way to liberation, immortality, equipoise, and mastery of the three worlds. Well, there are several more chapters to the book (please get yourself a copy) but right now I hope you are confused enough to remember to forget to remember what you assumed you knew before it changed for the better. Did the author of the *Kaulajñāna nirṇaya,* the famous Matsyendranāth, contradict himself? Is the book an assembly of various manuscripts at odds with each other? Or is the result of these mind-blowing complications that you can find and create cakras wherever you will?

Occult Anatomy

One of the important discoveries of early Tantra is the idea that the human body, the world, and the entire multiverse relate to each other. Body, in these systems, is not just connected with everything else, it can also be refined by meditation, mantra, mudrā, nyāsa, and a number of highly skilled physical exercises. This automatically influences the body on the large scale, i.e. the world you be-live in. There is only a difference of degree between your body as the microcosmic manifestation of the Great Body, which constitutes the worlds and everything in them. In the macrocosmic universe you may encounter cakras, places of energy and sentience, and the same goes for your own physical form. The nature, description, and amount of these cakras differs from time to time and system to system. To give you a basic idea what the reality of each cakra is, I shall now list a few descriptions.

Three cakras, sites of power/sentience, are at the core of most cakra models. You can find them in Chinese Daoism where they are described as alchemical ovens, furnaces, cauldrons, caves, courtyards, temple spaces, or palaces. Generally they are located in the belly (a little below the navel), near the heart, and in the head. It is useful to think of them as spheres, or as wide inner spaces. We are dealing with general realms of body and intelligence. It is interesting that these three correspond with the three major locations of intelligence in body. In the head we can find the brain, i.e. that miraculous bit of nervous tissue that makes you think that you are thinking. Near the heart is that complex web of nerves called the solar plexus, where the organs, such as lungs and heart are co-ordinated. If you ever got a fist in your solar plexus you'll know how essential its function is. In the belly is the seat of enteral intelligence, where the bowels do their highly complicated job. Enteral intelligence is a comparatively new discovery. It turned out that your guts make use of all the neurotransmitters of the brain. They have an enormously complex system of information-transmission. Just think about it. Every bit of food that goes down your throat has to be identified, dissolved, chemically transformed, and transported. Something goes into your body as nourishment; waste is restructured and evicted. Your belly uses an extremely lethal chemistry to dissolve food. Have you ever wondered why your body, which is able to digest meat, does not digest itself? There is a lot to gut-thinking, and also a lot that is influenced by your guts. It turns out that the guts are the third nervous system and that they are capable of doing their job independently from the brain. These three realms of intelligence and power have been recognised by several cultures, each of them making up its own lore and explanations.

In Hindu lore the body is divided into three units. Each of these may be divided into smaller units with specific functions, depending on the nature of the meditation. The bottom of the body is identified with fire. This is not the same idea as the 'fire element', we are on a different map here. From navel to throat is the realm of the sun, and everything above throat is the realm of the moon. This basic system lies behind a lot of complicated metaphors. When you encounter Tantric references to exchanging the positions of sun, moon, or fire, you are within the basic triple model. This system also appears in the eyes of Śiva and Kālī. Both of them have three eyes, corresponding to sun, moon, and fire. Sometimes fire is replaced by stars, indicating the influence from the outside. Now the model of the three planes is so ancient that it can be traced to the *Vedas*. It is so tied up with complex symbolism that I shall gladly leave it alone. A good introduction appears in White, 1996, chapter 2. If you want to explore the various cakra systems, you might start with the three zones of intelligence in your body by installing three deities, power beasts, spirits, or whatever representation of the divine you fancy. What will turn you on? Ask yourself, ask your deep mind, and ask your personal deities. Think of them daily. Install them with mantra and visualisation. Above all, lie or sit quietly and go travelling into each realm in your imagination. Repeated journeys to each inner space make it come alive. To reach full understanding, assume the form and consciousness of the deities of each realm.

Bhūta Śuddhi: the Purification of the Principles of your Body

A common system of meditation making use of five principles is called Bhūta Śuddhi. I first encountered it as part of the Kuṇḍalinī meditation, in the *Devī Bhāgawatam*, 11, 8. The text is in the translation of Swami Vijnanānanda (spelling slightly amended), who also wrote the commentaries (in brackets).

> *Nārāyana said:- 'O Great Muni! Now shall I tell you the rules of Bhūta Śuddhi i.e. the purification of the elements of the body (by respiratory attraction and replacement etc.) Firstly, think of the Highest Deity Kuṇḍalinī (the Serpent Fire) as rising up in the hollow canal Suṣumnā in the Spinal Cord from the Mulādhāra (the sacral plexus) to the Brahmarandra (the aperture supposed to be in the crown of the head).*
>
> *Next, the devotee is to meditate on the Mantra 'Haṁsa' and consider his Jīvātmā (the embodied soul) united with Para Brahma.*
>
> *Then think from leg to the knees in the form of a square Yantra (diagram as furnished with Vajra thunderbolt) (represented by 63 lines at the four corners) ; consider this square as the earth, of a golden colour and represented by the letter 'Laṁ', representing the Seed Mantra of earth. Next from the knee to the navel consider the semi-moon and at its two ends consider that the two lotuses are situated. Consider this as the circle of water,*

of white colour, represented by the letter 'Vaṁ' the Seed Mantra of water. Then again from the navel to the heart consider it as of a triangular form and the Svastik mark at its three angles and think it as of fire and represented by the letter 'Raṁ' its root Mantra, of red colour. Next from the heart to the centre of the eyebrows, consider as marked with six dots, with the Seed Mantra 'Yaṁ' of a smoke-coloured colour (dark red) and of a circular appearance and consider it as air. Then again from the centre of the eyebrows to the crown of the head consider as Ākāśa Maṇḍalam (a region of ether) beautiful and clear and with 'Haṁ' as its vīja letter. Thus thinking consider firstly the earthy principle originated from watery principle, dissolved in water. Then think water dissolved in fire, its cause; fire dissolved in air, its cause; and air dissolved in Ākāśa, ether, its cause; then consider Ākāśa dissolved in its cause Ahamkâra, egoism; then again Ahamkāra dissolved in the Great Principle (Mahattatva); and Mahattatva again in its cause Prakriti and consider Prakriti again diluted in its cause, the Supreme Self. Then consider your own self as the Highest Knowledge and only that.

Think, then, of the Pāpa Puruṣa, the Sinful Man, in your body. The size of this Man is that of a thumb and it is situated in the left abdomen. The head of him is represented by Brahmahatyā (murdering a Brāhmaṇ); his arm as stealing gold; his heart as drinking wine; his loins as going to the wife of his Guru, his legs as mixing with people who go to their Guru's wives, and his toes as representing other sins and venial offences. The Sinful Man holds axes and shield in his hands; he is always angry, with his head bent down and his appearance is very horrible.

Inhale air through the left nostril thinking of 'Vaṁ' the Root Mantra of air and make Kumbhaka i.e. fill the whole body with air, and hold it inside, purifying the sinful man; then repeating 'Raṁ', the Seed Mantra of fire, think the sinful man with his own body burnt down to ashes. Then exhale outside through the right nostril those ashes of the Sinful Man. Next consider the ashes due to the burning of the Sinful Man, as rolled and turned into a round ball with the nectar seed of the Moon. Think steadily this ball as transformed into a golden egg by the Seed Mantra 'Laṁ' of the earth. Repeat then 'Haṁ' the Seed Mantra of Ākāśa and think yourself as an ideal being pure and clear, and shape thus your body and the several limbs.

Create, then, fresh in an inverse order from the Brahma the elements Ākāśa, air, fire, water, earth and locate them in their respective positions.

Then by the Mantra 'Soham' separate the Jivātmā from the Paramātmā and locate the Jivātmā in the heart. Think also that the Kuṇḍalinī has come to the Sacral Plexus, after locating the Jivātmā, turned into nectar by contact with the Highest Self, in the heart.

Next follows a meditation on the Praṇā Śakti, quoted above in the chapter on breathing. This ends the exercise, the good book continuing with seven chapters on how to obtain sacred ashes. As you will have noticed, we are dealing with several exercises here. First the arousal of Kuṇḍalinī as an exercise of the imagination. It seems strange that this important matter is here a mere preliminary to the much more basic forms of inner purification. Wouldn't it make more sense to purify the body and the energy channels first and then to rouse Kuṇḍalinī? When I have done my Kuṇḍalinī practice, I am so spaced out that I wouldn't dream of doing something as basic as banishing the Sinful Man. That sort of stuff should happen earlier. So are we dealing with a full arousal of the Kuṇḍalinī in this section? Or is it merely a meditation on Kuṇḍalinī in a theoretical way? Both are possible. In many texts, the Bhūta Śuddhi has little to do with the arousal of the fire snake. It is a popular ritual that is performed by many Hindus every day. Perhaps the compilers of the *DB* were so busy putting odds and ends together that they did not bother to consider the syntax. I was a bit uneasy about the syntax of the ritual until I discovered what is probably the earliest recorded description of the matter. This is the *Jayākhya Saṁhitā*, a Vaiṣṇava text composed between the seventh and tenth century. You can find a translation of the relevant passages by Gavin Flood in *Tantra in Practice* (edited by David Gordon White, 2000: 509-520). The ritual is more detailed than in the account you read earlier. It begins with a number of preliminaries, such as purification of the place, seat, and body by mantra and mudrā, and a visualisation of *the god whose form is flames, whose splendor is like a thousand suns, covered with millions of flames, vomiting flames from his mouth*, who floods the entire universe (and the worshipper) with a blaze of heat and light. The Bhūta Śuddhi rite begins with an explanation that the body, like Indra's net, is composed of five principles. These are called earth, water, fire, air, and spirit. This sounds dangerously familiar. Indian sages generally use the term tattva, meaning 'thusness', principle, category for them. The tattvas are usually translated as 'elements' in European occultism. We owe this to the magicians of the Golden Dawn, who made use of some Indian texts, and introduced a practice of 'travelling in the spirit vision' that uses the tattva symbols as gates to the elements. This has led to the mistaken impression that the tattvas are identical with the five elements of Greek philosophy. A look at Greek philosophy is enough to show that this is not the case. The Presocratic thinkers worried a lot about the origin and nature of the world, and what it is made of. Thales, for instance, taught that the primal matter is water, and that from water, the earth and everything else appeared. Anaximandros stated that 'the eternal and unlimited' is the primal matter out of which everything arose. Anaximenes saw air as the primal element. Air is the source of all matter, the essence of the soul and the totality of the cosmos. Heracleitos disagreed (he liked disagreeing) and proposed that all things originate, end, and reappear from fire. In his lore, air is an expression of fire, and so are water, earth, the stars, planets, and souls. The primal fire is his idea of the divine. Empedocles rounded off the theory by adding earth to water, air, and fire and proposed that these four are eternal and keep changing and interacting in all matter, mainly through the two principal powers: love and disagreement.

As you can see, these philosophers were mainly interested in matter and things. Their elements are the stuff of which every thing consists, and in their quarrelling they paved the way for Democritus' atomic theory. The Indian term tattva means essence, principle, category. Western occult literature, thanks to the Theosophists and the Hermetic Order of the Golden Dawn, gives the impression that there are just five tattvas, but this is wrong - Indian lore has dozens of tattvas. The usual amount is twenty-five but some proposed thirty-six. The same error was committed when European scholars translated the Chinese concept 'movers' by elements. Now the Chinese movers: earth, water, fire, wood, and metal (gold) look superficially like the Indian principles and the Greek elements. Perhaps we can observe a bit of cultural exchange here. Nevertheless, the movers are not things or matter, they are the energies working change on matter. In short, fire is a thing in Greek thought, a principle in Indian lore, and a force of change in Chinese wisdom. All three make use of the symbol of 'fire' but each of them has a different meaning.

To make the rite of Bhūta Śuddhi work, we have to develop the concepts of the five tattvas. In the *Jayākhya Saṁhitā*, the ritual of purification begins after the invocation of five deities who correspond with the tattvas. This involves mantra and visualisation. To begin with, the worshipper expels *the Lord* through the right nostril and places the divine in the centre of a maṇḍala. S/he shifts awareness to the mantra-self in the highest place, i.e. above the top of the head. This is a matter of identification; you should look down from above your head. Gazing down from the height, the worshipper perceives the deities of the five tattvas, and further down the complete mantra body.

So much for the introduction. Let me summarise the process. If you want to study the classical method, read it up in Flood's presentation.

The first step is the invocation of the earth principle. Visualise a square of gold-yellow earth. Play around with the colours until you find a precise shade of yellow that appeals to you. Earth is woken by the sound of thunder. It is expands until it becomes as huge as the whole wide earth. Watch it developing mountain ranges, oceans, rivers and streams, vast forests, fertile plains, streets and settlements crowded with people. While you inhale, draw this vast living space into your body and locate it, tranquil and abundant, between the soles of your feet and the knees. Stabilise this image while breath rests. When all is well established, transform earth into the energy of smell and exhale, dissolving it. To dissolve something can mean several things. It can mean that earth, the firm, becomes fluid (water). It can mean that your awareness of dense body and matter moves into the realm of fluid thought and dreaming. It can mean that you cease thinking of the earth realm and gently move on to the next principle.

The same process applies to water. Here you visualise a half moon adorned with a lotus.Expand it until it becomes all the waters, fluids, and oceans in the world. See the swirling floods, the rich moisture, fill it with aquatic creatures, with fish, coral, squid, whales, diving birds, and seals. Build up your vision until you are almost lost in the wonder of the fluid world. When this is well developed, inhale and gently merge it with the symbol and locate it between your knees and the top of your thighs. Dissolve the water principle into the energy of taste as you exhale, and burn taste up in fire.

As you exhale, imagine fire as a red, upward pointing triangle. Expand this vision and fill it with all the fiery joy and passion you can think of. Imagine thunderstorms and lightning flashes, see sun and moon, planets and stars, watch household fires, torches, wildfires, and erupting volcanoes. Fire is inhaled into your body and established between the perineum and the navel. Note that this is not quite the same as described in the extract from the *DB.* Don't worry, all maps of occult anatomy show divergence. Choose what you will, and only what you will. Fire transforms into its mantra, and mantra dissolves into form and consciousness. Next, exhale the air principle. Visualise the wide realm of air, wind, breath, and speech and make up as much detail as you like. Be creative, it's no use if you simply repeat what others have found useful. When air is well established, inhale it into the region between your navel and throat. Wind is transformed into touch, as air touches everything, while you exhale. Exhaling, allow touch to transform into sound.

Imagine the space/spirit principle outside your body. This tattva is full of sound and vibration, it is all-pervading, omnipresent, sentient, and peopled by spirits, deities, and self-perfected entities. By inhaling space, you encounter the absolute. Settle it between your ears and the top of your head. When space and vibration are manifest within you, move them upwards through the top of your head. *Individualised consciousness, like a quivering star, is next to be meditated upon as at peace, departed from the cage of the elements (that is, the body).* At this point, the structure of the *Jayākhya Saṁhitā* ritual undergoes a change. Having left the terrene realm behind, your awareness should now be settled (more or less) outside the physical body. This takes a bit of practice, like all visualisations, so don't expect grandiose effects during your first tries. For some obscure reason, this step is repeated in what amounts to an early type of Kuṇḍalinī rising. As this is an early text, Kuṇḍalinī is not named nor described as a serpent. Also she rises from the heart and not the perineum. To begin with, attention goes to the heart. Here you can see your own self, which is identified with the deity. Rise from the cave of the heart in the fire of mantra. Rise along the central channel, the suṣumṇā, until you reach the top of your head, the aperture of the absolute. Leave body, gently, by the *wind of consciousness.* Now you are supposed to experience the supreme joy of becoming the divine.

In the next stage of the rite, the *sinful body* is burned up. It is not the material body which is sinful. Rather, people build up a 'body' out of their sins, restrictions, frustrations, and ignorance. This body manifests in muscular tension, as character armour in the sense of Wilhelm Reich, it also builds up in the shape of limiting concepts of oneself. This body is more than physical matter, it is a unit of belief that keeps you from being as happy and joyous as you would like to be. Whenever misery, frustration, and reduced expectations accumulate, they become a body of sin. This body can do with a bit of purification from time to time.

If you wish to clean and purify your body, you had better get out of it first. Having located your awareness outside of your body you are free to transform it. This is basic magick; if you wish to transform something you are stuck in, first get out. Seeing yourself beneath yourself, watch the fire of purification, fanned by mantra, surge out of the feet and blaze upward. Watch your body as it burns and see it reduced to ashes. Allow water to sweep the ashes away.

Next, imagine the primal milk ocean of elixir and poison. It contains the nectar juice of immortality as well as the worlds, realms, dimensions of the whole wide universe. Allow the milky fluid to pour down into the mantra body and establish it as a vehicle of the divine. Imagine the pale white showers cascading downwards, structuring your new flesh, hear the mantras fusing to form your new shape, see the tattvas, purified, combine to give flesh and substance to your being. Create a new body for your being, radiant with energy, filled with joy and laughter, adorned with celestial jewels, shining like the sun. What else turns you on? Find your own visions, this is your new body and you are free to make it as you will. When the radiant body is established, allow your awareness to descend. Go down through the aperture of the absolute, into your head, and gradually go deeper until you arrive at the centre of the heart. From there, let your awareness extend so that it brings the supreme consciousness into body/world manifestation. Come home to your new body and enjoy.

Let me emphasise an important magickal formula. In our meditation, we project a given tattva (such as earth or water) from ourselves. We visualise it in front of us - that is, outside of our body - and built up a vision that is elaborate and impressive. When the vision is fully developed, we bring it into our body again. Compare. In making a food offering, we obtain the material and bring it to the temple. The food is sacrificed and given to the deity, who transforms it. Then it returns to us and we may eat and enjoy it. Compare. When we draw a yantra, we project its deity (deities) from within ourselves. We locate them on specific points of the diagram and worship them. Then we dissolve the yantra and bring the deities back into ourselves. Compare. In generating the secretions, we make our offering in the womb/cauldron. Then the mingled essence is taken out of the yoni, ritually transformed, mixed with water or wine and re-ingested.

In each of these rituals, a given entity is created within, brought into the outside world for transformation and blessing, and re-assimilated into our system. Can you think of other rituals that follow this pattern?

A Look at Tradition

As you may have noticed, I am very much in favour of making up cakras according to personal needs. It is your job to discover how many cakras you can find in your body/mind system, how they fit together and function as a whole. There is a large amount of literature describing the nature and functions of cakras. Each of the cakra systems that are hallowed tradition nowadays used to be the personal and highly unique subjective experience of some crazed loony or saint. Each of them started out as direct experience, and became tradition by a process that discourages creativity and innovation. So let me offer an abridged summary of the cakras in the understanding that if you simply imitate what the authorities propose you'll never find what works best for you. What follows is based on the *Ṣaṭ-Cakra Nirūpaṇa*, translated by Woodroffe in his classic book *The Serpent Power* (1974), which I highly recommend. As you will notice, the text is not an early effort but a detailed account of each power zone with a highly complex structure.

Mūladhāra chakra Situated at the Mouth of the Suṣuṁnā, between genitals and anus. Four crimson petals, golden letters: Va, Śa, Ṣa, Sa. This lotus is hanging, its head (mouth) points down. Contains the yellow square of Pṛthivī, the earth tattva, and its bīja Laṁ, surrounded by eight spears pointing in eight directions. The spears are like Kulācalas, which may mean the breasts of women. Dharā (Indra) abides in this cakra. He has four arms, rides an elephant, and carries four-headed, four-armed Brahmā as a radiant, solar child on his lap. The Devī of the cakra is red eyed, beautiful, four-armed Dākinī, shining like a million suns, revealing pure intelligence. In the centre of the square is a downward pointing triangle, Traipura, which is Kāmarūpa, where dwells beautiful red Kāmadeva, the god of desire. Within the triangle is Svayaṁbhu (Self-Existent, a name of Śiva) in the form of a liṅga, like molten gold with his head turned down, or like a whirlpool. Coiled 3.5 times around the liṅga is Devī Kuṇḍalinī in her serpent form, asleep, shining like lightning-flashes, humming like a swarm of love-mad bees. Here is the source of all poetry and literature. *She is the world-bewilderer, gently covering the mouth of Brahma-dvāra by her own... It is She who maintains all the beings of the world by means of inspiration and expiration, and shines in the cavity of the root (Mūla) Lotus like a chain of brilliant lights.* (10, 11) She is the supreme, the Parameśvarī, the omnipotent kalā, the awakener. *She is the receptacle of that continuous stream of ambrosia which flows from the Eternal Bliss. By Her radiance it is that the whole of this Universe and this Cauldron is illumined.* (12). Meditating on the cakra (shining like ten-million suns) grants mastery of speech, learning, gives gladness, frees from disease, and makes the adept king among men and a lord of speech.

Svādhiṣthāna chakra Situated inside the Suṣuṁṇā at the root of the genitals, coloured vermilion, with six petals containing the letters from Ba, Bha, Ma, Ya, Ra, and La. Inside it is the oceanic realm of Varuṇa, in the form of a half-moon, white, shining, containing the bīja of the water tattva, Vaṁ, seated on a Makara (a crocodile-fish-dragon). Resting in the bīja is blue Hari (Viṣṇu), clothed in yellow, four armed, adorned with the auspicious breast curl, and a lustrous jewel on his heart. This is the home of Rākinī Devī, coloured like a blue lotus, clad in a celestial raiment, holding various weapons (spear, lotus, axe and ḍamaru-drum), drunk on ambrosia. Meditation on this cakra destroys enemies such as egoism, anger, lechery; activates yogīc power, and promotes inspired and well-reasoned discourse. Most of the cakras in this text tend to promote eloquence.

Maṇipūra chakra The cakra is located near the root of the navel. The lotus has ten petals, coloured like dark, rain-heavy clouds, adorned with the letters Ḍa, Ḍha, Ṇa, Ta, Tha, Da, Dha, Na, Pa, Pha. Here is the region of fire, an upward pointing triangle, red like the rising sun, surrounded by three svastikas and containing the bīja of Vahni (Agni, the fire god), Raṁ. Agni is seated on a ram and on his lap is Rudra, who is vermillion-red and also white from being smeared with funeral ashes. Rudra shows the gestures that dispel fear and grant boons. Here dwells Lākinī, who has a dark complexion, wears yellow, and is tipsy from swilling ambrosia. She holds the Śakti weapon, a thunderbolt, and shows the same gestures. Meditating on the navel cakra gives the power to create and destroy the world, and grants the blessings of Vāṇī (Sarasvatī).

Anāhata chakra The heart-lotus shines like a Bandhūka flower (Pentapoetes Phoenicea), it has twelve petals containing the letters Ka, Kha, Ga, Gha, Ṅa, Ca, Ccha, Ja, Jha, Jña, Ṭa, Ṭha, coloured vermilion. It is called Anāhata (self-sounding, i.e. sound not produced by striking two things together) and like the wish-fulfilling tree, it gives more than it is asked for. Inside it is a hexagram of grey smoky colour. Inside is the bīja of Vāyu, god of the air, Yaṁ, four armed, riding a black antelope. On his lap is three-eyed Iśa (the Lord, Śiva) who dwells in the *abode of mercy,* shines like the sun and makes the gestures of protection and boon-granting. This is the home of Kākinī Devī, the three-eyed, four-armed, yellow-skinned *benefactress of all.* Her gestures grant boons and dispel fear, the other two hands holds noose and skull and *her heart is softened* by consuming nectar. She dwells in the form of a downward pointing triangle containing a Śiva liṅga called Bāṇa, which is gold and has a gem-like orifice (bindu, here a hollow) on its top. This liṅga is the abode of Lakṣmī, goddess of prosperity. Meditation on this lotus grants eloquence and the power to destroy and create like Iśvara (the Lord, Śiva), whose seat it is. The cakra is also the seat of the jīvātmā, the incarnate soul, like the flame of a lamp in a windless place. Mastery of this lotus equals complete control of the senses (and passions), and makes the yogī wise, thoughtful of Brahman, do good deeds, and irresistible to women. The yogī becomes like Viṣṇu and gains the skill to enter the body of another (i.e. to assume another's point of view).

Figure 39 - Circles.
Top: Lotus ornament from a stone pillar.
Bottom: Makara, the crocodile / elephant / fish hybrid, sacred beast of the goddess Gaṇgā. From a stone pillar.

Viśuddha chakra At the throat is a smoky purple lotus of sixteen petals adorned with the sixteen vowels A, Ā, I, Ī, U, Ū, Ṛ, Ṝ, Ḷ, Ḹ, E, Ai, O, Au, Aṁ, Aḥ, in crimson. It contains the *Ethereal Region, circular in shape and white like the full Moon.* Aṁbara (Ethereal Region) sits on a snow-white elephant, holding noose and goad, his bīja is Haṁ. On his lap sits Sadā-Śiva (Everlasting Auspiciousness), snow-white, ten-armed, with three eyes and five faces, clad in a tiger pelt, embracing Girijā (Mountain-born, Pārvatī). Within the lotus, containing the whole region of the moon, dwells bone-white Śakti Sākinī, in yellow garb, holding bow, arrow, noose, and goad. For those who have purified their senses, this cakra is the gateway to liberation. It frees from disease and sorrow, prolongs life, gives knowledge of past, present, future, and promotes peace of mind for those who have direct experience of Ātmā (Brahman).

Who retains breath, fixing the mind on the cakra, may move the worlds and cannot be resisted by Brahmā, Viṣṇu, Hari-Hara, Sūrya, and Gaṇeśa.

Ājñā chakra Its location not mentioned in this text; usually it is the spot between and behind the eyebrows. Shining like the moon, the lotus has two petals with the letters Ha and Kṣa, radiant with the beauty of dhyāna (meditation). In its centre is a downward pointing triangle inscribed with the letters a, u, and ṁ (Oṁ), the pure mind, the seed-point (bindu), the nāda (vibration) diffusing the rays of the moon. It contains the Devī Hākinī, who exhibits six white moonlike faces, six arms holding book, skull, ḍamaru drum, rosary, and does the usual gestures. The cakra houses the subtle mind (manas). There is a yoni in the pericarp where Itara Śiva abides in phallic form. The worshipper *whose Ātmā is nothing but a meditation on this Lotus* gains the power to enter another's body (or house), and becomes an all-knowing and all-seeing Munī, who realises unity with Brahman and becomes creator, maintainer, and destroyer of the three worlds. The yogī *who closes the house which hangs without support* (shuts up the world and mind by doing yoni-mudrā) and dissolves the cetas by regular practice in this region of pure bliss, sees the fiery sparks above and within the triangle. From these appears a light like a lamp, like the morning sun between earth and heaven (Mūladhāra to Sahasrāra), the omnipresent Bhagavān. it is the abode of Viṣṇu where the yogī places the prāṇa at the time of dying to unite with the absolute.

Mahānāda chakra Located above the Ājñā is the place of dissolution of Vāyu (air). It manifests the lower half of Śiva, grants boons, banishes fear, and allows pure intelligence (Buddhi) to manifest.

Sahasrāra chakra The lotus of one thousand petals, radiant white like the full moon, has its head turned downward. Its petals are tinged with the hue of the red morning sun. At its centre (the crown of the head) is the stainless full moon, shedding its rays in abundance, moistening and cooling like nectar. Inside is a triangle, shining like lightning, containing the Great Void. Hidden within is the supreme 17th kalā, the root of liberation and abode of Parama Śiva, *the Brahman and Ātmā of all beings*, the sun that dispels ignorance and delusion, uniting attachment and detachment of worldly bliss. Shedding a constant stream of nectar, the incarnate and absolute self are realised as one. The sages call it the abode of Śiva, of Viṣṇu, of the Devī, the pure place of Prakṛti and Puruṣa. To know this cakra is to cease incarnating, as all bonds of attachment are severed. The yogī gains complete control of the mind and the ability to do as he wills, moving ever closer to Brahman. This is the location of Amā-kalā, the sixteenth kalā of the moon. She is radiant as the freshly risen sun, soft as the fragment of a fibre in a lotus stalk, and turns downwards. From her springs forth a stream of pure nectar, generated by Brahman (or by the blissful union of the supreme). Inside her is Nirvāṇa-kalā, much subtler than a hair, shaped like a crescent moon, the eternal Bhagavatī who grants divine knowledge and pervades all beings. Within her *shines the supreme and primordial Nirvāṇa-Śakti*, more subtle than the tenth-millionth part of the end of a hair, radiant like ten million suns, from whom streams of Prema (absolute love) cascade. Inside her is the supreme abode (or state) of Śiva, free from delusion, full of bliss and pure knowledge, known by some as Brahman and by others as Haṁsa, as the abode of Viṣṇu, and the place of liberation.

Kuṇḍalinī: Consciousness, Power, and the World Glamour

Kuṇḍalinī is one of the most misunderstood concepts (and experiences) in yoga and Tantra. Now I am sure that you have read a lot on this topic. It can't really be avoided, what with so many New-Age authors copying rubbish from each other. Even among the best informed researchers there are only a scant few who have ever had any practical experience of the subject. Instead, there have been loads of phoney guru figures selling all sorts of body-therapy techniques as 'Kuṇḍalinī yoga' to the innocent and the result-hungry. Not that such techniques are necessarily bad. Some of them involve jumping around, fast panting, and shouting. Good fun, great feelings of release, lots of oxygen, but just what has it got to do with Kuṇḍalinī? As the topic has been so thoroughly abused, I find it difficult to add my own estimates, let alone experiences. What follows is given in the understanding that when we deal with Kuṇḍalinī, we are dealing with highly subjective experiences. Some of my experiences may be similar to yours, some may differ considerably. Every person who wakes the Fire Snake creates a very unique and personal experience for her or himself. Do not take my comments as rules, they are more like guidelines. If you disagree, feel welcome. Kuṇḍalinī is such a perplexing topic that many opinions are essential.

On the simplest possible level, people think that Kuṇḍalinī is a serpent, often called the fire serpent, which lies coiled in a variety of places, such as the perineum, the base of the spine, the prostate gland, or the genitals. This serpent is woken by a number of techniques: yoga exercises, mantra, breathing, visualisation, ritual, until it rises along the subtle equivalent of the spine. In the process it passes through a number of cakras until it arrives at the top, where, hey, bingo! enlightenment is waiting for you. Some even entertain the belief that a skilled guru can do the job for them. All of this is a technical and materialistic way of thinking. It is a mechanical metaphor, instead of a spiritual one, where you have mechanisms within yourself that can be made to function in a specific way. It sounds as if you simply need a guru who installs the proper tubes and turbines and pulls the switch to make enlightenment surge through your system. Just what gives people the idea that somebody else could do the spiritual housework for them?

Kuṇḍalinī is a metaphor. Metaphor means literally 'to carry over', and Kuṇḍalinī is exactly this: a vehicle of consciousness/energy. And it is not the only one. This metaphor appears in many guises. Most people think that Kuṇḍalinī is a serpent. It can appear as a serpent, but this is just one form of manifestation. It can also be a pillar of energy, a vast tree of awareness, a ladder reaching to the stars. It can be a flame, it can be a flash of lightning, it can be the rising of sound-vibration within your hidden core. It can be the personal deity of the worshipper. Imagine your personal deity within your body. Not just in your heart but extending all the way. If you are standing or walking, the inner deity extends all the way through your body from your feet to the head. If you are sitting, the inner deity has her/his feet at your perineum and genitals extends upward. Here is the inner meaning behind the worship of the feet of the deity. Several arcane texts use the metaphor 'feet of the Goddess' to hint at the power zones of perineum and genitals. The *Saundaryalaharī* offers several examples, such as verse 2 stating that by *gathering a tiny speck of dust* from the feet of Lalitā Tripurā, the gods fulfil their functions of creating, maintaining, and destroying. Verse 4 tells us that all the other gods grant boons by their hands. *To protect from fear and grant fruits more than desired, in all the worlds, Oh! Refuge, Your feet alone are competent.* (trans. V. K. Subramanian 1993). The *Hymn to Mahiṣamardinī* (a late addition to the *KCT*, 7, 22-35), verse 29, trans. Finn, offers the following: *May the lustre (of your feet) which is like the antimony blackness of a rain cloud about to burst, be ever in our heart. From the sparkling, blazing womb of these feet (issue) the three gods who are of the nature of pure consciousness and bliss.* With this interpretation, it makes little difference whether Kālī is sitting or standing on Śiva, they still remain in congress.

What is it like with your deity standing within you? Perhaps your head and the head of the inner deity coincide, perhaps the head of the inner deity extends above your physical head. All of these are representations of a truth that cannot be adequately expressed in language, form, and feeling. Like all representations, these are totally artificial. They are not real, they are convenient. We are not dealing with things here, the things are just the keys to get you going. If you think that Kuṇḍalinī is really a serpent, an energy, a pillar of light, or a deity standing in your spine, you will miss the fact that Kuṇḍalinī is basically consciousness, attention, i.e. YOU.

Kuṇḍalinī asleep in the mūlādhāra cakra is a metaphor for everyday awareness: as your ego plods about, doing the various routines, tasks, and chores essential for your survival, Kuṇḍalinī is deep asleep. This is the state of most of humanity most of the time. It is a state where we start from and to which we return, unless we will to give up the body/mind/personality and join the absolute. Some yogīs did this. They went into the rapture to such an extent that they had to be called back. One good example is Rāmakṛṣṇa, who frequently lost himself in rapture. Some ascetics are said to have ended their incarnation this way: they went out of their physical shell and never returned.

There are, however, a lot of states where Kuṇḍalinī is active without being so extreme. Every time something really exalting, shaking, or shocking happened to you, Kuṇḍalinī moved. Some people get into samādhi by prayer, fasting, obsession, or loving dedication. Their

Kuṇḍalinī moves, no matter that they never bother to visualise serpents rushing up and down their spine. Others get into states of extreme exaltation through extended shaking trances, or by designing an enlightened consciousness (practical introductions to these approaches can be found in *Seidways*). When I developed the Taliesin Trance and wrote of the effects, Kenneth Grant told me that few practitioners would be able to hold their Kuṇḍalinī up for such extended periods. This amazed me, I had not done any thing remotely resembling Kuṇḍalinī yoga. All I had done was asked my deep mind to produce a highly specific consciousness for a few hours. It certainly changed my awareness and drew a lot of energy to the top of my head, but all of this happened spontaneously without any of the fireworks one tends to associate with fire-snake activity. Others get into such states by consuming psychedelic drugs. As you will notice, some of these approaches are spontaneous and happen naturally. This is an important point in Tantra: enlightenment can be approached in many ways. The natural approach is called Sahaja, meaning spontaneous and consisting of the syllable sa and ha, you know them as the one and only natural mantra (inhalation and exhalation). The technical approach is called Kuṇḍalinī. This, as you will be sure to know, is not one technique but quite a few of them. Some yogīs wake and move the fire snake by physical practices. It takes years of rigorous physical training before the yogī learns to direct the praṇā and apāna through postures, locks, contraction, breathing, and imagination. Woodroffe gives a good account in *The Serpent Power*, chapter 6, where you can find several physical methods and an introduction to the samaya school of Śri Vidyā, which prefers a more mental approach. Kuṇḍalinī yoga is not a single technique but a body of different approaches, techniques and visualisations that vary from school to school. What is valid is not any specific technique but your results. With Kuṇḍalinī we are in the realm of the totally subjective: the true method is simply the method that works for you. We have several choices in exploring Kuṇḍalinī, and some of them are traditional.

One way is to build up the cakras by visualisation. It's a slow process as each cakra corresponds to an understanding of the world and yourself, and constitutes, in a certain sense, the creation of a set of reality/identities. Your root-cakra, for example, is not just a spot at the perineum. It is also the totality of your experience of the manifest world. To wake Kuṇḍalinī in the root cakra is to wake up from the sleep that people call reality. It also means that you find your position and function in the world, that you purify and cultivate your physical universe, your body, your means of livelihood, that you assume responsibility for the life you live, and the world you be-live in. This is anything but escapism. Your journey to enlightenment begins and ends in the material world, and unless you learn to handle this cakra, you won't get far in the 'higher realms'.

Refining the sexual cakra involves not only an appreciation of the whole world as erotic play (As Austin Spare had it: *All things cohabit all of the time*) but also the creation of an erotic personality for oneself.

Sexuality and lust are brought under will, they become a sacred and wholesome part of your experience. Here we are miles away from ordinary lust, a force that makes fools out of most people. Coming to terms with this cakra may be simple for some and difficult for others; it depends on how many hang-ups and neurotic impulses you have. Cakra refining takes more than just imagining a lotus, some colours, geometrical shapes, and a few sounds. Nor will simple visualisation of that cakra in symbolic form be enough. The real refinement of this cakra is the development of a healthy, joyous, and inspiring sexuality that augments your spiritual evolution. The same goes for all the cakras; each of them is a complete reality and a personality that can handle it. Building up the cakras and learning to experience awareness of the higher ones is a process of gradual refinement that takes years. It is, essentially, not much different from the approach of western Qabalistic Magick, which has the practitioner ascend the Tree of Life, sphere by sphere, gradually refining and perfecting each energy/consciousness. Just as good training in Magick takes years, so does Kuṇḍalinī yoga. It's no use simply to excite Kuṇḍalinī and get her to rise unless you can cope with the experiences that result. There are people who had shifts of cakra awareness by chance or extreme exhaustion, disease, near-death experience, or drugs. Most of them did not become significantly happier by experiences they could not handle, and quite a few damaged their health or sanity in the process. If you think that Kuṇḍalinī is simply something to turn on and enjoy, you should better spend a few more years refining yourself. This, incidentally, is what most of Kuṇḍalinī yoga consists of. The technique is easy, but the preparation takes time. If you were so extremely lucky to find a genuine guru, it would still take at least a decade to explore Kuṇḍalinī. A decade sounds too much if you think that Kuṇḍalinī yoga is simply a technique. It is not much if you consider that Kuṇḍalinī is specifically You and more than you (or less, depending on how you see this), and that the technique is just a tiny part of the whole alchemy. Spending ten years to learn Magick isn't much, Druidry took twenty years if we can trust Caesar, hell, even a simple university degree (for what it's worth) can take ages. Thus, we have the approach 'one cakra after another', which takes years but has the advantage that what you achieve has a sound structure and a certain stability. Tantra and Magick are not just ways of mucking around with weird experiences; they are ways of life demanding total dedication.

The establishment and purification of the cakras may be an early form of Kuṇḍalinī yoga. You find it described in several early Tantras which do not even bother to mention Kuṇḍalinī. What we consider Kuṇḍalinī today is a conglomerate of experiences, metaphors, and myths that has been evolved over several centuries of Tantric practice. Not all schools made use of this method, nor did they have to. Kuṇḍalinī is just one approach to enlightenment and liberation (the way up), and to magickal changes and siddhis (the way down). There are many, many others. Kuṇḍalinī is not a must and it is not for everyone. People have different needs and desires, they also have different aims in life and different personalities. It is a pretty modern delusion, supported by tons of ill-informed books, that Kuṇḍalinī is the main thing in Tantra. There was a lot of Tantra before Kuṇḍalinī was even invented.

But what is Kuṇḍalinī precisely? Here you'll have to find your own explanation. In a sense Kuṇḍalinī is energy and sentience. In a sense it is the motion of all your power and consciousness at once. It is a coming-together of your whole being, it is your personal deity, and of course yourself way beyond your ego. Some authors claim that Kuṇḍalinī is sexual energy, which is supposed to be sublimated and refined until it is ready to blow your mind. Of course Kuṇḍalinī is sexual energy, but it is also all other energies in this wide and wonderful multiverse. Everything you can experience is Kuṇḍalinī, and Kuṇḍalinī is what produces every experience. The point is that Kuṇḍalinī is more than a little something in your bum. There is no serpent sleeping between your anus and genitals; if you want pets, seek them elsewhere. Strictly speaking, Kuṇḍalinī is the whole world and your experience of yourself. Kuṇḍalinī in the perineum creates, maintains, and destroys the material world, the 'real' world as some would have it, and its perception in your physical body/mind/personality. Everything you can see, hear, feel, smell, taste, and sense is Kuṇḍalinī manifesting the world glamour. When Kuṇḍalinī is active in your sexual centre, she is the force and awareness of your desire, lust, and sexuality (kāma). Mind you, it is Kuṇḍalinī and not your sexual centre that does the job; the very existence of a sexual centre is already an activity of Kuṇḍalinī. When Kuṇḍalinī manifests in your belly, her expression is praṇā, Qi, Ki, Pneuma, life-force, or whatever you may chose to call it. What you experience as vitality, power, and life energy in this consciousness is an activity of Kuṇḍalinī. And so it goes. In each cakra, Kuṇḍalinī creates an entire world of experience. She also creates a you who can experience these phenomena. All of this may sound complicated, but it isn't when you consider that Kuṇḍalinī is the YOU who weaves the world glamour on all levels. This is more than your ego, more than jīva and incarnate self. It is also less, in that what people think themselves to be is mainly a lot of misconceptions and delusions cluttering a pristine purity of pure experience. From a certain point of view, you do not exist. This is the true self, not a thing as such but sheer pre-conceptual formless consciousness. You shouldn't take my word for this. Words get in the way of experience, real learning, and bliss. Kuṇḍalinī is the supreme Śakti, Kuṇḍalinī is the inner deity, Kuṇḍalinī is the you beyond all definitions. Kuṇḍalinī is a mystique transcending the limits of your thinking. Kuṇḍalinī goes a long way beyond a scaly reptile snaking up and down your spine.

Nātha Lore

Before we look at the phenomena in a practical way, I would like to explore some of its forms in Tantric lore. To begin with, many of the earlier Tantras do not even use the term Kuṇḍalinī, nor do they seem to care much for the concept. In the *Kaulajñāna nirṇaya* you find hardly any reference to the matter. Remarkably, as the text is full of vivid descriptions of cakra systems and what siddhis can be obtained by meditation on each. We do not encounter the fire serpent here, instead there is the liṅga within your body. Like the Tree of Life, like Yggdrassil, or the pillar reaching to the North Star, this liṅga connects the height of heaven with the underworld. Along its height are various worlds, realms, and consciousness states, and it is to these that the *KJN* alludes when it describes the inner liṅga adorned with lotus blossoms. The inner liṅga has a similar function as the fire snake, as it connects all levels of awareness and being, and allows the sādhaka to move freely through all worlds. Let's look into the *Siddha Siddhānta Paddhati* of Gorakṣanātha, who was allegedly the star-student of Matsyendranāth. Compared with each other, the two 'founders' of the Nātha movement show vast differences in style and mood. Hardly surprising, as there were more than a hundred years between them. Gorakṣanātha presents a dry and highly intellectual system that became the basis of what constitutes Haṭha Yoga today. As his system goes back to the 11th century, his notion of Kuṇḍalinī differs from the modern one. Let's explore this in detail. Chapter 1 starts with a discussion of the primordial state, beyond Kula and Akula, beyond knowledge and definition, beyond cause and result. This state is defined as the inexpressible (anāma) who is identified as the Original Śakti (Nija Śakti). The Original Śakti has these qualities: eternity, she cannot be touched, she lacks vibration, does not permit creation to happen, and is of the nature of transcendental consciousness. When she is seen, she develops the Highest Śakti (Parā Śakti). The Highest Śakti is Being, immeasurable, undivided, complete, and unrevealed. She creates the Lower Śakti (Aparā Śakti) through vibration. The Lower Śakti is appearance, revelation, expansion, breaking-through, and manifestation through vibration. Through the sense of I-ness, the Lower Śakti becomes the Subtle Śakti (Sūkṣmaśakti). The Subtle Śakti is complete unity, constancy, immovability, firmness, and lack of differentiation. *And from this, the Kuṇḍalinī Śakti, who is of the nature of consciousness, has come forth.* (1, 7) *Never-ending fullness, the ability to project, strength, motion and pointing-upward are the qualities of the Kuṇḍalinī Śakti.* (1, 12). Kuṇḍalinī is primarily the motion and glamour weaving of consciousness. She is also the lowest and densest form of the primordial being/power/consciousness.

Let us take a look at the cakra system of this tradition. In 2, 1-9 we read that the first, the root cakra, is the thrice-twisted Brahmacakra in the form of a solar disk. Here is Kāmarūpa, and the meditation is on Śakti in burning, flaming form. In the second, the genital cakra is the sacred place Uḍyāna, and the meditation is on an upright liṅga like the branch of a coral. In the navel we find the abode of Kuṇḍalinī Śakti, five-times coiled, radiant like a million suns, the middle Śakti who grants siddhis. The heart cakra is described as a downward pointing eight-pedalled lotus. Inside it, meditation shapes light into the form of a liṅga, within the seedpod of the flower. This is the Haṁsakalā and the ruler of senses. The fifth cakra is in the throat, four thumbs in diameter. To its left is the moon-channel, the Iḍā, and to its right the sun-channel, the Piṅgalā. Within, you meditate on the Suṣumnā and listen to the Anāhata sound. (In more recent systems, this sound is heard in the heart.) The sixth cakra is at the palate where the nectar of immortality flows downward. Welcome to the tenth gate. Here one meditates on emptiness. It causes the dissolution of the organ of thought. The seventh cakra is located between the eyebrows. It is the eye of realisation. Here one meditates on a radiant flame. This causes perfection of language. The eighth is the Nirvāṇacakra in the Brahmarandhra. It is so fine that a needle tip could penetrate it. Here one meditates on a pillar of smoke. It contains the place Jālandhara, granting liberation. The ninth is the Ākāśacakra, a sixteen-petalled lotus turned upwards. Here dwells the upper Śakti. She abides in the seedpod of the lotus; she is supreme voidness and rests on three peaks. This is the site of the peak of the mountain of never-ending fullness where will is fulfilled.

So we have nine basic cakras in Gorakṣanātha's lore, each of them described very briefly as the author did not believe in burdening folks with excessive detail. Beyond the nine cakras, he describes sixteen points of energy (Adhārāḥ) and objects of meditation, some of them abstract, some localised in body. Primary to the whole method is the idea of the three Śaktis, located in perineum, navel, and above the head. All three Śaktis are a differentiation of one Śakti (4, 17). As you saw earlier, in this tradition the Kuṇḍalinī as a fire snake was associated with the navel, not with the root cakra. 4,16 quotes from the *Rūlaka*: *By waking the middle Śakti, contraction of the lower Śakti and the descent of the upper Śakti the highest is attained.* 4, 18- 30 details this teaching. Here is a brief synopsis. The lower Śakti consists of the activity of the senses and the manifold thoughts. The yogīns attain perfection by contracting the root cakra, the perineum. The root cakra itself is the world of moving and unmoving phenomena. Śivānanda is cited:

> *It is by expansion and contraction of all Śaktis that the world is created and dissolved. Therefore it is called the root. For this reason, all of the Perfect Ones (Siddhas) are devoted to the root centre. The middle Kuṇḍalinī is the Śakti who keeps the individual soul in its own consciousness/light. By nature, the individual soul is tossed around in the world or moves in useless confusion. As Kuṇḍalinī is the self-form of each soul, it appears in two states: the coarse and the subtle. The coarse Kuṇḍalinī is the self-form of all objects and their foundation. The subtle Kuṇḍalinī is the aimed for Kuṇḍalinī who gives supreme bliss to the yogīns. She is formless and awake. The subtle Kuṇḍalinī has to be woken to highest awareness in its self-form, a process requiring oral instruction from a true guru. The upper Śakti is beyond all principles of being. She is of the nature of the recognition of multiple perception and its own realisation of the highest. The descent of this Śakti is the denial of the double appearance of its self-form. The upper Śakti remains in its undivided self-form.*

Do I hear you sighing? All of this is an unusually clear and practical description of Kuṇḍalinī yoga. It connects with the work of Matsyendranāth, and the Trika teachings of Kashmir, where the three Śaktis are identified as Kriyā Śakti (the Śakti of right deeds and activity), Jñāna Śakti (the Śakti of true wisdom), and Icchā Śakti (the Śakti of true will). A very brief reference to their yoga appears in *Kaulajñāna nirṇaya* 2, 6-7, translated by Mike Magee: *Śakti dissolves within Śiva. Śiva dissolves within Kriya. Kriya dissolves within Jñāna. Jñana dissolves within Icchā. The Fire of Supreme Śakti is where Icchā Śakti is dissolved.* Give yourself time to ponder this deeply.

A Classical Approach

Let's take a look at the method. Vol. 11, chapter 1 of the *Devī Bhāgavatam* gives a brief description of the process in a chapter on morning rites which shyly introduces some Tantric practices. These are preceded by an injunction that Tantra is acceptable only when it does not contradict the *Vedas*. Sure. Thank you. You find such comments in a number of conservative scriptures. The commentaries in brackets are by Swami Vijnanānanda, who translated the text. I have slightly amended the spelling.

The day starts with a mild meditation. The sādhaka is advised to sit on a seat that is not too low, to put the tongue against the palate, to become quiet, to restrain the senses (introvert), and to visualise the self as a holy flame or light. Next follows a brief period of prāṇāyāma, as described in the chapter on breathing. The intervals are 2:4:1, i.e. two units inhalation, four units retaining breath, one unit exhalation. This is not the usual pattern used for general purposes. The worshipper recites and thinks AUM in the process.

> *After doing the prāṇāyāma as stated above, pierce the Six Chakras (i.e. plexuses) (called Ṣaṭchakra bheda) and carry the Kula Kuṇḍalinī to the Brahma Randhra, the brain aperture, or to the thousand petalled lotus in the head and meditate in the heart the Self like a Steady Flame...*
>
> *Within the body, the six nerve centres called Padmas (Lotuses) exist. They are respectively situated at the*
>
> *1. Mūlādhāra (half way between Anus and Linga Mūla), called Sacral Plexus;*
>
> *2. Linga Mūla (the root of the genital organs), called prostatic plexus; (this is also called Svādhiṣṭhāna)*
>
> *3. Navel, the Solar Plexus*
>
> *4. Heart, the cardiac Plexus,*
>
> *5. Throat*
>
> *6. Forehead, between the eye brows there the lotus in the forehead, called the cavernous plexus (Ajnā Chakra) has two petals; in these two petals the two letters 'Ham' and 'Kṣam' exist in the right hand direction...*
>
> *I bow down to these who are the two-lettered Brahman.*

The text proceeds to explain the cakras in terms of the sounds that are attributed to them. To summarise matters, each cakra has several syllables assigned in clockwise direction to its petals.

The throat cakra (viśuddhā cakra) contains the sixteen vowels **a, ā, i, ī, u, ū, ṛ, ṝ, ḷ, ḹ, e, ai, o, au, am, aḥ.**

The heart cakra (anāhata cakra) has twelve petals: **k, kh, g, gh, n, ch, cch, j, jh, ñ, ṭ, ṭh.**

The navel cakra (maṇipura cakra) has ten petals: **ḍ, ḍh, ṇ, t, th, d, dh, n, p, ph.**

The genital cakra (svādhiṣṭhāna cakra) has six petals: **b, bh, m, y, r, l.**

The root cakra (mūlādhāra cakra) has four petals: **v, ś, ṣ, s.**

> *Thus meditating on the Six Chakras or plexuses, meditate on the Kula Kuṇḍalinī, the Serpent Fire. She resides on the four petalled lotus (Centre of Śakti) called Mūlādhāra Chakra (Coccygeal plexus); She is of Rajo Guṇa; She is of a blood red colour, and She is expressed by the Mantra 'Hrīṁ', which is the Māyāvīja, she is subtle as the thread of the fibrous stock of the water lily. The Sun is Her face; Fire is Her breasts; he attains Jīvan Mukti (liberation while living) within whose heart such a Kula Kuṇḍalinī arises and awakens even once.*
>
> *Thus meditating on Kula Kuṇḍalinī, one should pray to Her:-*
>
> *Her sitting, coming, going, remaining, the thought of Her, the realisation of Her and chanting hymns to Her, etc., all are Mine, Who is of the nature of all in all; I am the Bhagavatī; O Bhagavatī! All my acts are Thy worship; I am the Devī; I am Brahma, I am free from sorrow. I am of the nature of Everlasting Existence, Intelligence and Bliss.*
>
> *Thus one should meditate of one's own self. I take refuge of that Kula Kuṇḍalinī, who appears like lightning and who holds the current thereof, when going to Brahmarandhra, in the brain, who appears like nectar when coming back from the brain to the Mūlādhāra and who travels in the Suṣumnā Nāḍī in the spinal cord.*

After this meditation follows a meditation on the guru in the head, identified with Brahmā, Viṣṇu, and Maheśvara (Śiva). You may have noticed that the meditation involved several methods, such as visualisation, imagination of sound, and free-style prayer and suggestion, expressed in the last part where the worshipper identifies with the goddess, Brahman, and so on. This ecstatic part of the rite may involve free speech, if you are up to it, or just rambling along with a few key phrases. In my experience, you have to come down a bit before you can speak again. Was the description too brief? Of course it was. However, considering that the entire rite appears as a short part of the morning meditation (!), we can count ourselves lucky to learn so much. And we shouldn't be too annoyed when the *DB* continues with topics of much greater interest. Such as the highly complex rituals required to pee and shit. The direction you face, how often you wipe your bum and the colour of the earth you use for wiping (which depends on your class, of course) were more important to the authors of the *DB* than a method to transcend human consciousness.

Kuṇḍalinī Yoga

There are many ways of waking the serpent power. Tantric literature does not always specify one, in Śri Vidyā worship is very much in the mind, while yoga systems generally tend to favour a lot of physical effort. I shall give a brief synopsis of these matters, a lot more can be found in Woodroffe's *The Serpent Power*. Simplifying things a lot, one yoga method is based on the system of the three channels. In the centre is the suṣuṁnā, just as it is in Tantric anatomy, but yoga emphasises the roles of the two ducts to the sides, the piṅgalā channel, associated with the sun, starting at the right nostril; and the idā channel, associated with the moon, starting at the left nostril. Generally, praṇā circulates in the two ducts to the sides. The lunar energy moves in the idā, moistening the body with nectar, while solar energy moves in piṅgalā, heating it. Using a system of difficult positions, locks, and motions, the channels to the left and right of the spine are closed so that the total of the yogī's power and awareness concentrates in the middle line. This requires skill in posture and in breathing. Now in some yoga systems, the energy/sentience of body is described in two forms: praṇā (breath, vitality, energy) and apāna, the downward moving energy of the lower body, including secretions, excrement, and gas. According to this model, praṇā, located in the heart, tends to move upwards (just as it ascends to heaven in the last breath of each person), while apāna, located at the perineum, moves down. In yogīc theory, these two forces are closely connected and each prevents the other from escaping from the body. Yoga inhibits such motions. By drawing up the muscles of perineum, and pelvic floor, apāna is prevented from moving down. By tilting the head forward at the joint of skull and spine, praṇā is prevented from moving up. The result produces an agglomeration of praṇā and apāna in the centre, which may be lead into the central channel at the root cakra, and made to move up. Combining, blending, and moving the two forces is what constitutes 'real prāṇāyāma' to some sages, all other practices being mere breathing exercises.

The yogīc method is highly complex as it appears in so many technical forms. The various traditions evolved as yogīs got effects from a range of postures, locks, and breathing intervals. The reason is that yoga activates the sleeping serpent in a highly physical form. Before the serpent power can be woken, the student spends years practising refined physical postures, breathing patterns, plus mental exercises. S/he assumes a lifestyle that is entirely devoted to the mastery of this yoga, involving a specific moral attitude, daily routine, and diet. All extremes of behaviour are avoided. Fasting, always popular among folks who love austerity, is prohibited, instead, the student eats small amounts every three hours during the day. Sexual abstinence is generally recommended, at least in the first stages, when the rush of energy can harm the body/mind complex. No, our yogīs were not necessarily prudish. In the first stages of Kuṇḍalinī yoga, the energy tends to move erratically. Sometimes it goes to the head in a way that reduces sexual impulses and lust, sometimes it goes into sensuous longing to the exclusion of rational thought. Sometimes it goes all over the place, resulting in a muddle. Not to mention all the problems that arise when a budding yogī wants to have a love-life in a disapproving, rigid society. Life was not very liberated in ancient India, most yogīs found it difficult to meet women, let alone have an affair with one. To keep things as simple as possible, abstinence is recommended until the new experience has been fully mastered and assimilated. Likewise, hard labour, long walks, and any strenuous activity are avoided, as exhaustion may be harmful to the budding snake-charmer. Plus a large amount of activities that the student should avoid, as they result in mental or emotional upset. Tradition recommends a lot of prohibitions, but in the real world it's much easier to consider just what upsets and enervates you. If something reduces your peace of mind or fills your thoughts with rubbish, avoid it.

A Practical Approach

The practice of this yoga is theoretically an easy matter. That is to say, the technique is simple and easy, but the preparation, the years of purification required before Kuṇḍalinī can ascend to the Sahasrāra is the difficulty. As Maggie Ingalls (Nema) expressed: *Ninety percent of Magick is trash removal.* What trash you will encounter, where this will happen, and how fast you'll proceed, depends very much on your spiritual attainment. Some Indian texts take the easy way. They propose that if you advance slowly, it must be due to the bad karman of your past lives. With this sort of attitude, even lousy gurus had a convenient explanation for the failure of a student. On the other hand, if a student advanced quickly, this was also due to karman. It prevented the guru from feeling overly proud. Whichever way you look at it, past life karman (real or imaginary) is a useful idea to reduce result orientation. Things happen in their own good time. Given your very own unique character with all its specific hang-ups and talents, it is not possible to give a precise technical format for the raising of the fire snake. Think of it as a work of art. Each practitioner has to undergo a highly personal period of transformation to wake, purify, and align even the lower cakras, let alone reach the pre-conceptual zones in and above the head. Not that a body metaphor makes sense in these realms of perception. The cakras are not 'above' each other in the physical sense. Each of them corresponds to a level of energy/manifestation. To 'raise' the fire snake implies shifting awareness from dense matter to energetic realms of perception which unfold with ever increasing degrees of subtlety. For a similar reason, descriptions of consciousness states during activation and union of Kuṇḍalinī in Sahasrāra are rarely more than garbled fragments of ill-fitting metaphors.

'Up there' there is no up 'there' any more, and words, images, symbols, visualisations cease to matter.

Perhaps it may be useful to give a brief technical description of my Kuṇḍalinī practice. I usually start after doing half an hour of sādhana including a bit of warm up exercise to limber up my body, some mild prāṇāyāma (without strain), and focusing on the personal deities in various body centres. The program varies according to mood and occasion.

Before I start exciting Kuṇḍalinī, I ask the deep mind and the personal deities whether they want me to. If the answer is yes, things will go easily. If no, I leave it for the day. Usually the deep mind knows quite well whether a given sort of ecstatic trance is fitting. Though I do not follow any classical yoga method of raising the fire snake physically, body is involved and there are days when the process is simply too exhausting. To raise Kuṇḍalinī you have to be fit, healthy, and well balanced. That's the main reason why many insist that the student leads a peaceful, healthy life, eats only food that is easy to digest, gets a lot of sleep, is not upset by worries, avoids reading newspapers or watching TV, and so on. One good time to do this practice is early in the day when the mind is not so cluttered with everyday matters. When all is well established, I introvert my awareness and sink into the core of my body. The main thing for the following yoga is a certain mood of longing. This is the crucial element that empowers the imagination. Longing. The longing of the incarnate self (jīva) to unite with the all-self, a return to the original fullness that predates incarnation. And a longing of the all-self to unite with the incarnate self to enjoy the world of form and energy.

A similar idea is suggested in an obscure passage of the *Toḍala Tantra,* 2, 9 (Sanjukta Gupta in White, 2000: 480-481). Here the divine serpent appears under the name Vāsukī (a serpent king of early Hindu myth) who is identified with Mahāmāyā. *The liberating (yogic duct, called nāḍī) Mahādhīrā ranges from rasātala to the end of satya, which exists inside the central (channel, that is, the spinal column, meru). Mahāviṣṇu Śiva resides in the satya region and Vāsukī is full of intense longing to meet him.* Rasātala is the lowest underworld below the root cakra, the satya region is the region of truth and pure being in and above the head.

Looking down from the inside of my head I see this tube descending to the depths of my body. I begin to call on Kuṇḍalinī, sometimes with words, sometimes with mantra, always with emotion. I like to use bījas such as Hrīṁ for this. Kenneth Grant recommended the bīja Oṁ for this stage (1999: 104), followed by Hrīṁ to wake and release the fire snake, Aīṁ to make it rise, Śrīṁ to make it rise further, and finally Kālī's Krīṁ upon reaching transcendence. This is a more detailed and refined option, but others are equally possible. Many bījas are associated with the rising fire snake; dare to experiment! Go for what turns you on (and don't expect bījas to work unless you have woken them and are well used to them). The vital thing is not the words or the vibration. It's the yearning of the absolute (heaven) for the particular (earth). Consider the cakras above your head as a form of the all-self and the root cakra as the manifestation of the particular self and you'll understand that the union of the two is the whole aim of Kuṇḍalinī yoga. Make this a strong emotion. Desire (Kāma) is useful here, and craving, and a vital urge to come together at last. Then I switch awareness to the bottom of the tube, to the root cakra at the perineum, between anus and genitals. Here I become the serpent of lust and awareness. I wake, and as I wake, body begins to pulsate. This usually means that the muscles of the perineum pull up and tense, as do the muscles of the pelvic floor. Sometimes the belly muscles follow. The entire bottom of my anatomy pulls upward in a surge of excitement and lust, while body begins to shake, sway, and tremble. These side effects may be soft or strong, depending on how relaxed I am. As I usually (not always) do this sort of sādhana while sitting, I do get a bit of motion. Not as much as I would if I were standing in a shaking trance, when belly and hips can pulsate freely.

A word on physical effects. A good many people imagine that body has to be stiff and immobile while Kuṇḍalinī goes up and down. This is not always the case. Swāmi Viṣṇu Tirtha (summarised in June McDaniel 1989: 118-119) gives a long list of ecstatic symptoms that may occur while Kuṇḍalinī rises. Shaking, shuddering, or trembling is just one possibility. Other options include hair standing on end, deep breathing or holding breath involuntarily, emotional outbursts such as weeping or laughing, visions, ejaculation, assumption of yogīc postures, vibrations in the spine, rolling eyes, convulsions, and so on. *Other symptoms include waves of bliss, hearing mantras, the body falling on the floor and rotating like a grinding stone, or squatting on the floor cross-legged and jumping from place to place like a frog, feeling as if dead or paralyzed, making animal sounds (jackals, dogs, tigers, birds), jerking and tossing of the body, a feeling of spirit possession, glossolalia, intoxication, energy and endurance, visions of deities and magical powers (siddhis).* As you can see, this is not simply a mind game nor is it a refined act of visualisation. It's much closer to shamanic obsession. When Kuṇḍalinī rises, pretty much anything can happen. Don't expect anything specific. Perhaps you will find yourself shaking, swaying, or falling around, but just as possibly your body may want to become still and minimise breathing. As Kuṇḍalinī rises, she makes things happen if you want it or not. If you accept the physical effects you'll get much further than if you try to control them.

As Kuṇḍalinī I glare up the tube, and as I wake, like the dark dragon Niddhöggr, like the monstrous Addanc of the deep, lightning flashes up and down my spine, earth shakes, and hissing and droning fills my mind. This is accompanied by the bīja Hrīṁ. I feel the longing to wake fully, to hurl upwards with all the power and awareness of the whole being. Here is the craving of the particular to unite with the absolute. Desire is the key, it doesn't work unless I feel a real hunger to shoot upwards into bliss. Keep in mind that Kuṇḍalinī is not willed upwards, nor is she directed. Kuṇḍalinī is a goddess, an expression of the personal deity, and you do not (usually) order gods around. Seen another way, Kuṇḍalinī is the motion of your true self, of the jīva, the incarnate divinity of your being. It is you, but a you who is free from the distortions of your life and personality. The motion of Kuṇḍalinī is an act of grace. Create a situation where Kuṇḍalinī wants to ascend.

Then I switch to head awareness again, and call for the deep to rise, looking downward the tube to the twisting, waking serpent. Then into serpent awareness again, getting ever more edgy and excited, and waking up to the point of eruption. I repeatedly switch awareness from the root cakra to the cakras in the head, going ever faster, building up the longing, the desire and the urge to unite. The important thing, for me, is *to be* the formless awareness in the crown cakra and *to be* the serpent looking up. Merely visualising a serpent going up and down (a dissociated vision) doesn't get me any effects. Maybe it will be different for you. Explore the visual submodalities and learn what turns you on! At some point the desire and longing become so extreme that I erupt upwards. Not an act of intent but one of release. It works when Kuṇḍalinī wants to go upward. Power rushes along the central channel, bearing upwards the lust and excitement of the up-drawn muscles, and corresponding to a reflex that makes my eyes go up and turn inward. Likewise, there is an urge for the tongue to go up and backwards, like swallowing it. The process is simply beyond description. It is usually fast, and I guess my body is tossed about a bit, and breathing may be strong and deep at times, but as you'll understand I don't have the brains to observe these matters while everything goes up in glory. The surge begins in serpent form, but what arrives in the head and shoots through the crown of the skull is hardly in a fixed form any more. Usually there are several surges of power and consciousness involved, it takes a while to allow Kuṇḍalinī to transcend humanity, and in this phase my body is not very still. There may be trembling or swaying; the natural pulsation of an organism resonating to energy and consciousness. With practice it tends to mellow out. If I allow Kuṇḍalinī to go up really high, ascending from heaven to heaven, body sensations become harder to discern. Sure, body remains down there, in a way, and seems to stay moderately upright, but all in all, awareness is quite a way from it. If I allow Kuṇḍalinī to retain its tail in my perineum, the swaying and shaking may continue all through the experience. If I draw the tail up so that it is rooted in one of the higher cakras, such as the heart or third eye, body calms. The upward progress often involves distinct phases: you could say that Kuṇḍalinī leaps (like a frog) from station to station. This is not the only option. June McDaniel (1989: 119) lists a wide range of possible styles of ascent: like ants (a slow, steady motion), like a frog (jumping in small leaps), like a snake in a zigzag path, like the flight of a bird (up and down), and like a monkey, who reaches the top in a few powerful leaps.

The important issue is that the motion should be natural. If you attempt to force Kuṇḍalinī you may run into difficulties. Result-orientation, hunger for achievement, stubborn determination and the like are counter-productive. When you find that Kuṇḍalinī only progresses to a certain point, keep it at that cakra for a while and then allow it to descend again.

In general, Kuṇḍalinī is not just busy transcending the human form but tends to shoot outwards into realms of perception where everything becomes, for want of better words, vibrations, rhythms, geometry, and colours. Fixed forms fade in these realms, and so do words to describe the whole thing. Excuse me for not putting it any better.

Sometime, somewhen, the whole thing goes down again. In a sense it is 'me' that goes down, only that it starts out as being, bliss, and awareness, and becomes 'me' the deeper it descends. Or goes in, the matter is not simply expressed as 'up and down' when outside and inside are just as essential. During the descent a flood of elixir drenches my body. It can be visualised, if you are in a mood for visualisation, but it may just as well happen naturally. Most Tantrics expect the elixir to come flowing and, as you know, people tend to get what they believe in. Some of this elixir looks like a shower in red and white, some of it appears physically in my mouth. I generally keep it there, under the up-turned tongue for a while before swallowing it. While the ascent is usually a swift matter, I generally descend slowly and step by step, making a pause in each cakra to stabilise and 'come down' gently. Settling awareness in body takes a while. I feel pretty stunned after such events and need to pause and put myself together before I can do anything. This usually involves nyāsa, i.e. touching various spots of the body while installing specific deities/energies/ Śaktis, spreading a vast, happy smile through my whole being, and a bit later full earthing, to allow the excess energy to surge down into the earth. Usually I just sit there for a while, and my scattered wits put themselves together again on a small enough scale to function in body on planet earth. Bringing Kuṇḍalinī down often means that my bladder fills. The urine has a special taste and is invigorating.

All of this may give the impression that Kuṇḍalinī yoga is the crowning pinnacle of trance technique. It sounds so dramatic and full of fireworks. I should add that the process can be a strain on the body-mind complex. There are less exhausting ways of inducing ecstatic states of awareness. The states I experience, for all their vividness, are not unlike things I may experience when in a really good shaking trance or when going on extended astral journeys, especially through Daath, to the back of the Tree, and upwards beyond Pluto/Yuggoth. And what of the Chinese method of 'Turning the Waterwheel'? In daily life, I find it much more beneficial (and less straining) to enjoy Daoist alchemy. Kuṇḍalinī is not a name for a specific experience but for an approach. The crucial question is not which approach you use but where it takes you. Sometimes, when raising Kuṇḍalinī in a seated position, the whole trance has a highly physical mood. Body is involved and resonates to emotion. It is even more physical when I do it standing and shaking, or after dancing for a while. When I do the trance lying on the floor in a state of deep relaxation, the physical effects are usually reduced. I still get some motion on occasion, but it is not half as much as when my torso can sway and shudder freely. All of which goes to show that Kuṇḍalinī yoga is just a crude term referring to a wide field of possible trances. Your trances. Some of them may involve serpents, mantras, and cakras, others may happen in any form that your deep mind invents, or even without a specific format. Up and down are not essential, remember that earth is round and that there really is no up and down in this amazing multiverse. All FORMS of Kuṇḍalinī yoga are convenient metaphors. You can use the ones favoured by the mad saints of India or you can find some that suit you better. The one and only important aspect of Kuṇḍalinī yoga is a process that dissolves you, transforms you, and returns you to your body and the world in a new and refined state. How you do this remains your choice.

12: A Feast of Five

Tantric sex

Here we come to a topic that many of you have been waiting for. Tantric sex has confused the minds of many. To orthodox Brahmins, many Tantric sects were suspect as their ritual included elements they could not sympathise with. Among them are such acts as drinking alcohol, eating meat, making no caste distinctions in ritual, cultivating magical powers, becoming obsessed by deities, and enjoying sex (real, symbolic, or imaginary) during worship. Even the worship of a goddess can upset a strict traditionalist, one of the reasons why many Śāktas did not openly confess to their real faith and pretended to be Śaivas or, more acceptable, Vaiṣṇavas in public. To the orthodox Hindu, most of the movements classed as 'Tantric' are more or less suspect. So is most of yoga. When you ask a traditional-minded Brahmin, you will learn that 'following the rites and duties of one's class' is sufficient to attain liberation eventually. Any extra effort, such as meditation, physical exercise, or Tantric sādhana, is not only unnecessary, it is also undesirable. This has been so for centuries and is still the case; to many Hindus, Tantra is a very dirty word indeed. People of other cultures were quite as intolerant. European missionaries made the mistake to assume that all the 'worship of genitalia' they sensed in Indian religion was Tantric, and consequently damned Tantra as a blasphemous orgy. Indian reformers soon came to agree with this opinion; as they sought to provide India with a monotheism modelled on Christianity and Islam they eagerly accepted the pet-hates of these religions. Most British scholars agreed with this attitude. Numerous European and American scholars rigorously condemned 'Tantra' as obscene, primitive, and superstitious before even a single authentic Tantric text had been translated. Woodroffe did that pioneering job with the *Mahānirvāṇa Tantra* and encountered any amount of resistance. There is a lot of literature on 'Tantra' that contains no good word for its adherents. Some of it is quite funny. Let me quote a few lines from a long essay published in *The Calcutta Review* XLVII, March 1855, written by H. H. Wilson, LLD and FRS:

> *The rites practised by the Vâmâchâris are so grossly obscene, as to cast into shade the worst inventions which the most impure imagination can conceive (unbridled debauchery with wine and women)... The devotees are now to repeat their radical mantra, but in a manner unutterably obscene. Then follow things too abominable to enter the ears of men, or to be borne by the feelings of an enlightened community; things of which a Tiberius would be*

ashamed, and from which the rudest savage would turn his face in disgust... The tenets of the Śāktas open the way for the gratification of all the sensual appetites, they hold out encouragement to drunkards, thieves and dacoits; they present the means of satisfying every lustful desire; they blunt the feelings by authorising the most cruel practices, and bad man (sic) to commit abominations which place them on a level worse than the beasts. The Śaktya worship is impure in itself, obscene in its practices, and highly injurious to the life and character of men.

Thank you, Mr. Wilson, for your enlightened presentation.

Next came the modern era with its demolition of prudish ideas in favour of a more hedonistic world-view. In the 1960's and '70's what the earlier authorities had considered sinful and debased was elevated to the height of glory and 'sacred sex' became a buzzword among hippies, intellectuals, and artists. In a philosophy where 'Make love, not war' is the supreme mantra (and not a bad one, either) gods who make love are highly popular. Of course the hippies simply reversed the ethical meaning, reclaiming as 'good' what had hitherto been 'evil'. This did not alter the fact that the 'Tantra' known in the industrial world was still a fable. Thanks to the efforts of orthodox Hindus, Christian missionaries, Indian reformers, prudish scholars, and a host of happy hippies what had been a general spiritual movement is nowadays irrevocably connected with 'sacral lovemaking' plus a lot of technical extravaganza. Finally the whole thing was completely distorted when a few clever guru figures with a sound head for business decided that sexual liberation could be sold as Tantra. One of them was 'Bhagwan' Shree Rajneesh, later called Osho, who sold a blend of simple hedonistic philosophy, free love, and modern Gestalt and body therapy as ancient Tantric lore. His Tantra is 'rebellious' and 'spontaneous', meaning you need no training, ritual, devotion, discipline, or brains. Indeed, Rajneesh is famous for stating: *Tantra is not a religion in the ordinary sense because it has no rituals, it has no priests, it has no scriptures.*(quoted in McDaniel, 2004: 268). Praising 'free sexuality', whatever that may be, and the destruction of all social conventions, Rajneesh possibly did more damage to the authentic traditions than all the missionaries and reformers put together. However, he certainly taught his followers to make money. Am I being too critical? Modern New Age Tantra, whatever that may be, does have a few advantages. A bit of basic sexual training is something direly needed by most inhabitants of Planet Idiot. Most people are result-oriented, serious, worried, and usually in a hurry. All of this is not very useful when you wish to enjoy leisurely lovemaking. The techniques sold as 'Tantric' at countless workshops all over the industrial world do have their value, as they teach people to make friends with their body and to extend and enjoy love-play. This is eminently useful and liberating and helps to make the world a better place. The problem is that it uses the term Tantra instead of calling it Reichian therapy, body therapy, or something honest. You only have to look at the shelves on 'Tantra' in any better book-shop and you'll be convinced that Tantrics had nothing but copulation in their minds. This, as I pointed out earlier, is a misconception. While there is a lot of sexual imagery and symbolism embedded in the rites and mythology of most Tantric cults, it is only a few that actually include lovemaking in their rites. Of these, the majority was quite content with lovemaking in the imagination or in symbolic form. What remains is a small section of a vast movement that actually did what others only thought about. These cults decided that lovemaking is divine. Even more so, they emphasised the importance of the sexual secretions as the fundamental sacraments of their worship. In many systems, the proper generation of secretions was a lot more important than postures, extended orgasms, and refined sensuality. Nevertheless, they were not as obsessed with the topic as so many modern would-be adherents of 'Tantra' would have it. Lovemaking was divine to such folk as the Kramas, Kaulas, Trikas, and other followers of the left hand path, but then, and this is the important issue, so was everything else. These people did not want to make any special fuss about making love, they just wanted to live their vision of no-difference within a world where all that exists and all that happens is divine. In this sort of reality, brushing your teeth, emptying the bowels, reciting hymns, eating a good meal, and having sex are all divine; there is no difference between the sacred and profane. The modern interpretation of Tantra as spiritual sexuality would have shocked and upset them, as it excludes so much.

Erotica

Most people think that the *Kāmasutra* is a Tantric work. This is error number one. The *Kāmasutra*, attributed to Vātsyāyana, is a work that seems to have been written (or compiled) between the third and fifth century CE. There were earlier authors of the same name, and so you can occasionally find the book attributed to earlier periods. We have no Tantric texts from this period, in fact, the philosophical and literary period known as Tantric only surfaced around the fifth or sixth century CE. Tantric texts are generally aimed at liberation. True, many of them contain large sections on mythology, religion, ritual, worldly duty, conduct, meditation, and the acquisition of magical powers, all of them supposed to make life easier in this uncertain world, but on the whole we have a frame where Śiva and Śakti have a discourse on how to master life and find release from its limitations. The *Kāmasutra*, by contrast, is aimed at an aristocratic audience. Its general purpose is to provide a catalogue of sexual and amorous techniques. Vātsyāyana tried to provide bored young princes with systematic training in the 'arts of love'. The intent of the work was to widen their erotic horizon, to give them a refined general ability to satisfy themselves and others, and to turn lovemaking into a sport and art-form for the wealthy connoisseur. If this program ever contained the idea of attaining liberation, the author concealed it really well. Instead, we have a work that seems almost cynical in its technical pedantry. Genital size is held more important for satisfaction than actual empathy and some of the positions are so demanding that I wonder how anyone can let go and have a good orgasm in between the cramps. If you look for poetry and tender feelings the *Kāmasutra* is not the work to inspire you. There is advice on how to cheat, tempt, deceive, and flatter potential lovers, sections on how to get rid of them after the fun, and there are even commentaries on how to seduce, force, and rape servants and social inferiors. If you need advice on how to poison a rival, you'll find it in the *Kāmasutra.* All of this is completely at odds with Tantric lore.

Closer to the Tantric spirit is the well known *Anaṅga Raṅga.* Unlike the *Kāmasutra,* this little book was compiled for married couples who want to liven up their love-life. The book contains some Tantric elements, such as the model of the four female temperaments and the charts attributing them to the sixteen kalās and to various power zones in body. If you need to know the days when 'elephant women' have good orgasms, look them up here. There are some magic spells, a discussion of types of anatomy, and apart from this, most of the text is dedicated to postures, a topic that is very rarely mentioned in genuine Hindu Tantras (it turns up more often in Tibetan Tantra of the Yogīnī tradition).

Then there is erotic Indian art. A few Indian temples are famous for their erotic sculptures, which are often classed as Tantric. Some of the flirting, embracing, and copulating figures show that love-play is divine, but there is often a deeper meaning behind the imagery. One fine example is the secret yantras of Lakṣmaṇa temple, Kajuraho, which are not openly displayed but suggested by the angle of bodies, arms, and legs of the erotic display (see M. Rabe in White 2000). The *Śilpa Prākāśa* explains that Kāma (god of desire) is the basis of all that exists, and that without the ecstatic union of Śiva and Śakti there would be no creation. As Śiva appears as liṅga and Śakti as yoni, they bring the world into being. The force that unites the two is Kāma. The text quotes some unnamed *Āgamas* that *a place devoid of erotic imagery is a place to be shunned,* and proceeds to give detailed rules on the art of laying out temple architecture and design on the groundplan of a secret yantra.

Now erotic elements appeared in temple interiors long before Tantra. Such images were usually concealed in some secret inner part of the temples. With the advent of Kaula Tantra, a number of royal families embraced the new creed (mainly as it promised magic powers and success in war) and began to erect ever larger temples dedicated to the Yogīnīs. This trend may have begun around the 7th century CE, when an ever-increasing number of kings sought to strengthen their ties with the countryside. While their prime deity usually remained Viṣṇu (as king of the gods) the kings began to embrace the worship of local goddesses. Most popular among these were goddesses showing a fierce, warlike nature. A good many of these goddesses were worshipped as Yogīnīs, with or without animal or bird-attributes and, for these, the kings began to erect ever larger temples. Royal Kaula patronage was at its height between the 9th and 12th centuries. In its wake the hidden erotic elements began to appear on the outside of the temples, much to the surprise of the population. The temples of Konarak, Bubanesvar, and Khajuraho are all world famous for their explicit sexual imagery. What they illustrate is not simply an orgy of divine love-play. Many of the images depict the

Figure 40 - Lovers.
Stone, Surya temple, Konarak, Orissa, 13th century.

kings and the highest ministers of the royal family, recognisable by the royal headwear, making love with a host of wives, concubines, servant girls, plus some Yoginīs. That these sculptures do not simply show a fantastic adolescent harem-heaven can only be told by the few participants that should not be present in a harem, namely, mendicants and priests who raise their hands in mudrās and who evidently conduct a ritual. In this Kaula phase of temple architecture, rituals were celebrated in successive stages, hence there is a sequence to the images. Another sign that the images are Tantric (and not simply hedonistic) is the appearance of 'forbidden' elements. One of these is images of women being licked by men, hinting at the extraction of the mingled fluids. After the 12th century, however, most Tantric systems began to decline. Royal patronage became ever rarer, and when the kings built temples with erotic imagery they did so for purely sensual reasons. The whole issue of openly advertised ritual sex took on the character of barely disguised boasting. Simultaneously temple prostitution began to thrive, no doubt with royal encouragement, and by this time we are a long way from what Tantra used to be all about..

By now I hope that you have given up the idea that erotic art is essentially Tantric. Most of the erotic art of India was not produced for ascetics striving to find liberation from desire. The usual customers were worldly people who got a kick from the images. There is an enormous amount of erotic art that shows a blissful ignorance of anatomy and is evidently made to stimulate the wealthy collector.

Where do you find sex in Tantric lore? The answer is not as simple as we might expect. Most original Tantras do not mention sex or lovemaking at all. A scant few mention the matter in passing, often using obscure metaphors to veil the meaning of the text, and only a tiny number dare to use clear language. One of these is the highly unorthodox *Yoni Tantra*, a brief work that is of great importance to any practitioner, as it happily praises congress and celebrates the sanctity of the female genitalia and menstrual blood. It makes such a point of this sacrament that all other requirements of worship, such as spiritual training and purification of the mind, are hardly mentioned at all. Such works are exceptions. Even the works attributed to schools that accept sexuality as divine are often shy about the topic. Some acknowledge the fact that congress is essential, and then go to great lengths to prove that physical congress is a lot inferior to spiritual congress, i.e. the union of the divine couple within the worshipper. Things are even more strict in the later schools of Buddhist Tantra. Here you can find vast religious movements that praise total asceticism and renunciation of the desires of body and mind. It wasn't always like this. Some early Buddhist Tantras of the Yoginī school survive, and these are astonishingly explicit. All the stuff that Hindu Tantrics were shy to speak about appears in very plain language in works such as the *Caṇḍamahāroṣaṇa Tantra*, the *Cakrasaṁvara Tantra* or the *Hevajra Tantra* all of them based on teachings from the good old days when Indian Tantric Buddhists met Hindu Kaula Tantrics for extended feasts on the cremation ground (see Miranda Shaw 1994). Those were the days when senior Buddhist adepts passionately worshipped and served female adepts. Their ideas on sexuality survive in Tibetan Buddhism to some extent, most of them hidden in cryptic symbolism. The later traditions of Tibetan Buddhism went to great lengths to delete this material. The role of women as initiatrixes was obscured, names of female teachers turned into their male form until, finally, the fact that half of Tibet's Buddhist pioneers were initiated and trained by high ranking Tantric women was forgotten. It is one of the great achievements of Miranda Shaw's study to bring these magnificent female gurus out of their obscurity and into our awareness. I wish someone would do a similar job for the forgotten female adepts of Hinduism. Nowadays, members of Tibet's leading Buddhist sect are sworn to celibacy and women have less to say than in any other form of Buddhism. When you think of Tantra as a religion of divine love-play, keep in mind that in our days the majority of its adherents have little or no sex-life at all.

Pañcamakāra

The pañca (five) ma (m) kāra (words), also known as the Five Ms, are the offerings given during a specific ritual. They have the name as each of the offerings begins with the syllable Ma. The usual list is māṁsa (meat), matsya (fish), mudrā (parched grain? spicy kidney beans? an unknown drug?), madya (wine from flowers and tree-fruit, alcohol), maithuna (coupling, lovemaking). We are on the level of vīratic (heroic) worship here, to the paśu and the divya the Five Ms were interpreted differently. In modern Hindu parlance the term Pañcamakāra has become a well known dirty word. Tāntrikas who do not wish to be abused tend to replace it by the less offensive Pañcatattva (Five Principles), or better still, keep their mouth shut.

The Five Ms did not develop overnight. In early Tantras, we usually only find three Ms, namely meat, wine, and lovemaking, and even these are not always systematically fused into a single ritual. Nor are all Tantras in favour of the Five Ms. Many traditions, such as the popular Śrī Vidyā, are strictly against them. In his classical treatment of the subject, Agehananda Bharati gave the impression that the Five Ms are the main thing in all Tantric worship. He proposed that the rite can be found in all Tantras, either as a must or as something that should not be practised at all, but I cannot agree with his estimation. Numerous Tantras only mention the subject in passing and some that do not mention it at all. The Five Ms are central to some traditions, but even in these, they were only performed rarely. As you will see, the ritual is so elaborate and complicated that it cannot be performed every other day.

Let us begin by looking at the ritual on the surface level. To begin with, the five offerings are all connected with what people like. They may be sacraments but they are also pleasures. If you read that worship involved drinking, feasting, and lovemaking, you might get the impression that Kaula worship is basically a cult that encourages the 'joys of the flesh'. To a certain extent t his is true. Through much of Indian

Figure 41 - Śiva and Pārvatī.
Stone. Parasuramesvar temple, Bhubanesvar. 8th century according to Leeson, 12th century according to Daniélou.

history eating of meat and fish was either prohibited or scorned among religious folk. Many worshippers were poor. Any meal that went beyond plain rice with lentils was a luxury for them. In this context, meat is 'power food' while fish, wine, and spicy beans were considered aphrodisiacs. Eating so many different things, drinking wine, and making love certainly constitute a pleasure, and indeed one of the aims of the ritual is to combine as many pleasures as possible. Śiva states in the sixth chapter of the *Mahānirvāṇa Tantra*: *Let the desire of the disciple determine what should be offered to the Devas. Whatsoever he himself likes, the offering of that conduces to his well-being.* A rather different interpretation can be found in several recent works on Tantra, where the taboo-nature of the substances is emphasised. Anyone celebrating with the Five Ms is upsetting a lot of religious regulations. Just look at it. Alcohol is forbidden to Hindus (at least in theory), as is the eating of meat and fish. The same goes for Jainas and Buddhists, who do their best not to harm living creatures. Muslims will object to alcohol and pork. Grains may be acceptable to all religions, provided they are really grains, which is the question. Lovemaking for religious reasons is frowned upon by everyone. In consequence, it has been claimed that anyone celebrating with the Five Ms is effectively sinning against the entire religious orthodoxy. This has produced the impression that left-hand Tantra is based on a personal rebellion against all religious norms and society itself. For the modern Indian Tantric this is certainly true. However, the rite of the Five Ms is not a recent development. We have to look at the rite in its original context. When early Tantra developed, Islam did not exist. Drinking taboos were not as strict as during the last centuries and even the meat of cows was occasionally eaten. Not a popular insight, to this day Indian scholars who propose such ideas may find themselves without a job.

Originally the Five Ms were not necessarily a revolt against social and religious restrictions, but nowadays they are. To understand the Five Ms, let's have a closer look at them.

Wine is usually heading the list, and there are more commentaries on it than about the other four Ms. The most extensive account of this sacrament appears in the *Kulārnava Tantra*. This early Kaula work contains several references on wine and, as the book is a compilation, there is any amount of confusion and contradiction. What is wine in the *KT*? Grain wines (beer) are called the roots of all sins and cursed. Wine, in this tradition, is not a product of grapes or grains. However, rice and rice water do appear in the recipes.

Now the *KT* offers several widely different attitudes. Long sections deal with plain prohibitions. For a start, worshippers of the paśu temperament, who are still bound by limitations and social conditioning, are not permitted to drink at all. Nor are all worshippers belonging to the three upper classes. If they see wine they have to stare into the sun to purify the eyes. If they smell wine they should do penance by standing in knee-deep water all day, plus three cycles of prāṇāyāma and fasting. Touching wine costs a whole day hip-deep in water plus fasting. Drinking the stuff needs harder penalties; the culprit has to burn his tongue (*KT* 2,127-129). Now the wines used for worship are made from tree fruit, flowers, and the like (*KT* 5, 11-43). They are called kula-dravya (dravya= substance, fluid). Here are a few mixtures.

Honey and twice as much water produce mead and bestow the love of the gods.

The liquor called gauḍī contains the bark of *Acacia arabica*, *Eugenia jambolana*, water, *Grislea tomentosa*, or *Cocos nucifera*, *Terminalia chebula*, *Solanum indicum*, lemon, ginger, *Piper longum*, *Piper nigrum* and molasses. All are mixed in a vessel for three days and then left to mature for twelve days. On the thirteenth day the broth is filtered and consumed; it allows the worshipper to enjoy the company of Śiva.

The favourite drink of the yoginīs contains one part ginger, two parts lemon-tree bark, three parts *Piper nigrum*, four parts *Grislea tomentosa*, five parts flowers (?), six parts honey, plus eighty parts molasses.

A wine beloved of the gods is made from curd, clarified butter of a she-buffalo, plus a hundred unripe *Mosa sapiensum* (seeds?). All are mixed, put into a bamboo, and left to ripen in a lotus pond for 48 days. The result is dried in the sun. The paste is mixed with water before use.

Inferior to these wines are simple broths made from tree barks, Madhūka flowers (*Bassia latifolia*), and fermented rice-water.

There is also a tradition of making pastes. A classical paste is obtained by mixing wine-paste with dried meat and vijayā (hashish). This paste is made into a pill, which may be dissolved in water for worship.

Now you may wonder about the effects of such elixirs. In *KT*, 8, 55-75 we learn of group worship where yoginīs and yogīs take food from each other and dance around with their drinking pots on their heads. They sing, tremble, stagger, make music, chant, weep, laugh, fall, and rise again. Women and men forget who they are and what they are doing. They embrace each other and make love, they feed each other mouth to mouth. The Śaktis sing songs that cannot be understood and stumble as they dance. They fall on men as they like, and men fall on women. All of this is loud, ecstatic, religious, and wild. It is also supposed to be really secret, making me wonder how such a rite can happen without half of the village being aware of it. In the state of Bhairava, the participants know no class or gender rules. All become as Śiva and Śakti. If we accept this account at face value, we observe a lot of happy celebrants who are blissfully out of their heads. Only on alcohol? Large doses of alcohol are not a good idea if you want to make love, nor do they promote spiritual sensitivity. So let's take a brief look at the chemistry of Tantric wines. *Acacia arabica* is the source of Arabian Gum, the basic glue used to make water-colours, Indian medicine considers it an aphrodisiac. *Cocos nucifera* is the coconut palm. The fermented juice may have up to 8% alcohol. As a well-known folk remedy for just about every sort of disease, the sap is also used as a disinfectant and as an aphrodisiac. *Terminalia chebula* is antiseptic and a tonic. *Solanum indicum* (Indian nightshade) is another tonic (especially for the heart), it is also a stimulant and an aphrodisiac. *Gingiber officinale* (common ginger) is a favourite of Siddha alchemy. Raw and powdered ginger are frequently eaten as a strong stimulant, or consumed as tea. The plant has so many uses in medicine and magic that I leave it to you to look them up. *Piper longum* (Indian long pepper) is another tonic, it is also used against afflictions of the lungs and as an aid of the digestion. It has anaesthetic effects and appears to produce psychoactive experiences. *Piper nigrum* (black pepper) is another powerful tonic. Indian medicine recommends it for people recovering from heavy maladies. Asian and European medicine consider it an aphrodisiac. Then there is the Honey tree with its gorgeous madhūka flowers (*Bassia latifolia*) - another tonic with heating qualities. And what of the other plants that keep appearing in Tantric rituals, offerings, and recipes? Hayāri (Sweet scented oleander; *Nerium odorum*) is a stimulant but also seems to have psychoactive effects, as it may be used for pain relief. Palāśa (*Butea frondosa*) is an aphrodisiac. Tantric wines were a lot more than mere alcohol. Large doses of alcohol lower blood pressure and reduce sensitivity, in other words, they tend to dull and sedate. In small doses, vijayā is a stimulant and aphrodisiac, large doses may lower blood pressure and induce drowsiness. To counteract such effects, Tantric wines are full of aphrodisiacs and stimulants.

The *KT* is a perplexing work. It gives strict rules regarding the amount you drink and a much wider scope of drinking etiquette. It is, for instance, good form to allow the guru to drink before the congregation, and to offer wine to the Śaktis before drinking oneself. To drink in a religious context is the way of the divyas, drinking in ritual is for the vīra and drinking for fun is the way of bondage. When paśus drink they go to hell, when vīras drink they gain enjoyment and when divyas drink the fruit is joy and liberation. Let's look into the drinking rules of *KT*, 7, 80-104. Viratic drinking is a tough job. You have to continue until hallucinations develop, but if you exceed this limit, you become a paśu and fall into bondage. The mouth should become deformed (?) and the senses agitated. More is not allowed. The fully initiated, however, should drink until they collapse. Rising again they should continue drinking, this way they are freed from rebirth. *Devī is satisfied by exhilaration; Bhairava himself is satisfied by swooning, and all the Devatās are satisfied by vomiting.* (*KT* 7, 101). It makes we wonder how they manage to make love in this state. Excessive drinking is in contrast to *KT*, 5, 89-114, which goes to great lengths to prohibit drinking outside of a religious and ritual context. Wine is elaborately condemned for the unqualified, as it is prone to destroy the knowledge of the self. People who are addicted to wine, women, and flesh live perpetually in hell. In verse 107 we read that the real wine drinking consists of moving (attention) from the perineum to the top of the head. When Kuṇḍalinī meets the moon of supreme consciousness, the true wine is released from the lotus of supreme spirit. Therefore consuming other substances is merely drinking booze; the hormonal secretions of your very own brain are not a substitute for alcohol, they are the real thing.

The *Mahānirvāṇa Tantra* mentions wine made from molasses, rice, madhūka flowers (or grapes), sap of Palmyra, and date trees. All of them are acceptable for worship, no matter who produced or brought them, provided they have been properly purified by ritual. Purification is the crucial issue. Purified wine gives all manners of siddhi to the worshippers; while ordinary wine is strictly forbidden, it is compared to poison and certain to cause disease and early death. This attitude is expressed in many Tantras.

Meat is classed according to origin (beasts of the earth, the waters, and the sky), but no matter who killed the animal or who brought it, it is pleasing to the gods. In ritual only male animals are sacrificed, as Śiva said that female animals should not be slain. Good thinking. Female animals may or may not be yoginīs in disguise. As in animal sacrifices, it is of highest importance that the animal is killed without pain. A goat that struggles or screams brings bad luck. In consequence, sacrificial animals are placated, soothed, and fed before they are slain, it is essential that the animal dies from a single, skilful blow. An unhappy sacrifice has dire consequences. In the *KT*, 5, 51 the sacrificer is Śiva and so is the sacrificial animal, hence, through the sacrifice, the animal attains to liberation. In this world-view, the animal may only find release from its animal incarnation, and become a higher being by being will-fully sacrificed. In the rite of the Five Ms meat is a stimulant. Only a small amount is eaten, after elaborate purification, in a strict ritual context. Eating meat as everyday food is condemned by most Tantric traditions. The same appears in several Daoist systems. Those who follow the Dao generally eat very little, if any, meat. They do not, however, make a fuss about it. Nothing is worse than fanaticism. A Daojia may not eat meat in her/his daily life, but when participating at important social occasions, will partake of small amounts out of politeness. And say 'Thank you!' to the animal. *KT* 2, 130-133 prohibits the killing and eating of animals for pleasure or selfish reasons. It classes eight sorts of animal killers, including those who buy, sell, dress or prepare the stuff, and promises as many days in hell as the animal had hairs. Regular eaters of meat are reborn as animals (and eventually sacrificed, *if* they are lucky). So much for heroic rites. Substitutes for meat are garlic and ginger. They may be used by worshippers who do not wish to injure animals, or by paśus, who are not allowed to eat meat anyway. Garlic and ginger were considered aphrodisiacs. Thus, they are supposed to stimulate, just like meat should. According to *KT*, 5, 109, real meat eating is to kill the animal of pride and shame (the ego) with the sword of knowledge. It releases your (personal) consciousness into the supreme spirit. Those who do so are the real partakers of meat. In a more refined (and secret) context proper meat-eating consist in feeding on the sexual secretions.

Fish does not appear as a sacrament in the earlier Tantras. It is classed according to species and all varieties may be eaten. In literature references to fish are rare. They obviously fall into a similar category as meat, and where it comes to eating them the same reservations apply as to the slaughter of animals. Eating fish for fun or outside a ritual context is prohibited. *KT*, 5, 110 states that the real eaters of fish are those who control the sense organs with the thinking faculty and yoke them with the self (ātmā). Others are only killers of animals. Another interesting interpretation of fish eating is linked to astrology. According to Hindu astrology, Pisces represents a pair of fish frolicking in the Ganges. The fish here represent inhalation and exhalation, and those who practice prāṇāyāma are the true fish-eaters. Finally, in secret code language, the fish, or fish-belly is often a term for the female genitals.

Parched grain is a special translation of the word mudrā. It is not a common term of everyday language. Superficially, the best quality is white rice, barley, and wheat, fried paddy is of medium quality, and all other grains inferior. The tricky issue is that the word mudrā has so many other meanings. There are authors who propose that it does not refer to food at all but to ritual gestures of the hands, or to positions of the body (as the word is used in yoga). The interpretation 'parched grains' is commonly found in Tantric literature. There are even authors who propose that Mudrā is not parched but fermented grains. This does not get us very far, fermented grains are in the 'wine' category, and condemned like beer. Others suggest that mudrā may be a code name for some unknown drug. This reminds me of the ergot fungus which can be found occasionally in wheat, rye, and several other grains. Ergot is dark and grows between the seeds, especially in years where the harvest got overly rain-drenched. This substance contains chemicals that are very close to LSD. In fact, LSD was developed when Albert Hofmann experimented with the chemistry of ergot. The problem with ergot is that it contains a lot of substances that are not psychoactive but simply lethal. The toxic alkaloids of ergot may cause massive diarrhoea, burning of the limbs ('sacred fire'), and gangrene; fingers or limbs become black and eventually fall off. In many cases this is accompanied by painful convulsions, mental disorder, and fits that resemble epilepsy. In the old days, when the toxin was unknown, ergot poisoning was a frequent occurrence and led to numerous deaths. Christian Rätsch (1998) claims that the psychedelic substances that occur in ergot are water soluble while the dangerous ones are not. Is it possible that Indian visionaries developed a way of distilling an elixir that retained the psychoactive drugs while extracting the deadly toxins? How come we hear of parched grains then, not of grains sodden in water?

Another possibility for mudrā is a dish of spicy kidney beans. This beverage was considered an aphrodisiac (Bharati 1983). In early Tantras, when the Five Ms were yet undeveloped, the mudrā-dish is rarely mentioned. Mudrā, in the language of early Hindu and Buddhist Tantra, is a term for the female genitals (lock, bolt). Mudrā can also mean a female ritual companion or an initiatrix.

Intercourse is an unpopular topic in India. As I write this, Hindu society is among the most prudish in the world. Apart from a handful of nude ascetics (an endangered species if ever there was one) people do not tolerate nudity. In Bollywood movies people remain partly dressed. They do not even kiss. Many traditional Hindus see sex as something that has to be endured, and this goes especially for women, who generally have not even heard of orgasm. Teenagers grow up in total ignorance about anatomy and what to do with it. Through most of Indian history, couples have not married for affection, indeed most couples never met before the marriage. They were selected and joined by the parents, who were interested in economical ties. If a young couple fits together this is an unexpected boon. Marriage is not supposed to be for love and pleasure. It is an economic institution based on work-division and (hopefully) a measure of respect. This is the climate in which all religions of India evolved. For the Tantric worshippers, who wanted to integrate love, sexuality, and religion in their worship, it was distinctly hostile. As a result, intercourse within a Tantric frame was only possible in rare cases. Some worshippers were happily married and did the rites with their partners. For this purpose, the partner was identified with the Paraśakti (i.e. the Paraśakti was superimposed on the form of the partner for the time of worship and congress). Those who were unhappily married occasionally took refuge in adultery or visited prostitutes. If the worshipper was unmarried these options were often the only ones. Tantric sādhana requires the woman to be initiated and spiritually competent. Making love with non-initiates is prohibited in most Tantric lineages, and for good reason. With the sort of ritual preferred by heroic worshippers, the partner has to be specially trained and capable of experiencing the divine. In some rites the woman is venerated as a goddess, in others she literally becomes the goddess, who obsesses her. Ordinary people simply could not be trusted to cope with the change of consciousness and to keep their mouth shut afterwards. Numerous Tantras advise the worshippers to be secretive and to veil their ritual in Vaiṣṇava forms, if only to escape persecution. As a result, the fifth M is usually the least mentioned in original Tantras. Several Tantras merely allude to meat and wine and leave the third important M unmentioned. Some texts only name it in passing, such as the *Mahānirvāṇa Tantra* which only comments: *O Great Devī! When the weakness of the Kali Age becomes great, one's own Śakti or wife should alone be known as the fifth Tattva... O Beloved of my Life! In this (the last Tattva) I have spoken of Svayambhū and other kinds of flower. As substitutes for them, however, I enjoin red sandal paste. Neither the Tattvas nor flowers, leaves and fruits should be offered to the Mahādevī unless purified.* Svayambhū is the menstrual blood of any woman, kuṇḍa the menses of a woman born from a married woman by a worshipper other than her husband, and gola the menses of a woman born by a widow. The *Mahānirvāṇa Tantra* does not say much about these issues, except to mention that yantras are consecrated by these flowers (5, 174-176). A similar mood can be found in several other Tantras. If you expect Tantras to be books full of erotic details, exciting techniques, and obscure positions, you will be disappointed. The majority of Hindu Tantra is shy. Very few of them even mention postures (apart from the occasional reference for viparīta maithuna in Kālī's rites). The same goes for the technique of lovemaking.

The *Yoni Tantra*, by contrast, goes into great detail regarding congress. As it is such an obscure and unusual work, we shouldn't assume that its regulations agree with those of other Tantras. We don't even know how old the good work is. I've seen estimations ranging from the eleventh to the seventeenth century, which makes a lot of a difference. In the basic ritual of the *Yoni Tantra*, a woman between age twelve to sixty is worshipped. This may sound shocking in our age, but keep in mind that only a century ago Indian reformers were struggling to outlaw child marriages. They weren't entirely successful to this day. In old India, the marriage of a twelve year old girl was not an exception but the rule. However, it was not expected that she was ripe enough to make love. Often a young bride simply moved into the house of her groom and spent a few years growing up before she learned about sex. If she was lucky. And when a twelve year old Śakti participated in worship this does not necessarily mean that she was involved in making love. In Hinduism, just as in some forms of Tantra, young girls are worshipped as representatives of a goddess. This is often a family affair. The girl receives adoration, flowers, sweets, and presents, and there is no sexual element involved. In the *YT* congress is only permitted during menstruation, which explains the age limits. Twelve and sixty are not taken as firm rules, the idea is that only women who are able to menstruate are competent for this sacrament.

The yoni pūjā begins by drawing a circle around the ritual space. No doubt there was a lot of preliminary ritual and meditation before this moment, but the *YT* is a brief work and takes a lot for granted which is not explained in detail. The Śakti is described as shameless, alluring, beautiful, and wanton. She receives vijayā (hashish boiled in milk and ghī) and is worshipped. She sits to the left of the devotee, who spends a long time adoring her yoni. For this purpose it is decorated with tree-blossoms and sandal. Her forehead is smeared with sandal, she is given purified wine and is identified with a goddess. I wonder whether she just sat there, spaced out and grinning happily, or if she actually became obsessed by a goddess. The devotee repeats a mantra (usually Aiṁ) 108 or 1008 times, recites a hymn with devotion, and caresses her breasts. Then he makes over the spiritual benefits to the guru, who is not present during the rite. Whether this pūjā involves intercourse is uncertain. It may have happened after the worship, or maybe the worship simply consisted of mantra recitation and adoration plus a bit of obsession thanks to the yoginī. Keep in mind that many Tāntrikas lived a celibate life. We often have such references. Most Tantras do not describe things explicitly. They hint and suggest, and generally they succeed in producing an atmosphere in which it is not even clear whether the worship happens physically or completely in the mind. This ambiguity is intended; the reader is supposed to make up her or his own interpretation of the rite, with or without the help of a guru. In a similar manner, the *KCT* 4, 56-58 manages to sum up an entire rite of congress in three verses. The sādhaka places cakras (does nyāsa) on Devīkuta (top side of the feet), Uḍḍīna (legs?), Kāmarūpa (genitals, possibly the external side), sloping ground (thighs), Jālandhara (breasts), Pūrṇa (stomach?), sacrificial ground (inner genitals), and repeats mantra eight times, ten times, a hundred times, or a thousand times while he takes his pīṭha (sacred place, here: penis) and enters the space of the pot (vulva). Neat, isn't it?

Figure 42 - Gaṇapati and Siddhī
Stone. Kajuraho, 10th century.

If we didn't have the secret attributions of the sacred places of the Devī to anatomy, we would hardly be aware what goes on. How does the rite continue? Next (verse 59) the sādhaka assumes the siddhāsana posture and worships the amulet pīṭha (his penis) and the pīṭha facing him (the vulva). He addresses the Śakti as the highly fortunate one, the giver of siddhi. She graciously accepts his behest. Then he worships her by offering the kula flower, perfume, and food which he has cooked himself. He places rice, meat, fish, ghī, honey, and other suitable foods in a bowl, consecrates them with the Paramī mudrā, and offers them to her. Then he meditates on his chosen deity and makes offering as prescribed by scripture (which one?). Finally, he divides a fruit in two. He offers half to the Kulaśakti and eats the other. So far, things seem simple enough. The next line, verse 66, states that if no woman is present, he should throw her food into the water. What was that? If no woman is present? What happened to her? Louise Finn proposes that the Śakti may have gone home. In the middle of the ritual? Was she there at all? Is this a ritual for two persons or is it an internal rite where the worshipper unites with a spirit Śakti, or perhaps with the personal deity, while he is all alone? This sort of ambiguity is typical for the *KCT*. The same question: does this happen in the manifest world or is it a meditation in the mind? appears in several rituals. Perhaps the most excessive is a worship of eight women who represent the Mothers. These 'mothers' are not very motherly, they are violent goddesses, many of them famed for slaying infants. The term can also mean matrixes, measures, and is used as a honourable title.

To summarise a long ritual (*KCT* 3, 22-58), the devotee prepares the following trifles: cakes of various flavours, milk, curds, ghī, buttermilk, sugared butter, sugar, various elixirs, coconut, 'elephant' fruit, lemon, citron, pomegranate fruit, more sorts of fruit, unguents, fragrances, sandalwood, musk, fresh leaves, borax, lodhra blossoms, water- and forest lotus, jewels from the mountains, water, blessed water, incense, silken clothes, sandals, jewels, ornaments, ointments, garlands, and a golden plate for offering. He prepares everything in a deserted place (probably in the jungle), and when the eight women arrive, they are dressed in new clothes, supplied with sandals, washed, perfumed, and fed with all sorts of delicacies. Then he invokes one of the Mothers into each of them and worships the Goddess in multifold form as she who dispels the need for mother and father, she who is both mother and father, she who is one in many, in the form of the universe. Then he offers betel to the Śaktis, gives them a garland scented with perfume and sandalwood, and *dismisses them!* What a surprise! What happens to the poor dears? How will they find their way home, 'dismissed' in the middle of the darknight jungle? Is our worshipper an unthinking brute? What will the neighbours say? And while we are at it, what did they say when those women sneaked out of their homes to come to the rendezvous? The whole event is highly suspect. India is not the sort of place where young women go for walks without attracting attention; it was hard enough to meet a single woman for a clandestine ritual, so eight are pretty much impossible (unless you happened to be king). And just how did he manage to prepare all those offerings and carry them to the 'deserted place' unobserved? How come he owned something as costly as a golden plate? If you see this as a 'real ritual' you are expecting a lot of unlikely things. The rite is most easily celebrated in the imagination. It is quite likely that none of the eight women was present as human beings - the only 'real' women appear after the dismissal. As *KCT* 3, 49-52 mentions, if there is a woman present at the time, be it his daughter, his younger sister, elder sister, aunt, mother, the co-wife with his mother, an old woman, or a casteless one, these are to be worshipped. Here we leave imagination and enter Kula family politics. These women are worshipped, whatever that may mean. Superficially it may be flowers, mantras, and scents. It could also mean intercourse. Is the *KCT* recommending incest? It is not the only work that seems to do so. At least, it may seem so to the uninitiated. In the world of Kaula adepts, the Kula (cluster, clan, family) is the real family of the adept. A mother is a female guru, an aunt a female guru who is not one's own guru, the sister is a female fellow student, the daughter is one's own female student. Likewise, a father is a male guru, a brother a male fellow student, a son one's own male student. The references suggest incest, as a literal interpretation, but they actually mean the company of the initiated. All of this goes to show that when Tantric literature actually bothers to describe ritual worship and intercourse, we still cannot be sure how much happens in the physical world and how much in the imagination. This situation appears in many works. And then there are those Tantras that do not mention worship or intercourse at all. All you read is that a given yantra should be drawn with a mixture of colour and menstrual blood. Now where does the red elixir come from? How was it generated? If the adept is male, where did he get it from? You may ask such questions, I hope, but you will rarely find an answer.

Orgasm

What is the aim of coupling? In new Age Tantra, which took a lot of useful ideas from the works of Wilhelm Reich, a basic aim is good orgasms. Reich discovered that natural orgasms and free pulsation require a happy, healthy body without tension or repressed neurotic impulses. He postulated that a cramped belly and 'frozen' hips promote such mind-sets as fascism, and was hounded and persecuted for this eminently true observation. Now Reich's ideas go a long way beyond such simple insights. Modern New Age Tantra picked some of them, plus a few techniques of Reichian body therapy, to teach people to have better orgasms. In some systems the emphasis is on learning to control the orgasm reflex. When men learn how to delay their orgasm, women get a chance to have several orgasms in the meantime. This sort of thing, quite a good idea, was classed as 'Tantric' and connected with several mistaken ideas. One common fable is that male adepts should have no orgasm, the entire sexual energy being withheld and transmuted into spiritual power. Women, by contrast, should have as many orgasms as possible, thereby increasing the male's spiritual energy, but as they come so often, they don't develop much spirituality themselves. This remarkable assumption did connect with some distorted forms of Yoga and Daoism. As mentioned earlier, several (not all) Daoist sects believed that the Jing (here: manifest life essence, seminal energy, the sexual fluids) should be preserved at all costs. To ejaculate, with or without orgasm, caused loss of vitality and shortened the life expectation. Others proposed that even the sensation of lust drains the life energy, no matter whether orgasm occurs. A few schools carried such ideas to ridiculous extremes. The Golden Lotus sect (founded in the 12th century) went for extreme celibacy. They also tried to reduce sleeping, as sleep carried the danger of wet dreams and involuntary emission (Hawkes 1985: 200-201). Not actually an old Daoist tradition; when you look into the Mawangdui manuscripts of the Huang Lao school, you will find that the occasional orgasm was still allowed, to relieve tension, in the second century BCE. Similar ideas appear in numerous schools of Tantra and Yoga. Hard-core adepts went for total celibacy in order to conserve their immortalising seminal energy. Some thought that doing without is not enough. They deliberately indulged in love-play and erotic visualisation to arouse their seminal energy, but instead of releasing it the usual way they held it back, reversed its direction, and moved it upward to the head.

A further development was to retain one's own energetic fluids but to feed on those of the partner. Here, the basic idea was that women feed on male secretions anyway. Men could stop this by retaining their sperm, or they could reverse the situation by consuming the fluids of their partner. It could happen orally, but it could also, so the books say, be done by sucking up the secretions by using the penis like a suction pump. Whether it is anatomically possible to reverse the flow of ejaculation is a matter I cheerfully leave to the experts. That fluids can be sucked up into the bladder seems possible, but it would be nice to know what it's good for. Anyway, such practices do appear in several Indian and Chinese systems, but generally they are frowned upon, as they can come close to vampirism. Not always, though. Several Daoist systems, such as the Western School founded by Li Xiyue, the Southern school attributed to Zhang Boduan, and the Eastern School of Lu Xixing permit such techniques provided they are used with the partner's permission. They may be useful if one of the lovers is old or of weak health and needs an energy burst to accomplish the basics of Daoist training. (Eva Wong, 1997: 2-6). Such methods were usually done cautiously, so as not to deplete the more vital partner in the process. Be that as it may, there were a lot of Far Eastern alchemists who went to great lengths to retain their vital fluids. Though sexual vampirism was practised by women and men, the general trend of male-oriented literature produces the impression that it was usually men who exploited women for their sexual secretions. Such misconceptions seem related to a fundamental error appearing in numerous academic books on Tantra: that men are adepts and women, though divine, are there to be used for higher purposes. You can find such rubbish in quite a few scholarly works. That a competent adept needs a competent ritual partner for ritual love-play seems to have escaped many researchers. Tantra is not an excuse for

Figure 43 - Lovers.
Stone. Kajuraho, 11th century.

random bed-hopping or spiritual one-night-stands; it takes training, training, training. Beyond that, it requires trust, respect, love, and a great deal of shared spirituality. Let me put this in very plain words. Unless there is lust (belly), love (heart), and friendship (head) between your partner and yourself, neither a meaningful relationship nor a ritual union are possible. 'Tantric union' should take you beyond your limited human personality.

If we follow the dogma of New Age Tantra we observe an obsession with control (holding back orgasm) and release (multiple orgasms); however, genuine Tantric literature does not bother about such topics at all. Orgasm is hardly ever mentioned, and even enjoyment is rarely discussed. White, in his excellent study on 'Tantric Sex' proposes that enjoyment was not an issue at all. I would not go quite as far, as there are a few hints, here and there, that at least a few adepts managed to combine union with joy. This is certainly not self-evident. Most treatises on Yoga or Tantra frown upon any sort of sensual pleasure. *Śiva Saṁhita* 5, 2-3 announces that the greatest obstacles to spiritual success are the enjoyments (bhoga), starting with women, beds, seats, dresses, riches, powers, music, dance, and family. It is a rare exception to the rule when the *Kulārnava Tantra* 2, 23-24 proposes that in the path of Kaula, yoga (union, liberation), and bhoga (enjoyment) have a happy union. Such a statement is a rarity, and even here we have a lot of additional material that condemns enjoyment without proper spiritual discipline. The majority of Tantras I have seen do not comment on the issue at all. The same goes for orgasm. If our Tantric authors had good orgasms, most didn't even hint at it. An exception to this rule is Kashmir's foremost Tantric saint; one of the most explicit commentaries on this matter comes from dear Abhinavagupta. Unlike so many fanatics, Abhinava made a point not to condemn the senses as an obstacle. Instead, he derided gurus who could not enjoy beauty, be it in art, nature, or humans. Several modern writers on Abhinava pretend that his contribution to Tantra was to make things more intellectual, philosophical, and remote. Some propose that thanks to Abhinava, Kaula, Krama, and Trika lost much of their physical nature and became a mind-game far beyond the flesh and blood of everyday worship. Again, I cannot agree. Abhinava writes like a heavyweight intellectual, but when you actually bother to read him (preferably in some lucid state of mind) you will find that he is a lot more practical than most writers. His 'philosophy' was the result of decades of training and practical experience. Mind you, he wrote mainly for advanced practitioners, so it's not surprising when academics cannot understand him. Here's a typical quote:

> *'In the case of both sexes sustained by the buoyancy of their seminal energy, the inwardly felt joy of orgasm in the central channel induced by the excitement of the seminal energy intent on oozing out at the moment of thrill is a matter of personal experience to every one. This joy is not simply dependent on the body which is merely a fabricated thing. If at such a moment it serves as a token of remembrance of the inherent delights of the Divine Self, one's consciousness gets entry in the eternal, unalterable state that it*

realized by means of the harmonious union with the expansive energy of the perfect I-consciousness which constitutes the venerable Supreme Divine Śakti who is an expression of the absolutely free manifestation of the bliss of the union of Śiva and Śakti denoting the supreme Brahman.' (Parātrīśikā Vivaraṇa, trans. Singh, 2002: 44-45)

Here, Abhinava said a lot more than you will find in most Tantras. Thanks to him, we are aware that to some Tāntrikas orgasm was an important matter. Nevertheless, they did not make an issue of it. What you can find with much greater frequency is the importance of the secretions. For most of the Kaulas, initiation was impossible without the ingestion of the clan-fluid. Sorcery, the cultivation of special powers, even the rites of enlightenment and liberation depended on the use of the clan-elixir. When a ritual involved congress, it usually did so to produce the desired secretions, and ingestion was the major point of the ritual.

Substitutes

As you read earlier, the use of meat, wine, fish, grains, and intercourse is restricted to the heroic worshipper (vīra) who has cast off the shackles of conventionality and class. This limits the rite to a small segment of possible worshippers. The paśu worshippers and the divine worshippers perform the rite without any of the original ingredients. Here we encounter the question of substitutes. In many (western) books on Tantra, the Five Ms are 'the real thing' and the substitutes are for those too weak-minded or spiritual to handle them. In this model, the heroic worshipper is the true Tāntrika. The paśu is simply a hero in training and the divya is a hero in retirement who has given up dramatic worship and internalised the rites. In other words, the paśu is a ignorant beginner, the vīra the expert/professional, while the divya is not up to drunken lovemaking on the cemetery any more. This model is misleading. When we propose that there is a 'real thing' in Tantra we also imply that all else is substitute. Now the one thing that is certain about the numerous schools and traditions of Tantra is the fact that they are all independently minded and cannot agree on any central teaching or rite. To some traditions, the imaginary, internalised worship of the divya is 'the real thing', to others, the Five Ms are simply the expression of five principles on different planes of meaning. In this sense I would like to offer a few of the 'substitutes', asking you to consider that the vīratic form is also a substitute, and the real thing the essence behind all forms. Here is what paśus make do with:

Wine: Brahmins use milk, warriors ghī, traders honey, and Śūdras enjoy a drink made from rice.

Meat: Ginger, garlic, salt, sesamum, wheat and beans.

Fish: Aubergine (egg-plant), red radish, red sesamum, and some water plants.

Mudrā: Grains such as paddy, rice, wheat.

Congress: Flower offerings or mudrās (hand-gestures) denoting intercourse.

In divya worship, the sacraments are a lot more refined. Internal or spiritual worship has a few advantages over the heroic form. The ritual in its classical form is a complicated and extended affair that can easily take all day. More so, memorising all formula and understanding each gesture, act, word, or element can involve years of preliminary learning. The adepts who invented the rite made it absolutely clear that this is not a short road to feast and fuck. They created a grand, complex, and mind-blowing ritual that works much like an initiation. You don't do this sort of ritual on any other day, it was designed to be something special and unusual. As the rite is so complex and demanding it acquired the typical notoriety of things that are not available to anybody. It may have produced the impression that it is so central to Tantra. I see this in a different light. Things that only happen every few months or years may be important for special occasions of identity transformation. They may provide a break-through experience or permit you to make a quantum leap into another personality/world-view. This is especially the case when the ingredients of the rite are prohibited by your society. To a devout Hindu such taboo acts contain power, and when the worshipper accepts them in a ritual context, the pent-up energy of prohibition and damnation is released, transcended, and may produce a moment of divine grace that can break down the imaginary barriers between the human and the divine. Such acts of 'forbidden ritual' work when they remain special. Done too often, the power of the forbidden wanes, and what remains is just another set of habits. I very much doubt that a non-Indian get such a strong effect from doing the Five Ms. In western culture you can eat meat, fish, grains, you can drink alcohol in a hundred forms, and make love as much as you like, with and without marriage. To a culture that allows such acts, the Five Ms are much weaker than to traditional Hindus. A Westerner is not liberated by the acts that release the Hindu from a straight-jacket of socio-religious regulations. Nor does s/he get a kick from transgressing classes and castes. The Five Ms lose importance when taken out of their Indian context. If you want to design a similar rite for your own culture, look for the taboos. The important issue is to recognise useless conditioning and to free yourself from it. This does not mean that you do everything that society forbids. In Hindu culture, acts such as deceit, rape, murder, and theft are prohibited, and the Tantras do not approve of them either. It is the useless restrictions, the ones that obscure the simplicity of primal self-nature, that are transcended by the heroic worshipper, who usually makes a big, dramatic thing out of it. Drama, excitement, transcendence of fear and revulsion... such moods make rituals appear important that may only be peripheral in the long run.

More central to daily life is what you can do every day. Here we encounter the versions invented by the divyas. These rites can and should be practised every day, they form an inner alchemy that refines the initiates from within. Woodroffe cites *Kaivalya* (1972: Chapter CXIX)

Wine: The intoxicated bliss that comes from union with the supreme.

Meat: The offering of all things to the divine.

Fish: The sense of identification through which the worshipper sympathises with the pleasure and pain of all beings.

Mudrā: Giving up all acts that result in bondage.

Congress: Union of Kuṇḍalinī and Śiva within the body of the worshipper.

The *Āgamasāra* (Woodroffe 1972: Chapter CXIX) proposes:

Wine: Somadhārā, the lunar elixir generated in the lotus of the head.

Meat: Controlling the tongue (i.e. speech as a divine power). 'Eating meat' means cultivating silence.

Fish: The two fishes are the rivers Idā and Pingalā. Eating fish means to control the circulation of vital energies in the two channels. The process requires prāṇāyāma, the fish are 'eaten' when breath rests, and the energy moves into the central channel.

Mudrā: The awakening of true knowledge when Kuṇḍalinī unites with the Ātmā in the highest centre.

Congress: Gaining the supreme knowledge of Brahman in pure bliss in the highest cakra.

Of course there are further possibilities. Here are some of my ideas. **Wine** can refer to any sort of inner secretion, to colours and fluids that saturate the body of the worshipper. **Meat** can be the offering of the body and the whole world of flesh and form. It can be the practice of posture, and the identification of the yogīc body with the world mountain, and indeed the whole world. **Fish** can be the pulsation of in-breath and out-breath, of tension and relaxation, of hard and soft, of tonification and sedation. **Mudrā** can be grains (bīja mantras) scorched by continuous recitation. If you heat your grains before ingestion they are easier to digest. And **union** is everything that takes you out of your narrow little human reality into the wider wisdom of the all-consciousness. It can be union with your personal deity or with some spirit, but it can also be any meditation that makes the mind open up. What other interpretations can you invent, develop, discover, and cultivate?

A Day in the Life of a Neo-Kaula

To perform the full ritual of the Five Ms is quite an achievement. Most books do not set down the details of the rite, and leave it to the guru to explain the fine-tuning. We are happy to have that popular Neo-Kaula work, the *Mahānirvāṇa Tantra*, which sets down the entire ritual timetable in almost pedantic detail. Of course the rite is still far from clear, but then, we can count ourselves lucky that we have the text at all. Doing the Five Ms requires training. A few mantras and gestures are not enough. The practitioner needs an almost encyclopaedic knowledge of numerous deities and spiritual entities, including their myths, meanings, iconography, plus a lot of cosmology and hidden lore. Each step of the rite is accompanied by mantras and visualisation of figures, activities, symbols, and so on. To build up the necessary store of knowledge requires an excellent memory and the ability to understand (or invent) deeper interpretations. After all, simply calling a deity by name is not enough, nor is it much use to rely on mantras that have not been properly woken. The ritual also requires yoga, such as Kuṇḍalinī meditation and prāṇāyāma. All in all, the student needs several years before being competent to do the ritual in its full form. The decision whether the student is competent does not rest with the devotee but with her or his guru. Let's have a brief summary of the Five Ms. Yes, it's a long, long text. In the original, translated by Woodroffe and published in 1913, the ritual is summarised in chapters five and six (1972 edition, pp. 60-137). Even this extended treatment is but a summary lacking many important details. Any lovemaking, for instance, is barely hinted at. To make matters comprehensible, I had to leave out some (I hope) minor details. Please forgive my errors. I have also taken the liberty of dividing the ritual into units and to number them. Like so many Tantras, the text addresses the male reader. Sorry about this linguistic convention and all the sexism it implies. Let me ask your consideration that things may just as well be the other way around. One day we'll have Tantras without sexism, inspired works transcending male/female role-games and social conventions. I look forward to it.

1. The worshipper crawls out of bed before dawn and seats himself to meditate on the guru and his Śakti who are imagined as embracing in the white lotus within the head. There is worship in the mind and repetition of the Vāgbhava (Sarasvatī) bīja (Aīṁ). The benefits of the repetition is made over to the guru with gesture and mantra.

2. Worship of the personal deity follows including repetition of mantra, visualisation and giving the benefits of the worship to the personal deity. As our text is strongly influenced by the worship of Kālī, she is invoked frequently.

3. The worshipper leaves the house (left foot first) to empty bowels and bladder and to clean teeth. He approaches a body of water and walks in. There is one immersion, the recitation of mantra to clean the mouth, a little sip of water, mantra, more sips, more mantra, and drawing the kula-yantra on the water with mantra (twelve repetitions) in the centre. The water is imagined to be fire, is offered to the sun and sprinkled over body. All seven openings are sealed with the water, then follow three further immersions (*'for the pleasure of the Devī'*).

4. The devotee leaves the water, dries, ties the hair, and draws the sacred marks on the brow (usually three horizontal lines plus a central red dot, for Śaivas and Śāktas), all the time repeating a Tantric version of the Gāyatrī.

5. Tantra Sandhya. Mouth rinsing, invocation of the sacred rivers into the ritual water. Several mantras and mudrās follow, the worshipper sprinkles himself, invokes the bījas Haṁ, Yaṁ, Vaṁ, Raṁ, Laṁ over a

little water held between the palms, imagines the water to be fire, draws it through the left nostril and expels it through the right nostril to wash all impurities away (does this happen in the imagination?). The water is dashed three times against an (imaginary) adamant (the palm) while exclaiming 'Phaṭ!' Then follow mouth rinsing and offering of the water to the sun with mantra.

6. Morning meditation on the Supreme Devī as Brāhmī, midday meditation on Vaiṣṇavī, evening meditation on Śaivī, all accompanied by the Devī gāyatrī. Offerings of water with both hands to the devī, the devas, seers, and forefathers.

7. Invocation of the Supreme Devī (here: Ādyā Kālikā) with Hrīṁ, Śrīṁ, Krīṁ, and prayer. Mantra and japa, the benefit is given to the goddess.

8. The devotee collects water for the ritual and goes to the ritual space, meanwhile meditating and reciting hymns of praise to Kālī.

9. Arriving, hands and feet are washed and a simple yantra (a triangle surrounded by a circle surrounded by a square) is drawn on the doorstep. The water-vessel is set on the triangle and worshipped. The water vessel needs elaborate preparation, including purification by mantra and mudrā, identifying the water with the sacred rivers, and scattering flowers into it. This constitutes the sāmānyārghyā, the common or universal offering. The deity of the entrance of the ritual space is worshipped with water and flowers. The text lists eight deities starting with Gaṇeśa.

10. The worshipper enters, meditates on the lotus feet of the goddess, and blesses the space with sacred water. The deity of the site is worshipped, as well as Brahmā (in the south-west corner) and all obstacles are banished by stamping on the ground with the left heel, uttering 'Phaṭ!'

11. The place is consecrated by burning incense (sandal, aloe, musk, and camphor).

12. A rectangular space is marked as the seat, within it a triangle is drawn and identified with Kāma-rūpa, the yoni of Satī. Over this rectangle a mat (āsana) is spread and the Ādhāra (support) Śakti is invoked with Klīṁ. She is the deity of the lotus seat and by sitting on the dedicated space, the devotee symbolises the union of liṅga and yoni.

13. The devotee assumes a posture kneeling on one foot, facing east or north, and consecrates the vijayā. See the chapter on mantra for details of this procedure. After dedication to the guru in the head, the goddess in the heart, the mouth of the Kuṇḍalinī, and praising Sarasvatī, the devotee drinks the sacrament. As it can take more than an hour before the vijayā works, the sādhaka has plenty of time for the following meditation. Let me add that vijayā is mentioned in very, very few Tantras. It is by no means a standard element of worship.

14. The devotee bows to guru, Gaṇeśa, and the primordial Kālī and meditates on the devī.

15. The articles of worship are placed on the right of the devotee, the articles of kula worship (wine, meat, etc.) are placed to the left. They are blessed with mantra and sprinkled with sacred water.

16. The devotee draws a circle of water around himself and the ritual space. The water circle is transformed into a circle of fire with the bīja Raṁ. The palms of the hands are purified by rubbing a flower and sandal paste between them, the crushed flower is cast away ('Phaṭ!').

17. Now the quarters are purified. First mudrā and finger snapping ('Phaṭ!'), then Purification of the Elements of the Body (bhūtaśuddhi).

18. The devotee meditates on the root-cakra (at the perineum) and wakes Kuṇḍalinī using the bīja Hrīṁ. He leads her upwards, together with the earth-category (solidity) to the sexual cakra by means of the Haṁsa mantra (the breath-sound); here the Earth-category and the sense of smell are dissolved into water (fluidity). As Kuṇḍalinī rises, water (and taste) is dissolved into fire, and fire (energy) as well as sight and vision are dissolved into air (subtlety). Air and touch are dissolved into ether, ether and sound are dissolved in aham (conscious self, ego, identity), aham in mahat (intelligence), mahat dissolves in Prakṛti (Before-Creation. Primal matter, also nature) and finally Prakṛti dissolves in pure Brahman (all-consciousness).

19. The worshipper imagines an angry black man with red hair, armed with sword and shield, as big as a thumb, and the personification of all sins within his left abdomen. Now the devotee inhales through the left nostril sixteen times, meanwhile imagining the purple, grey, smoky Vāju bīja (Yaṁ), as the breath dries up the sinful body. Next, imagining the red Agni bīja (Raṁ) in the navel, where fire burns up the sinful body during sixty-four times of holding-breath. Last, the white Varuṇa bīja is imagined in the brow. It releases a pure white elixir that showers down the (burned) body during thirty-two units of exhalation and revives it. This creates the divine body. The devotee now strengthens the body with the yellow earth bīja (Laṁ) imagined in the root-cakra and by a steady gaze. He places a hand on his heart and recites *Aṁ, Hrīṁ, Kroṁ, Haṁsaḥ, So'haṁ* and places the vital airs of the devī in his body. This concludes the jīva nyāsa and the purification of the body. Our text deals very briefly with the matter, a more detailed account can be found in the chapter on Kuṇḍalinī.

20. Next follows the nyāsa (placing) of the matrixes (the letters of the alphabet) on body. This procedure is quite complex and cannot be given in detail. Sarasvatī as goddess of speech and learning is invoked and the entire alphabet is placed, imagined, and vibrated in the six cakras. After this, the letters are placed on the outer body, such as brow, face, eyes, and ears.

21. More prāṇāyāma. Breath goes in through the left nostril (repeat sixteen Hrīṁ), is held for sixty-four Hrīṁ and exhaled through the right nostril (thirty-two Hrīṁ). Then the other way around, three repetitions.

22. More nyāsa applying Hrīṁ, Śrīṁ, Krīṁ to all parts of the body. The hands are passed three or seven times over the whole body from bottom to the top and from top to bottom. Various bījas are combined.

23. More nyāsa, this time not of body but of the fingers, which are identified with various mantras.

24. More nyāsa. Now the heroic worshipper places within his heart lotus the Support-Śakti, tortoise, the serpent-king, the earth-goddess, the ocean of ambrosia, the gem-island, Indra's pārijāta tree, the chamber of wish-fulfilling gems, the jewelled altar, and the lotus seat. Other items and qualities are located in shoulders and hips. Finally in the other heart lotus (not one of the six cakras but the seat of the personal deity a little below the normal heart cakra) sun, moon, and fire are placed, plus the three guṇas, the eight nāyikās (attendants of Durgā) in the petals of the lotus, and the eight Bhairavas (terrifying forms of Śiva) in the tips of the leaves.

25. The worshipper takes two flowers and, holding them close to the heart, meditates on the goddess. This worship can be of two sorts: formless (for advanced devotees) or with form. Here we find an extensive meditation on the primordial Kālī: *'I adore the Ādyā Kālikā whose body is of the hue of the (dark) rain-cloud, upon whose forehead the moon gleams, the three-eyed One, clad in crimson raiment. Whose two hands are raised - the one to dispel fear, and the other to bestow blessing - Who is seated on a red lotus in full bloom, Her beautiful face radiant, watching Mahā-Kāla, Who, drunk with the delicious wine of the Madhūka flower, is dancing before Her.'* The worshipper places a flower on his head and proceeds to offer the articles of mental worship to his personal deity. The lotus of the heart is offered as her seat, the white elixir of the thousand-petaled lotus is offered to wash her feet, the mind becomes her purified food, and so on. Flowers are offered, and as this is mental worship, the flowers are qualities such as absence of egotism, absence of pride, absence of anger, and so on. Fifteen flowers are listed, which adds a lunar symbolism to the verse.

26. More offerings. This time, there are allusions to secret mysteries, as the offerings are: 'the ocean of ambrosia (wine), a mountain of meat and fried fish, a heap of parched food, grain cooked in milk with sugar and ghī, the kula-nectar (*'nectar produced by means of the Śakti'*, Woodroffe), the kula-flower (menses), and the water which has been used for the washing of the Śakti (i.e. her yoni)'. This is the first reference to the five sacraments in the entire ritual. You will notice that the text mentions several sacraments that go beyond the basic five. Sadly, it does not tell us how these are acquired. Where does the worshipper obtain menses, love-juice, and the like? So far, the ritual partner (Śakti) has not even appeared in our ritual!

27. After so much mental excitement, the worshipper sits down for a lengthy period of repeating mantras by combining various phonemes in ingenious ways. Mental prostration of the eight parts of body. This ends the stage of mental worship.

28. The next step is the preparation of the viśeṣārghya, the special offering. This cup of offerings is so pleasing that at its sight the Yoginīs, Bhairavas, and all gods dance with joy and give siddhi.

29. The worshipper takes water from the sāmānyārghyā vessel and draws a yantra on the ground. First a triangle with the Māyā bīja (Hrīṁ) in its centre. Around the triangle a circle, around the circle a square. He worships the Support-Shakti and washes the support (here a tripod) and places it in the centre of the yantra. Then follows worship of the region of fire and the circle of fire with its ten kalās (units, digits).

30. After washing the arghya vessel with mantra (Phaṭ!) it is placed on the support and worshipped with the twelve kalās of the sun.

31. The vessel of worship is filled to three quarters with wine and one quarter with water, plus flowers and spice. The main mantra of the personal deity is recited and the sixteen kalās of the moon are worshipped. Before the special offering (water and wine) bael leaves dipped in red sandal paste, dūrvā grass, flowers, and sun-dried rice are placed. These items, together with hibiscus blossoms, constitute the arghya. Here, the ritual instructions become extremely brief and obscure.

32. First the devī and then the arghya is worshipped, the devī with incense, flowers, and mantra, the arghya by calling the sacred rivers into the fluids, plus more mantra and mudrā. Some of the fluid is sprinkled (using a special vessel) over ritual space, equipment, and worshipper. This ends the consecration of the special offering.

33. A yantra is drawn. First a triangle with Hrīṁ in its centre. Around it a circle, and around that another. In between the circles there are sixteen filaments, outside them eight lotus petals, and around the periphery of the blossom a square with doors to the four directions. The worshipper recites the root-mantra of the personal deity while drawing the image. By preference, the yantra should be drawn on gold, silver, or copper with a gold needle, or with the thorn of the bael tree. The yantra is consecrated with svayambhū-, kuṇḍa- or gola flowers (three types of menstrual blood), or with sandal, fragrant aloe, red sandal paste, or the red powder used on Holī. This yantra is a permanent item, it is kept inside the house to banish evil influences and to invoke peace and plenty. During the rite, the yantra is placed on a jewelled altar (!) and used for the worship of the deity of the place and the personal deity of the devotee.

34. The placing of the kalaśa jar. This is a vessel with a circumference of thirty-six finger-breadths and sixteen finger-breadths high. The neck is four, the mouth six, and the bottom five finger-breadths. The vessel is made of gold, silver, copper, bell metal, mud, stone, or glass, it should be beautiful as it is to please the deities and in its making, all costs should be disregarded. The worshipper draws a hexagon with a point (bindu) in its centre, around the hexagon a circle, and around the circle a square. These figures are either executed in red colour or using menses. The deity of the support is worshipped with various mantras and the support (usually a tripod) is placed on the yantra and the jar on the support.

35. The kalaśa jar is filled with wine and more mantras are recited, including the matrix letters, plus Hrīṁ, in the reverse order. The devotee should be intoxicated and obsessed by the personal goddess by now and

worships the sun, moon, and fire in jar, support, and wine. The jar is decorated with red colour and crimson flowers.

36. The five ceremonies. **Wine**. First there is a complex ceremony to purify the wine in its vessel. The rite involves mudrā, mantra, invocation, visualisation and several complex gestures you should read up in the original. The wine is consecrated in the name of the supreme Brahman, to remove his curse from it, and identified with amā-bīja, the sixteenth kalā of the moon. Using a lot more ceremony, the curses of Brahmā, Śukra, and Kṛṣṇa are removed. Then the Ānanda Bhairava (the Blissful Terrifying One) and the Ānanda Bhairavī are worshipped using the mantras **Ha Sa Kṣa Ma La Va Ra Yuṁ** (for him) and **Sa Ha Kṣa Ma La Va Ra Yīṁ** (for her). The love-play of the deities is visualised within the wine, which becomes ambrosia. Twelve repetitions of the root mantra of the personal deity. The wine has now become a deity and is worshipped with more mantra, waving of lights and incense etc..

37. The **meat** is placed on the triangle, purified with 'Phaṭ!' and consecrated with air (Yaṁ) and fire (Raṁ). It is covered with the gesture of the veil, reciting Hūṁ, protected with 'Phaṭ!', blessed with Vaṁ and the cow-gesture, and blessed in the name of the devī who is in the breast of Viṣṇu and Śankara (Śiva).

38. The **fish** is consecrated much like the meat, calling upon Tryambaka (the Three-eyed One, Śiva) who causes nourishment, is all-present, and grants liberation.

39. The **parched grain** is purified with a mantra that calls upon the sun (the eye of heaven) and the foot of Viṣṇu.

40. Here ends the fifth joyful message . The author is kind enough to point out that, should the worshiper lack time, the mantras for purification may be replaced with the root mantra of the personal deity and everything offered to the devī. The fifth tattva, **maithuna** (congress), is not mentioned at all. How do you explain this? And just where did the worshipper get the secretions and the menses from?

41. Now begins the sixth joyful message with a short description of the Five Ms. Śiva details types of meat, fish, grains, wine but devotes only a single line to **maithuna**; nowadays, during the Kali age, only one's own Śakti or wife should be the fifth tattva (principle). He adds that the menstrual flowers can be replaced by red sandal paste.

42. The auspicious cup is placed next to the *virtuous Śakti* and she is sprinkled with purified wine or water of the offering while a mantra is recited to purify her.

43. The worshipper draws a triangle, surrounded by a circle, a hexagon, and a square inscribed with Hrīṁ between himself and the ritual yantra, and worships the four basic pīṭhas (places of pilgrimage, parts of the body of Satī) with mantras.

44. The six parts of the body are worshipped in the corners of the hexagon.

45. The triangle and its deity is worshipped with the root-mantra.

46. The receptacle is washed with mantra and placed on the maṇḍala.

47. The **ten kalās of Vahni** (Agni) are worshipped within the receptacle. These are (1) Smoky Red, (2) Flame, (3) Shining, (4) Subtle, (5) Burning, (6) Shining with Sparks, (7) Beautiful, (8) Well-formed, (9) Tawny, (10) That Which Carries the Offerings to the Gods.

48. The offering vessel is purified with mantra, placed on the placed on the receptacle and the **twelve kalās of the sun** are worshipped within: (1) Containing Heat, (2) Emanating Heat, (3) Smoky, (4) Ray-Producing, (5) Burning, (6) Lustrous, (7) Smoky Red/Purple, (8) Granting Enjoyment, (9) Universal, (10) Which makes Known, (11) Quality productive of Consciousness, (12) The Ability to Draw Water from Earth and to let it Rain again.

49. The cup is filled to three quarters with wine from the jar and to one quarter with the special offering while mantras are recited.

50. Within the cup the **sixteen kalās of the moon** are worshipped by combining their names with the vowels. The kalās are: (1) Ambrosial, (2) That which Nourishes the Drug Producing Plants, (3) Shame-producing, (4) Pleasing, (5) Nourishing, (6) Playful, (7) Constancy, (8) Containing the Hare of the Moon, (9) That Which Produces Joy, (10) Charming, (11) Ray-producing, (12) Prosperity-giving, (13) Affection-producing, (14) Body -purifying, (15) Complete, (16) Full of Nectar.

51. Dūrvā grass, red flowers, sun dried rice, sacred basil, and the aparājitā flower (the clitoria flower, looking much like the yoni, sacred to Durgā) are thrown into the vessel and the sacred waters are invoked into it.

52. The fluid is covered with the veil-mudrā, protected with the armour and the weapon bīja, and the offering is transubstantiated with the cow mudrā, and covered with the fish-mudra.

53. The root-mantra is repeated ten times, then the personal deity is invoked and worshipped with flowers held between the palms.

54. The fluid is charged with the mantra:

> *O Kula-rūpinī! (Goddess of the shape/form/truth of the Group) Infuse into the essence of this excellent wine which produces full and unbroken bliss its thrill (trembling, pulsating) of joy.*
> *Thou who art like the nectar which is in Ananga (Kāma), and art the embodiment of pure Knowledge, place into this liquid the ambrosia of Brahmānanda (Bliss of Brahman).*
> *O Thou, who art the very image of That (Tat: being) ! Do Thou unite (sexual union) this arghya with the image of self of That, and having become the kulāmṛta, blossom in me.*
> *Bring into this sacred vessel, which is full of wine, essence of ambrosia produced from the essence of all that is in this world, and containing all kinds of taste.*
> *May this cup of self, which is filled with the nectar of self, Lord, be sacrificed in the Fire of the Supreme Self.*

55. After this consecration, the union of Sadāśiva and Bhagavtī is visualised within the fluid. Incense and lights are waived before it.

56. Between the common offering and the auspicious cup, the cups of guru, enjoyment, Śakti, the yoginīs of the vīra, sacrifice, washing feet, and rinsing mouth are placed, nine cups altogether.

57. Each cup is filled to three quarters with wine from the jar.

58. Holding the cup in the left between thumb and fourth finger, śuddhi (meat, grains etc.) is added and oblation is offered to the Ānanda Bhairava and to Ānanda Bhairavī with the right hand and mantra.

59. Oblation is offered from the guru-cup to the guru and his wife, sitting on a thousand petaled lotus, and to the three gurus and their wives who came before them, with the bīja Aiṁ.

60. Wine is offered from the cup of enjoyment to Ādya-Kālī with her bīja Krīṁ and svāhā thrice.

61. Wine from the cup of Śakti is offered to gods of the parts of her body and their attendants.

62. Wine of the yoginī-cup is offered to Ādyā-Kālikā, her weapons and worshippers.

63. Next follows Tattva śuddhi, i.e. the purification of the elements that constitute body, the emotions, sentiments, senses, and the worshipper declares his freedom from sin.

64. Further ritual follows, in fact a lot of it. First a sacrifice to Vaṭuka to the east of a rectangle, containing wine, meat, and other things, then a sacrifice to the yoginīs of the south, to the deity of the ground in the west, to Gaṇeśa in the north, and the Bhūtas in the centre.

65. Then follows a sacrifice to the sivās, the jackals. This part of the rite has a divinatory aspect. *Oṁ, O Devī! O Śivā, O Exalted One, Thou art the image of the final conflagration at the dissolution of things, deign to accept this sacrifice, and to reveal clearly to me the good and evil which is my destiny. To Śivā I bow.*

66. The tortoise-mudrā is made and a flower scented with sandal, musk, and aloe is taken to the heart centre where the primordial Ādyā is worshipped.

67. The Devī moves along the Suṣuṁnā Nāḍī, which is the highway of Brahman to the great Lotus of a thousand petals, and made joyful. Then the goddess is brought through the nose and into the flower, the flower is placed on the yantra.

68. Mantra and prayer to the personal deity. In our text, this is Kālī, who is called, invoked, seated, and welcomed. She is sprinkled with water of the special oblation. Nyāsa of the six parts of her body.

69. The personal deity is worshipped with sixteen offerings: feet-washing water, water of the offering, mouth rinsing, bath-water, garments, jewels, perfume, flowers, incense, lights, food, mouth washing water again (offered to guests before and after a meal), nectar (wine), pān (a rolled betel leaf filled with up to sixty-four spices, or a synonym for menstrual blood), waters of oblation (satisfaction), and obeisance. Each offering requires specific gestures, mantras, and ritual acts.

70. The goddess is worshipped in various forms of the yantra, then the line of gurus, then the eight mothers on a lotus of eight petals, and the eight Bhairavas in the tips of the petals plus several gods and their weapons.

71. Now follows an animal sacrifice, which may be a real animal (the text lists deer, goat, ram, buffalo, hog, porcupine, hare, and iguana, always the male of the species) or an undesirable quality of the worshipper, such as pride, greed, cruelty, etc. This rite is given at length and involves worship of the animal, mantras, and plenty of ritual.

72. The next rite is a fire offering (homa) made within a square (four gods are invoked) containing a triangle surrounded by a hexagon and a circle and eight petals. The preparation is much as in the auspicious cup ritual, the yantra is full of deities, and the kalās of sun and moon.

73. The worshipper meditates on Sarasvatī who has taken her purification bath (after menstruation). She has eyes like blue lotus blossoms and sits on the seat of fire in the embrace of Brahmā.

74. Fire is brought, gazed into, and Agni is invoked into it. The ritual space is dedicated to Kālī and its centre to Sarasvatī.

75. The Fire is kindled and a share of raw meat is offered to the rākṣasas (man-eating demons). Fire is touched, invoked, identified with Śivas's sperm and various mantras and salutations. Agni is worshipped by his seven tongues, by his six limbs, his eight forms, eight Śaktis, the eight treasures of Kubera, the ten regents of the quarters, and so on.

76. The sacrificial ghī (clear butter) is prepared and the three major nāḍīs are imagined into it. The ghī is offered to the fire with salutations.

77. The personal deity is visualised in the fire in union with Agni, and the worshipper contemplates his identity with the two. A lot of oblations follow.

78. The personal deity is reclaimed from the fire with a mudrā and the fire god is politely dismissed.

79. Japa follows. The worshipper locates guru in his head, the goddess in the heart, and fire on his tongue. Bījas and prāṇāyāma. The mālā (rosary) is worshipped as *the image of all Śaktis* and *the repository of the fourfold blessings.* Various mantras are recited, the most important of them 1008 times (or at least 108).

80. More prāṇāyāma follows as the fruit of all offerings, mantras, oblations, flowers, etc. are given to the goddess. Then a *Hymn to Kālī* is recited and her mantra of protection.

81. The sādhaka now circles the goddess (clockwise) holding the special oblation in his hand and offers himself to her: *Oṁ, whatsoever ere this I in the possession of life, intelligence, body, or in action, awake, in dream or dreamless sleep have done, whether by word or deed, by my hands, feet, belly, or organ of generation, whatsoever I have remembered or spoken - of all that I make an offering to Brahman. I and all that is mine I lay at the lotus-feet of the Ādyā Kālī. I make the sacrifice of myself Oṁ tat sat.*

Figure 44 - Lovers.
Stone. Devi Jagadamba temple, Kajuraho, 11th century.

82. The worshipper then ends the rite by reciting Hrīṁ, stating that he has worshipped Kālī with all his powers and devotion, asks her forgiveness, and bids her go. He holds a flower in the mudrā of dissolution and places it at his heart.

83. A triangle is drawn at the north-east corner where Nirmālya-Vāsinī is worshipped. Nirmālya are the (sacred) leftovers after the ritual and she is their goddess.

84. Food is offered to Brahmā, Viṣṇu, Śiva and all other deities. Then the worshipper may partake of it.

85. The Śakti (here, the ritual partner) takes a seat to the left of the worshipper or sits on the same seat, on his left side. A cup made of gold, silver, crystal, or coconut is placed on the support to the right of the food and filled with wine.

86. The food and wine are served (food first). When there are several people present at the rite, the congregation partakes of the offerings. The food is served on plates, each participant has a cup for wine. There are no caste distinctions in congregations.

87. Each person meditates on the Kulakuṇḍalinī (here: personal Śakti), the divine intelligence extending from the root cakra to the tip of the tongue; all food and drink are offerings to her.

88. The Śakti, if she is the worshippers wife (as this Tantra insists), merely smells the wine. If she is not, she may drink, but the *Mahānirvāṇa Tantra* does not encourage this. Also, wine is allowed in small amounts, only five cups are permitted, and only if mind and eye are not affected. To drink beyond this is beastial. In these matters, the ritual shows the influence of Vaiṣṇava orthodoxy. Quite a break from earlier Kaula traditions.

89. The worshippers, after partaking of food and drink, clean their hands with cloth and a little water. They place a flower from the leftovers on their heads and draw the brow sign from the remnants of the yantra. Now *the intelligent worshipper may roam the earth like a Deva.* This ends the sixth joyful message and the ritual.

What a day. As you noticed, the *Mahānirvāṇa Tantra* is very shy regarding sexual secretions, lovemaking, and wild, ecstatic behaviour. Perhaps, when the ritual allows for several participants the necessary elixirs are refined before the rite commences. When it is done in private, this need not be the case. However this may be, our text is a guideline. Any worshipper seeking to do this ritual needs advice from the guru, and where it comes to the fifth tattva, quite a lot of it. The *MT*, for all its detail, is prudish. It likes to replace objectionable acts and substances with harmless symbolic alternatives. Likewise, allowing the ritual Śakti only a sniff of wine is sort of mean. Her entire function remains questionable. When does she enter the ritual space? What does she do during the hours needed to perform every little detail? In the *Mahānirvāṇa Tantra*, she seems hardly an active participant. She represents the goddess, but if the worshipper has Kālī as his personal deity, as the text makes abundantly clear, how can we reconcile the idea of a Śakti incarnating

Kālī with one who seems to take little part in the proceedings? If she is worshipped as the goddess, does she abide like a living statue, or is she shaking and ranting in delirious obsession? This is what obsession in India looks like and plenty of women are good at it. You find loads of it in folk worship, which often overlaps with Tantric rites (read the books by June McDaniel for excellent accounts). Judging from the prudish and slightly conservative tone of this text; I guess the author left out a lot that simply wasn't acceptable. Remember that the *Mahānirvāṇa Tantra* is a rather late Tantra; the legal chapters seem to include ideas gained from British law, as proposed by Goudriaan and Gupta (1981), and it is one of the few Tantras which are respected by a wide range of worshippers, which is often a bad sign. It even tries to be acceptable to Vedic worshippers, which of course does not work. The text is not as detailed as you and I would like, but I am sure that you can improve on it. Just ask your inner guru, your personal deity, and your partner! As you noticed, the whole rite is so complicated and extensive that it requires years of training to be properly performed. Even then, it is obvious that sensual indulgence and the joys of the flesh are a small part of the package. I wouldn't call so much ritual hard work, as good ritual inspires and is highly enjoyable in a mad sort of way. Good ritual can carry you away. You may have noticed that the schedule does not allow for a single meal until the whole rite is complete (after nightfall). Our worshipper is acting on an empty stomach and with a steadily falling blood-sugar level, which amplifies the effects of the vijayā for good or ill. After such a long day I am sure that even a few morsels of food and a few drops of wine are enough to produce an ecstatic experience. All in all, the rite is good evidence that the infamous Five Ms are not an excuse for loose living or happy hedonism. Getting drunk, having a meal, and making love can all be had in easier ways.

13: Red and White

The Yoni Shrine

Remember how Viṣṇu dissected dead Satī, and how her limbs, falling to the ground, created a myriad of sacred places all over India? The yoni (vulva) of Satī fell to the ground in Kāmākhhyā, in Kāmarūpa (Form/Shape of Desire/Love), modern day Assam. Kāmākhhyā is also the name of a goddess who is frequently called the Yoni-Goddess. Kāmarūpa is a land with a highly mixed population. Legend has it that one Naraka, conceived by Viṣṇu, and the goddess of the earth while she was menstruating, received the country from his father, who commanded him to exile the local population, the Kirātas (wild people, hunters, fishers, mountain dwellers), to repopulate it with Brahmins and to adore no other goddess than Kāmākhhyā. In the *Devī - Bhagāvatam*, Kāmākhhyā is listed as one of the places which are prominent, sacred, worth visiting, and beloved by the goddess.

> *The Yonimandala Kāmākhhyā, the place of Srimatî Tripurâ Bhairavî, excellent of all the places in this earth, where the Devî Mahâ Mâyâ always dwells. There is no other place better than this on the earth. Here the Devî becomes every month in her course of menstruation and where the virtuous men are seen. Here all the Devas remain in the form of mountains and where on the mountains the excellent Devas inhabit. The sages say: That all the places there are of the nature of the Devî; there is no better place than this Kāmākhhyā Yonimandala. (7, 38)*

Sorry about the English, it seems our translator got a little overexcited.

This brief reference contains a lot of unusual information. To begin with, the place of Kāmākhhyā is identified as the holiest of all the sites of pilgrimage (pīṭha). These places are so sacred that the mere recitation of their names is sufficient to burn up all sins, hence it is to be practised every morning. The place Kāmākhhyā is characterised by mountains (or hills) who are gods, but the gods also appear on the tops of the mountains, high above the earth and below the wide wind-swept sky where heaven and earth meet. Kāmākhhyā has a cult involving a series of highly specialised deities, all identified with specific heights. Kāmākhhyā's main sanctuary is a temple on a mountain called Nīla, Kāmagiri and Kubjikā - pītha.

> *Nīla has three angles, is deep (hollow) in the centre and identical with Sadāśiva. The mountain which is Brahmā is of white colour, the mountain-shape of Śiva is blue (nīla)... in its*

centre is a beautiful mandala with 30 Śaktis. There is the cave Manobhavā which was created by Manobhava... Here is the purest of all pīthas, the petrified yoni of Satī, so powerful that a human who touches it gains immortality while those who already dwell in the world of Brahmā attain mokṣa. (Kālikāpurāṇa, trans. from Stapelfeldt, 2001)

The sacred yoni is protected by a temple. The present one goes back to the 16th century, but there were earlier buildings on location. The first one is said to have been built by Kāma, the deity of lust and desire, as a condition for being allowed to reincarnate. The inner sanctuary of the temple is only open to Hindus. It is said to contain a stone with a furrow which is constantly moistened by the waters of a spring. The stone is richly adorned with flowers, sacrificial offerings and red colour. Next to it are two smaller stones representing Mātangi and Kamalā.

The menstruation of the goddess is celebrated once every month. This is not unlike a number of other temples of India that acknowledge a period when the local goddess is supposed to menstruate. This constitutes a marked difference to ordinary Vedic worship. In orthodox religion, upper class goddesses do not menstruate nor do they give birth. To the traditionally minded Brahmin, these are two periods when women are unclean, dangerous, and to be shunned. Folk traditions see this differently. There is a public ceremony at Travancore (Walker, 1965: 62), performed up to ten times a year which involves the veiling of a goddess. When the cloth is removed, red stains are discovered and the image of the deity is moved into a shed. The reddened cloth is ritually examined, cleaned by a washerwoman, and used as a talisman. A south Indian class, the pokunātivaru, believe that they originated from such a stained red cloth which had been thrown away by the mountain goddess Pārvatī.

In Kāmākhhyā, the goddess Kāmākhhyā menstruates regularly, though at these days the temple is closed and no worship is performed. Once a year, after the rainy season, the menstruation of the goddess is a special event. The water of the spring turns red, possibly due to a higher level of subterranean water, which might release mineral deposits (iron?). The temple is closed for three days, and then a feast ensues to which thousands of pilgrims assemble. Those who suffer from lack of blood anoint themselves with the red water. The feast is officially supposed to celebrate the renewed purity of the goddess after her days. I'd guess it is merely a reinterpretation that makes the dreaded idea of menstruation acceptable to the Brahmin population and the aristocracy. In everyday life, men shun women who menstruate. If the menstruation of the goddess attracts *virtuous men*, as quoted above, it may well be that the *Devī Bhagāvatam* is relating unorthodox teachings of a highly Tantric quality. The *Kaulajñāna nirṇaya* adds: at the sacred place of Kāmākhhyā female worshippers are dwelling, who are experts in yoga (yogīnīs).

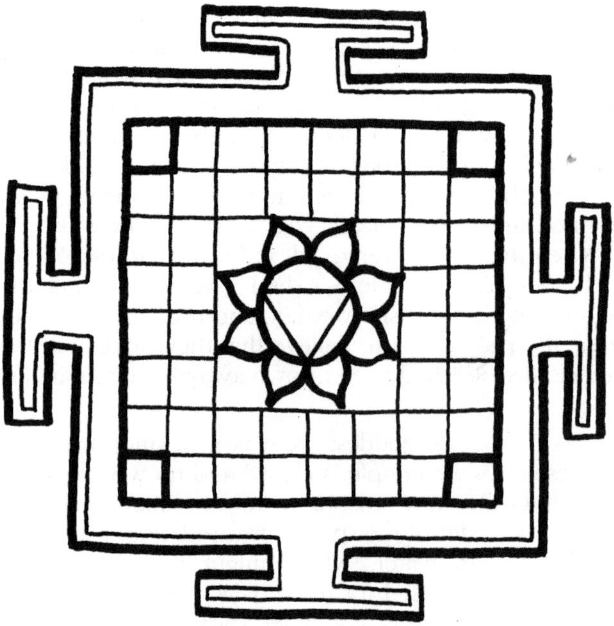

Figure 45 - Yantra of the Kula ritual.
Based on the description by Abhinavagupta (Tantrāloka, 29, 52-54) and Jayaratha's commentary (54 D.2).
Top: Reconstruction by Dupuche, Bottom: my reconstruction.
Abhinava tells us that the square is made of a grid of 8 x 8 spaces. The text does not mention that these are erased (as Dupuche assumes) after the yantra is drawn. The direction of the triangle is not given and the placement of the four squares is enigmatic. Dupuche's version places them towards the cardinal points, which upsets the symmetry of the grid. I follow a vague allusion to 'diagonals' in my interpretation. According to Abhinava, eight goddesses and eight Bhairavas are worshipped in the petals and spaces. Fifty-six masters are installed in the spaces.

Those who join them gain consciousness, mind, shape-shifting skills, mastery of the eight siddhis, and whatever they will. You can think about these initiatrixes in several ways. In one sense, they were spiritual entities, like spirits or half-gods, who enabled the adepts to find liberation and/or magical power. In another sense they were real women who had chosen to take the path of asceticism and inner alchemy to refine themselves. In a third sense, think of real women who become semi divine entities by manifesting them in their own bodies. You'll meet more Yogīnīs further on.

Menstruation

In mainstream Hindu thought, all secretions of the body are dangerous, impure, and endowed with powerful magical virtues. This goes for excrement, semen, spittle, sweat, urine, female discharges, and any form of blood. We find the first references to the dangers of blood in the Vedic period. Marriage was a dangerous time, a passing period of ritual pollution, and one of the most dangerous items of the ceremony was the cloth that soaked up the virgin blood of the bride's deflowerment. This soggy rag was so dangerous that it had to be given to a high-ranking priest, who performed a lengthy ritual to avert evil influences. You can find references to this belief in *ṚV 10, 85* and in first two songs of the *AV, 14.* In either case we learn that marriage is an exceedingly dangerous occasion and that the young bride can be lethal to her husband. Clinging to her is a blue or red fiend who threatens spouse, household, clan, and cattle. By giving the stained garments to a high-ranking priest, the evil influence is banished and the bridal pair faces a life of docile happiness. It might be argued that with the blood-soaked cloth, the more independent-minded aspects of the bride are exorcised. In Indian thought, unmarried women are dangerous. They have a hot temperament that can only be cooled by male influence. For this reason women are represented by the sun, and men by the moon. When a woman bleeds, she is twice as hot, and twice as dangerous. Menstrual blood, though not quite as dangerous as the blood of the marriage bed, continues as one of the most terrible taboo-substances in Hindu life.

According to the *Taittirīyasaṁhitā* 2.5.1 (trans. F. Smith, in Leslie 1992) thunder god Indra slew the god Viśvarūpa, a son of the divine craftsman Tvaṣṭṛ, who happened to be of Brahmanic rank. Another version of the tale replaces Viśvarūpa with good old serpentine Vṛtra, who began as a dragon/serpent/bank of rainclouds and eventually became a Brahmin. Now killing of Brahmins is frowned upon, especially by Brahmins, and Indra was guilty of a serious crime. You might think that a god, especially a mighty thunder god like Indra, is superior to a mere Brahmin, but in old India, it was the Brahmins who ordered the gods around. The deed polluted Indra, who managed to transfer the pollution (and guilt) to earth, to trees, and to women. All three bring forth fluids. The pollution appears in earth as water, in trees as sap, and in women as menstruation. It's an ambiguous pollution, as, after all, living beings depend on the earth's water to survive. Likewise, the menstrual fluids of women are not only 'pollution', they are also the source of life-to-come. In ancient Hindu medicine, the two substances that form an embryo are sperm and menstrual blood. *When the female is fertile it (the human body) is conceived during the union of man and woman. The soul enters during the fusion of male seed (bindu) and female fluid (rajas).* (*Siddha-Siddhānta-Paddhati* 1, 69-70) Red and white fuse to become a human being, hence, they are literally elixirs of life. They are also the prime materials that shape the universe, as with each new human, a new perception of reality is born. This idea features prominently in the Tantras of the Left Hand Path, where the substances are not feared but cherished, worshipped, and ingested. In mainstream Hinduism this is definitely not the case.

But menstrual blood is more than the female contribution to the production of an embryo. When women are pregnant, they (usually) do not menstruate. Instead, their breasts fill with milk. It was assumed that in pregnant women menstrual blood transforms into milk. In this world-view infants feed on transformed menstrual blood. Here the polluting fluid, the dangerous, hot sap, becomes a source of nourishment. Due to such ideas there are some obscure Tantric rituals where mother's milk is consumed or blended with the menstrual blood of another woman. Think about it. To drink from the breast of a woman is to become a child, or her child. Becoming a child is an essential stage in many systems that aim at extending life or creating immortality (advanced Daoist alchemy keeps emphasising this point). Consider also how Śiva was breast-fed by Tārā after he had drunk too much of the lethal milk ocean poison. Yes, and think of the milk ocean itself. Are we talking of milk at all?

For fundamentalists the good points of these fluids are hardly worth mentioning. The *TS* proclaims that one should not converse with a woman with 'stained garments', nor sit with her, or eat the food she has prepared. If a menstruating woman participates in a ceremony half of the sacrifice 'dies'. Any child conceived during menstruation is cursed. You might argue that it is by no means easy to conceive during menstruation. Normally, women cannot conceive at this time, but there are (very rare) cases where women become fertile on the sixth day after the beginning of menstruation. Just as seldom a glue-like slime develops during the last days of menstruation, which may keep sperm alive for up to six days (Brater, 2003: 245). It's a possibility, but it is not what the ancient Hindus had in mind.

In general parlance, menstruation is given a wide range of names, most common being 'rajas'. Vātsyāyana, author of the *Kāma Sutra* (quoted by Walker, 1965: 61) calls menstruation *that illness that comes without being called, cannot be concealed, cannot be revealed, and yet is always present.* Good evidence that the teachings of the *Kāma Sutra* cannot be classed as proto-tantric. Tāntrikas do not consider menstruation an illness, nor do they try to conceal it. Things are a lot different among orthodox Hindus. A woman who menstruates partakes of Indra's curse and is considered dangerous and polluted. Traditionally, women had to leave the house during the time. They retired to a hut or to a secluded room, in extreme cases to a tree house, so they were not likely to injure others. They had to remain alone, if possible in darkness, and they were not supposed to speak or to look out of a window. Sunlight had to be avoided (as sunlight can impregnate women). Sexual activity was especially dangerous. When a woman is in her rajas phase, she is liable to be more erotically inclined than usual. Good thinking, when you consider that menstrual cramps may be reduced by lovemaking, especially when the woman is sitting on top. However, old Manu did not approve at all. In his opinion, a menstruating woman can destroy a man's sanity, health, and virility simply by thinking (!) of him, while actual congress was deemed a lot more dangerous. Religious activity was also forbidden. As Walker points out, the *Manusmṛiti* and the *Mahābhārata* forbid menstruating women to see an image of a deity, or even to think of the gods.

The (traditional) three days of menstruation result in different degrees of impurity. On the first day she was as polluted as a class-less 'Untouchable'. On the second day as polluted as a killer of Brahmins. The third day was somewhere between the first two. On day four menstruation was supposed to be over. Women had to undergo rites of purification, such as ablutions with cow-dung and water, saffron and water, and finally just water. After a drink containing the five jewels of the cow, the woman was clean enough to return to her home. This sort of thing is still happening. In 2005, the Nepalese government passed a law that makes it illegal to throw menstruating women out of the house or to lock them in cow sheds. We live in enlightened times. From the fourth to twelfth day (except for the unlucky eleventh) she was in the ṛitu ('right') time for congress. Congress, though not especially popular among traditionalists, was encouraged only during this time. In fact it became an obligation. To waste the time of ṛitu was considered a serious offence. It was only through congress that the dangerous powers of the fertile woman could be calmed and controlled. Kauṭilya's famous book on statesmanship proposes that men who do not cohabit after the menstruation of their spouses are to be fined heavily. Kauṭilya's work was considered a genuine law text for centuries, and numerous rulers shaped their decrees in accordance with it. Nowadays it has turned out that the book is a fiction, or really a model of what laws might be like in a better world. Regarding couples who miss their fertile days, we have no evidence if penalties were ever effected.

When a girl becomes old enough to menstruate she is also ripe for ṛitu. In some parts of India she also acquires gender, and some make a point of casting a horoscope for the first menstruation (White 2003: 69). If she has no husband at the time, trouble and ill-fortune may result - the ancestors may suffer. Traditional Hindu laws condemn parents to hell if they have not married their girls before they menstruate. Just as dangerous were young widows, who still have their menstruation but no husbands to have fun with. It was claimed that unmarried women, or those with absent husbands, could make love with men of their choice rather than allow the fertile days to pass unused. Or so it is said. If it ever happened is one of those questions. However, you can find the idea expressed in the *Mahābhārata*, and as we know, the *Mahābhārata* contains everything. All of which shows that traditionalists considered sex a matter of procreation. Sex for pleasure was not encouraged, nor is it encouraged today.

Mothers, Seizers, and Yoginīs

When the Aryans arrived at the shores of the Indus, they had already developed a number of terrifying female spirits. Best documented of them are the Apsarases and the Yakṣinīs or Yakṣīs. **Apsarases** appear in modern Hinduism as alluring heavenly girls, denizens of Indra's warrior heaven, where they sing and dance and make love with the slain warriors. Their power to seduce is so devastating that even the gods may fall under their spell, and humans, unless they are advanced seers of the grumpy old austerity school, are even more likely to succumb. When you look at Vedic lore you will find that the Apsarases did not begin as popstars of paradise. The *AV* contains several long hymns to exorcise them. Why exorcise a heavenly nymph? In Vedic times the Apsarases had a sinister side. They were known to lead men to excesses of drink, gambling, fornication, and violence. They also went for women, and assaulted the embryo in the womb. This function was shared by their mates, the Gandharvas, the heavenly youths, the celestial musicians of Hindu times. In the Vedic period, the Gandharvas were sinister spirits who slew women in childbirth, crushed the baby, or attacked young children.

A similar range of activities was attributed to the tree-spirits, the **Yakṣinīs**. Here we find a link between the Indus valley folk and the Aryan invaders. A few seals of the Indus people show what looks like vegetation deities, leading to the proposition that, perhaps, the Yakṣis and Yakṣinīs of Hinduism were venerated long before the Aryan invasion. However, very similar spirits appear in Indo-European myth, just look at the dryads of Greek myth or the goddesses appearing out of trees in central European folk-lore. Many of them are a lethal lot.

Male tree spirits (Yakṣis) tend to be guardians of nature's wealth. They hold the secrets of nourishment and fertility, they know the secret medicines of the forests, the magic of plant lore, and the hidden wealth of ores and minerals deep within the earth. Their king is Kubera, usually shown as a fat man of dwarfish proportions, who is the lord of wealth and prosperity. The female tree spirits, the Yakṣinīs, are a popular motif of early Indian art, whenever a sculptor thought that a few big breasted females might liven up a building. However, the Yakṣinīs are by no means as harmless as they appear. Several early statues show them standing on dwarf-like beings, much like Śiva dances on a malevolent dwarf (the human ego) and Kālī dances on Śiva. And when you look into early Yakṣinī lore you may find them among the most dangerous spirits of the wilderness and forest. The jungle was a place of fear and danger. Few people went into the wild, unless they had to, and these, hunters and woodcutters, did it with great caution and under the protection of numerous amulets and spells. When travellers had to pass through jungle country, they were prone to be assaulted by wild beasts, venomous serpents, bandits, outcasts, not to mention malaria and a wide range of diseases. The latter were thought to come from evil minded spirits, such as the Yakṣinīs. Lone men were attacked by Yakṣinīs, who appeared as helpless women, lost far from the village. Such beauties easily seduced their victims, with or without an informal and brief marriage ceremony. Then the male was spell-bound, sexually drained, and finally the seductress drank his blood and devoured his flesh until death set in. This could happen literally, but it could also appear as a disease which simply wasted the man away. As White (2003: 63-66) mentions, in Sri Lanka, almost all diseases are called Yakas, a form of Yakṣa. Let me recommend *The Kiss of the Yoginī* for further reading. In Kerala folk belief, women who die violently, before their time, by suicide or while giving birth, become Yakṣinīs. Hungry for revenge they ride the nightways hunting for prey. Their victims are usually men, babies, and children. Similar ideas were once popular in ancient Europe, just look at the startling amount of young women (died in childbirth?) who were treated as 'dangerous dead' by the Celts and buried accordingly (see my previous book *Cauldron of the Gods*). That Yakṣinīs slay infants is of importance. If the image (see illustration) of the woman with baby under that tree does not show a human mother but a Yakṣinī (as I suspect) the infant in her arms is a stolen one. And, while their seductive and dangerous nature made the Yakṣinīs unpopular for most of the population, it also made them attractive to heroic Tantric worshippers dwelling in or near the jungle. There are several rites and mantras to evoke a Yakṣinī, a ritual that no sane Hindu would bother considering.

These beings are by no means the only dangerous females of India. As mentioned earlier, Vedic lore mentions hordes of frenzied women, the **Grahīs** (male: Grahas) or Seizers who accompany Rudra when he rides the stormwinds. The Grahīs are Seizers and Devourers, they clutch and hold and tear. In their early form they often appeared as birds or serpents. White (2003: 43) points out that these two shapes, which are also among the most popular for the later Yoginīs, have their reflection in the Kuṇḍalinī and the Haṁsa. Kuṇḍalinī is the primal creatrix in serpent shape, Haṁsa may be a term for the breath-mantra, or for the divine gander or swan who is the vehicle of the highest. To seize may also mean to obsess. In this sense, the seven planets of astrology are called Graha, as their influence obsesses people.

Next, let's take a brief look at the **Mātṛkās**, a complex term that may mean Mothers, but can also mean Matrixes, Measures, and the alignments of numbers, sounds, and vibrations in advanced Tantric lore. Usually, the Mātṛkās appear in groups. Best known are the Seven Mothers (Sapta Mātṛkā), who made their appearance in the *Devī Māhātmyam* around the 5th or 6th century. As the story goes, each of the male gods cast off his own Śakti, who appeared on the battlefield as a frenzied warrior woman. This well known tale may be a 5th century

Figure 46 - Woman or Yakṣī holding her own (or a stolen) child.
Stone, no details available. Today in Berlin.

attempt to give a male origin to a few selected Mothers of the emerging Śākta cults. Well, in the real world the Mothers are much older. They were not cast off from male gods and if you think of them as mothers at all you are in for a few surprises. White offers a range of tales relating to the birth of Skanda. Skanda is nowadays acknowledged as the son of Śiva and Pārvatī, but in earlier texts this is not always the case. In book 3 of the *Mahābhārata*, we learn that Agni was seduced by six wives of the Seven Rśi (the constellation Ursa Major, the Wain). Not the real wives, however, it turns out that all six goddesses were forms assumed by the elder goddess Svāhā. After making love, each of them took her share of Agni's sperm and dropped it into a golden basin on the peak of White Mountain. Out of the elixir Skanda / Kārrtikeya was born. Indra, hearing of the birth of the invincible wonder child, feared that one day Skanda might usurp his position. So he sent a range of Lokasya Mātaraḥ (World Mothers) to destroy Skanda. These assaulted Skanda and did their best to slay him. When they realised that they could not defeat the infant, they made a peace with him. As their anger had faded and their breasts had become swollen with milk, they asked Skanda to acknowledge them as his 'Mothers', and, henceforth, they were addressed by this title.

Various Mātṛkā cults surfaced during the first century CE. At the time, the Mātṛkās were either thought to be innumerable, or they were classed in small groups. These early Mātṛkās are a long way from what is considered a 'mother-goddess' today. All of them are dangerous, and where it comes to children, they don't have any, and they kill those of others. Among the Mātṛkās of the Skanda episode, two are described in detail. One of them was born of anger, she wields a spike. The other comes from the deep sea, she has a red face and drinks blood. But there are more mothers in the tale. In another episode (Kinsley 1988:152) Indra tries to slay Skanda with a well aimed thunderbolt. It does not hurt Skanda, but makes him give birth to a range of lethal goddesses whom he also acknowledges as mothers. While the text tries to divide them into auspicious and inauspicious goddesses, it turns out that all of them steal and kill children. Finally the wives of the Seven Seers come round, who had been accused of adultery and kicked out by their husbands. These, too, ask Skanda to be his mothers, and beg for two boons. First, to be worshipped as great goddesses and, second, as they are now divorced and cannot have children of their own, to slay the children of others. Skanda is not too happy about all those child-killing ladies in his company. He grants them powers over every child under sixteen years and allows them to have a violent, indestructible nature. This being settled, he asks them to take some children under their protection. The Mātṛkās agree gladly, but there are even more child devourers to come. The next episode offers another range of ten Mātṛkās, all of them lurkers of birth-chambers, slayers of children, eaters of flesh, and drinkers of alcohol. Further on we learn that among Skanda's army, as he sets out to fight demons, are no fewer than 92 terrifying, child-killing Mothers. Actually there are more, but the *Mahābhārata* only mentions 92 by name. By now you should have guessed that the Mothers were primarily

Figure 47 - Yakṣī.

worshipped in order to avoid them. To make them honorary mothers of a sickly child is to turn their nature from hostile to protective. Such goddesses abound in Hindu myth, no doubt due to the sanitary conditions under which children were born and reared. One well known example is Pūtanā (The Smelly One) who tried to kill baby Kṛṣṇa by offering him an infected nipple dripping with poisonous milk. To her surprise, the toxins did not affect the babe at all. Young Kṛṣṇa sucked the demoness dry, an act that killed her but also turned her into a goddess. Pūtanā appears among the mothers of the Skanda episode. She is a dark goddess, black, with gaping mouth, horrible tusks, tangled hair, and filthy clothes (if any) who lives in desolate buildings. Sometimes she appears as a bird. She affects children with smallpox and a wide range of diseases. To win her affection, she is given sacrifices of fish, rice, cow manure, sesame, and alcohol. Pūtanā appears several times in literature. Sometimes she is called a Seizer, sometimes a Yogīnī, and in the *Brahmāṇḍa Purāṇa*, the Pūtanās are an entire group of Mothers including Ḍākinī and Kālī. It is for their dangerous qualities that the Mothers appear in the odd Tantric ritual (see *KCT* 3). The cult of the Mothers, whoever that may be, peaked around the seventh century CE and disappeared around the 10th century (Finn 1986: 22-25). A few of their stone-hewn images remain in Hindu temples, but their worship has long ceased.

So far we had Apsarases, Yakṣīs, Grahīs, and Mātṛkās. While most of them lost importance around the tenth century, a new class of divine beings emerged who continued their functions. These new spirits, or goddesses, were called **Yogīnīs**, a term that became popular around the seventh century CE, in the dawn of the Tantric period. The Yogīnīs began as dangerous, otherworldly beings. Like their ancestresses, they are associated with child killing and with dangerous diseases of all sorts. They were even known to bring plagues. In the world of humans, the Yogīnīs appear in numerous guises. Most popular among them are animal forms. *KJN* 23, 1-7 gives a catalogue of their favourites. The text lists the following female animals as the favourite vehicles of the Yogīnīs: dove, vulture, swan, hen, other (female) birds, bitch, she-wolf, owl, hawk, bee, beetle, jackal, she-goat, buffalo, cat, camel, mongoose, tigress, elephant, peahen, and cuckoo. They also appear as horses, cocks, serpents, stags, scorpions, bulls, mice, and frogs. As you noticed, a few of these are male. In the Yogīnī Kaula it is strictly prohibited to harm or eat these animals. They are to be worshipped, as there may be a Yogīnī playing in their form. If you accept this belief, you'll find that just about any animal may be a vehicle of a Yogīnī. Even the most insignificant insect can house a magnificent, magical, and absolutely lethal spirit. And you may realise that the animals you meet have a lot to teach. A Yogīnī may be an initiatrix into the most advanced realms of Kaula Tantra, and who knows whether that spider, that pigeon, or that wasp is really a Yogīnī watching you watching her. More so, Yogīnīs may appear as human beings. Here we leave the realm of spiritual entities and enter the world of humans. A Yogīnī may be a witch. This is close to the Ḍākinī, who is much the same as a Yogīnī, only that the former is

Figure 48 - Yoginī with serpents.
Wooden statuette, South India, c. 1800, 30 cm high

more popular in Tantric Buddhism. She may also be a woman who practices yoga, or sorcery, or austerities. A Yoginī may come from any class. She may be a princess or a beggar woman, a recluse, a warrioress, a courtesan, a barber's daughter, a washerwoman, an Untouchable, or a trader.

Perhaps she is a spirit or goddess who has assumed human form. Perhaps she is a human being who has evolved a spiritual form. Perhaps she is both or neither, or simply a woman who manifests a dangerous goddess. The complexity of the term is part of the magick. The worldview of the Yoginī Kaula thrives on multiple interpretations, and so do you.

But there is more to the magick of the Yoginīs. Some Yoginīs appear in a highly abstract form: they manifest as complex arrangements of phonemes in mantras. This is not to say they are just sounds or only formula. In Yoginī Kaula, the sounds and their arrangement have more reality to them than the shapes of actual living beings, or anything manifest in the gross realm of form. Here, sound (vibration) is at the root of all manifestation. But the Yoginīs also have a lot to do with menstruation. It is the nether mouth of the Yoginī which produces the Kulamṛta, the Nectar of Immortality of the Clan, the fluid gnosis that initiates the worshipper. It may be that the Yoginīs, never on good terms with children, initiate those whose life is not aimed at procreation. Those worshippers who favoured menstruation for lovemaking and elixir generation were not likely to have children. They could keep their attention on their spiritual evolution instead of falling into the duties and restrictions of the householder's life.

Others, favouring internal worship, may not have gone for physical lovemaking at all. These, worshipping the circle of sixteen Yoginīs, all of them young, black skinned, dressed in radiant red, smeared with blood, smiling, with gleaming eyes (*KJN* 19, 2-5, also 23, 12-16 and 24, 4-12), find their bliss in the pure company of spirits.

What was that? Childless worshippers in India invoking the Yoginī goddesses into their ritual partners? Women, adept in yoga, who transformed into Yoginīs to initiate and teach their consorts? And what of those who never had a physical consort and lived with a dream partner, a **Spirit Lover**? Such forms of internal worship were widely known in Tantric circles. A good many lonely worshippers chose to live with such spirits and learned a lot from them. A spirit lover may be your creation, in that you invent a shape, but the consciousness that comes through is not a creature of your thinking. Like all spirits, a good shadow lover is an expression of the deep mind, or of the all-self, and as such a being from whom you can learn a lot. The test is predictability. If your dream lover does just as you think it is not much of a spirit, but simply a creature of your ego. If the spirit has original ideas, contributes surprises, and is not too predictable, you two may evolve in company. This sort of relationship was considered inferior to a real partnership, but it was accepted and respected, especially when the conditions of life forced the initiate to lead a solitary life. Several Tantras include rituals with one or several consorts that would have been very difficult for any adept living on the road. Some even offered ritual formats to evoke such a partner, such as the *KCM* which proposes the evocation of a heavenly woman (an Apsaras?) or a serpent maiden from the underworld. The same phenomena appears in the Tantric Buddhism of Tibet. Miranda Shaw (1994: 147-148) cites the first Dalai Lama, who proposed that superior practitioners will prefer to enact the required rituals with an imaginary partner (jñānamudrā), while dull minded, inferior folk need to have a living human being as a ritual consort. Mind you, this attitude comes from a religious environment that aimed at celibacy and considered lovemaking with real human partners a threat to monastic discipline. Another interpretation, also found in Tibetan Buddhism, counsels that novices enact the rites with an imaginary partner, while advanced worshippers and gurus were entitled to a living, human consort. Some of the stricter traditions even insist on a human partner for the final initiations. In their opinion, beginners are too concerned with their own problems, so that a human partner would necessarily be a distraction, and increase the confusion. Once the novice has become an adept, and mastered the basics of meditation, ritual, and visualisation, a human partner becomes a necessity.

All of this may remind you of what were known as incubi and succubi in medieval Europe. Sure, the church has always condemned such spirits as evil phantasms born of wishful thinking and sick fantasies. I am sure they knew what they were talking about. Nevertheless, there were sorcerers in Europe who thought otherwise. So there are dream-lovers. How do they connect with the Yoginīs? If you research Greek and Near Eastern myths, you may find a lot of closely related spirits. What about Lamia (the Hungry One), a simple girl who dallied a bit with old Zeus, only to be cursed by Hera? She was turned into an insane winged monster who devoured her own children, and those of other women as well. What of the bird women on Celtic coins? Where do the harpies fit in? How about the Valkyrie, the lethal swan maidens, daughters of Odin, haunters of the battlefield and Choosers of the Slain? And what of the violent bird women of Chinese myth? You may be familiar with the Yellow Emperor, Huangdi, of Chinese prehistory. According to legend, he lived at the beginning of civilisation, some 4500 years ago, and unified the country. Which took a lot of fighting. When he realised that these fights were getting him nowhere, he ascended the Taishan mountain and disappeared for three days on the fog shrouded peak. Up there, in the bleak, pale gloom, he met Xuannü. She had the head of a woman and the body of a bird. The Yellow Emperor fell on his knees. 'What do you want from me?' asked Xuannü. 'I desire ten thousand victories, if I have to fight ten thousand battles. I wish to be successful ten thousand times, even if I have to lurk in ambush ten-thousand times. What shall I do first?' So Xuannü taught Huangdi battle strategies, and the Yellow Emperor brought peace to the land (*Quan shang gu sandai qinhan liu chao wen*, *Anthology of Ancient Literature,* in Ding 1991: 19).

Alone with Lilith

One of the earliest proto-yoginīs is the eldritch woman of the dark. She does not come from India, but you will soon see how much the seizers, Mothers, tree-, bird-, and serpent women have in common with her. Say welcome to the joy and terror of the elder night.

For a start a brief look at a medieval tale that has been retold numerous times. The original is in the *Alpha Bet Ben Sirra.* In the beginning, God created Adam out of dust, and Lilith out of dirt and filth. Lilith was married to Adam but the two began to quarrel almost immediately. For one thing she insisted on being equal to him, for another she didn't want to lie under him all the time. Well, who could blame her? When he attempted to force her, she spoke the unutterable name of God and flew away to spawn a race of demons and devils in a cave near the Red Sea. Adam, being angry and very much alone, appealed to God allmighty for a new mate. God, knowing that Adam wouldn't get along with anybody (that's the human ego, folks!), put him to sleep and did a bit of surgery. Taking a rib (or in some versions, Adams's foreskin), God created Eve. The two fell in love, which wasn't too difficult, as they were both the same anyway. In short, mankind developed out of a single hermaphrodite and is in love with itself. Lilith remained way off and refused to return.

This story made her a favourite goddess of feminists, who took it as evidence for the primal male-female conflict, and consider Lilith as the first woman who said 'No!' to a man. While this is certainly a good show of independent-minded free will, I see it as something that goes beyond gender. The primordial Adam was not a man, it was hermaphrodite, male-female at once. In fact it was simply human, and it is humanity itself which always wants to be on top and boss other beings around. Lilith, by contrast, is neither male nor female nor human at all. It's her skill that 'she' can assume any form, gender, or character that you may desire or fear. She can haunt and confront you with the very stimuli that make you shake with longing or dread. In her appearance she can blend both, and bless you with an experience you won't forget in a hurry. Lilith appears as a winged human, but this is only her mask, a shell of her essence. It's a hard shell, and it contains emptiness within. Adam and Lilith are not a model of male-female gender politics: we are talking of humanity meeting extraterrestrial awareness. As humans turned out to be bloody bad at getting along with other forms of intelligence, God decided they had better stick to each other. Adam was split in two, a male (Adam) and a female (Eve) part, and these were left to get along as well as they could. Which wasn't very. And while Eve brought forth human children, Lilith spawned millions of darksome demons every day.

Now before Lilith was considered 'Adam's first wife', she already had an impressive history. The Hebrew Lil (Night) derives from Babylonian/Assyrian Lîlû, which might mean 'Maiden of the Night'. Alternatively, her name may come from Lilu. Lil is the wind in Babylonian and Assyrian, this would make her the 'Maiden of the Wind'. Look into the *Gilgamesh* epos, dating c. 2500-2200 BCE. Gilgamesh was the Thearch of Uruk in ancient Sumeria. The Sumerians were the first ancient culture that built huge, well organised cities, several of them housing more than a million inhabitants. They also discovered what a wide range of diseases you get when so many people live together without much hygiene. Diseases, for the Sumerians, were the product of evil sorcery or the malevolent work of spirits. One of them was Lilit. Our first reference to her comes from an episode where the goddess Inanna (or a priestess of hers) discovered a sacred huluppu tree, uprooted by the river Euphrat. Inanna wished to have a throne and bed made of the wood, so she had the tree fetched to her temple in Uruk. The tree was planted in the courtyard and for ten years the goddess tended it carefully. Alas, by the time the tree had matured it was already withering. A dragon-serpent had built its lair among the roots of the tree, the Zû bird was nesting and rearing its hatchlings in the crown, and, in the very centre of the tree, dark lady Lilit had made her house. This turned out to be a real problem for Inanna: all three realms of existence (underworld, world, and heaven) were infested with demons. She turned to Gilgamesh, who took shield and bronze axe and set out to rescue the tree. With a mighty blow he slew the dragon-serpent. Then the Zû bird and its young escaped into the mountains, while Lilit, shaken with fear, destroyed her home and disappeared into the wilderness. We don't know much about the snake-dragon, but the Zû bird appears in a fragmentary story from Assurbanipal's library. He is a storm demon who once stole the tablets of fate to conquer the gods. After freeing the huluppu tree from its inhabitants, Gilgamesh had it cut down. Inanna made two mysterious objects from the wood, the pukku and the mikku (a drum and its beater?), which delighted Gilgamesh for a while, until they happened to fall into the underworld.

So we have Lilit alive and well in the third millennium BCE, where she is already associated with darkness, night, diseases, and a sacred tree. Lilit began as a seductive, child slaying bird woman who haunted jungles, deserts, and bedrooms. Her primary victims were embryos, babies, and infants. There are numerous talismans with Lilith's name that can force her to spare a sickly child. Sometimes she was a queen of nightmares, or she appeared in seductive form to haunt the dreams of lonely men and take away their seed. In Lilith you can meet your worst fears and deepest desires at once, and with a bit of luck you can learn to transcend both. Jewish tradition contains many scattered hints at Lilith, all of them unfriendly. In the *Talmud* she has wings, long hair, and seizes those who sleep alone in a house. The *Old Testament* rarely mentions her by name, but kindly identifies her as a screeching night owl. Now for the next centuries we don't hear much of Lilith, but she certainly made a return with the publication of the *Zohar* in 13th century Spain. The book, a compilation of elder texts and more recent commentaries, became the most influential work on Qabalah in Europe. In the *Zohar*, Lilith is a hot, flaming, female spirit dwelling in the depth of the abyss (3,19 a). She is a snarer of men and the ruin of the world. *Zohar* 1, 148a claims that Lilith and her mate Samael arose together like a hermaphrodite out of the dregs of wine, red like a rose, spreading outwards into all paths and ways, and calls her Serpent, Harlot, End of all Flesh, and End of Day. *Zohar* 1, 34 says that she is the soul of every creeping creature and of every beast of the field. At night, the animals are chanting to her. In *Zohar*, 1, 19b God brought Lilith out of the depths of the sea and gave her power over all children who may be punished for the sins of their fathers. She has the nature of a revolving sword and wanders through the world slaying infants. In *Zohar* 1, 148a-b she lurks at crossroads, dressed like a courtesan, to seize men and feed them a wine of viper's gall. Then she puts on her seduction-outfit. Long red hair, pale skin, six ear pendants, Egyptian and Eastern jewellery, and a scarlet dress adorned with 39 ornaments. Her mouth is like a narrow door, her tongue is a sharp sword, her lips are red, and her words are oily and enchanting. Or she assumes a more sinister form. Her dress becomes a cloak of fire, her eyes terrify, and a sword appears in her hand, dripping bitter venom. In this shape she kills those whom she has ridden. She is also known to breed demons from the sperm she gathers when she haunts men's dreams. When couples make love in the nude or (oh dear) by candlelight, this is sure to attract Lilith, who hungers for the secretions that may stain the bed (*Zohar* 1, 14b). It takes a spell plus some ritual to keep Her who is Wrapped in a Black Velvet Robe from the marital bed (*Zohar* 3, 19a in Black Koltuv 1986). According to the *Sefer Ḥasîdîm* she lives in trees and makes them bleed (Bächtold-Stäubli 2000: Vol. 5, 1302-1304). While Lilith was by no means popular in Jewish myth, she was certainly notorious. It may be thanks to the numerous European Jews, and the medieval European Qabalists, that Lilith entered Christian folklore. When the church tortured witches, the clergy frequently asked if Lilith had been worshipped. There are even folk-tales and sorceries that identify her with the Germanic Helja, Holle, and Hel. For good reason, such goddesses share a single nature.

When you look for elder relations of hers, you will soon come upon the Babylonian Lamashtu (Wallis Budge 1978: 104-117). In early translations her name was sometimes rendered Labartu, modern scholars read the name as Lamashtu. Like Lilith, or the 'Queen of the Night', Lamashtu appears as a nude woman with wings and bird claws instead of feet. Unlike her later form, Lamashtu usually has the head of a lion (or stands on a pair of them). Like Lilith, Lamashtu is a slayer of infants. The Babylonians feared to utter her name. All miscarriages were attributed to her baleful influence. Sorcerers called her up to bring fever and destruction to their enemies, see the *Maklû spells* (Ungnad 1921: 243-258). Sorcerers and witches made images of people and sent Lamashtu after them, but with the proper ritual knowledge, and the help of the fire god, her baleful influence could be returned to the spell-caster. *You have given pictures of me to Lamashtu, the Daughter of Anu, in vain!* goes one banishing. In some exorcisms images of Lamashtu herself were burned. A text from the library of Assurbanipal associates Lamashtu with sadness, heartache, headache, toothache, and unspecified serious diseases. The late Assyrian collection *Evil Fiends* calls her a night-demon and states that she fills the body with pain (Ungnad 1921: 280, 281). To placate her, and to make her return to the wilderness or underworld from which she came, she received a range of offerings. These include jewellery, a cloak, a spindle, foodstuff (provisions for the journey), water and grain (for beer), sandals for her feet, and oil for annointment. Thus, she was beseeched to travel westwards across the mountains that block the way to the underworld, or return to swamp and jungle, far from human habitations. We are exceptionally lucky to have several cheerful inscriptions praising her. Here is my favourite (slightly paraphrased after Wallis-Budge):

The Six Names of Lamashtu

Lamashtu, Daughter of Anu (God of the Stars) is thy first name.
The second is Sister of the Gods of the Streets.
The third is Sword which Splittest the Skull.
The fourth is She who Kindleth a Fire.
The fifth is Goddess, (the sight) of Whose Face causeth Horror.
The sixth is Committed to the Hands.

The six names are useful for meditation. They can also be identified with the six sides of a dice, should you wish to develop a pretty sinister oracle. Afraid? Desirous? Lilith can take you beyond both.

This is all good evidence for a sinister nightside goddess who has a lot in common with the Yoginīs and many drastic Tantric goddesses. Which may remind you of Lalitā, the most popular goddess of several Tantric systems. Is she related to Lilith? Here I can only offer a sigh and a shrug. In her own, charming way, Lilith is a very specific goddess. By contrast, Lalitā is such a cosmic, all-including goddess that pretty much anything can be argued regarding her nature. A few of her thousand names have similarities to Lilith, but then, with a thousand names, Lalitā has something in common with any deity. That's her job specification.

Secret Sacraments

To combine lovemaking with ritual is an ancient idea. You can find traces of it in the early *Vedas.* Ritual coitus appeared in some of the Soma rites. It was not the main thing in generating Soma, but it was certainly part of the extensive ritual schedule. When we come to the Upaniṣadic period, things had cooled down a little. The rites had undergone a lot of refinement and what used to be coupling for higher purposes turned into symbolic coupling. You might call this prudish. However, a lot of the rites found in the early *Vedas* are a bit simple and direct. Mock battles, ritual haggling for the Soma plant, beating up the seller of Soma and suchlike fun had a certain crude appeal. The seers of the *Upaniṣads* went a long way to reduce such elements. They also reduced the importance of Soma itself by replacing drugged glory with cultivation of the mind. When we look into the *Upaniṣads* we encounter a few references that point at sacred sexuality. Here we are talking about symbolism. The *Upaniṣads*, as a whole, are not very keen on lovemaking, in fact, most of them are strictly against anything that might be fun. Now the thing about ancient Indian literature is that it never went out of fashion. Each movement went to extremes when it came to proving that its teachings (no matter how freshly invented) can be found in earliest literature. In this sense, the few brief references to sacred sexuality may have been just the sort of thing that certain proto-Tantric lineages needed to make up a past to be proud of. Take, for instance, the identification of the yoni with the fire altar, as in the *Chāndogya Upaniṣad*:

> *1. Women, verily, O Gautama, is the (sacrificial) fire, of this the sexual organ is the fuel, what invites is the smoke, the vulva is the flame, what is done inside is the coals, the pleasures the sparks.*
>
> *2. In this fire the gods offer (the libation of) semen; from this offering arises the foetus. (5, 8. 12)*

But life goes a lot beyond mere procreation. Fire creates, but fire also maintains, and provides you with food, warmth, and light. Beyond this, fire destroys. Every Indian knew that after death, the body goes into the pyre.

> *When born, he lives whatever the length of his life may be. When he has departed, they (his friends) carry him to the appointed place for the fire (of the funeral pyre), from which indeed he came, from which he arose. (5, 9, 2)*

Yoni, sacrificial fire, and funeral fire are interchangeable. The vulva brings forth, nourishes, maintains, devours, hides in potential, and brings forth again. Seen in this light, a simple gesture, like pouring ghī into a flame, may contain an amazing wealth of hidden meaning.

Well, the seers of the *Upaniṣads* were still open minded enough to discuss such matters. With the advent of early Hinduism, things became a lot more prudish and many spiritual seekers successfully eliminated lovemaking from their lifestyle. When we reach early Tantra, around the middle of the first millennium CE, lovemaking returns into ritual. From the little we know of the earliest Tantric systems it appears that several of them made a point of including sexuality (along with everything else) in their spiritual discipline. Just how this happened and what it was like remains an open question. The early centuries of Tantra remain shrouded in obscurity. We know that some folks, such as the kāpālikas, included wine, meat, and lovemaking in their quest for liberation, and that some kāpālikas lived in relationships that may be loosely classed as marriage. The happy couples may have lived out on the road, begging for alms, and often getting into trouble with followers of the mainstream religions. So we do have folk who made love for spiritual reasons. But just what does this expression mean? Modern New Age Tantra, for what it's worth, tends to emphasise beauty, orgasm, refined sensuality, deification of gender, and silly postures. If our early tāntrikas went for such things, they certainly forgot to mention them. What emerges more frequently is the magic of the secretions.

Figure 49 - Skanda / Kārrtikeya.

As you read earlier, menstrual blood (rakta, rajas), vaginal secretions (rasa), and sperm (śukra), not to mention urine and faeces, are among the most dreaded substances in Hinduism. All of them are mightily polluting, dangerous, and abhorred. This, of course, made them interesting for any free thinking sorcerer. Now several early systems, such as the Kaulas, made a point of exploring taboos by breaking them. This goes for cremation place ritual just as it goes for body-chemistry. The generation of magically potent sexual secretions is one of the most important matters in Kaula. Indeed, it is the thing that makes Kaula possible at all. Kaula, and its relation, Kula, are based on the concept of the clan, group, or cluster, and the goddess who represents them. We encounter her as the Kuladevatā, the goddess who represents the cluster, group, or lineage. From the Kula-goddess, the fluids flow which make the group a continuity. Kaulas were initiated with these sacraments. Indeed, the lineage of each group is an oral tradition, a tradition of fluids passed to and from each mouth.

Science of Rasa

Here we encounter the wonderful term rasa. Rasa is an amazingly complex idea. On the simplest level, rasa is fluids of all sorts, including sap, juices, water, and a wide range of body products. As fluids connect with emotion, rasa can also be a term for feelings, passions, and the like. Rasa is also the taste of something, or its flavour, in the same sense that music or a painting have a certain 'flavour' (call it 'mood' if you like). Sexual secretions also come under the heading of rasa, good thinking, as they combine fluid qualities with intensely emotional experience. Finally, rasa came to be used as a term for mercury.

Here we encounter a lovely bit of confusion. I am sure you'll like this one. India has a long tradition of alchemy. The first alchemists, if we may call them that, were seers of the Vedic age who sought to extend their lifespans by several strategies. Magic was one, sacrifices was another, and a third was mucking about with plants. The *Vedas* abound with plant lore. Plants were spirits, of course, but they were also substances to experiment with. Many were worn as amulets but some were ingested. Surely there must exist a herb somewhere which could extend human life over a hundred years? Such dreams were also entertained by Chinese sorcerers. Unlike their Vedic colleagues, the Chinese also explored a wide range of minerals. Powdered stalactites and stalagmites, sea shells, metals, ores, minerals, coral, and pearls were tested, plus a wide range of flowers, plants, parts of trees (pine was a favourite), and animal products. What we know as 'alchemy' is a Chinese invention. There were loads of enterprising sages who sought to extend their lives by collecting dew, breathing sunlight, eating minerals, ingesting mercury, and refining their true self-nature. A good many of them poisoned themselves in the process. Most of them were crazy loners but there were also some noblemen and even a few emperors who died in the hope of attaining a long life. One of the reasons for this is the fact that mercury and cinnabar (red mercury sulphite) have strong, observable effects on the body and that, unless you overdose them, death comes slowly. Both minerals were available in China, but they are extremely rare in India. The Indian alchemists imported them from China, together with the lore on how to use them. It must have caused them a lot of trouble.

If you look into early Chinese alchemical literature you will soon discover that none of its authors bothered to speak in simple terms. Such texts abound in enigmatic symbolism. Green dragon, white tiger, celestial mercury, true lead, heaven and earth, moon and sun, weaving girl and herding boy, true yang born out of total yin in the hour of the living midnight... all of these were mystifying enough to the Chinese reader. I wonder what the Indian seers made out of them. You can spend a lot of time struggling through classics like the *Cantong Qi* without comprehending what Wei Boyang was really talking about. Often enough, symbols can be exchanged for each other, and what looks like mineral chemistry in one verse is treated as a family relationship, crazy mythology, numerology, or entirely abstract meditative transformation in another. When you read of the union of red and white it's entirely your guess whether the term refers to sperm and menstrual blood, cinnabar and mercury, or the circulation of coloured vapours in the ovens of your body. The same problem appears in Indian alchemy. There is a wide range of Tantras which deal with the chemistry of immortality. Some of them may be chemical textbooks, others might refer to meditation and visualisation or suggest ritual. It is by no means easy to work out what's really going on. This has a simple reason. Many seers did not give a damn for any approach as such. They simply wanted to extend their lives, gain magic powers, become free to do their will, and went for anything that looked promising. Thus, when the *KJN* details how one should keep the rasa in the mouth while breathing in a certain way, we have no way of knowing whether Matsyendranāth was talking about sexual secretions or mercury. Both answers are not only possible but likely. The alchemy of minerals was not an obscure side-aspect of Tantric practice, in several systems it was the main thing. The Siddha saints in particular attempted to blend medical drugs, and mercurial alchemy with Haṭhayoga and complex inner visualisations. For a brilliant study of this topic, see White 1996.

Fluid Gnosis

While the alchemy of minerals is a fascinating subject, it may also be a little unhealthy for people who like to explore Tantra practically. While countless Indians, ranging from obscure saints to mighty Mogul princes, were keen on munching mercury, nowadays people would much prefer if there was less of the stuff polluting our environment. So let us return to substances that can be generated in the laboratory of the body. They are not all there is to Tantric rasāyana, the science of fluids, but at least they are available.

Figure 50 - One way of doing Yoni-mudrā.
Stone. Kajuraho.

What is so special to secretions of the body? For one thing, the Hindu scholars believed sperm and menstrual blood are the fluids that form a child. In this sense they are literally the materials of life. What could be better to extend life than to feed on the raw materials that make up every living being? Next, they are highly polluting, hence magically potent. This sort of thing appealed to the Kaulas. When I say Kaulas you are probably thinking of obscure worshippers dwelling hidden in society or living as ascetics on the fringes, haunting cremation places and jungle hermitages. Not a bad idea but certainly not good enough. Remember that there was a period, between the 9th and the 13th century, when a number of Indian kings went for Kaula rituals. Some of them openly displayed their excesses as erotic sculpture on temple walls. Others sought trained priestesses for rituals that were meant to subjugate their rivals. A lot of Tantra is concerned with magic. Again and again you read that certain practices grant siddhis (here: magical skills) such as the power to subjugate kings, conquer kingdoms, or shake cities. Such goals were rarely attractive to lone, ash-smeared nutters looking for liberation. They appealed primarily to regents who wanted to stabilise their realm and crush their enemies. In general, kings are not a very spiritual lot, and they usually want to profit from religion. Divine blessings may be well and good, but what counts to a regent is political power. White gives a magnificent example (1996: 308-9). Meet king Cakravarman, who won the throne of Kashmir in 936 CE and ruled for just one year. One bonny night Cakravarman was entertained by an outcaste Ḍom singer called Raṅga and his two daughters Haṁsī and Nāgalatā, both of them accomplished dancers. Their names are interesting: Haṁsī is the female form of Haṁsa, the breath-soul-spirit of the height, often represented as a goose, gander, or swan, while Nāgalatā, rendered 'Serpentina' by White, refers to the subterranean Nāgas, the serpent spirits who influenced the Kuṇḍalinī concept so much. Indeed, what appears as a serpent when dormant in body becomes the free breathing water-bird of the soul when it awakes and rises. The two dancers quickly enchanted the king. One of them began to hug and kiss the columns in the king's hall while the other, while singing with trembling earrings, mimed sexual frenzy in the viparīta posture. It blew the king's mind. He soon married the two and made them his queens. This was not an entirely wise move, as the two girls came from one of the lowest classes. Partners from the Ḍom class may be esteemed among crazy Tāntrikas, but they were certainly not respected by the Brahmins and warriors of the court. Indeed, it is said that the two introduced their families and relations to the court and that the whole place, just like the king, became irrevocably polluted. The king saw this in a different light. He adored his new wives and tried to enforce their high rank. White records that it became a great honour to feed on the leftovers from their plates, and that their relations, all of them Ḍoms, attained ministerial rank and proudly wore the mens-stained clothes of the queens over their splendid courtly costume. In the end, so disapproving historians noted, the king became totally mad. Allegedly he raped a Brahmin woman and executed a number of his allies. The survivors were not amused. One night they assassinated king Cakravarman in the royal latrine, and flayed his body as it was lying on one of his queens. Cakravarman got a lot of bad press. Nevertheless, the episode, real or imaginary, shows that some regents went for 'pollution' in order to win power.

So what were the secretions used for? The normal use is to dissolve them in water or wine, bless them with ritual, and ingest them. Let's look into the *KJN*. As an early Tantra the good book is astonishingly outspoken and to the point. Chapter 11, verse 11 informs us that the five pure and eternal substances of the Kaula Āgama are ashes, wife's nectar (female discharge), śukra (sperm), rakta (menstrual blood), and ghī (clarified butter). These are offered in daily ritual and in special rites for the fulfilment of desire (12). It is the 'Great Discharge', elsewhere symbolised by the letter ḥ, which produces the desired magical powers.

Verse 32 says: *One should always consume the rajas and the śukra.*

One should pour Rakta and Śukra in equal proportions, using either Kuṇḍa, Gola or Udbhava, mixed with wine and ghee. Rakta is the Vāmāmṛta; mixed with wine and Śukra ist is the absolute itself. (KJN, 18, 7-8, trans. Mike Magee). The mixture is fermented with buk flowers and black flowers to produce a ritual wine (9). In general worship, equal amounts of rakta and śukra should be offered (15). Taking the mixture directly from the (lower) mouth of the Yoginī one gains siddhi (22). What remains is placed in a pot of conch as a general offering (22).

Extracting the fluids from the yoni of the yogīnī is a vital part of the rite. One way is to allow them to drip on a special leaf. Another is to extract them by tongue.

> *'Those who desire to acquire a supernatural power should consume the ejaculated form. Then they should worship with it alone since it is a most pure substance because of its proximity to consciousness and the [ejaculated form], since it is stated to go especially from mouth to mouth, in reciprocal fashion, being intent on bestowing eternal youth and immortality, is designated as kula. It is supreme.' (Abhinavagupta,Tantrāloka, in Dupuche 2006:268-69)*

In shared rituals, the secretions go from the yoni to the mouth of the worshipper, who passes them to the mouth of the Śakti, who returns some to the worshipper, who passes the remnant in a bowl for other worshippers. Hence, the mingled fluids of the two, being of the essence of Brahman, can feed and enlighten the whole group (kula). The whole rite echoes a cyclic process. Abhinavagupta again:

> *''Emanation', 'Permanance', 'Reabsorption' and 'the Nameless' constitute the set of four in the krama [tradition]. He should worship [the set of four] in connection with 'sacred sites' and 'cremation ground' with a view to enjoyment and liberation.' (Dupuche, 2006:218)*

Here, the 'sacred sites' are the genitals while 'cremation ground' is the voidness of the heart, and its eternal, vibratory pulsation. Extracting the rasa by oral stimulation happens in a posture that may be called yoni-mudrā. This term has a lot of different meanings in various traditions. Feeding from the lower mouth appears prominently in erotic temple sculptures of the Kaula tradition. When the act does not appear among the images, you can be fairly sure that the whole thing was commissioned by a king who wanted to boast about his sexual achievements, but had no Kaula training nor any sort of sense. The mixture was sometimes washed or combed out of the sādhikā's pubic hair. A complicated method appears in the *Picumata* where a ritual circle with eight segments is drawn. The phonemes are assigned to the segments. The Śakti is brought to excitement and lays down in the centre of the sign. Next, the sādhaka should perform his personal ritual, satisfy her with gifts and *having brought his Śakti to excitement, he should wash her generative organ; he should collect all the water, with the blood, into a vessel.* (Goudriaan & Gupta 1981: 44) Did they have intercourse at all? Who knows?

Others propose that the sacrament should be kept under the tongue so that its essence can go directly to the brain. In my experience, a mouth full of mingled secretions is a wonderful way of getting all gods excited. They just come roaring up the spine and cluster in head and throat to get their share. Often enough trembling happens spontaneously. In private worship, both participants partake of the sacrament. In larger assemblies, the leaders of the rite generated the substance in private, mixed it with water or wine, and shared it with the assembly.

The sacrament is not only used internally. As a truly magical substance, it was involved in countless rites and sorceries. *KJN*, 11, 38-40 has it that repeatedly making a brow mark of kuṇḍa, gola, or udbhava menses heals leprosy and smallpox, and frees the sādhaka from all diseases just as a serpent sheds its skin. The three types of menses appear in several texts. According to Woodroffe (1972: 92) svayambhū is the kula flower of any woman, kuṇḍa the menses of a girl whose mother conceived her in adultery with a Tāntrika, and gola the menses of the daughter of a widow. Louise Finn (1986: 87) cites the *Śyāmārahasya*, where kuṇḍa is simply the mingled sexual fluids, and gola the menses of a widow. She adds the comments of a contemporary Tāntrika, according to whom kuṇḍa is the blood of the first menstruation of a girl conceived in adultery, and gola is the first menstrual blood of a girl after the death of her father. According to Śrī Batohi Jha (also cited by Finn), svayambhū is the blood of any woman's first menstruation. Here we can be sure that the fluids were not ingested for purely biochemical reasons. The blood of a widow or an illegitimate girl is especially favoured as it contains, in normal Hindu thought, a lot of extra pollution. For the daring Kaula adept, such special 'flowers' contain an extraordinary amount of sheer power.

Menstrual blood or sexual secretions appear prominently when it comes to drawing yantras. *KCT* 4, 35 recommends drawing a Kālī yantra on a Tuesday night at the cremation ground using a kula stick (?) and kula vermillion. Likewise, the *Vāmakeśvara Tantra*, chapter 2, discusses various ways of drawing the Śrī Yantra. It recommends a lot of substances for painting the sign, among them, depending on how you read the code words, menstrual blood and sperm. There is more to such sorceries but I'm sure you can make up your own.

Finally, there is the matter of astrology. Some Tāntrikas attached great importance to the lunar stations, to the fifteen kalās of the waxing and the fifteen kalās of the waning moon. Put very simply, kalā is a digit, a unit. This is not a Tantric idea, it is a basic of Indian astronomy. The moon has kalās, but so has the sun, fire, and all of the planets. Anything that can be calculated in units appears as kalās. A list of the kalās appears in the schedule of the Five Ms ritual (for which see the previous chapter). Now, some Tāntrikas thought that there should be a 16th kalā, a unit of perfection that includes all others. This supreme kalā appears on the night of the 15th, but only under special circumstances and in very special states of awareness. Others thought that sixteen kalās are not good enough and added a 17th. The sixteen kalās may be related to the phases of the moon, but there is more to them. To each Kalā corresponds one of the sixteen vowels. These, in turn, have a lot of symbolic meaning. In the *Parātrīśikālaghuvṛttiḥ*, Abhinavagupta explains that the vowels are called 'lunar stations' as they fill the stations of the 'moon of consciousness'. A refers to anuttara (the ultimate), Ā to ānanda (bliss), I to will (icchā), Ī to domination (īśanā), U is opening (unmeṣa),

Ū is decrease (ūnatā). The phonemes Ṛ, Ṝ, Ḷ, Ḹ arise when objects appear in will and domination. The phonemes E and Ai appear out of the union of will and domination with the ultimate and bliss. The phonemes O and Au appear when opening and decrease unite with the ultimate and bliss. Finally there appears bindu as ṁ, representing the knowing subject. Last of the lot is visarga, Ḥ, the emissional state or the great discharge, which is inherent in the other 15. Using such attributions, the nights of the lunar fortnight could be identified with all sorts of magical qualities. So could the nights of the personal fortnight of the Śakti, i.e. her menstrual cycle. The result is a complex science of astrological energies. Using such calculations, the adepts were able to evoke specific powers, depending on the night of the Śakti's menstruation. These topics are treated in great detail in the works of Kenneth Grant. However, not all Tantric lineages made use of them. A good many lineages did not care for astrology at all and boldly proposed that for ritual, or pūjā, any time is good and any place is suitable. I can only agree.

Last, let's have a bit of common sense. I am sure you are all eager to experiment with these matters. However, this is the age of AIDS and other unpleasant diseases. It may be possible to catch an infection when you ingest sexual secretions. Use your brains (not the glands) for thinking. I know this is hard, especially for males. All the blood required for a stable erection goes missing in the brain. However, it might be a good idea to do your sādhana with a partner you have been together with for a while. Or to have an AIDS test. If you go for bed-hopping, things may be a little risky. For this reason, some magical organisations make a point of baking the fluids into cakes. Heating the stuff in an oven is one way of destroying the virus.

The Partner for You

Tantric literature is very specific about the people qualified to do these rituals. After all, the secretions in themselves are not good enough. Having an orgasm is not good enough. It is only when your mind fuses with the mind of your partner, when both of you experience a state of bliss and rapture and the whole thing happens in a spiritual frame that takes you beyond your sorry little ego that the sacraments have any power at all. Without a proper charge, the secretions are power in potential. Produced properly, in a state transcending mere copulation, they take on the consciousness and power of the act. This is more than repeating a mantra or imagining something holy (or desirable) during orgasm. All of the act goes to inform the fluids with a specific energy/consciousness. Loveplay does not begin in bed, it starts a long time earlier. When there is love and sharing between your partner and yourself, you both leave the arena of separate human stupidity and open up to something larger and wiser than either of you. This is the beginning of the rite, and if you can't do this properly you may well forget about the rest. The rite needs a minimum of two participants if done on the physical plane. If you are on your own you may simply awake the parts of you that are of the other sex and make love within yourself. Anyway, it takes two to do this right. When I say 'two' I mean two competent worshippers. It's not enough to do the Crowley thing, to sleep with some uninformed (and often drunk) prostitute, to visualise one's desire during orgasm, and to feed on the secretions without offering her any. Just look at Crowely's sex-magick diaries. In Crowley's highly initiated opinion, things imagined during orgasm are supposed to manifest (sorry for putting the GREAT SECRET so simply). The old goat went to great lengths to prove the efficiency of his method. Sadly, the statistics show that usually it didn't work at all. Most of his operations were for money, which he rarely got and soon spent, for fame, which eluded him most of his life, and good looks... well, you'll be the judge of that. Focusing your mind on a desire during orgasm is not good enough. Doing such magick with an inexperienced partner is plain irresponsible. The Kaulas were quite aware of this point. Just as there are long catalogues on what a guru should be like, there are specifications of the qualities of a student. And there are specifications on the qualities of the Śakti. All participants have to be qualified. All have to travel actively on the spiritual path of their choice, all have to be independently minded enough to get along on their own. More so, daily practice is a must. The discipline you need to learn what really matters to you, and the joy of clearing up your mind, taking out the garbage and reorganising the personality to make it a vehicle for the greater self. Unless you sort yourself out for many years, and your partner does the same, you two won't be competent for Tantric union.

Last, a word on consciousness. Abhinavagupta distinguishes between 'the risen', which is your awareness focused on the sacred sites of the partner, and 'the resting', which is your awareness resting within yourself. In coupling, 'the risen' and 'the resting' alternate, as awareness expands and contracts, again and again. Here we have two who experience self, in themselves and each other. But as self is undivided, it is one consciousness, and indeed one self (or non-being) which comes together. *'The expression of differentiated thought subsides for the pair who are in that state ...'* recorded Abhinavagupta. *'... it is the universal, generous bliss which is composed of both. The supreme kaula is neither 'rested' nor 'risen'; it is the cause which produces the 'rested' and 'rise' ... the nature of consciousness, i.e. of the goddess, is in the highest meaning of the word undivided.' (Dupuche 2006:260-61)*

14: Mahāvidyās

Ten Principles of Wisdom

Many Indian religions have gone to considerable lengths to make their favourite deity the supreme and all-including divinity. There are also a few movements who chose to promote a supreme selection of deities. In these cults we find clusters of deities that share the same or a similar essence, flavour, and mode of manifestation. Gods can be grouped according to similarity, but usually our worshippers went beyond this and proposed a group that is similar but also different, to provide a range of choices and options. Viṣṇu's ten (or more) incarnations are such a case. They are alike in that they share a certain amount of Viṣṇuness, but they are also different, as the god appeared and acted differently in each of his manifestations. The worshipper enjoys a range of choices. Some incarnations are good for one object, some for another. The worshipper can select a form of the deity that suits her or him, and proceed to other incarnations of the deity to learn more and more aspects of a complex and fascinating totality. Whoever has celebrated, worshipped, and become all ten incarnations stands a good chance of understanding the essence of them all. This is a crucial step. The clusters of deities stand between the single and the multiple expression of divinity. There are numerous groups of deities in Hindu religion. Think of the nine Durgās, the ten Yoginīs, the sixty-four Yoginīs, the eight Bhairavas, the five to thirteen Kālīs, the Mātṛkās, and a good deal more. Why do some prefer nine Durgās or eight Bhairavas to a single one?

People tend to think in terms of individuality. They like to imagine their gods as persons, just as they personify pets, places, and vehicles. The gods thrive on this, to an extent, as it makes contact with humans more emotional and direct. The disadvantage lies in the fact that any personality is limiting. Whatever mask you wear, as long as it is the only one, you are stuck in it. Well, the gods have as much need to break out of their personalities as humans do. In Indian religion this seems to be easier than in other faiths. Gods often share attributes and appearances; they blend into one another, change gender, swap titles, myths, and functions, and as long as there is no single dogma to religious practice, will continue to do so. Names, symbols, and definitions of behaviour are all well and good for limited purposes and specific occasions. When it comes to liberating yourself from restrictions, do yourself a favour by transcending the limits of personality, both of your gods and your own. Now the divine can be approached personally (one specific god) or universally (all gods in a single package). Between them, and easier to handle, are specific groups or clusters of deities. In this chapter we will explore the ten Mahāvidyās. The word Mahāvidyā consists of mahā = great and vidyā = supreme knowledge, science, magic formula, wisdom, liberating experience. Like the Gnosis of the European mystics, vidyā is direct experience beyond the need to think or deliberate. A vidyā is both a store of divine knowledge and an experience that liberates from delusions. Now, the ten Mahāvidyās appear as a group of powerful goddesses that were especially popular among followers of the Left-Hand path. As a group they may be almost a thousand years old, but several of them are considerably older. They are best-known and most popular in northern India, Bengal, and Nepal. Half of them share a certain aggressive temper, the others are supposed to be benevolent. Don't underestimate the ones with gentle appearance, all Mahāvidyās have their own little ways of transforming and transcending what you consider your personality. They are all personified as goddesses, which does not mean that they are women, just as the gods are not males. If you believe that any god is male or female you don't even understand a quarter of it. Gods have appearances, and as long as humans make such a fuss about gender, the gods will appear in humanoid shapes including gender attributes. This does not mean that they are male or female nor human at all: don't mistake the package for the contents. Divine form is a convenience.

To begin with, let's have a look at the ten Mahāvidyās. As you probably guessed the lists do not agree. If you feel like including other deities in your personal worship, ask them. Whoever brought the Mahāvidyās together did so in the interest of uniting several distinct religious movements. Some of the goddesses are popular in Kaula and Krama, others have strong links to the Tantric Buddhists of the Himalayas, to folk worship, and to the Śrī Vidyā tradition.

The 14th century *Toḍala Tantra* was and is especially popular in Bengal. It gives the following list of Mahāvidyās. 1. Kālī, especially Dakṣiṇā Kālī. 2. Tārā, also called Tāriṇī. 3. Tripurasundarī. 4. Bhuvanasundarī or Bhuvaneśvarī . 5. Bhairavī. 6. Chinnamastā. 7. Dhūmāvatī. 8. Bagalā. 9. Mātaṅgī. 10. Kamalā. The text also mentions Durgā, who is not usually a member of the group.

The *Muṇḍamāla Tantra* gives the same list, but replaces Tripurasundarī with Śoḍaṣī. The *Mahābhāgavatapurāna* (8, 62) gives the following order: 1. Kālī. 2. Tārā. 3. Kamalā 4. Bhuvaneśvarī 5. Chinnamastā. 6. Śoḍaṣī. 7. Sundarī. 8.Balāmukhī. 9. Dhūmāvatī. 10. Mātaṅgī.

In the late *Yoni Tantra*, patala 3, the Mahāvidyās are attributed to different parts of the female genitals. You find Devī at the base of the yoni and Naganandini within. Kālī and Tārā are in the yoni cakra (circle), the pubic hair is the abode of Cchinnamastaka. Bagalamukhi and Mataṅgī appear on the edges. Mahālakṣmī, Śoḍaṣī, and Bhuvanśvarī are within. Candalī is in the centre. Again, we arrive at eleven Mahāvidyās. Here the attribution of the goddesses to different parts of the female genitals is an aid for meditation. In patala 8, a different list appears: 1.

Kālī. 2. Tripurā. 3. Śoḍaṣī. 4. Bhuvaneśvarī 5. Chin-Tārā. 6. Mahālakṣmī. 7. Mātaṅgī. 8. Sundarī. 9. Bhairavī. 10. Dakṣiṇā. 11.Tārinī.

In the *Kubjikā Upaniṣad* (Schoterman 1992: 318) we find 1. Kālikā. 2. Tārā or Ugratārā. 3. Śoḍaṣī or Rājarājeśvarī 4. Bhuvaneśvarī 5. Bhairavī or Caitanyabhairavī or Annapūrṇā 6. Chinnamastā or Pracaṇḍacaṇḍikā or Pracaṇḍogracaṇḍikā 7. Dhūmāvatī. 8.Bagalāmukhī. 9. Mātaṅgī or Mātaṅginī. 10. Kamalā or Siddhilakṣmī.

The *Devī Bhāgawatam*, 7,28 goes beyond this. It does not even attempt to limit the number to ten and offers the following: 1. Kālikā. 2. Tāriṇī. 3. Śoḍaṣī. 4. Tripurā. 5. Bhairavī 6. Kamalā 7. Bagalā 8. Mātaṅgī 9. Tripurā Sundarī10. Kāmākṣī 11. Tulajā Devī. 12. Jambhinī. 13. Mohinī. 14. Chinnamastā. Plus ten-thousand armed Guhya Kālīs. This list, though impressive, is not all we can find in the good book. Book 10, chapter 8 mentions quite a few of the Mahāvidyās in a hymn of praise to Bhagavatī, who had just saved the world by destroying an army of Asuras with the help of black bees and hornets. The names appear in the following order, with praise and salutations in between: 1. Kālikā. 2. Nīla Sarasvatī. 3. Ugra Tārā. 4. Mahogrā. 5. Tripura Sundrī. 6. Bhaiarabī. 7. Mātangī. 8. Dhūmāvatī. 9. Chhiṇṇamastā. 10. Śākambharī. 11. Rakta Dantikā. 12. Lakṣmī. 13. Vijayā. 14. Gangā.

There are more lists scattered through literature. An interesting addition occurs in the fairly young *Viśvasāratantra*, which includes Kāmākhyā, goddess of menstruation. According to Stapelfeldt's invaluable study, there are shrines for the Mahāvidyas on the hills around the central sanctuary of Kāmākhyā at Kāmarūpa.

Last, there is a brief reference to the Mahāvidyās in the late *Mahānirvāna Tantra*, 9, 276. Here we find a short selection of them in a Kaula marriage rite in Śaiva form. During the wedding ceremony, and with the blessings of Kālikā and the Kaula community, the lord of the Cakra (here: ritual circle) sprinkles the bridal pair with water of oblation and the mantra: *May Rāja-rājeśvarī, Kālī, Tāriṇī, Bhuvaneśvarī, Bagalā, Kamalā, Nityā, Bhairavī, ever protect thee both.* This marriage form is frowned upon by a good many orthodox upper class folk, as it ignores class and age restrictions. It can be performed in two ways: for the purpose of the specific ritual cakra (this marriage is dissolved after the woman menstruates again, showing that she is not pregnant) or for life.

The Mahāvidyās are closely related to the tale of Śiva and Satī. This story occurs in countless variations. The one given here is based partly on the *Bṛhaddharma Purāṇa*, summarised by Sanjukta Gupta (in White 2000). It is not quite the usual form of the tale, as it portrays a Satī who is very much in control of her own fate. As you will remember, Satī was the daughter of the ancient god Dakṣa. Dakṣa was not pleased that Satī had married the ash-smeared, semi-nude Śiva, a deplorable drop-out who spent much of his time wandering in the desolation of mountains and wilderness, consuming drugs, and practising yoga. In his eyes Śiva was a social failure and Satī a disobedient child. Consequently, the couple was not invited to the great sacrifice that Dakṣa was giving for all other gods.

Figure 51 - Tārā.

Figure 52 - Tārā yantras.
Top: *Mantramahodahtiḥ,* also used to invoke Dhūmāvatī; bottom, contemporary India.

Hearing the news, Satī became raging mad. She declared that she was going to the sacrifice with or without invitation. This worried Śiva, who did not much appreciate social events and feared that Satī would be insulted or ridiculed. He tried to placate her, but this only aroused her anger and made her appear in her true form, as black Mahākālī. Now Śiva had not known that his wife was really Kāli, and that the personality of Satī had been a mask assumed for incarnation. Scared, he turned and ran away. She shouted after him, but confused as he was he just kept running. Trying to stop him, she assumed another form and blocked his way. Śiva turned again and ran in another direction. Ten manifestations of Satī appeared in the process: Kālī before him (east); Tārā above him; Chinnamastā (south); Bagalā (west); to his left (north) Bhuvaneṣvarī; to the south-east Dhūmāvatī; to the south-west Sundarī; Mātaṅgī to the north-west; Śoḍaṣī to the north-east and within himself Bhairavī. Encompassed by the goddess, Śiva stopped, considered and apologised. He now understood that his wife was sure to go where she wanted and to do as she willed. And so she did. Satī went to Dakṣa's feast, with disastrous consequences.

Another geometrical layout appears in the yantra described in the *Kubjikā Upaniṣad* where Siddhilakṣmī (The Lakṣmī who grants Perfection/Magical Power) occupies the central spot. Around her are Kālikā and Tārā or Ugratārā, plus Śoḍaṣī or Rājarājeśvarī, who form the central triangle. It is surrounded by a hexagon with the other goddesses on the points. Around the hexagon is an eight-petaled lotus surrounded by an octagon and a square with four gates. This is the principal yantra used in the worship of Kubjikā, the Curvaceous, Crooked, or Coiled One, the Lady of the Western Tradition.

Let's take a closer look at the Mahāvidyās. The following account leans heavily on the *Mantra Mahodhadhiḥ*, the *Toḍala Tantra* and the odd reference here and there. In the *Toḍala Tantra*, the description is altogether too short. It does, however, provide each of the goddesses with a specific form of Śiva as a partner. In meditation, the two are usually visualised together, and the worshipper identifies with both at once. Several Tantras, such as the *Toḍala Tantra* and the *Muṇḍamāla Tantra* also offer lists of Viṣṇu's ten incarnations and how they relate to the Mahāvidyās. Attempts to integrate followers of Viṣṇu? Personally, I find that these correspondences make less sense than the Śaivite forms. However, as you have a brain of your own you'll be delighted to think about this for yourself. The order given in the *Muṇḍamāla Tantra* (*MT*) appears at the end of each section. As you can see, some of the goddesses are so popular that they have long histories of independent worship, while others are little known and hard to research. (Note: two years after writing this chapter, I came upon David Kinsley's *The Ten Mahāvidyās - Tantric Visions of the Divine Feminine*. I have added a few items from that book but leave it to you, for completeness sake, to get your own copy for more details.)

Kālī is the best known deity of the group. She is also identified, one way or another, with several goddesses of the cluster. Some even propose that the entire group consists of Kālī manifestations (or Tripurā, or Lakṣmī). Her iconography among the ten Mahāvidyās shows her black, naked, intoxicated, with dishevelled hair, lolling tongue, and a range of items such as cleaver, severed head, skull cup, scissors, serpents, plus a necklace of skulls, and a girdle of severed hands. Usually she stands or sits on Śiva, who lies like a corpse beneath her. This also goes for several Mahāvidyās. Among the corpse-sitters, habitual or occasional, are Tārā, Tripurā, Bagalā, Dhūmāvatī, and Mātaṅgī. Kālī has a wide range of appearances. As the next chapter is devoted to Kālī's Kula, she is only briefly introduced in this one. If you want more, close your eyes and embrace the dark. When you can breathe darkness, eat darkness, and drink darkness you will understand. Night is not the absence of light, it is the primal void of the pre-create. Kālī is making love with Bhairava Mahākāla, i.e. the Fear-Inspiring Great Time/Devourer. This is a dark form of Śiva with bulging eyes, huge teeth, gaping mouth, adorned with skulls and serpents. He is one of the few male gods modelled on a goddess: Mahākāla is the expression of Mahākālī in male form. The two are lovers; in meditation, she is often visualised sitting on him, having one earth shaking orgasm after another. The *MT* couples Kālī with Kṛṣṇa, mainly because both are black.

Tārā is a popular goddess of Northern India and Nepal. The Hindu Tārā is not identical with the Buddhist goddess Tārā, of whom exist a wide range of variations, aspects, and specific manifestations. It is by no means easy to determine her origin. Buddhists texts give the first references to her in the 7th century CE. The Buddhist Tārā is usually a beautiful young girl of sixteen years, playful and benevolent, who often acts as a saviour. This is not unlike some Hindu descriptions of Kālī and Ṣoḍaśī, both of whom may appear like playful sixteen year old girls. The number sixteen may be a direct reference to the lunar kalās, it is also a number denoting completeness. Fifteen units make up a fortnight, the 16th is beyond them and, in essence, beyond time. She has some fierce and sinister shapes but is generally worshipped as the essence of compassion. Tārā, green and white, was also identified with the wives of the Tibetan king Songsten Gampo who attempted to introduce Buddhism into his country in the seventh century. In spite of royal patronage, the locals did not take to the new creed and continued to practice their native shamanism. Tārā became a popular goddess in Tibet around the eleventh century, when Buddhism was firmly established. In the process, a native folk legend had to be re-constructed. Originally, so the Tibetans believed, their people had been born out of the union of a monstrous rock giantess and a monkey. Buddhism identified the ogress with Tārā, and the monkey with Avalokiteśvara, the Buddha of compassion. Another Buddhist tale claims that Tārā was born out of a tear of Avalokiteśvara. Hence, the Buddhist Tārā is the essence of compassion.

The Hindu Tārā, by contrast, is generally worshipped as a wild and dangerous deity. In Hindu iconography, Tārā is very similar to Kālī. Both are generally nude or only clad in a tiger skin, both hold swords, skull cups, heads, serpents, both stand on corpses and generally exhibit a terrifying countenance. Sometimes Tārā is shown with a pregnant belly, which is rarely the case with Kālī. Kinsley claims that the only specific difference is that Kālī wears her hair open and dishevelled while Tārā has hers in a single red braid. I can't agree, there are plenty of exceptions to the rule. Tārā is sometimes shown standing on a funeral pyre or a corpse, laughing madly. Ugratārā, the Tārā who rescues her devotees from the grave (ugra) is usually blue, has three eyes, and wears a crescent moon and one or several coiled serpents on her head. In her hands are sword and knife, skull, and a blue lotus. She sits on a corpse resting on a white lotus. She is the Empress of the Three Worlds. The main function of Tārā is to save her devotees. She is associated with the secret lore of cheating death, a topic dear to the Kaulas and Nāthas, and also popular in Tibetan mysticism. She is called upon to rescue her devotees from danger, oppression, and death. The Hindu Tārā is frequently associated with the obscure Mahācīna (Great China) tradition, and with the science of alchemy, which was imported, along with the much needed mercury and cinnabar, from China. It is a possibility that she represents a Chinese goddess of alchemy. The Hindus may have accepted the new goddess, but as she lacked iconography, equipped her with the appearance of the most formidable deity in evidence: Kālī. In Bengali devotional poetry, Kālī and Tārā are not only similar but exchangeable.

Oṁ hrīṁ trīṁ hūṁ phaṭ was a popular Tārā mantra. Saint Vasiṣṭha spent considerable time with its recitation. When he could not achieve success, he cursed the goddess and the power of the mantra disappeared. Years later, the sage reconsidered. He renounced his curse and added the letter **s** to the formula. This made the mantra *as auspicious as a bride*: **Oṁ hrīṁ strīṁ hūṁ phaṭ** . Tārā was henceforth called by the *bride-like* bīja **strīm**, though some worshippers prefer the earlier bīja **trīṁ**. The second of her mantras is associated with Ekajaṭā: **hrīṁ trīṁ hūṁ phaṭ**, the third is for Nīla Sarasvatī: **hrīṁ trīṁ hūṁ.** Let's return to saint Vasiṣṭha. There are several accounts of his life, as he was one of those practical minded saints who went for Hindu and Buddhist Tantra, and achieved success (siddhi) in both disciplines. His difficulties with Tārā appear in several tales (Bharati 1983: 66-70; Kinsley 1998: 96-97). Vasiṣṭha performed tapas for a millennium but got no success. Then Brahmā told him of Tārā, the goddess who grants power to all gods, and equipped the saint with a mantra. Vasiṣṭha travelled to Kāmākhyā in Assam, to the yoni temple of the goddess, and spent another thousand years reciting the mantra. It did not work. This made the saint raging mad. In his wrath, he was about to curse the mantra, the goddess, and the world at large. Luckily, the goddess appeared. She told him that he was doing it all wrong. If Vasiṣṭha wanted to do it properly, he should go to China to learn the proper worship in the Cīna-tārā style from Viṣṇu, who was residing there in the form of the Buddha. Vasiṣṭha packed his bags and began travelling again. When he reached Tibet, he had a vision of the Buddha in the company of numerous girls. They were all naked, drunk, and having an ecstatic orgy. Vasiṣṭha almost had a heart attack. A voice from the skies told him 'This is how Tārā should be adored'. Grudgingly, Vasiṣṭha gave in. He took refuge in Viṣṇu in the form of the

Buddha, who initiated him into the Kaula Mārga and taught him the way of non-duality. And Vasiṣṭha learned. He learned that there is no difference between purity and pollution, that superior worship is internal, that women should be worshipped in ritual and respected in daily life. When Vasiṣṭha returned to Bengal, he set up a temple to Tārā at Tārāpur (today Tārāpīṭh) right next to the cremation ground, and had a happy and long life.

Tārā's worship is full of magical and morbid elements. She is a terrifying deity who grants great sorcerous powers. Her worship should preferably be done in a lonely temple, some hidden place in the forests or mountains, or at the cross-roads, at cremation places, battlefields, or in a dark and desolate house. The place should be sanctified by setting up a skull. *The Sādhaka must be looking, touching and carnally enjoying a woman while offering sacrificial oblations at midnight. He should never be envious of women. On the other hand, he should always try to keep them in good humour.* (*Mantra Mahodhadhiḥ*, 4). This is not all there is to it: just look into the good book for a stunning amount of complicated ritual details. Several are a little eccentric. Occasionally the worshipper sat on a corpse or on a dead infant. More on this further on. Tārā comes from the root tāra: carrying across (the ocean of illusory existence), a saviour, a protector (also applied to Rudra), translucence, star, meteor, and a lot of other things (see glossary). Tārā is a ruthless goddess whose prime function is to liberate the self from the demon of you. In this sense she is a microcosmic manifestation of the macrocosmic Mahākālī; where Kālī demolishes ages, cultures, planets, and (occasionally) the universe, Tārā is more concerned with the personal death of You. If you can sit on your own corpse and enjoy it, you'll learn what liberation is all about. Tārā is accompanied by Akṣobhya (Unagitated). This is usually a name of Śiva, but it can also be the title of a Buddha worshipped in Nepal and Tibet. When the cosmic milk-ocean was churned, part of the fluid turned into a lethal poison. None of the gods could handle it, apart from Śiva, who, well used to all sorts of drugs, drank the lot and remained unagitated. Only his throat turned deep blue. It earned him the title Nīlakaṇṭha (Blue-Throat). The poison-drinking is one of the more recent elements of Hindu myth, it does not appear in the original legend in the *Mahābhārata*. What poison arose from the cosmic milk-ocean? What is the most lethal toxin in the world? In several accounts the poison is sheer egoism. This toxin can be found all over the world, and pretty well in anybody, so if Śiva within is so kind as to swallow it, we can only be grateful. There are several versions of the tale. Some myths claim that Śiva became so intoxicated that he collapsed and fainted. And here we meet Tārā again, who picked up the unconscious god, bared her breasts, and fed him on her milk (transmuted menstrual blood) until his health was restored. You can occasionally find this scene in Tārā's iconography. The Śiva in her arms often appears as a youth or child.

Usually Akṣobhya is visualised in love play with Tāriṇī, goddess of delusion, but sometimes he appears as a great serpent coiled around her head. Other serpents coil around her legs, arms, fingers, they form her ear-rings, girdle, and garland. In iconography these serpents, like her

Figure 53 - Lalitā Tripurā Sundarī.

Figure 54 - Lalitā Tripurā Sundarī yantras.
Top: Contemporary India, bottom: Traditional design used in Śrī Vidyā. Also a yantra of Śrī Lakṣmī.

Figure 55 - Bhuvaneśvarī.

Figure 56 - Bhuvaneśvarī yantras.
Contemporary Northern India.

lotus, are often painted blue. Worship of Tārā is sometimes influenced by Buddhist rites, more often there is a Chinese influence (the Cīnācāra style). In the *MT* Tārā is accompanied by (or identical with) Rāma.

Lalitā Tripurasundarī is well known from the Śrī Vidyā tradition. As Lalitā Tripurasundarī she became the main goddess of that arcane tradition, see the chapter on mantra. She is the goddess of the city Śrīpura, the jewel-island Maṇi dvīpa, and the Śrī Yantra. As a highly inclusive goddess, she assimilated a lot of other deities and their mythology. In her cult, she is called Tripurā (Three Cities), Sundarī (Beautiful), Lalitā (The Playful, Wanton One), Śoḍaṣī (The Sixteenth, or Sixteen-year-old), Rājarājeśvarī (Queen of Kings), Kāmeśvarī, Pañcamī, and similar titles. Sometimes she is a triple goddess. Her followers, nowadays mostly adherents of the right-hand-path, generally worship her abstract form, i.e. her mantra and her yantra. Anthropomorphic representations exist, but are less popular as they are considered gross. Tripurā is visualised red as a mountain of cinnabar (a reference to alchemy), three eyed, and four handed, holding a bow (mind) of flowers (desire), five arrows of flowers (the senses), a book, and a mālā. Another version equips her with a flower-arrow, a sugarcane bow, an elephant-goad, and a noose. She is red, as radiant as a thousand suns, nude, long-haired, and stands on a corpse lying on four corpses. Her rites are often associated with Kāma, the god of desire and lust, who dwells in the hearts of all living beings. Tripurā is not just the main goddess of the Śrī Vidyā tradition. The name (Three Cities) in its male form (Tripura) refers to a demonic Daitya who was eventually slain by Śiva. The two share a name but very little else. Śiva called Tripurāri (Enemy of Three Cities) is the opponent of the demon, not of the goddess.

Her second form, Tripurabālā, sits in a stream of human blood, shining like the sun. She is a joyous and benevolent goddess holding book and mālā, her other hands show the gestures that dispel fear and grant boons. She is young, nude, slim, and wears strings of pearls, jewels, and a necklace of heads. She is happily drunk and smiles. The third form is called Tripurabhairavī, see below under Bhairavī.Triple goddess Tripurā is one of the elder deities of the Tantras and has assimilated an enormous amount of lore, ritual, and enlightened interpretation. Her main mantra is the celebrated

ka e ī la hrīṁ -

ha sa ka ha la hrīṁ -

sa ka la hrīṁ.

This mantra is sometimes prefixed or ended with the bījas **śrīṁ hrīṁ klīṁ aiṁ sauḥ** in various combinations. Each ingredient of the great fifteen-syllable mantra can be rearranged in order to produce specific magical effects, hence, the mantra is considered a vidyā, a supreme knowledge and a science. As Kulasundarī her mantra is **Aiṁ klīṁ sauḥ**. Tripurā is invoked by the bījas **Klīṁ** or **Aīṁ**. Her name Tripurā associates her with Three Cities, these are the cities underworld, earth, and heaven; belly, heart, and head; coarse consciousness, subconsciousness, and unconsciousness. Another interpretation makes her Tripurā as she is worshipped by the three main gods Brahmā, Viṣṇu, and Rudra/Śiva. She is the support of the three worlds. Tripurasundarī is accompanied by the five faced Śiva. For his five faces (see below), she is called The Fifth. The *MT* has Nṛsiṁha, Viṣṇu as a lion-man, as her mate.

Bhuvanasundarī or **Bhuvaneśvarī** (Queen of the Earth, Mistress of the World) holds a piece of fruit, a goad, and a noose. She has a friendly smile, her complexion is bright and she nourishes the three worlds with her huge, oozing breasts. She is sometimes associated with creation in all three worlds. This is not a singular event: in Hindu philosophy, creation is ever-present and continuous. She is also the maintainer and the destroyer of the world, in fact, she is the world herself. In this sense she may be called Sarvarūpa: She Whose Form is All. In the *Devī Bhāgavatam,* 3,3 we find her worshipped by Brahmā, Viṣṇu, and Śiva. She appears to them in the highest celestial realm, on the jewel-sparkling island Maṇi Dvīpa where insects hum and trees are laden with flowers, gems, and pearls. Here the goddess sits on a couch whose legs are formed by the main gods, adorned by rainbows, smiling blissfully. She wears red, is coloured with red sandal-paste, her red lips shine like ten millions lightning bolts, her red eyes sparkle with delight. Her bīja is **hrīṁ** and the birds of her paradise island repeat it incessantly. The gods, struck with awe, are immediately turned into goddesses and begin to worship her lotus feet.

The text identifies her with Mahāmāyā, the creatrix of the world-play, the one who is both eternal and temporal, the full, the cause of all, the one who can only be seen by yogīs. In *Devī Bhāgavatam* 11, 18 she is also identified with Mahāmāyā. It tells us that the devotee who writes her root mantra **Hrīṁ Bhuvaneśvaryai Namaḥ** with 'red sandalpaste' on the leaf of the bilva tree and offers it to her 'lotus feet' becomes Manu. Her gāyatri mantra is **Oṁ nārāyaṇyai vidmahe bhuvaneśvaryai dhīmahi. Tanno devī pracodayat** (Oṁ. Let us think of Nārāyaṇa, let us meditate on Bhuvaneśvarī. May Devī direct us). Karapātrī, in the *Śrī Bhagavatī Tattva* (Daniélou 1991: 279-280) describes her as golden, adorned with golden ornaments, and adds regarding her headdress: *With the ambrosia made from the lunar essence, that is, the seed, the sacrificial offering, soma, she quenches the thirst of the world. This is why the all-powerful goddess has the moon, the cup of soma, as her diadem... On her head are a serpent, a liṅga, and a yoni.* It is an interesting detail that the goddess who is the form of the world is beautiful. This is a typical idea of Hindu Tantra. It implies that the world, no matter whether real or unreal, true or illusionary, should be place of joy and beauty. In the *TT,* the Śiva at her side is called Tryambaka, meaning Of Three Mothers or with Three Eyes. It refers to the triple appearance of the goddess in heaven, earth, and underworld. There is also a male form of the goddess called Bhuvaneśvara, Lord of the Earth, who is usually considered a form of Śiva (*Mhb*). In the *MT* you can find her accompanied by Varāha, Viṣṇu as the primal boar-man who raised the earth out of the waters after the deluge.

Bhairavī is The Fear-Inspiring Lady, beloved of **Bhairava**, the Fear Inspiring One (Śiva). Both are terrifying deities who do their best to scare their worshippers out of their heads. Once the adherents of the cult have left the false security of their individual personality, they become Bhairavas themselves. Bhairavī appears as partner of Bhairava-Śiva. This is a highly complex form of Śiva. In literature there are quite a few Bhairavas. Some of them appear in the petals of the lotus of the heart, others are manifestations of Śiva or even his son. Bhairava and Bhairavī are widely popular in Kashmir, northern India, and Nepal. I wonder whether thy started out as independent deities and became identified with Śakti and Śiva during the early Tantric period. Both of them are universal deities. Kinsley wondered whether she is a goddess of destruction, but when I look into the Tantras that celebrate her, I cannot agree. In Abhinavagupta's lore, she is all-encompassing consciousness itself and the very essence of the heart. In the *KJN* (trans. Magee) Bhairava addresses her by numerous titles, including Devī, Lady worshipped by Vīras, Sweet Faced One, You Worshipped by the Yoginīs, Mother of Yoginīs and Heroines, Beauteous Eyed One, Self of Kula, Great Wisdom, One of Bounteous Womb, Dearest, plus some names of other goddesses, such as Pārvatī and Umā. It does not sound very destructive. Sadly, she is rarely described in much detail. Kinsley (1998: 169) quotes a ninth century hymn allegedly composed by Abhinavagupta's guru Lakṣmaṇa Deśikendra:

> *You are so subtle that the gods cannot describe you. You are the source of the world and have no beginning. You have three eyes, a beautiful face, and four hands in which you hold a book and a rosary and with which you make the signs of assurance and granting favours... After worshipping you, the wives of the siddhas become red eyed because of drinking too much wine... We worship you who as a coiled serpent goes to the city of Śiva after passing along the suṣumnā nāḍī making all the lotuses bloom. We worship you who are bathed with a flow of nectar... your form is consciousness itself...*

This is just a small sample. The hymn continues at length and identifies the goddess with all form, the major gods, the *Vedas*, and so on. One description of hers appears in the *Tripurā - Bhairavī Tantra* (Daniélou 1991: 282) where her hands show the gestures of victory, of wisdom, of giving boons, and dispelling fear. Gently smiling, the goddess shines in crimson like a thousand newly risen suns. She is adorned with a veil, a garland of skulls, her breasts are blood-smeared, and above her three eyes shines the crescent of the moon. Her hymn from the *Tantrasāra* (Woodroffe 2001: 23-30) identifies her with the world-creating Kuṇḍalinī:

Figure 57 - Bhairvī.

Figure 58 - Bhairavī yantras.
Top, also yantra of Durgā. Both yantras are contemporary Northern India and Nepal.

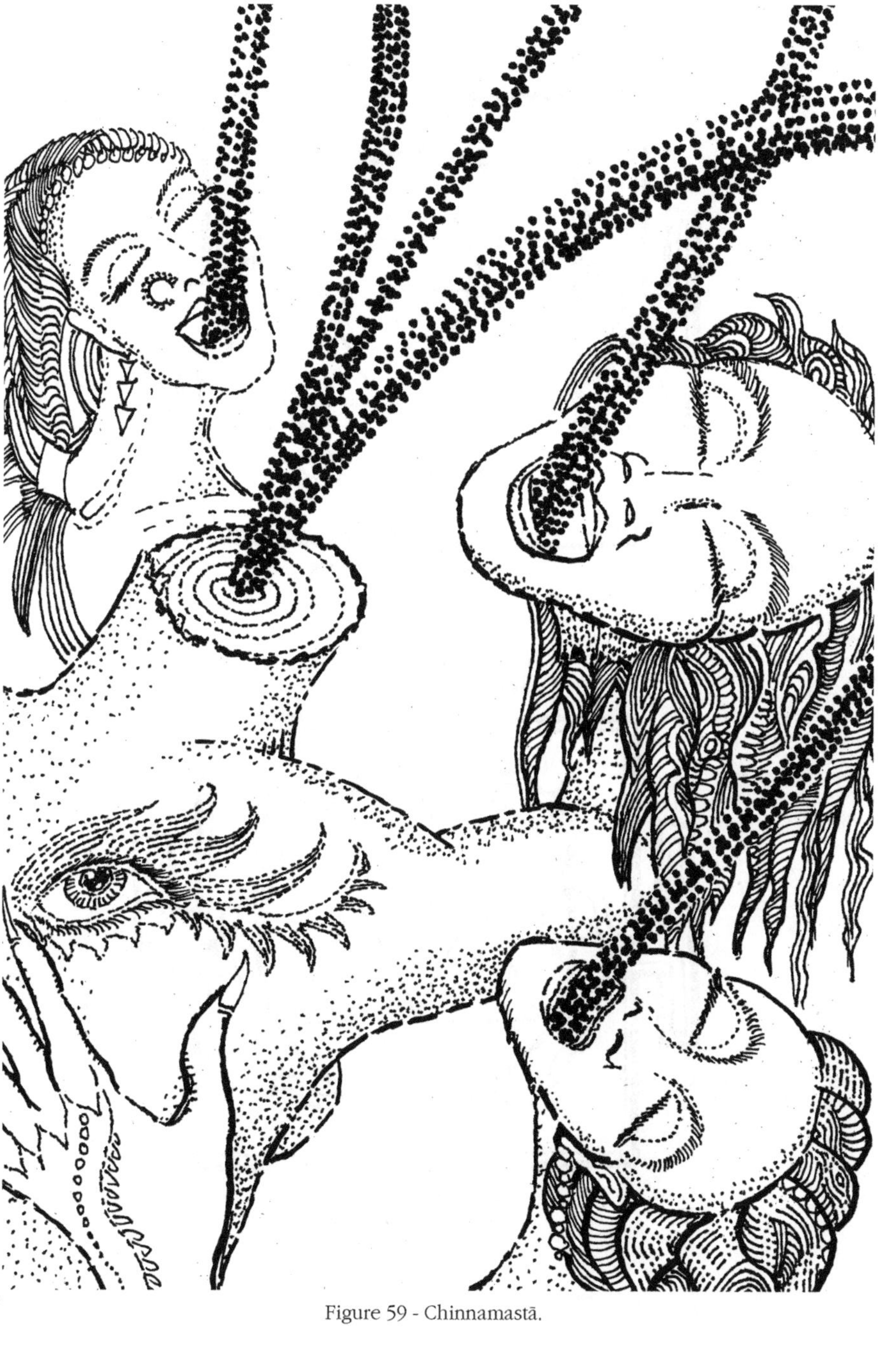

Figure 59 - Chinnamastā.

Figure 60 - Chinnamastā yantras.
Top: Mantramahodhahtiḥ, also for Gaṇeśa and Agni. Bottom: Contemporary India.

In company with the wives of the Kinnaras,
The Siddha women, whose eyes are reddened by wine
Having worshipped Thee with the flowers of celestial trees
In Thy pītha in the caverns of the golden mountain,
sing Thy praises.
I worship in my heart the Devī whose body is moist with nectar,
Beauteous as the splendour of lightning,
Who, going from Her abode to that of Śiva,
Opens the lotuses on the beautiful way
of the suṣuṁnā. (11, 12)

The *MM* gives her gāyatri mantra: **Oṁ tripurāyai vidmahe mahābhairavyai dhīmahi. Tanno devī pracodayat** (Oṁ. Let us think of Tripura, let us meditate on Great Bhairavī, may Devī direct us). Her bījas are **Klhrīṁ** or the heart mantra, **Sauḥ**.

In the Śrī Vidyā tradition, Bhairavī appears as Tripurabhairavī. She is a fear-inspiring deity, red like the china-rose and sits on the heart of Sadāśiva, who lies dead and stiff beneath her. She laughs madly, delights in blood, and wears a necklace of alternating skulls and red lotus blossoms. Apart from this, she is nude. The Śiva below her is called Dakṣiṇāmūrti, who has five faces. These five faces have different names and colours: Sadyojāta (crystal-white), Vāmadeva (yellow), Aghora (blue-black), Tatpuruṣa (red), Īśāna (green). The heads are associated with five mantras (or a mantra of five syllables), the five 'elements', and the five functions of Śiva: creation, maintenance, destruction, veiling, and revealing (tearing the veil of ignorance). Bhairavī does not appear in the MT (which lists both Tripurā and Ṣoḍaśī, the latter accompanied by Kalki), but a more recent source (Kinsley 1998: 255) connects Bhairavī with the deified constellation Halī.

Chinnamastā appears as the goddess of wisdom around the twelfth century. Kinsley mentions a number of much earlier goddesses who seem to be related to her: the statues show a nude, squatting torso with exposed genitals, arms lifted, but without a head. Not that the head came off: these statues were never intended to have one. As the story goes (*Śakti-saṁgama Tantra* 4, 5), after love-play with Śiva she went to take a bath in a river. With her were her attendants, two minor goddesses called Ḍākinī and Varṇinī. When the three returned, Śiva wondered why Chinnā looked so pale. The goddess replied that, after the bath, her two friends were hungry. To provide a nourishing meal, Chinnamastā cut off her own head. Three fountains of blood jutted from her neck, feeding Ḍākinī to the left, Varṇinī to the right, and her own severed head in the centre. In this form the goddess appears in (not very popular) iconography. She is usually shown standing on a pair of copulating lovers: Madana or Kāma, god of (sexual) desire lying on his back and his wife Rati (sexual lust) on top of him. In the *Prāṇatoṣinī Tantra*, we find Pārvatī going for a bath with her companions Jayā and Vijayā. As Pārvatī is sexually aroused, she becomes black (Kālī!) and, when her companions ask for a bit of food, she decapitates herself with her fingernails. Another version of the tale, from the same source, begins when Śiva and Mahāmāyā make love on Mount Kailāsa. When Śiva has an orgasm, the goddess frowns and emits Dākinī and Varṇinī. The three go for their bath and bloody breakfast, but when they return, the goddess, now called Caṇḍikā, looks terribly pale. Śiva immediately suspects that she has been abused. He becomes angry, and from his anger, Krodha Bhairava, a wrathful deity, is born (Kinsley 1998: 147-149)

The *Chinnamastā Tantra* (Daniélou 1991: 281) states: *Naked, she drinks voluptuously the stream of the blood-nectar flowing from her beheaded body. The jewel on her forehead is tied with a serpent. She has three eyes. Her breasts are adorned with lotuses. Inclined toward lust, she sits erect above the god of love...*

Consider the three streams of blood. Could they be a representation of the three major energy channels in the yogīc body?

In the *MM*, Chinnamastā is visualised seated in the centre of the sun. Her mantras are:

Oṁ śrīṁ hrīṁ hrīṁ vajravairocanīye hrīṁ hrīṁ phaṭ svāhā. Oṁ aiṁ chinnamastāyai namaḥ. Oṁ aiṁ dākinyai namaḥ. Oṁ aiṁ vārṇinyai namaḥ. These mantras have been 'nailed' or 'sealed' by Śiva. To pull out the nails or unseal them, the mantra **Oṁ hrīṁ Oṁ** is recited 108 times before and after the main mantras. Her bījas is usually **hūṁ**, **Oṁ**, or **aiṁ**. The main mantra shows Buddhist influence. The goddess appears in Tantric Buddhism under such names as Vajrayoginī and Vajra Varāhī. The iconography is similar, but for some mysterious reason the copulating couple beneath the goddess tends to be missing. Chögyam Trungpa (1991: 132) praised her: *Experiencing the vajra mind of Vajrayoginī is so deep and vast that if thoughts arise, they do not become highlights: they are small fish in a huge ocean of space.*

Chinnamastā worship abounds with special sacrifices (*MM*). Once the mantras are awake, the worshipper uses them while offering various substances for magical ends: jackal-flesh for wealth; milk, sugar and rice for writing skills; ghī-smeared goat-flesh to captivate kings, and so on. Many offerings are flowers: cāmpa and bilva flowers for happiness, white karavīra flowers for health, red ones to captivate kings and ministers, menstrual blood to captivate everyone. The goddess is adored in several colours: white for worldly pleasures and liberation, blue for aversion, red to captivate, smoky to eradicate, and gold to paralyse. This connects Chinnamastā with the notorious six rites. The goddess is also worshipped by lovemaking on midnight of the 14th day of a dark fortnight in total darkness, after the recitation of ten-thousand mantras. The same rite, replacing lovemaking with fasting, is said to produce erudition. Chinnamastā is called upon in dangerous situations: while gambling, in forest, and wilderness, in the royal palace, on the battlefield, and when confronting an enemy. The consort of Chinnā is Kabandha, the Headless Trunk. Worship of this Śiva gives great siddhi. In the *MT*, her mate is Paraśurāma.

Figure 61 - Dhūmāvatī.

Figure 62 - Dhūmāvatī yantras.
Top: Traditional, Nepal; bottom: Contemporary Nepal. Contains the Dhūṁ bīja.

Figure 63 - Bagalā

Figure 64- Bagalā yantras.
Top: Mantramahodhahtiḥ, bottom: Contemporary India.

Dhūmāvatī is a widow. As such she is unaccompanied by any manifestation of Śiva and, indeed, the story goes that she devoured him one jolly night in a fit of hunger. Apparently he did not like it much. Widows are not very auspicious in Hindu thought and neither is Dhūmāvatī. She represents the idea that women can be independent from their husbands and that they can survive without males to protect and order them around. In general Hindu philosophy, this is a distinctly unpleasant idea. Many rich widows 'voluntarily' burned with the corpses of their husbands, often for reasons of inheritance, others chose to become nuns, attaching themselves to temples, shrines, communities, or became wandering ascetics. They were supposed to pray for the well-being of their deceased husbands, their sons, and families. This implies spiritual power, and such power was not always appreciated by the family. In old India, widows were persons who did not fit into the social system. The law books place them outside of society and general custom decreed that widows, especially from high-class families, could not remarry. Hence, Dhūmāvatī was dreaded as a bringer of bad luck. The goddess is usually depicted as a tall, sickly figure with dark complexion, filthy hair, and clothes that come straight from the cremation ground. Her face is wet with perspiration, her three eyes are dry, her teeth huge, her breasts are withered, and her appetite is immense. She is restless, lonely, hungry and is said to enjoy quarrelling and strife. Her attributes are winnowing basket, winnowing fan, pot, and broom. According to the *Śākta Pramoda*, she crushes bones in her mouth, makes the (warlike) sound of drums and bells, wears a garland of skulls, quaffs blood and wine (the favourite Kaula drink), and chews the corpses of the demons Caṇḍa and Muṇḍa. With so many unpopular attributes it seems strange that people should worship her at all. Those who do, know her as one of the most fear-inspiring deities of the left-hand path. They also know that there is love behind the smoke-screen of terror. However, the goddess is not only worshipped by heroic Tāntrikas. She has a few minor temples, as Kinsley reports, and the locals appeal to her for blessings, wealth, and sons, just as they appeal to any other goddess. The goddess is usually shown as an old woman, living on cremation places, the essence of ugliness and pollution, and sometimes she is identified with Śmaśāna Kālī. Its not her only form. Who says that widows must be old? Kinsley shows several pictures which portray her young, well-dressed, adorned with jewels, and beautiful. I have a Nepali print showing her around twenty years old, wrapped in a white robe, sitting in a golden, winged chariot. Such images hint at the dangers inherent in young widows, in women who have survived their husbands and remain sexually active. In consequence, some sources hint that she likes sex and favours worship involving the Five Ms. She may even openly display her yoni. Would you like to guess how many young widows, cast out by their families, with nowhere to go, met charming young sādhakas at the cremation places?

Dhūmāvatī's name may be related to the root dhūma- smoke, vapour, mist, cloud. The *Śaktisaṁgama Tantra* proposes that Dhūmāvatī appeared as black smoke when Satī burned herself. Hence, the goddess receives plenty of burned offerings, including cigarettes and bhāng.

Daniélou 1991: 282 proposes that she connects with the four months of the rainy season when terribly torrents of water prevent travelling and activities such as marriage and initiation. Her mantra is **dhūṁ dhūṁ Dhūmāvati svāhā**, her bīja is **dhūṁ**. She is visualised riding a crow in the cremation place, or sitting in a horseless chariot under the banner of a crow. The worship is nude and nocturnal. The devotee has to fast at a desolate place, in the forest or wilderness, food being allowed once each night. 100,000 repetitions of her mantra are said to destroy all enemies, i.e. the imaginary ones outside and the real ones within. She is sometimes identified with the dark goddess Jyeṣṭhā. This name may mean most excellent, pre-eminent, chief, best or greatest (is this a dangerous deity who needs placation and flowery compliments?), while a less common identification is with Jyeṣṭhā-Lakṣmī, or Alakṣmī who is the goddess of misfortune. As she is a widow, there is no Śiva to accompany her in the TT. The MT names Vāmana, Viṣṇu in his dwarf-form, as her mate.

Bagalā or **Bagalamukhī** is sometimes considered a form of Tripurasundarī, and connected with the Śrī Vidyā tradition. Her mantra is **Oṁ hrīṁ Bagalāmukhī sarva-duṣṭānaṁ vācaṁ mukhaṁ padaṁ stambhaya jihvāṁ-kīlaya buddhiṁ vināśaya hlīṁ oṁ svāhā**. The name may be loosely connected with the word baka, meaning a heron or crane. In Indian folk-tales, cranes are creatures of cunning. They are famed for deception and cheating, but they are also admired for the patient and circumspect way they stalk their prey. In folk art, Bagalā sometimes appears with the head of a crane or heron. Like these birds, the goddess can be very still, almost invisible, poised to strike and devour. Other images show her with a flag bearing the image of a duck, goose, or water bird. She is a dangerous three-eyed goddess who sits on a golden throne, with golden complexion and yellow clothes. This hints at another name of hers: Pitāmbara-Devī (She Who is Dressed in Yellow). Yellow and gold colour are essential in her worship. She wears a crescent moon on her head and a garland of campā flowers. In her hands are club, noose, thunderbolt, and the severed tongue of an enemy. The enemy, in this case, was an Asura called Madan. He practised austerities until he attained the power that whatever he said became true. This gave him the ability to terrorise the world (just like the mass-media do). With a few words he could kill anyone! Consequently, the goddess had to take hold of (paralyse) his tongue before she could club him to death. Paralysis is Bagalā's speciality. She has the power to paralyse the three worlds. In this context, paralyse can also mean to calm, soothe, bring to rest. It can also imply self-paralysis, expressed by the yogī who sits or rests completely still, lost in deep meditation. Bagalā's power to be still wakes extraordinary sensitivity, eloquence, and penetrating insight.

Let's look into the *MM*. For the worship of Bagalā, the devotee dresses in yellow, applies yellow sandal to the body, and sits on a yellow seat, preferably in a forest, on a mountain, at the confluence of rivers, or in a Śiva temple. Offerings of yellow flowers accompanies the japa, the mālā should be of turmeric. Her sorceries include a number of fire sacrifices (homa). Offerings of salt with the three sweets captivates people; nīma leaves mixed with oil cause disagreement. Drinking consecrated milk of a unicolour cow, mixed with sugar and honey, gives the power to slay enemies. There are also recipes for travelling instantly to far places and becoming invisible. Her yantra is drawn on sandalwood as a talisman, on a skull (buried near the home of an enemy) to paralyse, on a shroud and placed in the mouth of a frog to paralyse speech. I'll leave out the sorry details of these spells. If you really think you have to work such delusions, you are obviously not qualified for them. Her yantra may be drawn on the ground to paralyse supernatural manifestations, there is even a spell to paralyse water by consecrating a root. At her side is the earliest form of Śiva, the Vedic god of the wilderness, Rudra the archer, who annihilates delusion. The Viṣṇu form of the *MT* is Kūrma, the tortoise who became the pivot when the milk ocean was churned.

Mātaṅgī, **Mātaṅginī**, or **Mātaṁgī** is the mother of the elephants (*Mhb*). Mātaṁga can mean an elephant or the plant ficus religiosa, a mātaṁga-kumārī is a young girl from the much despised Caṇḍāla class. In the cult of Śrī Vidyā, she is a dark form of Lalitā who teaches poetry. The *Mātaṅgī Tantra* (Daniélou 1991: 284) calls her *the elephant power, delight of the world.* She is a dark goddess wearing a moon-crescent on her head who sits on a jewelled throne, holding noose, sword, shield, and elephant hook. *She shines like a blue lotus, resembling the forest fire which consumes the abode of the demons.* In Indian lore elephants have a complex symbolism. They are associated with the dark rain clouds, with irresistible forces, success in warfare and especially with the sovereign power of kings. Anyone who has known elephants closely will be aware that they are highly intelligent beings who move their massive bodies with grace and elegance. Those I worked with were a playful and sometimes mischievous lot much given to playing little tricks. Elephants are also among the animals that enjoy to get drunk. Feasting on over-ripe fruit, elephants may become thoroughly tipsy and playful. Another tradition makes Mātaṅgī a goddess of pollution. According to the *Śaktisaṁgama Tantra*, Viṣṇu and Lakṣmī went to visit Śiva and Pārvatī. When they exchanged food, a few bits fell to the ground and from these, a beautiful girl arose who asked for the leftovers (ucciṣṭa). Leftovers are polluting, especially when they have fallen to the ground. This gave her the name Ucciṣṭa Mātaṅgī. As Kinsley documents, the goddess is associated with very low classes, with Caṇḍālas and some jungle tribes way outside of Hindu society. In Nepal, according to Kinsley (1998: 218), the lowest classes, i.e. fishermen, sweepers, garbage collectors and latrine cleaners are sometimes known by the caste name Mātaṅgī. The goddess Mātaṅgī is also associated with the worst rubbish, the very sort that is traditionally left at the cross-roads where no one picks it up. He notes (1998: 274-275) that in many folk festivals in south India, a low class woman called a Mātaṅgī personifies the goddess: *Possessed by the goddess, she dances wildly, uses obscene language, drinks intoxicants, spits on spectators, and pushes people about with her backside. She seems to take special delight in abusing members of the high castes.* It seems only natural that a goddess who transgresses purity laws became a darling of the Kaula folk.

According to the *MM*, Mātaṅgī is seated on a lotus on a jewelled pedestal, playing on a vallakī (an ancient lute) chatting with a parrot. Her complexion is black, she wears bright red clothes and is so intoxicated that she reels. In this inspired state, words cascade from her lips. In her hands are lotus and noose, she makes the gesture that dispels fear. Her worship involves numerous offerings of flowers, fruit, salt, bamboo and food for specific enchantments. There are sorceries that involve making small puppets out of salt, honey or flour, burned on special woods or cremation ashes, to captivate and control people. A special panacea of hers is to offer red sandal, karcūra, jatāmāṁsī, kuṁkuma, gorocana, white sandal, agara and camphor, eight substances called gandhāṣṭaka. According to Monier-Williams, these are eight fragrant (gandha-) substances varying according to the deities to whom they are offered, including sandal, agallochum, camphor, saffron, valerian and fragrant grasses. As you'll guess, several of these may be code names for sexual secretions. When offered, they captivate the whole world, when crushed into powder and worn as a brow mark the worshipper becomes popular and well-loved. Mātaṅgī is a goddess who grants wishes and fulfils desires. She is much involved with the world and its beauty. Her mantra is **Oṁ hrīṁ aiṁ śrīṁ namo Bhagavatī ucchiṣṭa cāṇḍāli Śrī Mātaṅgeśvari sarvajana-vaśaṁkari svāhā**. Or the Mātaṅgī Gāyatrī: **Aiṁ śukapriyāyai vidmahe klīṁ kāmeśvarīṁ dhīmahi. Tannaḥ śhyāmā pracodayāt**. This mantra captivates and controls kings, princes and inebriated women. It protects from various evil spirits, fulfils all desires and makes the worshippers as gods. The devotees are warned never to speak ill of women and to respect them like the goddess herself. As Mātaṅgī is generally a benevolent goddess, her companion is Mātaṅga Śiva, who represents universal bliss.

Her association with song, music and string instruments associates Mātaṅgī with Sarasvatī. Both of them give poetic talent, true speech, knowledge of scriptures, skill in music and great learning. In the *Kubjikā Upaniṣad* (Schoterman 1992: 318-320) she is called The Blue One. Her colour is blue, her body is blue, and so are her garments, throne, parrot and even the perfumes on her skin. Her yantra is a central bindu (dot) surrounded by a triangle, an octagon, a sixteen petal lotus and a square without gates. She is worshipped at midnight with the Five Ms and with menstrual blood. Her mantra is **Oṁ hrīṁ klīṁ Mātaṅginyaī phaṭ svāhā**:

With blood of ram and tomcat,
with the red flower spontaneously grown;
with flesh from pit and bulb
one should sacrifice to Mātaṅgī.

The translation is by Schoterman, who points out that the red flower which grows spontaneously (svayambhū: self-existing, independent) is

Figure 65 - Mātaṅgī.

Figure 66 - Mātaṅgī yantras.
Top: Mantramahodhahtiḥ, bottom: Contemporary Nepal.

Figure 67 - Lakṣmī yantras.
Top: Lakṣmī, bottom: Kamalā. Both contemporary northern India.

Figure 68 - Contemporary Lakṣmī yantras.
Typical women's art, traced in chalk or colour.
Top left: Lakṣmī's spiral star with feet of the goddess. Floor painting, Alpona, Bengal.
Top right: a section of a lengthy Path of Lakṣmī with the footprints of the goddess in the centre. Floor painting, Himachal Pradesh.
Bottom left: Design for Lakṣmī showing a number of her symbols, from a ritual seat, Alpona, Bengal.
Bottom right: Three variations of the footprints of Lakṣmī (or the house goddess), floor paintings, Alpona, Bengal.
After Mode and Chandra.

menstruation. The kuṇḍagola in the next line is ambiguous. Kuṇḍa is a vessel, bowl, basin, waterpot, pit, well or simply a hole in the ground, such as used in various rituals; it can also be a personal name, a name of Śiva or of Śakti, or it could mean an adulteress, the son of a widow or a mystical figure. In general language, kuṇḍagola can be a sort of sour rice, a gruel. It can also be the food found in the vessel, guess what. According to Louise Finn (1986: 87) the *Śyāmārahasya* states that kuṇḍa is the mixture of female and male sexual fluids while gola is the menstrual secretions of a widow. She cites another, contemporary source, a Śākta pundit who informed her that kuṇḍa is the first menstruation of a girl conceived in adultery, while gola is the first menstruation of a girl after the death of her father. As you can see, this interpretation emphasises the role of the absent father. The secretions are not only revered for their own sake but gain special power by coming from a source that is, effectively, outside of society and essentially polluting. In the *MT* you can find Mātaṅgī associated with Viṣṇu as the Buddha, which makes great sense, provided you ignore everything we know of the historical Buddha.

Kamalā (Lotus) and **Śrī Mahālakṣmī** (Great Prosperity, Great Fortune) are two titles of the same goddess. The story begins with a goddess called Śrī, whose first appearance is in the Vedic period. Śrī as a noun means well-being, good luck, prosperity. Originally, the goddess was associated with wealth, well being and authority. Kinsley (1988: 20-34) gives an excellent account of the goddess. Her ten boons are: *food, royal power, universal sovereignty, noble rank, power, holy lustre, kingdom, fortune, bounteousness and beauty.* It made her popular with the noble and wealthy. But there is another side to her which is closely connected with agriculture, cow-herding and the incomparable generosity of nature. The goddess was born of a lotus that arose from the milk-ocean. She lives in all sap and juice, is a giver of rain and growth, her sons are mud and manure. *In the Śri-sūkta she is described as moist (13,14), perceptible through odor (9),abundant in harvest, and dwelling in cow-dung* (Kinsley 1988: 20). Here we have a real fertility goddess, frequently invoked by farmers to make the fields fertile, the rains fall and the cattle increase. In ritual, she was often represented by a basket full of grains. Quite early she fused with the goddess Lakṣmī, which produced the form we know today: Śrī Lakṣmī. Apart from her agricultural blessings, she is a giver of success, love, beauty and charm. Few deities are as popular as Lakṣmī, especially in the country. The goddess is imagined radiant and shining. She sits gracefully on a lotus, at her flanks are elephants showering water (blessings) on her. Elephants are among her earliest attributes, they can symbolise rain, strength and royal privilege. Modern Indian art often shows her in the company of elephant-headed Gaṇeśa. Another animal companion, popular in Bengal, is the white owl. In her hands she holds lotus flowers and makes the gestures that grant boons: showers of coins fall from her palms.

As the goddess of beauty she is also its manifestation. Whenever you sense something beautiful, this quality is Lakṣmī. Other attributes are closely connected with the cult of Viṣṇu: conch, mace, pot, discus and so on. Śrī Lakṣmī was consort of a wide range of gods, including Agni, Indra, Soma, Dharma, a few demons and the fabulously rich Kubera. Evidently the goddess of beauty, wealth and royal authority was far too beneficial to be confined to a single mate. Most of her mates were only powerful and rich due to her blessings. It is only in the later sections of the *Mahābhārata*, c. 400 CE, that she was equipped with a single mate: shape-changing Viṣṇu, who appears in ten or more forms, thereby providing enough excitement for such an all-embracing goddess. As a Mahāvidyā, Lakṣmī tends to appear alone. She is not worshipped as Śakti of Viṣṇu but as a beneficial goddess with a head of her own. The same happens in the Pāñcarātra tradition.

The *Lakṣmī Tantra* shows her as the all-powerful creatrix, ruler and destroyer of the multiverse. There is a Viṣṇu at her side, true, but his nature and appearance are veiled by the fireworks-radiance of the goddess. In rituals of left-hand Tantra, Śrīlakṣmī is associated with the veneration of bodily excrement and fluids. Mahālakśmī's mantra is **Oṁ śrīṁ hrīṁ śrīṁ kamale kamalāye prasīda prasīda śrīṁ hrīṁ śrīṁ oṁ mahālakṣmyai namaḥ**, her bīja is **śrīṁ**. Siddhalakṣmī's mantra is **Aiṁ klinne madadrave kule hsrauḥ**. She grants magical power and unusual skills. In some popular texts, the goddess is only identified with a range of worldly blessings. This is a misunderstanding. Lakṣmī is generosity herself, and her greatest gifts are not wealth and fame but liberation. Another folksy idea is that Lakṣmī and Sarasvatī are enemies: the rich are not learned and the learned will never be rich. Another misunderstanding. Great knowledge and wisdom are forms of prosperity. People can be wealthy, prosperous and rich in their ideas, their wisdom and their experience even if they live in mud hovels. It does not happen often but it does. Lakṣmī is a capricious and unreliable goddess, so some believe, as wealth, joy, beauty and prosperity never last for long enough. Already in Vedic times, there is an unpopular sister of hers called Alakṣmī, goddess of need, unhappiness, hunger and misfortune who is petitioned to stay away. And Lakṣmī is certainly more than a well-meaning pretty girl. Her hymn refers repeatedly to her terrible forms, including that which destroyed the Asura Kola (Woodroffe 2001: 229-232).

Lakṣmī is exclusively accompanied by Viṣṇu in modern Hinduism. To associate her with a form of Śiva, the *Toḍala Tantra* relates that Viṣṇu is really a form of Sadāśiva. The *MT* proposes Matsya, i.e. Viṣṇu in his fish-form.

Annapūrṇā. An obscure goddess who appears in the *TT* as an extension of the ten. Annapūrnā is a provider of food. Her insignia are a rice bowl and a spoon, those who worship her will never face starvation. She is accompanied by a cosmic form of Śiva, who is the manifest Brahman, ten faced, and bestower of liberation.

Durgā, the Unapproachable One, is not usually one of the Mahāvidyas. She has her own group of nine personifications, the Nava Durgās, all of them born on the battlefield, and an amazing amount of mythology. However, the *TT* mentions her as number twelve. The Śiva at her side is Nārada, who is supposed to create (nā), destroy (ra) and protect (da).

Naganandinī has little mythology. She is called Durgā-with-the-smiling-Face in the *Yoni Tantra*, where she appears as the consort of Śiva; the text is revealed at her request. Hence she is specifically associated with the worship of the vulva.

Kāmākhya only appears in one list of Mahāvidyās, in the *Mahābhāgavata Purāṇa* (Stapelfeldt, 2001: 68). Here she occupies position number one, replacing Kālī. Kāmākhya is a form assumed by red Mahāmāyā in order to make love with Śiva. Kāmākhya is the goddess of the yoni, closely related to menstruation; her sacred place, the yoni-piṭha, is famous Kāmarūpa (Form of Desire) in modern Assam, where the yoni of Satī fell. The goddess is saffron yellow, she stands on a white corpse, makes the gestures that grant wishes and banish fear, her other two hands hold a mālā and a magical rope (siddhasūtra) (*Kālikā Purāṇa* 72, 63). In 76, 91-92 she is visualised radiant like a red lotus, the mālā is replaced by a sword. Kāmākhya overlaps with two Mahāvidyās. She is occasionally identified with Tripurā and with Tripurā Bhairavi (Stapelfeldt, 2001: 70-72).

The Mahāvidyās and You.

After so many types of playful divinity we come to the vital question: what is it good for? Please pause now and consider. Each of the ten is a goddess representing a science, a form of magick, a stream of elder wisdom. What are their functions, what are their arts and skills in the daily glamour of the world? To answer these tricky question, I recommend you get to know them closely. For a start, decide on a basic group. Ten is a good number, and allows you to identify them with the decimal system, which may be useful if you wish to cook up a new numerology. Other numbers are just as useful. If you wish to add to the selection or merge several deities in one, be so kind and ask them for permission. Gods like to be asked about such matters. Relax. You don't have to decide for eternity, it is enough to have a selection that seems workable for the time being. There is always time to change names and order of appearance should you will to do so later on. The gods dance many personalities and so do we. Once the deities are memorised, cautiously include them in your daily worship. One good approach is when you do your breathing and meditation. I like to do this in the morning, when I still feel dazed and tired, the Mahāvidyās tend to wake me up. It's nice to start the day with something worthwhile. My preference is a gentle sort of prāṇāyāma with closed eyes. Inhale in silence, recite the name while holding breath, exhale in silence, pause briefly. The whole thing is done without strain, force or haste. It should be gentle, refreshing and pleasant. If you find yourself tensing or forcefully exhaling, you are doing it wrong. While holding breath I pull up the muscles of my perineum and the entire pelvic floor. The first three breaths invoke Kālī, the second three breaths Tārā and so on. This gives you three breaths for each Vidyā, and a chance to visualise each briefly as she appears before you. The first set starts as dualistic worship. After going through the whole range, repeat, with the difference that now the Vidyā is within you.

If you are up to a third set (only for those who are skilled in prāṇāyāma), assume the form of the Vidyā and become her. This little ritual will fix the order and appearance of the Vidyās in your memory. It will build up images that can be explored at length once you have mastered this short form. Later on it may be useful to invoke only one Vidyā at a time, and to explore that very intensely. It is easier to start out with short visualisations than to burden your mind with detailed and lengthy ones. If you persist in this exercise for a few weeks, the Mahāvidyās will gradually assume a form that suits you. The experience of each depends very much on you. It may be useful to start out with a classical description of appearance, insignia, colours, animal vehicles and the like. Before long you will find them changing and assuming forms that are closer to your heart. Go for your own vision! Make use of the visual, acoustic and kinaesthetic submodalities when you invoke and invite: this is your mind, your imagination and your chance to create something that impresses or even shakes you. This sort of meditation is best done when your body lies at ease on the ground, deeply relaxed, breath flowing gently and your mind in a pleasant trance state. Invocation is very graceful when done in the astral (i.e. the imagination). You can meet them in your heart, deep in the empty core of yourself. Or you could go 'outside'. Imagine that you leave your body. Float out of your body and imagine that you can see it resting on the ground. Imagine that you travel through doorways and passages until you come to an Indian otherworld. Take your time, imagination needs a while to develop. Things may seem hazy or disrupted during the first visualisations, they will become more solid and enduring when you have made the journey a few times. Call on the Mahāvidyās. Meet them at lonely cross-roads and wind-swept cremation places, in humid jungles a-drip with moisture, in lush flower gardens, desolate shrines, at springs and lakes sparkling under wide skies, between snow covered mountains, deep within breath-cold caverns and in the twilight of your awareness. Meet them, learn, understand, and integrate. This process can take months or years, but it is certainly worth it.

The next step is to learn about the functions of each Vidyā. As you will have noticed, several goddesses have more than one function or name, and some seem to overlap regarding appearance and activity. Nevertheless, you could work out what function and form each of them has for you. Each Vidyā has several meanings and offers a choice of yoga and trance activities. A single interpretation is never enough, two are still a bit shallow but when we find three or more we are ready to take off. Here are some of my interpretations, given with the understanding that you do not simply imitate them but go out and learn for yourself. They are not hallowed by Indian tradition, as far as I know, but then we are here to create something new.

Figure 69 - Kālī & Śiva yantras.
Top: Kālī - Mahāvidyā yantra. The goddesses gave this one to me one shaky night when I was spaced out on my own brain chemistry. You wouldn't believe what the brain can cook up given a bit of training and enthusiasm. Not traditional (yet).
Bottom: Śiva yantra, contemporary India.

Direct Experience

Kālī and her rituals will be explored in the next chapter. You can do them, but you could also use this opportunity for something more specifically you. Who is Kālī for you? How does she relate to your liberation? Maybe the easiest spiritual exercise for Kālī is to invoke her into your mind, body and life and to ask her to sort you out.

Think about this deeply. Are you up to it? Observe the 'parts of your mind'. Who is afraid and who is eager? Who goes ahead and who slows you down?

One thing that I would like to recommend regarding Kālī awareness is the art of not-doing. Consider. In yoga, Tantra, magick and similar disciplines, the practitioner needs a certain amount of will and intent to get anywhere. This means daily practice. Sounds like work, doesn't it? In the beginning it usually is. It's not easy to sit upright when you have spent years slouching on padded chairs. It's not easy to breathe fully when your belly is tense due to emotional pressure. It's not easy to clear your thinking when you have filled your head with everyday garbage. Its not easy to know and do your true will when your being is tied up in wishes, fears, frustration and desire. It takes a while to sort out the human personality. All self development needs phases of gradual refinement. Call it discipline if you like, I prefer dedication. Then, however, comes a point when you find that you enjoy doing your exercises. Before long you may feel that something is missing from your life when you have to pause a day or two. It is at this point that your attitude undergoes a remarkable change. When you enjoy doing what used to need effort, you have come half of the way. You will still have a lot of effort-oriented patterns in your sādhana: the very patterns you needed to start. To get rid of these behaviour structures, cultivate not-doing. Sometimes it's good to do breathing in a comfortable posture. Sometimes it's good to stop thinking and controlling and to allow the deep mind to go it's own way. Sometimes it's absolutely essential to forget technicalities and rules. Let body breathe you. Let mind find its own way. Let your true nature unfold. Things can be really easy when you are ready for them. Some of the best initiations happen when you are well prepared, ready, and then stop controlling and interfering and allow things to go their own way. Ride the Kālī current by going with the flow.

Tārā, Tāriṇī, though she is similar to Kālī the functions differ. Kālī has much to do with dissolution and liberation on a large or even cosmic scale, while Tārā tends to have a more personal approach to this subject. She liberates the worshipper from the fear of death, be it by ritual or trance experience of dying, be it by the development of an immortal consciousness. According to the *MM* much of her secret ritual involved sitting on a corpse, especially the corpse of an enemy or an infant. The worship can be performed in a real cremation ground or one built up in the imagination. The sādhaka should visualise a wish-fulfilling tree with a jewelled pedestal at its root, which becomes the seat of Tārā, who is blue and laughs madly. Everywhere, s/he visualises corpses, bones, skulls and jackals in a happy, playful mood. In sorcerous rites, similar aesthetics abound. One such rite is to bury a skull, anointed with sandalpaste, on a Thursday or Saturday night and to sit above it for a thousand repetitions of mantra. This makes the worshipper the human counterpart of the wish-fulfilling tree. Or one brings a corpse home (sounds more simple than it is) and buries it under the threshold. Eight days of mantra repetition produce various siddhis. Another bit of sorcery involves wrapping funeral cinders in black cloth to throw them into the house of an enemy. Likewise, a bone may be inscribed with mantras. It can be thrown into the house of an enemy or buried in a field to make it barren.

Why do we keep finding references to corpse-rituals in texts related to Kālī and Tārā? One interpretation is that the corpse is you. Can you imagine your own death? This is a useful and popular meditation. It is also a great chance to enact something with your whole being. Play-act your own death. Twist around on the ground, then let go, give a last groan and relax. Allow all tension, all thought and all effort to drain out of your body. Let go. Then imagine yourself going stiff, decaying, coming apart. Imagine animals feeding on you, maggots wriggling, flies buzzing, crows pecking and jackals devouring. Imagine the bones that remain, and see them wither and disappear. This is a useful trance you can find in many magickal systems. Austin Spare called it the Death Posture. The Golden Dawn included a ritual simulation of death in its initiation ceremonies and Tantric Buddhists are especially fond of the matter. Just look at the high art of Chöd (see *Cauldron of the Gods* for more details). Salvador Dalí, when still a cute little lad, began day-dreaming his own death and disintegration and practised it with great persistence, just look what became of him. Such meditations can be done regularly, they can be refined and perfected until they become a pleasure and a relief. Death is something to be savoured. It's good to let go once in a while – in fact it's sheer joy to get out of the confines of body, mind and personality. The absence that follows is highly refreshing, and when you put yourself together again, re-shaping a new body out of mantras, the essence of the gods and rainbow-radiance, you'll return to life feeling much better than before. Reincarnation can be experienced lots of times, and a physical death is not always required for it.

Lalitā Tripurasundarī may appear in a playful form. Usually she is a benign goddess who likes to play in and with the world. Lalitā means playful (or wanton). A good trance is to consider yourself a player and your life a play. In Tantric worship, a player is a devotee. The worshipper plays the gods, the gods play the worshipper. Often during voluntary obsession, when the human form invites, manifests and enacts a divine consciousness. Are you up to shaking? The gods love to play in human bodies, just as some humans love to play in divine awareness. Playing, in Tantric thought, is a lot more essential that in European philosophy. Something can be a play, but this does not mean that it is not real. Some forms of play are a lot more real than serious normality. Well, you can play when you enact or manifest a deity. You can also play when you participate in the game that people consider real life. Most people play all the time, they just don't know they are doing it (and hate to be reminded of that). How can you bring playfulness into your life? This does not mean that you act silly or irresponsibly (unless you really want to), the main thing is that you interpret the events of your life, and your activity, as a glamour, a story, maybe a comedy or a drama. The actor is unreal, the stage is everywhere, your role is a glamour, the acting is imagination, the play is a fiction expressing deeper truths. Who writes the play? Who selects the actors? Who defines the roles? This world is full of wonderful actors. Look at the people you meet! Watch folks in shops, on the road, in public spaces. See them hurrying, haggling, arguing, flirting and bringing up the kids. Everybody is amazingly typical. No real actor could be so convincing as the very common people you encounter everywhere. They playact roles they have created or accepted for themselves, and like all good actors, they go into their part so deeply that it seems real. You are such an actor. You are a player, participating in the divine glamour. You can also be audience, playwright, director and critic. You can decide which play you want to be in. Whatever you decide to do, it begins when you realise that the play is really a fiction. The same goes for the part you chose. Who is the real self behind the masks? Can you look behind the masks of others? Can you seriously play with a light and happy heart? Lalitā is the Playful One, so the trance of playing suits her. As Tripurasundarī she is the goddess of three realms. Here you could explore the three levels of experience, be it underworld, world and heaven; roots, stem and branches or belly, heart and head. What is the intelligence and wisdom of the three realms? What is their siddhi, and how can they change your consciousness? How can you create a vidyā out of them? Ask Tripurasundarī and learn.

Bhuvanasundarī, Bhuvaneśvarī is the Lady of the World. In this function she is all-creating, all-maintaining and all-destroying Mahāmāyā, the personification of the world glamour. There are many trances to experience her glamours, joys and deceptions. As Māyā is not only the glamour but also the substance, all trances that enchant your awareness, all experiences that reveal the beauty and terror of 'reality' are part of her divine play. The key to this formula is the question of reality. Māyā deceives by being so utterly 'real', she binds by fetters called 'important', 'substantial', 'true', 'serious', 'consequential', 'crucial', 'essential' and so on. Whenever you stop questioning and accept some part of reality for 'real', you are getting entangled in the glamour. Whenever you find a 'might be' becoming a 'must', the glamour has become a chain. Whenever you chose that another 'reality' applies, old bonds disappear and new attachments are formed. Bondage to reality is called necessity, freedom of reality is possibility. Both of them are flesh and blood of Mahāmāyā, who binds and releases continuously. Think of the elephant goad that prods and pulls, the sling that binds and frees, the bow of the mind, strong under tension, the flowery arrows of the senses, exhausting themselves in the wide world of experience. Here are some trances to explore.

For one day, dedicate your awareness to necessity. Observe how your body is bound by need, by hunger, thirst, sleep, motion and rest. Observe how your mind is bound by conditioning. Observe how your activity is limited by past history, conditions of life, work, social norms, society. Watch how others influence your awareness, and how they themselves follow some strange set of rules and necessities. When do they function automatically and when do you? List all the necessary things, the things that are vital to your survival, essential to your well being, important to the doing of your true will. Ask yourself: What do I need this for? And observe the needs and cravings of other people. How do they compare to the needs and habits of yourself?

For one whole day, delight in possibility. Find choices, opportunities, mind spaces of voluntary pleasure. What is extra to your life? What is special to this moment? What can you enjoy right now, in this very instant? Find the opportunities for doing things differently. Eat different food, rest in a new way, read something unusual, go to a new place or enjoy something old in a new state of mind. Turn necessity into possibility, break your routines or change them gradually. Explore something different, be someone different. Assume a new mask (personality) and do something habitual in that new persona. Go for a walk and be a stranger or an alien.

For one whole day, invoke the goddess continuously. The Lady of the World is the world, s/he is also you, as you are the world you believe and identify with. Identify all events as the love-play of Bhuvaneśvarī with your consciousness. Female or male, you are Śiva awareness in Śakti-body. See all form as Bhuvaneśvarī and understand her continuous necessity, possibility and go beyond. As you enter her form and withdraw from it, you are weaving the māyā and creating a magick that fills the world with new inspiration. For more trances and mind-blowing experiences relating to Bhuvaneśvarī, explore the play of kula and akula awareness. You can identify your self so intensely with the world that its forms are parts of your body. You can disengage from form to such an extent that your environment and even your body, personality and sense of identity disappear. Freedom means enjoying a choice.

Bhairavī offers an exercise in sheer terror. It's not her only enchantment, but it is certainly a good one. If you approach her properly, you will get a good helping of your very best fears. Sure, Bhairavī may look horrible. This does not necessarily mean stuff like sharp teeth and evil eyes. The real Bhairavī looks a lot worse. She is the expression of your very own nightmares, and when you invoke her regularly, you will learn a lot about the things that really scare you. Here we are close to what usually happens when people invoke the Ancient Ones. Before these primal entities can manifest, they need a dose of energy to get started. This is usually fear-energy. It can give an amazing kick, and indeed you can observe stranded 'black magicians' and similar folk at the edges of the occult movement who have become habituated to scaring themselves or others in order to produce energy. Fear can give a good initial blast to scare you out of your habitual mind-space (and reality). It is not the sort of thing that can be relied on forever. If you are wise, approach Bhairavī with simple humility (and humour). She'll give you a good tour through your private hells. You'll get used to them. Eventually, the horror will be replaced by awe, wonder, astonishment and later even by affection and love. Yes, it is possible to love blood and bones, wriggly tentacloid space monsters, entities that devour ego or deconstruct your reasonable world-order. Such experiences are bread and butter to the heroic worshipper. What of the things that are even more scary? The pressure of consensual reality, the necessity to behave 'normal' just to keep a job? How about the horrors of blind routine, everyday-dullness and the mind-killing entertainment industry? To some worshippers, the terrors of the chaos demons are less troublesome than the dread of holding a stupid, steady job for a few years. Or how about the commitment it takes to raise kids? And what of the horrors of aging, weakening, of physical limitation or sheer loneliness? Whoever you may be, your greatest fear is always diametrical opposed to your preferred state of mind. The dramatic can be as terrifying to the normal as the normal to the dramatic. Bhairavī can appear in many forms, just as your fears do, and though you may drain them of their potential of terror, you will find that deeper within there is still lots of stuff to get excited about. Meeting and integrating fears is not something that ends, you'll come to meet Bhairavī quite often in your life. Use the chance, embrace and become her. You'll be surprised!

Chinnamastā has a lot to offer: once the head comes off, all sorts of things are possible. Behind the image of the self-decapitating goddess lies a wealth of spiritual treasure. Some of this is a little obscure. Several writers have misunderstood the matter. Chinnā is not a goddess of self-mutilators, if only for the reason that the goddess can take off her head and put it on again with no harm done to anyone. She is not a masochist or a self-sacrificer, nor does she sacrifice herself to a higher ideal or entity. Chinnā takes her head off to feed on its essence, she also feeds her friends on the showering red elixir. Have you noticed how the three spumes of blood resemble the three vital nāḍīs in the spiritual body? Metaphorically, cutting off one's own head is the surest road to wisdom. Those stuck to a single point of view will never understand anything. Chinnā's wisdom derives from the ability to be a head without body, a body without head or both of them together. She nourishes herself and the world by creating a void between personality and being. This void space of belief is the source of her elixir. Think about these matters deeply, or better still, invoke the goddess, become her and find out. For the competent mind-explorer she incarnates one of the most vital formulas of magickal change. She also shows that even deities need to get out of the rigid boundaries of the personality from time to time. When you identify with her and become her (use your imagination!), you may find that your awareness changes when you detach your head from your trunk. As the head goes up, unhindered by your body, consciousness changes. What else can the detached head teach? How about assuming different points of view? Can you see yourself from the side, below or above? Can you remember a memory in a new way by going in and out of it? How does it change your experience? When is the proper time to take your head off and to put it on again? What else can Chinnā teach to you?

Dhūmāvatī may well be on her way to becoming the goddess of singles. Living alone is something increasingly popular in the industrial world, while more traditional people find this hard to understand. Several years ago while visiting Kurdistan, I recall rural Kurds asking why I was living on my own. Have I done anything evil? Have I been cast out of my family? What meant freedom to me meant isolation to them. In many parts of the world, family and clan are safety while loneliness equals wretchedness. There are many people alive who have never been really alone. There are even more who can't handle loneliness, and prefer a bad relationship to the silence of an empty home. Before you read on, take a chance to explore. Are you living on your own? Do you have a partner? When did you last feel really alone? How did you produce this sensation? Loneliness is not simply something that exists, it is essentially a state of mind. You have to think certain things in a specific form and sequence to produce a feeling of loneliness. What do you see in your imagination? What do you hear, what do you tell yourself? How to you produce the sensation of isolation? Make notes and explore. Knowing how to be miserable is always useful, if only to avoid it. The difference between being happily alone and miserably alone is completely in your head. For those who work magick or explore themselves, being alone from time to time is essential. Other people can be such a distraction. No matter whether you love, like or abhor them, they do tend to catch your attention. If your attention is in the outside world you will find it difficult to go inward. Some folks use this to avoid introspection. They go out with anyone, they watch any sort of garbage on TV and chat away for hours on the phone without ever really saying anything. Most methods of wasting time have the advantage of keeping attention away from yourself. If you wish to change yourself, to explore your mind or to enchant yourself and others with creativity and beauty, regular opportunities to retire within are a must. A competent mind explorer needs many hours of loneliness. For the same reason it may be useful to spend a few years living on your own. Sure, it's nicer to have someone around whom you love. But have you ever considered the sense of freedom, self-responsibility and will power you develop when there is no-one around to look after you? Those who can live alone win freedom of choice. When you can cope with loneliness, you won't be confined to bad relationships. You won't depend on a partner or mate, and you certainly won't have to accept anybody who comes along. Of course the price of this freedom is the ability to handle isolation. Not always an easy task but certainly a rewarding one. In this sense Dhūmāvatī manifests a formula of introspection, freedom from bondage and an exit from the exciting world of the social trivia. She also provides a chance to encounter the usual fears that arise with loneliness. What single does not worry about the future from time to time? Who is really beyond the fear of old age, disease, poverty and utter desolation? Come and meet Dhūmāvatī. She knows how to handle these fears, how to go on living under averse conditions, and how to enjoy life nevertheless.

Bagalā has several arts to offer. One of the first is the siddhi of becoming totally still. Yellow often symbolises paralysation in Kaula Tantra, but instead of taking this for granted I suggest you visualise the colour, and yourself within, to find out if this works for you. If not, replace it with another colour or find some approach more suited to your nature. Everybody is unique. To learn Bagalā's arts, watch animals that make a living by being still or practising camouflage. Look at a heron stalking fish. It moves ever so slowly through the cold water, its outline dark against grey skies. Instead of going after prey it chooses a place where the prey will go to naturally. It waits until the fish is practically swimming between those long, reed-like shanks. Then the pointed beak shoots down, piercing flesh and scales, and pins the intruder to the ground. One skilled flick of the head and the fish is tossed up and caught, head first, and disappears. Or look at a spider waiting in it's web. Becoming still is not the same thing as being passive. The heron chooses its hunting site with as much care and consideration as the spider does. It waits patiently, but it does not wait forever. The siddhi of Bagalā is to know when to wait and when to act. You can practice this art. Go somewhere in the wild and become totally still. Calm those muscles, relax, find the axis of your body-balance, empty your mind, slow down. There is a special power in being really still. When your head, especially the eyes become still, you will find all sorts of visual effects happen. They can be like shifting fields of colour, you may find items of the scenery disappearing or becoming especially vivid, the ground rippling, some objects may become bigger or maybe the air is full of sparkles or drifting fog. All of this happens all the time, but usually your eyes do a fast, regular motion (circadian rhythms) to keep the images steady and your mind filters out all odd elements. When you become still you can see what you really see, or what you would see if you wouldn't edit your vision all the time. And just what happens to your breathing?

Being still means moving the lungs as little as possible; small motions at an increased rate. You can get into minimal breathing by being as still as possible. It's not an act of control but one of release. Real stillness can only last when it is relaxed. Come to rest within yourself. This, in itself, is already a meditation. People are rarely still and many seem to be instinctively afraid of it. Few like to wait, to do nothing, but when you observe them you'll see that they do not really wait, they fidget, and they are not really still, either. A tense body may seem still but it is full of muscles working against each other. Relaxing into a moment and enjoying it is one of the hardest siddhis you can master, precisely as it is based on not-doing instead of control, activity and effort. I once asked Mogg Morgan what his favourite meditation is. 'Just being' was his smiling reply. If you can enjoy that, you've come a long way. It's worth it. But stillness of body has further advantages. It is no surprise that Bagalā is associated with such skills as travelling in the imagination: when your body is really still (and fully relaxed), the sensation of the body periphery becomes diffuse. Soon the whole thing is forgotten and you are free to imagine, visualise and dream with greater clarity. Being really still changes the mind just as being regularly in motion. You get this effect when you shake, sway or tremble at a regular rhythm for a while. Pulsating, rhythmic motion is another way of being still. Both resting and shaking are states that blur the awareness of the confines of the body, both tend to dissolve the limits of yourself. What else can Bagalā teach? Shut up, calm down and learn.

Mātaṅgī is in charge of ecstatic arts such as music and poetry. Now real music happens and real poetry manifest naturally. We have to make a distinction here. Consider learning music. The usual approach is to burden the beginner with theory, posture and program. All of this means conscious intent. In extreme cases it means learning notes and trying to repeat a given melody. Complicated and disappointing. It's much more rewarding to pick up a given instrument and to produce sound for the fun of it. Beginners progress faster when they ignore melody and begin by developing rhythm. Everybody has rhythm. There is rhythm in your heart, your breathing, your eye motions, your brain activity, your sleeping, waking and daily routines. If you learn playing a flute, for example, forget about all those holes and fingers. Close the holes. Move only one finger if you have to. Breathe rhythmically, and move that one finger to produce variation. Two sounds are enough to get carried away. Move! Dance! Feel that rhythm; move to that rhythm, let the rhythm move you. Go into it deeply. You'll learn a lot about breathing, motion, air-supply and all the rest. You'll learn without thinking. This is just like small children learn. Have you ever considered that adults and small kids have different approaches to learning? Adults tend to think and consider a lot, even while they are doing things. They take a large task, break it down into segments, practice these units separately and try to put the lot together again. Small kids do it the other way around. They see something done by an adult and imitate the lot, in one go, including posture, dynamics and personal characteristics. They do everything at once and then they begin to fine-tune the various parts needed to do the job properly. Can you remember how you used to slip into the role of a character when you were small? Adult learning is often a lot of preparation and deliberation; child-like learning is often doing everything at once without thinking. This may produce accidents, but it is fast. Adult learning may seem safer, but is slower and less elegant. It takes a long time to fuse together a skill that has been learned as many separate units. Now look at Mātaṅgī. She is so drunk that she reels. This is the very state to shut up thinking and enjoy doing. Now I'm not suggesting that you do your daily sādhana with a bottle of scotch. It is, however, not a bad thing when overly controlled people get out of their heads once in a while. If you are serious about your sādhana, daily discipline can make the mind a little too one-pointed. It's easy to get stuck by continuous, determined effort, especially when it goes on for months and years. Some Tantric experts recommend getting drunk from time to time. Gurdjeff got his pupils into states of extreme exhaustion and then filled them up with vodka, all the while forcing them to do complicated mathematical calculations. Chögyam Trungpa recommended alcohol for the over serious seeker:

For the conscious drinker, or for the yogī, the virtue of alcohol is that it brings one down to ordinary reality, so that one does not dissolve into mediation on nonduality. In this case alcohol acts as a longevity potion. Those who are overly involved with the sense that the world is a mirage, an illusion, have to be brought down out of their meditation into a state of nonmeditation to relate with people. In this state, the sights, sounds, and smells of the world become overwhelmingly poignant with their humour. (1991: 189).

There is a vast difference between drinking for anaesthesia and drinking as a spiritual practice. But alcohol is by no means the only approach. Alcohol can be a metaphor for anything that takes you out of the confines of deliberation and control. It can mean other drugs, provided they are strong enough to shake the ego to the core, but it can also refer to any consciousness of such an ecstatic nature that it dissolves the rigid limits of your personality. Your brain is capable of producing an amazing amount of enlightening and bizarre consciousness states. This provides a wide field for experiment. When you assume the posture, motion and identity of Mātaṅg, you may learn that playacting drunkenness can lead to real states of intoxication. The same happens in drunken style Kung fu. Moving like a drunk can change awareness. Think of Rāmakṛṣṇa. Bengal's wonderfully mad saint was often considered drunk, when he was delirious with divine rapture. Likewise, he often confused real drunkards with divine ecstatics. The same misunderstanding can be found in the poetry of Rāmprasād Sen. Being drunk, drugged or spaced out are all states of mind. They depend far more on your mind than on the substances you ingested. Try moving, playacting and dancing Mātaṅgī. Can you move like a drunk? Can you speak faster than you think? Welcome to bardic poetry. The way to be oracular is to express yourself without censorship. Not quite the thing to practice in company but excellent when you are on your own. Record what you are ranting and explore it the next day for spontaneous poetry and deeper meaning. Can you draw faster than you think? Can you act with abandon without all the hang-ups of a reasonable, sensible person? When it comes to breaking out of the confines of reason and discipline, Mātaṅgī is the deity of your choice. Welcome to chance and coincidence! Welcome to happy madness, intoxication and playful unpredictability!

Last, think of the goddess as the divine state of pollution. Just what is disgusting to you? What makes you feel abhorrence? Most people begin to cultivate dislikes in early childhood. Some learn disgust from copying their parents or relations. A lot of dislikes are irrational and have little use in real life. Take spiders for instance. Can you get close to them and admire their beauty? How come infants play with their own shit unless they are taught to loathe it? And what about body secretions? Āyurvedic medicine recommends urine drinking every morning. Would you like a cup of your own secretions? What else comes to mind? Are there things that disgust you for no useful reason? You can liberate the emotional energy that is stored in such sentiments.

Kamalā or **Lakṣmī** offer a wide range of choices and experiences. Her role in the world-play is to support, maintain and nourish. Nourishment means a lot more than preserving a specific situation. In nature, things are not stable. Balance is a dynamic process involving change, and this means that things appear, last, disappear and make space for new development. The play of Lakṣmī is adaptation to changing circumstances. May I propose three trances to discover the meaning of this lila?

Think of the autumn forest. After a few days of rain and drizzle, the grey clouds are swept away by fresh winds and the sun appears shining and radiant. Earth warms, little plumes of steam spiral from moist ground, and only a few hours later, the first mushrooms shyly emerge out of their subterranean lairs. Golden leaves cascade and litter the ground with a jewelled mosaic of ochre, sepia, umbra and auburn. All nature is aflame. Look for those mushrooms. It takes a while before you see the first. It's colour is too close to the variegated browns. Then you find another, then a third. If you go slowly and slower still and give yourself time, more and more mushrooms will leap into your field of visions. You will see a dozen where before only a single one was visible. Somehow you are telling your deep mind to identify mushroom shapes, and before long you'll be stunned by the mushrooms thriving everywhere. You are standing right in the middle of the lot, and have been doing so all the time without ever noticing. Consciousness is selective. You tell it what to select for you and it does the job. People who look for beauty become acutely aware of beauty, people who look for filth will discover filth. Someone with a phobia for bees and wasps will be acutely aware of many little flying creatures you wouldn't even bother to notice. Consciousness is selective, it is always selective. If you want to change what you are aware of, ask your deep mind to search for something else. To get started, a bit of conscious doing can help.

Dedicate a walk in the country or forest to Mahāmāyā. Do a bit of prayer, meditation or mantra repetition if you like and invoke the force that creates, innovates, surprises and brings forth sudden changes. Then go for a slow walk (fast walking may be fun but it reduces the quality of your perception a lot) and look for anything new. In spring you'll be stunned by the amount of new things you'll discover, but even in autumn and winter there will be changes and fresh developments. There are surprises in every season if you open your mind sufficiently. Treat yourself to several hours of delighting in the new.

Next, dedicate a walk to Mahālakṣmī. Her formula is maintenance and you can observe her in things that endure and last. Look for things that flourish, look for the beauty of the developed, enjoy the reliability of things that have been with you all through life. Think of what you enjoyed in past lives and what you'll enjoy in future incarnations. Though mountains change, there will always be mountains. Though stars move, there will always be stars out there, shining in frozen splendour across the voids of space. The winds will always move across the earth, rains will fall here and there, waters will flow and life itself is continuous.

Look for the things that happen again and again, through age after age, and learn how they change is part of the stability.

Last learn about dissolution, erosion and destruction by going for a walk with Mahākālī. In every biotope, the majority of life-forms are destructive. You can hardly see the myriad of hungry mouths feeding on falling leaves, rotting wood and decaying matter, but they are always there. The destruents turn the waste of nature into food for fresh life. Without the hordes of minute bugs, the forest would suffocate in an ever growing layer of dead vegetation; without the humble rainworm, soil would be rock-hard and infertile. So go for a walk with Mahākālī and learn about dissolution. Look for the tree fungi and mosses that indicate a tree is rotting. See fallen leaves, withered blossoms, dried stalks and bleached bones. Watch where nature dissolves matter to make way for fresh growth. See how animals and plants feed on each other, think of disease and age and death. Beasts die, plants die, trees die and so do humans. Watch them taking their place in the great flow of evolution, see them playing their parts and disappearing again. All of the people you see on the street today will be dead and memory in a few decades. What is their contribution to history and evolution? What story will they leave behind? Some change the flow, others obstruct it, still others live their life and do little more than pass their DNA to the next generation. All of this may make for a strangely morbid mood. It can also be a delightful mood when you understand the beauty and perfection of it all. Creation, maintenance, destruction, hiding and re-creation are full of beauty.

What else can the tenth vidyā reveal? Think of her as **Siddhilakṣmī**, the one generous in skills, powers and perfection. A good trance for her can be found in the chapter on gurus. It's the trance of perfect behaviour. Observe how everything that animals, plants and people do functions. It may not function well but it usually functions sufficiently. Look at every piece of behaviour as a skill. What is it's function? What is it's context? When happens what and how is it done? There are more skills around than you and I will ever be aware of. Maybe some of them are not the skills we'd really be happy with, but in certain circumstances and for certain beings, even these may have their use. There is a wealth of learning available for those who open their minds and observe that, for good or bad, the world-play functions perfectly. Mind you, some bits could certainly be improved. The tenth vidyā also appears as Kamalā, seated on a lotus, showered by elephants. Her magick is the art of beauty.

Find something beautiful. How do you know it is beautiful? How do you recognise it, how do you tell its difference from something that isn't beautiful? People usually have hierarchies of values in their deep mind, they also have criteria by which they measure something as abstract as beauty. Now play around with it. Make it bigger, smaller, distort it, move it, see it from different points of view, hear it in a new way, change its elements and so on. How could you make a situation more beautiful? What would reduce its beauty? Think of the different sorts of beauty.

Figure 70 - Siddhilakṣmī Kamalā.

There is aesthetic beauty, for example, but there are many other sorts of beauty that are rarely considered. A thing may be ugly but it can have a functional beauty. Others may have a negative beauty, a suggestive beauty, a symbolic beauty, a hidden beauty or a beauty that brings out the beauty in other things. How many sorts of beauty can you recognise or invent? Look for examples, learn to enjoy unusual sensations. Watch Lakṣmī in her playful dance!

15: Kālī's Kula

Nirṛti

Our first reference to a black goddess comes from the earliest periods of recorded Vedic religion. In the *Ṛg Veda* you can find numerous brief references to a goddess called Nirṛti whose name (or title) can be translated as Destruction, Doom, Disorder, Perdition and Dissolution. Nirṛti was such a terror-inspiring deity that she was rarely invoked and never praised. Her rites, most of them unknown, were performed to placate her, to calm her dangerous temper and to ensure good luck for the living and especially the dead. For this reason we can find her mentioned quite a few times, but never in any detail or with much sympathy. *Ṛg Veda* 10, 59 states: *Let Nirṛti depart to distant places*, 10, 36 has: *Let not malignant Nirṛti rule over us. We crave to-day this gracious favour of the gods... May ringing press-stones keep the Rākṣasas afar, ill dream, and Nirṛti, and each voracious fiend.* 10, 18, 10 asks that the deceased should be saved from the bosom of Nirṛti, while other passages assign liars and sinners to that sinister spot. As you may guess, the yoni of the black goddess is the darkest place conceivable. It seems that Nirṛti was in charge of the dead who had offended the divine order. 10, 10, 11 associates her with the end of the world. In 10,164, 1 an unknown god, the Master of Thought is asked to go far away, to tell Nirṛti about the nature of human thought. The passage is a mysterious and unexplained part of a spell, perhaps against the evils of wrong thinking and sinful daydreams. 7, 37, 7 has *Though Nirṛti the Goddess reigneth round him, Autumns with food in plenty come to Indra.* 5, 41, 17 proposes that Nirṛti should devour the old age of the seer, perhaps to make him young again. In the *Atharva Veda*, the goddess appears just as prominently. 7, 70 is a spell against the enchantment/sacrifice made by an enemy: *1. Whatsoever he yonder offers with mind, and what with voice, with sacrifices, with oblation, with sacred formula, that let perdition (Nirṛti), in concord with death, smite, his offering before it comes true.* 6, 63 is a mysterious spell to release some person from Nirṛti: *1. The tie that the divine Nirṛti bound upon thy neck, (and) that was unreleasable, that do I untie for thee, in order to long life, splendor, strength; do thou, quickened, eat un-injurious (?) food. 2. Homage be to thee, O Nirṛti, thou of keen keenness; unfasten the bond-fetters of iron.*

Nirṛti's ceremonies are performed with black grains, her fire altar is made of black stones and black earth (the earth of the dead) is her home. Childless women are human representatives of Nirṛti, during the consecration of kings his childless wives represent the goddess. She is also associated, somewhat vaguely, with dice, women and doves (see

Figure 71 - Statue of Kālī as a young woman.
Stone. Sorry, no details available.

Gonda 1960). Dice, in Vedic times, were no trivial entertainment but had a serious ritual use (see the crucial dice game in the *Mahābhārata*), they also appear prominently in divination, as shown in Mogg Morgan's work *The Tantric Knuckle Bone Oracle* in *Tantra Sādhana*, 2008. Nirṛti's dove, flying innocently into the house, is called a messenger of destruction and a winged spear who threatens the lives of humans, beasts and the survival of the household. This theme is elaborated in the *Atharva Veda*, where we find a whole series of incantations to chase a pigeon out of the house. The dove is not her only harbinger of doom; owls are also dreaded as her winged missiles. In the *Atharva Veda*, Nirṛti occasionally appears in the company of Mṛtyu and Yama (Death), with whom she co-operates closely. Nevertheless she is not called a death-goddess, perhaps she is more closely associated with trance and sleep. The similarities between Nirṛti and the North-Germanic underworld-goddess Hel are rather striking. These are not the only ties between Hel, Helja, the Cailleach and Vedic religion. Coincidence or common origin?

Kālī Rising

The next reference to a black (Kālī) goddess comes from the *Muṇḍaka Upaniṣad*. This text, roughly dated around 500 BCE and included in the *Atharva Veda*, was written to reform the nature of worship. Elder *Upaniṣads* prescribed lengthy and often completely obscure ritual formulas for worship. The *Muṇḍaka Upaniṣad* (from muṇḍ = to shave) proposed to cut off the superfluous and to reinstate worship as an inner and meditative discipline. All scriptural knowledge, all external worship and customs of sacrifice are deemed secondary to the Higher Knowledge, which is direct experience of the Undecaying (Brahman). The Undecaying is invisible, un-hearable, beyond family, caste, body, all pervading, omnipresent, the bhūta-yoni (source of all being). The text, while not explicitly denying the validity of traditional worship, points out that ordinary ritual in itself is not enough, as it only produces temporary benefits, and argues that the true worshippers ought to return to the seclusion of the wilderness and the forest, through the door of the sun to the dwelling place of the immortal, indestructible self. This proved to be a refreshing new attitude; it also provided the background for our altogether too brief and obscure reference to the black goddess. In a passage describing the fire sacrifice, we learn that there are seven tongues of Agni, the deity of fire. Remember that fire is not just the phenomena you know from hearth, campsite and candle-flame but also the heat of hunger, life and lust that burns in all beings, humans, beasts and deities. Fire can be destructive, but it can also have a liberating function. Fire receives the offerings of the worshipper and transmits them to the gods. Likewise, fire devours the dead body of the worshipper and liberates the spirit.

The seven moving tongues of fire are the black, the terrific, the swift as mind, the very red, the very smoky-coloured, the spark-blazing, the all shaped (all-tasting?) goddess. (1, 2, 4) It's not much of a reference. Are we dealing with seven goddesses or with a single goddess arising as

Figure 72 - Kālī in folk religion.
Terracotta statue, Madhya Pradesh.

seven tongues from the same mouth? Whatever the nature of these fire-goddesses may have been, the first one among them is called Kālī. We cannot know whether this Kālī has much in common with the later forms of the goddess, apart from her blackness, the tongue symbolism and the fact that fire devours, transforms and liberates, but at least it is a start.

For the next millennium, hardly anything was recorded regarding Kālī. Few people bothered to write about the terrifying black goddess. Instead, we see the emergence of the early *Purāṇas*, most of them concerned with the worship of Viṣṇu and Śiva, with a kind word for goddesses here and there. Kālī is mentioned on occasion, but rarely in any detail or in any active role. However, we have her appearing in a Buddhist text of the first century. Its author, Aśvaghoṣa, wrote one of the many biographies of Buddha, the Enlightened one. You know the story, I hope, of how the ascetic renouncer sat down under his tree and decided not to leave before enlightenment happened? In his trance, Gautama was severely tried by hunger, thirst, pain, exhaustion, doubt and by a series of dramatic visions and temptations. The lord of evil himself, Māra, appeared to shake the seer out of his samādhi. So far, most Buddhist myths agree. When it comes to the nature of the temptations we encounter great variability. In several old versions, the last ordeal is the encounter of Māra's daughters, who try to seduce and scare. Now Aśvaghoṣa introduced a new element. In his *Buddhacarita*, the final and supreme ordeal are not Māra's daughters but the black goddess Kālī herself. As Cynthia Humes (in McDermott & Kripal 2003: 152) summarises: *...the great demon Māra sends in 'a woman named Meghakālī, bearing a skull in her hand,' whose intent was 'to infatuate the mind of the sage.' Instead of shaking the Buddha, however, she herself 'flitted about unsettled and stayed not in one spot, like the mind of a fickle student over the sacred texts.'* The passage has several implications. For one thing, it associates Kālī with ritual skull-bearing. Here the goddess herself is a Kāpālinī, a skull bearer, much like the later Tantrik movement of ascetic worshippers who used to feed and drink from a skull-cup. Their role-model is usually Śiva, who had to carry one of Brahmā's heads for a few eternities, but on a deeper level, a person who feeds from a skull-cup is essentially one who has learned to feed on the hormonal essences produced within her or his very own skull. The goddess, in our account, has the name Meghakālī. Humes proposes that this may come from time (kāla) of clouds (megha), a reference to the rainy season. It could also mean black (kāla) clouds. Black clouds and the rainy season-two ideas that contain a lot of associations to the Indian literati. In India, the rains are devastating, catastrophic and overwhelming. They are also eagerly desired. When the clouds burst and the streets are flooded hip-deep, the scorching heat of summer has ended and life begins anew. The bursting of the monstrous black clouds has a sexual undertone, much like the erotic metaphors of China and Japan. And while the Kālī of the *Buddhacarita* is essentially a silly woman who can't trouble Buddha one bit, the fact remains that she is the toughest ordeal and temptation that the universe could direct against him. While making fun of her, Aśvaghoṣa unconsciously tells us that Kālī was well known in Buddhist circles and had a powerful reputation, otherwise he would never have turned her into the ultimate temptation of the Buddha.

In the *Mahābhārata* Kālī appears a few times. This formidable work of epic literature contains a lot of old material, its core (the original *Bhārata*) may well have been composed around 1000 BCE. It was expanded by later generations of storytellers and scribes until it reached its basic form in the fourth century BCE, but this does not mean that it wasn't edited and altered in later periods. The text was refined till the fourth century CE. We encounter Mahiṣamardinī, identified with Kālī, who is in turn identified with Durgā in the episode when Yudhiṣṭhira asks her blessing before departing to the city of king Virāta (4, 6 trans. Kisari Mohan Ganguli). This prayer is one of the earliest appearances of Śākta or Kaula belief, predating the *Devī Māhātmya* by maybe one hundred years. Here is an interesting passage:

> *O Goddesss, thou shinest with a face that challengeth the moon in beauty. With an excellent diadem and beautiful braid with robes made of the bodies of snakes, and with also the brilliant girdle around thy hips, thou shinest like the Mandara mountain encircled with snakes. Thou shinest also with peacock-plumes standing erect on thy head, and thou hast sanctified the celestial regions by adopting the vow of perpetual maidenhood. It is for this, O thou that hast slain the Mahiṣāsura that thou art praised and worshipped by the gods for the protection of the three worlds. O thou foremost of all deities, extend to me thy grace, show me thy mercy, and be thou the source of blessings to me. Thou art Jayā and Vijayā, and it is thou who givest victory in battle. Grant me victory, O Goddess, and give me boons also at this hour of distress. Thy eternal abode is on Vindhya - that foremost of mountains. O Kālī, O Kālī, thou art the great Kālī, ever fond of wine and meat and animal sacrifice. Capable of going everywhere at will, and bestowing boons on devotees, thou art ever followed in thy journeys by Brahmā and the other gods. By them that call upon thee for the relief of their burdens, and by them also that bow to thee at daybreak on Earth, there is nothing that cannot be attained in respect either of offspring or wealth. And because thou rescuest people from difficulties whether they are afflicted in the wilderness or sinking in the great ocean, it is for this that thou art called Durgā by all. Thou art the sole refuge of men when attacked by robbers or while afflicted in crossing streams and seas or in wilderness and forests. Those men that remember thee are never prostrated, O great Goddess. Thou art Fame, thou art Prosperity, thou art Steadiness, thou art Success, thou art the Wife, thou art men's Offspring, thou art Knowledge, and thou art the Intellect. Thou art the two twilights, the Night, Sleep, Light - both solar and lunar, Beauty, Forgiveness, Mercy, and every other thing. Thou dispellest, worshipped by the devotees their fetters, ignorance, loss of children and loss of wealth, disease, death and fear. I, who have been deprived of my kingdom, seek thy protection.*

The other famous passage occurs just prior to the beginning of the *Bhagavad Gītā* where Kṛṣṇa asks Arjuna to invoke Durgā before the final battle. Arjuna utters a hymn that begins with the praise of Kālī, Umā and Durgā. Let me quote the passage extolling Kālī (*Mahābhārata*, 6, 23, trans. Kisari Mohan Ganguli, diacritical marks and comments added). As much of the *Mahābhārata* is devoted to the worship of Kṛṣṇa and Vaṣudeva, who had just been made incarnations of Viṣṇu, care is taken to put the goddess in a Vaiṣṇava setting, to call her the sister of Vaṣudeva and to identify her with Kṛṣṇa:

I bow to thee, O leader of Yogīns,
O thou who art identical with Brahman,
O thou that dwellest in the forest of Mandāra,
O thou that are free from decrepitude and decay,
O Kālī, O wife of Kāpāla (Śiva),
O thou that art of black and tawny hue, I bow to thee.
O bringer of benefits to thy devotees (Bhadrakālī),
I bow to thee, O Mahākālī,
O wife (Caṇḍī) of the universal destroyer (Caṇḍa),
I bow to thee.
O proud one,
O thou that rescuest from dangers (Tārinī),
O thou that art endued with every auspicious attribute,
O thou that art sprung from the Kata race,
O thou that deservest the most regardful worship,
O fierce one,
O giver of victory (Vijayā),
O victory's self (Jayā),
O thou that bearest a banner of peacock plumes,
O thou that art decked with every ornament,
O thou that bearest an awful spear,
O thou that holdest a sword and a shield (made of skin),
O thou that art the younger sister of the chief of cow-herds (Kṛṣṇa)
O eldest one,
O thou that wert born in the race of the cowherd Nanda!
O thou that art always fond of buffalo's blood,
O thou that wert born in the race of Kuśika,
O thou that art dressed in yellow robes,
O thou that hadst devoured Asuras assuming the face of a wolf,
I bow to thee that art fond of battle!

The age of these passages is open to debate. The *Gītā* is one of the most recent additions to the work. So are the two hymns to the goddesses, they do not appear in the elder South Indian manuscripts. However, they show that much of Kālī's nature and appearance was developed before the fifth century. Apart from these references, there are few signs of the worship of Kālī. This does not necessarily mean that she was unknown, it could well be that she was worshipped by people far removed from the literary world, among tribal people, outcasts and folk belonging to low classes. In historical times, these fringes of society have been her favourite haunts. She re-emerges around the year 500 CE. Here we find her in the *Devī Māhātmya*, taking a prominent part in several great battles against demonic Asuras. The text celebrates her primarily as Bhadrakālī, more on her further on.

In the *Bhāgavata Purāṇa,* 5, 9, 12-20 (c. 10th century CE), Kālī is associated with thieves and criminals. As many bands of outlaws haunted the forest, jungles and mountains, the goddess came to be associated with wild, desolate and dangerous places. Numerous worshippers of Kālī chose to worship the goddess in the wild. However, if we look closely into the *BP*, it turns out that the story is not as simple as it seems. The bandits, worshippers of Bhadrakālī, decide to perform a human sacrifice so that their chief may have a son. For this purpose, they catch a Brahmin called Bhārata. Well, Bhārata is a devotee of Viṣṇu and one with Brahman. Wrong choice! During the ceremony, the image of Bhadrakālī goes up in flames and the goddess and her attendants appear. They are raging mad, destroy the bandits, gorge themselves on blood and play ball with their heads. (see Patricia Dold in MacDermott/Kripal 2003) The worship of Kālī, as performed by the bandits, is a fatal mistake, and our story, far from making Kālī a goddess of killers, turns out to be pro-brahmanical.

As you can imagine, Kālī represented a lot of different ideas to her followers. We see her active in literature composed for the religious mainstream, but we can also trace her in the less popular literature of Tantric adepts. Here, Kālī has a good many functions which go a long way beyond the simple, anthropomorphic image favoured by folk religion. Goudriaan and Gupta give an excellent summary of Kālī-related Tantras (1981: 75-92). Typical for Kālīnian scripture is a bias towards heroic worship, including meditations at cremation places and horrible locations, encounters of the divine in its terrible shape and offerings of the usual secretions, wine and meat. Kālī Tantras tend to have cruder language than the Tantras of Śrī Vidyā, indicating that the folk who wrote them were not always upper-class literati. As Goudriaan remarks, the Kālī Tantras seem to be older than the literature of Śrī Vidyā. However, he does not give even a tentative date for the first Kālī Tantras, mainly as they have not survived. One of the first we know of, the *Kālīkula*, is mentioned by Abhinavagupta around the year 1000 BCE. Before that date, we already have the *KCT* which gives an invigorating meditation on Bhadrakālī in chapter 4 which is highly recommended. Goudriaan proposes that perhaps the oldest surviving Kālī Tantra is the *Yonigahvara* ('Recess of the Womb'). In this work, Bhairava is questioned by Bhairavī on a cremation ground in Uttarapiṭha, the northern seat. Kālī is often associated with the north, as is the Krama system which made so much of her transmutations. The *Yonigahvara* is already a highly developed Tantra. We learn that Kālī has thirty-five aspects (!) and that she is *beyond the senses, inconceivable, of free volition, free from defects, identical with the stainless supreme sky, without desire, (residing in) the sphere beyond the sky* (trans. Goudriaan). It also mentions Śakti as a coiled serpent within the yogīc body of the worshipper, lists the requirements of a vīra and gives a diagram of fifty sections (corresponding to the fifty phonemes) to construct mantras.

Kālī appears in several *Purāṇas*, but usually not in much detail. Indeed there is good evidence that many seers were busy smoothing her rough and dangerous appearance. In this sense, and especially during the last centuries, she has suffered from a certain amount of Vaiṣnavisation. A typical example from the *Devī Bhāgawatam* (9, 1):

> *Now come the lotus-eyed Mâheśvarî Kâlî who when angry can destroy all this universe in a moment, who sprang from the forehead of the Mûlâ Prakriti, Dûrgâ to slay the two Demons Śumbha and Niśumbha. She is the half-portion of Dûrgâ and qualified like Her, fiery and energetic. The beauty and splendour of whose body make one think as if the millions of suns have arisen simultaneously. Who is the foremost of all Śaktis and is more powerful than any of them, Who grants success to all persons, Who is superior to all and is of Yogīc nature, Who is exceedingly devoted to Krisṇa and like Him fiery, well-qualified, and valorous, Whose body has become black by the constant meditation of Śrî Krisṇa, Who can destroy in one breath this whole Brahmâṇḍa, Who is engaged in fighting with the Daityas simply for sport and instruction to the people and Who, when pleased in worship can grant the four fruits Dharma, Artha, Kâma and Mokṣa.*

Now Kālī means black or dark, and so does Kṛṣṇa, and in this sense they are related. However, the playful deity of cow-herders, Kṛṣṇa, who only became a major god by being identified with Viṣṇu in the last stages of the *Mahābhārata*, has little to do with the goddess. The *DB*, though supposedly a Śākta work, has many such episodes, where you can read how major goddesses became divine thanks to the good efforts of Kṛṣṇa. By contrast, Śiva is mentioned in remarkably few places. A similar trend appears in devotional Bengali poetry, where the two dark deities are occasionally identified with each other. The worshippers of Kālī retaliated by telling myths which show Kṛṣṇa as Kālī's inferior, or even make her his mother. Most of these developments happened after the 16th century CE, when a Vaiṣṇava revival flowered in north-east India. In its wake, a number of Kālī Tantras sought to incorporate Viṣṇu/Kṛṣṇa, or were extended by the addition of chapters on Viṣṇu. They popularised the new idea that Kālī is Kṛṣṇas mother. One of them, the *Kālīvilāsatantra* (Goudriaan & Gupta 1981: 82-83), is an excellent example how left-hand Tantra was corrupted by the religious heterodoxy. It includes the idea that only the twice-born classes are allowed to recite Oṁ and Svāhā, thereby excluding Śūdras and women. For the sake of tolerance, there is a rite that turns Śūdras into Vaiśyas of sorts, but this is unofficial and recitation of Oṁ remains prohibited. This is by no means a minor problem. Oṁ is the sound-form of Brahman, meaning that women and the lower classes are not permitted contact to the all-self. You have to believe in a very selective, upper class Brahman to invent such rubbish. The *Kālīvilāsatantra* is strongly opposed to the imaginary worship of the divyas and the wild worship of the vīras, and proposes that in this age of evil, both methods are forbidden. Thinking of the Five Ms? It's hello to substitutes instead. In the last section we learn that Kālī gave birth to Kṛṣṇa, one of the very rare cases where Kālī appears as a mother at all. Reversing the usual pattern, we read that Gaurī (the Golden One) became black (Kālī) when Kāma's arrow hit her, i.e. she turned from bright to dark to bring forth a dark (Kṛṣṇa) child. Her two breasts produced two qualities of amṛta, white and black. It might remind you of the two sorts of blood (life-giving from the right and death-dealing from the left) produced by the body of Medusa (Apollodor, *Bibl.* 3, 10, 3 in Lücke 2005). Creeping Vaiṣṇavisation also appears in popular worship. Sanjukta Gupta (in McDermott/Kripal 2003) gives an thorough study how Kālī's worship at the great temple of Calcutta has been softened by her priests, who happen to belong to a Vaiṣṇava family tradition. As a result, her statue is not nude but well dressed in an expensive sari, she bears a Vaiṣṇava mark on her nose-ridge, and her face is so densely covered by flowers that the terrifying details are well concealed. Unlike traditional worship, the goddess receives animal offerings only twice a year, and during her most important ritual, the Kālīpūjā, she receives no animal offerings and is addressed as Lakṣmī.

Indian literature is certainly uneasy about Kālī. To many learned Brahmins, sages, reformers and intellectuals, the divine, naked, blood-covered madwoman was the very epitome of a past they would much rather forget. Jainas complained about the bloody sacrifices of goats and animals at her temples, mind you, they complained about most goddesses for the same reasons. Others took an apologetic attitude and toned down the myths to make her a deity who could be mentioned in better society. This usually involved a massive reinterpretation of her insignia and appearance. Usha Menon and Richard Shweder (in MacDermott & Kripal, 2003: 80-99) give an excellent account how Kālī was transformed into a submissive little woman in the 15th century *Caṇḍī Purāṇa*, which turned out be highly influential on the modern opinion on Kālī in India and Nepal. Cynthia Ann Humes gives a fascinating study on such transformations in MacDermott & Kripal, 2003: 145-168 and introduces six models on how the goddess was considered, or interpreted. **Devotional**, as expressed by Śākta worshippers and Tantrics; **apologist** (learned Brahmins and Vedic worshippers apologising for certain aspects of the cult or explaining them away); **disbelieving** (outsiders, such as Buddhists, Christians and Jainas, who consider the deity a dangerous delusion); **demonizing** (here the goddess is real and evil), **dismissive** (making little of the importance of the deity) and **sensationalizing/scandalizing**, generally involving blood, guts and sexual excess. These six approaches appear in most treatments of Kālī. Useful when you look into Indian literature, or into the texts composed by Western authors.

Kālī had a popular revival thanks to a number of Bengali poets who made her the special focus of their devotion. These poets made strong use of Tantric imagery and poetry, and showed an obvious passion for worship in the sense of bhakti. They usually did not take a heroic or divine attitude but considered the goddess as the Mother and themselves as her child. This made a humble and very humane approach possible: the poet, though obviously an inspired seer, does not completely withdraw from social rules and regulations but attempts to relate the vision of his all-embracing love to his fellow humans. Many devotional poets alluded to the fact that everybody thought them mad. How far they participated in Tantric forms of worship remains an open and much discussed issue (see McDermott in White 2000, and McDermott 2001 for an inspiring selection of devotional hymns). Many poets practised meditation, raised the Kuṇḍalinī, got drunk on the secretions of their minds and saw the goddess in all and everything. Lovemaking, however, is conspicuously absent from their poetry. Best known of these poets is the incomparable Rāmprasād Sen (c. 1718-1775 CE), the son of a medical doctor. After a singularly devout childhood, Rāmprasād was educated by two gurus in succession. He wished to devote his life to religion, but the untimely death of his father set an end to his spiritual career and forced him to seek employment. Caring little for prestigious occupations, he preferred to become a clerk for a wealthy landowner. Doing figures all day did not really suit his religious temperament. He spent much of his time jotting down devotional hymns on the edges of the account books. Eventually, these poems were discovered and so was their shy scribe. It is claimed that his employer was quite impressed (or was that worried?) and decided that business is safer when saints leave their fingers out of it. Rāmprasād was sent home to his village but his wages continued to be paid. This allowed the poet to compose (allegedly) more than a thousand hymns to his favourite deities Kālī, Tārā and Umā. Of these hymns, some three hundred survive. They inspired a tradition of devotional poetry that was so influential that more than two hundred authors took up the genre, using Rāmprasād's style and metaphors to celebrate a wide range of deities. To this day, Rāmprasād's songs are highly popular and frequently sung in Bengal.

Kālī Abroad

With the occupation of India, Kālī entered Western thought. She caused such a stir that you can find her, alive and well, in numerous books, movies, TV programs and even a few political movements. During the British occupation, Kālī became the essential symbol of what was incomprehensible to the European mind. Many saw her primarily as a deity of sex and violence. The fact that these forces were represented by a *female* deity did not make things better. Numerous European writers made her the epitome of sin and saw in her the soul of an India which they could never completely control. To them, Kālī was the personified Orient: dark, desirable, dangerous, debased and essentially destructive. The mere fact that Kālī was often shown nude was enough to turn her into a deity of sex-craving maniacs. Others saw her as the goddess of criminals, bandits, killers and ultimately, of those revolutionaries who did not really feel happy under British rule. Frequently she was called the goddess of the Thugs. Here we encounter a difficult topic.

According to popular myth, the Thugs were a cult of killers who used to strangle their victims (usually innocent travellers) with a silken scarf (rumal). Most of what we know regarding the thugs is hearsay evidence. According to William Sleeman, authorised to solve the Thug problem in 1826, Thugee goes back to the myth of Kālī's fight with Rukt Bij-dana (Raktabīja). As this mighty Asura doubled each time a drop of his blood fell to earth, Kālī was faced with millions of demonic opponents and soon exhausted. She created two humans out of the sweat running down her arms and gave them the rumal. The humans killed all the replicas of the Asura without spilling a single drop of blood. When they had slain the lot, they wanted to give the rumal back to Kālī. According to Sleeman, the goddess asked them to keep it and to kill all people who were not of their own kin. (Sleeman in Sen 1993). The basic idea behind this tale is that Thugs are allowed to kill strangers. In the process, the goddess receives the life of the victim while the happy Thug absconds with the valuables.

All of which may be misleading. Whether the Thugs really existed in the way that Sleeman portrayed them is a difficult question. That some people were occasionally robbed and murdered is certain. Whether this was done with Kālī's blessing is less certain, let alone whether the Thuggee 'cult' existed at all. Let's take a look into Cynthia Humes and Hugh B. Urban's researches (MacDermott & Kripal, 2003: 145-168 and 169-195). It was, first of all, Captain Sleeman who made the Thug-cult famous. His sources, as he was reluctant to admit, were not witnesses or victims but H. H. Wilson, a translator of Indian myths and folktales, Major General Sargent Leger and Dr. Richard C. Sherwood. The latter imagined that there exist a class of hereditary stranglers who serve the goddess 'Cali'. The northern branch of this movement was supposedly called 'T'hegs' meaning deceivers. Sherwood claimed to have inside knowledge of the cult and even made up a cute little dictionary of Thug slang, which was widely read by the British. His data, however, turned out to come from early medieval folktales (such as Somadeva's famous compilation) dramas and stage-plays, most of them with highly fantastic contents. None of it was factual or contemporary. William Sleeman made use of these works to support his own gory tales of Thuggee. In his opinion, *it is the imperious duty of the Supreme Government of this country to put an end in some way or other to this dreadful system of murder, by which thousands of human beings are now annually sacrificed upon every great road throughout India.* Sleeman believed that each goddess temple was a meeting place of murderers who planned their crimes under the protection of Brahmins. Now you might ask whether there is any proof of these remarkable accusations. It turns out that there isn't. Perhaps Sleeman had some evidence and perhaps he didn't. He said that he had, but it had been eaten by white ants. At the time being we have no way of knowing whether Thuggee and human sacrifice for Kālī ever happened. This did not deter the British from taking violent action. Sleeman was authorised to crush the Thugs and made a bloody job of it. A large number of innocent Śāktas were arrested, questioned and sentenced, not to mention numerous Muslims who were assumed to worship 'Davey'. To the British, most of whom did not make much of a difference between one heathen idol and another, Kālī was identical with Durgā and many other dangerous goddesses, whose followers were automatically suspected of all sorts of crimes and perversions. Soon enough, the British discovered Thugs everywhere. Thuggee became the national paranoia, much like the terrorism-craze of our time, and just like today, we have no way of estimating how much happened in reality and how much in the imagination. Only idiots believe in the mass media. As Cynthia Humes expressed: *Eliminating Thugs was precisely the rationale for the British to enter new areas, demand cooperation from princely states, and countermand standard Muslim law, which required greater proof than mere accusations by cohorts.* The Thug-hunt went on for several years. In the process, the British but also the Indian population were convinced that Thuggee was real. Then Sleeman officially declared 'victory' over the terrible Thugs (mission accomplished!) and claimed that the problem had been solved for good. Indeed it seemed so, as from that point onwards, there were no further reports of Thuggee. However, a few years later, the Thugs reappeared. Strangely, they were not interested in murdering Indians any more. Instead, they were a subversive force that sought to get rid of the British themselves. The new Thugs were sexually crazed and a threat to the numerous British women who were, by then, coming to India for marriage. The sexual element is worth considering. Numerous British writers had claimed that Indian males suffer from degeneration, cowardice and slave mentality and that Hindu culture was corrupt due to masturbation, phallus worship and sexual indulgence. By contrast, Hindu women were obviously dangerous, sexually-overactive seductresses. Such women were, so the British assumed, aptly represented by Kālī, Durgā, Devī and others. The British were scared of the 'cult' and assumed that Thuggee lurked not only behind the odd murder on the road but also behind all attempts to subvert their enlightened rule. Kālī, always good when a symbol is needed, was soon considered a goddess of rebellion, terrorism and social unrest. Soon enough, Hindus picked up the notion and when the Bengalis began to fight for independence, they found solace in a Kālī who scared the Europeans out of their wits. In fact she became the personification of pretty much everything abhorred by the European establishment. Politicians, missionaries and reformers, British or Indian, found their own repressed urges and instincts reflected in the dark goddess and did not like it one bit. Their ignorance formed the foundation of the modern Kālī.

In the Western world, Kālī has become a goddess associated with a good many ideas that rarely appear in Indian lore. To the British occupation force, Kālī was synonymous with murder, rebellion and sex (evil!). A few decades later the Hippie movement turned the world around and sex suddenly became good. This made Tantra (previously evil) a good thing, and the nude gods Śiva and Kālī popular as proto-hippies. Nowadays many see Kālī as a goddess of sex and sexual

Figure 73 - Kālī and Śiva making love.
Brass statuette, Rajasthan, 18th century, height 12.5cm.

liberation. This is not what the scribes of the *Mahābhārata* had in mind, nor is it quite what Kālī's Tantric worshippers assumed. Then some feminists decided that any goddess who tramples on a male god has to be a deity of gender liberation, and made her a goddess of free women. All of a sudden Kālī had gained a lot of new devotees. Few of them had any idea of her background (or any spiritual training), especially not such experts as Barbara G. Walker, who introduced the idea that Oṁ is Kālī's sound, that Kālī invented Sanskrit and incidentally the very idea of the Logos, which was later stolen and adopted by Christians. To Walker, Kālī appears as the 'archetypal triple goddess' (virgin, mother, crone, as set out in Robert Graves' *The White Goddess*) who is the origin of pretty much all elder religions, including the Christian trinity (McDermott in Hawley & Wulff, 1996: 297-304). In the wake of such rubbish came the idea that Kālī is one of the earliest mother goddesses, or better, the very Great Goddess of prehistoric matriarchy. The common feminist myth goes that the black goddess was originally the all-goddess, who was loved and worshipped by everyone, until aggressive patriarchal cults destroyed matriarchy and made the goddess a creature of evil and horror. Kālī's symbols, such as skulls, snakes, weapons, blood and corpses are part of the evil reinterpretation of a goddess who was once nice and friendly to all. None of this is based on any sort of research. Kālī did not start out nice and became nasty, nor can I agree with David Kinsley's notion that Kālī started horrible but became more benign later on (Kinsley 1988: 125). We encounter a lot of fierce and destructive Kālīs in early art and literature. By contrast, the modern Kālīs of popular art tend to be sexy little girlies who wield their sword more for fun than for effect. However, to see this as a development from horrible crones to little darlings is to postulate a linear development. It turns out that while most early Kālīs are savage nightmares, there are several who do not fit the pattern. Just look into the *Mahābhārata* sections quoted above - which Kinsley seems to have conveniently ignored. To put it simply, to her worshippers, the black goddess appears terrible and beautiful, while the outsiders didn't understand anyway. But this is not all. Thanks to the Internet, there is more dubious information available than ever. Kālī as a prominent and enigmatic goddess has been adopted as a symbol of all sorts of markets, including Chaos Magick and Satanism. As she seems to idealise violence, she is also prominent among people yearning for the end of the world. On the other hand, Kālī is appearing in softcore mainstream esoteric publications. Rachel Fell McDermott gives some delightful examples she found in the Internet. In one, Kālī is invoked by mantra to do the housework (*Om Namo Kali Om... I praise you when I scrub the toilet*), in others, she is invoked to improve sex life and to 'liberate the female orgasm'. And while the Western world is busy discovering all sorts of repressed urges under Kālī's dripping loincloth there are also neo-Indian movements that attempt to reduce the goddess to the status of a saintly girl. For instance Swami Satyananda Saraswati and Shree Maa, who compiled a little book *Kali Puja*, 1998, out of various original texts. They manage to mistranslate the name of the goddess from its original 'Black' or 'Dark' to 'She who takes away Darkness'. Kālīkā, meaning 'Little Black One' or 'Blackie' is rendered by them 'She Who is the Cause of Removing Darkness'. We are witnessing the birth of many new Kālīs who have remarkably little to do with their own past.

Masks of Kālī

Like several other Indian deities, Kālī was not only worshipped in a single shape. Indian gods tend to multiply. Sometimes a single deity appears in several aspects, sometimes a whole bunch of deities are collected under a similar name. There is a cluster of goddesses who are supposed to be appearances of Kālī. You may think of them along several lines. When you have a group, such as the eight Kālīs, the group can be considered a specific (and specialised) aspects of the main goddess. Or you could propose that the eight are a collection of local goddesses who began independently and came to be identified with Kālī in an attempt at unification. What other interpretations can you think of? Invent some more.

One of the most famous assortments of Kālīs are the eight Kālīs. Here is the selection given by the *Toḍala Tantra.*

Dakṣiṇākālikā is the goddess who grants boons. Dakṣiṇākālikā is presently the most popular form of Kālī. She appears as a beautiful young woman standing on the breast of a Śiva who is lying blissfully on the ground beneath her. This picture contains a lot of symbolism, so much, that I hope you'll forgive me for giving only a few interpretations. One meaning of the picture is that Śiva is passive, formless consciousness while Kālī is consciousness in force, form and dynamic activity. In other words, when Kālī is in action, Śiva becomes passive like a sleeper or a corpse. As the *TT* points out, he nevertheless remains stiff. In another interpretation, the standing posture is a replacement for all those early Kālīs who used to sit on Śiva. Feet can be a symbol for the two lowest cakras, i.e. for perineum and genitals. A third interpretation, which I have heard a few times, goes as follows. One bonny day Kālī was busy destroying evil-minded Asuras. She went over the battlefield like a screeching fury and slaughtered all demons who got in her way. Soon the surviving Asuras fled but Kālī had only just warmed up properly and wouldn't stop. In her ecstasy, she was demolishing the universe! The gods despaired. Only Śiva knew how to calm her and laid down in her path of destruction. As Kālī was happily rampaging along she inadvertedly stepped on him. This is not the way Indian wives are supposed to treat their husbands. She instantly stopped, said 'oops!' and stuck out her tongue, much as north Indian ladies do, as a sign of shame. This tale is widely popular in India and Nepal. It comes from the 15th century *Caṇḍī Purāṇa,* a work that went to considerable lengths to domesticate the fierce dark goddess.

Let's look at the word dakṣiṇa. Dakṣiṇā is a goddess in purāṇic myth. She is so similar to Svāhā that I won't bother to re-tell her myth. As you'll remember, Svāhā is the goddess who transfers the sacrifices to the gods. Without her, no sacrifice is considered efficient. Now Dakṣiṇā is very similar. In Vedic times, a dakṣiṇa was an extra fee, gift or present for the officiating sacrificial priest, originally a minimum of one cow. This gift was believed essential to make the major sacrifice efficient. A cow is great value, you can see this idea comes from a period when only the very rich were able to afford a sacrifice. In later times, the value of the gifts went down a good deal, but they are still present in modern ritual. By giving a dakṣiṇa, the good effects of the sacrifice are actualised and merit finds reward. Without a dakṣiṇa, so the priests taught, the greatest sacrifices remain barren and fruitless. The dakṣiṇa was personified and became a goddess. According to the *DB* she was married to a god called Sacrifice. Dakṣiṇa can mean 1. a fee for the sacrificial priest. 2. a prolific, fertile cow. 3. a gift, a donation. 4. the completion of a rite. 5. a reward. In this sense, Dakṣiṇākālikā is the Kālī who is benevolent, who gives to the worshipper what s/he deserves, who grants the results of prayer, worship and spiritual discipline. She is a goddess of manifestation. The term dakṣiṇa connects with another stream of meanings. Dakṣiṇa is the southern direction. When you sit facing east (as Śiva is supposed to do), your left hand is to the north, the dark direction, and your right hand to the south, the bright, visible world. Hence, dakṣiṇa can also mean 6. Right, to the right. Note that Dakṣiṇa Kālī usually steps on Śiva with her right foot. There are a few representations where she uses her left foot, but these are rare and only used for magical purposes. 7. Southern, to the south, in the south. 8. Deosil motion. Going sun-wise (or clockwise) around something is to keep it to the right. Like the old Irish, the Indians have it as a sign of politeness to approach with the right side first. 9. Able, clever, dextrous - references to the superiority of the right hand in most people. The association of right and proper is not far. However, the term dakṣiṇa can also have a sinister meaning. When dakṣiṇa is the south, it is also the location of Yama, the lord of death. Here south is the direction of heat, hence of the funeral fire, and traditionally, cremation places used to be to the south of each settlement. In this sense, the goddess could be seen as the deity of the burning ground. Those who prefer this interpretation claim that Dakṣiṇa-Kālī is the goddess who liberates from the fear of death.

Siddhikālikā is the Kālī who gives siddhi. Siddhi is a highly complex term. To sum up some of the meanings: 1. accomplishment, achievement, success, attainment etc. 2. hitting a mark. 3. healing, to cure by. 4. validity, coming into force, actualisation. 5. settlement, payment. 6. proof, result. 7. decision. 8. preparation, cooking, ripening, maturing. 9. prosperity, well-being, good luck, advantage. 10. emancipation, perfection. 11. acquisition of magical power. 12. unusual skill, talent. The latter two points are the most important when the word is used in a Tantric context. The siddhis are a range of unique skills or magical powers, and for many, they are the main object of worship, meditation and ritual. Eight of them are especially famed. Aṇima, mahimā, garīmā, laghimā prāpti, prākāmya, iṣitva, and vaṣitva are the powers to become *very small, vast, light, heavy, power of vision and movement, power of creation and control over the worlds and their Lords* (Woodroffe 2001: 18)

Guhyakālikā has her name from guhya: 1. covered, hidden, concealed, secret, private. 2. a tortoise (name of Viṣṇu). 3. the genitals. 4. the anus. Śiva appears as Guhyaguru, the Mysterious Guru, and when Kālī manifests as guhya, she is mysterious, hidden, revealing and hiding as she weaves will and consciousness. She is the Kālī who lurks behind the play of appearances, and who reveals her true nature to all who pass through the veil of form. According to the *Tantrasāra* (quoted in Kinsley 1998:67) Guhyakālī is not nude but wears black clothes. She is fond of serpents and wears them as her 'sacred thread' (traditionally, women are not entitled to the second birth, and hence, to wear the sacred thread). Over her head looms the thousand-headed serpent Ananta (usually Viṣṇu's couch) and she sits on a bed made of serpents. Though she is dreadful and terrifying, she laughs wildly and is accompanied by a Śiva who appears as a young boy (perhaps this idea comes from Tārā's cult).

Śrīkālikā is a benevolent goddess. Śrī appears first in Vedic texts, where she is the goddess of generosity, radiance, beauty and grace. The term śrī means 1. bright, radiant, shining. 2. light, splendour, glory, grace, beauty, loveliness. 3. welfare, prosperity, success, good fortune, wealth, high rank, majesty, power. 4. intellect, understanding. 5. speech. The word is not only the name of a goddess, it is also applied to other deities. Before the advent of early Hinduism, the goddess Śrī had merged with the similar goddess Lakṣmī, creating the popular form Śrīlakṣmī. Other gods are more loosely associated with Śrī. Sometimes the title is given to Sarasvatī. More often it is used as an honorific prefix, and gods, elders and venerable persons are addressed with it. In Kālī's cluster, Śrīkālikā is not only a benevolent and generous goddess. She is also a link to the cluster of deities that emerge from Lakṣmī. Consider the mixed goddess Lakśmīkālikā. Here is a benevolent, generous Kālī who grants joy, pleasure and luxury to her devotees.

Bhadrakālī is one of the elder Kālīs. She appears a few times in early shāktic literature. In the *Devī Māhātmyam*, that famous work on the Devī's battles against various demons, she plays a major part. She is named twice in the *Kūrma Purāṇa* (1, 12, 100 & 148) in the thousand names of Pārvatī. It also names Mahākālī, Guhyaśakti, Ādyā, Siddhā and Śrī. In the *KP*, 1, 15, 43 we learn that at Dakṣa's sacrifice, *Bhadrakālī, Maheśvarī was created angrily by Umā.* She is described briefly in *Devī Mahātmyam* 11, 26: *'Terrible with flames, exceedingly sharp, destroyer of all asuras, may your trident guard us from fear. Salutation be to you, O Bhadrakālī'*

Bhadra is a cheerful term that seems to appeal to the devotee. It means 1. blessed, auspicious, fortunate, happy and prosperous. 2. good, gracious, kind, friendly. 3. beautiful, excellent, fair, lovely, dear. 4. skilful. Sounds good, doesn't it? You might get a wrong impression of the goddess if you prefer words to experience. Bhadrakālī is one of the most terrifying Kālīs in evidence. She joins the Devī to slaughter demons on the battlefield. Her name is a polite term to placate the goddess. Just look at the *DM*. It is composed of three distinct episodes. In the first, we find the Asuras Madhu and Kaiṭabha attacking Brahmā. In his panic, Brahmā tries to wake Viṣṇu, who sleeps in mystic slumber. When Brahmā praises

Mahāmāyā, she allows Viṣṇu to wake and defeat the oppressors. Episode two offers the battle against the terrible buffalo demon Mahiṣāsura (originally an enemy of Skanda). Here the Devī makes her first appearance in written myth. She is created by Śiva and Viṣṇu, and equipped with arms of all varieties by the rest of the gods. Episode three contains the battle against the Asuras Śumbbha and Niśumbha, Caṇḍa, Muṇḍa and Raktabīja. All three episodes are distinct stories. In the much later version of the *DB*, episode two and three are combined, and this is the version that is most popular nowadays. We find Bhadrakālī appearing in episode two (3, 9) where she destroys the general Cikṣura with her pike. In a vague way, she is identified with the Devī (or the Devī with her?). It's a crazy thing. Nowadays, many Indians believe that Kālī and similar goddesses are merely angry aspects of one great goddess called Devī. Or that, as the *DM* indicates, Kālī was created out of the dark, frowning forehead of Ambikā. You may notice that in her first appearance in the *DM*, Bhadrakālī is not created or evoked by any deity. She simply exists. Where she came from and how she got involved in the fight remains an open question. In chapter 5, 83-88, it is Pārvatī who goes to the Ganges for a bath. Stepping into the blessed waters, a beautiful goddess sprung from her body, the blessed Ambikā. *After she had issued forth, Pārvatī became dark and was called Kālikā and stationed on mount Himalaya.* So we have a Kālī who simply exists, one who arises out of Ambikā, one who comes out of Pārvatī, and one who is addressed as the Devī.

In 4, 35-37, the gods praise the goddess for saving them.

> *4, 35 'And if a boon is to be granted to us by you, O Maheśvarī, whenever we think of you again, destroy our direct calamities'.*
> *38-39: The Ṛṣī said: O King, being thus propitiated by the devas for the sake of the world and for their own sake, Bhadrakālī said, 'Be it so' and vanished from their sight.*

Please stop a moment and consider. In the primary 'holy writ' of the Śākta movement, it is not radiant Devī, magnificent Durgā or beautiful Ambikā who promises the worshippers to come and help. It is fierce and savage Bhadrakālī who makes the crucial promise that links her eternally with those humans (and deities) who have the brains to comprehend her blessings. It gets more complicated in chapter 7, 5. Caṇḍa and Muṇḍa approach the graciously smiling Ambikā. What happens now can be found in the next section.

Cāmuṇḍākālikā When Caṇḍa and Muṇḍa tried to capture Ambikā, she became terribly angry. Her face turned black.

> *6. Out from the surface of her forehead, fierce with frown, issued suddenly Kālī of terrible countenance, armed with a sword and a noose.*
> *7-9. Bearing the strange skull-topped staff, decorated with a garland of skulls, clad in a tiger's skin, very appalling owing to her emaciated flesh, with gaping mouth, fearful with her tongue lolling out, having deep-sunk reddish eyes and filling the*

regions of the sky with her roars, and falling upon impetuously and slaughtering the great asuras in that army, she devoured those hosts of the foes of the devas.

Lines 10-15 describe in gory detail how Kālī devours elephants, the entire demon cavalry and most of the raging Asuras. Caṇḍa attacks her with a storm of arrows, Muṇḍa hurls thousands of discusses, but the missiles all end in Kālī's gaping mouth. *19. Thereat Kālī, who was roaring frightfully, whose fearful teeth were gleaming within her dreadful mouth, laughed terribly with exceeding fury.* Cutting down both enemies with her sword, she sends the Asuras into panic flight. Returning to the Ambikā (here called Caṇḍikā, i.e. the Wild One, with a diminutive ending), she exclaims, laughing aloud, *24. 'Here I have brought you the heads of Caṇḍa and Muṇḍa as two great animal offerings in this sacrifice of battle'.* For making this offering, Kālī received the title Cāmuṇḍā, meaning the Slayer of Caṇḍa and Muṇḍa. Such action did not go unnoticed. The demonic Śumbha and his hosts attack Ambikā and Kālī, who roars a terrifying 'Hūṁ' filling all quarters of the world (8, 10). At this instant, Śaktis arise from the bodies of Brahmā, Śiva, Kārtikeya, Viṣṇu and Indra. This is the first appearance of a group of Seven Mothers: Brahmānī riding a swan; Māheśvarī, riding a bull, adorned with serpents and the kalā of the moon; Ambikā Kaumārī on a peacock; three female forms of Viṣṇu's: Vaiṣṇavī riding Garuḍa, Vārāhī in boar shape, Nārasimhī in lion-form; and Aindrī with her thunderbolt. These goddesses, here called Mātṛs (mothers, principles, matrices) have the time of their lives slaughtering foes. Finally the great Raktabīja (Blood-seed) approaches. He had been granted the siddhi that whenever a drop of his blood fell to the ground, a new Raktabīja appeared. As the ferocious ladies hurl their weapons at him, the earth is splattered with his blood and soon there are millions of Raktabījas arising from the soil. This scares the gods out of their minds. *53-54. Seeing the devas dejected, Caṇḍikā laughed and said to Kālī, 'O Cāmuṇḍā, open out your mouth wide; with this mouth quickly take in the drops of blood generated by the blow of my weapon and (also) the great asuras born of the drops of blood of Raktabīja. 55. 'Roam about the battle-field, devouring the great asuras that spring from him. So shall this daitya, with his blood emptied, perish.'* And so it happened. Kālī sucked the invincible Raktabīja dry and glutted herself on his spawn. *63. Thereupon the devas attained great joy, O King. The band of Mātṛs who sprang from them danced, being intoxicated with blood.* Well, the slaughter continues for quite a while. I can only recommend that you get yourself a copy of the text and recite it aloud, it's a wonderful celebration full of drama and intensity. Good for the immune system. The nine-syllable mantra of Cāmuṇḍā Devī is **Aiṁ, Hrīṁ, Klīṁ, Cāmuṇḍāyai vicce**.

Śmaśānakālikā is the Kālī of the cremation place. Śmaśāna is usually an elevated cremation place, where corpses are burned with great ceremony. It can also be a place where the ashes and bones of the burned are buried. In another sense, śmaśāna can be an oblation for the ancestors. Some burning-places are of great beauty. A cremation can be

Figure 74 - Bhadrā Kālī.
Stone (partly eroded), Rāngaṛh, Rajputana, 12th century.

an elaborate rite involving guests, celebrants, offerings, choice wood and incense and a whole group of qualified priests. Other cremation places, and these are the ones frequented by heroic worshippers, were hidden at the fringes of the jungle. I say were, as there is very little jungle left in modern India. Here, poor people were burned, such as those without relations, executed criminals and plague victims. Others were simply buried with no cremation at all. Low budget cremations imply that the job is badly done, and the burial of the remnants is a swift and sloppy job. Such śmaśānas were macabre sites where jackals feasted on the remnants of corpses. For the viratic worshipper, a śmaśāna is just the place to encounter a great range of nightside horrors and to come to terms with them. Tantric literature is full of references to nocturnal worship at cremation places. The term can be taken literally, i.e. the worshipper goes to a place of fear, evil, disgust and impurity to find a bit of peace and quiet. It can also be a cremation place in the imagination. Here you may come upon the mother of all cremation places, the sheer, mind-stunning essence of death and transcendence. I suggest you build up a good and dramatic cremation place in your imagination. Make it as dark and dreadful as you can. Indian poets occasionally give good descriptions. Look at this account. It comes from two versions of the wonderful *Vetālapañcaviṁśatikā,* by Somadeva and by Śivadāsa. We meet King Vikramasena, who is oath bound to visit a sorcerer on the cremation place.

> *Early in the night of the new moon he swathed his head in a dark-blue cloth and left the royal residence, bearing his sword in his hand. Free of fear and confusion he entered the cremation place. In the terrifying deep, dense darkness it appeared a dirty grey, lit by the flickering flames of smouldering pyres. The ground was littered with countless human bones, skulls and skeletons. Everywhere, dreadful Bhūta spirits and Vetāla-Demons were moving, who gave themselves with abandon to their terrifying pursuit, their mouths full of meat, their minds intoxicated by strong drink. The shrill howl of the jackals echoed far and wide, so that the cremation place appeared like a second form of Śiva in his cruel form as Bhairava.*

At the end of the book, the king has to return to the cremation place:

> *Finally, King Trivikramasena, bearing the corpse on his shoulders, reached the beggar-monk Kṣāntiśīla. The renouncer was sitting at the foot of a tree, alone and desolate, eagerly awaiting the return of the king. He sat within a circle made of white bone-powder. The inside of the circle was smeared with blood and in all directions, vessels of blood were set up. The curve was brightly illuminated by lamps feeding on human fat. Nearby, a sacrificial fire was burning. All sacrificial gear stood ready. The ascetic worshipper was venerating his personal deity.*

How the king managed to deceive the sinister adept is something you ought to read for yourself. The *'Tale of the Vetāla'* is one of the most important early Indian collection of stories and is available in numerous translations.

But cremation places are more than sites to work dark rituals or to transcend one's feelings of revulsion, horror and disgust. For one thing, the morbid and macabre have their own beauty. To meditate at the cremation place implies discovering the beauty, the superb aesthetics of inevitable decay. Some worshippers chose this as a discipline. Others identified the whole manifest universe as a vast cremation place. Death and decay are not restricted to the places set aside by humans. Dissolution and destruction are part of the play of life, and can be observed everywhere. Every place on this bonny earth has seen the death of countless creatures. Whatever exists builds on the foundations of what has been before. Whatever follows, builds on what is happening now. Every single thing in the world is bound to rot and disintegrate eventually. Just look at yourself! You came here with nothing. All that you own is borrowed, including your name and body. Your property? It was never yours. Your achievements? They are all in the mind. Your history? Ripples on the lake, foam on the sea. You have the right to use and enjoy them for a while. One day you will leave, and others will use them. Your atoms will go into the winds, the earth, the waters, the plants and animals who lent them to you. It's good to travel lightly. When you can see the whole world as a cremation place, when you can watch the end of all that is you and yours, when you can say goodbye to the fancies and beliefs that constitute what you consider yourself and enjoy the freedom that arises from this release, the cremation ground becomes a womb of new beginnings. The bone-strewn ground, haunted by ghosts and demons, becomes the flower-strewn, fragrant yoni of the dark goddess, out of whose elixirs fresh life manifests. This is a lot more than a flowery metaphor. Those who see Tantra as a religion of joy, beauty and divine eroticism are not going deep enough. Body has its beauty, but beauty is subject to age and eventual decay. The cremation place is the nightside counterpart of the dayside dream of joy and beauty. Both belong together, both are the same truth seen from different points of view. In left-hand Tantra, the vision of lust and beauty must be balanced with the vision of dread and destruction. They fuse, they blend and become one. Beyond this point comes transcendence, and freedom from conventions. Don't agree, don't disagree, don't talk so much. The easy answer misleads. The facts of life should be experienced. Sex and death are the strongest drives in the human mindset. You can think of them as much as you like. Can you embrace them with your entire being?

Mahākālī is the cosmic manifestation of Kālī. Mahā means great, strong, mighty, abundant. or light, lustre, brilliance, while Kālī means black or time. In this latter sense, Mahākālī can be radiant, brilliant black. A third meaning is a buffalo or a cow. The last reference might be cosmic again, just think of the symbolism that all gods are manifest in one great cow, or the idea that the universe is one vast bovine. As Mahākālī, the goddess is creator, maintainer, destroyer, suspender and re-creator of the cosmos. Mahākālī has ten heads, ten mouths, ten feet and holds in her ten hands club, bow, bolt, trident, bhuśuṇḍī, sword, discus, skull, conch and arrow. Her colour is blue-black, she has three eyes and her body is adorned with sparkling ornaments like the stars in the nightsky.

Eight Kālīs are all well and good, but why stop? Abhinavagupta and the Krama cult decided on thirteen, one more than usually worshipped in Kashmir. And thirteen is not much either. There are several hymns extolling the hundred names of Kālī, plus a few that managed to offer a thousand. Just a few of them to give you some food for thought:

Haṁsa Kālī: Haṁsa, as you will recall from the chapter on mantra, is the supreme mantra, the only one uttered without effort, as it is the sound of out-breath and in-breath. The meaning of Haṁsa goes beyond breathing, however. It also refers to the supreme spirit and to the natural pulsation within the manifest universe.

Kāmakalā Kālī: Kāmakalā is the 'Unit of Desire'. Imagine a hexagram representing the union of female and male (the two triangles symbolise the genitals). It can also be seen as a glyph of the goddess, each angle being a power zone in her body. And it can be the sign that is used in spells of attraction. You can even project this image on your body.This Kālī is much concerned with energising sorceries and making desires come true.

Ādyā: primordial, ancient, original. She is a black Kālī clad in a red robe, reclining on a couch.

Klīṁ-kārī: Creatrix of the bīja Klīṁ, the seed of desire (Kāma) and sexual lust (Rati), associated with the root and sexual centres in body.

Digambarī: Sky-clad. Nude. Kālī is nude as she is free of deception, illusion and the glamour of separate consciousness. She wears no masks - her nude body is the naked truth. The same goes for Śiva, and consequently, the title can be used for both.

Araṇyā: has the name Forest, Jungle. She is identified with Kālī in the *Kulacūḍāmaṇi Tantra* 5, 67-70, where we read that their identities, mantras, rituals and worship are identical. She is not only associated with forests but also with water, see 5, 33, where the devotee declares his familiarity with kula matters in the forest and near water. Araṇyā is worshipped at night for the evocation of a ritual partner, who happens to be a divine female or a serpent woman from the underworld. The partner is described as a supernatural being, not as a lover in flesh and blood. Why is this so? First of all, the rite is performed by a forest dwelling ascetic, and there were few women available in the dense heart of the jungle. Consequently, a good many ascetics invoked a spirit, be it a vegetation goddess (Yakṣī), a serpent girl from the deep or a celestial maiden from the height as an imaginary companion. Such spirits are close to the Christian concept of the succubus, with the exception that the classical succubus is an evil demon who vampirises and kills males, while the spirit of our forest ritual is a ritual partner. The spirit lover is dangerous, but not a demon. Demons are simply gods who have no place and function in the divine plan. The spirit lover has a place in the world, and for many lonely adepts, it is quite an important one. She is

Figure 75 - Two classical Kālī yantras.
Top: Śmaśana Kālī, bottom: Dakṣiṇā Kālī

respected, worshipped and helps the adept to achieve liberation. In short, lonely Tantric worshippers found a way to integrate their sexual urges while the Christians were scared and tried to banish them.

There is, however, more to these spirits. The divine female is a Śakti, the naga-maiden can be a form of the Kuṇḍalinī. Both of them need not be human women at all. Nevertheless they can manifest as human women, and in this sense the rite is open. It evokes a ritual partner. How, and on what plane this partner manifests, depends very much on the circumstances. As the ritual is described very briefly, and the text abounds with twilight language, it may take a bit of creative contemplation to make sense of it. The worshipper places a conch in the north-east direction and draws a yantra. North-east is the direction of deepest darkness from where the first, faint glow of the dawn emerges. The *well controlled sādhaka* repeats the mantra 108 times on the eighth night, and repeats the ritual till the 14th night. What happens in these nights? *73. Naked, with betel in his mouth, his hair loose (but) his senses under control, with eyes rolling from the effect of wine and in union with a woman other than his wife, 74. the jewel of the kulas and the beloved of heroes should worship with scents and flower(s) the naked ladies; and he should worship the yantra which has a name inscribed within.* This evokes the maiden, who comes to the sādhaka, wherever he may be, full of sexual longing and desire. The sādhaka offers her wine and meat, dedicates some to the guru, and eats the reminder himself after bowing and asking her permission. *79. Or else, the object of worship may be honoured with the 'nectar' from the top of the head. It is the wine drunk by yogīs; the wine (drunk) by the best of yogīs. 80. The wine to be drunk is not that wine which is produced from molasses and meal.*(trans. Louise M. Finn). I am sure you noticed that the 'woman other than his wife' is the Paraṣakti, the supreme Śakti, who is not any incarnate woman, man or ritual partner but the Śakti-Being to the Śiva-Consciousness-You. 'Para' as you recall, can mean 'supreme' but it can also mean '(of) another (man)'. As mentioned earlier, this tricky term has caused a lot of trouble. There are Tantras that seem to encourage promiscuity and adultery when they are really only talking about a meditative union with the supreme energy/form/consciousness in an internal and solitary rite. When things are not solitary, the adept takes care to identify his wife with the supreme Śakti, a ritual that installs her as the highest goddess. Not that this is the case in our forest ritual, where the adept is pretty much alone. Here, the Paraśakti creates the ritual partner, who may be considered a manifestation of the supreme. The 'jewel of the kulas' can be the sādhaka, the 'beloved of heroes' the goddess, scents and flowers various vibrations and offerings. On the physical plane, a flower may be menstrual blood, on the inner plane, it is a quality such as non-violence, peace, tolerance. 'Ladies', in the *Kulacūḍāmaṇi Tantra* are usually vidyās, i.e. mantras, sciences and formulas of magic power, who are identical with goddesses (a vidyā is the manifestation of a goddess in her sound/vibration-body). Wine is the state of ecstasy that releases the elixirs of the cakras in the head, i.e. the rejuvenating and enlightening secretions of the glands. Line 79 is a clear indication that none of the elements in the ritual is to be taken at its literal value. What reads like a drunken sex orgy with the wife of another guy turns out to be a solitary ritual focusing on inner worship. Consider the description of the sādhaka, who is called *well controlled*; quite at odds with the delirious frenzy described in line 73. If we take the rite as it appears to the uninitiated, we have to make up a scenario where an adept and the wife of another make love in the middle of the jungle at night to produce a spirit lover for him! Why should she bother to do this? Just how did she manage to get away from her husband anyway, without the entire village being aware of it? And why should he need a spirit lover when he already has a human lover? Texts like these are responsible for making Tantra so unpopular with the religious mainstream. All of which makes Araṇyā a hard-core goddess of the left hand path. She did not start quite that wild. Araṇyā is a shortened form of the Vedic forest goddess Aranyānī, who is celebrated in *Ṛg Veda* 146 (trans. Griffith). Could it be that Araṇyānī, the Forest herself, became identified with Kālī as so many of Kālī's worshippers lived in or near the forest?

1. Goddess of wild and forest who seemest to vanish from the sight.

How is it that thou seekest not the village? Art thou afraid?

2. What time the grasshopper replies and swells the shrill cicada's voice,

Seeming to sound with tinkling bells, the Lady of the Woods exults.

3. And, yonder, cattle seems to graze, what seems a dwelling place appears:

Or else at eve the Lady of the Forest seems to free the wains.

4. Here one is calling to his cow, another there hath felled a tree:

At eve, the dweller in the wood fancies that somebody has screamed.

5. The Goddess never slays, unless some murderous enemy approach.

Man eats of savoury fruit and then takes, even as he wills, his rest.

6. Now have I praised the Forest Queen, sweet-scented, redolent of balm,

The Mother of all sylvan things, who tills not but hath stores of food.

All of these names are worth exploring at length. They can be combined with the usual mantras and whatever forms of breathing, dreaming and visualisation you prefer. But you can do more. What happens when you draw a star of eight points by combining two squares and install a Kālī at each? When you visualise Dakṣiṇākālikā in the south, how do the other directions work out? You could do it the simple way and simply assign a Kālī to each point as you go around. Or you could assign the first four Kālīs to one square and the second four Kālīs to the other. Does this layout make more sense? And can you project them on the cakra system? What happens when you locate Dakṣiṇākālikā as the all-manifesting goddess in the mūlādhāra cakra/perineum and Mahākālī as the cosmic, all-encompassing goddess in the sahasrāra cakra at the crown of the head (or above it)? How do the Kālīs fit the cakras on the central pillar? Or would you prefer another selection? Choose a selection of Kālīs that suit your self, your will, your knowledge and your deeds.

Figure 76 - Aranyā.

Hymn to Kālī - Karpūrādi-Stotra

Verse 1

O Mother (She who measures and gives)
and Spouse of the Destroyer of the three cities (Tripurāri= Śiva),
they who thrice recite Thy Bīja
formed by omitting from Karpūra (camphor),
the middle and last consonants and the vowels (Kr),
but adding Vāmākṣi (ī) and Bindu (ṁ) (= Krīṁ),
the speech of such, whether in poetry or prose,
like that of men who have attained all powers (siddhi),
issues of a surety with all ease from the hollow of their mouth,
O Thou who are beauteous with the beauty of a dark rain cloud.

Verse 2

Oh Maheśi, even should one of poor mind
at any time recite but once another doubled Bīja of Thine,
composed of Iśāna (H), and Vāmaśravaṇa (ū),
and Bindu (ṁ) (=Hūṁ); then,
O Thou who hast great and formidable ear-rings of arrow form,
who bearest on Thy head the crescent moon,
such an one becomes all-powerful,
having conquered even the Lord of Speech (Bṛhaspati)
and the Wealth-Giver (Kubera),
and charmed countless youthful women (vidyās?) with lotus-like eyes.

Verse 3

O Kālikā, O auspicious Kālikā with dishevelled hair,
from the corners of whose mouth two streams of blood trickle,
they who recite another doubled Bīja of Thine
composed of Iśa (H), Vaiśvānara (r), Vāmanetra, (ī),
and the lustrous Bindu (ṁ) (= Hrīṁ),
destroy all their enemies,
and bring under subjection the three worlds.

Verse 4

O Destructress of the sins of the three worlds, auspicious Kālikā,
who in Thy upper lotus-like left hand holdest a sword;
and in the lower left hand a severed head; who
with Thy upper right hand maketh the gesture which dispels fear,
and with Thy lower right hand that which grants boons;
they, O Mother with gaping mouth,
who reciting Thy name,

meditate in this way upon the greatness of Thy mantra,
possess the eight great powers (siddhi) of the
Three-Eyed One (Tryaṁbaka= Śiva) in the palm of their hands.

Verse 5

O Mother, they who recite Thy charming Bīja,
composed of the first of the group
of letters (K), followed by Vahni (r), Rati (ī),
and beautified by Vidhu (ṁ), thrice,
the Kūrca (armour) Bīja twice (Hūṁ),
and thereafter, O Smiling Face, the Lajjā (modesty) Bīja twice (Hrīṁ),
followed by the two Thas (Svāhā),
(Krīṁ, Krīṁ, Krīṁ; Hūṁ, Hūṁ; Hrīṁ, Hrīṁ; Dakṣiṇé Kālike,
Krīṁ, Krīṁ, Krīṁ; Hūṁ, Hūṁ; Hrīṁ, Hrīṁ; Svāhā)
they, O Spouse of the Destroyer (Śiva) of the Deva of Desire (Kāma)
contemplating Thy true form,
become themselves the Deva of Love (Kāma)
whose eyes are as beautiful as the petals of the lotus
which Lakṣmī holds in her playful dance.

Verse 6

O Devī of full breasts,
whose throat is adorned with a garland of heads,
They who meditating recite any one or two or three
of Thy very secret and excelling Bījas
or all thereof together with Thy name,
in the moonlike face of all such
the Devi of Speech (Sarasvatī) ever wanders,
and in their lotus-like eyes Kamalā (Lakṣmī) ever plays.

Verse 7

O Mother, even a dullard becomes a poet
who meditates upon Thee raimented with space,
three-eyed, Creatrix of the three worlds,
*whose waist (*buttocks*) is beautiful with a girdle*
made of numbers of dead men's arms,
and who on the breast of a corpse,
as Thy couch in the cremation-ground, enjoyest Mahākāla (Śiva).

Verse 8

Those who truly meditate on Thee, the Spouse of Hara (Śiva),
*who art seated (*entered*) in the cremation-ground*
strewn with funeral pyres, corpses, skulls, and bones,
and haunted by female jackals howling fearfully;

who art very youthful (without childhood or old age*),*
and art in full enjoyment upon Thy Spouse,
are revered by all and in all places.

Verse 9

*What, indeed, O Mother (*Origin of the three worlds*),*
can we of so dull a mind say
*of Thee whose True Being (*reality*)*
not even Dhātā (Brahmā), Iśa (Śiva*), or Hari (Viṣṇu) know?*
Yet, despite our dullness and ignorance,
our devotion towards Thee makes us talk of Thee.
*Therefore, O Dark Devi (*Unlimited One*), forgive this our folly.*
Answer towards ignorant creatures such as we,
is not befitting Thee.

Verse 10

If by night, Thy devotee unclothed, with dishevelled hair,
*recites whilst meditating on Thee (*seeing in the heart*),*
Thy mantra,
when with his Śakti youthful, full-breasted, and heavy-hipped
such an one makes all powers subject to him,
*and dwells on the earth ever a seer (*poet*).*

Verse 11

*O Spouse of Hara, should (a Sādhaka) daily (*always*)*
recite Thy mantra
for the space of a year meditating the while
with knowledge of its meaning
upon Thee intent upon Thy union
with the great Mahākāla,
above whom Thou art, then such a knower has
every pleasure that he wills upon the earth
*(*wandering freely on earth*),*
and holds all great powers in the grasp of his lotus-like hands.

Verse 12

O Mother, Thou givest birth to and protectest the world,
and at the time of dissolution dost withdraw to Thyself
the earth and all things;
therefore Thou art Brahmā,
and Lord of the three worlds,
the Spouse (Viṣṇu) of Śri (Lakṣmī),
and Maheśa (Śiva),
*and all other beings and things (*moving and unmoving things*).*
Ah Me! How, then, shall I praise Thy greatness?

Verse 13

O Mother, people there are who worship
many other Devas than Thyself. They are greatly ignorant,
and know nothing of the high truth,
(but I) of my own uncontrollable desire for Thee approach Thee,
the Primordial Power (Ādyā),
who dost deeply enjoy the great Bliss
arising from union (with Śiva),
and who art worshipped
by Hari, Hara, Viriñci (Viṣṇu, Śiva, Brahmā),
and all other Devas.

Verse 14

O Kālī, spouse of Giriśa (Śiva),
Thou art Earth, Water, Fire, Air and Ether.
Thou art all.
Thou art one and beneficent (Kalyāṇi).
What can be said in praise of Thee, O Mother?
Of Thy mercy show Thy favour towards me, helpless as I am.
By Thy grace may I never be reborn.

Verse 15

He, O Mahākālī, who in the cremation-ground,
naked, and with dishevelled hair,
intently meditates upon Thee and recites Thy mantra,
and with each recitation
makes offering to Thee
of a thousand Ākaṇḍa (sun/mind) flowers
with seed (sperm*),*
becomes without any effort a Lord of the earth.

Verse 16

O Kālī, whoever on Tuesday at midnight,
having uttered Thy mantra,
makes offering even but once with devotion to Thee
of a hair of his Śakti in the cremation-ground (?),
b. of the (pubic?) hair of the wife
which has been combed straight at home (?);
c. of the blend of secretions produced by the Liṇga/penis
in the abode of Kāma, the Yoni/vulva (?)
becomes a great poet, a Lord of the earth,
and ever goes mounted upon an elephant.

Verse 17

The devotee who, having placed before himself,
and meditated and again meditated upon,
the abode, strewn with flowers (the yoni),

of the Deva with the bow of flowers (Kāma),
recites Thy Mantra,
Ah! he becomes on earth
the Lord of Gandharvas (celestial musicians),
and the ocean of the nectar of the flow of poesy,
and is after death in Thy supreme abode.

Verse 18

He who at night, when in union with his Śakti,
meditates with centred mind on Thee,
O Mother with gently smiling face,
as on the breast of the corpse-like Śiva,
lying on a fifteen-angled yantra
deeply enlisted in sweet amorous play with Mahākāla,
himself becomes the destroyer of the God of Love
*(*excels in beauty the God of Love*).*

Verse 19

*O Dark One (*Unbound One*),*
wondrous and excelling in every way,
becomes the accomplishment,
of those worshippers who living in this world
freely make offering to Thee
in worship of the greatly satisfying flesh,
together with hair and bone (the totality),
of cats (greed), camels (envy),
sheep (delusion), buffaloes (anger),
goats (lust), and men (pride and arrogance).

Verse 20

O Mother, he who, being a controller of his passions,
eats haviṣyānnaṁ (sacrificial food)
and, being proficient in meditation on Thy feet (yoni),
rightly recites Thy mantra a hundred thousand times by day,
and he who afterwards naked at night,
when united with his Śakti,
rightly recites Thy great mantra
another such hundred thousand times,
becomes on earth like unto the Destroyer (Śiva) of Smara (Kāma).

Verse 21

O Mother, this Hymn of Thine is the source
from whence originates Thy mantra.
It sings of Thy real self,
and contains injunctions
for the worship of Thy two lotus Feet (genitals & perineum).
*He who reads (*recites*) it at midnight or at time of worship*

even his random (meaningless, delirious) *talk*
becomes the nectar juice of poesy.

Verse 22

Numbers of women with large eyes,
like those of the antelope,
impatient for his love, ever follow him.
Even the King becomes subject to his control.
He becomes like unto Kubera himself.
An enemy fears him as if he were a prison.
Living in continuous bliss
the devotee is liberated when yet living,
and is never again reborn
(the devotee experiences the Devatā directly
and is reborn life after life as her devotee).

Here ends the Hymn by Śrī Mahākāla, entitled *Karpūrādistotra.* Commentary and alternative translations in brackets.

The *Hymn to Kālī* is one of the most important texts of the left-hand path. Bharati (1983: 72) proposes that it comes from between the ninth and eleventh century CE and remarks that it *has given much pain to non-tantric Hindus.* It is also my favourite Tantric hymn, as it is so magnificently poetic, deep and concise. You can recite it aloud, read it silently and meditate on the meanings hidden in each single word. Like the wish-fulfilling gem, it yields treasures when you put your life into it. Not that it is entirely easy to understand, let alone put into practice. Each verse can be interpreted on at least three levels. The translation is by Sir John Woodroffe, I have added a few comments (in brackets) and alternative translations (non-italicised text). As I encourage creative thinking I shall refrain from writing an extended commentary. Here it should suffice to look at a few aspects of the text. To begin with, the *Hymn to Kālī* takes its name from Karpūraṁ, which is camphor. Camphor has a lot of qualities that can do with a bit of meditation. In ritual, camphor is the fuel of sacred fires. It is a fierce disinfectant with a stunning scent, it keeps moths away, and was used for medicine. Cautiously. The stuff is pretty poisonous when ingested. Sometimes, tiny amounts were used to flavour wine, or to fresh up the breath before reciting mantra, but then, it is quite possible that it wasn't actual camphor that went into the drink but the sexual secretions. When we look into the wonderful world of twilight language, camphor is a code word for the blend of rakta (blood, here menstrual blood) and śukra (a blend of sperm and female secretions in early Tantra; just sperm in later periods), the elixir of immortality. Vimalānanda calls it *Saguṇa-Brahman, the Kalpaka or fashioner of the World.* The *Hymn* has a lot of references to this subtle alchemy. The beginning of the text is full of mysterious allusions. The first six verses give the mantra-yoga of the cult, and as the text is fairly late, the mantras are given in code. Very secretive, considering that the bījas that make up the secret mantra are well known from numerous other works. For those who really want to know, Vāmākṣi means the left eye and is the letter ī, while Bindu, as you will remember from the chapter on mantra, is the nasal NG vibration which is written as ṁ. Verse 2 has Iśāna, a reference to Śiva ('the Lord') and the syllable Ha, and Vāmaśravaṇa, the left ear, ū. In verse 3 you find Iśa ('the Lord'), Śiva again, and syllable ha; Vaiśvānara, the Lord of Fire (Agni) whose sound is the syllable ra; and Vāmanetra, the left eye, ī. In verse 4 Kālī's name is inserted. The verse does not say which one (choose what you will) but Woodroffe proposes Dakṣiṇā Kālī, whose name is recited in the vocative (Dakṣiṇé Kālike). Verse 5 alludes to Vahni/Agni who is the god of fire and the syllable ra. Rati ('Lust') is a wife of Kāma and the letter ī. Vidhu is the moon, and the nasal ṁ. The Kūrca bīja is Hūṁ. The Lajjā bīja is Hrīṁ. Tha (ṭ) is the moon letter, the two Thas are Svāhā, the goddess who mediates between the worlds and manifests the fruits of all karma (see the chapter on mantra). Thus the full form of the mantra is

Krīṁ, Krīṁ, Krīṁ; Hūṁ, Hūṁ; Hrīṁ, Hrīṁ; (Dakṣiṇé Kālike),

Krīṁ, Krīṁ, Krīṁ; Hūṁ, Hūṁ; Hrīṁ, Hrīṁ; Svāhā.

This mantra is not peculiar to the *Hymn to Kālī*, it also appears in one of the versions of the 14th-15th century *Kālītantra* and several late texts, such as the *Mahānirvāṇa Tantra* contain variations of it. As Woodroffe remarks, there seems to be a relation between the 22 syllables of the mantra and the 22 verses of the *Hymn*. Can you discover it, or make it up? As you noticed, the *Hymn to Kālī* is by no means a simple song of praise but a detailed set of instructions for practical worship. In most cases, the imagery has several meanings. This is of special importance when we come to the verses treating mutual worship. All practices mentioned in the hymn can be done physically, but they can also be performed in a symbolic form or entirely in the imagination. All three approaches have the same validity, though they tend to produce different effects. You can invite your lover for this celebration, but you can also do the rites with your personal deity. This is especially important for solitary worshippers. Śakti can manifest in others, Śakti can manifest within yourself. The Śakti of the practitioner can be a ritual partner, or a ritual partner obsessed by a deity; in solitary ritual s/he is the inner deity, the Kulakuṇḍalinī, or the deity who manifest in the world at large. When Kālī and Mahākāla make love, this serves as an example for the worship. I am sure you guessed that Śiva as Mahākāla is not simply 'Great Time' or the 'Great Devourer', as the name means. It is also a reference to making love with lots of time - and indeed, outside of time as well. Here we find Kālī sitting on Mahākāla in the posture called viparīta maithuna (reverse coupling). Good evidence that the divine lovers know how lovemaking can be fun for both. This is certainly not self evident. Orthodox lovemaking in Hinduism has the man on top, hence the interpretation of viparīta as 'reverse' or 'upside down'. Hinduism, like Islam and Christianity go to considerable lengths to prohibit and damn this posture. How come so many 'world-religions' are terrified of women who enjoy orgasm? But when we see it as a reference to solitary practice, viparīta means a reversal of the current of consciousness, a trance of awareness detaching itself from the world of phenomena and returning to its nameless, incomprehensible and essentially void source. Ordinary coupling, in this interpretation, joins you with the world via the senses. Reversed coupling reverses the flow of attention. This is the true heart and the state before conception. You can find it by introversion.

The flower offering of verse 15 does not refer to the Indian 'sunflower' but to the flowers of the mind, such as non-injury, compassion, peace, benevolence. The animals offered in verse 19 are bad habits such as greed, pride, arrogance, stupidity and anger. In a non-dualist context, offerings are not only given to the gods, they are also transformed by the deities and returned to the worshippers. It is typical for this sort of worship that the worshippers consume what was given to the gods, as the offering, the offerer, the act of offering and the gods are all one. Verse 16 is very enigmatic. Are you ready for a bit of scholarly confusion? The line *makes offering even but once with devotion to Thee of a hair of his Śakti in the cremation-ground* is not a translation. Woodroffe made use of several versions of the text and as it so happens, at this crucial passage they disagree. In all fairness he wrote *The English translation is somewhat abbreviated with the object of giving only so much as all renderings are agreed upon*. The problem with the line is that several words can be read quite differently. The original reads: *grihe sammārjanyā parigalitabījam hi cikuram samūlang madhyāhne vitarati citayām kujadine.* The gṛhe can be taken as 'at home', it can also mean grihinī 'wife'. It can also refer, according to the initiated tradition of the commentary used by Woodroffe, to manmathagrihe, i.e. the home of Kāmadeva, the yoni. If the line refers to hair, it is pubic hair, and if we read sammārjanī as 'comb' and parigalita as 'removed', we arrive more or less at an offering made of the wife's (pubic) hair from which the curls (?) have been removed with a comb. Hair could also mean 'restlessness', which does not make things easier, nor does the interpretation of hair as 'thinking' (i.e. what has grown out of the head). Is it the Śakti who is restless, is her restlessness offered or is it a thought of the Śakti? Or is it the secretions clinging to pubic hair after coitus which may have been combed out ? Luckily Woodroffe hastens to add what the initiated commentary says: *Śaktisādhakayoh gṛhe maithunasamaye yoniliṁgasaṁgharṣavaśāt śaktiyonipatitaṁ vīryaliptaṁ loma devyai samarpitaṁ bhavati... According to Vimalānanda, Gṛhe parigalita-vīryaṁ, is that produced by the union with the Sādhaka's svaśakti or wife.* He adds the commentary of Durgārāma Siddhāntavāgiśa: *The whole phrase then means Wife's hair, root and all, combed out straight with a comb or b) Sammārjanya parigalita-vīryaṁ means Śukra produced by Sammārjani here meaning Liṅga of the Sādhaka; gṛhe means in the abode of Kāma that is Yoni of Śakti together with hair, root and all.* Note that in early Hindu and Buddhist Tantra, sukra is not only sperm but the blend of sexual secretions. The word can also mean 'bright'. I am sure the whole matter could have been expressed a lot more clearly, but then, in Woodroffe's time such topics were practically unprintable and we can be happy to get any interpretation at all.

Bharati (1983: 72), referring to these passages, shows a lot more daring. Instead of honest plain English he translates them into Latin! Verse 17 continues in this mood, and proposes meditation on the yoni/vulva, and verse 20 points out that the sacrificial food, the haviṣyānnaṁ ought to be eaten. Usually haviṣyānnaṁ is clarified butter (ghī) which is poured into the fire as an offering, a worshipper who eats this offering makes her/himself equal to the gods and in particular identifies with Agni, the god of fire. In another sense the haviṣyānnaṁ is not pure ghī but a special food whose ingredients include rice, ghī and milk. which is specially prepared for the gods, again, to eat the food of the gods is to be one with them. And finally, as you hopefully guessed, haviṣyānnaṁ can be a code word for the refined and dedicated sexual secretions. Here the fire altar is cognate with the yoni, an identification that predates Tantra and can be traced to the *Chāndogya Upaniṣad*, 5, 8. 1-2. The lotus feet of the goddess refer, in the initiated context, to the worship of her yoni. Meditations on the genitals are a common routine in left-hand Tantra. Strictly speaking, the worship of her two feet is the worship of the centres at the perineum and the genitals. Many Tantric systems consider the two lowest cakras as something that ought to be transcended. Unlike these sects, the worshippers of Kālī prefer to experience the goddess in body, mind and spirit. Your body, the body of your partner and the world at large. All of this is the piṇḍa, the sum of body, manifestation and experience that constitutes your reality. Verse 22 contains an interesting translation problem, as the last line can either be read that the worshipper attains liberation and is never reborn (the goal of most Hindus) or that the worshipper is reborn life after life with direct experience of the goddess. Such ambiguity is certainly no coincidence but a work of art. There is a great deal more to the *Hymn*, but I won't spoil your fun by attempting to explain everything. However, it might be useful to take a look into the *Mantra Mahodhadhiḥ* by Mahidhara. His section on the worship of Kālī bears some close similarities to our text. First, the reader is told that he will become like Bṛhaspati, the divine priest and sacrificer of the Vedic age, by repeating Kālī's mantra ten thousand times whilst looking at the vulva of a beautiful woman:

> *Sitting naked on the heart region of a corpse in a cremation ground, if the Sādhaka devotedly worships the Goddess with one thousand Arka flowers, each smeared with his own semen, and uttering each time the Mūla-mantra, he very soon becomes the Lord of the earth.*
>
> *If a naked Sādhaka meditates upon the menstruating sexual organ of a woman and devotedly repeats the mantra ten thousand times, he will be able to enchant others with his excellent poetic capacity.*
>
> *If the Sādhaka meditates upon the Goddess seated on the chest of a corpse, placed on a big pedestal of fifteen corners, and engaged in amorous union with her husband, the Mahākāla, with a pleasant smile on Her face, and also himself engaged in sexual intercourse while meditating upon the Goddess, and performs one thousand Japas of the mantra, he becomes equal to Lord Śaṁkara (Śiva).*

On the eighth day of the dark fortnight at midnight, if a Sādhaka offers oblations of flesh of a cat, sheep, camel or buffalo, together with the bones, hides and hairs, he is able to subjugate all creatures.

The text goes on to recommend japa on the cremation ground and sitting on a corpse. The corpse, as you hopefully guessed, is your own corpse. The rite of Kālī can only be celebrated by offering yourself. When you sit on the dead body of your identity, of your beliefs, hopes, fears and ambitions Kālī comes to manifest in your heart.

Rites of Kālī

The primary worship of any deity is union with her/him/it. You can build up energy and passion by worship in a dualistic way, but if you want the full, uncensored, overwhelming totality of the experience, you have to become that deity. There are three basic approaches to this union. One is on the sexual level: it uses the metaphors of flirting, loveplay and coitus to find a union with the divine, who is here imagined or identified as a ritual partner. This rite can be celebrated in the imagination, it can also be done in living flesh should you have a competent ritual partner who can manifest that deity. This can be a difficult matter as a competent partner is not easy to find. It can also cause problems when the level of human relationship, the dance and interaction of egos is not thoroughly brought under will. You have to get rid of a lot of rubbish to go beyond the human persona. Your rubbish, explicitly.

The second approach is union by being devoured by the deity. You dedicate and give yourself, you transform and devour yourself, you bring yourself forth anew. Here we have the joys of drama, passion, fierce hunger and lust and raging madness. You are the prasāda, the sacrifice, the sacrificer, the one to whom the sacrifice is made, the one who returns the sacrifice to you, and the transformed essence of the rite. When you understand that you are the totality of the act of giving and receiving, that all life feeds on itself, you will begin to understand what offering is all about. This practice can include dramatic visualisation, if you do it by ritual, prayer and imagination. It can also appear as crisis, as terrible events and circumstances that take you beyond whatever you assumed yourself to be.

The third approach is to become the deity by imagination and playacting. If you build up a good, strong vision of the deity, you can imbue it with so much life and emotion that the image becomes a manifestation of the divine. Done over a few weeks or months, a deity can assume a lot of form. When the image is well developed, step into it and become it. Here I am talking about power and sentience. This identification is more than just a bit of intellectual play, it should be an experience that touches, shakes and transform you. If you think 'O how well I am doing', something went wrong. Magick begins with playacting, but it soon goes beyond pretence. When you unite with a major god, or your personal deities, you may find your ego scared. This is an excellent sign; you can trust your ego to feel uneasy when it encounters something much stronger and wiser. Now to identify with a deity requires practice and playacting. It starts out with a bit of effort and maybe it needs some time to develop. Some gods want to be invited over a few weeks, others just come in and take over. As a side effect, you may find your body shaking, swaying, trembling or staggering around. Wonderful! Welcome to the world of primal vibration! Anything that upsets ego and confuses your usual perception may be just the key to learn something radically new. Or would you like to have it the other way around? You can induce shaking or swaying and make use of the power that wells up when your body-armour (muscular and psychic tension) disintegrates. The very earth beneath Kālī shakes and trembles (*KCT* 4, 41) and so may you, once you shake off the shackles of control and purpose. Good shaking can free from inhibitions, it can dissolve cramp, produce a rich aura of sheer vitality and induce a lucid trance awareness that is perfectly suited for long periods of intense experience.

Here we leave the realm of the expressible. There are insights in Tantra that make sense when you stand shaking in ecstasy. That your body is Śakti and your consciousness is Śiva may seem like philosophy. If you think that thinking this is enough, you'll miss most of the essential. Such insights should be the quintessence of direct experience - they should not be discussed but lived. If Kālī does not take you out of the immediate confines and configurations of your belief in yourself and the world, you have not given enough.

In Tantric worship, all three approaches can be found with some regularity. They are not inferior or superior to one another. In the cycles of your transformation they will naturally appear again and again. Some situations need a bit of drama, other occasions need regular persistence and steady effort, or maybe an act of release by giving up control and taking refuge in something much vaster than anyone can comprehend.

In traditional ritual, there are some basic elements of worship. These elements form a tradition. Some worshipper found this or that mantra beneficial, another did not, and before long there is a whole range of mantras, yantras and ritual acts. Each of them is presented as eminently efficient, but when you look at the range of choices, you'll come to appreciate that people need variation and freedom of choice. What you need is not the sacred mantra of hallowed tradition. You need the mantra that works specifically for you. You may need even more than that, maybe you'll discover mantras that work even better when you experiment and play around with an open mind. Whether these mantras are ancient, recent, or whether you have just made them up matters very little. Ask your inner guru, ask your personal deity, find out for yourself.

Here are some of the mantras associated with the worship of Kālī. Wake them, explore them, change them according to your needs. Put life into them and allow them to transform you from the core.

The primary mantra of Kālī is the 22 syllable pattern given above. In the *Toḍala Tantra* the same mantra appears, called the *Queen of all Vidyās*. Again, without a specification of Kālī's name. What happens when you insert the other names of Kālī? Now the *Toḍala Tantra* offers quite a range of mantras. Here they are:

By reciting the vāgbhava mantra, the bīja of Vāc, the goddess of speech (**Aīṁ**) before the 22 syllable mantra, it becomes the mantra of Śrīkālī.

By preceding the main mantra with **Oṁ**, it becomes the mantra of Siddhikālikā.

The mantra of Cāmuṇḍākālikā to bring about success: **Krīṁ, Krīṁ; Hūṁ.**

Of equal power is the six-syllable mantra**: Krīṁ, Krīṁ, Krīṁ; Phaṭ; Svāhā.**

The fourteen syllable mantra worshipped in the three worlds is: **Krīṁ, Krīṁ, Krīṁ; Śmaśānakālike; Krīṁ, Krīṁ, Krīṁ; Svāhā.**

For the eight names of Kālī recite: **Krīṁ**, (name in the vocative), **Krīṁ; Svāhā**.

In the *Mantra Mahodhadhiḥ* even more variations appear:

The bestower of all siddhis is the bīja of Kālī: **Krīṁ.**

The twenty-one syllable mantra that grants siddhis when recited 100,000 times sitting under a bilva tree, a baṭa tree or on a corpse: **Oṁ; Hrīṁ, Hrīṁ; Hūṁ, Hūṁ, Krīṁ, Krīṁ, Krīṁ; Dakṣiṇé Kālike, Krīṁ, Krīṁ, Krīṁ; Hūṁ, Hūṁ; Hrīṁ, Hrīṁ.**

The fourteen syllable mantra that attracts men and gods: **Krīṁ; Hūṁ; Hrīṁ; Dakṣiṇé Kālike; Krīṁ; Hūṁ; Hrīṁ; Svāhā.**

The king of mantras, used in rites of subjugation (100,000 repetitions required): **Hūṁ, Hūṁ, Krīṁ, Krīṁ, Krīṁ; Hrīṁ, Hrīṁ; Dakṣiṇé Kālike, Hūṁ, Hūṁ, Krīṁ, Krīṁ, Krīṁ; Hrīṁ, Hrīṁ; Svāhā.**

The fifteen syllable mantra, called the great mantra: **Hūṁ, Hūṁ, Krīṁ, Krīṁ, Krīṁ; Hrīṁ, Hrīṁ; Dakṣiṇé Kālike; Svāhā.**

The six syllable mantra: **Krīṁ; Kālike; Svāhā.**

The three syllable mantra: **Krīṁ; Hūṁ; Hrīṁ.**

The five syllable mantra: **Krīṁ; Hūṁ; Hrīṁ; Hūṁ; Phāṭ**.

The seven syllable mantra: **Krīṁ; Hūṁ; Hrīṁ; Hūṁ; Phāṭ; Svāhā.**

These mantras have the power to withhold and uphold.

As you probably guessed, the ṛṣi of these mantras is Bhairava. Well, this should suffice for a lot of experiments in sound and rhythm. I hope you go beyond the scope and explore further possibilities. Real Kālī worship arises from the crossroads of your heart.

An old Kālī mantra appears in the *Kulacūḍāmaṇi Tantra* 4, 36, where the goddess is worshipped on a Tuesday night at a cremation place. The worshipper makes a yantra using a Kula stick (?), writes the mūla (root) mantra **Spheṁ Spheṁ Kiṭi Kiṭi** in its centre and adds the Fierce Mantra **Phaṭ**! to start a meditation on Bhadrakālī. The mantra is also used for rites of enchantment, by 'threading' it with the name of the person who is to be influenced, or the spirit to be conjured. Quite simply, you insert the name between each two words of the mantra and repeat the mantra 800 times whilst holding white mustard seed (?) and worshipping the goddess in the *crossroads of the heart*. Kiṭi, by the way, means 'wild boar', hence it may refer to the goddess in her fiercely screaming, tusked form. If you have ever met fighting boars in the forest you'll never forget it.

Some Kālī mantras from the *Mahānirvāṇa Tantra*:

The vidyā of seven letters of the supreme Kālikā:
Hrīṁ, Parameśvarī, Svāhā.

The vidyā of the supreme Devī in ten syllables containing all mantras:
Hrīṁ, Śrīṁ, Krīṁ, Parameśvarī, Svāhā.

The vidyā of the supreme Devī of sixteen syllables concealed in all the Tantras:

Hrīṁ, Śrīṁ, Krīṁ, Parameśvarī Kālike, Hrīṁ, Śrīṁ, Krīṁ, Svāhā.

Figure 77 - Heads and hands for Kālī.

As the Kālīka (little Kali) mantra **Hrīṁ, Śrīṁ, Krīṁ**, the pattern reflects the Trimūrti, i.e. the three divine functions of creation, maintenance and destruction which are usually personified by the gods Brahmā, Viṣṇu and Śiva/Rudra, and the goddesses Māyā/Sarasvatī, Lakṣmī and Kālī. The vidyā given in the *Karpūrādi Stotra* gives the 'nightside' of the Trimurti. Here we have dissolution (Krīṁ) first, then voidness and absence (Hūṁ) followed by recreation or rebirth (Hrīṁ). How about adding śrīṁ to complete the circuit?

Ādyāyai vidmahe Parameśvaryyai dhīmahi:
tannaḥ Kālī prachodayāt

This is the Devī Gāyatrī: 'Let us think upon Ādyā, let us meditate on Parameśvarī, may Kālī direct us.'

Kālī Yantra

There are several popular yantras associated with the dark goddess (see illustration). As in all yantras, each point, angle and space is identified with a divine principle. We have one such pattern in the *KCT* 5, 56-67. The account is brief, sketchy and enigmatic. Most of the time we do not know whether the ritual is solitary or performed with a partner, real or imaginary. The worshipper starts with nyāsa. He imagines the limbs of the deity together with the root seed of Kālī (Krīṁ) and the six long vowels, this yields the mantra **Ā Krīṁ Ī Krīṁ Ū Krīṁ O Krīṁ AI Krīṁ AU Krīṁ**. Next, the fourteen letters (the vowels) are placed (nyāsa) separately on heart, hands and feet. Then the root mantra (here **Spheṁ Spheṁ Kiṭi Kiṭi Phaṭ**) is placed all over the body fifty times, followed by a meditation on the goddess in her terrifying aspect. This meditation, I am sure you guessed, is really an identification: the goddess is you. The pīṭha (usually 'seat', occasionally 'genitals', here 'yantra') is worshipped by invoking Dakṣiṇā on lotus blossoms of fifteen petals and by sacrificing to her who is the Jewel of the Kulas (the goddess or the ritual partner?). After this stage there is sacrifice to Mahākāla and to the Śakti of the pīṭha. Who is this Śakti? The goddess herself, the ritual partner or a goddess associated with the location? In the yantra, the first (inner) triangle is inhabited by Kālī (Black), Kāpālinī (Skull-carrier) and Kullā. The second triangle is Kurukullā, Virodhī and Vipracitta (Vibration-consciousness?). The third triangle houses Ugramukhī, Ugraprabhā and Pradīptā. The fourth Nīlā (Blue), Ghanā and Balākā; the fifth Mātrā, Mitā and Mudrikā. All constitute the fifteen-angled seat of the goddess. They also provide a calendar for the lunar fortnight. Around it, there are eight lotus petals, identified with Brahmāṇī in the east, followed by Maheśvarī, Kaumārī, Vaiṣṇavī, Vārāhī, Indrāṇī, Cāmuṇḍā and Mahālakṣmī. The installation of the yantra completed, the worshipper proceeds to utter the mantra 100,000 times by day and 100,000 times by night, eating only haviṣyānnaṁ (sacrificial food) and maintaining purity. The sādhaka may not think or worship another young woman than the vidyā herself. This is a solitary ritual. As an alternative, *KCT* 5, 67 proposes that Kālī is worshipped as Araṇyā and a spirit is evoked for ritual, you read about this rite earlier.

Kālī's Flowers

Offerings of flowers, garlands and lavish bouquets are an essential part of Indian temple decoration. Flowers are freshly picked or bought at temple shops to decorate the images of deities and I have seen some of the long stemmed ones, in particular carnations, in use to sprinkle sacred water over the participants of pūjās. As flowers do not last long, they have to be replaced ever so often, this makes them part of the daily discipline of worship. In ritual usage, there is a whole range of symbolism to species and colours. When Rāmakṛṣṇa was still young, and entrusted with the duty to look after the daily flower decoration of the Kālī shrine, it often happened that his passionate vision of the dark goddess spaced him out of his human consciousness. In these states he became the goddess so intensely that he placed the flower offerings not before and on the statue but on his own head, much to the annoyance of less enlightened worshippers. In late life he gave up offering flowers, as each wild growing flower is in itself a bouquet to the goddess and too perfect to be picked and used for decoration. All of this goes for flowers in general. In the twilight language of left hand Tantra, flowers have a lot of meaning that goes far beyond their nature as plant genitalia. Take the ākaṇḍa flowers which feature so importantly in the worship of Kālī. Ākaṇḍa flowers are literally sunflowers, but the Indian sunflower is not the same species as the European sunflower. A sunflower is a flower that radiates warmth and light. As the sun is the heart, i.e. mind & awareness, the sunflowers are the best the mind can yield. According to Woodroffe such flowers are compassion, wisdom, forgiveness, control of the senses, charity, religious merit, non-injury to any being, bliss and worship. Who offers the heart/mind itself gives a supreme gift. In another interpretation, the flowers are the lotus blossoms representing the cakras. Each blossom you offer is another level of body/mind/reality offered to the liberation of all. This is your offering, as ultimately the only thing you can really offer is yourself. On another level of interpretation, the ākaṇḍa flowers are stemless. This means that they have not grown from a plant and are in fact not plants at all. Here we encounter the sweet-smelling yoni of the entranced priestess. Flowers are often synonyms for menstrual fluids, and menstruation is the 'flowering' of the woman. As Śiva observes in the *Kaulajñāna nirṇaya* (24, 4-12) flowers without scent are terrible. Hardly surprising, as they lack pheromones. Seen from the perspective of those Tantrics who use arousal as a ritual force but avoid congress, the stemless flowers remain virgin. When the stemless flowers are offered with seed this may be a reference to bīja mantras, to magically charged sexual fluids or to the elixir trickling from the crown of the head in rites of inner alchemy. What else could flowers mean to you?

Tribute to the Jackals

Remember those jackals haunting cremation places, howling fearfully? Feeding them is part of a complex of cremation ground rites that appears in several early Tantras. For the heroic worshipper this rite is a meeting with the dark goddess in her terrible form. Also, it should appeal to animal lovers world-wide. The female jackal or fox (Śivā, not identical with the god Śiva) is an incarnation of Pārvatī, Umā, Tārā and Kālī. Worshippers used to feed the jackals in the middle of the night on the 14th, i.e. the darkest night of the moon. This was usually done at cross-roads, at cremation grounds, in the deep jungle, far from human habitations or in any convenient wilderness. One version appears in the *Mahākālasaṁhitā* (Goudriaan & Gupta 1981: 79), a fragmentary text dedicated to the worship of nine manifestations of Kālī. The rite begins by obtaining Kāmakalākālī's permission. Then the heroic worshipper, completely nude, with loose hair, wearing only a garland, invites the jackals *of terrible forms and blazing mouths* in a low voice by uttering a mantra. When the beasts approach the offering, great care is taken to observe when and how they come close. When *bearing Kālī's form*, they arrive immediately, this is an auspicious sign, if not, it signifies failure. They are to be worshipped with reverence from a distance, uttering mantras containing the words: *'take, take, devour, devour, create create success for me, destroy destroy, kill my foes'*. The jackals are manifestations of Kālikā, and from what delicacies they choose first and which they neglect, oracular advise may be gained. The topic is elaborated in *KCT* 7, 40-52. In the evening, the worshipper approaches a lonesome bilva tree or a cremation ground and makes an offering consisting mainly of meat. Crying 'Kālī, Kālī!' Umā appears in her jackal shape. If she feeds and howls towards the north-east, the offering has been accepted and the worshipper will enjoy good fortune. Those who do not regularly feed the goddess in her jackal form have all the merit of pūjā, good works and japa instantly destroyed: *the jackal grabs them and uttering a curse she goes off to weep in a solitary place.* Just a single rite of jackal feeding is sure to grant the blessings of all Śaktis and to make ritual, which had hitherto been futile, effective. The animal Śakti, the human Śakti and the bird Śakti (?) are worshipped in this fashion. The rite is also done as a form of divination in times of danger and trouble.

If we take this rite at its face value, a little zoology may be useful. If you want cheerful jackals to come out of the night to gobble up your offerings, you had better train them patiently to accept your presence, scent and mantra-mumbling. Without such preparations, it is not very likely that the oracle will be auspicious. The same goes for other scavengers. If you have no jackals or hyenas in the neighbourhood you will have to find alternatives. Foxes are excellent, and the same goes for other carrion eaters, such as crows. Also, you had better approach the spot of worship before darkness falls, as stumbling around nude in jungles and cremation places in pitch black darkness isn't very auspicious either. And while we are at it, how distinctly can anyone see a *blazing mouth* in the middle of a forest on a new moon night? This is not really an oracle. Either you train the jackals to like you, in which case the oracle is not an oracle at all, or you go there in the hope of being lucky. Is this an animal feeding rite at all? You will observe that there are any amount of loaded terms involved. Just think of the meaning of crossroads, cremation grounds, wildernesses, the north-east and similar concepts in twilight language and consider that all female animals, and especially carnivorous ones, may be manifestations of yoginīs. A yoginī may be a dangerous spirit of forest and wilderness, a deity who appears in animal form or a human woman who is an expert in yoga. What happens when you interpret the rite as a meditation or as a shared ritual? What if you go into the voidness of your heart and offer your own body, form and personality?

Playing in Guyana

Another interesting example how Hindu religion may transform comes from the Caribbean (see Stephanides and Singh). In 1838, the British began to settle Hindu labourers in British Guyana, where they had to work on sugar plantations that had formerly been worked by slaves. This continued to 1917 and today more than half of the Guyanese population is of Indian origin, though most of them do not speak their native languages any more. The Hindu workers were recruited mainly in Bengal and northern India but also in the southern, Tamil-speaking districts.

The recruitment was not a nice matter. Most labourers came from very poor sections of society. They were badly informed regarding the country and work waiting for them, many were tricked or coerced and many did not even survive the incredibly insanitary conditions on the ships transporting them to their new homeland. Arriving in Guyana, they were stationed in what had formerly been slave barracks and made to toil much like the slaves they had replaced. It is hardly surprising that under these conditions, most of the social regulations of Hindu society began to disintegrate. The forced labour soon led to disease, misery and crisis. To survive, the old gods were direly needed. The Hindu workers responded to the situation by identifying a local river with the sacred Ganges. They performed a ritual procession to the riverbank, made sacrificial offerings to Mā Gaṇgā, intoned mantras and sacred chants and before long, several of the participants 'got vibration'. As in so much Indian folk worship, they started to tremble and became obsessed. Talking through an obsessed woman, the goddess Kālī appeared and gave instructions on her worship and how her temple should be constructed. Think about it: though Mā Gaṇgā had been invoked, Kālī appeared. As a result, the Guyanese form of Kālī is closely connected with the river goddess Mā Gaṇgā, and often appears in semi-aquatic forms. The worship of Kālī took on several innovative forms. In Guyanan Hindu religion, Kālī tends to be worshipped as a rather fair-skinned and beneficial goddess called Kalimai, *Mother Kali.* Her darksome and sinister nature has been give form as her black skinned little sister Kateri (*Little Mother*), who regulates menstruation, prevents miscarriage, and may well derive from the nightmarish Hindu goddess Churyl. Several other deities

Figure 78 - Gate after Gate.

are involved in the worship, some of them well known from Indian tradition, such as Śiva, Kṛṣṇa, Durgā and a serpent god called Nag, while others were made up or redefined in the new homeland. Religion in Guyana developed non-brahmanically. As the labourers came from many widely distinct locations and ethnic groups, the religion they developed in Guyana is largely syncretistic and involves elements from numerous local traditions. This is not unlike the way Voodoo developed in Haiti and elsewhere. When you force people of many places to live and labour under conditions of extreme poverty and misery, they have to come to some consensus if they want to survive. The African slaves that worked on the plantations came from numerous cultures and were mixed on purpose to keep them under control. It forced them to disregard their native tradition and to focus on mutual beliefs and things that really work. This is how West Indian Voodoo began, and why it is so much more creative and pragmatic than the many traditional religions in Africa.

In Guyana, the labourers had to transcend the rigid limits of traditional Hindu thought to create a religion suited to everyone. The worshippers are called marlo pujaras, they are of either sex and of any caste, and their religion is based on very few sacred texts and lots of direct obsession. The pujaras dedicate their bodies as physical vehicles to the deities. Prior to great festivities, they spend weeks or months purifying themselves with ritual baths, prayer, worship, meditation, they abstain from sex and alcohol, they assume a completely vegetarian diet and work themselves into a state of excitement that simply wants to release itself on the great occasion. Dangerous occasions such as births, marriages and funeral ceremonies are avoided if possible. Each pujara is devoted to one or more personal deities. Obsession starts in the sacred temple premises, when the worshippers have left worldly space and time, by swaying and shaking. The process is called 'getting vibration'. The devotees are called 'players' and the ritual is a form of the divine play, the līlā of divine manifestation that people call reality. *Devotees 'play' when they are possessed by the rhythm vibration of a deity and fall into a trance-like state.* (Stephanides & Singh 2000). They become the 'players' of the divine, just as the divine plays through them.

Consider this deeply. In recent times, the New Age movement has successfully turned a lot of magic into 'work'. People do 'trance-work', 'aura-work', 'circle-work', 'divination-work', 'body-work', 'work a ritual', 'work a healing', and generally sound as if they had to make up for doing silly stuff by seeming serious and sober. Perhaps things become more real in the modern world when they are classed as work. Nevertheless, it takes a lot of fun out of the act. To *play*, on the other hand, is really much more efficient. Work, as we all know, eventually exhausts. It takes effort, determination and discipline. Play, in contrast, is fun and functions thanks to obsession and joy. Just think of the effort it takes to make a child do some 'work'. Getting it to play is much easier. And what about you? Are you serious enough about your magick that you can afford to call and consider it play?

Now 'work' also has its place in Guyanese Hindu religion. The act of making offerings is called 'work'. There is 'sweet work' consisting of offerings of sweets, flowers, fruit and incense. There is a wide range of plants associated with the various deities. Kālī receives double rosed oleander, mango, neem leaves and marigold, the bright yellow and saffron colours of the leaves being sacred to her and Durgā respectively. Pomegranates are sacred to Durgā, hibiscus is attributed to several deities according to the colours of its leaves and Śiva receives calatropis, a plant of the morning glory family. The other variety is 'life work', which is the sacrifice of cigarettes, cigars, alcohol and blood. Goats are occasionally slaughtered at great festivities, though on a much smaller scale than in some Indian temples, and their hides are used for the ritual drums. Drumming, music and chanting feature prominently in the pūjās. One unusual aspect is the use of the uddukai, a small hand-drum. The worshippers tap the skin with the fingers while singing into the bottom of the drum, thus increasing the resonance of their voices. The marlo pujaras are obsessed by their deities. They shake, tremble and sway, they rock to and fro, and when the deity of their choice is fully integrated, they dance in the particular style of that deity, which may involve spinning, leaping and fast turning. In full obsession, the players receive the requests of the worshippers and perform blessings and healings. Others take oaths by placing burning camphor on the tongue or receive whiplash blows on the arms during obsession. A particular issue seems to be obsession simply for the joy of it. On the second night of the 'big pūjā', the women of the temple lead the devotees to the riverside. The moon shines brightly and the black waters glisten. There is prayer and offering of sweetmeats to the river, then the frenzy comes over the congregation and the players jump into the dark waters where they dance among floating garlands of flowers and little fires of burning camphor set on floating lotus leaves. *In their ecstasy, some Marlos writhe in reptilian movements or undulate like water as they emulate Kali's aqueous and alligator forms* (Stephanides and Singh). This is the climax of the ritual. Afterwards, the players and worshippers slowly return to the temple premises. As you can see, the worship of Kālī is alive and well in Guyana, from where it subsequently spread to the Hindu population of Trinidad. It may be far from several traditions that define worship in India, but it is all the same wonderfully alive.

Figure 79 - Kālī rising.

Appendixes

Appendix One: Language and Pronunciation

Here is a rough guide to pronouncing Saṅskṛt. Spelling Saṅskṛt words in Latin letters requires a lot of diacritical marks, which, so I've heard, are not very popular among general readers. Luckily, you happen to be an exception. Excellent training for tackling more scholarly works.

Writing started fairly late in India (if we ignore the enigmatic script of the Indus culture), we find the first Saṅskṛt inscriptions around the end of the third century BCE under the reign of emperor Aśoka, who had his edicts engraved into rocks and pillars. Aśoka wanted to make sure that everybody got the message, hence he used all scripts of his period. Aramaic, Kharoṣṭhī, Brāhmī and, in the western realms, Greek. Brāhmī was the source out of which the Devanāgarī script developed, plus a good dozen other scripts which happily do not concern us here. Brāmī is already a highly developed script. Unlike the Roman alphabet, which shows very little reasonable organisation, Brāhmī is divided into several groups of letters based on the way each sound is formed. The principles behind this organisation continued in Devanāgarī, and as they form an important part of many Tantric systems, we'll take a brief look at the organisation. To begin with, the script is based on phonemes, not on letters, as Brāhmī started out as a syllable script. When you see a consonant, such as 'k', this sound is actually pronounced 'ka' (with a short 'a'), unless otherwise indicated. Useful should you wish to do the classical mantra routine of reciting all phonemes of Devanāgarī in order and reverse.

The script begins with sixteen **vowels**, which appear prominently in the obscure gnosis of Kashmir Śaivism and several other traditions. The vowels, the first group of phonemes, correspond to the stations of the moon, and to an entire science of secret elixirs, vibrations and energy currents. You should not think of this as an esoteric extra to a system of sounds. Indian religion and philosophy have for a long time proposed that it is the sounds themselves which constitute the matrix of consciousness, or the entire universe, if you like. More so, sound is the most subtle manifestation of the all-consciousness. Sound, or rather vibration, is the beginning of form. For this reason you will encounter numerous Tantras where the sounds themselves are the Mothers, the Yoginīs and the vidyās that manifest the worlds and those who experience them. We do not discuss anthropomorphic deities here, nor humans who manifest them. Vibration is the essence of the entire play of manifestation. Vibration produces sound, sight, sensations. A similar idea appears in the term Devanāgarī, which may mean the houses or cities of the gods.

After the first group, the vowels, follow several groups of **consonants**.

Laryngal sounds: ka kha, ga, gha, ṅa form the second group. These sounds are formed in the back of your mouth and throat.

The third group consists of **palatal** sounds, i.e. sounds produced by the interaction of the upper surface of your tongue with the palate. Here you pronounce ca, cha, ja, jha, ña.

Group four consists of **retroflex** sounds: ṭa, ṭha, ḍa, ḍha, ṇa, they are formed by the backward bent tongue against the hard palate.

Group five are the **dental** sounds: ta, tha, da, dha, na, shaped by the tip of the tongue against the upper, cutting teeth.

Group six offers the **labial** sounds: pa, pha, ba, bha, ma, which are shaped by the lips.

Group seven are **half-vowels**: ya (palatal), ra (retroflex), la (dental) and va (labial).

Group eight consists of **hissing** sounds: śa (palatal), ṣa (retroflex), sa (dental).

Finally, there is the sound ha and in some systems, the letter kṣa, denoting Śakti.

Plus a few odd sounds, which were added to the vowels.

The Devanāgarī script is a remarkably well organised form of writing. As you recall, there are attributions of sounds to the cakras. The sound range of most cakras corresponds to the groups of letters, hence with the motion of sound from the back of the throat to the lips. The same pattern is used to organise the vowels, mind you, it does not quite follow the same structure, as it moves the labial vowels to the middle of the sequence. First come the simple vowels: a and ā are laryngal, I and ī are palatal, u and ū are labial, ṛ and ṝ are retroflex while dental vowels are ḷ and ḹ. The vowels continue with the diphtongs e and ai (palatal), o and au (labial), all diphtongs count as long vowels. This yields fourteen vowels, to make up the much desired sixteen, ṁ (aṁ) and visarga (aḥ) are added.

Now for a simplified guide to pronunciation. The vowels are pronounced much as in most European languages, apart from English. The consonants are often close to the English ones. What you encounter in this list is the pronunciation of classical Saṅskṛt. As Saṅskṛt is still a living language (though only a few thousand people can speak it fluently) there are still new words being made up and the pronunciation is not quite the same as is used to be. The guidelines given below do not apply to Hindi, Nepali or other modern languages.

As you'll recall from the chapter on mantra, there are several code names for each letter which may or may not convey a hidden meaning to the initiate. Here I would like to introduce some of the attributions that the phonemes have in Abhinavagupta's synthesis of Kashmir Śaivism.

Comments marked with AB are based on Abhinavagupta's *PTV* and *PTLV* and exceedingly simplified. I have (sorry about this) only bothered to give Abhinava's commentaries to the sixteen vowels, as they are still fairly comprehensible. In his blend of Kaula, Krama and Trika lore, he also arranged the consonants in various patterns and interpreted them in more ways than you or I will ever comprehend. In Trika lore, the phonemes basically follow two patterns. One is called Mātṛkā (Little Mother) and follows the usual sequence of the alphabet. In Mālinī (She Who Wears a Mālā) the letters follow an esoteric pattern and appear confused. Abhinava comments on the Mātṛkā (ordinary order) of the letters:

> *The letters from 'a' to visarga denote Śiva tattva, those from ka to ṅa denote the five elements from the earth up to the ether; those from ca up to ña denote the five tanmātras from smell up to sound; those from ṭa to ṇa denote the five karmendriyas (organs of action) from the feet up to the tongue; those from ta to na denote five jñānendriyas from the nose up to the ears; those from pa to ma denote the group of five i.e. manas, ahaṁkāra, buddhi, prakṛti, and puruṣa; those from ya to va denote through vāyu bīja, agni bīja, jala bīja and indrabīja, raga, vidyā, kalā and māyā tattvas. (PTV, trans. Jaideva Singh, 2002: 98).*

To give you at least a very basic idea of the range of thought that went into the consonants and their correspondence with the patterns of consciousness, I have added the key terms attributed by Abhinava to them in the order of Mātṛkā. These concepts were drawn together from Abhinava's *PTV*, Jaideva Singh's commentaries and the tables of attribution given by John Dupuche (2006: 351-352), based on Gnoli and Padoux. It is one attribution, but there are several such lists, depending on how the principles are assigned to the sounds and the order of the alphabet. Don't ask me to explain. It's much better fun to explore the sounds in the voidness of the heart and to learn what effects they have on you. All vowels and consonants appear in a sequence manifesting the entire universe and those who weave its fabric by consciousness, will, knowledge, action and belief. The vowels form one such cycle and the consonants another. Where the vowels refer mainly to consciousness (Śiva), the consonants describe a journey from the crude, manifest reality of everyday life to ever more subtle ranges of experience, at least in the Mātṛkā sequence.

Vowels

There are short and long vowels, the latter indicated by a bar atop the letter. Long vowels are pronounced approximately twice as long as normal ones.

a: **a**rrive, rur**a**l, s**u**n (AB: a is cit, pure consciousness, anuttara: the Ultimate, All-Pervasive, *an inner massive I-consciousness abiding in the Transcendent*) ā: **fa**ther, cr**a**ft (AB: ā is ānanda, pure bliss)

i: **li**ly, w**i**ll (AB: i is icchā, the subjective will towards manifestation)

ī: pol**i**ce, fr**ee** (AB. ī is īśana, lordship, mastery, domination, sovereignty. Here icchā becomes objective)

u: p**u**t, f**u**ll, b**u**ll (AB: unmeṣa, opening; arising of knowledge; jñāna, knowledge as direct experience, gnosis, expansion)

ū: r**u**de, f**oo**l (AB: ūnatā, decrease, is lack of or deficient knowledge, leading to objective appearance, 'reality'. Diminution of pure awareness, increase of manifest awareness)

ṛ is a vowel as there is a short i after the r: mer**ri**ly, **ri**d.

ṝ has a long i (ī) after the r: ma**ri**ne. The phoneme never appears at the beginning of words. It has a lot of symbolic meanings however: breasts; memory; Mother of the Gods and Non-Gods (asura); and the two divine families of the Dānavas and Bhairavas.

ḷ has a short I or e attached to the l: stab**le**, tang**le** . Not a common letter either. It symbolises, among other ideas, earth; mountain and the Mother of the Gods (Elvira Friedrich, 1999: 34-36).

ḹ does not occur in writing or speech. It was invented to add an l-sound with a long i (ī) to the script, mainly for reasons of symmetry. Its meanings are complex: mother; divine woman; female nature; a name of Śiva; Mother of the Dānavas; Mother of the Wish-Fulfilling-Cow.

According to Abhinavagupta, the letters ṛ, ṝ, ḷ and ḹ are the imperishable letters. They do not effect change nor are they affected by it. They are called amṛtabīja, seed of the elixir of immortality, due to their timeless and place-less presence. Another term is void-vowels, or the essential nature of Śiva. Their nature is restful, immortal, essential. The ṛ and ṝ also signify luminosity while ḷ and ḹ signify immobility. This is based on r as the fire sound and l as the sound of earth.

e: th**e**re, r**a**re (AB: aspuṭha kriyāṣakti, indistinct power of activity. Śiva without Śakti.)

ai: **ai**sle, r**ai**n (AB: spuṭha kriyāṣakti, distinct power of activity. The eternal union of Śiva and Śakti, hence the Heart of Bhairava/Bhairavī.)

o: **o**rder, n**o** (AB: spuṭhatara kriyāṣakti, increasingly distinct power of activity)

au: h**ou**se, s**ou**r (AB: spuṭhatama kriyāṣakti, most distinct power of activity, the process of knowing, the sum of the vowels, the trident of Trika, fusion of icchā, jñāna and kriyā)

ṁ: the anusvāra is a nasal vibration, much like 'ng'. (AB: the bindu of Śiva, the undivided, all-inclusive knowledge of all, the knowing subject)

ḥ: a strongly aspirated 'h', the sound of exhalation. The letter ḥ is written as two dots (:). According to AB, the upper dot represents Śiva as the I-consciousness of all beings and things, itself void in essence, while the lower dot represents Śakti as the form and force of the manifest universe in the process of expansion. Both of them are points of view. The letter can also refer to the pulsation of the heart; opening and closing; rest and activity; to the essence of Bhairava/Bhairavī; the Rudra

Yāmala or union of Śiva and Śakti; the totality of all sounds expressing all-being; to female and male discharge and their mixture; the Emissional State; the inherent form in all fifteen vowels plus a great deal of similar ideas. This is the sixteenth kalā, the quintessence of the fifteen.

Consonants

In general, the vowels are manifestations of Śiva as consciousness-without-form while the consonants represent Śakti as consciousness-in-form-and-energy. Remember that the consonants are not really consonants but phonemes beginning with a consonant. There is, unless deleted, always a short 'a' behind each consonant.

When the letter h is added to a consonant, it adds an element of aspiration. Buddha, for example, is pronounced Budd-ha, Bhairava as B-hairava, phaṭ as p-haṭ. There is no English th in Saṅskṛt, though the 'd' is sometimes pronounced with a slight lisp, a little like the letter ð.

Laryngal (AB: mahābhūta, gross elements or principles)

k: **k**ing, **k**ick (AB: Pṛthivī, goddess and principle of earth, matter, density)

kh: in**kh**orn (AB: jala, principle of water)

g: **g**oat, **g**ive (AB: Agni, god and principle of fire, heat, hunger)

gh: lo**gh**ut (AB: Vāyu, god and principle of air, wind, breath)

ṅ: ri**ng**, sti**n**k (AB: ākāśa, principle of space and spirit)

Palatal (AB: tanmātras, subtle elements)

c: **ch**est, **ch**eers (AB: gandha, smell)

ch: chur**chh**ill (AB: rasa, sap, juice, here taste)

j: **j**ungle, **j**oint, occasionally **du**ty (AB: rupa, form, essence)

jh: he**dgeh**og (AB: sparśa, touch)

ñ: cri**ng**e, si**ng**e, opi**ni**on (AB: śabda, sound)

Retroflex (AB: karmendriyas, organs of action)

ṭ: **t**rue, **t**ree (AB: upastha, procreating)

ṭh: an**th**ill (AB: pāyu, excreting)

ḍ: **d**rum, **d**ream (AB: pāda, walking)

ḍh: re**dh**aired (AB: pāṇi, grasping)

ṇ: **n**one, **n**ever, u**n**der (AB: vāk, speaking, voice)

Dental (AB: jñānendriyas, organs of knowledge)

t: wa**t**er (AB: prāṇa or ghrāṇa, smelling)

th: ra**th**ole (AB: rasanā, tasting)

d: **d**ice, **d**ame (AB: cakṣus, seeing)

dh: lan**dh**ouse (AB: tvak, touching)

n: **n**ot, **n**ut (AB: śrotra, hearing)

Labial (AB: antaḥ karaṇa, inner faculties)

p: **p**ound, **p**erson (AB: manas, mind)

ph: u**ph**ill (AB: ahaṁkāra, I-principle, ego)

b: **b**ear, **b**all (AB: buddhi, intelligence)

bh: a**bh**or (AB: prakṛti, matter, primordial nature)

m: **m**ind, ra**m** (AB: puruṣa, soul, individual)

Half-Vowels (AB: dhāraṇās, concentration, elemental seeds)

y: **y**et, **y**ou, **y**es (AB: Vāyu bīja, seed of air; rāga, attachment)

r: **r**ight, **r**eal, ve**r**y (AB: Agni bīja, vidyā, knowledge, magic seed of fire; niyati, necessity)

l: **l**earn, **l**eap (AB: salila bīja, seed of earth; kāla, time)

v: i**v**y, **v**odka (between v and w) (AB: Indra bīja, seed of thunder and rain; Māyā, craft, illusion)

Hissing (AB: brahmapañcaka, Brahman's five)

ś: **s**ure, **sh**iver (soft sh) (AB: Mahāmāyā, the Great Craftful Illusion)

ṣ: **sh**ut, wa**sh, sh**ow (sharp sh) (AB: Śuddha vidyā, here corresponding to kriyā, action)

s: **s**alad, **s**erpent, hi**ss** (AB: Īśvara, Śiva as 'The Lord', here corresponding to jñāna, true knowledge)

h: **h**ead, **h**ope (AB: Sadāśiva, Eternal Śiva, here corresponding to icchā, will)

kṣ: ri**cksh**a (AB: Śakti, force, form, here corresponding to ānanda, bliss)

Appendix Two: A Brief Glossary of Saṅskṛt Terms

The following glossary was assembled to make life easier for you. Luckily, not all of the terms had to be used in writing this book. They may, however, be of use when it comes to exploring other texts. The words are usually explained in the forms commonly used in Hindu Tantric literature. Their interpretation in Buddhist, Jain and Moslem Tantras may be widely different. Spelling is another question: the original texts are full of variation. The translations are always the simplest possible. I have aimed at usefulness, not at giving complete definitions. For the full meaning of the terms, consult a good dictionary, the passages where they appear within the text and as much original literature as you can lay your hands on. Tantra is not supposed to be exact science. You may need the mind of an artist or a poet to find or create a meaning that is perfectly suited to your will. A given term may have a several literal meanings but also a lot of deeper ones in religion, yoga and Tantric 'Twilight Language'. The latter are marked TL. Multiple interpretations are part of the fun. Many are known from antiquity, others have long been lost and forgotten, and some of the best are yet to be invented.

Sarvaṁ sarvātmakaṁ: Everything consists of everything else. (Abhinavagupta)

A

abhaya-mudrā: the gesture that dispels fear.

abhiṣeka: from siñc, to sprinkle, moisten, soak. 1. In ritual, statues, objects and the ritual space are anointed, often using generous amounts of fluids (usually milk, fruit juice, ghī, oil, honey etc.); 2. initiation; 3. impregnation.

ācārya: teacher, instructor.

ādhāra: foundation, base, support, often a reference to the perineum.

adhikāri: competent.

Advaita: non-dual. A philosophy emphasising the unity of the worshipper, the divine and everything else.

ādyā: primordial.

ādyā bīja: primordial seed: Krīṁ.

Ādyā Kālī: the Primordial Kālī.

ādyā Śaktī: 1. the primordial Śaktī; 2. the wife or mate of the worshipper.

Āgama: a class of religious scripture & ritual instruction, often proposing a dualist philosophy, starting c. 500 CE. Usually a teaching given by Śiva at the request of a goddess.

Agni: Vedic god of fire, heat, light, life energy, hunger and the sacrificial fire that transmits the offering to the gods.

aham: 'I am'. An important element in some mantras and basis of much metaphysical speculation.

ajaya: 1. defeat, non-victory; 2. unconquerable, invincible; 3. a name of Viṣṇu; 4. Māyā, illusion; 5. a friend of Durgā; 6. hemp, hashish.

ajapa: 1. one who does no japa; 2. one who recites heterodox works; 3. the not-recited mantra Haṁsa (out-breath and in-breath).

ājñā cakra: the consciousness/energy centre between the eyebrows, seat of the inner guru.

akala: not in parts, entire.

ākaṇḍa flowers :1. the Indian 'sunflower'; 2. TL flowers without stem (yoni), 3. TL flowers of the mind (sun): various qualities such as bliss, charity, wisdom, non-injury etc.

ākāśa: ether, spirit.

Akṣobhya: Unagitated. The blue throated Śiva who drank the poison of the cosmic ocean.

Akrama: without succession, not in sequence (see Krama). The formless principle of consciousness that goes through life without change.

Akula: 1. without clusters/groups ; 2. Śiva (pure consciousness) as partner of Śaktī who is kula; 3. a trance of total liberation from everything, dissolving all clusters; 4. not of good family; 5. a name of Śiva, a name of Pārvatī.

amākalā: the 16th kalā, the blend of the nectar generated by the union of Śakti and Śiva.

ambuvācī: the feast of Kāmākhhyā's menstruation and subsequent renewal.

amṝta : from 'death-less', ambrosia, elixir of life. May be plants, brain-hormones, sexual secretions or alchemical medicine, depending on the context.

anāhata: the cakra of the heart region (not identical with the cakra that forms the seat of the personal deity slightly below the heart).

ānanda: bliss.

ānanda kanda: the eight petaled lotus of the personal deity in the heart.

aṇḍa: 1. egg, testicle; 2. scrotum; 3. sperm; 4. a bag of musk; 5. a name of Śiva.

aṅkuśa: 1. A hook; 2. elephant goad; 3. A Jaina goddess; 4. a mudrā to prod, hook and pull.

Annapūrṇā: She who is Full of Food. A goddess who bestows food on worshippers.

anuttara: a key concept of Krama, Trika, Kaula in Abhinavagupta's lore. It means essential nature, supreme reality, divine consciousness. It is timeless, unbound by any conditions, all-inclusive, luminous. The realisation that the experience of being and the 'objective world' are an expression of undivided true consciousness. And a lot more.

apāna: downward moving 'wind'. In body: gasses, urine, sexual fluids and excrement; also energy tending towards birth, externalisation and manifestation.

Aparājitā: A black Śakti in black clothes armed with club and shield, riding a chariot, inspiring fear by her screams.

Apsaras: in Vedic times a demonic seductress, associated with obsessions and dicing; in Hinduism a beautiful water-nymph dwelling in the heavenly realm of Indra. Often busy seducing seers and ascetics.

Aranyānī: Vedic goddess of forests and waters. As Aranyā (Forest) she became a form of Kālī.

āratī: a ritual involving the waiving of a lamp or some holy object in a circle before the image of a deity. Usually accompanied by recitation, song or ringing a bell.

Ardhanārīśvara: a deity who is half woman, half man, representing Śiva and Śakti and the cosmic totality in union with itself.

argha: 1. vessel; 2. TL sexual fluids, pure or mixed with wine. One of the three essentials of the Kula sacrifice. The others are dipa (lamp) and dhāman (sacred place, genitals).

arghya: offering a little rice, consecrated water and tips of durvā grass to a deity.

artha: wealth.

aruṇa: blood, menstrual blood.

āsana: 1. Posture. 2. Seat.

Asitā: 1. Dark One; 2. Unbound One (Kālī).

astra: 1. missile; 2. bow and arrow.

Asura: In Vedic times, a tribe of powerful and respectable deities (including Agni, Soma, Varuna, Uṣas, Rudra, the Maruts, the Ādityas etc.). In Hinduism, a class of demons, giants and monsters, eternal enemies of the Devas. Often a symbol for antisocial, egoistic tendencies and imagined in animal form.

Aśvins: Pertaining to Horses. Divine twins, each of them half-human, half-horse; Vedic deities of healing.

Atharvan (from **athar**: fire): 1. Name of a priest who instituted the worship of fire and soma; 2. a priest worshipping fire and soma; 3. name of Śiva, Soma, prāṇa; 4. one major author of the *Atharvaveda.*

ātman: A Vedic concept for the individual self, identified as breath and life force. Later the immortal, eternal self-essence. Sometimes a term for the world-soul, the all-being.

avatāra: 'descent', a deity who has descended to earth and manifests in a human or beastial incarnation.

avidyā: ignorance.

B

Bagalā : Fierce goddess of sorcery, sometimes with a crane-head, who is specialized in magical rites of paralysis.

bali: 1. a tribute, gift, offering, oblation; 2. a food offering made before a meal by arranging the oblation in a circle or by throwing it into the fire; 3. an animal sacrificed for a goddess; 4. a Daitya demon, a ruler of the underworlds.

Bhadrā: Gracious (Śiva).

Bhadrākāḷi: Gracious Kālī, a particularly angry and terrifying form of the goddess.

bhaga: 1. love, sexual lust, 2. vulva.

bhaga-aṅkura: 'sprout of the womb' i.e. clitoris.

Bhagamālinī: She who wears a garland of vulvas.

Bhagavati: The Blessed One, a benevolent form of Kālī.

Bhairava: Frightful, Horrible, Terrible, Formidable, 1. a name of Śiva, very popular in Kashmir and Nepal; 2. a son of Śiva; 3. a worshipper who identifies with Śiva in his terrifying aspect; 4. eight Bhairavas: eight aspects of Śiva residing in the petals of the lotus of the heart; 5. a name of Nirṛti; 6. a class of Apsarases.

Bhairavī: 1. Terrible One. A popular goddess of Kashmir and Nepal. 2. a ritual partner.

bhakta: a religious devotee.

bhakti: partaking. Total loving devotion to a deity, an ecstatic form of worship often associated with the cults celebrating Viṣṇu.

bhāng: the lower leaves of the hemp plant.

bhāvanā: imagination, visualisation, conceptual thinking, pondering, contemplation.

bandha: 1. bondage; 2. manacle; 3. connection; 4. grip; 5. a position that locks, binds and controls the energy flow within body.

Bhava: from 'world', 'universe'. A title of Śiva.

bhāva: becoming, being. Identifying with a deity.

bodha: universal divine consciousness, characterised by being free of thoughts and all-inclusive, full, complete (pūrṇa). Totally unlimited and free of all conditions of existence. Its counterpart is abodha: empirical, differentiated consciousness.

bhoga: 1. enjoyment, feeding on; 2. use, application; 3. sexual enjoyment; 4. experiencing, feeling, perception; 5. profit, advantage, delight; 6. property, wealth.

Bhūcarī: One who moves in the sphere of existence (bhū), i.e. manifests the divine energies on earth and elsewhere. Her sphere is the world of objective existence, but as Krama lore insists, her nature is truly identical with the Khecarī.

bhukti: enjoyment, pleasure.

bhūtaśuddhi: the purification of the elements of the body. A meditation involving the rising of awareness within body, from the coarse to the subtle, involving complex visualisation.

Bhuvaneśvarī: Lady of the Earth. A red goddess who rules the multiverse. She is occasionally identified with Mahāmāyā and Kuṇḍalinī.

bīja: 1. seed; 2. syllable which manifests a given deity, energy or sentience. 3. TL sperm.

bilva, **bel**: a tree sacred to Śiva and Durgā.

bindu: 1. point; 2. dot; 3. drop; 4. TL central point of a yantra and focus of ritual; 4. TL sperm.

Bodhi: enlightenment.

Brahmā: Minor four faced deity, associated with creation. An attempt to personify the Brahman.

Brahmamayī: Essence of Brahman, a title of Kālī.

Brahman: all-consciousness, the absolute, the Being of all that is. Formless, nameless, without attributes. Source of all consciousness in humans, gods, beings, things. Ultimate reality.

Brahmāṇī: female form of Brahmā.

Brahma-pura: the city of Brahman. TL The human body.

Brahmarandhara: the Gate of Brahman. A cakra at the top of the head, to pass through this aperture is to transcend incarnate humanity.

Bṛhaspati: the guru of the gods. A deity representing the Brahmins and their function.

Buddha: The Enlightened One. In Buddhism, the historical Gautama, 6-5th century BCE, founder of the cult; in Hinduism, a reincarnation of Viṣṇu.

C

cakra: 1. circle, wheel, disk; 2. TL a ritual circle, an assembly 3. TL an energy/consciousness centre in the human body. May have been a circle of goddesses originally.

Cakravartin: Turner of the Wheel/Circle. A title of the king who makes a ritual circuit around the periphery of the kingdom to install himself in the centre. If the king is false, the rite may secretly be done by some Tantric adept, who usurps divine and royal authority.

Caṇḍa: 1. fierce, violent, cruel, hot, passionate; 2. a name of a goddess/Durgā/Kālī; 3. a name of a Daitya demon; 4. name of a cloud that enclosed the earth during the deluge; 5. name of a being who had 20 demonic daughters; 6. a fond name given to a mistress.

Caṇḍī: 1. the Fierce One, a name of Durgā as the destroyer of demons. 2. a title of the *Devī Mahātmyam*.

Cāmuṇḍā: Kālī as the killer of the Dānava demons Caṇḍa and Muṇḍa. Usually she appears as a hungry, frenzied, blood-swilling hag.

caryā: ritual action, action, ceremony, ritual.

Cidambara: cid = consciousness, ambara = sky. 1. geographically a special place of Śiva. In the Tillai forest of Cidambara, the original, first liṅga, made of pure crystal, and a ruby figure of Śiva Naṭarāja were worshipped. The site is considered the heart cakra of India (i.e. the world).2. a metaphor for the heart as the seat of consciousness.

Chinnamastā: self-decapitated goddess of wisdom. She holds her own head and a sword, three streams of blood jet from her neck, feeding her two attendants and herself.

cit (cid): pure consciousness.

citi: universal mind, consciousness/energy of the absolute.

citta: (individual) mind, consciousness, heart, awareness.

D

Ḍākinī: 1. flying female spirit who mediates between the worlds, usually dangerous and keen on blood; 2. witch, sorceress; 3. a female initiate, especially in Tantric Buddhism.

Dakṣiṇā: 1. a gift or offering to the Brahmins, who represent the incarnate gods. Nowadays a fee or small sum, in Vedic times at least one fertile cow. Given in addition to the sacrifice to make the offering fruitful. 2. the goddess who grants fulfilment. She makes sacrifices and offerings fruitful and gives people what they deserve. 3. to the right, to the south, deosil.

dakṣiṇabhāva: orthodox worship, usually associated with benevolent goddesses. In the dakṣiṇa path, the so called right hand path, physical ritual, lovemaking, intoxication, obsession etc. are replaced by inner, symbolic and imaginary worship. It also tends towards making friends with the Brahmanic orthodoxy. As Abhinavagupta said *The Dakṣiṇa path is full of terrible practices*. (in *PTV*, 2002:85).

Dakṣiṇā Kālī: The aspect of Kālī who grants liberation. Usually portrayed as standing on Śiva, right (dakṣiṇa) foot forward, who is lying inert, like a corpse, beneath her.

ḍamaru: hourglass-shaped small drum with two skins and two beads on strings. Played by rotating. An emblem of Śiva and a symbol of the heart. An image of the yogīc body.

Dānava: a class of Asuras. Originally followers of Śiva, today well known as demons.

darśana: seeing. A ritual of meditation holding eye-contact with an image of a deity.

devī: shining one, goddess.

Devī: Shining One. The major goddess, or just a general term for a goddess of the Śāktas, an agglomerate of earlier goddesses fused into a single deity in an attempt at monotheism.

Devī-pīṭha: sacred place of a devī, usually associated with a part of the body of Satī.

dhāman: 1. sacrificial place; 2. the genitals.

dharma: 1. religious, moral and social duty (truth, rightness, tradition, law etc.) thought to reflect the true order of the universe. 2. these qualities personified as a deity.

Dhātā: Brahmā as dispenser of the fruit of karma.

Dhūmāvatī: Sinister dark goddess representing a widow, outside of society.

dhyāna: focusing of thought, visualisation, meditation.

Digambarī: space clad i. e. nude, a name of Kālī.

Dikcarī: one who moves in space (dik) i.e. the outer senses, the energy which moves sensual perception.

dīkṣā: ritual initiation.

dīpa: 1. lamp; 2. edible ritual lamp made of paste and secretions, saturated with ghī, with a red wick. Large numbers of these are set up during the Kula ritual. They represent human flesh, their number represents the phonemes or the Yogīnīs. At the end of the rite they are consumed.

dravya: substance, matter, ingredient (fluid).

Durgā: Unapproachable, Inaccessible, Untouchable. Possibly from durga: fortress, stronghold. A beautiful, fierce goddess, riding a lion of tiger, who fights evil and grants peace. Her ten weapons manifest the essences of all deities. Often identified with Kālī and Mahāmāyā. Her cult was eagerly embraced by Hindu kings after the 7th century, who adorned their fortresses with Durgā images and made her the protectress of their kingdoms.

Durgāpūjā: Durgā-worship; one of the most important Indian rituals, lasting between five and nine days, generally in September or October. In the old days, after the celebration the season of warfare began.

Dūtī: 1. a female messenger; 2. a female adept, a semi-divine yogīnī; 3. a ritual partner or consort.

dvāpara-yuga: one-half-yuga. The third world age when virtue and goodness had decreased by one half. It lasted for 864 000 human years.

G

Gaurī: Bright, 1.a name of Pārvatī; 2. An eight year old girl.

Gandharva: In Vedic times, a class of malevolent demons who harm women. In later Hinduism, a class of celestial musicians, occasionally a guarding spirit.

Gaṇeśa: the elephant-headed god, destroyer of obstacles, protector of beginnings, lord of literature, patron of merchants. Accompanied by a rat to show that great strength should be coupled by craftiness, cunning and subtlety.

Garuḍa: bird-shaped vehicle of Viṣṇu. Originally (*Mhb.*) a destructive heavenly force, a meteor. Traditional foe of serpents.

ghāṭ: the steps descending to a sacred river or to the water-tank within a temple.

ghī: 1. clarified butter (used as sacrifice, to purify, as medicine etc.). In Vedic rites it is usually poured into the sacred fire; 2. TL the sexual fluids.

Giriśa, Giriśā: Lord or Lady of the Mountain (Śiva & Pārvatī).

Gocarī: One who moves in Sense (go), i.e. the seat of the senses, the mind. Traveller in the psychic apparatus. Her sphere is the mind and all thinking, remembering, contemplation etc.

gopī: a cow girl. Usually a lover of Kṛṣṇa, who is often shown playing the flute among gopīs or stealing their clothes. A symbol for the human worshippers longing for the divine.

granthi: knot. A vague term that is synonymous with 'cakra' in several early texts. In others, the granthi are obstacles between the cakras. Their number varies widely. Sometimes there is a granthi above and below each cakra (including one under the root cakra, i.e. below the torso!). In modern yoga, there are only three knots that obstruct the ascent of the Kuṇḍalinī. Each is an essential locus of crisis and ordeal in the transformation of consciousness.

guṇa: 1. thread; 2. quality. One of the fundamental ideas in Hindu philosophy. Prakṛti (nature, matter) is thought to consist of three guṇas: sattva, rajas and tamas. All phenomena partake of all three guṇas in varying amounts, which activate and/or suppress each other. The concept was borrowed by Muslim philosophers and reappears in European alchemy as the three essential substances mercury, sulphur and salt.

guru: 1. teacher, initiator, spiritual parent; 2. venerable, respectable (title given to parents, elders etc.); 3. excessive, high in degree, difficult; 4. heavy on the stomach, hard to digest.

gurupāraṁparya: one teacher after another. A spiritual lineage.

H

Haṁsa: 1. the supreme mantra (out-breath and in-breath) 2. a name of Śiva; 3. A gander, goose or swan, symbolising the divine spirit. 4. the rising Kuṇḍalinī.

Hara: Bandit, Destroyer. A Vedic title of Rudra, later applied to Śiva.

Hari: Lion, a name of Viṣṇu in his lion-man incarnation.

Havih: the ghī (clarified butter) poured into the fire-sacrifice.

haviṣyānnaṁ: the pure food 1. the sacrificial ghee; 2. TL the consecrated sexual secretions.

Hlādinī Śakti: Blissful Energy, a name of Rādhā.

Homa: a fire sacrifice.

hṛdaya: 1. the heart as the organ; 2. the heart as the seat of consciousness, thought, vision, cognition, the senses etc.; 3. centre, core, middle; 4. a trance of introversion, descending into the original source of being and non-being; 5. the union and true nature of Śiva and Śakti; 6. the central void from which all being arises and into which it returns. (A highly complex key-experience developed in some *Upaniṣads*, refined by Kashmir monism). 7. TL the suṣuṁnā; 8. TL the consecrated sexual fluids; 9. TL A code word for the mantra 'namaḥ' (homage).

I

Icchā: 1. will; 2. the Śakti of true will.

Idā: the nādī of the moon, starting at the left nostril.

Indra: Vedic god of thunder and rainstorm, fighter of the dragon/serpent, inaugurator of kings, lord of battle, destroyer of foes. King of the gods in Vedic times.

Iṁ: core-sound of many bījas. The essence of the turīja state.

Īśa: The Lord, the Ruler (Śiva).

iṣṭadevatā: chosen deity, personal deity of a worshipper.

Īśvara, **Īśvarī**: The Lord; the Lady.

Īśvaratattva: the Principle of the Lord.

J

Jagaddhātrī: Mother of the World, title of several goddesses.

Jagannātha: Lord of the World, a title of Viṣṇu.

japa: to recite (often silently); repetition of mantra.

japamālā: a rosary used for meditation, to count and offer the recitation of a mantra.

jati: station in society according to one's origin, class, relationship, membership in religious, ethnic or professional groups. Part of the 'caste' concept.

Jayā: Victorious. 1. a white Śakti seated on a corpse, holding club and shield, the possessor of mantras; 2. Śiva's doorkeeper; 3. hashish; 4. a Śakti of Śiva or Viṣṇu.

Jayāntī: A golden Śakti in yellow clothes, holding bell and club and riding a horse.

jīva: the incarnate divinity/soul/consciousness.

Jīvanmukti: liberation of the jīva; liberation while incarnate.

jīvātmā: embodied consciousness.

Jñāna: 1. true wisdom, insight, direct experience, gnosis; 2. the Śakti of true wisdom.

jñānamārga: the way of true wisdom.

Jyeṣṭhā: Eldest, the most Ancient. 1. title of a goddess of a triad formed with Vāmā and Raudrī.2. eldest lady of a Kula community, an honorary title corresponding to the male form jyeṣṭha.

K

ka: 1. head, skull; 2. Brahman; 3. Body.

Kailasa: Śiva's sacred mountain.

kāla: time.

kalā: digit, unit. In astrology, each heavenly body has a number of kalās. The sun has 12, fire/stars has 10. In left-hand path worship, the important ones are the 16 kalās of the moon (the month consists of twice 15 kalās. The 16th is generated on the night of the 15th, full moon.) The 16 was considered the summit of perfection (the whole summarised in one), later Kashmiri traditions increased the number of lunar kalās to 17 and 18.

kālacakra: the wheel of time.

Kāla-Mātā: Mother of Time (Kālī).

Kali: 1. Vedic god of decadence, gambling and corruption; 2. the worst throw of the dice (#1); 3. the god of the present world age.

Kālī: The Black One; a dark goddess usually shown in a terrifying form, with a garland of heads, a lolling tongue, haunting jungles, cross-roads and cremation places. The name may also be read as 'Time'.

Kālīkā: Little Kālī, 'Blackie'.

Kālīkula: Kālī's cluster, a group of goddesses and their devotees.

Kali-yuga: the age of corruption. It started 3120 BCE when Viṣṇu ended his eighth incarnation and lasts for a total of 432 000 human years.

kalpa: world cycle, aeon. A day of Brahmā. It lasts 4 320 000 000 human years.

Kalyāṇi: The Beneficent one. The goddess of the Malaya mountain, a title of Kālī.

Kāma: 1. Wish, desire, longing, affection, lust, love etc. 2. Pleasure, enjoyment, sensuality etc. 3. The god of desire.

Kāmadeva: The god of desire, lust and love, also called Manmatha (the Whisk of the Mind) and Madana (Intoxicator).

Kāmabīja: desire/lust seed, Klīṁ.

Kāmakalā: 1. Unit of Desire. Usually a hexagram which is drawn in the centre of a yantra or visualised within your body. Sometimes a symbol of the body of a goddess. 2. The arts of Desire/Love.

Kāmākhhyā: possibly from kāma: the Place of Love/Desire. 1. the devī of the yoni (Mahāmāyā); 2. the sacred place in Kāmarūpa; 3. the genitals.

Kamalā: lotus. A name of Lakṣmī.

Kāmarūpa: Form/Body of Desire, also called Kāmagiri, Kāmapīṭha and Kāmākhya. 1. a sacred place in Assam, associated with the yoni of Satī. 2. the genitals. 3. the part of your body on which you sit. 4. a mat used in meditation.

Kāmarūpinī: She Who Assumes All Forms As She Likes, a name of Kāmākhhyā.

Kāmeśvarī: six-faced goddess standing on a lotus sprouting from the navel of a corpse lying on a lion. Occasionally identified with Kāmākhhyā.

kampa: 1. trembling, shaking, quivering. Can be a sign of divine possession, of Śaktipāta (descent of power), an effect of dīkṣa (initiation), of Kuṇḍalinī rising, of the penetration of body by mantra etc.. 2. a column.

kanda: bulb. 1. the lower part of the lotus on which Śiva sits; 2. sacred spot at the perineum; 3. an egg-shaped sacred site surrounding the navel. 'To squeeze the bulb' usually means to contract the muscles around genitals, perineum and anus and to pull up the force within the central channel.

kāpālika (fem. Kāpālinī): skull-bearer. Member of an early sect that used to carry a begging bowl made of a Brahmin's skull and a skull-topped staff. Well known for obscure rituals at cremation places. Their archetype is Śiva, who calls himself a kāpālika in the *Kālikāpurāna* (61.3-10) and proposes that this is what made Dakṣa so mad at him.

kāpilasnāna: a form of purification. After a partial bath and washing with a wet cloth, the worshipper recites mantra while visualising that a fire arises from the (right) big toe which burns up all impurities. When the fire reaches the head, it releases the nectar of immortality which pours down the body and rejuvenates it.

karamālā: the hand and fingers used to count repetitions of mantra.

karaṇa: 1. instrument of perception or activity, organ of the senses; 2. practice involving body; 3. a posture of the body (often emphasising the torso, arms and head); 4. ritual tool or utensil.

kāraṇa: 1. Cause. Several systems attributing a variety of deities (kāraṇeśvaras are the 'causers') to parts of the body (cakras, granthi). 2. wine or alcohol used in worship. 3. a name of Śiva. 4. initiation and other intense experiences leading to (eventual) liberation.

Karaṇeśvarī: the goddess of the senses, hence of the perceivable universe and what we believe to know about it.

karman: action, doing, work. The 'Law of Karma' implies that each action and non-action causes results which bind or release from the phenomenal world. Thus, karman is all development arising from past impulses. In early thought, a subtle principle that attaches itself to the jīva and accompanies it from life to life. Later interpreted in terms of moral values.

karmasāmya: 1. balance due to blockage of karman. In Saiddhāntika lore, karman can become blocked when several impulses of equal power obstruct each other. A descent of power (Śaktipāta) can unstop the impasse, this is experienced as a moment of grace. 2. egalisation of karman by equipoise and indifference. 3. balancing of the evil and good deeds of a worshipper, invalidating both, and freeing the jīva for spiritual evolution.

karmayoga: the yoga of right activity

karpūram: camphor. Can also be a general term for a mixture of several perfumes. TL 1. Kālī; 2. sperm and menstrual blood; 3. Saguṇa-Brahman, The Fashioner of the Worlds; 4. The moon.

Kaula: 1. union of kula & akula, 2. of the clan, of the tribe; 3. A cluster of early cults belonging to the left hand path; 4. The hidden essence of several traditions.

keśara: 1. hair, mane; 2. fibre; 3. name of several plants; gold; 4. iron-sulphate.

kha: sky. Also void and Brahman. TL: the consciousness of the void.

Khecara, **Khecarī**: Sky traveller, One-who-moves-in-the-Void, a spiritual being or a human who has attained the highest form of transcendence and is not bound by worldly matters any more. A Khecarī may be synonymous with a Yoginī in all her benevolent and lethal aspects. In Krama lore (and Abhinavagupta), the Khecarī is the highest manifestation, presiding over the sphere of the self, her nature being pure anuttara. The power of consciousness on the plane of pure universal awareness. Related to Gocarī, Dikcarī and Bhūcarī in descending order.

Khecarīcakra: 1. a ritual circle or assembly of those Yoginīs who have attained the consciousness of the void; 2. the highest cakra in the five-cakra system, located above the head and containing three maṇḍalas of twenty-four, thirty-two and eight Khecarīs.

Khecarī-samatā: a state of awareness in which the divine presence is experienced in all events, forms, energies etc. including those which are repugnant. An exercise in non-dualistic awareness that should be cultivated every day.

Klīṁ-Kārī: Creatrix of the bīja Klīṁ (Kālī). see Kāmabīja.

Krama: 1. tradition, succession, lineage; 2. a specific tradition from Kashmir which emphasises cyclic development represented by four (or five) phases and 12 or 13 Kālīs.

Kramamudrā: Joy (mud-) of progression, sequence (Krama): a trance where consciousness alternates between inward and outward. Keeping awareness within while perceiving the outside world and keeping awareness outside while realising what is within, in rapid alternation, until a blend of both occurs. The loveplay of internalisation and externalisation, the outside being 'devoured' and the inside 'emitted'. Key mantras: 'I am that' and 'That am I'.

Kriyā: 1. (right) action, activity; 2. the Śakti of right action.

Kṛtakas: members of a Kaula cult that believes in worldly activities and worships dualistically (i.e. deities and worshippers remain apart).

Kṛṣṇa: black, an incarnation of Viṣṇu. A highly popular deity who is often shown playing a flute in the company of the cow-girls or making love with his Śakti Rādhā. In older literature he has a more pronounced warlike character.

Kṣemaṅkarī: The Kind One (Kālī).

kṣetra: 1. sacred space; 2. TL: sexual union.

Kubera: the lord of wealth and fertility, king of the Yakṣas, early mate of Lakṣmī.

Kubjikā: Crooked, Curved, Curvaceous, Hunchbacked One. The major goddess of the 'western transmission', originally a dangerous tree goddess worshipped by a class of hereditary potters. Her name is enigmatic and has given rise to any amount of bizarre mythology. Such as that she became hunchbacked to lick her own yoni.

Kula: 1. cluster, group, family, clan, tribe, flock; 2. An organism, any self-contained unit of various elements; 3. a specific Tantric tradition of northern India and Kashmir (or the hidden essence of several influential linages); 4. Śakti as partner of Śiva (who is Akula, i.e. without clusters); name of a goddess; 5. a trance of total union with everything; when Śaktī is realised as identical with the jīva. 6. a Cakra. 7. the suṣuṁnā. The term is extremely complex.

kulācāra: the specific ritual practice of a given tradition.

Kulakuṇḍalinī: 1. the kuṇḍalinī experienced as kula, i.e. as the personal Śaktī or as the consciousness that creates groups, clusters, structures and connections. 2. or the kuṇḍalinī of a specific group (kula). 3. a name of Kālī.

Kulāmṛta: 1. the nectar of the sahasrāra released by the ascent of the Kuṇḍalinī; 2. the nectar manifest as sexual secretions; 3. the sacrament of the Kulas.

Kulaśakti: Śakti of the Kulas.

Kumārī: 1. a young (virgin) girl; 2. name of a goddess.

Kumārī pūjā: the ritual worship of an eight year old girl.

Kumbhaka: from 'kumbha': vessel, pot. In yoga, the art of holding (or resting) breath with full or empty lungs.

kuṇḍa: 1. pit, hole, fire pit; 2. TL: vulva.

Kuṇḍalinī: coiled, bent 1. a consciousness/energy creating various forms of 'reality' in various stations (cakra) of the mind/body complex. Usually represented as a serpent coiled at the perineum, which arising, winds its way up the human spine to attain union with all- consciousness above the head. This union releases the nectar of immortality which pours down the body, saturating it. Its 3.5 coils represent the consciousness states sleeping, dreaming, waking and turīya. 2. a world creating and dissolving goddess, occasionally identified with Mahāmāyā; 3. the Supreme Śakti. 4. the inner Śaktī of the practitioner. 5. the Mother of the Kulas (groups).

kusuma: 1. flower, blossom; 2. TL: menstrual blood.

L

Lakṣmī: Good Fortune. A goddess of joy, wealth, prosperity, fertility, beauty, authority and success. A maintainer of the multiverse, nowadays associated with Viṣṇu. Usually shown rising out of the milk ocean, holding lotus blossoms and scattering coins, often accompanied by elephants. In Bengal, her animal is the white owl.

Lakṣmī bīja: Śrīṁ.

lalanā-cakra: cakra above the palate.

Lalitā: 1. sporting, playful, wanton, amorous 2. innocent, artless, gentle, charming, lovely etc. 3. quivering, tremulous. 4. the universal goddess of Śrī Vidyā.

Lāsya: Śiva's slow and graceful dance, maintaining the phenomenal world.

laya-yoga: the yoga of dissolution, the upward path of the Kuṇḍalinī, dissolving the worlds and the human person on the way towards simplicity.

līlā: play. The spontaneous, divine play of creation that manifests as the phenomenal world.

liṅga: 1. characteristic; 2. sign, form; 3. pillar, axis, spine. 4. penis; 5. Śiva's emblem and self-form; 6. TL the suṣuṁnā; 7. TL the subtle body.

M

Mā Gaṇgā: goddess of the river Ganges.

Mahācīna: Great China. A vague term referring to any country to the north or east of India, coined by scholars who had very little geography. Allegedly the place from where a number of left-hand-path traditions were imported, as well as alchemy and the goddess Tārā.

Mahādevī: Great Goddess, a title attributed to lots of goddesses.

Mahākāla: Great Time or Great Devourer 1. a form of Śiva closely modelled on Mahākālī: black, with huge eyes, terrifying teeth, semi-nude, adorned with skulls and serpents; 2. a son of Śiva; 3. a form of Śiva popular in Himalayan Buddhism.

Mahākāmakaleśvarī: Great Lady of the Arts of Desire/Love. A Kaula goddess.

mahāliṇga: great liṅga.

Mahāmāyā: Great Māyā. The red goddess of world-creating glamour, the world-mother.

Mahāpreta: great corpses: the Devī's couch made of five corpses (Sadāśiva, Īśāna, Rudra, Viṣṇu, Brahmā). Their bīja is Hsau.

Mahāsiddhi: Great Siddhi, a name of Lalitā.

mahāśūnya: the great void.

Mahāvidyās: a group of ten or more goddesses, most of them fierce and dangerous, who represent magical powers, formulas and esoteric wisdom.

mahā-yuga: great ages. A cycle of four yugas (Satya, Tretā, Dvāpara, Kali), totalling 4 320 000 human years.

Maheśvara, Maheśvarī: King, Queen. Titles of Śiva and Pārvatī, Kālī etc.

Mahiṣamardinī: Slayer of Mahiṣasura. Pre-Tantric goddess riding a lion or tiger, who eventually blended with Durgā.

Mahiṣāsura, Mahiṣa: the water-buffalo demon, the opponent of Durgā. Originally opponent of Skanda.

maithuna, mithuna: 1. coupling, pairing; 2. action & reaction (Woodroffe); 3. Congress, union (often in a sexual sense).

makāra: M-word. The five M-words are references to specific sacraments in rituals of the left-hand path, usually māṁsa (meat), matsya (fish), mudrā (parched grain, kidney beans, spiced vegetables, a drug ?), madya (tree-fruit wine, alcohol), maithuna (coupling, lovemaking). Each of the M-words has a lot of alternative interpretations.

mālā: a necklace. The ones used for ritual are called japa-mālā.

mānasa japa: mental recitation of the bīja letter by letter, keeping their meaning in mind.

manas-cakra: cakra high on the brow, above the ājñācakra.

maṇipūra: the cakra of (or near) the navel.

maṇḍala: circle. A symbolic representation of the cosmos used in ritual meditation. Originally an administrative unit, a political unit, a country or a part of it.

mantra: liberation by thought. A sacred formula, such as a holy word, sound-pattern or spell. Mantras are repeated, often silently, in meditation, worship, ritual and sorcery.

mantra-caitanya: giving consciousness (caitanya) to a mantra, waking it.

mantra yoga: attaining union with the absolute, liberation from bondage, sorcerous powers or material success through the recitation or repetition of a mantra.

Manu: a legendary ancestor of the human race, a law giver. There were at least ten of them.

martya: earth.

Maruts: Vedic gods of wind and storm, singers and bards of the gods, sons of Rudra.

Mātā: 1. Mother; 2. She who Measures and Rules; 3. a honorific title given to goddesses (whether thy are mothers or not) to imply that the speaker is their child; 4. a title given to priestesses who are regularly obsessed by a goddess.

Mātaṅga: Elephant. A benevolent form of Śiva.

Mātaṅgī: Elephant. A dark goddess of poetry, song, music and intoxication, mostly friendly.

Mātṛkā: 1. mother; 2. matrix.

Mātṛkā Devīs: Mother/Matrix Goddesses. 1. Usually a group of dangerous, child-killing goddesses (the lists vary) who become the spiritual mothers of the practitioner. Their cult flourished up to the 10th century and declined, today, they receive very little veneration. In recent literature, they are often (and falsely) identified with fertility and child-bearing. 2. also the goddesses associated with the alphabet, the sound-matrixes that manifest the universe.

Māyā bīja: Hrīṁ.

māyā: a Vedic concept involving, according to a range of disagreeing scholars, such ideas as 1. glamour; 2. deception; 3. illusion; 4. cunning, cleverness; 5. to make something, to create; 6. to measure. It probably evolved by incorporating two different word-roots, one of them involving glamour, the other the ability to craft something.

melaka: union, meeting, mating, coming together, company.

mokṣa: spiritual liberation, emancipation, release.

mudrā: possibly from 'mud' : to please 1. seal; 2. bolt; 3. postures that seal the orifices of the body in yoga; 4. gesture of fingers and hands in ritual; 5. In early Hindu and Buddhist Tantra a female companion or simply her vulva and what is generated within; 6. parched grain (?) and other 'aphrodisiacal' beverages such as spicy beans; 7. the wooden earrings of the Nāths; 8. A trance state; 9. a state or method of obsession.

mukti: spiritual liberation.

mūla bīja: root seed, usually Hrīṁ.

mūlādhāra: 'root-support'. The root cakra, situated by various texts at several places in the lower belly, usually identified with the perineum.

Mūlaprakṛiti: the Root of Nature/Primal Matter, i.e. the creatrix of the world, a title of Mahāmāyā.

mūrti: an image or statue of a deity.

mūtra: urine.

N

nāda: vibration. In music, the term can mean sound.

nāda-bindu: vibration-point, the letter ṁ, pronounced NG.

nāḍī: energy 'nerve'. There are 72 000 of them within the subtle body.

Nāga: serpent spirits of the underworlds.

nāla: stalk; 2. energy channel; 3. the central channel.

Naraka: 'demonic' son of Viṣṇu and the menstruating earth, first legendary ruler of Kāmarūpa.

Naṭarājā: Lord of the Dance, a title of Śiva. The dance of Śiva first appears in the 10th century *Sūta Saṁhitā*, the theme was elaborated in the 12th century *Cidambara Māhātyma*.

Nātha: 1. Lord, a title of Śiva; 2. someone who identifies with Śiva; 3. a follower of the Nātha school.

Navarātrī: nine nights. The major festival celebrating Durgā and her defeat of the water-buffalo demon. Celebrated widely and in numerous variations in India.

Nāyikā: 1. an attendant of Kālī or Durgā; 2. a 14 year old girl worshipped as Śakti in ritual.

nigama: a Tantra format in which some form of Śiva or Viṣṇu asks questions and a goddess answers. The opposite of an āgama.

Nīla: blue, sacred mountain of Kāmākhhyā.

nirguṇa: without qualities. Usually identified with the ultimate reality, Brahman, or with deities who are considered absolute and beyond description.

nirmālya: Stainless, dirtless. The leftovers (flowers, foodstuff etc.) after the ritual.

Nirmālya-Vāsinī: the goddess of the leftovers.

nirvān: 1. cessation, end of existence; 2. liberation, freedom from rebirth. Interpreted by some as total cessation, by others as pure bliss.

nitya: ever, always, daily, daily ritual.

Nityaklinnā: She who is always wet. A Kaula goddess.

nyāsa: placing, laying down. Locating mantras, phonemes and deities in various parts of the body using touch, visualisation and ritual. Can be applied to your own body, to the body of another or to the points of a yantra.

O

Oṁkāra: the sound or letter Oṁ.

ojas: vital energy, magical energy.

P

Padmā: Lotus, a name of Lakṣmi.

paṇḍita: learned. A Brahmin with traditional knowledge, one who recites sacred writ for pilgrims.

para: 1. supreme; 2. another, of another.

Parameśvari: the supreme goddess.

Paraśakti: 1. Supreme or Another Śaktī (a ritual partner). As the Supreme Śakti, she is the highest consciousness, creatrix of all gods and everything, and manifests everywhere. The term can also be translated as 'the Śakti (partner, mate, wife) of another (man)'. In this case, union with the Paraśakti can be understood as adultery. The ambiguity of the term has produced many confusing passages in Tantric literature. 2. the inner Śaktī; 3. Kuṇḍalinī Śaktī.

Parayoṣit: 'Supreme Woman', 1. the Supreme Śakti (absolute reality); 2. the consecrated Śakti, i.e. the ritual partner or mate who embodies the supreme Śakti; 3. the woman of another man, *the latter interpretation being the one given by the opponents of the tantric tradition* (Bharati, 1983:73)

Pārvatī: She who was Born of the Mountain. The Daughter of the Himalayas, a mountain goddess.

pāśa: noose.

paśu: 1. domestic animal; 2. layperson, an ignorant person, a person bound by fetters; 3. the most common class of Tantric worshippers.

Paśupati: Śiva as the Lord of Domestic Animals.

pātāla: the underworld/s.

piṇḍa: 1. body, matter, mass. 2. TL body as a whole, the entire unit of being/experience that constitutes your material reality. 3. TL the mūlādhāra as manifestation of all worlds.

piṅgalā: the nādī of the sun.

pīṭha: 1. bench; 2. footstool; 3. sacred place, 4. seat, 5. yantra; 6. TL the genitals.

pīṭha-yātrā: pilgrimage.

Prajāpati: Vedic god of creation, who shaped the world, time, space, the rituals and all beings out of himself. In early literature a form of the creative all-self, in later myth occasionally identified with Dakṣa.

Prajnā: wisdom. In Tantric Buddhism, a goddess or female ritual partner.

Prakṛti: pra = before, kṛti = creation 1. primal matter; 2. nature; 3. the primordial creatrix, identified with Mahāmāyā, Kālī and other goddesses.

pralaya: dissolution; the Time of Dissolution at the end of a cycle.

praṇā: life energy, vital breath, wind.

praṇava: the syllable Oṁ, spelled AUṀ, the greatest mantra of the *Upaniṣads*, vibration of Brahman.

prāṇāyāma: 1. extension, lengthening of prāṇa; 2. cessation of prāṇa. Usually mistaken for 'breath-control'.

prasāda: purity, grace. Food that has been dedicated to a deity, which is returned partially to the worshipper after the ritual as a sacrament.

Pratyabhijña: re-cognition. A system of Kashmir Śaivism that aims at the realisation that the incarnate self (jīva) is essentially the manifestation of Śiva, by recognition of one's divine nature.

pūjā: veneration, worship. Usually a complex ritual lasting from a few minutes to several days.

Purāṇa: ancient. A class of encyclopaedic literature starting with early Hinduism. Each purāṇa deals with several standard topics, such as mythology, cosmology, geography, history, royal genealogies, religion, social order, astronomy etc.. The earliest were compiled during early Hinduism, the last attained their final form only two centuries ago.

pūrṇa: 1. the experience-whole; 2. filled, full, rich, abundant; 3. accomplished; 4. complete, ended; 5. satisfied, contended; 6. strong, capable. 7. name of a goddess, title of Kālī.

Puruṣa: 1. the primordial man/human. A Vedic deity who became the first sacrifice and who was dismembered, the parts being used to fashion the world, all life forms and human society; 2. Supreme Spirit; 3. person. 4. consciousness as counterpart of Prakṛti (nature, matter); 5. the personal principle in all beings; 6. 'soul' or 'spirit', identified with Śiva, Brahmā, Viṣṇu or Śakti/Durgā/Kālī.

R

Rādhā: Kṛśṇa's Śakti, one of the gopī girls. Often considered a role model for the worshipper loving, yearning for and adoring the deity.

Rāja-yoga: 1. nowadays the 'royal' yoga, a system blending posture, do's & don'ts, physical exercise and meditation. 2. earlier, the union (yoga) of rajas, here hot female secretions (menstruation).

rajas: 1. the dynamic, active and changeful guṇa. It is associated with the colour red, the heroic (virā) temperament and strong emotions such as courage and sorrow. 2. TL: female secretions, in particular menstrual blood.

rakta: blood; TL menstrual blood.

Raktabīja: Blood-seed. A demonic enemy of the gods, killed and sucked dry by Kālī. Sometimes interpreted as 'Seed of Desire'.

rasa: 1. flavour; 2. liquid extract, fluid, juice, sap; 3. the highest degree of bhakti. 4. passion, temperament; 5. sexual secretions; 6. mercury, as used in alchemical medicine.

Rati: goddess of sexual lust, wife of Kāmadeva.

rati: 1. lust; 2. joy; 3. the joy of making love.

retas: sperm.

ṛṣi: a seer, a poet. Some ṛṣis had a higher status than the gods, especially in the Vedic period. Others are deities, such as the Seven Ṛṣis (the stars of Ursa Major).

Rudra: (etymology uncertain). The Destroyer, dangerous Vedic god of mountains and wilderness, protector and slayer of cattle, lord of poisons and medicines. Originally a minor deity, later popular under his name Śiva.

rūpa: self, form, body, shape.

S

sādhaka, **sādhikā**: worshipper (male & female).

sādhana: 1. spiritual practice; 2. worship; 3. practice to attain obsession by a goddess.

sādhu: an ascetic worshipper. Usually of Śiva, tending a sacred fire, smoking bhāng and living on alms.

saguṇa: with qualities, opposite of niguṇa.

sahaja: 1. spontaneity 2. union of Sa (Śakti) and Ha (Śiva); 3. the spontaneous experience of enlightenment, as opposed to the technical approach (Kuṇḍalinī).

Sahajas: members of an esoteric Kaula cult that believes that the worshipper and the worshipped are one.

Sa'haṁ: I am She (Śaktī).

Sahasrāra Cakra: the thousand petalled lotus, usually a cakra located at the crown of the head, the petals stooping downward. Some locate it above the head.

Śaiva: 1. a worshipper of Śiva, 2. pertaining to the worship of Śiva.

sākṣāt darśan: direct sight. Personal experience of a deity without any outside help.

Śākta: a worshipper of Śakti. The name became popular around the 10th or 11th century.

Śakti: energy, power, force (this includes matter & form), personified as a goddess or as the ritual partner. In Hinduism, the active principle, counterpart of Śiva, who is passive consciousness. In Śaiva thought, the personified energy/form of Śiva. In Śākta thought, the supreme consciousness who creates Brahman, out of which the gods arise, including Śiva, who creates manifest Śakti as form/energy. In Tantric Buddhism, the female, passive principle of various active male deities and spiritual beings.

śaktimān: holder or possessor of śakti (energy/form). In Kashmir Śaivism, Śiva is the śaktimān, as pure consciousness holds the energies/forms of all reality. Not necessarily a reference to male/female divinities or sexist concepts.

śaktipāta: descent of energy. A tremendous experience or initiation that liberates and enlightens simultaneously, destroys the bonds of past karman and produces, according to Abhinavagupta, the distinct signs of blissful ecstasy, lightness of the body, trembling or shaking of the body, sleep of the outer sense-organs and a certain reeling or staggering.

sama: equipoise.

samādhi: absorption (in meditation, the deity, the absolute etc.).

sāmānyārghyā: the common or universal offering, usually a vessel full of sacred water. It is located outside of the ritual space, in contrast to the viśeṣārghya.

Śambhu: Origin of Happiness (Śiva).

śāmbhavī-mudrā: the seal of Śambhu, a consciousness that unites outer and inner perception of the divine.

sampradāya: tradition, transmission.

samsāra: flowing together. The phenomenal universe, the world of appearances, the cycles of reincarnation. To some ascetics, the entire range of manifest reality, to others, merely the house-holder's life of people being born, growing up, marrying, having children and ultimately dropping dead.

sandhyābhāṣa: a language of codes and allusions, reserved for initiates. The term may mean 'twilight Language', as the codes are deliberately obscure while also suggestive, or 'intentional language', as the terms are supposedly used in a systematical way. In the real world, most lineages made up their own codes and no two systems or texts are in full agreement with each other.

śanta: 1. rested, placid, tranquil; 2. in the Kula rite, a state that transcends the universe, completely focused on the self. Out of the supreme Kaula, both śanta and udita arise at once.

Santoṣī Mā: the Mother of Satisfaction. A minor goddess who became one of the most popular modern goddesses thanks to the Bollywood movie industry.

sannyāsin, sannyāsinī : a renouncer ascetic who has left the worldly life, dead to the family, without caste, social station, property and religious faith, equal to the guru.

Sarasvatī: 1. In Vedic times, a powerful river goddess who granted success in war and healing. In early Hinduism, merged with the goddess Vāc, she became goddess of speech, music, learning and literature; 2. The most sacred river of Vedic times. Originally the Indus, later a major river that is dry nowadays.

śāstra: book, treatise, teaching, lore.

Sat: 1. being, truth, virtue; 2. blessings accumulated by a satī through selfless sacrifice.

Satī: 1. virtuous woman; 2. Śiva's wife, who burned herself in yogīc fire. As he carried her corpse, parts of it dropped all over India, creating up to 108 sacred places and identifying her body with the whole land.

ṣaṭkarmāṇi: six deeds, six rites. A group of magical practices: to appease, to subjugate, to paralyse, to cause enmity, to eradicate and to liquidate.

sattva: from 'sat': 1. that which exists; 2. what is good (divine). The blissful, truth-revealing, joyous guṇa. It is associated with the colour white, the spiritual, semi-divine temperament (divyabhāva) and ecstatic, enlightened consciousness.

satya-yuga: the first world age, a time of innocence, virtue, truth and beauty when people were huge and lived in full health as long as they liked. It lasted 1 728 000 human years.

śava: corpse; TL Śiva as passive consciousness

savārī: vehicle. A person who embodies or is obsessed by the goddess Śerāṇvālī (She who rides a Lion, Durgā).

śavāsana: the posture of the corpse. Lie on the back, the arms at the sides and play dead.

Siddha: Perfected Being. 1. in early literature a celestial spirit, wise in sorcery. 2. later, a human follower of the Siddha tradition which incorporated elements of several Tantric movements, plus alchemy, yoga, medicine etc.. Today, a thriving movement, with numerous contrasting traditions, especially popular in Southern India.

siddhasūtra: magical string.

siddhi: (magical) power, success, accomplishment, perfection, proof, unusual ability, skill.

śiṣya: student, pupil of a guru.

Śiva: The Auspicious One, The Gracious One. Originally a title of the Vedic Rudra. Semi-nude, ash-smeared, serpent-carrying god of liberation, yoga, dance, austerities, sexual activity etc. Identified as pure formless consciousness in the *Upaniṣads*. Counterpart of Śakti.

Śivā: 1. female jackal; 2. a title of Pārvatī, Kālī, Umā.

śivābali: tribute to the jackals. A ritual involving the worship and feeding of jackals in the forest or at the cross-roads at night, generally for divination, blessing and magical purposes.

śloka: verse.

Smara: sexual union, a title of Kāmadeva.

Smarahara: Śiva as the destroyer (and re-creator) of Kāmadeva.

śmaśāna: 1. cremation ground, funeral pyre; 2. total dissolution of the world and oneself; 3. TL: the pause between out-breath and in-breath; 4. TL: the yoni of a devī.

Śmaśāna Kālī: the terrifying Kālī of the cremation ground.

So'haṁ: I am He (Śiva).

Soma: 1. Vedic deity of intoxicated rapture; 2. the personified moon; 3. an intoxicating, hallucinogenic drink made of a mysterious plant. Maybe fly agaric, rue or some unknown herb, the texts are full of contradictions. 4. in later periods used metaphorically for elixirs of mind and body.

Soma-cakra: the cakra above the manas-cakra.

sphuraṇa: vibration, pulsation, tremor, shaking. The essential pulsation that underlies all existence, i.e. whatever exists, vibrates.

Śrī: Radiance, Splendour. Vedic goddess of wealth, abundance, fortune and fertility, later fused with Lakṣmī.

Śrīkula: the cluster of Śri, a group of goddesses and their devotees.

Śrī Vaiṣṇava: a worshipper of Viṣṇu and Śrī who approaches the divine totality from the feminine side (i.e. by worshipping her, he is worshipped as well).

Śrī Vidyā: 1. auspicious wisdom/principle/knowledge/magic. 2. An early Tantric school, focused on a cluster of goddesses, the Śrī Yantra and a complex mantra. In its early phase, it was close to Kula worship. Later, it became increasingly abstract and for the last centuries, it favours worship in the mind (opposed to in physical form). This made it one of the very few forms of Tantra respected by Brahmanic society. Very popular in Southern India.

Śrī Yantra: the most famous yantra of the Śrī Vidyā, composed of five downward pointing (yoni) triangles, four upward pointing (liṅga) triangles, the circle of Māyā and the square of earth with its four doors and the central bindu.

sruk, sruva: 1. the large and the small ladle in sacrificial ritual, used to pour ghī into the fire pit; 2. TL: a ladle represents the penis when the fire pit is the vulva and the ghī is sperm.

sthūla: gross.

stotra: hymn.

Śūdra: the fourth and lowest class. Craftspeople, servants, artisans, menial labourers, hired hands.

sūkṣma: subtle.

śukra: 1. in early Tantras, Hindu and Buddhist, a term for the blend of sperm and female secretions. 2. in later Tantras, a word for sperm. 3. in general usage, bright.

Sūrya: Vedic sun god.

suṣumṇā: usually the energy connection between the perineum and the cakras above the head, path of the Kuṇḍalinī, within the spine but not identical with it. Occasionally one of the side channels within the subtle body.

suṣupti: one of the three basic consciousness states: dreamless sleep.

svādhiṣṭhāna: the cakra of the genitals.

Svāhā: 1. Vedic mantra concluding sacrificial fire offerings. 2. goddess ('Beloved of Fire') who transmits offerings to the gods and blessings to the worshippers. She manifests the results of each offering. 3. in modern interpretations, sometimes ' I am God' (from sva = to be, being and ha = Hara (Śiva), Hari (Viṣṇu) or simply breath, consciousness, divine spirit).

svarga: heaven.

svarūpa: essential form. The true appearance of a deity.

Śyāmā: Black One, a title of Kālī.

T

tamas: the veiling, dark, dense and inert guṇa. It is associated with black and brown colour, delusion, ignorance, materialism, the temperament of the paśu (beast, lay-person) and a consciousness that is bound in veils of māyā.

tāṇḍava: Śiva's violent dance that destroys the phenomenal world.

Tantra: 1. woven material, textile, 2. An extension, to lengthen and stretch something, 3. A class of literature starting c. 5th century CE. 4. A text.

Tāmbūla: 1. betel leaf, a popular drug, often flavoured with spices (pān); 2. TL: menstrual blood and sperm.

tantrasādhanā: Tantric spiritual exercises.

Tāntrika, Tāntrikā: practitioner of Tantra. A late term, the folk who invented 'Tantra' did not call it by that name.

tapas: heat. 1. the fire of inner heat generated by yoga; 2. austerities; 3. religious fervour attained by intense discipline.

Tāra: 1. carrying across, a saviour, protector. 2. a high and shrill tone. 3. shining, radiant. 4. clean, clear. 5. good, excellent, well-flavoured. 6. clearness (of a pearl), translucence. 7. a star, a fixed star, a meteor. 8. the pupil of the eye. 9. descent to a river (bank). 10. name of a goddess (Tārā), a Daitya, a monkey general, a class of gods etc.

Tārā: a terrifying, protecting goddess who appears much like Kālī in northern Hindu Tantra. Saviouress. Said to be of Chinese origin. Also several highly popular goddesses of Tantric Buddhism.

tattva: 1. 'thusness'; 2. principle; 3. category. There is a succession of 'principles' ranging from dense, material earth to the universal consciousness. Some schools have 25 tattvas, others expand the system to 36. Consider them a map of evolution.

tejas: 1. splendour, glory, brilliance; 2. sperm; 3. name of the fire tattva.

tīrtha: ford, crossing (of a river). A sacred place of watery nature or a place where the 'river of life' can be crossed to reach the absolute.

tretā-yuga: three-fourth yuga. The second world age, when humans were still three-quarters good. It lasted for 1 296 000 human years.

Trika: a highly refined Kashmirian system based on triads and the mantra sauḥ.

Tripura: Three Cities (heaven, earth and underworlds), a Daitya Asura destroyed by Śiva.

Tripurā: 1. triple goddess, uniting Brahmī, Vaiṣṇavī and Raudrī; 2. triple goddess uniting Tripurā, Tripurabālā and Tripurabhairavī; 3. triple goddess uniting Vāmā, Jyeṣṭhā and Raudrī; 4. Goddess of the Three Cities 'Coarse Consciousness', 'Sub-consciousness' and 'Un-consciousness'. 5. Goddess of heaven, earth and underworld. 6. Goddess of belly, heart and head.

Tripurāri: Enemy of the Three Cities-Asura (a name of Śiva).

Tripurasundarī: great goddess of the Śri Vidyā.

trimūrti: a trinity composed of the functions of creation, maintenance and destruction, identified with various deities.

Tryaṁbaka: the Three-Eyed One or the One with Three Mothers (Śiva).

Tumburu: the white, four faced, eight armed, bull-riding Śiva, of the *Vīṇāśikhatantra*. He sits in the centre, surrounded by Jayā (east), Vijayā (south), Jayantī (west) and Aparājitā (north).

turīya: the supreme consciousness state. It includes the other three (sleeping, dreaming and waking) and transcends them.

U

udita: 1. risen, appeared, manifest; 2. in the Kula ritual, the focusing on the self and body/genitals of the other. During the rite of union, both participants experience udita and śanta simultaneously, hence Śakti and Śiva are one.

Umā: a form of Pārvatī, sometimes unmarried, sometimes mate of Śiva.

unmanī: an enlightened state of awareness which is defined quite differently in various works.

Upaniṣad: a class of religious and philosophical literature starting c. 8th century BCE

V

vajra: 1. thunderbolt, 2. a ritual sceptre and/or weapon, 3. an image of sudden, spontaneous enlightenment.

Vāc, Vāk: 1. Voice, Speech; 2. Vedic goddess of speech and letters, occasionally wife of Prajāpati or Mahāviṣṇu. Identified with Sarasvatī in the late vedic period, in early Hinduism, the two deities had fused already.

vām: 1. left; 2. opposite; 3. reversed, 4. slanted; 5. bad, evil.

vāmā: beautiful woman.

vāmabhāva: heterodox ritual, often associated with terrifying goddesses, 'unclean' substances, ritual intoxication and obsession, worship of and with women. The so called left-hand-path.

Vānī: a name of Sarasvatī.

varada-mudrā: the gesture that grants boons: open hand, fingers pointing down.

varṇa: 1. inherited station in society, usually mistranslated as 'caste'. There are four classical varṇas: Brāhmaṇa (priests, teachers, scholars), Kṣatriya (warriors, aristocracy), Vaiṣya (merchants) and Śūdra (farmers, servants, artisans). Though their theoretical station in society is part of Vedic law, their real status may vary, depending on jati and income; 2. class; 3. colour; 4. letters.

Varuṇa: Vedic god governing wide spaces, sky, oceans, the whole earth. Law-keeper, punisher of evildoers. Later reduced to god of the oceans and the great deep.

Vāyu: Vedic wind god.

Veda: the earliest recorded Indian literature, a body of four works dating between c. 1200 BCE and 500 BCE.

Vedānta: the end of Veda, i.e. the final part (or quintessence) of Vedic lore, a name of the *Upaniṣads.*

vedha: penetration. A vital concept of Kula initiation. The initiant is 'penetrated' by 1. mantra directed at the heart; 2. sound directed at the mind; 3. flames directed at the bindu between the eyebrows or the heart; 4. energy (śakti) directed at the perineum and projected outward through the entire universe; 5. cobra (Kuṇḍalinī) arising in sheer bliss from womb to the supreme, or by contemplation of the mind until the mind has faded away, leading to supreme bliss; 6. supreme penetration, i.e. the awareness that there are no faculties, no prāṇa, no mind, no object or subject, no thought or thinking, no beings etc.: the total negation of every-thing.

vidyā: 1. esoteric lore, wisdom tradition, ritual knowledge, science; 2. mantra associated with a goddess; 3. A young woman.

Vijayā: 1. A terrifying red goddess, seated on an owl, bearing a bow and wine, meat and fish, granting success; 2. hashish as a ritual drink; 3. songs chanted on the 9th and 10th day of Durgā pūjā.

viparīta maithuna: reversed or upside down coupling. 1. lovemaking with the female sitting on top; 2. TL a reversal of the current of consciousness, turning awareness inwards to its nameless, formless, undefined source. 3. TL Entering the heart.

vīra: hero; TL the heroic worshipper who approaches the deity in her terrible form.

vīrya: potency, sperm, seed.

Viriñci: a name of Brahmā.

visarga: 1. the phoneme ḥ (audible exhalation); 2. emission, a key concept of Trika and Krama; 3. TL: the sexual secretions.

viśeṣārghya: the special offering of the inner ritual space (in contrast to sāmānyārghya).

Viṣṇu: Originally a minor Vedic god who helps Indra by creating space (three steps for heaven, earth and underworlds) to fight the rain-binding, world encompassing dragon-serpent. Later, major god who maintains the worlds, to which end he incarnates up to 22 times. Installer of kings, supporter of divine order.

viśuddhi: the cakra in the throat region.

Y

Yakṣa: a virile spirit or deity associated with plants, trees and abundance.

Yakṣī or **Yakṣinī**: an alluring female spirit or deity associated with vegetation, trees and water. Usually benevolent in Hinduism, earlier on such spirits were feared as seductive killers of men and infants. In Kerala folklore, a seductive, homicidal and bloodthirsty demoness.

Yama: Twin. In Vedic times, first human being, child of the sun. Later god of death and the underworlds, punisher of evildoers.

yāmala: union, mating, coupling, pairing.

yantra: instrument of control. A diagram of a specific deity, usually composed of angles, circles, blossoms and often letters. In TL a map of the human body/mind/energy system or a map of a ritual assembly.

yoga: union (with the gods, the absolute etc.).

yogīn: practitioner of one of the paths of yoga.

yoginī: 1. female practitioner of yoga; 2. sorceress; 3. dangerous and sexually attractive goddess, often in the form of a female bird, beast or human.

yoni: 1. vulva, the female genitals as a whole. 2. a source, womb, cakra in its creative function.

yoni-bīja: Aiṁ.

yonimaṇḍala: the place and goddess Kāmākhhyā.

yonimudrā: the posture or gesture of the yoni, 1. various shapes of the hands folded to resembling a triangle or the female genitalia; 2. to please the yoni; 3. union of the self with the absolute; 4. an alignment of the hands across the face so that thumbs close ears, index fingers eyes, ring fingers mouth etc. used to perceive the primordial sound; 5. a meditation on the mūlādhāra, a rising flame and the release of the heavenly nectar (*Śiva Saṁhita*)

yonipūjā: ritual worship of the vulva.

yonitattva: 1. yoni-principle, essence of the vulva. Blend of sperm and female secretions or menstrual blood. The supreme sacrament of several cults. 2. a pink elixir generated in the head, cascading down the body, healing and rejuvenating.

Bibliography

Note: Primary source texts are listed by title and also by name of editor or translator.

Abhinavagupta: *The Short Gloss on the Supreme; The Queen of the Three, Parātrīśikālaghuvṛttiḥ*, in Muller-Ortega 1989

Abhinavagupta: *Parātrīśikā-Vivaraṇa. The Secret of Tantric Mysticism.* Trans. and comments by Jaideva Singh, ed. Bettina Baumer, Motilal Banarsidass, Delhi 2002 (1988)

Abhinavagupta: *The Kula Ritual, as Elaborated in Chapter 29 of the Tantraloka*, trans. & ed. John R. Dupuche, Motilal Banarsidass, Delhi, 2006 (2003)

Akashanath: *The Elements of Puja: An Introduction to Tantric Puja* in *Thelemic Magick II, Being the Proceedings of the Tenth International Symposium of Thelemic Magick* (1995, Carfax, Oxford), Golden Dawn Publications, Mandrake Press, Oxford, 1996

Andreas Alberts & Peter Mullen, *Psychoaktive Pflanzen, Pilze und Tiere*, Kosmos Verlag, Stuttgart, 2000

Altchinesische Hymnen, trans. Peter Weber-Schäfer, Jakob Hegner Verlag, Köln, 1967

AMOOKOS: *Tantra Magick*, Mandrake of Oxford, Oxford, 1990

Atharva-Veda Saṁhitā, trans. William D. Whitney, revised by Nag S. Singh, Nag Publishers, Delhi, 1987

Hanns Bächtold-Stäubli (ed.): *Handwörterbuch des deutschen Aberglaubens*, Weltbild Verlag, Augsburg, 2005 (1927 - 1942)

Bagley, Robert (ed.). *Ancient Sichuan. Treasures from a Lost Civilization.* Seattle Art Museum, Princeton University Press, 2001

Richard Bandler, *Unbändige Motivation, Angewandte Neurodynamik*, (*Applied Neuro Dynamics*) Junfermann Verlag, Paderborn, 1997 (1996)

Richard Bandler: *Using your Brain for a Change*, Real People Press, Moab, 1985

Richard Bandler: *Time for a Change*, Meta Publications, Cupertino, Cal, 1993

Richard Bandler: *Richard Bandler's Guide to Trance-formation*, Health Communications Inc., Deerfield Beach, 2008

Richard Bandler & John Grinder: *Trance-formations*, Real People Press, Moab, 1981

The Brahmāṇḍa Purāṇa, trans. Ganesh Vasudeo Tagare, Motilal Banarsidass, Delhi, 1983

Agehananda Bharati (pseud. Leopold Fischer): *The Tantric Tradition*, B. I. Publications, New Delhi, 1983 (1965)

Anne Birrel (trans.): *The Classic of Mountains and Seas*, Penguin Books, London, 1999

Barbara Black Koltuv: *The Book of Lilith*, Nicolas-Hays, York Beach, Maine 1986

Jürgen Brater: *Lexikon der Sexualirrtümer*, Eichborn Verlag, Frankfurt M., 2003

Douglas Renfrew Brooks:*Auspicious Wisdom, The Texts and Traditions of Śrīvidyā Śākta Tantrism in Southern India*, State University of New York Press, Albany, 1992

E. A. Wallis Budge: *Amulets and Superstitions*, Dover Publications, New York, 1978 (1930)

Suzanne E. Cahill: *Transcendence and Divine Passion, The Queen Mother of the West in Medieval China*, Stanford University Press, Stanford, Cal. 1993

Chang, Kwang-chih: *Art, Myth and Ritual. The Path to Political Authority in Ancient China*, Harvard University Press, Cambridge, 1983

Chang, T.T.: *Der Kult der Shang Dynastie im Spiegel der Orakelinschriften*, Otto Harrassowitz, Wiesbaden, 1970

Chögyam Trungpa: *The Heart of the Buddha*, Shambhala, Boston & London, 1991

Chuang Tzu: *The Complete Works*, trans. Burton Watson, Columbia University Press, New York, 1971 (1968)

The Classic of Mountains and Seas Trans. Anne Birrel, Penguin Books, London, 1999

Thomas Cleary: *Vitality, Energy, Spirit. A Taoist Sourcebook.* Shambhala Publications, Boston, 1991

Thomas Cleary (ed. & trans): *Sex, Health and Long Life*, Shambhala Books, Boston, 1994

Thomas B. Coburn: *Devī / The Great Goddess*, (in: Hawley and Wulff, 1996)

Aleister Crowley: *Eight Lectures on Yoga*, Sangreal Foundation, Dallas, 1969

Aleister Crowley: *Magick*, John Symonds & Kenneth Grant (ed.), Samuel Weiser, New York, 1977 (1973)

Alain Daniélou: *The Myths and Gods of India*, Inner Traditions international, Rochester, 1991 (originally : *Hindu Polytheism*, 1964)

Lynn Teskey Denton: *Varieties of Hindu Female Asceticism*, (in Leslie 1992)

Phoolan Devi: *Ich war die Königin der Banditen (I, Phoolan Devi. The Autobiography of India's Bandit Queen),* Gustav Lübbe Verlag, Bergisch Gladbach, 1996

Devī-Māhātmyam or Śrī Durgā-Saptaśatī, trans. Svāmī Jagadīśvarānanda, Sri Rāmakṛṣṇa Math, Madras, 1955

Robert Dilts , T. Hallbom, S. Smith: *Beliefs: Pathways to Health and Well-Being,* Metamorphous Press, Portland, 1990

Ding Wangdao (trans.): *100 Chinese Myths and Fantasies,* Zhong Guo dui wai fan yi chu ban gong si, Beijing 1991 (1988)

The Rig Veda, An Anthology, trans: Wendy Doniger O'Flaherty, Penguin Books, London, 1981

Pschyrembel: Wörterbuch Sexualität, Dressler & Zink (ed.), Walter de Gruyter Verlag, Berlin, 2003

J. J. L. Duyvendak (trans.): *Tao Te Ching, The Book of the Way and its Virtue,* John Murray, London, 1954

Werner Eichhorn: *Die Religionen Chinas,* Kohlhammer Verlag, Stuttgart, 1973

Mircea Eliade: *Yoga, Unsterblichkeit und Freiheit,* Suhrkamp Taschenbuch, Insel Verlag, Frankfurt M., 1985 (1960)

Milton H. Erickson, *My voice will go with you,* W. W. Norton & Co., 1991

Stephen Eskildsen: *Asceticism in Early Taoist Religion,* State University of New York Press, Albany, 1998

Louise M. Finn (intr., trans., & annotated): *The Kulacūḍāmaṇi Tantra and The Vāmakeśvara Tantra with the Jayaratha Commentary,* Otto Harrassowitz Verlag, Wiesbaden, 1986

Jan Fries: *Visual Magick, A Manual of Freestyle Shamanism,* Mandrake of Oxford, Oxford, 1992

Jan Fries: *Helrunar - A Manual of Rune Magick,* Mandrake of Oxford, Oxford, 1993

Jan Fries: *Seidways; Shaking Swaying and Serpent Mysteries,* Mandrake of Oxford, Oxford, 1996

Jan Fries: *Living Midnight, Three Movements of the Tao,* Mandrake of Oxford, Oxford, 1998

Jan Fries: *Cauldron of the Gods - A Manual of Celtic Magick,* Mandrake of Oxford, Oxford, 2003

Kisari Mohan Ganguli (trans.): *Mahābhārata,* 1889-1896

Margot Gatzlaff-Hälsig: *Handwörterbuch Hindi - Deutsch,* Helmut Buske Verlag, Hamburg 2002

Helmuth von Glasenapp (ed., trans.): *Indische Geisteswelt, I & II,* Holle Verlag, Baden-Baden, 1958

Jan Gonda: *Die Religionen Indiens I,* Kohlhammer Verlag, Stuttgart, 1960

Karuna Goswamy: *The Glory of the Great Goddess, an illustrated manuscript from Kashmir from the Alice Boner Collection in the Museum Rietberg,* Zurich, 1989 (illustrations of the Devī Mahātmya)

Teun Goudriaan *(trans.): The Vīṇāśikhatantra, A Shaiva Tantra of the Left Current*, Motilal Banarsidass, Delhi, 1985

Teun Goudriaan (ed.): *Ritual and Speculation in Early Tantrism, Studies in Honor of André Padoux*, State University of New York Press, 1992

Teun Goudriaan & Sanjukta Gupta: *Hindu Tantric and Śākta Literature*, Otto Harrassowitz Verlag, Wiesbaden, 1981

Kenneth Grant: *Cults of the Shadow*, Samuel Weiser, New York, 1976 (1975)

Kenneth Grant: *Beyond the Mauve Zone*, Starfire Publishing, London, 1999

Ralph T. H. Griffith (trans.): *The Rig Veda*, Motilal Banarsidass, Delhi, Special Edition for Book of the month Club, NY, 1992

Sanjukta Gupta: *Women in the Śaiva / Śākta Ethos,* (in: Leslie 1992)

Sanjukta Gupta (trans. & intr.): *Lakṣmī Tantra, a Pāñcarātra Text*, Motilal Banarsidass, Delhi, 2003

John Stratton Hawley and Donna Maria Wulff (ed.): *Devi, Goddesses of India*, University of California Press, Berkeley and Los Angeles, 1996

David Hawkes (trans.): *The Songs of the South, An Ancient Chinese Anthology of Poems by Qu Yuan and other Poets* (*Chu Ci*), Penguin Books, London 1985

Lex Hixon: *Mother of the Universe, Visions of the Goddess and Tantric Hymns of Enlightenment.* Quest Books, Theosophical Publishing House, Wheaton, IL, 1994 (paraphrased poems, Ramprasad Sen)

Ellic Howe: *The Magicians of the Golden Dawn, A Documentary History of a Magical Order 1887-1923*, Samuel Weiser, New York, 1978 (1972)

Hu Bin: *A Brief Introduction to the Science of Breathing Exercise*, Hai Feng Publishing Company, Hong Kong, 1983 (1982)

Hu, Hou Xuan: *Zhan Hou Suo Jian Jia Gu Lu*, 6 vol. Beijing, 1951

Georges Ifrah: *Universalgeschichte der Zahlen*, Zweitausendeins Verlag, Frankfurt M., 1993 (1981)

Veronica Ions: *Indische Mythologie*, Emil Vollmer Verlag, Wiesbaden, 1967

B. K. S. Iyengar: *Licht auf Pranayama (Prāṇāyāma Dīpikā)*, Otto Wilhelm Barth Verlag/Scherz Verlag, Bern, 1984 (1981)

Svāmī Jagadīśvarānanda (trans.): *Devī-Māhātmyam or Śrī Durgā-Saptaśatī*, Sri Rāmakṛṣṇa Math, Madras, 1955

Jean-François Jarrige: *Die frühen Kulturen in Pakistan und ihre Entwicklung*, in: *Vergessene Städte am Indus*, Verlag Phillip von Zabern, Mainz, 1987

Jean-François Jarrige: *Vorzeit und Induskultur*, in: Heinrich Gerhard Franz (ed.): *Das alte Indien, Geschichte und Kultur des indischen Subkontinents*, Bertelsmann, München, 1990

Katon Shual, *Sexual Magick*, Mandrake of Oxford, Oxford 1995

The Kaulajñāna nirṇaya, ed P.C. Bagchi, trans. Michael Magee, Prachya Prakashan, Varanasi, 1986

David N. Keightley: *The Ancestral Landscape*, University of California, Berkeley, 2002

Wilhelmine Keyserling (trans.): *Vijnana Bhairava Tantra, Das Tantra der Befreiung*, Verlag Bruno Martin, Südergellersen, 1994

David R. Kinsley: *Hindu Goddesses - Visions of the Divine Feminine in the Hindu Religious Tradition*, Univ. of California Press, Berkeley, 1988 (1986)

David R. Kinsley: *Kali/ Blood and Death out of Place*, (in Hawley and Wulff, 1996)

David R. Kinsley: *The Ten Mahāvidyās, Tantric Visions of the Divine Feminine*, Motilal Banarsidass, Delhi 1998 (1997)

Kṣemarāja: *Pratyabhijñāhṛdayam, The Secret of Self-Recognition*, trans. & ed. Jaideva Singh, Motilal Banarsidass, Delhi, 1980 (1963)

The Kulacūḍāmaṇi Tantra and The Vāmakeśvara Tantra with the Jayaratha Commentary, intr., trans., annotated by Louise M. Finn, Otto Harrassowitz Verlag, Wiesbaden, 1986

The Kulachudamani Tantra, abridged trans. Michael Magee, available on the Internet

Kulārṇava Tantra, ed. John Woodroffe, summarised translation M. P. Pandit, Motilal Banarsidass, Delhi, 1984 (1916)

Kulārṇava Tantra, trans. Ram Kumar Rai, Prachya Prakashan, Varanasi, 1999

Kūrma - Purāṇa, translation by Ganesh Vasudeo Tagare, Motilal Banarsidass, Delhi 1981

Lakṣmī Tantra, a Pāñcarātra Text, intr, and trans. Sanjukta Gupta, Motilal Banarsidass, Delhi, 2003

Hans Lamer, *Wörterbuch der Antike*, Alfred Kröner Verlag, Stuttgart, 1963

Julia Leslie (ed.): *Roles and Rituals for Hindu Women*, Motilal Banarsidass Publishers PVT. LTD. Delhi 1992

David N. Lorenzen: *A Parody of the Kāpālikas in the Mattavilāsa*, in White (ed.) : *Tantra in Practice*, Princeton University Press, Princeton & Oxford, 2000

Hans-K. & Susanne Lücke: *Antike Mythologie*, Marix Verlag, Wiesbaden, 2005

Mahābhārata, trans. Kisari Mohan Ganguli, 1889-1896

Michael Magee (trans.): *The Kaulajñāna nirṇaya*, ed P.C. Bagchi, Prachya Prakashan, Varanasi, 1986

Michael Magee (trans.): *The Kulachudamani Tantra,* abridged, available on the Internet

Michael Magee (trans.): *Vamakesvarimatam*, Prachya Prakashan, Varanasi, 1986

Michael Magee (trans.): *Yoni Tantra*, Worldwide Tantra Project, vol. II, 1995 (internet)

Mahidhara: *Mantra Mahodadhiḥ*, trans. Ram Kumar , Prachya Prakashan, Varanasi, 1992

Trilok Chandra Majupuria & Rohit Kumar: *Gods, Goddesses & Religious Symbols of Hinduism, Buddhism & Tantrism (including Tibetan deities) (most authentic & exhaustive)*, M. Devi, Lashkar (Gwalior), 2004

June McDaniel: *The Madness of the Saints. Ecstatic Religion in Bengal.* University of Chicago Press, 1989

June McDaniel: *Offering Flowers, Feeding Skulls. Popular Goddess Worship in West Bengal.* Oxford University Press, 2004.

Rachel Fell McDermott: *The Western Kali*, (in Hawley and Wulff, 1996)

Rachel Fell McDermott & Jeffrey Kripal (ed.): *Encountering Kālī in the margins, at the center, in the west.* University of California Press, Berkely, 2003

Rachel Fell McDermott: *Singing to the Goddess. Poems to Kālī and Umā from Bengal.* Oxford University Press, 2001

Hans-Georg Möller (trans.): *Tao Te King, Nach den Seidentexten von Mawangdui*, Fischer Verlag, 1995

Sir Monier Monier-Williams: *Sanskṛit-English Dictionary*, new edition, Munshiram Manoharlal Publishers Pvt. Ltd. New Delhi, 1976 (1899)

Ajit Mookerjee: *Kali: The Feminine Force*, Thames & Hudson, London 1988

Kris Morgan: *Medicine of the Gods, Basic Principles of Ayurvedic Medicine*, Mandrake of Oxford, Oxford 1994

Mogg Morgan: *The English Mahatma*, Mandrake of Oxford, Oxford 2001

Mogg Morgan: *The Tantric Knuckle Bone Oracle*, in: *Tantra Sādhana*, Mandrake of Oxford, 2008

Mogg Morgan: *Isis in India*, unpublished

Mudras (in Symbols), Bharatanatya Manual, Center for the Promotion of Traditional Arts, Madras, no year

Paul Eduardo Muller-Ortega: *The Triadic Heart of Śiva. Kaula Tantricism of Abhinavagupta in the Non-Dual Shaivism of Kashmir*, University of NY Press, 1989

Klaus Mylius, *Handwörterbuch Deutsch-Sanskrit*, Langenscheidt, Berlin, München, 2001

Nema: *Maat Magick, A Guide to Self-Initiation*, Samuel Weiser, York Beach, 1995

Nema: *The Way of Mystery; Magick, Mysticism & Self-Transcendence*, Llewellyn Publications, St. Paul, 2003

H. Parker: *Village Folk Tales of Ceylon*, Vol. 3, Tisara Prakasakayo, Dehiwala, 1910, 1973

Bhagwan Shree Patañjali: *Aphorisms of Yoga*, Faber and Faber, London, 1973 (1938)

James J. Preston: *Cult of the Goddess, Social and religious change in a Hindu Temple*, Waveland Press, Prospect Heights, Illinois, 1985

Pschyrembel: Wörterbuch Sexualität, Dressler & Zink (ed.), Walter de Gruyter Verlag, Berlin, 2003

Radhakrishna (trans.): *The Principal Upaniṣads*, George Allen & Unwin, London 1953

Ram Kumar Rai (trans.): *Kulārṇava Tantra*, Prachya Prakashan, Varanasi, 1999

Christian Rätsch: *Heilkräuter der Antike*. Diederichs Verlag, München, revised edition 1998

Navjivan Rastogi: *The Krama Tantricism of Kashmir, Historical and General Sources*, vol. I, Motilal Banarsidass, Delhi, 1979

Israel Regardie: *An Account of the Teachings, Rites and Ceremonies of the Hermetic Order of the Golden Dawn*, Llewellyn Publications, Saint Paul, 1978 (revised edition 1971)

Wilhelm Reich, *Die Entdeckung des Orgons, 1. Die Funktion des Orgasmus (1972), 2. Der Krebs (1985)*, Fischer Verlag, Frankfurt M.

The Rig Veda, An Anthology, trans: Wendy Doniger O'Flaherty, Penguin Books, London, 1981

The Rig Veda, trans. Ralph T. H. Griffith, Motilal Banarsidass, Delhi, Special Edition for Book of the month Club, NY, 1992

Gerhard Roth, *Aus der Sicht des Gehirns*, Suhrkamp Verlag, Frankfurt / M. 2003

Dietmar Rothermund (ed): *Indien. Kultur, Geschichte, Politik, Wirtschaft, Umwelt. Ein Handbuch*. C. H. Beck Verlag, München 1995

Yogī-Raj Boris Sacharow: *Das große Geheimnis, Die verborgene Seite der Yoga-Übungen*, Drei Eichen Verlag, München, 1954 (trans. and commentary on the *Gheranda Samhita*).

Michael Saso: *The Gold Pavilion, Taoist Ways to Peace, Healing and Long Life*, Charles E. Tuttle, Boston, 1995

Swami Satyananda Saraswati & Shree Maa: *Kali Puja*. Devi Mandir Publications, Napa, CA, 1998

Saundaryalaharī, trans. V. K. Subramanian, Motilal Banarsidass Publishers, Delhi, 1993 (1977)

Saundarya-Laharī, The Ocean of Beauty, trans. S. Subrahmanya Sastri & T. R. Srinivasa Ayyangar, Theosophical Publishing House, Adyar, Madras, 1985 (1965)

Jan A. Schoterman: *The Kubjikā Upaniṣad and its Atharvavedic Character*, in: Teun Goudriaan (ed.) *Ritual and Speculation in Early Tantrism, Studies in Honour of André Padoux*, State University of New York Press, Albany, 1992

Schultes, Richard & Hofmann, Albert: *Plants of the Gods*, Mcgraw-Hill Books Co., Maidenhead, 1979

Mala Sen: *Bandit Queen. Die Geschichte der Phoolan Devi (India's Bandit Queen - The True Story of Phoolan Devi)* Goldmann Verlag, München, 1993

Sex, Health and Long Life, ed. & trans. Thomas Cleary, Shambhala Books, Boston, 1994

Dr. Swami Shankardevananda Saraswati: *Amaroli*, Bihar School of Yoga, Monghyr, 1978

Miranda Shaw: *Passionate Enlightenment, Women in Tantric Buddhism*, Princeton University Press, New Jersey, 1994

T. R. Sharma: *Studies in the Sectarian Upaniṣads (Metaphysics, Ethics and Rituals)*, Indological Book House, Varanasi, 1972

Madanjeet Singh: *Arte Himalaya*, Silvana - Editoriale d'Arte, UNESCO, 1968

Śivananda; *Tantra Yoga, Nada Yoga and Kriya Yoga*, The Divine Life Society, Shivanandanagar, Tehri-Garhwal, 1982 (1955)

The Śiva Saṁhita, trans. Rai Bahadur Srisa Chandra Vasu, Oriental Books Reprint Corporation, New Delhi, 1975 (1914-1915)

William Skene, *The Four Ancient Books of Wales*, Edmonston and Douglas, Edinburgh, 1868

David James Smith: *The Dance of Śiva: Religion, art and poetry in South India*, Cambridge University Press, 1996

Frederick M. Smith: *Indra's Curse, Varuna's Noose, and the Suppression of the Woman in the Vedic Śrauta Ritual*, (in Leslie 1992)

The Songs of the South, An Ancient Chinese Anthology of Poems by Qu Yuan and other Poets (*Chu Ci*) trans. David Hawkes, Penguin Books, London 1985

Peter Stafford, *Psychedelics Encyclopaedia*, Ronin Publishing, 1992

Sylvia Stapelfeldt: *Kāmākhyā - Satī - Mahāmāyā: Konzeptionen der Großen Göttin im Kālikāpurāṇa.* Peter Lang GmbH, Europäischer Verlag der Wissenschaften, Frankfurt/ M, 2001

Stephanos Stephanides and Karna Singh: *Translating Kali's Fest. The Goddess in Indo-Caribbean Ritual and Fiction*, Cross/Cultures, 43, Rodopi, Amsterdam 2000

Heinrich von Stietencron, *Die Erscheinungsformen des Hinduismus* (in Rothermund 1995)

Strabo, *Geographica*, trans. A. Forbiger, Marix Verlag, Wiesbaden, 2005

V. K. Subramanian (trans.): *Saundaryalaharī*,Motilal Banarsidass Publishers, Delhi, 1993 (1977)

S. Subrahmanya Sastri & T. R. Srinivasa Ayyangar (trans.): *Saundarya-Laharī, The Ocean of Beauty*, Theosophical Publishing House, Adyar, Madras, 1985 (1965)

Ganesh Vasudeo Tagare (trans.): *The Brahmāṇḍa Purāṇa*, Motilal Banarsidass, Delhi, 1983

Tāntrikābhidhānakośa II, A Dictionary of Technical Terms from Hindu Tantric Literature, Ed: H. Brunner, G. Oberhammer, A. Padoux, Verlag der österreichischen Akademie der Wissenschaften, Wien 2004

Tao Te Ching, The Book of the Way and its Virtue, trans. J. J. L. Duyvendak, John Murray, London, 1954

Tao Te King, Nach den Seidentexten von Mawangdui, trans. Hans-Georg Möller, Fischer Verlag, 1995

Teachings of the Tao, trans. & ed. Eva Wong, Shambhala Books, Boston, 1997

Victor & Victoria Trimondi: *Der Schatten des Dalai Lama, Sexualität, Magie und Politik im tibetischen Buddhismus*, Patmos Verlag, Düsseldorf, 1999

Tripurā Rahasya, in: *Śakti Sādhanā, Steps to Samādhi*, trans. Pandit Rajmani Tigunait, intr. Swami Rama, Himalayan International Institute of Yoga Science and Philosophy of the USA, Honesdale, PA, 1993

Heinrich Uhle (trans.): *Vetalapantschavinsati*, die fünfundzwanzig Erzählungen eines Dämons, 1924, Wissenschaftliche Buchgesellschaft Darmstadt, 1966

Arthur Ungnad (ed. & trans.): *Die Religionen der Babylonier und Assyrer*, Diederichs Verlag, Jena, 1921

Vamakesvarimatam, trans. Michael Magee, Prachya Prakashan, Varanasi, 1986

Rai Bahadur Srisa Chandra Vasu (trans.): *The Śiva Saṁhita*, Oriental Books Reprint Corporation, New Delhi, 1975 (1914-1915)

Vetalapantschavinsati, die fünfundzwanzig Erzählungen eines Dämons, trans. Heinrich Uhle, 1924, Wissenschaftliche Buchgesellschaft Darmstadt, 1966

Vijnana Bhairava Tantra, Das Tantra der Befreiung, trans. Wilhelmine Keyserling, Verlag Bruno Martin, Südergellersen, 1994

Vīmalānanda, *Introduction and Commentary to the Karpūrādi-Stotra*, in John Woodroffe: *Hymns to the Goddess and Hymn to Kālī*, Ganesh & Company, Madras, 2001 (1922)

The Vīṇāśikhatantra, A Shaiva Tantra of the Left Current, trans. Teun Goudriaan, Motilal Banarsidass, Delhi, 1985

Benjamin Walker: *Hindu World – An Encyclopaedic Survey of Hinduism*, 2 vols., George Allen & Unwin, London 1965

Peter Weber-Schäfer (trans.): *Altchinesische Hymnen*, Jakob Hegner Verlag, Köln, 1967

David Gordon White (ed.), *Tantra in Practice*, Princeton University Press, Princeton, 2000

David Gordon White: *The Alchemical Body, Siddha Traditions in Medieval India*, University of Chicago Press, 1996

David Gordon White: *Kiss of the Yoginī. "Tantric Sex" in its South Asian Contexts*, University of Chicago Press, 2003

William D. Whitney (trans): *Atharva-Veda Saṁhitā*, revised by Nag S. Singh, Nag Publishers, Delhi, 1987

Friedrich Wilhelm: *Geschichte, Staat und Gesellschaft*, in: Heinrich Gerhard Franz (ed.): *Das alte Indien, Geschichte und Kultur des indischen Subkontinents*, Bertelsmann, München, 1990

Herbert Wilhelmy: *Kulturraum*, in: Heinrich Gerhard Franz (ed.): *Das alte Indien, Geschichte und Kultur des indischen Subkontinents*, Bertelsmann, München, 1990

Eva Wong (trans. & ed.): *Teachings of the Tao*, Shambhala Books, Boston, 1997

John Woodroffe (Arthur Avalon) trans.: *Tantra of the Great Liberation (Mahānirvāna Tantra)*, Dover Publications, N.Y., 1972 (1913)

John Woodroffe (Arthur Avalon) trans.: *Hymn to Kali*, 1922 (included in *Hymns to the Goddess* 2001)

John Woodroffe (Arthur Avalon) and Ellen Woodroffe trans.: *Hymns to the Goddess*, Ganesh & Co., Madras, 2001 (1913)

John Woodroffe (Arthur Avalon): *The Serpent Power, The Secrets of Tantric and Shactic Yoga , being the Ṣaṭ - Cakra Nirūpaṇa and Pādukā-Pañcaka*, Dover Publications, New York 1974 (1919)

John Woodroffe (Arthur Avalon): *The Garland of Letters. Studies in the Mantra-Śāstra.* Ganesh & Company, Pondicherry, 1979 (1922)

John Woodroffe (Arthur Avalon): *Śakti and Śākta, Essays and Addresses*, Ganesh & Co, Madras, 2001 (1927)

Yoni Tantra, trans. Michael Magee, Worldwide Tantra Project, vol. II, 1995 (internet)

Kamil V Zvelebil: *The Siddha Quest for Immortality*, Mandrake of Oxford, Oxford, 1996

Index

Abhaya-mudrā ... 520
Abhinavagupta...17, 20, 23, 95, 127, 133, 137, 156, 186, 194, 195, 225, 257, 283, 286, 288, 290, 292, 366, 384, 407, 408, 410, 426, 470, 486, 515, 516, 517, 520, 522, 525, 531, 539, 547, 552
Adam ... 397
Aditi ... 51, 60
Adultery..102, 103, 359, 391, 408, 445, 488, 537
Ādyā ... 520, 521
Ādyā Kālī ... 272, 286, 378, 521
Āgama ... 406, 521
Āgamasāra ... 369
Agni..13, 44, 47, 48, 49, 50, 51, 55, 59, 78, 206, 240, 241, 251, 257, 270, 310, 327, 372, 376, 378, 391, 430, 446, 465, 497, 499, 518, 519, 521, 522
Ahiṁsa ... 69
Aīṁ..243, 250, 341, 360, 370, 377, 424, 502, 546
Ajapa ... 521
Ājñā Cakra ... 521
Ākaṇḍa Flowers ... 506, 521
Ākāśa ... 229, 254, 518, 521
Akashanath ... 222, 547
Akkā Mahādevī ... 168
Akṣobhya ... 419, 521
Akrama ... 137, 521
Akula.. ... 95, 131, 288, 335, 521, 532
Alchemy..87, 119, 123, 124, 133, 142, 143, 146, 147, 153, 154, 252, 293, 294, 295, 302, 333, 344, 355, 368, 385, 386, 403, 404, 418, 424, 496, 506, 527, 533, 541
Alpha Bet Ben Sirra ... 397
Alphabet..89, 271, 272, 372, 514, 516, 535
Ammaiyār, Kāraikkāl ... 167
Anāhata ... 284, 285, 307, 338, 521
Ānanda..285, 286, 408, 517, 519, 521
Ānanda Kanda ... 521
Anaṅga Raṅga ... 349
Aṅkuśa ... 521
Annapūrṇā ... 413, 446, 522
Āṇṭāḷ ... 167
Anuttara ... 408, 516, 522, 531
Apāna..55, 206, 232, 281, 283, 332, 339, 522
Aparājitā ... 24, 254, 255, 522, 544
Apsaras ... 58, 166, 396, 522
Aranyānī ... 51, 489, 522
Ardhanārīśvara ... 269, 522
Artha ... 251, 271, 522
Arthur Avalon ... *See* John Woodroffe
Aryans..37, 41, 42, 47, 51, 58, 63, 77, 388
Āsana ... 139, 185, 200, 371, 522
Aśoka ... 43, 73, 514
Assam..17, 87, 147, 382, 418, 447, 530
Astrology..20, 73, 357, 358, 389, 408, 409, 529
Asura..25, 55, 254, 438, 446, 474, 522, 543
Aśvaghoṣa ... 467
Aśvins ... 47, 55, 78, 522
Atharvan ... 56, 522
Atharvaveda..22, 46, 55, 56, 58, 205, 385, 388, 522
Ātman..56, 58, 60, 64, 65, 66, 67, 205, 522

Autogenic Training 226, 229
AV........................ See *Atharvaveda*
Avatāra 81, 169, 523
Ayyangar, T.R. Srinivasa.....249, 553, 554
Bagalā..14, 412, 413, 416, 417, 435, 436, 438, 456, 523
Bagchi, P.C.........................244, 551
Bali 286, 523, 541
Bandler, Richard.........6, 7, 228, 259, 296, 300, 547
BāUp,........... See *Bṛhad-āraṇyaka Upaniṣad*
Beans..200, 352, 354, 358, 367, 534, 535
Bel 524
Bengal..70, 87, 100, 113, 114, 162, 177, 245, 275, 412, 419, 444, 445, 458, 473, 508, 533, 552
Betel 362, 377, 488, 543
Bhadrā 14, 286, 483, 523
Bhadrākāḷi 523
Bhagavad Gītā.......................... 469
Bhāgavata Purāṇa................... 470
Bhairava..13, 24, 96, 98, 120, 127, 129, 131, 182, 195, 225, 247, 254, 257, 270, 278, 282, 283, 288, 290, 303, 305, 314, 355, 356, 375, 377, 417, 426, 432, 470, 484, 503, 517, 518, 523, 551, 555
Bhairavī..14, 114, 127, 247, 251, 254, 257, 277, 283, 290, 375, 377, 412, 413, 416, 424, 426, 428, 431, 453, 470, 517, 523
Bhakti..80, 82, 87, 167, 169, 170, 191, 473, 523, 538
Bhāng 437, 523, 539
Bharati, Agehananda..141, 142, 352, 358, 418, 496, 499, 537, 548
Bhoga 366, 523
Bhūcarī 524, 531
Bhukti 524
Bhūtaśuddhi 184, 372, 524
Bhuvaneśvarī..14, 412, 413, 422, 423, 425, 452, 453, 524
Bīja..26, 198, 223, 224, 233, 238, 239, 249, 250, 251, 253, 254, 257, 265, 266, 290, 326, 327, 328, 341, 342, 369, 370, 372, 374, 375, 376, 377, 418, 425, 434, 438, 446, 486, 497, 502, 506, 516, 519, 520, 524, 531, 533, 534, 535, 546
Bilva Tree 425, 502, 507
Bindu..211, 251, 253, 254, 255, 257, 272, 327, 329, 374, 386, 409, 440, 517, 524, 535, 542, 545
Birrel, Anne.........................143, 548
Boar.............. 81, 277, 425, 482, 503
Books of the Late Han Dynasty..150
Brahmā..25, 27, 54, 60, 71, 101, 104, 105, 129, 182, 211, 224, 230, 233, 240, 241, 247, 249, 251, 254, 255, 270, 307, 310, 326, 329, 338, 371, 375, 378, 380, 382, 418, 425, 467, 468, 480, 482, 493, 494, 505, 524, 526, 529, 534, 538, 545
Brahmacārya 173
Brahman..26, 60, 64, 66, 67, 80, 83, 85, 92, 101, 103, 127, 131, 155, 182, 203, 207, 231, 236, 250, 255, 257, 269, 284, 287, 289, 305, 310, 311, 327, 328, 329, 337, 338, 367, 369, 372, 375, 376, 377, 378, 407, 446, 465, 469, 470, 471, 496, 519, 524, 529, 531, 536, 537, 539
Brāhmaṇa......22, 59, 64, 65, 99, 101, 207, 544
Brahmarandhara 524
Brahmaṇī, Bhairavī....................169
Brahmī 104, 543
Brahmins..44, 47, 59, 61, 64, 69, 74, 75, 76, 77, 78, 83, 97, 115, 116, 140, 169, 191, 253, 270, 308, 310, 346, 367, 382, 385, 387, 406, 472, 474, 524, 525
Bṛhad-āraṇyaka Upaniṣad.........22, 206, 280
Bṛhaddharma Purāṇa..............413
Bṛhaspati....47, 241, 253, 261, 499, 524
Brooks, Douglas Renfrew..139, 140, 245, 250, 548
Brunner, H. 555
Buddha..67, 68, 69, 79, 81, 113, 121, 141, 417, 418, 419, 445, 467, 518, 524, 548

Buddhacarita 467

Buddhist..68, 69, 73, 113, 114, 121, 123, 124, 125, 129, 136, 141, 142, 152, 179, 201, 351, 358, 417, 418, 424, 432, 467, 498, 520, 535, 542

Budge, E.A. Wallis 399, 400, 548

Cahill, Suzanne E. 144, 145, 548

Caitanya Caritāmṛta 192

Cakra..21, 28, 43, 55, 89, 94, 126, 133, 139, 178, 182, 183, 184, 195, 214, 215, 239, 250, 283, 284, 285, 286, 305, 307, 308, 309, 314, 315, 317, 318, 319, 320, 326, 327, 328, 329, 331, 332, 333, 334, 335, 336, 338, 339, 341, 342, 343, 344, 369, 372, 373, 380, 412, 413, 489, 521, 524, 525, 527, 531, 532, 533, 534, 535, 539, 541, 542, 545, 546

Cakrasaṁvara Tantra 351

Camphor 22, 496

Cāmuṇḍā 482, 505, 525

Caṇḍa..286, 437, 469, 481, 482, 524, 525

Caṇḍamahāroṣaṇa Tantra 351

Caṇḍī 22, 469, 472, 478, 525

Caṇḍī Purāṇa 472, 478

Cantong Qi 302, 404

Chāndogya Upaniṣad..66, 181, 255, 261, 401, 499

Chang, T.T. 148, 153

China..68, 73, 123, 142, 143, 146, 147, 150, 152, 153, 179, 196, 275, 404, 418, 467, 533, 548

Chinnamastā..14, 254, 412, 413, 416, 429, 430, 431, 432, 454, 525

Chinnamastā Tantra 432

Chöd 451

Chu Ci 550, 554

Chuang Tzu 548

Cidambara 103, 525, 536

Cidambara Māhātyma 103, 536

Cinnabar..21, 143, 403, 404, 418, 424

Circle..94, 139, 153, 177, 196, 204, 215, 253, 255, 257, 268, 294, 311, 314, 320, 360, 371, 372, 374, 375, 378, 395, 407, 412, 413, 484, 510, 522, 523, 524, 531, 534, 542

Cit 516, 525

Cleary, Thomas..146, 223, 303, 548, 554

Cluster..95, 119, 131, 159, 161, 239, 287, 308, 310, 363, 403, 407, 416, 478, 480, 529, 531, 532, 541, 542

Coconut 199, 355, 362, 380

Consonants 491, 515, 516, 518

Corpse..27, 28, 95, 114, 129, 173, 186, 188, 191, 229, 243, 254, 277, 417, 418, 419, 424, 447, 450, 451, 478, 484, 492, 495, 499, 500, 502, 525, 528, 530, 540, 541

Cow..45, 51, 52, 60, 61, 76, 80, 90, 99, 102, 116, 168, 170, 254, 263, 375, 376, 387, 393, 439, 445, 469, 471, 479, 485, 489, 525, 527, 532

Cremation Place..54, 90, 107, 131, 179, 212, 403, 438, 482, 484, 485, 503

Crowley, Aleister..123, 188, 189, 197, 222, 224, 266, 410, 548

Daitya 424, 523, 524, 543

Dākinī 525

Dakṣa..9, 25, 26, 27, 60, 413, 416, 480, 530, 537

Dakṣiṇā..244, 412, 413, 478, 487, 497, 505, 525

Dakṣiṇā Kālī 525

Dalai Lama 180, 396, 555

Dalí, Salvador 451

Damaru 130, 327, 329, 525

Dānava 25, 525

Dance 93, 457, 536, 554

Daniélou, Alain..353, 425, 426, 432, 438, 439, 548

Dantian 214

Daodejing 145, 147, 293

Daoism..122, 123, 145, 146, 153, 154, 196, 214, 217, 292, 294, 303, 319, 364

Dasyus 41

DBh,.......... See *Devī Bhāgavatam Purāṇa*

Denton, Lynn Teskey.........172, 173, 174, 548

Deśikendra, Lakṣmaṇa 426

Desire..25, 29, 64, 66, 68, 79, 80, 90, 135, 169, 179, 181, 184, 194, 200, 212, 240, 248, 250, 251, 254, 270, 280, 293, 305, 310, 326, 334, 343, 347, 349, 351, 354, 383, 396, 397, 406, 407, 410, 424, 431, 450, 470, 486, 488, 494, 529
Devanāgarī.................251, 514, 515
Devī..22, 29, 61, 87, 90, 94, 101, 103, 139, 155, 162, 207, 223, 240, 243, 244, 245, 246, 254, 269, 271, 303, 305, 316, 318, 320, 326, 327, 329, 337, 338, 356, 359, 362, 370, 371, 377, 382, 383, 389, 412, 413, 425, 426, 431, 438, 468, 470, 471, 475, 480, 481, 482, 492, 503, 505, 525, 526, 534, 548, 549, 550
Devī Bhāgavatam Purāṇa.. 22, 101
Devī Māhātmya.... 22, 468, 470, 480
Dharma..71, 74, 75, 77, 80, 122, 134, 247, 251, 271, 526
Dhātā.................................493, 526
Dhūmāvatī..14, 412, 413, 415, 416, 417, 434, 437, 455, 526
Dhyāna........ 247, 261, 285, 329, 526
Di 147
Digambarī..........................486, 526
Dikcarī...............................526, 531
Dilts, Robert.......................304, 549
Ding Wangdao.......................... 549
DM................. *See* Devī Māhātmya
Dold, Patricia 470
Dragon 294
Dravya...............................355, 526
Dupuche, John R..17, 384, 407, 410, 516, 547
Durgā..6, 22, 85, 87, 103, 116, 171, 199, 203, 245, 253, 277, 309, 311, 373, 376, 412, 428, 446, 447, 468, 469, 475, 481, 510, 511, 521, 524, 525, 526, 534, 536, 538, 541, 545, 549, 550
Duyvendak, J.J.L. 147, 549, 555
Dyaus 51
Earth..22, 25, 47, 50, 51, 52, 55, 56, 58, 59, 64, 78, 79, 81, 92, 105, 114, 147, 148, 149, 150, 160, 182, 194, 202, 205, 229, 237, 249, 250, 255, 269, 276, 278, 288, 293, 304, 311, 315, 316, 317, 320, 321, 322, 323, 325, 326, 329, 339, 341, 342, 344, 345, 357, 372, 373, 380, 382, 385, 386, 388, 404, 417, 424, 425, 459, 463, 474, 482, 485, 493, 494, 495, 499, 501, 516, 517, 518, 519, 523, 524, 525, 534, 536, 542, 543, 544, 545
Eberlein, Gisela..............5, 226, 228
Elephant..26, 34, 35, 202, 203, 242, 253, 277, 326, 328, 349, 362, 393, 424, 439, 445, 452, 494, 521, 527
Eliade, Mircea..88, 129, 130, 131, 549
Ergot..358
Erickson, Milton H............178, 228, 549
Eskildsen, Stephen 146, 549
Eve 397
Evil Fiends 399
Fang Shi 152
Finn, Louise M..5, 194, 197, 223, 276, 331, 362, 393, 408, 445, 488, 549, 551
Fire..55, 240, 241, 261, 281, 320, 324, 330, 337, 338, 376, 378, 400, 401, 465, 494, 497, 542
Flowers.. 12, 115, 174, 373, 506, 552
Food..76, 183, 199, 209, 241, 380, 522, 537
Fox 277, 507
Gan Bao 150
Gandharva 95, 527
Gandharva Tantra.......................95
Gaṇeśa..13, 123, 128, 155, 242, 245, 253, 270, 329, 371, 377, 430, 445, 527
Gaṇgā.........................328, 508, 533
Ganges..42, 80, 89, 110, 270, 358, 481, 508, 533
Ganguli, Kisari Mohan.......468, 469, 549, 551
Garuḍa 104, 243, 482, 527
Gaurī 25, 26, 28, 472, 526
Gheraṇḍa Saṁhita.............22, 186, 233, 285

Ghī..99, 183, 230, 240, 245, 360, 362, 367, 373, 378, 401, 406, 432, 499, 520, 526, 527, 528, 542
Gilgamesh 397
Ginger 355, 357
Glasenapp, Helmuth von.......30, 97, 169, 284, 549
Gnoli 516
Gocarī.................................527, 531
Gold..32, 45, 73, 97, 143, 145, 247, 252, 265, 293, 309, 321, 323, 326, 327, 374, 380, 432, 438, 531
Golden Dawn..123, 301, 311, 322, 323, 451, 547, 550, 553
Golden Pavilion 294
Gonda, Jan..30, 45, 52, 55, 58, 69, 465, 549
Goose 406, 438, 527
Gośāla 69
Goudriaan, Teun..178, 381, 407, 470, 471, 507, 550, 553, 555
Grahīs 389, 393
Grain..200, 271, 352, 358, 373, 375, 400, 534, 535
Grant, Kenneth..332, 341, 409, 548, 550
Graves, Robert 477
Grinder, John 547
Griffith, Ralph T.H..30, 56, 280, 489, 550, 553
GS ....See *Gheraṇḍa Saṁhita*
Gu Sorcery 151
Guṇa.... 104, 105, 527, 538, 540, 542
Guoyu.. 149
Gupta, Sanjukta..72, 100, 167, 168, 178, 381, 407, 470, 471, 472, 507, 550, 551
Gurdjeff..................................... 457
Guru..20, 47, 100, 108, 115, 120, 121, 125, 126, 131, 132, 134, 137, 140, 155, 156, 157, 158, 159, 160, 161, 162, 163, 165, 168, 169, 170, 172, 173, 174, 175, 178, 194, 197, 224, 233, 237, 238, 239, 241, 245, 253, 268, 270, 271, 308, 310, 314, 330, 333, 336, 338, 340, 347, 356, 360, 363, 369, 370, 371, 377, 378, 380, 381, 410, 426, 488, 501, 521, 524, 527, 540, 541
Guyana................. 12, 508, 510, 511
Hair..35, 52, 56, 92, 130, 135, 138, 143, 145, 167, 168, 170, 173, 178, 179, 182, 183, 184, 192, 202, 225, 233, 247, 263, 276, 329, 330, 342, 370, 372, 393, 398, 399, 407, 412, 417, 418, 437, 488, 491, 493, 494, 495, 498, 507, 531
Haṁsa..211, 212, 224, 234, 237, 249, 261, 266, 320, 330, 372, 389, 406, 486, 521, 527
Hara..52, 82, 101, 243, 277, 329, 492, 493, 494, 527, 542
Harappa 32, 34
Hari..80, 233, 249, 327, 329, 493, 494, 528, 542
Hashish..245, 355, 360, 521, 528, 545
Haviṣyānnaṁ 495, 499, 505, 528
Hawkes, David . ..153, 364, 550, 554
Hawley, John Stratton........477, 548, 550, 551, 552
Heart..17, 18, 19, 23, 25, 66, 159, 182, 186, 189, 194, 195, 198, 206, 207, 208, 209, 214, 217, 221, 225, 232, 234, 238, 239, 244, 245, 246, 251, 259, 265, 272, 273, 276, 280, 281, 283, 284, 285, 286, 287, 288, 289, 290, 292, 293, 294, 295, 296, 301, 302, 304, 307, 318, 319, 321, 324, 325, 327, 331, 335, 337, 338, 339, 343, 355, 366, 371, 372, 373, 377, 378, 380, 407, 418, 424, 426, 431, 448, 452, 457, 486, 493, 498, 499, 500, 503, 505, 506, 508, 516, 517, 521, 523, 525, 528, 543, 545
Hevajra Tantra..........................351
Hexagram 247, 327, 486, 530
Himalaya....................... 26, 481, 554
Homa 251, 528
Horse..37, 41, 47, 78, 81, 114, 115, 131, 194, 269, 277, 522, 528
Howe, Ellic 301, 550
Hṛdaya 242, 280, 284, 528
Hrīṁ..26, 161, 197, 198, 223, 241, 242, 243, 244, 245, 250, 254, 258, 272, 338, 341, 342, 371, 372, 374,

375, 380, 425, 482, 491, 492, 497, 502, 503, 505, 535
Hu Bin........................217, 229, 550
Hūṁ..244, 254, 258, 375, 482, 491, 492, 497, 502, 503, 505
Humes, Cynthia Ann..467, 472, 474, 475
Hypnosis...........6, 20, 226, 227, 228
I Ching.....................149, *See* Yijing
Icchā........... 133, 243, 317, 336, 528
Iḍā.....................................369, 528
Ifrah, Georges............274, 275, 550
Immortals..122, 143, 145, 146, 286, 294
Inanna...................................... 398
Indra..41, 44, 47, 50, 51, 52, 55, 58, 59, 66, 78, 79, 80, 82, 166, 181, 182, 207, 231, 244, 254, 255, 261, 270, 310, 322, 326, 373, 385, 386, 388, 391, 446, 463, 482, 519, 522, 528, 545, 554
Indus..9, 13, 32, 33, 34, 35, 36, 37, 39, 40, 51, 71, 388, 514, 540, 550
Indus Culture......32, 34, 35, 37, 514
Initiation..17, 20, 29, 61, 69, 77, 100, 114, 126, 131, 140, 145, 156, 172, 173, 194, 196, 197, 254, 278, 314, 367, 368, 438, 451, 520, 526, 530, 539, 545
Īśa..................................63, 66, 528
Īśa Upaniṣad.............................. 66
Iṣṭadevatā..155, 285, 310, 311, 313, 528
Īśvara..................182, 257, 519, 528
Īśvarī... 528
Iyengar, B.K.S......209, 210, 223, 550
Jackal...114, 276, 277, 393, 432, 507, 541
Jade..........................143, 145, 303
Jagadīśvarānanda, Svāmī....549, 550
Jain.. 520
Japa..107, 108, 173, 212, 223, 240, 251, 254, 261, 263, 267, 268, 271, 272, 273, 274, 371, 438, 500, 507, 521, 528, 534
Japamālā............................223, 528
Jarrige, Jean-François.......... 35, 550
Jati...............................75, 528, 544
Jayā..24, 85, 254, 255, 431, 468, 469, 528, 544
Jayāntī......................................528
Jayaratha....................384, 549, 551
Jing..153
Jīva..92, 202, 281, 334, 341, 342, 372, 529, 531, 532, 538
Jīvanmukti.................................529
Jñāna.....133, 243, 249, 317, 336, 529
Jyeṣṭhā..........168, 309, 438, 529, 543
Kailāsa...............................183, 432
Kaivalya.................63, 83, 198, 368
Kajuraho..111, 349, 361, 365, 379, 405
Kalā..249, 326, 329, 375, 408, 482, 516, 518, 521, 529
Kāla..104, 129, 417, 467, 492, 493, 495, 496, 497, 499, 505, 519, 529, 533
Kālī..10, 12, 14, 18, 19, 22, 23, 27, 51, 85, 87, 89, 94, 102, 103, 105, 107, 114, 115, 130, 131, 133, 135, 136, 138, 143, 147, 160, 167, 168, 169, 171, 183, 192, 194, 195, 198, 199, 202, 203, 223, 242, 245, 250, 251, 254, 261, 265, 271, 272, 276, 283, 304, 309, 311, 320, 331, 341, 359, 370, 371, 373, 377, 378, 380, 388, 393, 408, 412, 413, 416, 417, 419, 431, 437, 447, 449, 450, 451, 463, 464, 465, 466, 467, 468, 469, 470, 471, 472, 473, 474, 475, 476, 477, 478, 479, 480, 481, 482, 483, 485, 486, 487, 489, 491, 494, 496, 497, 499, 500, 501, 502, 503, 504, 505, 506, 507, 508, 511, 512, 521, 522, 523, 524, 525, 526, 529, 531, 532, 534, 536, 537, 538, 541, 542, 543, 552, 555
Kālīkā...............................477, 529
Kālikāpurāṇa....... 22, 383, 480, 554
Kālīkula...........................470, 529
Kālītantra..................................497
Kālīvilāsatantra..........................471
Kali-yuga...................................529
Kāma..28, 29, 58, 68, 79, 179, 198, 245, 247, 249, 250, 251, 270, 271, 280, 342, 349, 371, 376, 383, 386,

424, 431, 472, 486, 492, 494, 495, 497, 498, 529
Kāmadeva..13, 225, 254, 305, 306, 307, 326, 498, 529, 538, 541
Kāmakalā 486, 530
Kāmākhhyā..382, 383, 521, 530, 536, 546
Kamalā..14, 257, 383, 412, 413, 443, 445, 459, 460, 461, 492, 530
Kāmarūpa..28, 197, 326, 335, 360, 382, 413, 447, 530, 536
Kāmasutra 348, 349
Kāmeśvarī....................139, 424, 530
Kampa 194, 530
Kāpālika 530
Kāpālinī....... 129, 167, 467, 505, 530
Karman..27, 29, 64, 65, 66, 67, 68, 69, 71, 75, 77, 116, 175, 232, 340, 530, 531, 539
Karpūrādi Stotra..........22, 103, 505
Karpūram 531
Kashmir..11, 17, 87, 94, 127, 133, 135, 138, 140, 168, 183, 257, 283, 286, 287, 336, 366, 406, 426, 486, 514, 515, 523, 528, 531, 532, 538, 539, 549, 552, 553
Kaula..9, 11, 17, 18, 19, 20, 23, 24, 76, 94, 95, 101, 102, 103, 123, 125, 129, 131, 132, 133, 134, 135, 138, 139, 140, 141, 196, 246, 248, 283, 287, 305, 349, 351, 352, 354, 363, 366, 369, 380, 393, 395, 403, 405, 406, 407, 408, 412, 413, 419, 437, 440, 456, 468, 516, 522, 531, 532, 533, 536, 539, 540, 552
Kaulajñāna nirṇaya..19, 22, 93, 102, 132, 143, 155, 177, 178, 192, 244, 278, 303, 305, 308, 309, 315, 317, 319, 334, 335, 337, 383, 393, 395, 404, 406, 408, 426, 506, 551
Kaulāvali Tantra 102
Kauṣītakī Brāhmaṇa Upaniṣad. 22, 207
Kavirāja, Kṛṣṇadāsa.................... 192
KBUp..See *Kauṣītakī Brāhmaṇa Upaniṣad*
KCT.......See *Kulacūḍāmaṇi Tantra*
Keightley, David 148, 551
Kerala 389, 546
Keśakambalin, Ajita 71
Khecarī....................318, 524, 531
Kingston, Maxine Hong.............6, 7, 299
Kinsley, David R.........113, 391, 416, 418, 426, 431, 432, 437, 439, 445, 477, 480, 551
KJN..........See *Kaulajñāna nirṇaya*
Knot 201, 264, 305, 527
Koltuv, Barbara Black.........399, 548
Konarak 109, 349, 350
Kośa 183, 184
Kongzi (Confucius) 150
KP.................... See *Kālikāpurāṇa*
Krama..9, 13, 17, 18, 19, 20, 94, 101, 124, 135, 136, 137, 138, 140, 177, 258, 286, 366, 412, 470, 486, 516, 521, 522, 524, 531, 545, 553
Krīṁ..161, 198, 223, 251, 254, 258, 272, 341, 371, 372, 377, 491, 492, 497, 502, 503, 505, 520
Kripal, Jeffrey..467, 470, 472, 474, 552
Kriyā.....133, 243, 249, 317, 336, 532
Kṛṣṇa..80, 81, 100, 102, 155, 162, 167, 170, 192, 240, 241, 243, 254, 375, 393, 417, 469, 471, 510, 527, 532
KS ....See *Karpūrādi Stotra*
Kṣatriya 59, 61, 99, 544
Kṣemarāja 283, 551
KT.................... See *Kulārṇava Tantra*
Kubera..242, 244, 247, 378, 388, 446, 491, 496, 532
Kubjikā..58, 108, 127, 382, 413, 416, 440, 532, 553
Kuhū 51
Kula..9, 10, 12, 14, 19, 20, 22, 23, 95, 101, 131, 132, 134, 135, 136, 138, 141, 182, 195, 242, 271, 272, 276, 277, 278, 280, 286, 287, 288, 289, 314, 335, 337, 338, 362, 363, 376, 384, 403, 417, 426, 463, 503, 522, 526, 529, 532, 540, 542, 544, 545, 547
Kulacūḍāmaṇi Tantra..22, 109, 133, 153, 179, 194, 195, 197, 223,

238, 276, 278, 283, 331, 360, 362, 363, 393, 408, 470, 486, 488, 501, 503, 505, 506, 507, 549, 551
Kulāmṛta.. 532
Kulārṇava Tantra..23, 94, 105, 124, 133, 156, 181, 194, 236, 237, 238, 239, 261, 263, 265, 266, 354, 355, 356, 357, 551, 553
Kumārī.. 532
Kumbhaka..................221, 321, 532
Kuṇḍa.........359, 374, 408, 445, 532
Kuṇḍalinī..11, 18, 23, 24, 43, 89, 110, 169, 170, 184, 194, 195, 202, 210, 214, 224, 236, 245, 254, 271, 272, 276, 302, 303, 307, 315, 317, 320, 321, 322, 324, 326, 330, 331, 332, 333, 334, 335, 336, 337, 338, 339, 340, 341, 342, 343, 344, 356, 369, 370, 371, 372, 389, 406, 426, 473, 488, 524, 527, 530, 532, 533, 537, 539, 542, 545
Kunlun.. 152
Kūrma Purāṇa..................310, 480
Lakṣmī..10, 13, 14, 23, 25, 26, 52, 79, 87, 99, 101, 111, 124, 127, 197, 198, 202, 242, 244, 254, 257, 261, 263, 269, 304, 327, 413, 416, 417, 421, 438, 439, 443, 444, 445, 446, 459, 462, 472, 480, 492, 493, 505, 530, 532, 533, 541, 550, 551
Lakṣmī Tantra..23, 99, 100, 124, 197, 254, 269, 446, 550, 551
Lakṣmīdhara......................139, 141
Lalitā..14, 24, 87, 139, 141, 245, 246, 247, 249, 331, 400, 420, 421, 424, 439, 451, 533, 534
Lallā Ded.................................. 168
Lamashtu...........................399, 400
Lamp......68, 263, 327, 329, 522, 526
Laozi..................145, 146, 147, 293
Laws of Manu........................ 41, 97
Laya-yoga.................................. 533
Leftovers.............380, 406, 439, 536
Leslie, Julie..97, 99, 100, 167, 168, 385, 548, 550, 551, 554
Liexian Zhuan.......................... 146
Liji... 149
Līlā.............................163, 510, 533
Lilith.......11, 397, 398, 399, 400, 548
Liṅga..41, 82, 84, 92, 93, 194, 243, 315, 316, 326, 327, 335, 349, 371, 425, 525, 533, 542
Liubo..144
Loki..50
Lorenzen, David N............129, 130, 551
Lotus..104, 178, 182, 208, 246, 250, 255, 268, 269, 283, 285, 286, 304, 305, 307, 316, 317, 318, 323, 326, 327, 328, 329, 333, 335, 336, 337, 338, 355, 356, 362, 369, 370, 371, 373, 374, 377, 378, 416, 418, 424, 425, 426, 431, 439, 440, 445, 447, 460, 471, 491, 492, 493, 495, 499, 505, 506, 511, 521, 523, 530, 533, 539
LT......................See *Lakṣmī Tantra*
Lü Bu Wei..................................150
Lü Dongbin................................303
Madhūka flowers.......................355
Mādhurya Bhāva........................170
Magee, Michael..155, 194, 337, 406, 426, 551, 552, 555, 556
Mahābhāgavatapurāna.............412
Mahābhārata..23, 42, 73, 78, 79, 80, 85, 166, 191, 387, 388, 391, 419, 446, 465, 468, 469, 471, 477, 549, 551
Mahācīna..9, 18, 141, 142, 154, 418, 533
Mahākāla...................................533
Mahākālasaṁhitā.....................507
Mahānirvāṇa Tantra..23, 102, 104, 108, 135, 162, 198, 223, 245, 286, 346, 354, 356, 359, 369, 380, 497, 503
Mahāvīra.......................................69
Maitrī Upaniṣad..................66, 181
Makāra Devī......................135, 137, *See* Mangalā Devī
Maklû Spells..............................399
Mālinī..516
Māṇḍūkya Upaniṣad...........23, 255
Mangalā Devī.....................135, 137
Mantra..5, 18, 24, 29, 76, 103, 107, 108, 110, 114, 119, 124, 126, 132,

139, 140, 173, 175, 192, 194, 195, 196, 197, 198, 200, 207, 211, 212, 217, 218, 219, 222, 223, 224, 225, 229, 234, 236, 237, 238, 239, 240, 241, 242, 243, 244, 245, 249, 250, 251, 252, 253, 254, 255, 257, 259, 261, 262, 263, 264, 265, 266, 267, 268, 272, 273, 276, 277, 283, 289, 290, 292, 296, 319, 320, 322, 323, 324, 325, 330, 332, 341, 346, 347, 360, 370, 371, 372, 374, 375, 376, 377, 378, 389, 409, 413, 418, 424, 425, 431, 432, 438, 440, 446, 451, 459, 477, 482, 486, 488, 492, 493, 494, 495, 496, 497, 499, 501, 502, 503, 505, 507, 514, 515, 521, 527, 528, 530, 534, 537, 542, 543, 545

Mantramahodhadhiḥ..23, 239, 240, 241, 264, 268, 309, 431, 432, 438, 440, 450

Manu 74, 81, 97, 387, 425, 534

Mātā 529, 535

Maruts.. ..47, 52, 55, 78, 79, 522, 535

Mātaṅgī...412, 412, 416, 417, 439, 440, 441, 442, 445, 457, 458, 535

Mātaṅgī Tantra 439

Mathers, MacGregor 301

Matriarchy 35, 477

Mātṛkā . ..22, 318, 389, 391, 516, 535

Matsyendranātha 22

Mattavilāsa..................129, 130, 551

MāUp.......See *Māṇḍūkya Upaniṣad*

Mawangdui..146, 147, 217, 223, 293, 364, 552, 555

Māyā..26, 54, 198, 251, 254, 257, 272, 341, 425, 432, 447, 452, 453, 459, 481, 516, 519, 524, 526, 530, 533, 534, 535, 537, 543, 554

McDaniel, June..21, 85, 169, 170, 174, 178, 192, 342, 343, 347, 381, 552

McDermott, Rachel Fell........89, 467, 472, 473, 477, 552

Meditation..22, 24, 46, 66, 67, 87, 93, 95, 104, 113, 115, 117, 122, 123, 133, 141, 158, 161, 165, 169, 173, 175, 177, 178, 179, 185, 186, 188, 189, 191, 196, 212, 215, 217, 221, 223, 225, 229, 231, 236, 238, 247, 262, 269, 272, 280, 285, 286, 287, 294, 303, 304, 305, 307, 308, 309, 318, 319, 320, 322, 325, 329, 335, 336, 337, 338, 346, 348, 360, 362, 369, 370, 371, 373, 396, 400, 404, 412, 416, 417, 438, 447, 448, 451, 456, 458, 459, 470, 471, 473, 479, 495, 496, 499, 503, 505, 508, 510, 524, 526, 528, 530, 534, 538, 539, 546

Medusa.......................................472

Meluhha 32

Menon, Usha..............................472

Menstrual Blood..22, 24, 284, 308, 351, 359, 363, 374, 377, 386, 403, 404, 405, 406, 408, 419, 432, 440, 488, 496, 522, 531, 533, 538, 543, 546

Menstruation..272, 360, 378, 382, 383, 385, 386, 387, 395, 408, 409, 413, 445, 447, 506, 508, 521, 538

Mercury..21, 142, 143, 403, 404, 418, 527, 538

Meru.....139, 182, 183, 194, 272, 315

Mesopotamia 32, 34

MHB.................. See *Mahābhārata*

Midnight..404, 419, 432, 440, 494, 495, 500

Milk..26, 45, 81, 183, 245, 251, 271, 303, 304, 325, 360, 362, 367, 373, 386, 391, 393, 419, 432, 439, 445, 499, 520, 533

Mithra 50

MM.........See *Mantramahodhadhiḥ*

MNT....... See *Mahānirvāṇa Tantra*

Mohenjo Daro.............32, 33, 39, 48

Monier-Williams, Sir Monier......440, 552

Mookerjee, Ajit...................104, 552

Moon..43, 50, 51, 55, 59, 64, 92, 159, 178, 182, 183, 202, 205, 206, 224, 225, 230, 231, 232, 240, 241, 247, 249, 257, 263, 265, 275, 304, 305, 309, 320, 323, 324, 327, 328, 329, 330, 335, 339, 356, 373, 374, 375, 376, 378, 385, 404, 408, 418, 425, 426, 438, 439, 468, 482, 484, 491, 497, 507, 511, 514, 528, 529, 531, 541

Morgan, Mogg. ..5, 73, 456, 465, 552

Moslem.......................................520

Mothers..11, 51, 133, 362, 388, 389, 391, 393, 397, 425, 482, 514, 544

Mudrā..14, 24, 126, 195, 196, 200, 201, 202, 203, 204, 225, 274, 307, 308, 319, 322, 329, 352, 358, 362, 371, 372, 374, 375, 376, 377, 378, 380, 405, 407, 521, 534, 535, 540, 544

Mukti.......................................535

Mūlādhāra..307, 331, 338, 489, 535, 537, 546

Muller-Ortega, Paul Eduardo.... 194, 225, 257, 283, 547, 552

Muṇḍa.................437, 481, 482, 525

Muṇḍaka Upaniṣad........23, 65, 465

Muṇḍamāla Tantra...........412, 416

Mup......... See *Muṇḍaka Upaniṣad*

Music..44, 68, 79, 109, 123, 153, 160, 227, 260, 264, 312, 355, 366, 403, 440, 457, 511, 535, 540

Nāda..251, 253, 254, 257, 284, 329, 535

Nāḍī.....................315, 341, 426, 536

Nāga.......................................536

Nāgārjuna.................................142

Naraka...............................382, 536

Naṭarājā...................................536

Nātha..11, 22, 24, 123, 127, 334, 335, 536

Navarātrī...................................536

Nema..................5, 6, 266, 340, 552

Nepal..125, 132, 142, 179, 412, 417, 419, 426, 428, 434, 439, 442, 472, 478, 523

Nigama...........................22, 23, 536

Nightshade................................355

Nīla.....................382, 413, 418, 536

Nine Songs...............................153

Nirguṇa....................................536

Nirmālya...................................536

Nirvān......................................536

Noose..26, 104, 105, 208, 246, 247, 327, 328, 424, 425, 438, 439, 440, 481, 537

Nü Ji...146

Nü Wa...59

Nyāsa..195, 196, 197, 198, 199, 239, 319, 344, 360, 372, 373, 505, 536

Oberhammer, G.........................555

Obsession..23, 56, 68, 76, 102, 132, 138, 154, 160, 169, 174, 200, 214, 239, 252, 261, 266, 331, 342, 366, 381, 451, 510, 511, 525, 535, 539, 544

O'Flaherty, Wendy Doniger..56, 60, 549, 553

Ojas.............. 29, 238, 284, 312, 536

Old Testament............................398

Oṁ..44, 110, 224, 241, 242, 243, 244, 245, 246, 247, 248, 250, 255, 256, 257, 329, 341, 377, 378, 418, 425, 431, 432, 438, 440, 446, 471, 477, 502, 536, 537

Orgasm..146, 147, 175, 177, 349, 358, 363, 364, 366, 367, 401, 409, 410, 417, 432, 477, 497

Owl 253, 393, 398, 445, 533, 545

Padmasaṁbhava........................103

Padoux, André.. ..516, 550, 553, 555

Pādukā Pañcaka..........................23

Pan Gu...59

Pandit, M.P........... 23, 236, 551, 555

Parameśvari.......................272, 537

Paraśakti..25, 102, 133, 153, 179, 198, 359, 488, 537

Parasympathetic Nervous System 216, 217, 221

Parātriśikā Vivaraṇa 23, 95, 283, 292, 367, 516, 525

Parātriśikālaghuvṛttiḥ 23, 283, 408, 547

Pārvatī..13, 28, 29, 54, 72, 103, 104, 194, 199, 242, 245, 276, 311, 328, 353, 383, 391, 426, 431, 439, 480, 481, 507, 521, 526, 527, 534, 537, 541, 544

Paśu..105, 107, 108, 110, 178, 266, 352, 354, 356, 367, 537, 543

Paśupati 37, 266, 537

Pātāla...537

Patañjali........185, 186, 232, 234, 552

Peacock................ 38, 468, 469, 482

Penis..92, 93, 94, 121, 179, 197, 318, 360, 362, 364, 494, 533, 542
Perineum..206, 218, 229, 294, 302, 303, 307, 308, 315, 324, 330, 331, 332, 334, 336, 339, 342, 343, 356, 372, 447, 478, 489, 495, 499, 520, 530, 532, 535, 542, 545
Phonemes..20, 23, 24, 89, 126, 239, 267, 318, 373, 395, 407, 409, 471, 514, 515, 516, 518, 526, 536
Phoolan Devi 170, 171, 549, 554
Picumata 407
Piṇḍa 126, 305, 499, 537
Piṅgalā 224, 339, 537
Pīṭha..28, 137, 138, 360, 362, 382, 505, 526, 537
Play..78, 95, 97, 108, 110, 129, 130, 133, 135, 145, 150, 158, 162, 163, 166, 188, 228, 254, 259, 260, 276, 289, 290, 296, 298, 299, 304, 308, 309, 311, 316, 332, 347, 349, 352, 364, 375, 419, 425, 431, 451, 452, 453, 458, 459, 460, 470, 480, 485, 495, 500, 501, 510, 514, 533, 541
PP .... See *Pādukā Pañcaka*
Prajāpati..58, 59, 60, 64, 181, 537, 544
Prakṛti..104, 127, 240, 254, 267, 329, 372, 527, 537, 538
Praṇā 332, 334, 339, 537
Prāṇāyāma..10, 114, 205, 206, 207, 208, 210, 211, 220, 223, 229, 232, 233, 255, 261, 308, 337, 339, 341, 354, 358, 369, 370, 372, 378, 447, 448, 537
Prasāda 116, 273, 500, 537
Pṛthivī 51, 326, 518
PTL .... See *Parātrīśikālaghuvṛttiḥ*
PTV .... See *Parātrīśikā Vivaraṇa*
Pūjā..360, 409, 472, 507, 511, 526, 532, 538, 545
Purāṇa..22, 245, 393, 447, 538, 548, 551, 554
Pūraṇa Kāśyapa 71
Puruṣa..58, 59, 60, 127, 267, 321, 329, 538
Pūtanā 393
Qi 294, 295
Rādhā ... 100, 102, 170, 528, 532, 538
Radhakrishna 230, 232, 553
Rākā 51
Rai 94, 134, 194, 265
Rai, Ram Kumar 23, 551, 553
Rajas..104, 105, 107, 233, 249, 386, 387, 403, 406, 527, 538
Rakta 403, 406, 496, 538
Raktabīja 474, 481, 482, 538
Rāmakṛṣṇa..100, 162, 169, 195, 331, 458, 506, 549, 550
Rāmāyaṇa 23, 73, 81
Rasa..248, 284, 403, 404, 407, 518, 538
Rastogi, Navijivan..136, 137, 138, 553
Rati..29, 79, 309, 431, 486, 492, 497, 538
Rätsch, Christian 45, 358, 553
Regardie, Israel 301, 553
Reich, Wilhelm..190, 216, 324, 363, 553
Reincarnation..43, 46, 64, 65, 67, 69, 75, 77, 165, 184, 524, 540
Ṛgveda..23, 30, 41, 43, 46, 50, 51, 52, 54, 55, 56, 59, 60, 63, 280, 385
Rosary..223, 267, 271, 274, 329, 378, 426, 528
Ṛṣi 46, 239, 503, 538
Rudra..13, 20, 37, 50, 52, 53, 54, 55, 56, 58, 81, 105, 182, 243, 247, 254, 255, 270, 287, 327, 389, 419, 425, 439, 505, 517, 522, 527, 534, 535, 538, 541
Rudrayāmala 23, 283
ṚV .... See *Ṛgveda*
RY .... See *Rāmāyaṇa*
Sādhaka..156, 179, 197, 272, 307, 335, 337, 360, 362, 371, 378, 407, 408, 450, 488, 489, 505, 539
Sādhana..22, 124, 140, 171, 174, 341, 342, 346, 359, 409, 450, 457, 539
Sādhikā 407, 539
Saguṇa 104, 539
Sahaja 539

Sa'haṁ 211, 539
Sahasrāra Cakra 539
Śaiva..24, 63, 83, 85, 100, 120, 123, 138, 168, 178, 413, 539, 550
Śaivī 103, 104, 371
Śākta..22, 63, 68, 87, 101, 120, 121, 123, 138, 174, 192, 276, 391, 437, 445, 468, 471, 472, 481, 539, 548, 550, 556
Śākta Pramoda 437
Śakti..9, 13, 25, 26, 52, 58, 71, 85, 88, 89, 92, 93, 94, 95, 100, 102, 103, 104, 127, 131, 178, 180, 182, 185, 194, 195, 197, 198, 207, 208, 211, 236, 239, 242, 249, 250, 251, 253, 254, 257, 265, 266, 272, 277, 288, 289, 291, 292, 307, 308, 310, 314, 317, 322, 327, 328, 330, 334, 335, 336, 338, 348, 349, 355, 359, 360, 362, 367, 370, 371, 373, 375, 377, 380, 389, 407, 409, 410, 426, 431, 445, 446, 453, 470, 488, 493, 494, 495, 497, 498, 501, 505, 507, 515, 517, 518, 519, 521, 522, 528, 529, 532, 533, 536, 537, 538, 539, 541, 544, 555, 556
Śaktimān 539
Śaktipāta 539
Śaktisaṁgama Tantra 437, 439
Samādhi..197, 234, 266, 331, 467, 539
Sāmānyārghyā 371, 374, 540
Śambhu 540
Saṁhāra 136
Samsāra 540
Saṁvit 136
Sandhyābhāṣa 540
Sannyāsin 162, 540
Sannyāsinī 540
Śāradā Devī 170
Sarasvatī..25, 50, 51, 55, 79, 89, 202, 249, 253, 309, 327, 370, 371, 372, 378, 413, 418, 440, 446, 480, 492, 505, 540, 544
Saraswati, Swami Satyananda ... 477, 553, 554
Saso, Michael 295, 553
Sastri, S. Subrahmanya.......249, 553, 554
Sat..26, 27, 28, 29, 162, 371, 375, 382, 383, 413, 416, 437, 447, 526, 530, 540, 554
Satī..26, 27, 28, 29, 371, 375, 382, 383, 413, 416, 437, 447, 526, 530, 540, 554
Ṣaṭkarmāṇi 309, 540
Ṣaṭ Cakra Nirūpaṇa 24
Sattva..104, 105, 107, 233, 245, 249, 527, 540
Saundarya Laharī ..13, 24, 249, 252
Śavāsana 186, 188, 229, 541
Schoterman, Jan A.......413, 440, 553
ṢCN.......... See *Ṣaṭ Cakra Nirūpaṇa*
Secretions..75, 76, 122, 133, 135, 146, 147, 180, 263, 271, 276, 283, 284, 325, 339, 348, 356, 357, 364, 367, 375, 380, 385, 399, 401, 403, 404, 405, 406, 407, 408, 409, 410, 440, 445, 458, 470, 473, 488, 494, 496, 498, 499, 521, 526, 528, 532, 538, 542, 545, 546
Seed..44, 196, 197, 198, 200, 212, 223, 238, 239, 251, 253, 254, 255, 257, 280, 318, 321, 329, 386, 398, 425, 482, 486, 494, 503, 505, 506, 517, 519, 520, 524, 529, 535, 538, 545
Sefer Ḥasîdîm 399
Sen, Mala 474, 554
Sen, Rāmprasād..89, 195, 458, 473, 550
Senses..26, 29, 60, 110, 112, 135, 170, 178, 182, 186, 206, 207, 230, 232, 247, 259, 261, 280, 281, 285, 287, 296, 302, 303, 327, 328, 335, 336, 337, 356, 366, 377, 424, 452, 470, 488, 498, 506, 526, 527, 528, 530
Serpent..18, 50, 78, 89, 121, 135, 162, 302, 303, 317, 324, 326, 330, 331, 334, 335, 339, 341, 342, 343, 373, 385, 389, 396, 397, 398, 406, 408, 419, 425, 426, 432, 470, 480, 486, 510, 519, 528, 532, 536, 541, 545
Shāstri, Haraprasād 88
Shāstri, Vidushekar 88

Shaking..5, 20, 52, 54, 55, 56, 58, 66, 191, 192, 194, 195, 213, 238, 318, 331, 332, 342, 343, 344, 381, 417, 451, 457, 467, 501, 510, 530, 539, 541
Shamanism..6, 123, 148, 153, 154, 163, 229, 317, 417
Shang dynasty............143, 144, 147
Shaw, Miranda..180, 351, 352, 396, 554
Shree Maa............................477, 553
Shujing..................................... 148
Shweder, Richard...................... 472
Siddha..24, 127, 155, 182, 206, 335, 355, 386, 404, 431, 541, 555, 556
Siddha Siddhānta Paddhati......24, 182, 206, 335
Siddhāntavāgiśa, Durgārāma.....498
Siddhi..240, 245, 250, 277, 357, 362, 373, 406, 418, 432, 452, 456, 479, 482, 491, 492, 534, 541
Śilpa Prākāśa............................ 349
Sima Qian...................148, 150, 151
Sinīvalī... 51
Singh, Jaideva..292, 508, 510, 511, 516, 547
Singh, Karna............................. 554
Śiṣya 155, 156, 163, 541
Śiva..9, 13, 14, 16, 24, 25, 26, 27, 28, 29, 37, 48, 52, 54, 60, 63, 71, 72, 74, 78, 79, 81, 82, 83, 84, 85, 88, 90, 92, 93, 94, 95, 100, 101, 102, 103, 104, 105, 108, 114, 120, 127, 129, 130, 131, 135, 138, 139, 141, 155, 167, 168, 169, 178, 182, 186, 188, 190, 195, 198, 202, 203, 207, 211, 223, 224, 225, 233, 239, 241, 242, 243, 247, 248, 249, 250, 254, 255, 257, 266, 269, 270, 272, 276, 283, 287, 288, 290, 303, 307, 308, 310, 314, 320, 326, 327, 328, 329, 331, 337, 338, 341, 348, 349, 353, 354, 355, 357, 366, 367, 369, 373, 375, 380, 382, 386, 388, 391, 413, 416, 417, 419, 424, 425, 426, 431, 432, 437, 438, 439, 440, 445, 446, 447, 449, 453, 467, 469, 471, 475, 476, 478, 479, 480, 481, 482, 484, 486, 488, 491, 492, 493, 494, 495, 497, 499, 501, 505, 506, 507, 510, 511, 516, 517, 518, 519, 521, 522, 523, 524, 525, 527, 528, 529, 530, 532, 533, 534, 535, 536, 537, 538, 539, 540, 541, 542, 543, 544, 546, 552, 554, 555
Śiva Saṁhita..24, 182, 225, 250, 307, 366, 546, 554, 555
Śivadāsa 484
Śivananda...................191, 220, 554
Śiva-sūtra....................................283
Sixteen..140, 223, 224, 233, 241, 249, 250, 257, 269, 283, 304, 305, 308, 309, 317, 318, 328, 336, 338, 349, 372, 374, 376, 377, 391, 395, 408, 417, 440, 503, 514, 515, 516
Skanda ...14, 391, 393, 402, 481, 534
Skene, William...................222, 554
Skull..26, 31, 104, 114, 129, 130, 167, 169, 188, 190, 208, 220, 243, 303, 304, 318, 327, 329, 339, 343, 417, 418, 419, 439, 451, 467, 481, 486, 529, 530
SL................ See *Saundarya Laharī*
Sleeman, William...............474, 475
ŚLS.......See *Śrī Lalitā Sahasranāma*
Smara 249, 495, 541
Śmaśāna 212, 482, 484, 541
Śmaśāna Kālī..............................541
Smith, David James...............93, 554
Smith, Frederick M........99, 385, 554
So'haṁ 94, 211, 372, 541
Soma..9, 34, 43, 44, 45, 47, 50, 51, 52, 54, 55, 58, 59, 99, 129, 130, 261, 310, 400, 446, 522, 541
Somadeva 474, 484
Songsten Gampo 142, 417
Soul..56, 60, 64, 65, 67, 68, 69, 71, 79, 92, 94, 114, 116, 151, 153, 154, 169, 181, 204, 205, 232, 266, 270, 272, 280, 320, 322, 327, 336, 386, 399, 406, 473, 519, 522, 529, 538
Spare, Austin..95, 281, 310, 332, 451
Sperm..97, 99, 146, 147, 175, 181, 200, 308, 364, 378, 386, 391, 399, 403, 404, 405, 406, 408, 494, 496, 498, 521, 524, 531, 538, 542, 543, 545, 546

Sphuraṇa 541
Square..34, 144, 179, 320, 323, 326, 371, 374, 375, 378, 384, 416, 440, 489, 542
Śrī..9, 10, 22, 24, 52, 79, 99, 139, 140, 161, 178, 183, 198, 243, 244, 245, 246, 247, 249, 252, 257, 258, 272, 341, 352, 371, 372, 408, 412, 421, 424, 425, 431, 438, 439, 440, 445, 446, 470, 480, 496, 503, 505, 533, 541, 542, 549, 550
Śrī Lalitā Sahasranāma 24, 245
Śrī Vidyā..24, 139, 140, 141, 246, 247, 424, 470, 542
Śrī Yantra 24, 424, 542
Śrīkula 541
Śrīṁ..161, 198, 243, 244, 257, 258, 272, 341, 371, 372, 503, 505, 533
Sṛṣṭi 136
ŚS .... See *Śiva Saṁhita*
SSP............. See *Siddha Siddhānta Paddhati*
Stafford, Peter 45, 554
Staggering 20, 195, 501, 539
Stapelfeldt, Sylvia..383, 413, 447, 554
Stephanides, Stephanos.....508, 510, 511, 554
Sthiti 136
Submodalities..6, 259, 260, 261, 265, 296, 297, 298, 299, 300, 301, 302, 304, 343, 448
Subramanian, V.K. 331, 553, 554
Śūdra 44, 59, 99, 114, 542, 544
Śukra 403, 406, 496, 542
Sumeria 32, 36, 398
Sunflower 498, 506, 521
Sūrya 48, 78, 243, 329, 542
Suṣumṇā 66, 324, 542
Suṣupti 542
Svādhiṣṭhāna 338, 542
Svāhā..10, 161, 240, 241, 244, 245, 258, 272, 391, 471, 478, 492, 497, 502, 503, 542
Śvetāśvatara Upaniṣad 287, 289
Swaying..28, 191, 192, 194, 195, 218, 221, 342, 343, 501, 510
Sword..196, 203, 204, 357, 372, 399, 418, 439, 447, 469, 477, 481, 482, 484, 486, 491, 525
Śyāmā 542
Śyāmārahasya 408, 445
Sympathetic Nervous System 216, 217, 221
Taittirīyasaṁhitā 99, 385
Talmud 398
Tamas..104, 105, 107, 233, 249, 527, 542
Tāṇḍava 104, 543
Tantra Kalpadruma 251
Tantrāloka..17, 20, 195, 384, 407, 547
Tantrasāra 426, 480
Tāntrikā 175, 543
Tāntrika..20, 115, 119, 127, 143, 367, 408, 543
Tao Te Ching 147, 293, 549, 555
Taoist .. ...548, 549, 553, *See* Daoism
Tapas..25, 46, 54, 55, 59, 78, 123, 124, 174, 418, 543
Tārā..14, 103, 114, 141, 142, 143, 145, 147, 257, 265, 386, 412, 413, 414, 415, 416, 417, 418, 419, 424, 447, 450, 451, 473, 480, 507, 533, 543
Tattva..269, 322, 323, 324, 325, 326, 327, 375, 380, 516, 543
Tejas 253, 543
The Classic of Mountains and Seas 548
Thugs 474
Tiger 294
Tigunait, Pandit Rajmani 555
Tirodhāna 136
Tirumantiram 93
Toḍala Tantra..24, 189, 251, 341, 412, 416, 425, 438, 446, 478, 502
Tongue..182, 200, 209, 225, 234, 245, 253, 294, 302, 337, 343, 344, 355, 369, 378, 380, 399, 407, 417, 438, 467, 478, 481, 511, 515, 516, 529
TR .... See *Tripurā Rahasya*

Tree..13, 35, 36, 82, 100, 112, 176, 194, 244, 263, 268, 269, 285, 315, 327, 331, 352, 355, 356, 360, 373, 374, 387, 388, 389, 397, 398, 450, 451, 460, 467, 484, 489, 502, 518, 524, 532, 534
Triangle..38, 108, 139, 324, 326, 327, 329, 371, 374, 375, 378, 380, 384, 416, 440, 505, 546
Trika..18, 19, 23, 94, 127, 138, 286, 336, 366, 516, 517, 522, 543, 545
Trimondi, Victor & Victoria 103, 555
Trimūrti 543
Tripurā..14, 24, 133, 139, 178, 181, 247, 251, 277, 331, 413, 416, 420, 421, 424, 426, 431, 447, 543, 555
Tripura..170, 269, 413, 424, 431, 543
Tripurā - Bhairavī Tantra......... 426
Tripurā Rahasya...24, 178, 181, 555
Tripurāri 424, 491, 543
Tripurasundarī..412, 424, 425, 438, 451, 543
Trungpa, Chögyam......432, 457, 548
Tryaṁbaka 492, 544
*TT*See *Toḍala Tantra*
Tumburu 24, 254, 544
Turīya..110, 112, 113, 254, 255, 265, 533, 544
Umā..72, 130, 245, 310, 426, 469, 473, 480, 507, 541, 544, 552
Ungnad, Arthur 399, 555
Unmanī 234, 544
Upaniṣad..60, 64, 65, 66, 83, 229, 230, 255, 287, 413, 416, 440, 465, 544, 553
Urban, Hugh B. 474
Urine..45, 66, 115, 181, 182, 206, 208, 344, 385, 403, 458, 522, 535
Ūrmyā 51
Ursa Major 391, 538
Uṣas 47, 50, 78, 522
Utpaladeva 283
Vāc 52, 58, 79, 502, 540, 544
Vaiṣṇavī..104, 286, 371, 482, 505, 543
Vaiṣya 59, 99, 544
Vajra 99, 432, 544
Vāk 58, 79, 249, 544
Vāmabhāva 544
Vāmakeśvara Tantra..24, 120, 139, 408, 549, 551
Varadā Tantra 251, 253
Varada-mudrā 544
Varanasi..172, 173, 551, 552, 553, 554, 555
Vardhamāna 69
Varṇa 75, 76, 544
Varnāśrama Dharma 97
Varuṇa..47, 50, 56, 66, 78, 257, 261, 326, 372, 544
Vasiṣṭha 76, 141, 418
Vasu, Rai Bahadur Srisa Chandra 307, 554, 555
Vāta 50, 257
Vātsalya 170
Vāyu..79, 257, 261, 327, 329, 518, 519, 544
VBT ....See *Vijñana Bhairava Tantra*
Veda..9, 10, 23, 30, 41, 42, 43, 44, 45, 46, 47, 51, 58, 63, 71, 76, 78, 82, 205, 254, 255, 280, 285, 463, 465, 489, 545, 547, 549, 550, 553, 556
Vedas..22, 30, 41, 42, 43, 46, 47, 50, 51, 52, 54, 61, 63, 67, 68, 74, 77, 78, 79, 97, 99, 123, 140, 252, 255, 270, 280, 320, 337, 400, 403, 426
Veśya 175
Vetālapañcaviṁśatikā 484
Vibration..47, 54, 90, 92, 194, 195, 211, 236, 237, 239, 240, 251, 253, 254, 259, 264, 289, 290, 296, 307, 318, 324, 329, 331, 335, 341, 395, 488, 497, 501, 508, 510, 514, 517, 535, 537, 541
Vidyā..229, 238, 240, 241, 244, 249, 250, 412, 424, 446, 449, 452, 460, 488, 503, 505, 516, 519, 545, 548
Vijayā..24, 245, 253, 255, 286, 413, 431, 468, 469, 544, 545
Vijñana Bhairava Tantra............24
Vimalānanda 103, 496, 498

Vīṇāśikhatantra..24, 254, 255, 544, 550, 555
Viparīta Maithuna........359, 497, 545
Vīra..69, 107, 108, 110, 308, 356, 367, 377, 471, 545
Viriñci.................................494, 545
Visarga................409, 515, 516, 545
Viśeṣārghya................373, 540, 545
Viṣṇu..24, 25, 27, 28, 50, 60, 71, 73, 78, 79, 80, 81, 82, 83, 85, 100, 101, 102, 103, 105, 127, 155, 168, 182, 211, 224, 233, 243, 245, 247, 249, 254, 255, 267, 270, 310, 327, 329, 338, 342, 349, 375, 380, 382, 411, 416, 418, 425, 438, 439, 445, 446, 467, 469, 470, 471, 480, 482, 493, 494, 505, 521, 523, 524, 527, 528, 529, 532, 533, 534, 536, 538, 542, 545
Viśuddhi.................................... 545
Viśvasāratantra........................ 413
Voodoo 510
VŚT................ See *Vīṇāśikhatantra*
VT.......... See *Vāmakeśvara Tantra*
Vulva..55, 92, 93, 147, 253, 307, 360, 362, 382, 401, 447, 494, 499, 523, 532, 535, 542, 546
Walker, Barbara G. 477
Walker, Benjamin..383, 386, 387, 555
Waterwheel 294
Wei Boyang................302, 303, 404
Wei Huacun 294, 295
White, David Gordon..21, 115, 119, 125, 129, 132, 143, 147, 168, 189, 192, 309, 320, 322, 341, 349, 366, 387, 389, 391, 404, 405, 406, 413, 473, 555
Whitney, William D........30, 206, 547, 556
Widow..270, 359, 408, 437, 438, 445, 526
Wilhelm, Friedrich..43, 67, 190, 216, 324, 550, 553, 556
Wilhelmy, Herbert 556
Wodan 50, 52
Womb..13, 101, 157, 164, 289, 325, 331, 388, 485, 523, 545, 546
Woodroffe, John...23, 103, 108, 119, 184, 198, 236, 245, 253, 254, 272, 315, 316, 326, 332, 339, 346, 368, 369, 370, 373, 408, 426, 446, 479, 496, 497, 498, 506, 534, 551, 555, 556
Wu..144, 147, 148, 149, 150, 151, 152, 153, 154, 188, 212
Wu Peng 149
Wu Xian 148, 150
Wulff, Donna Maria..477, 548, 550, 551, 552
Xiwangmu..143, 144, 145, 146, 150, 214, 294
Xuannü 396
Yakṣa 389, 545
Yakṣī 14, 390, 392, 486, 545
Yakṣinī 388, 545
Yama..79, 207, 244, 270, 276, 465, 479, 546
Yāmala 546
Yantra..107, 114, 126, 139, 200, 271, 286, 325, 349, 363, 370, 371, 374, 375, 377, 378, 380, 384, 408, 416, 421, 424, 428, 439, 440, 449, 488, 495, 503, 505, 524, 530, 536, 537, 542, 546
Yijing.................................149, 152
Ymir 59
Yoga..22, 23, 24, 46, 54, 55, 66, 68, 78, 93, 100, 123, 124, 133, 137, 139, 156, 157, 166, 173, 174, 175, 178, 181, 185, 186, 188, 191, 192, 205, 210, 212, 214, 221, 228, 229, 232, 236, 239, 240, 250, 261, 262, 264, 265, 284, 287, 302, 303, 307, 308, 315, 317, 318, 330, 332, 333, 336, 337, 339, 340, 341, 342, 344, 345, 346, 358, 366, 370, 383, 395, 413, 448, 450, 496, 508, 520, 527, 531, 532, 533, 534, 535, 538, 541, 543, 546
Yogīn..125, 132, 133, 137, 143, 147, 169, 174, 182, 200, 283, 308, 309, 355, 357, 360, 377, 383, 397, 407, 508, 526, 546
Yogīnī..125, 137, 147, 169, 200, 283, 360, 377, 407, 508, 526, 546
Yoni..24, 28, 38, 93, 121, 179, 200, 253, 286, 307, 308, 318, 325, 329,

349, 360, 371, 373, 376, 382, 383, 401, 407, 412, 418, 425, 437, 447, 463, 465, 485, 494, 495, 498, 499, 506, 521, 530, 532, 541, 542, 546
Yonigahvara 470
Yonimudrā 189, 546
Yonitantra........................... 24, 360
YT............................ See *Yonitantra*
Zhang Boduan 303, 364
Zhouli 149
Zhuangzi............ 143, 149, 150, 293
Zohar 398

CPSIA information can be obtained
at www.ICGtesting.com
Printed in the USA
BVHW041746170321
602785BV00003B/164

9 781905 297375